BLANCHOT AND THE MOVING IMAGE
FASCINATION AND SPECTATORSHIP

LEGENDA

LEGENDA is the Modern Humanities Research Association's book imprint for new research in the Humanities. Founded in 1995 by Malcolm Bowie and others within the University of Oxford, Legenda has always been a collaborative publishing enterprise, directly governed by scholars. The Modern Humanities Research Association (MHRA) joined this collaboration in 1998, became half-owner in 2004, in partnership with Maney Publishing and then Routledge, and has since 2016 been sole owner. Titles range from medieval texts to contemporary cinema and form a widely comparative view of the modern humanities, including works on Arabic, Catalan, English, French, German, Greek, Italian, Portuguese, Russian, Spanish, and Yiddish literature. Editorial boards and committees of more than 60 leading academic specialists work in collaboration with bodies such as the Society for French Studies, the British Comparative Literature Association and the Association of Hispanists of Great Britain & Ireland.

The MHRA encourages and promotes advanced study and research in the field of the modern humanities, especially modern European languages and literature, including English, and also cinema. It aims to break down the barriers between scholars working in different disciplines and to maintain the unity of humanistic scholarship. The Association fulfils this purpose through the publication of journals, bibliographies, monographs, critical editions, and the MHRA Style Guide, and by making grants in support of research. Membership is open to all who work in the Humanities, whether independent or in a University post, and the participation of younger colleagues entering the field is especially welcomed.

ALSO PUBLISHED BY THE ASSOCIATION

Critical Texts
Tudor and Stuart Translations • *New Translations* • *European Translations*
MHRA Library of Medieval Welsh Literature

MHRA Bibliographies
Publications of the Modern Humanities Research Association

The Annual Bibliography of English Language & Literature
Austrian Studies
Modern Language Review
Portuguese Studies
The Slavonic and East European Review
Working Papers in the Humanities
The Yearbook of English Studies

www.mhra.org.uk
www.legendabooks.com

MOVING IMAGE

Editorial Committee
Professor Emma Wilson, Corpus Christi College, Cambridge (General Editor)
Professor Erica Carter (King's College London)
Professor Robert Gordon (Gonville and Caius College, Cambridge)
Professor Jo Labanyi (New York University)
Nikolaj Lubecker (St John's College, Oxford)

Legenda/Moving Image publishes cutting-edge work on any aspect of film or screen media from Europe and Latin America. Studies of European-language cinemas from other continents, and diasporic and intercultural cinemas (with some relation to Europe or its languages), are also encompassed. The series seeks to reflect a diversity of theoretical, historical, and interdisciplinary approaches to the moving image, and includes projects comparing screen media with other art forms. Research monographs and collected volumes will be considered, but not studies of a single film. As innovation is a priority for the series, volumes should predominantly consist of previously unpublished material.

Proposals should be sent with one or two sample chapters to the Editor, Professor Emma Wilson, Corpus Christi College, Cambridge CB2 1RH, UK.

APPEARING IN THIS SERIES

1. *Spanish Practices: Literature, Cinema, Television*, by Paul Julian Smith
2. *Cinema and Contact: The Withdrawal of Touch in Nancy, Bresson, Duras and Denis*, by Laura McMahon
3. *Holocaust Intersections: Genocide and Visual Culture at the New Millennium*, edited by Axel Bangert, Robert S. C. Gordon and Libby Saxton

Managing Editor
Dr Graham Nelson, 41 Wellington Square, Oxford OX1 2JF, UK

www.legendabooks.com

Blanchot and the Moving Image

Fascination and Spectatorship

Calum Watt

LEGENDA
Moving Image 8
Modern Humanities Research Association
2017

Published by Legenda
an imprint of the Modern Humanities Research Association
Salisbury House, Station Road, Cambridge CB1 2LA

ISBN 978-1-78188-537-6 (HB)
ISBN 978-1-78188-538-3 (PB)

First published 2017

All rights reserved. No part of this publication may be reproduced or disseminated or transmitted in any form or by any means, electronic, mechanical, photocopying, recording or otherwise, or stored in any retrieval system, or otherwise used in any manner whatsoever without written permission of the copyright owner, except in accordance with the provisions of the Copyright, Designs and Patents Act 1988, or under the terms of a licence permitting restricted copying issued in the UK by the Copyright Licensing Agency Ltd, Saffron House, 6–10 Kirby Street, London EC1N 8TS, England, or in the USA by the Copyright Clearance Center, 222 Rosewood Drive, Danvers MA 01923. Application for the written permission of the copyright owner to reproduce any part of this publication must be made by email to legenda@mhra.org.uk.

Disclaimer: Statements of fact and opinion contained in this book are those of the author and not of the editors or the Modern Humanities Research Association. The publisher makes no representation, express or implied, in respect of the accuracy of the material in this book and cannot accept any legal responsibility or liability for any errors or omissions that may be made.

Trademark notice: Product or corporate names may be trademarks or registered trademarks, and are used only for identification and explanation without intent to infringe.

© Modern Humanities Research Association 2017

Copy-Editor: Charlotte Brown

CONTENTS

	Acknowledgements	ix
	Abbreviations	x
	List of Figures	xi
	Introduction: Maurice Blanchot and Cinema	1
1	Reading the Ontology of Film After Blanchot	14
2	Appropriations of Blanchot in Godard's *Histoire(s) du cinéma* and Deleuze's *Cinéma* volumes	61
3	Experiencing the Absence of Time: *Satantango*	103
4	*Irréversible*, Disidentification, and Disastrous Responsibility	132
	Conclusion: On a Disappearing Art	163
	Bibliography	171
	Index	183

ACKNOWLEDGEMENTS

This book could not have been written without the exemplary guidance of my PhD supervisors at King's College London, Sarah Cooper and Patrick ffrench. I am very grateful to Martin Crowley and James S. Williams for their encouragement of the project and the stimulating discussions at the viva of the doctoral thesis on which this book is based. I owe thanks to Josh Cohen for inspiring my initial interest in Blanchot and to Jeri Johnson for encouraging me as an undergraduate. For discussions on various topics touched on in the book, I wish to acknowledge my fellow researchers at King's and elsewhere: Carla Ambrósio Garcia, Anna Batori, Sophie Corser, Tom Gould, Beth Guilding, Richard Mason, Jacob McGuinn and Barbara Plotz.

I am grateful to Gaumont for permission to use screengrabs from *Histoire(s) du cinéma* in Chapter 2 and to Iris Crey for designing the book's cover image.

c.w., Paris, June 2017

ABBREVIATIONS

For material in French, I have used existing translations where available. Occasionally I have modified them and indicated this in the text. Where no English version of a text is indicated the translation is my own. All emphases in quotations are in the original unless otherwise stated.

Abbreviations are used to refer to the following works, all of which are by Maurice Blanchot unless otherwise stated:

AO — *L'Attente l'oubli* (Paris: Gallimard, 1962); *Awaiting Oblivion*, trans. by John Gregg (Lincoln: University of Nebraska Press, 1997)

LV/BC — *Le Livre à venir* (Paris: Gallimard, 1959); *The Book to Come*, trans. by Charlotte Mandell (Stanford, CA: Stanford University Press, 2003)

FP — *Faux pas* (Paris: Gallimard, 1943); *Faux Pas*, trans. by Charlotte Mandell (Stanford, CA: Stanford University Press, 2001)

A/F — *L'Amitié* (Paris: Gallimard, 1971); *Friendship*, trans. by Elizabeth Rottenberg (Stanford, CA: Stanford University Press, 1997)

EI/IC — *L'Entretien infini* (Paris: Gallimard, 1969); *The Infinite Conversation*, trans. by Susan Hanson (Minneapolis: University of Minnesota Press, 1993)

D/ID — Jacques Derrida, *Demeure: Maurice Blanchot* (Paris: Galilée, 1998); Maurice Blanchot and Jacques Derrida, *The Instant of My Death/ Demeure: Fiction and Testimony*, trans. by Elizabeth Rottenberg (Stanford, CA: Stanford University Press, 2000)

EP/PW — *Écrits politiques: 1958–1993* (Paris: Léo Scheer, 2003); *Political Writings, 1953–1993*, trans. by Zakir Paul (New York: Fordham University Press, 2013)

EL/SL — *L'Espace littéraire* (Paris: Gallimard, 1955); *The Space of Literature*, trans. by Ann Smock (Lincoln: University of Nebraska Press, 1982)

SHB — *The Station Hill Blanchot Reader*, ed. by George Quasha, trans. by Lydia Davis, Paul Auster and Robert Lamberton (New York: Station Hill Press, 1999)

PD/SNB — *Le Pas au-delà* (Paris: Gallimard, 1973); *The Step Not Beyond*, trans. by Lycette Nelson (New York: State University of New York Press, 1992)

TO1 — *Thomas l'obscur: première version, 1941* (Paris: Gallimard, 2005)

TO2 — *Thomas l'obscur* (Paris: Gallimard, 1950)

PF/WF — *Le Part du feu* (Paris: Gallimard, 1949); *The Work of Fire*, trans. by Charlotte Mandell (Stanford, CA: Stanford University Press, 1995)

ED/WD — *L'Écriture du désastre* (Paris: Gallimard, 1980); *The Writing of the Disaster*, trans. by Ann Smock, new edn (Lincoln: University of Nebraska Press, 1995)

LIST OF FIGURES

Figures 2.1–2.23 are screengrabs from Jean-Luc Godard, *Histoire(s) du cinéma*, DVD (London: Artificial Eye, 2008). Copyright: "Histoire(s) du cinéma", un film de Jean-Luc Godard. © 1989/1999 Gaumont.

Figures 3.1–3.8 are screengrabs from Béla Tarr, *Satantango*, DVD (London: Artificial Eye, 2006)

Figure 3.9 is a drawing by the author

Figures 3.10–3.11 are screengrabs from *Journey on the Plain*, from Disc 4 of Béla Tarr, *Satantango*, DVD (Chicago: Facets, 2008)

Figure 4.1 is a screengrab from Gaspar Noé, *Irreversible*, collector's ed., DVD (London: Tartan Video, 2006)

INTRODUCTION

Maurice Blanchot and Cinema

One of the last texts of the French writer and philosopher Maurice Blanchot (1907–2003) is the extremely short and enigmatic *L'Instant de ma mort* [The Instant of My Death] (1994). This is a narrative describing how a young man — who may or may not be Blanchot — narrowly avoids being shot by soldiers during the Second World War. The text has subsequently been twinned with a long commentary by Jacques Derrida, entitled *Demeure* (1998), in which he reflects on the 'spectral' nature of this event: a summary execution is interrupted and a seemingly inevitable death does not come (*ID* 92/*D* 123). Derrida is constantly questioning the reality of the testimony in Blanchot's text, and much of his analysis is concerned with the distinction between reality and fiction in general. Derrida associates this testimony with fiction, hallucination, and by extension other 'imaginary' forms, in which it persists (*demeure*) in spite of its falsity. For Derrida, this question comes to hinge on the notion of the *instant*:

> La mort a déjà eu lieu, tout inéprouvée qu'en demeure l'expérience dans cette accélération absolue d'un temps infiniment contracté à la pointe de l'instant. Le scénario est si clair, et il en décrit le déroulement, en deux lignes, de façon tellement explicite que le programme est d'avance épuisé. On sait tout d'un savoir absolu. Tout, tout ça, s'est déjà passé parce qu'on sait ce qui va se passer. On connaît le scénario, on sait ce qui va se passer. C'est fini, c'est déjà fini dès l'instant du générique. Ça commence par la fin; comme dans *La folie du jour*, ça commence par la fin. On sait que c'est arrivé. 'Comme si tout était déjà accompli', c'est déjà arrivé. La fin des temps. (*D* 79)

> [Death has already taken place, however unexperienced its experience may remain in the absolute acceleration of a time infinitely contracted into the point of an instant. The screenplay is so clear, and it describes the action so explicitly in two lines, that the program is exhausted in advance. We know everything with an absolute knowledge. Everything, all of it, has already happened because we know what is going to happen. We know the screenplay; we know what is going to happen. It is over; it is already over from the instant of the credits. It begins with the end; as in *The Madness of the Day*, it begins with the end. We know it happened. 'As if everything were already done,' it already happened. The end of time.] (*ID* 62)

It is remarkable that Derrida describes this event in terms of a 'scénario'. This idea of a film or script is not obviously present in Blanchot's text. What relation does this event have to film? Does Derrida see Blanchot's text as cinematic, or the described events themselves? The text is not conventionally 'dramatic'. It is narrated as if its central event is instead almost banal: the soldiers take the young man out of his house and line him up to be shot, but a noise of battle is heard and the soldiers rush away before carrying out the shooting. The 'programme' would seem a strange term for an account of what is seemingly something of a non-event. There is a sense in which we could say that 'nothing happens'. The 'action', such as it is, that is described seems almost beside the point: it revolves around the feeling of the death still to come, described by Blanchot as 'toujours en instance' (*ID* 10) ('henceforth always in abeyance', *ID* 11). There is a repetitive insistence to the 'on sait' in Derrida's commentary quoted above, and to the idea of knowing more generally. This seems to belie the event's essential opacity. Indeed, following on from this, the reference to 'un savoir absolu' seems calculated to evoke the Hegelian absolute knowledge, which appears almost parodic as, within the context of the text, the titular instant seems to dissolve the rational subject of consciousness. In Philippe Lacoue-Labarthe's commentary on Blanchot's text, he remarks that '[l]a clarté de cette écriture est son énigme même' [the clarity of this writing is its very enigma].[1] In this text, opacity seems to become a species of this 'clarté'. In the same way, it is as 'si clair' that Derrida characterizes the 'scénario' in the quotation above, as if to suggest that the particular textual form of the screenplay has something to do with clarity. Clarity is both a word and effect that is called upon and set against its opposite 'obscurité' in some of the texts making up Blanchot's collection *L'Entretien infini* [The Infinite Conversation] (1969), as well as the later fragmentary text *L'Écriture du désastre* [The Writing of the Disaster] (1980), to refigure the dialectic of light and dark; clarity is thus understood etymologically in the sense of brightness.[2] Clarity also calls to mind Blanchot's classic text on Alain Robbe-Grillet, 'La Clarté romanesque' [The Clarity of the Novel] (1955), in which he describes Robbe-Grillet's novel *Le Voyeur* [The Voyeur], published in the same year, as marked by a clarity that seems to reveal everything: 'Il semble que nous voyions tout, mais que tout ne nous soit que visible. Le résultat est étrange' (*LV* 195) ('It is as if we were seeing everything, without anything being visible. The result is strange', *BC* 159).

This is not the only time that Derrida makes a comparison between Blanchot's writing and film. In the essay 'Survivre' [Living On] (1986), Derrida, commenting on it as if it were a translator's note written by himself, suggests the 'bande' running along the bottom of the pages of the essay should be read 'comme un télégramme ou un film à développer (to be processed?)' ('as a telegram or a film for developing (a film *to be processed*, in English?)'). He goes on to discuss the reflexivity of Blanchot's *récit* entitled *La Folie du jour* [The Madness of the Day] (1973) as a 'surimpression' ('a "double-exposure", a superimprinting').[3] Double-exposure here carries the sense of the filmmaking technique of recording twice with the same strip of film, thus exposing it twice to light. The two images recorded appear superimposed on one another. In this way the written text is figured as a strip of celluloid and, by extension, the process of marking the page with writing is analogous to exposure to light.[4]

This analogy with film reaches a climax in *Demeure* when Derrida describes the outstanding moment of *L'Instant de ma mort*, the moment of the suspended death:

'Cet instantané ressemble à un tableau [...] Arrêt sur image dans le déroulement d'un film en caméra: les soldats sont là, ils ne bougent plus, le jeune homme non plus, un instant éternel, un autre instant éternel' (*D* 96) ('This instantaneous seizure resembles a painting [...] Freeze-frame in the unfolding of a film in a movie camera: the soldiers are there, they no longer move, neither does the young man, an eternal instant, another eternal instant', *ID* 74). The reference to the freeze-frame as well as the film camera creates a slightly mixed metaphor: the unfolding of film in a movie camera suggests that we situate this analogy within the moment of recording, but the freeze-frame evokes something seen on a screen during playback or projection, as does the earlier reference to the credits. If the *déroulement* takes place in the camera, how does this give us to understand the freeze-frame? A freeze-frame is the name for the technique whereby the same frame is repeated on a film strip, giving the impression of stasis when played back. In other words, it is a feature of post-production rather than shooting. One might imagine a false freeze-frame, in which that which is before the camera is completely still. However, in this quotation the freeze-frame is syntactically anterior to the detail that the soldiers 'ne bougent plus', as if to suggest that it is not their standing still that creates the perception of a freeze-frame, but the freeze-frame that occasions their halt. The lack of a verb in this line mimics the stasis it describes. The difficulty in disentangling this passage is partly due to the complexity of the metaphor (recording or playback), and partly to the enigmatic nature of Blanchot's text and how Derrida understands it, standing between fiction and testimony. This question of fiction and testimony begs the question of the camera metaphor: does its recording equate to the events as they 'happened' or as they are recounted in the text? Is recording a hypothetical moment of the text or of history? It would also seem that the running of the hypothetical film whose end inheres in itself implies a relation between life and death such that death is already present, though not in terms of predestination or fatalism. *Déroulement* or the unfurling of the film is presented as a way of understanding the stream of time, and the freeze-frame the instant, the *arrêt*. By the same token, if we read *déroulement* as in reference to playback or projection, would that playing refer to a moment of reading or to the happening of events? With the reference to the screenplay, the film is in addition already textualized, as if a film could be 'read' from Blanchot's text. More basically, we must ask: is Derrida interpreting his own or Blanchot's vision of the *récit* as cinematic? And is the freeze-frame itself a moment of the hypothetical film, an interruption in an imagined playback, one seen through a viewfinder, or one stipulated in a screenplay? At a certain level these categories become impossible to distinguish effectively.

Derrida's use of the French *arrêt sur image*, in this context, cannot but contain an echo of the title of Blanchot's earlier *récit*, which Derrida has also written about, *L'Arrêt de mort* [Death Sentence] (1948). Reading these two phrases together, the death of that story is brought into an essential relationship with the freeze-frame in *L'Instant de ma mort*. More importantly, death as a concept becomes entangled with that of the image, and both with the idea of suspension of *arrêt*. Already from this brief reading we have come across many of the key ideas of this study, such as the instant, the image, death, and stasis. Yet the question remains: what is at work in this relation between film and the instant that Derrida identifies in Blanchot's thought? To answer this, we need to return to earlier in Blanchot's writings.[5]

★ ★ ★ ★ ★

This book explores the relation between Maurice Blanchot and film. The inspiration for the book comes from the apparent discrepancy between Blanchot's avowedly exclusive concern with literature — his life being 'wholly devoted to literature and to the silence unique to it' (*BC* ix) — and the interest filmmakers and writers on film have taken in his work. This is the book's animating paradox, something of which I have tried to evoke in the foregoing discussion of Derrida. One must begin by saying that Blanchot himself rarely touches on film, despite living a long life in the century in which film came to prominence as an art form and a cultural institution. Indeed, as Serge Zenkine remarks, 'à s'en tenir à ses essais on doute s'il est jamais allé au cinéma' [to go by his essays, one doubts he has ever been to the cinema].[6] Before outlining the direction this book will take, I want to briefly draw out some biographical connections between Blanchot and film.

Through his association with the Rue Saint-Benoît group (which included Marguerite Duras, Robert Antelme, and Dionys Mascolo), Blanchot was in close contact with Duras, who, in addition to her writings, made nineteen films. Laura McMahon has adumbrated the relevance of Blanchot to the contextual and theoretical understanding of certain films of Duras, especially *Détruire dit-elle* [Destroy, She Said] (1969) and *India Song* (1975).[7] Mascolo wrote contemporaneously that the latter film 'permet d'imaginer comment certains récits-limites (de Maurice Blanchot par exemple) pourraient devenir films sans s'appauvrir [...]. Avant ce film, les moyens d'une telle audace manquaient évidemment au cinéma' [allows one to imagine how certain limit-récits (such as those of Blanchot for example) could become films without being the poorer for it [...]. Before this film, the means of such an ambition were evidently missing in cinema]. For Mascolo, this is achieved by making speech sovereign and letting the image speak through silence.[8] In this context, Duras's films are the screen on which a connection between Blanchot and film has to an extent already been played out. Blanchot himself has a role in this. Writing about *Détruire dit-elle* in 1970, Blanchot asks: 'est-ce un "livre", un "film"? l'intervalle des deux?' (*A* 132) ('is it a "book"? a "film"? the interval between the two?', *F* 113).[9] Blanchot's biographer, Christophe Bident, points to a connection between Blanchot and the characters in *Détruire dit-elle*, notably in the figure of Stein.[10] The idea of a slippage between book and film is echoed by Blanchot in another context, when, on the occasion of the anniversary of *La Quinzaine littéraire* in 1986, he chose to quote, from the preceding 20 years, 'parmi tant de livres mémorables, un livre qui n'en est pas un, *Shoah* de Claude Lanzmann [1985]' ('amongst so many memorable books, one book that is not a book at all, but a film, Claude Lanzmann's *Shoah*').[11]

Blanchot's most direct statement on cinema appears to have been given to a filmmaker, Dominique Emard, in 1986, who sought permission to show a short film inspired by a part of *L'Arrêt de mort*. Blanchot refers to a key essay to which we will return at length in Chapters 2 and 3: 'Parler, ce n'est pas voir' [Speaking is Not Seeing], first published in *La Nouvelle Revue française* in 1960 and collected in *L'Entretien infini*. It is from this text that comes 'mon appréhension, lorsque je vois l'écrit passer au visible' [my apprehension when I see the written pass to the visible]. Even reading aloud is painful to him. Yet the experience of unauthorized film versions being made of his texts (see below) made clear to him that 'je n'étais pas "propriétaire" de ces textes' [I was not the 'owner' of these texts]. Blanchot ends the letter with the poignant request: 'ne m'en demandez pas. Faites comme si j'étais mort depuis fort longtemps et donc incapable de vous donner un avis d'outre-tombe. [...] Agissez comme si j'avais, sinon les dons, du moins l'âge d'Homère' [do not ask it of me. Act as if I had been dead for a very long time and thus incapable of giving you an opinion from beyond the grave. [...] Act as if I was at least as old, if not as gifted, as Homer].[12] Dismissive of the notion of copyright, Blanchot abdicates the position of any controlling authorial persona at the same time as indicating the primacy of the silence of the text. It is clear from what he writes that to make an adaptation of his work is to misread it — there can only be new texts, and if they engage with his they do so across an impossible distance.

In spite of Blanchot's lack of enthusiasm for films being made of his works, the novel *Thomas l'obscur* [Thomas the Obscure] (1950) did have a kind of cinematic afterlife. Benoît Jacquot made a curious short film of a chapter of the book and reports that he found it to be a testing experience.[13] One filmmaker who has subsequently drawn on Blanchot is the American video artist Gary Hill, notably with the work *Incidences of Catastrophe* (1988), which is also based on *Thomas l'obscur*.[14] As Michel Chion describes it, this film '"interprets" [the text] in very fluid images that show the material substance of Blanchot's book itself — the pages being flipped in close-up and following the thread of the written discourse — in alternation with sights of shifting sands and ocean waves, agitated by many visual movements that have the rapidity of a text'.[15] The only full-length study relating Blanchot to film in a systematic way has as its specific focus the relation between Blanchot and Gary Hill.[16]

Perhaps the most suggestive biographical detail concerning Blanchot and cinema is an anecdote told in a recent interview with Jacqueline Laporte. In the summer of 1964, she and Roger Laporte were spending the day in Paris and decided to go to the cinema. All of a sudden in the street, Blanchot appeared on the other side of the road, accompanied by a woman. They crossed to say hello. The cinema was also on the other side of the road. But he went straight into the cinema. They were confused. The next day they received a letter from Blanchot, saying that for him they were:

> comme deux figures amicales d'un rêve, et il était beau que je puisse vous saluer sans tout à fait pouvoir vous atteindre et ainsi sans rompre l'inaccessible du rêve — cela, un instant, dans le grand jour anonyme de la rue.[17]
>
> [like two friendly figures from a dream, it was beautiful that I could greet you without being able to reach you and thus without breaking the inaccessibility

of a dream — there, for an instant, in the great anonymous daylight of the street].

According to Laporte:

> Le film que nous avions vu, ensemble, séparés: *Le Silence* d'Ingmar Bergman. Nous n'en parlâmes jamais alors que, souvent, sachant ma passion cinéphile, il m'interrogeait sur des films que j'avais vus et aimés, d'autant qu'après 1970 il ne fréquenta plus les salles.
>
> Ses goûts cinématographiques étaient classiques: Murnau, Ophuls, Orson Welles, Ozu, Bergmann [*sic*], nous l'avons vu. Peu de cinéma français, à l'exception notable (il les évoqua plus d'une fois) des *Enfants du Paradis* et de *Casque d'or*. Il aimait beaucoup certaines comédiennes, et me dit un jour qu'il avait rencontré quelques fois Brigitte Bardot et Jeanne Moreau, à Èze j'imagine. Je me souviens aussi d'une longue discussion sur les cauchemars que provoquaient en moi certaines images, et il fit un long développement sur la différence entre l'imprégnation par des images vraies (c'était peu après l'assassinat de J.-F. Kennedy), et celle par des images de fiction, en concluant par 'un jour je vous emmènerai voir un terrible film d'horreur'. Ce qu'il ne fit pas.[18]
>
> [The film that we had seen, together, separately: Ingmar Bergman's *The Silence*. We never spoke about it, even though, often, knowing my love of cinema, he would ask me about films that I had seen and liked, especially as after 1970 he no longer went to the cinema.
>
> His taste in films was classical: Murnau, Ophüls, Orson Welles, Ozu, Bergman, we saw it. Not much French cinema, with the notable exception (he mentioned them more than once) of *Les Enfants du Paradis* and *Casque d'or*. He very much liked certain female actors and one day he told me that a few times he had met Brigitte Bardot and Jeanne Moreau, in Èze I imagine. I also remember a long discussion about the nightmares which certain images caused me to have, and he discussed at length the difference between how one internalizes real images (it was shortly after the assassination of J. F. Kennedy) and those of fiction, concluding by saying 'one day I will take you to see a terrifying horror film'. He didn't.]

The faintly deadpan final sentence does not appear intended to undercut the foregoing sketch of Blanchot's interest in film. However, these are personal recollections and likely tell us more about Blanchot's friendship with the Laportes than about his thoughts on film, such as they may have been. I cite this passage primarily to mitigate the suspicion expressed above by Zenkine that Blanchot was entirely aloof from cinema.[19] The biography of this notoriously private individual is not, however, what is at stake in this study, nor adaptations of his work, but his thought and writing.

Arguably the most notable moment in Blanchot's published output in which he engages with the cinema is one that he subsequently revised out of the text as part of a drastic abridgement. This is a passage in the first version of *Thomas l'obscur* (1941) in which the characters Thomas, Anne, and Irène go to watch a film in a cinema.[20] The passage describes Irène sitting in the darkness near Thomas and describes her perceptions. Irène touches Thomas's hand and thinks back to her husband holding her hand. The cinema is the place where a kind of revelation takes place for Irène, a strange experience much like many of those described in both versions of the text. At the moment that she touches Thomas's hand, an extended and disturbing hallucination begins in which she comes to imagine a phantom body in the darkness:

> C'est une absence de corps qu'elle s'appropriait comme son propre corps délicieux et dont la douceur, bouleversante et déchirante, la grisait. [...] Pendant la première partie du spectacle, comme si la fantasmagorie des images l'eût projetée en dehors d'elle-même, tout le mystère d'une telle existence lui fut voilé et elle n'éprouva en Thomas, son corps, aucune des souffrances qui eussent pu lui en faire connaître les contours et la chair redoutables. Elle n'arrivait pas à savoir qu'il y avait auprès d'elle, qu'il y avait en elle des organes qu'on pouvait appeler poumons, estomac ou cœur mais dont la réalité dissimulait des essences, ombres d'une tragique dureté. Ce n'est qu'après un écoulement très long du temps qu'elle commença de sentir une différence de température et de tension entre les deux corps, jusque-là parfaitement identiques, qu'elle avait. On eût dit que les rayons inconnus, la vie inassimilable qui convenait aux figures déjà à moitié consumées de l'écran réussissaient à le toucher et l'embrasaient silencieusement. Une chaleur qui était comme la chaleur paradoxale du fond de l'être, l'image lourde et grossière de la chaleur plutôt que la chaleur même, flottait au-dessus de Thomas. (*TO1* 176–77)

> [It was an absence of body that she took on as her own delicious body and whose sweetness, overwhelming and heart-breaking, intoxicated her. [...] During the first part of the spectacle, as if the phantasmagoria of images had projected her outside of herself, all the mystery of such an existence was veiled to her and she could not feel in Thomas, his body, any of the sufferings that could have made known to her the contours of his body and fearsome skin. She did not know that there were close to her, that there were within her organs that one could call lungs, stomach or heart but whose reality concealed essences, shadows of a tragic stiffness. It was only after a very long passage of time that she began to feel a difference in temperature and in tension between the two bodies, until then perfectly identical, that she had. It was as if the unknown rays, the inassimilable life which pertained to the figures already half consumed by the screen managed to touch him and engulf him in a silent conflagration. A heat which was like the paradoxical heat at the base of being, the heavy and crude image of heat rather than heat itself, floated above Thomas.]

Something is trying to take form here, a body 'réduit en cendres et se révélant dans sa destruction' (*TO1* 178) [reduced to ashes and revealing itself in its destruction]. The knowledge of this 'autre corps' [other body] is said to be fatal:

> Comme il ne lui était pas possible d'aller au fond de ce mystère, elle accepta l'idée que, dans l'atmosphère étouffante où elle était, le pouvoir de décomposition qui émane de certaines images particulièrement perverses et insinuantes, agissait comme un cancer étincelant et mettait à nu, sous une forme extraordinaire de sensibilité, les parties insensibles et obscures de l'être. Par la dévastation et la mort un corps très tendre, d'une merveilleuse délicatesse, se construisait. (*TO1* 178)

> [As it was not possible for her to go to the heart of the mystery, she accepted the idea that, in the suffocating atmosphere where she was, the power of decomposition

which emanates from certain particularly perverse and insinuating images acted like a brilliant cancer and laid bare, under an extraordinary form of feeling, the unfeeling and obscure parts of being. From destruction and death a very tender body, marvellously delicate, was constructed.]

This is after 'une demi-heure de cinéma' [half an hour of cinema]. After an hour, she is in a state of 'l'euphorie':

> Déjà un par un les organes que la maladie avait éclairés s'éteignaient. Un rêve les remplaçait. Il y avait un estomac de rêve, une tête de rêve, une langue de cauchemar. Tout de Thomas était visible. Il rayonnait parfaitement une dernière fois. Il n'y avait plus sur lui la moindre taie d'accoutumance qui empêchât son corps d'être pour Irène, après dix ans de mariage, après une heure de cinéma, un corps glorieux. Il se séparait d'elle, il devenait un corps étranger, un corps ami, il mourait. Le film était fini. Les lumières éclairèrent la salle et Anne qui ignorait tout présenta son ami à Irène. (*TO1* 179–80)

> [Already one by one the organs that the malady had illuminated spread out. A dream replaced them. There was a dream stomach, a dream head, a tongue of nightmare. All of Thomas was visible. He shone perfectly a last time. There was no more on him the cover of habit which stopped his body being for Irène, after ten years of marriage, after an hour of cinema, a glorious body. He separated from her, he became a foreign body, the body of a friend, he died. The film was finished. The lights came up in the auditorium and Anne, who had not seen all of this, presented her friend to Irène.]

One cannot say that all of this is occasioned only by the cinema. Before she touches Thomas's hand, it is said of Irène: 'Nulle femme ne paraissait aussi distante, aussi intouchable' [No woman had appeared so distant, so untouchable]. The strangeness that typifies Blanchot's narratives is already present before the film starts to play. Already before the touching of the hand events are taking place 'dans des temps abolis' (*TO1* 175) [in abolished times]. Irène is said to be like 'une très antique épouse' [a very ancient wife] of the very darkness concealing Thomas and 'il était sans doute qu'elle avait épousé ce bras depuis des années' (*TO1* 176) [it was without doubt that she had been wedded to this arm for many years]. The hand evokes its associations for her in memories of childbirth and adultery. She imagines these memories marked on her like a tender skin while on his like a callus. In other words, a full analysis of this scene would have to take into account the complexities of desire that are written into Irène's character before this.[21] But while the abrupt switch in which the lights go up and suddenly Anne is presenting Thomas to Irène indicates how quickly the moment of what I am soon to call 'fascination' can dissipate, this change also makes clear the extent to which cinema is what *perpetuates and maintains* this strange, protracted experience. These last lines are the last lines of a paragraph spanning seven pages. Through the play of lights the cinema potentiates the power of darkness itself. Readers of the second version of *Thomas l'obscur* may be reminded of the second chapter, in which Thomas enters 'une sorte de cave' (*TO2* 15) ('a sort of vault', *SHB* 59), a dark place in which he is placed 'en rapport avec une masse nocturne qu'il percevait vaguement comme étant lui-même et dans laquelle il baignait' (*TO2* 16) ('in contact with a nocturnal mass which he vaguely perceived to be himself and in which he was bathed', *SHB* 60). As with Irène, this relationship with this darkness is one of strange intimacy in which time seems distorted and unknowable. In both passages, the darkness opens a space in which the body in particular becomes exterior to itself. With Thomas, we read that: 'Son œil, inutile pour voir, prenait des proportions extraordinaires, se développait d'une manière démesurée [...] c'était donc le regard et l'objet du regard qui se mêlaient. Non seulement cet œil qui ne voyait rien appréhendait quelque chose, mais il appréhendait la cause de sa vision' (*TO2* 17) ('Useless for seeing, his eye took on extraordinary proportions, developed beyond measure [...] it was sight and the object of sight which mingled together. Not only did this eye which saw nothing apprehend something, it apprehended the cause of its vision', *SHB* 60). In the case of Irène, the lights of the cinema seem to illuminate the phantasmal shapes and half-formed beings which emerge from the darkness and which are the images of real things and bodies. The 'spectacle' takes on a double sense of being both what is on the screen, which is never described as such, and the vision in the darkness, the manifestation of an 'other' body. The text repeatedly suggests that these images give contact with unknown regions of 'being', begging the question of whether the experience described is an illusion or authentic access to a real as yet unknown.

Throughout, the present study examines discussions of Blanchot in relation to film as they appear within English language scholarship in both film and French studies. It also attempts to bring into discussion writing in French on this topic that has not received extensive coverage in English. To this extent, I mention at the outset two French scholars to whom I will make recurring reference and who have substantially used Blanchot's work in speculative writing on cinema: Raymond Bellour (b. 1939) and Marie-Claire Ropars-Wuilleumier (1936–2007). Large portions of the work of these two writers — especially Ropars-Wuilleumier — remain untranslated into English. As well as several books and many other publications, Ropars-Wuilleumier was a regular contributor to *Esprit* throughout the 1960s and 70s, and in 1983 she founded the revue *Hors Cadre* with Pierre Sorlin and Michèle Lagny, which ran until 1992. Translations of her work in English appeared during the 1980s in journals such as *Camera Obscura*, *Diacritics*, *Enclitic*, and *Wide Angle*, though to date none of her books has been translated in full.[22] Bellour is arguably the better-known of the two. While his more recent work has been less widely translated, his readings of Hitchcock in the 1970s, several of which appeared in *Screen*, were particularly influential in Anglophone film theory. With Serge Daney he was involved in establishing the revue *Trafic* in 1991, to which he continues to contribute.[23] Detailed examinations of both writers' work would require studies of their own. Let it suffice to say that while this book aims to expand upon what little writing on film there is in relation to Blanchot in English, this relation has been explored more extensively in the French context.

This book is inspired by a desire to follow Blanchot's line of thought beyond his own parameters, in order to consider film as an art according to his writings on art. In doing this, the book aspires to revitalize the Blanchotian notions of the *image* and *fascination*. Films are made of what are commonly called 'images', and are sometimes said to inspire 'fascination', yet Blanchot's terms have specific meanings. Chapter 1 consists in setting out the context and sense of these terms. At the same time as I suggest that the concept of the image opens a horizon in Blanchot's text, it must be said that the subject of the image is also more generally of ongoing interest in the French context.[24] At the end of the chapter I return to the question I have set out above in relation to *L'Instant de ma mort* and Derrida's filmic metaphors. This chapter also introduces several further key terms and ideas that will be used in the course of the book, notably the notions of *désœuvrement*, the 'disaster' and the 'primal scene'.

A question asked throughout is why Blanchot keeps on appearing in the margins of works by figures associated with film today. This is the question guiding Chapter 2, which examines the uses of Blanchot made by Jean-Luc Godard in his video work *Histoire(s) du cinéma* (1988–98) and by Gilles Deleuze in his *Cinéma* volumes (1983–85). As Nicole Brenez writes:

> Revenant encore et toujours sur le caractère non-liquidable de la disparition, la théorie du cinéma, dont il est frappant qu'elle est aujourd'hui produite par des individus isolés et non par des écoles ou des laboratoires comme c'est le cas dans d'autres champs, est, collectivement et qu'elle le sache ou non, blanchotienne. Les deux œuvres majeures de ce temps sont d'ailleurs structurées comme *L'Arrêt de mort* de Maurice Blanchot.[25]

> [Returning again and again to the persistent nature of disappearance, the theory of cinema, of which it is striking that it is today produced by isolated individuals and not by schools or laboratories as is the case in other fields, is, collectively and whether it knows it or not, Blanchotian. The two major works of this time are structured, furthermore, like Blanchot's *L'Arrêt de mort*.]

The 'deux œuvres majeures' Brenez is referring to are *Histoire(s)* and the *Cinéma* volumes. While I do not press the comparison with *L'Arrêt de mort*, this chapter is devoted to exploring the Blanchotian influences and resonances in the works by Godard and Deleuze, beginning by looking at a key moment in Godard's film in which Blanchot is quoted before examining his relevance to the film more generally. I suggest that Blanchot's presence is not limited to this single quotation. Later in the chapter the use of Blanchot at various moments in Deleuze's *Cinéma* volumes is discussed. I argue that, although the work is highly remarkable for bringing Blanchot into a philosophy of cinema, Deleuze's use of Blanchot to some extent dilutes the force with which Blanchot's concept of the image puts ontology into question.

Chapter 3 continues the engagement with Deleuze by moving on to an analysis of the Hungarian director Béla Tarr's film *Satantango* (1994). Tarr's film is chosen in part precisely because it has no direct connection to Blanchot, to demonstrate the validity of the theory of cinematic fascination beyond the immediate national or theoretical context. While others could have been chosen, I argue the film's distinctive stylistic properties make it a good case study of fascination. I examine the secondary literature surrounding Tarr, notably including that by Jacques Rancière, and suggest, somewhat more speculatively than the previous chapter, the relevance of Blanchot in interpreting *Satantango*. Key to this chapter is the consideration of the long take as a stylistic feature, which I use to develop Deleuze's analyses of waiting and tiredness in *Cinéma 2*, where Deleuze considers these ideas through reference to Michelangelo Antonioni. In my argument the long take opens an unusual relation to time, which I theorize in this and the following chapter.

Chapter 4 examines Gaspar Noé's controversial film *Irréversible* (2002) in relation to the question of the Other, as discussed in both Blanchot's writing and that of Emmanuel Levinas. Noé's is a film *maudit*, a 'problem film', emblematic of the so-called 'new extremism' in cinema and therefore a symptom of a putative epochal malaise. Following on from the discussion in the previous chapter of 'slow cinema', with which Tarr has been linked, I thus begin to suggest a way of thinking Blanchot's writing in congruence with contemporary European art cinema more generally. I argue that these trends — the 'new extremism' and 'slow cinema', ultraviolence and inertia — are not to be seen as opposites, but rather as different aspects of, or reactions to, the same phenomenon. In this chapter I consider the problem of spectatorial response to extreme images, as well as how the Other is made manifest in film.

Finally, the Conclusion summarizes the findings of the study and indicates the implicit politics of reading Blanchot in relation to film studies. Scholarship continues to demonstrate that Blanchot is critically relevant to our epoch and our relation to history itself. This study thus touches on the relation of film to technological modernity. Film is a dominant art of our time, at once archaic and undergoing digital transformation, and our fascination is partly symptomatic of historical change. In the Conclusion I also reflect on what is perhaps the most radical implication of Blanchot's writing, indicated both in Chapter 1 and even already in the foregoing discussion of *L'Instant de ma mort*, which is that the imaginary is found to dwell at the heart of the real. A central aim of this work is to demonstrate how cinema can make this visible.

Notes to the Introduction

1. Philippe Lacoue-Labarthe, *Agonie terminée, agonie interminable*, ed. by Aristide Bianchi and Leonid Kharlamov (Paris: Galilée, 2011), p. 75.
2. See for example *EI* 41 & 82; *IC* 29 & 57. What is troubling, as Blanchot says of Sade, is the 'alliance' of clarity and obscurity (*EI* 325; *IC* 218).
3. Jacques Derrida, *Parages* (Paris: Galilée, 1986), pp. 122 & 146; *Parages*, ed. by John P. Leavey, trans. by Tom Conley and others (Stanford, CA: Stanford University Press, 2011), pp. 106 & 127.
4. In a similar metaphor, Blanchot reflects on the title of his essay 'Traces' (1963): '*Spuren*, traces, pistes (par exemple, celles des bandes de magnétophone, où les voix sont contiguës sans se mêler), paroles discontinues, affirmations, non pas seulement fragmentaires, mais se rapportant à une experience du fragmentaire' (*A* 246, n. 1) ('*Spuren*, traces, tracks (for example, those on magnetic tape, where voices are contiguous yet do not mix), discontinuous words, affirmations, not only fragmentary but related to an experience of the fragmentary', *F* 303–04, n. 1).
5. For a broad consideration of the relation between Derrida's writings and film theory, see Peter Brunette and David Wills, *Screen/Play: Derrida and Film Theory* (Princeton, NJ: Princeton University Press, 1989).
6. Serge Zenkine, 'Blanchot et l'image visuelle', in *Blanchot dans son siècle*, ed. by Monique Antelme and others (Lyon: Parangon, 2009), pp. 214–27 (p. 214).

7. Laura McMahon, *Cinema and Contact: The Withdrawal of Touch in Nancy, Bresson, Duras and Denis* (Oxford: Legenda, 2012), pp. 74–97.
8. Dionys Mascolo, 'Naissance de la tragédie', *La Quinzaine littéraire*, 202, 15 January 1975.
9. For Marie-Claire Ropars-Wuilleumier: 'Sans doute, le rapport de l'essai et de la fiction tient-il dans l'œuvre de Blanchot le rôle que joue, chez Duras, la relation du film et du texte: mise en écart de l'œuvre et renvoi incessant, réversible, où s'oublie le commencement' [Without doubt, the relation between essay and fiction takes on in the work of Blanchot the role played, in Duras, by the relation between film and text: a process of separation in and of the work and incessant, reversible return, in which the beginning is forgotten]. Marie-Claire Ropars-Wuilleumier, *Écraniques: le film du texte* (Lille: Presses Universitaires de Lille, 1990), p. 58, n. 3.
10. Christophe Bident, *Maurice Blanchot: partenaire invisible* (Seyssel: Champ Vallon, 1998), pp. 555–56. For a discussion of this film see for example Leslie Hill, *Marguerite Duras: Apocalyptic Desires* (London: Routledge, 1993), pp. 88–93.
11. Maurice Blanchot, *La Condition critique: articles 1945–1998*, ed. by Christophe Bident (Paris: Gallimard, 2010), p. 432; 'Responses and Interventions (1946–98)', *Paragraph*, 30:3, 'Blanchot's Epoch', ed. by Leslie Hill and Michael Holland (2007), 5–45 (p. 35).
12. Maurice Blanchot, 'Lettre à un jeune cinéaste', *Trafic*, 49 (2004), 139.
13. Jacquot's film, *Lecture du chapitre X de* Thomas l'obscur *de Maurice Blanchot* (1975), was screened at the conference 'Maurice Blanchot: La littérature encore une fois' in Geneva in May 2017. For more on this, see the texts by Jonathan Degenève, Leslie Hill and Daniel Wilhelm in the conference proceedings, forthcoming from Éditions Furor.
14. For a discussion of Hill's work *In Situ* (1986), also based on *Thomas l'obscur*, in relation to Blanchot, see Raymond Bellour, *L'Entre-Images: photo, cinéma, vidéo* (Paris: La Différence, 2002), pp. 226–31; *Between-the-Images*, ed. by Lionel Bovier, trans. by Allyn Hardyck (Zurich: JRP/Ringier, 2012), pp. 268–73. See also George Quasha and Charles Stein, '*Liminal Performance*: Gary Hill in Dialogue', in *Gary Hill*, ed. by Robert C. Morgan (Baltimore, MD: John Hopkins University Press, 2000), pp. 243–68 (pp. 258–60).
15. Michel Chion, *Audio-Vision: Sound on Screen*, ed. and trans. by Claudia Gorbman (New York: Columbia University Press, 1994), p. 163.
16. Paul-Emmanuel Odin, *L'Absence de livre: Gary Hill et Maurice Blanchot — écriture, vidéo* (Marseille: La Compagnie, 2007).
17. Jacqueline Laporte and Éric Hoppenot, '"Le meilleur des amis": Jacqueline Laporte avec Éric Hoppenot', in *Maurice Blanchot*, ed. by Éric Hoppenot and Dominique Rabaté (Paris: Éditions de l'Herne, 2014), pp. 99–102 (p. 102).
18. Ibid.
19. See also the recently unearthed material in which we can see Blanchot writing a report of a film premiere in 1931 and serving on the jury of a prize for acting in the theatre and cinema, Michael Holland, 'L'Archive introuvable', *Cahiers Maurice Blanchot*, 3 (2014), 164–74 (pp. 166–67, 172–73).
20. *Thomas l'obscur* was first published in 1941 and republished in a considerably abridged form in 1950. The original was then only republished in 2005 after Blanchot's death.
21. For a discussion of this episode in relation to theories of haptic visuality, see Crispin T. Lee, *Haptic Experience in the Writings of Georges Bataille, Maurice Blanchot and Michel Serres* (Bern: Peter Lang, 2014), pp. 152–59.
22. For an account of the work of Ropars-Wuilleumier, see D. N. Rodowick, *Reading the Figural, or, Philosophy after the New Media* (Durham, NC: Duke University Press, 2001), pp. 89–106. The editor provides a clear outline of the stages of Ropars-Wuilleumier's career in Marie-Claire Ropars-Wuilleumier, *Le Temps d'une pensée*, ed. by Sophie Charlin (Paris: Presses Universitaires de Vincennes, 2009); for a bibliography see pp. 423–31.
23. For an introduction to the work of Bellour, see Michael Goddard, 'Raymond Bellour', in *Film, Theory and Philosophy: The Key Thinkers*, ed. by Felicity Colman (Montreal & Kingston: McGill-Queens University Press, 2009), pp. 256–65. On Hitchcock, see Raymond Bellour, *The Analysis of Film*, ed. by Constance Penley (Bloomington and Indianapolis: Indiana University Press, [1979] 2000). For a recent volume collecting many texts from *Trafic*, see Raymond Bellour, *Pensées du cinéma*, (Paris: P.O.L., 2016).

24. For a range of recent perspectives on the image, see *Penser l'image*, ed. by Emmanuel Alloa (Dijon: Les Presses du réel, 2010).
25. Nicole Brenez, *De la figure en général et du corps en particulier: l'invention figurative au cinéma* (Paris: De Boeck Université, 1998), p. 422.

CHAPTER 1

Reading the Ontology of Film After Blanchot

'la fin du livre'

In a key essay, Marie-Claire Ropars-Wuilleumier, who has done much to bring Blanchot into discussions of film theory, writes that Blanchot 'écarte tout rapport de l'image avec la fabrique médiatique de l'audiovisuel' ('dismisses any relation between the image and audio-visual production').[1] It is important to note at the outset the difficulty and complexity of the relation between Blanchot's writing, his concept of the image, and cinema. To attempt to think the relation between Blanchot's writing and film in a theoretical sense would not be a case of reconstructing an approach to film from its latency in his writings, nor any kind of 'application' of his writings to fictional films.[2] We certainly could not say straightforwardly that the business of filmmaking corresponds to Blanchot's understanding of writing. It would rather be to try to understand how film fits in with Blanchot's writing on the questions of art, the image, and fascination. It would be to try and think film at the same time as pursuing the thought of Blanchot. At the same time it would be a case of understanding the influence of Blanchot's thinking of literature for writers and philosophers working on film.

In addressing Ropars-Wuilleumier's claim we must turn to the moments when Blanchot seems to allude to film to imply its relation to his broader argument about art and history. The following lines, from the 'Note' that opens *L'Entretien infini*, are a case in point:

> Lorsque je parle de 'la fin du livre' ou mieux de 'l'absence de livre', je n'entends pas faire allusion au développement des moyens de communication audiovisuels dont tant de spécialistes se préoccupent. Qu'on cesse de publier des livres, au bénéfice d'une communication par la voix, l'image ou la machine, cela ne changerait rien à la réalité de ce qu'on nomme 'livre': au contraire, le langage, comme parole, y affirmerait encore davantage sa prédominance, sa certitude d'une vérité possible. Autrement dit, le Livre indique toujours un ordre soumis à *l'unité*, un système de notions où s'affirme le primat de la parole sur l'écriture, de la pensée sur le langage et la promesse d'une communication un jour immédiate ou transparente. (*EI* vii)
>
> [When I speak of 'the end of the book,' or better 'the absence of the book,' I do not mean to allude to developments in the audio-visual means of communication

with which so many experts are concerned. If one ceased publishing books in favor of communication by voice, image, or machine, this would in no way change the reality of what is called the 'book'; on the contrary, language, like speech, would thereby affirm all the more its predominance and its certitude of a possible truth. In other words, the Book always indicates an order that submits to *unity*, a system of notions in which are affirmed the primacy of speech over writing, of thought over language, and the promise of a communication that would one day be immediate and transparent.] (*IC* xii)

Blanchot is explicitly drawing out what is at stake in literature as such: 'la question du langage' (*EI* vii) ('the question of language', *IC* xi). Through this question comes another question which 'peut-être la renverse' (*EI* vii) ('perhaps overturns it', *IC* xii), which is writing. This is writing as 'force aléatoire d'absence' ('the aleatory force of absence'): that which 'semble ne se consacrer qu'à elle-même qui reste sans identité' ('seems to devote itself solely to itself as something that remains without identity') and that which:

peu à peu, dégage des possibilités tout autres, une façon anonyme, distraite, différée et dispersée d'être en rapport par laquelle *tout* est mise en cause, et d'abord l'idée de Dieu, du Moi, du Sujet, puis de la Vérité et de l'Un, puis l'idée du Livre et de l'Œuvre. (*EI* vii, my emphasis)

[little by little brings forth possibilities that are entirely other: an anonymous, distracted, deferred, and dispersed way of being in relation, by which *everything* is brought into question — and first of all the idea of God, of the Self, of the Subject, then of Truth and the One, then finally the idea of the Book and the Work.] (*IC* xii)

Clearly, Blanchot is discussing writing as theorized in his prior works *L'Espace littéraire* [The Space of Literature] (1955), *Le Livre à venir* [The Book to Come] (1959), and 'La Littérature et le droit à la mort' [Literature and the Right to Death] (1947–48), which he explicitly invokes at the beginning of the 'Note'. At this point comes the quotation above, in which the reference to 'moyens de communication audio-visuels' about which so many 'spécialistes' are at present concerned seems in part to be a veiled allusion to the work of French film critics and theorists in the 1960s. What Blanchot makes clear is that in his vocabulary *livre* does not literally mean 'book', at least not always. As he writes at the beginning of this text, 'il y aura encore des livres, longtemps après que le concept de livre sera épuisé' (*EI* vi) ('there will still be books a long while after the concept of book is exhausted', *IC* xi). He does not mean by this simply that books will still exist as relics even after physical publishing has stopped, and that books will still anyway come to us in an as yet unknown form (a situation rather more readily imaginable today than in 1969). The word *livre*, in addition to its literal referent understood as a physical object with paper pages, works in something like a metonymical relation to the aspiration of the dialectic to totality and unity. It is in a similar fashion that Blanchot will sometimes refer obliquely to the 'System', which can be understood as shorthand for Hegelian totality; another example is the 'Whole'. In the third 'proposition' of 'L'Absence de livre' [The Absence of the Book] (1969), the text that closes *L'Entretien infini*, we find a series of definitions of what is meant by the word *livre*. There is the 'livre' and the 'Livre' and '[l]e livre est le Livre' ('the book is the Book'). There is first the 'empirique' ('empirical') book; then there is the book as 'l'a priori du savoir' ('the *a priori* of knowledge'); and then there is '[l]'absolu du livre' ('the absolute of the book'). The third possibility is referred to as 'totalité' ('totality') or 'Œuvre' ('Work'). Blanchot notes that what links these three is the promise of *presence*. The absence of the book, conversely, names the 'unworking' or *désœuvrement* — a term I shall come to shortly — of that Book or Whole (*EI* 621/*IC* 423). The impossibility of the System is a key idea around which many of Blanchot's ideas constellate. In the closing lines of the 'Note', Blanchot suggests that it may be that writing requires 'la fin et aussi l'achèvement de tout ce qui garantit notre culture' ('the end and also the coming to completion of everything that guarantees our culture') in order to 'aller au-delà' ('go beyond') the totality of this System, which is here coterminous with history (*EI* vii/*IC* xii).

The audio-visual means of communication are part of 'le livre'. Therefore, despite the prima facie lack of any relevance of film for Blanchot, these lines can be read as implying its inclusion within his broader argument about history and the book, if only tangentially and to subsume it within a wider horizon. The remoteness or technicality of the phrase 'moyens de communication audio-visuels', in preference to the more familiar 'film', bespeaks an estrangement from its object. In itself this implies a need to consider that object according to a certain manner of its ontology; in other words, the language with which the (multiplicitous) object is described connotes its unfamiliarity. Film, before being particular films or a familiar pastime, is first to be considered as a technological means of *communication*. It is therefore always to be understood in relation to the Book, which is to say in relation to the ultimate communication that would always be to come, to the totality of knowledge.

Blanchot writes in 'La Parole quotidienne' [Everyday Speech] (1962) that the means of communication 's'usent et perdent leur force médiatrice' ('are wearing out and losing their mediating potential') and now have the character of 'une prolixité ressassante qui ne dit rien et ne montre rien' (*EI* 358) ('an insistent prolixity that says and shows nothing', *IC* 240). In this text Blanchot is discussing the everyday as such. Blanchot notes in parenthesis what is meant by the phrase 'moyens de communication': 'langage, culture, puissance imaginative' ('language, culture, imaginative output'). Yet with the sense of 'prolixité' the phrase gives a hint that it sometimes carries the sense for Blanchot of what might be called today 'media' or 'communications de masse'; in other words, the sense played on in the title of the journal *Communications*. This echo is made manifest as Blanchot, in a footnote to 'La Parole quotidienne', refers the reader to Roland Barthes's essay 'Le Message photographique' [The Photographic Message], which first appeared in *Communications* in 1961 (*EI* 363, n. 1/*IC* 456, n. 4).[3] Blanchot's footnote comes during a passage describing how in the newspaper 'tout se fait image' (*EI* 363) ('everything has become image', *IC* 243), while Barthes's essay provides a semiotic analysis of an advertizing image. What is clear is that Blanchot is concerned at this point with popular, visual media.

Thus it seems that the phrase 'moyens de communication' cannot simply stand for all of language and culture, though it is perhaps moving too fast to read it as referring specifically to 'communications de masse'. Breaking the phrase down to its constituent parts, it is firstly to be observed that 'communication' is itself a charged idea in Blanchot's writing. In the essay 'Le Demain joueur' [Tomorrow at Stake] (1967), Blanchot writes: 'La communication — pour employer ce mot douteux — est communication avec l'inconnu' (*EI* 600) ('Communication — to employ this dubious word — is communication with the unknown', *IC* 409). Why is communication a 'mot douteux'? In this piece Blanchot is discussing surrealism. Considering, in a somewhat allusive manner, the various surrealist 'initiatives', he finds 'moyens de communiquer tout nouveaux' ('new means of communicating') through which one can communicate 'sans passer par la parole normale et sans s'isoler dans l'écriture' ('without passing through ordinary speech and without isolating oneself in writing'). Blanchot is critical of 'formes de sociabilité médiocres' ('mediocre forms of sociability'), including 'ce pur bavardage' ('pure chatting') and public demonstrations, but states that communication 'exige la pluralité' ('requires plurality'). Communication is closely associated with 'la parole' ('speech') (*EI* 599–600/*IC* 408–09). While as we saw in the 'Note' Blanchot writes that the Book indicates the promise of a future communication that would be immediate, communication here seems to be a 'mot douteux' on account of the possibility of its taking inadequate forms; that is, of not always equalling the presence that it nominally connotes.

The sense of the word communication becomes a little clearer when one goes back to earlier writing by Blanchot. In the section of *L'Espace littéraire* entitled 'La Communication' [Communication] (*EL* 207–16/*SL* 198–207), originally published in 1953, communication refers to a *relation* a reader can have with a text. When a poem is read, the reader opens a space in which the poem becomes 'la communication ouverte entre le *pouvoir* et l'*impossibilité*, entre le pouvoir lié au moment de la lecture et l'impossibilité liée au moment de l'écriture' (*EL* 207) ('communication opened between *power* and *impossibility*, between the power linked to the moment of reading and the impossibility linked to the moment of writing', *SL* 198). Communication in this sense is not the readability of a text, rather almost the opposite: access to the impossibility at work in its creation. Communication is a matter of access, in a space and across times ('moment[s]'), to this origin of the work.

Expanding on the idea of the 'inconnu' above, it can be said that communication means communication in which there is experience of alterity as such, understood as an 'excess' which 'affects or changes thought'.[4] In this sense, Blanchot's avowedly exclusive concern with literature is not as clear-cut as it might first appear. As Jean-Luc Nancy has recently observed in an interview in *Lignes*:

> Je ne sais pas encore comment considérer cette 'littérature' qui semble toujours appeler sa propre reprise interprétative et donc *en fin de compte être plus allégorique que littéraire* — littéraire voulant dire précisément ce qui ne produit pas une allégorie, mais qui dit (l'existence, la vie, etc.).[5]
>
> [I still do not know how to consider this 'literature' which seems always to

call for its own interpretative response and *which is thus ultimately more allegorical than literary* — literary meaning, here, precisely that which does not produce an allegory, but which speaks (existence, life, etc.).]

Nancy goes on to ally literature with the absence of sense, with love and madness, in contrast to politics.

In the essay 'Sur une approche du communisme (besoins, valeurs)' [On One Approach to Communism (needs, values)] (1953), communication comes to stand for an even broader relation, a relation 'à l'homme' ('to man') that is not a power and one arrived at only 'lorsque l'homme se sera accompli (*supprimé*) comme pouvoir' (*A* 110, n. 1) ('only when man will have completed (*removed*) himself as power', *F* 296, n. 2):

> La 'communication', telle qu'elle se dévoile dans les rapports humains privés et se retire dans les œuvres que nous appelons encore œuvres d'art, ne nous indique peut-être pas l'horizon d'un monde dégagé des rapports trompeurs, mais nous aide à récuser l'instance qui fonde ces rapports, nous forçant à gagner une position d'où il serait possible de n'avoir pas de part aux 'valeurs'. (*A* 113)

> ['Communication,' such as it reveals itself in private human relations and such as it withdraws itself in the works that we still call works of art, perhaps does not indicate to us the horizon of a world free of deceptive relations but helps us to challenge the authority that founds these relations, forcing us to reach a position from which it would be possible to have no part in 'values'.] (*F* 96)

It is partly in this sense of withdrawing from established values that Nancy later writes in *La Communauté désœuvrée* [The Inoperative Community] (1986): 'La communication est le désœuvrement de l'œuvre sociale, économique, technique, institutionnelle' ('Communication is the unworking of work that is social, economic, technical, and institutional').[6]

Le désœuvrement is one of the 'concepts', Blanchot writes towards the end of 'Le Demain joueur', 'échappant à toute conceptualisation' (*EI* 617) ('escaping every conceptualization', *IC* 420). The word can be translated as 'worklessness', 'unworking', or 'unemployment', and Blanchot's translator Ann Smock calls it 'the absence of the work'.[7] It is in a related formulation that Lacoue-Labarthe and Nancy refer to the 'œuvre de l'absence d'œuvre' [work of the absence of work]. According to them, the work of the absence of work would constitute the most essential — most romantic and most modern — gesture in romanticism, and refers to the way in which the work gets lost and undoes itself even in its pursuit of the project of the Work.[8] This is a dynamic that is discussed according to various scales — from an individual work of art to the Work of history, the Book. To put it simply, it would refer to the way in which all 'true' works have already been compromised and unravel themselves. Blanchot discusses this idea at great length in *L'Espace littéraire*, finding it in his account of the most intimate psychological valences in the work of the writer, who is paradigmatic in being idled out of work by the very work he is trying to accomplish. But *désœuvrement* also refers to an historical condition, an epoch. It is thus that the Italian philosopher Giorgio Agamben, with a look back to Nancy's text referred to earlier, notes that the term can be understood as designating 'inoperativeness as the figure of the fullness of man at the end of history'. Agamben observes that the term's first use was by Alexandre Kojève in 1952 in a review of novels by Raymond Queneau.⁹ Work is the work of history and *désœuvrement* is that history as it were under arrest. This is the reverse of the idea that, to quote Kojève himself: 'Là où il y a Travail, il y a donc nécessairement changement, progrès, évolution historique' [Where there is Work there is necessarily change, progress, historical evolution].¹⁰ For Blanchot, we are in some sense at the end of history, and this would partly account for how we are to understand the 'changement radical d'époque' (*EI* vii) ('radical change of epoch', *IC* xii) he sometimes alludes to, such as in the 'Note'. As Leslie Hill has shown, the change of epoch suggests that all historical eras are constituted by something ahistorical, rendering them alien to themselves.¹¹ It is thus that 'ce qui mettait en branle la dialectique, l'expérience inexpérimentable de la mort, l'arrêtait aussitôt, arrêt dont tout le procès ultérieur garda une sorte de souvenir, comme d'une aporie avec laquelle il fallait toujours compter' (*ED* 112) ('the experience which initiates the movement of the dialectic — the experience which none experiences, the experience of death — stopped it right away, and that the entire subsequent process retained a sort of memory of this halt, as if of an aporia which always had still to be accounted for', *WD* 68). This is why Blanchot describes the *disaster* as 'le hors de l'histoire historique' (*ED* 68) ('outside history, but historically so', *WD* 40).¹²

Michael Holland suggests an approach to Blanchot's writing in which that writing can be regarded not simply as the work of a single individual but as 'the site of a huge and fundamental change in Western values themselves (which is how successors like Foucault and Derrida approached it)'. In the course of the Occupation, the very relation between literature and thought changes. The writer in this time seeks in the work a withdrawal from the events of the time, but this becomes 'a falling away that affects everything: the world, the work, and the subject who seeks through language to bring them into relation [...] it disrupts the basic convergence of the discourses of thought, literature and politics within a single value system'. Drawing out the connection between this historical moment and what will later come to be named by Blanchot the disaster, Holland writes that '[i]t is this catastrophe that will turn the historical moment of France's defeat into a turning point for the very idea of history and the worldview it underpins'.¹³

In relation to the events of May 1968, we find this thought of disaster or change of epoch articulated as a need to 'affirm the rupture'. The crucial statement of this comes in the first (and only) issue of *Comité*, appearing in October 1968: 'Quelle rupture? La rupture avec le pouvoir, donc avec la notion de pouvoir, donc en tous lieux où prédomine un pouvoir' (*EP* 104) ('What rupture? The rupture with the powers that be, thus with the notion of power, thus with all places where power predominates', *PW* 88). To affirm the rupture first means to state that 'nous sommes en état de guerre avec ce qui est, partout et toujours, n'ayant de rapport qu'avec une loi que nous ne reconnaissons pas, avec une société dont les valeurs, les vérités, l'idéal, les privilèges nous sont étrangers' (*EP* 104) ('we are in a state of war against what exists, everywhere and always; that we exist only in relation to a law that we do not recognize, within a society whose values, truths, ideals, and privileges are foreign to us', *PW* 88).¹⁴ Echoing the idea of the end of the book, Blanchot writes:

> En Mai, il n'y a pas de livre sur Mai: non par manque de temps ou par nécessité 'd'agir', mais par un empêchement plus décisif; cela s'écrit ailleurs, dans un monde privé d'édition, cela se diffuse face à la police et d'une certaine manière avec son aide, violence contre violence. Cet arrêt du livre qui est aussi arrêt de l'histoire et qui loin de nous reconduire avant la culture désigne un point situé bien au-delà de la culture, voilà ce qui provoque le plus l'autorité, le pouvoir, la loi. Que ce bulletin prolonge cet arrêt, tout en l'empêchant de s'arrêter. Plus de livre, plus jamais de livre, aussi longtemps que nous serons en rapport avec l'ébranlement de la rupture. (*EP* 119–20)

> [In May, there is no book on May — not due to a lack of time or due to the necessity 'to act,' but because of a more decisive obstacle: it is written elsewhere, in a world devoid of publication; it is distributed with the police and in a certain way with their help, violence against violence. This arrest of the book is also an arrest of history that, far from leading us back before culture, designates a point well beyond culture, and this is what most provokes authority, power, and the law. May this bulletin prolong this arrest, while preventing it from being arrested, suspended, ended. No more books, never again a book, so long as we maintain our relation with the upheaval of the rupture.] (*PW* 95)

Blanchot here as throughout emerges as the thinker of the interruption or the *arrêt*, and these lines show how the political exigency that arises from his thought of the disaster is a need to affirm the break. These lines also make clear how the interruption can be 'le hors de l'histoire historique'. They also give an indication, paradoxically, that *désœuvrement* is something one can seek. Blanchot in a piece about the *Revue internationale* discusses 'comment réintroduire le "désœuvrement"' (*EP* 69) ('how to reintroduce "worklessness"', *PW* 66) into the periodical, as if to suggest that it can somehow be engineered. I will suggest that cinema may be a mode in which, through the image, the rupture may be affirmed. There is an echo of this exigency in Derrida's use of the trope of the *arrêt sur image* as the form in which the instant as interruption is affirmed.

Returning to 'moyens de communication', it is necessary to ask what is the significance of their wearing out. Is there a connection between the wearing out of the means of communication and the 'unworking' that Nancy links to communication? Blanchot writes that, in this time of mass media: 'Nous sommes quittes du souci des événements, dès que nous avons posé sur leur *image* un regard intéressé, puis simplement curieux, puis vide mais *fasciné*' (*EI* 358, my emphasis) ('We are no longer burdened by events as soon as we behold their *image* with an interested, then simply curious, then empty but *fascinated* look', *IC* 240). A fundamental condition today, it seems, is one of *fascination*. If the change of epoch relates to the absence of the book, and the contemporary means of communication are the mode in which this is historically registered as an ever-imminent turning and a relation to alterity, then today this means a vigilance with regard to the cinema as a dominant means of communication. This is because the context of mediatization — that is, the *disappearance* of older forms — is one in which Blanchot can be demonstrated as being of contemporary relevance. To say that the present work is about fascination means that it aims to tell us something about how we relate to the world today and about that relation as a relation to what Blanchot calls the Outside.

Existing Between Two Slopes: A Proviso on the Word 'Blanchotian'

Before going on to discuss the crucial terms of this book it is necessary to make some broadly methodological remarks. To appropriate Blanchot's terms in general involves committing a conceptual violence against his work and especially his later work, which seeks to avoid an easy conceptual articulation. Both the substance and the style of this thought resist this appropriation. We must concur with the assessment of Christopher Fynsk that Blanchot's 'last steps' can be characterized first as a refusal of the 'postwar technopolitical order', but one that moves to 'engage that crossing of a wasteland that Heidegger, in his meditation on nihilism, claimed would necessitate a change of language'.[15] This notion of a change in language gestures towards the extreme stylistic density of the late works, especially *Le Pas au-delà* [The Step Not Beyond] (1973) and *L'Écriture du désastre*. Fynsk indicates the affirmative quality of the late writing, which bears out the trajectory of moving beyond dialectical thinking and beyond the negative. It is in a similar mood that Leslie Hill writes:

> As the world threatens increasingly to move into a new and perhaps even final epoch, dominated by globalised exploitation, technological uniformity, and cynical nihilism, it has arguably become more urgent than ever to draw on the resources of Blanchot's still neglected rethinking of the fragment.[16]

Both of these important recent studies have emphasized the formal qualities of Blanchot's later texts, yet it is striking that they identify the relevance of that form in relation to an era of ostensible nihilism and technological advancement. Though not concerned with fragmentary writing per se, this study is informed by the later texts and will refer to their terms even as they resist such an appropriation.

Yet at the same time the study of Marlène Zarader is useful for articulating the need (at the same time as treating the work and the difficulties of its style with the extreme care it requires) to avoid excessive deference to Blanchot and to be ready to take him at his word: 'bref, substituer à la deference l'usage du questionnement' [in brief, to substitute deference with questioning].[17] We could say that Blanchot's work itself is subject to the 'double relation' that he sometimes makes reference to. As Blanchot writes in a piece on Georges Bataille, each event can be lived by way of a double relation. It can be lived as something comprehended and mastered, related to a good or value, to Unity; or 'comme ce qui se dérobe à tout emploi et à toute fin, davantage comme ce qui échappe à notre pouvoir même d'en faire l'épreuve, mais à l'épreuve duquel nous ne saurions échapper' (*EI* 308) ('as something that escapes all employ and all end, and more, as that which escapes our very capacity to undergo it, but whose trial we cannot escape', *IC* 207). Again, in a letter addressed to Bataille in the same year (1962), he writes that there is 'la passion, la realization et la parole du tout, dans l'accomplissement dialectique' ('the passion, the realization, and the speech of the whole in dialectical accomplishment'), as well as a nondialectical movement which does not tend towards power. This double relation implies 'un double langage' ('a double language'): 'l'un en parole d'affrontement, d'opposition, de négation [...] l'autre est parole qui parle avant tout, et en dehors de tout [...] sans concordance, sans confrontation et prête à accueillir l'inconnu, l'étranger' ('one is a speech of confrontation, opposition and negation [...] the other is the speech that speaks before all, and outside of all [...] without concord or confrontation, and ready to welcome the unknown, the stranger'). In simplest terms: 'L'un *nomme* le possible et veut le possible. L'autre *répond* à l'impossible' ('One *names* the possible and wants the possible. The other *responds* to the impossible').[18] Blanchot makes the point that despite their impossible tension, neither of these approaches can be renounced. Their direct correlative is the notion of literature's 'deux versants' ('two slopes') described in the seminal essay of 1947–48, 'La Littérature et le droit à la mort': one side of literature is directed towards a movement of negation by which things are named, known, destroyed, and referred to an imaginary totality; the other seeks not to appropriate but to persist amongst a material substratum and without revelation or meaning (*PF* 318–22; *WF* 330–34). In the present study it will be a question of moving between the two as mutually implicated, of using both a totalizing register and one open to discontinuity. Occasionally the lexicons of Hegel, Heidegger, and Levinas will be invoked, seeing as they are frequent reference points in which Blanchot's 'philosophy', such as it is and to such an extent as one can be spoken of, is articulated. We might say that Blanchot's work is almost unique in how far he moves in this latter direction, were it not oxymoronic, the second movement being opposed to the very ideas of direction and progress.

It is therefore essential to acknowledge the ambiguity of the uneasy adjective 'Blanchotian'. Perhaps we can talk of two ambiguities. The first would be a question of 'which Blanchot'? It would be impossible to speak of all of Blanchot's writing. The present study does not engage, for example, very much with the *récits*, and the opening remarks are as close as it will come to approaching the political writings, which have in recent times attracted increasing critical attention. Crucial texts for this study are those on the image and the texts on art in the abstract, especially those of the 1950s — the texts themselves, that is to say, but also insofar as they persist and undergo an afterlife in certain strains of French thought. They have been given crucial elaboration in the works of such writers as Nancy, Bellour and Ropars-Wuilleumier. 'Blanchotian' would then imply not simply that written by Blanchot, but that overtly inspired by Blanchot and that which is consonant with, or 'continues', his thought.

The second, related ambiguity would involve writing on Blanchot at all as a risk of not having taken him sufficiently at his word in the first place. If one 'lesson' of Blanchot is essentially bound up with not only the notion of naming as the work of the negative, nomination as erasure (as Blanchot interprets Hegel), but also the cancellation of the namer and therefore the effacement of the proper name, then as an epithet 'Blanchotian' would appear to be a contradiction in terms. This would be partly to announce pre-emptively the impossibility of the present study:

there can be no such thing as a Blanchotian approach to film. Of necessity the natural mode will be working along the totalizing slope; by common definition the academic voice is totalizing and utilitarian, and tones of discontinuity may be seen as affectation, stylistic contamination, the internalization of thought's very disintegration. This would be to draw attention to how what ensues will involve a necessary and unavoidable reduction.

The Image and Fascination

Film is an audio-visual means of communication; it is also an art form. As art it is intimately related to what Blanchot calls 'image'. The critical text, and one to which this study will return frequently, is 'Les Deux Versions de l'imaginaire' [The Two Versions of the Imaginary], a text first published in *Les Cahiers de la Pléiade* in 1951 before being revised as an appendix to *L'Espace littéraire*.[19]

It is through reference to Heidegger that Blanchot shows the notion of *use* to be involved in the process by which we come to deal with images, and I want to sketch firstly how this complex phenomenological category has its roots in material things. Early on in *L'Espace littéraire*, Blanchot opposes the image to signs, value, reality, and truth (*EL* 15; *SL* 24). To illustrate this, Blanchot adopts the famous example of the tool from Heidegger's *Being and Time* (1927). Heidegger uses the example of the hammer to explain the distinction between *Vorhandenheit* ('presence-at-hand') and *Zuhandenheit* ('readiness-to-hand') — roughly speaking, the distinction between things in the world appearing as objects to consciousness and things appearing as there to be manipulated in some way (in the case of the hammer, as equipment). Heidegger writes: 'the less we just stare at the hammer-Thing, and the more we seize hold of it and use it, the more primordial does our relationship to it become and the more unveiledly is it encountered as that which it is — as equipment'.[20]

However, when the tool is damaged or is in some way obstructive, it becomes 'conspicuous' and slips out of the 'ready-to-hand' mode.[21] Blanchot does not use Heidegger's technical terminology from *Being and Time*, but instead refers to a relation of appearance and disappearance. As he phrases this, the tool, when damaged, becomes its image — 'ne disparaissant plus dans son usage, *apparaît*' ('no longer disappearing into use, it *appears*') — and this is 'si l'on veut, son double' ('the object's double, if you will') (*EL* 271; *SL* 258). As so often in Blanchot, the qualifying subclause should give us pause to think that it is not so simple. Blanchot moves from the simple dynamic in this fleeting reference to Heidegger to then claim:

> La catégorie de l'art est liée à cette possibilité pour les objets d'"apparaître', c'est-à-dire de s'abandonner à la pure et simple ressemblance derrière laquelle il n'y a rien — que l'être. N'apparaît que de qui s'est livré à l'image, et tout ce qui apparaît est, en ce sens, imaginaire. (*EL* 271)

> [The category of art is linked to this possibility for objects to 'appear,' to surrender, that is, to the pure and simple resemblance behind which there is nothing — but being. Only that which is abandoned to the image appears, and everything that appears is, in this sense, imaginary.] (*SL* 259)

Certainly at this stage at least Heidegger does not sanction this invocation of art, but what he would consider the more unorthodox reading of his tool passage would surely be, without considering the rest of the piece, Blanchot's use of the terms 'being' and 'nothing', and especially that dash which threatens to equate them. Yet it is just this collapse that is in fact at stake. The appearance that marks the present-at-hand — 'just staring at the hammer-Thing' — is for Heidegger as a mirage that veils the object and blinds Dasein from a primordial relationship with the world, while for Blanchot the image seems to open up the world onto an abyss, an absence. To put it in other words, while Heidegger may be concerned that the hammer needs fixing, so to speak, for Blanchot what is alarming about the image is that it points to the nothingness behind it. At the level of the prose styles a different relation to the image can be seen, such that while Heidegger seems to bear closely to a ground and is attentive to revelations that may be at hand, in Blanchot there is a careful, even aloof approach to that which is 'at hand'. As in the remoteness of the phrase 'moyens de communication', there is a sense of distance inscribed in the writing itself. Indeed, Blanchot's distinction from the phenomenological approach is even clearer when compared with Jean-Paul Sartre's *L'Imaginaire* (1940), in which the image is essentially indicative of a relationship of intentionality. If for Sartre the image represents an unreal object that in consciousness *stands for* a real thing in the real world, in Blanchot the image is ontologically disruptive of that world and is not readily available to consciousness; in contrast to Sartre's explicit invocation of psychology, Blanchot banishes such terms as consciousness so as to radicalize the unreality of the image.[22] Looking ahead to how the argument will develop in relation to cinema, we can note how Ropars-Wuilleumier draws the distinction:

> Si le cinéma peut figurer le travail de l'imaginaire, ce n'est pas en suscitant des images absentes, mais bien parce qu'il donne à lire, dans la présence même de l'image, l'aptitude à l'absence. En extrapolant cette remarque hors champ du cinéma, on serait conduit à cerner l'intrusion de l'imaginaire dans le réel comme le moment où le défaut de réalité ne tient pas au manque de l'objet, mais au contraire à sa présence, dont la perception serait affectée d'un coefficient de nullité; à la différence de l'imagination sartrienne, en laquelle les objets que fait paraître la conscience sont frappés d'irréalité parce qu'absents, l'imaginaire se définirait comme cet instant singulier où s'abolit, dans la présence affirmée du réel, le principe même de réalité. Découvrir l'image en l'objet, recouvrir d'absence la présence — tel serait alors le facteur qui départage l'imaginaire de l'imagination.[23]
>
> [If cinema can figure the work of the imaginary, it is not by giving rise to absent images, but rather because it allows us to read, in the very presence of the image, the aptitude for absence. Extrapolating this remark out of the field of cinema, one can understand the intrusion of the imaginary in the real as the moment in which the default of reality is not due to the lack of the object, but on the contrary its presence, the perception of which would be affected by a coefficient of nullity; unlike Sartrean imagination, in which objects which appear to consciousness are marked by unreality because absent, the imaginary would be characterized as this singular instant, in the affirmed presence of the real, in which the very principle of reality abolishes itself. To discover the image

> in the object, to recover presence in absence — such would be the factor which distinguishes the imaginary from the imagination.]

This sense of the imaginary being bound up with the real will be a recurring idea as we proceed.

It is thus that for Blanchot it is not only things qua discrete, useful objects that can 'founder', but as it were things in general, things themselves, things as such: 'si nous fixons un visage, un coin de mur, ne nous arrive-t-il pas aussi de nous abandonner à ce que nous voyons [...]? Il est vrai, mais c'est qu'alors la chose que nous fixons s'est effondrée dans son image' (*EL* 267) ('if we fix upon a face, the corner of a wall — does it not also sometimes happen that we abandon ourselves to what we see [...]? Indeed, this can happen, but it happens because the thing we stare at has foundered, sunk into its image', *SL* 255). As we saw above, objects are said to appear when they abandon themselves to resemblance. Taking these lines together, the image seems to involve a notion of *abandonment*. In both cases it is a passive, reflexive abandonment, but in one case on the part of objects ('s'abandonner à la pure et simple ressemblance') and in the other on the part of the observer ('nous abandonner à ce que nous voyons'). Furthermore, this latter example establishes a connection between appearance and seeing: the image is at least in some sense visible. It is both as abandoned that it can be seen and we are able to see it if we abandon ourselves. These phrasings bring out both sides of *relation* that one can have with the image: the image is both a property of things and something like a disposition on the part of the viewer. With the apparently arbitrary examples of the face and the wall, it might also be conceived that Blanchot is extending the notion of use to all things, such that anything can become image. Considering how far this idea extends, it should be remembered that use also implies the notions of value, sign, truth, reality — all of the aspects we saw above to be opposed to the image. Blanchot goes on to write: 'Dans l'image, l'objet effleure à nouveau quelque chose qu'il avait maîtrisé pour être objet, contre quoi il s'était édifié et défini' (*EL* 268) ('In the image, the object again grazes something which it had dominated in order to be an object — something counter to which it had defined and built itself up', *SL* 256). This would in a sense be to extend the Heideggerian use to encompass all that can be an object for consciousness — to all that can be understood as contained in the world. Thus the object turned image has its meaning suspended and 'le monde l'abandonne au désœuvrement' (*EL* 268) ('the world abandons it to idleness', *SL* 256). Strictly speaking, the object ceases to be a thing in the world for me. The logical conclusion of this motif of abandonment is not just that the world abandons things to their idleness, but the world as such is abandoned and rendered idle or imaginary. When this happens, 'l'élémentaire le revendique' (*EL* 268) ('materiality, the elemental, reclaims it', *SL* 256). The image in this way is *unearthly*.

There are several points to be drawn from this. This elemental materiality refers to the substratum of being that Levinas calls the 'il y a'. This is 'underneath' the world. Blanchot defines this in a footnote to 'La Littérature et le droit à la mort', referring to it as:

> ce courant anonyme et impersonnel de l'être qui précède tout être, l'être qui au sein de la disparition est déjà présent, qui au fond de l'anéantissement retourne encore à l'être, l'être comme la fatalité de l'être, le néant comme l'existence: quand il n'y a rien, *il y a* de l'être. (*PF* 320)
>
> [this anonymous and impersonal flow of being that precedes all being, being that is already present in the heart of disappearance, that in the depths of annihilation still returns to being, being as the fatality of being, nothingness as existence: when there is nothing, *il y a* being.] (*WF* 332)[24]

When the thing becomes image, we are in a milieu:

> où l'image, d'allusion à une figure, devient allusion à ce qui est sans figure et, de forme dessinée sur l'absence, devient l'informe présence de cette absence, l'ouverture opaque et vide sur ce qui est quand il n'y a plus de monde, quand il n'y a pas encore de monde. (*EL* 25)
>
> [where the image, instead of alluding to some particular feature, becomes an allusion to the featureless, and instead of a form drawn upon absence, becomes the formless presence of this absence, the opaque, empty opening onto that which is when there is no more world, when there is no world yet.] (*SL* 33)

This is the intimate relation of the work of art with the fundament of being that is close to nothingness. When the world abandons itself, this is what is left. It is what 'there is' when there is nothing. Later texts, especially *L'Entretien infini*, develop the Levinasian aspect. In a text on Gaston Bachelard, 'Vaste comme la nuit' [Vast as the Night] (1959), Blanchot states that the words image, imaginary, and imagination:

> ne désignent pas seulement l'aptitude aux phantasmes intérieurs, mais l'accès à la réalité propre de l'irréel (à ce qu'il y a en celui-ci de non-affirmation illimitée, d'infinie position dans son exigence négative) et en même temps la mesure recréante et renouvelante du réel qu'est l'ouverture de l'irréalité. (*EI* 476–77)
>
> [not only an aptitude for interior phantasms, but also access to the proper reality of the unreal (its unlimited non-affirmation, the infinite position of its negative exigency) and, at the same time, the recreative and renewing measure of the real, which is the opening of unreality.] (*IC* 325)

The double aspect replicates the dual structure of the image already indicated. This is very dense and at times even apparently oxymoronic (how can there be a reality of the unreal?), but for now the crucial aspect here is the link of the image and imaginary to unreality. Later examples will show that the *il y a* — a notion originating in the 1940s — is a persistent figure and always implicit in discussions of the image.

One crucial consequence to observe in the above lines is that this zone of the imaginary is said to *precede* being. If it was not already implicit, at this point it becomes clear that Blanchot's theory of the image entails an ontological argument. Blanchot's conception of the image is thus one that reverses the secondary nature of the image (the original necessarily anterior to the copy), a philosophical standard going back to Plato. The image, it is important to note, is not the object's double, but 'le dédoublement initial qui permet ensuite à la chose d'être figurée' (*EI* 42) ('the initial division that then permits the thing to be figured', IC 30). As Ropars-Wuilleumier writes, the image is borne of a gaze cast upon the object which 's'insinue au cœur de l'objet' [insinuates itself into the heart of the object].[25] The most important point to make is that, for Blanchot, when a thing appears or an event takes place before us, it appears *both as itself and as an image of itself.* There is always something like an 'originary doubling'. This indicates, as in Levinas, a fundamental split in being. We must be wary of elevating this 'originary' aspect to an idealism or essence that is behind phenomenal reality — it should rather tell us something *of* phenomenal reality. As such it does not mean that we cannot tell the difference between the image and the object (a strict distinction in classical thought), rather that the object itself is never as stable as it might at first seem. In a strong articulation of this theme, Blanchot writes that the image in this way stands for the absence of origin as such (A 205; F 180). This would be the sense of the following line: 'L'image, présente derrière chaque chose et comme la dissolution de cette chose et sa subsistence dans sa dissolution, a aussi, derrière elle, ce lourde sommeil du trépas dans lequel il nous viendrait des songes' (EL 267) ('The image, present behind each thing, and which is like the dissolution of this thing and its subsistence in its dissolution, also has behind it that heavy sleep of death in which dreams threaten', SL 255). In Zarader's gloss, 'l'image est *l'autre côté* des choses: ce qui, de la chose, résiste à sa constitution en chose' [the image is the *other side* of things: that which, in the thing, resists its constitution as a thing]; this looks back to the idea that objects need to build themselves up against something in order to properly 'be', and which returns in the image.[26] Georges Didi-Huberman writes: 'L'image n'est donc pas l'autre du neutre. Plutôt son *antre*, dans *l'entre* de la chose et du néant' [The image is thus not the other of the neuter, rather its *lair*, in *between* the thing and nothingness]. He writes too that Blanchot found in Sartre and in Bachelard the elements of a re-evaluation of the imaginary as a concept and in Rilke and Kafka 'la mise en pratique — la mise en texte — de cette "ouverture opaque" qui caractérise, selon lui, une image *au sens fort*' [the putting into practice — putting into text — of this 'opaque opening' which characterizes, according to him, an image *in the strong sense*].[27] This notion of a 'strong sense' in which the term 'image' can be taken is important. The key terms in Blanchot's conceptual vocabulary — such as 'image', 'passivity', 'other' — tend to be terms which have a familiar and commonplace meaning, but whose use by Blanchot implies a specialized usage. They are also frequently terms that, in their common usage, form one part of an opposition, but in the specialized usage step outside of or erase that opposition. The 'autre nuit' [other night] is a good example, being neither the day in its association with action nor the night of rest, but the agitated, insomniac night of the *il y a*.

The reason it is important to state this idea of a strong sense is that Blanchot's terms are liable to be appropriated in a *weak sense*, not far departed from their familiar meaning, rather than in a *strong sense*, fully implying the erasure of that familiar meaning. This is key to appreciating the difficulty of Blanchot's writing. When Blanchot writes that what Narcissus sees is not his own reflection but an *image*, and the characteristic of the image is that it 'ne ressembler à rien' (ED 192) ('resembles nothing', *WD* 125), this can be taken in a strong sense as well: nothing qua nothingness. This slippage is one that can be found in Blanchot's writing style itself, in which a term may be introduced according to its familiar meaning, and over the course of the text's tergiversations be redefined and re-presented with its familiar meaning erased. 'Les Deux Versions de l'imaginaire' is a case in point. In this way we can see appearing at the level of the surface of the writing the work of erasure described by that writing. At the same time as Blanchot's terms have strong senses and undergo the play of erasure in their deployment, it should also be noted that their sheer number and multiplication works to oppose the sedimentation of terms into concepts and the erection of shibboleths, as per much of post-war French deconstructive philosophy.

So, just as there are two relations in thought — totalizing and discontinuous — and two slopes of literature, there would a fortiori also be two versions of the imaginary. This duplicity, says Blanchot, is a result of the 'double sens initial qu'apporte avec soi la puissance du négatif et ce fait que la mort est tantôt le travail de la vérité dans le monde, tantôt la perpétuité de ce qui ne supporte ni commencement ni fin' (*EL* 274) ('the initial double meaning which the power of the negative brings with it and from the fact that death is sometimes the work of truth in the world and sometimes the perpetuity of that which admits neither beginning nor end', *SL* 261, translation modified). These parallels — the two relations, the two slopes, the two versions of the imaginary — all suggest the overall coherence of Blanchot's thought as always orbiting around a relation to death. Given this, it is perhaps only logical that Blanchot's exemplar of the imaginary is the 'ressemblance cadavérique' ('cadaverous resemblance'), the uncanny moment in which 'le défunt regretté commence à *ressembler à lui-même*' (*EL* 270) ('the mourned deceased begins to *resemble himself*', *SL* 257).

The relation that one has with the image is what Blanchot calls 'fascination'. It is essentially opposed to comprehension. A relatively clear statement of fascination can be found thus:

> Vivre un événement en image, ce n'est pas se dégager de cet événement, s'en désintéresser, comme le voudraient la version esthétique de l'image et l'idéal serein de l'art classique, mais ce n'est non plus s'y engager par une décision libre: c'est s'y laisser prendre, passer de la région du réel, où nous nous tenons à distance des choses pour mieux en disposer, à cette autre région où la distance nous tient, cette distance qui est alors profondeur non vivante, indisponible, lointain inappréciable devenu comme la puissance souveraine et dernière des choses. Ce mouvement implique des degrés infinis. (*EL* 274)

> [To live an event as an image is not to remain uninvolved, to regard the event disinterestedly in the way that the esthetic version of the image and the serene ideal of classical art propose. But neither is it to take part freely and decisively. It is to be taken: to pass from the region of the real where we hold ourselves at a distance from things the better to order and use them into that other region where the distance holds us — the distance which then is the lifeless deep, an unmanageable, inappreciable remoteness which has become something like the sovereign power behind all things. This movement implies infinite degrees.] (*SL* 261)

These important lines summarize several of the ideas outlined above. They describe the passage from the first version of the imaginary to the second. They also draw attention to the essential aspect of *passivity* in fascination, according to which we are held by the fascinating object. In a realm in which the real and image lose their distinction, the 'I' also loses itself. In engendering passivity, it will be argued by the same token in Chapter 4 that the Levinasian *visage* is structurally similar to the image in Blanchot. Blanchot will later write that, if Narcissus falls in love with the image, it is because the image 'est attirante, attrait du vide même et de la mort en son leurre' (*ED* 193) ('exerts the attraction of the void, and of death in its falsity', *WD* 125). According to Kevin Hart's analysis of fascination, there is first an active approach to art in which one tries to decipher what it means. Then there is a passive relation, in which one learns from it. And finally one is in a state of fascination, when it is no longer experience. Citing the example of watching a DVD, Hart writes that this is not an experience, rather an experience of non-experience in that one is utterly passive, 'vanish[ing] into images that appear only to have no use at all'.[28]

Though it is not directly connected to his analysis of the tool, or by extension to the experience of images, Heidegger's own use of the idea of fascination (Heidegger's translators Macquarrie and Robinson's rendering of *Benommenheit*) is yet relevant. Heidegger writes of Dasein 'losing itself' in the world and becoming fascinated. This 'inauthenticity' is the case for Dasein most of the time. Inauthenticity means 'a quite distinctive kind of Being-in-the-world — the kind which is completely fascinated by the "world" and by the Dasein-with of Others in the "they"'.[29] However, fascination carries the possibility of a break with itself. In anxiety, Heidegger writes:

> Dasein is taken all the way back to its naked uncanniness, and becomes fascinated by it. This fascination, however, not only *takes* Dasein back from its '*worldly*' possibilities, but at the same time *gives* it the possibility of an *authentic* potentiality-for-Being.[30]

So for Heidegger fascination names a mystification that is inauthentic (the German carries the sense of being dazed or confused, while the French, like the English, etymologically relates more closely to bewitchment), like Dasein's engrossment or absorption in 'idle talk'. It can nevertheless, in the unusual case of anxiety, lead to a more profound way of Being. Anxiety is remarkable in that it makes clear one's existential situation — '*That in the face of which one has anxiety is Being-in-the-world as such*' — and therefore can bring out the Being of Dasein as that of Being-possible or, more simply, free.[31]

The experience of the Outside in fascination bears some relation to experience of *Angst*. Certainly some of the formulations are very similar:

> That in the face of which one is anxious is completely indefinite [...] [it] is characterized by the fact that what threatens is *nowhere* [...] it is so close that it is oppressive and stifles one's breath, and yet it is nowhere.[32]

(We might note how Irène found the atmosphere in the cinema to be suffocating.) But what activates anxiety for Blanchot (and it is perhaps doubtful that 'anxiety' is the correct word) is not Being-in-the-world as such but the intrusion of the Outside. The world itself is capable of being abandoned. 'Si, parmi tous les mots, il y a un mot inauthentique, c'est bien le mot "authentique"' (*ED* 98) ('If there is, among all words, one that is inauthentic, then surely it is the word "'authentic'", *WD* 60). There is for Blanchot no 'authentic' Being to which we might awaken ourselves. It is therefore that, although he does not phrase it as such, there is for Blanchot something akin to two versions of fascination: on the one hand, the inauthentic absorption in idle talk (compare the 'pur bavardage' mentioned above) that Heidegger designates as fascination; and, on the other, the anxious experience of the abandonment of the world in the image which is for Blanchot, unlike Heidegger, still not something that can be called 'authentic'.

By the same token, this will go some way to explaining the difference between Heidegger's and Blanchot's use of the idea of 'they'. 'The They' (*das Man*) in Heidegger refers to the public world and the everyday Others.[33] Blanchot's use of 'on' or the They is not the same as Heidegger's, in which it carries the sense of a social order, but stands for an anonymity related to death. As it is put in a provocative fragment: 'Il y a mort et meurtre (mots que je mets au défi de distinguer sérieusement et qu'il faut cependant séparer); de cette mort et de ce meurtre, c'est un "on" impersonnel, inactif et irresponsable, qui a à répondre' (*ED* 115–16) ('There is death and murder (words which I defy anyone to seriously distinguish and which must nonetheless be separated); but there is no designated or designatable dealer of death. It is an impersonal, inactive, and irresponsible "they" that must answer for this death and this murder', *WD* 71). (The They as plural is an anomaly: in both the French and German it is the third person singular). This fragment in *L'Écriture du désastre* is a key one beginning 'On tue un enfant' [A Child is Being Killed], concerning the impossibility of situating death in time, and clearly the use of the pronoun 'on' in its title likewise makes the identification of death's agent unclear. 'They' are most extensively referred to in *Le Pas au-delà*, and in that text they, whose arrival is anticipated but never seems to come, effectively stand for death. What is important about this is that for Blanchot, fascination is 'fondamentalement liée à la présence neutre, impersonnelle, le On indéterminé, l'immense Quelqu'un sans figure' (*EL* 24) ('fundamentally linked to neutral, impersonal presence, to the indeterminate They, the immense, faceless Someone', *SL* 33). Fascination is developed by Blanchot as a concept drawing on both the everyday fascination that Heidegger writes of and the *Angst* that offers a way out of it, so as to posit a new reading in which there is still an everyday absorption; but this can be disturbed by Blanchotian fascination in which things become image, others become 'They' and death becomes impossibility. In this fascination the world is abandoned and the subject is held at a distance, an image which is like an impersonal presence or Other.

A further point to be made on the philosophical status of fascination concerns Kant. At the end of his study on Kant, and in particular Kant's style, *Le Discours de la syncope* [The Discourse of the Syncope] (1976), Nancy describes Blanchot as 'le plus rigoureux commentateur de Kant' ('Kant's most rigorous commentator').[34] Nancy quotes from a short essay on Maurice Merleau-Ponty in which Blanchot writes that '[l]e discours philosophique toujours se perd à un certain moment: il n'est peut-être même qu'une manière inexorable de perdre et de se perdre' ('Philosophical discourse always gets lost at a certain point; perhaps it is even nothing but an inexorable way of losing and of losing oneself').[35] As Hill notes, this is a surprising remark given that Blanchot 'hardly ever mentions Kant'.[36]

While the relation between Kant and Blanchot may not be immediately clear, Kant has been a point of reference for discussions of the concept of the imaginary in Blanchot. In the first book-length study of Blanchot, Françoise Collin writes that Blanchot's thought invites us to reflect on Kant's remarks on the irreducibility of the aesthetic Idea to the concept in the *Critique of Judgement* (1790).[37] This would lead us to think that the image entails a relation which is qualitatively different from that of knowledge. More recently, Ian Maclachlan has tantalizingly suggested that, despite appearances to the contrary, a 'reworked version' of the Romantic concept of imagination may be helpful in thinking about what Blanchot understands by the related terms of image and imaginary, even if 'imagination' is a word Blanchot tends to eschew.[38] While drawing on Blanchot's early essays on William Blake, Maclachlan looks to Kant for a sense of this reworking: not the Kant who discusses aesthetic experience in the *Critique of Judgement*, as Collin suggests, but the Kant of the 'transcendental imagination' of the first edition of the *Critique of Pure Reason* (1781) (A95–130).[39] Kant published two versions of this foundational text. In his famous words in the first version, the imagination is 'a blind but indispensable function of the soul, without which we should have no knowledge whatsoever, but of which we are scarcely ever conscious' (A78/B103). The imagination is 'transcendental' in Kant's terms in that it makes experience possible; in other words, it pertains to 'the mode of our knowledge of objects in so far as this mode of knowledge is to be possible *a priori*' (A11). The imagination is prior to apperception (the fact of 'I think', of my representations being objects of my thought and belonging to my consciousness) and is thus a precondition of all knowledge, including knowledge of being. Maclachlan writes that 'the peculiar priority of the transcendental imagination in relation to sensibility and understanding is such as to endow it with what we might call, after Blanchot, a neutral status'.[40]

As Maclachlan notes, the first edition of the *Critique of Pure Reason*, and in particular the transcendental imagination, is an important reference for Heidegger, providing a basis for seeing finitude as Dasein's fundamental condition.[41] As sensation and understanding (the two forms of knowledge) are underpinned by the imagination, so too the intuition of time is bound up with the transcendental imagination. In Heidegger's reading of Kant, at the heart of knowledge lies a kind of nothing, a transcendental object where the transcendental imagination is no longer a power but represents the very capacity of things to appear (see A108–09 & 250).[42] For Kant, the anterior dimension of experience is that which presents and combines or schematizes thought and intuition into a unity, allowing things to appear and be experienced (A138/B177). Yet it presents 'nothing'. It is a limit that cannot be approached or got back to. As Thomas Carl Wall writes in a suggestive commentary on the later importance of Heidegger's account for Agamben:

> Thought is originally purely exposed, purely presented, purely *there*, and it is 'able' to hold itself just *en deçà du temps*, or *l'entretemps*, prior to its 'work' of figuration. Thought, in short, before it is captured in the world, 'thinks' the place of art, *l'espace littéraire* [...] This 'ability' is a passivity. It is a pure passion.⁴³

This, we might suggest, is the process of 'losing' oneself in philosophy that Blanchot writes of — fascination as a reduction to passivity.

Bernard Stiegler has taken up the question of the transcendental imagination in relation to cinema in the most recent volume of his series *La Technique et le temps* [Technics and Time]. Stiegler is concerned to critique Kant in light of what he considers the tertiary or technical constitution of consciousness. For Stiegler, Kant's unity of consciousness is never fully achieved:

> 'Je' ne suis peut-être pas [...] je ne suis peut-être, comme 'je', qu'une fiction, qu'une projection, qu'une phantasme de moi [...] je me néantise en me faisant du cinéma [...] *je ne cesse de devenir moi-même en tant que milieu rétentionnel de moi-même*'.
>
> ['I' am perhaps *not* [...] I am not, perhaps, an 'I'; but only a fiction, a projection, a phantasm of me [...] I negate myself in making myself cinematic [...] I never cease to become myself as the retentional medium of myself.]⁴⁴

The nothingness or passivity in which the 'je' is lost at the heart of the transcendental imagination lies behind what Stiegler hypothesizes as '*une structure essentiellement cinémato-graphique de la conscience en général*, comme si elle avait "toujours fait du cinéma sans le savoir" — ce qui expliquerait la singulière force de persuasion du cinématographe' ('an *essentially* cinemato-graphic structure for consciousness in general, as if it had 'always had cinema without realizing it' — which explains the singular power of cinemato-graphic persuasion').⁴⁵ The point I would like to make here is that the passivity in the accounts of Heidegger and Stiegler is also that of Blanchot's fascination. As I have shown elsewhere, Stiegler refers to *L'Instant de ma mort* at a key point in his argument that film is both a temporal object (an object that can only exist given a certain time) which can synchronize the time of the spectator's consciousness with the time of film's playing, and a technical object, like photography and writing, which records experience, exteriorizes memory, and is thus 'mnemotechnical'.⁴⁶ If passivity is brought out in cinema, this is also for Stiegler because the 'I think' is itself cinematic. As Stiegler puts it:

> Ce *présavoir* [of the 'instant of death'] qu'il emmène partout avec lui, et en particulier au cinéma, accompagne toutes les représentations cinématographiques comme la réalité effective de son 'Je pense', et ce présavoir qu'il sait de toujours est aussi bien une *réminiscence* (une 'recognition') qu'un *non-savoir*.
>
> [This *pre-knowledge* the spectator carries everywhere, in particular to the cinema; it accompanies every cinematic representation as the effective reality of the 'I think'; it is also just as much a reminiscence (a 'recognition') as a *non-knowledge*.]⁴⁷

What is significant here is that Blanchot's position in relation to debates surrounding the image, though often veiled or merely alluded to, appears both on the side of the subject's interiority (in the imagination) and externally (in the cinema), thus bearing out the two sides of the relation described in 'Les Deux Versions de l'imaginaire'. Stiegler's conception of one's subjective (non-)constitution as essentially cinematic vividly suggests the importance of the category of the image in Blanchotian fascination, which in some sense refers us to a region of the real before the world and before the 'I' — as if the very core of my subjectivity could be figured as a film screening inside an empty cinema.

Fascination and Vision

At this point it becomes necessary to ask about the visibility of the image in fascination. In fascination we are faced with 'vision qui n'est plus possibilité de voir, mais impossibilité de ne pas voir' (*EL* 23) ('vision that is no longer the possibility of seeing, but the impossibility of not seeing', *SL* 32). Drawing on Blanchot's account of the image, what Ropars-Wuilleumier calls 'l'idée d'image' [the idea of the image] is 'le paradoxe constitutif d'une notion qui comporte tous les attributs de l'invisibilité et néanmoins ne sera dite image qu'à condition de demeurer visible' [the constitutive paradox of a notion which comprises all the attributes of invisibility and nevertheless will only be called an image on the condition of remaining visible].[48] Zarader goes as far as to write that 'la fascination soit moins une vision qu'un aveuglement' [fascination is not so much a vision as a blinding].[49] As part of the generalized abandonment it entails, the image in a sense sacrifices visibility, or at least ocular objectivity. On this point the pages of 'Les Deux Versions de l'imaginaire' have to be thought of in conjunction with the text 'Parler, ce n'est pas voir'. In this essay we read that in fascination 'nous sommes peut-être déjà hors du visible-invisible' (*EI* 42) ('we are perhaps already outside the realm of the visible-invisible', *IC* 30). The image holds us at the limit of these two 'domains'. Speech is said in this text to free thought from vision, from an imperialism of the notion of light in the Western metaphysical tradition, vision being essentially bound up with light as the condition of visibility. In this essay, which takes the form of a dialogue between two interlocutors, Blanchot is positing a relation in which thought could escape vision through speech, a relation he seeks to affirm.

This idea of visibility is a question that puts Blanchot much in line with Derrida, and which the latter explores through the figures of the spectre and blindness. Derrida's remarks on the invisibility of the visible, that 'La visibilité n'est pas visible' ('Visibility is not visible'), are in negotiation with Blanchot's suspicion of the means by which light conceals itself while disclosing other entities.[50] It is a question of *clarity*, an idea we have come across in the Introduction, where the word named an effect of Blanchot's writing in which what was described was seemingly both transparent and profoundly opaque. The question of visibility here invokes the dialectics of light and obscurity that Blanchot discusses over the course of the later work, notably in *L'Entretien infini* and *L'Écriture du désastre*. In a commentary on Nietzsche, 'Réflexions sur le nihilisme' [Reflections on Nihilism] (1966–67), Blanchot discusses the 'tromperie' ('deception') of light, which is that, in illumination, light conceals itself. What light illuminates appears as an immediate presence while the light itself 'se dérober en une absence rayonnante' ('slips away in a radiating absence'). It is thus that 'l'œuvre de lumière ne s'accomplit que là où la lumière nous fait oublier que quelque chose comme la lumière est à l'œuvre' (*EI* 244) ('the work of light is accomplished only when light makes us forget that something like light is at work', *IC* 163). This gives us confidence in 'l'acte de voir comme à la simplicité, et nous propose l'immédiation comme le modèle de la connaissance' (*EI* 244) ('the simplicity of the act of seeing, proposing im-mediation to us as the model of knowledge', *IC* 163). Clarity, then, can be defined as 'la non-lumière de la lumière; le non-voir du voir' (*EI* 244) ('the non-light of light, the non-seeing of seeing', *IC* 163). The difference between the accounts of Derrida and Blanchot, which are very close in several respects, lies in this notion of a 'non-lumière', in which Blanchot posits a neutral light, light (as a positive value) turning into a non-light. The different choice of metaphorics — visibility in Derrida, light in Blanchot — may appear to be the same thing described in different terms but in fact reveals subtle distinctions. For Derrida visibility (the possibility or condition of the visible) itself is invisible, giving invisibility a spectral relationship with the visible as its own condition of possibility: the visible 'produirait ainsi d'aveuglement, par émanation, comme s'il secrétait son propre médium' ('by emanation, and as if it were screening its own *medium*, the visible would produce blindness').[51] The possibility of seeing always implies a concomitant impossibility (as it were, the impossibility of seeing seeing) as constitutive of that seeing, such that there is never a pure seeing. In Blanchot, the 'non-lumière' is not the same as this invisibility as condition or possibility of seeing, but rather is as that 'absence rayonnante'. So while in Derrida there is a non-seeing in seeing, in Blanchot there is a seeing in non-seeing: even as light slips away something seems to shine. Clarity is redefined as not so much seeing in a clear light but, in an aporetic formulation, seeing when there is no light. Blanchot writes: 'Le jour est un faux jour' (*EI* 244) ('The day is a false day', *IC* 163, translation modified). This is not because there could be a truer day or a clearer day, but because the light always dissimulates. Thus clarity is bound up with non-seeing and with dissimulation. An aspect of fascination is the way light operates a basic deception. The movement of clarity and obscurity appears to be a mode of fascination. It is thus that, in one of the very few pieces that relate the notion of fascination after Blanchot to cinema, Blanchot's notion of fascination is said to be about 'visualizing obscurity'.[52] This metaphor of luminescence as meaning is one that is alluded to elsewhere by Blanchot. For example, he will write that when we are left with meaninglessness in literature, 'maintenant s'affirme la possibilité même de signifier, le pouvoir vide de donner un sens, étrange lumière impersonnelle' (*PF* 318) ('what asserts itself now is the very possibility of signifying, the empty power of bestowing meaning — a strange impersonal light', *WF* 329). If in fascination we are put into contact with the fundament of being or the *il y a*, it is striking that this is figured as a kind of light.

This metaphor of light and its connection to fascination is perhaps made clearer when considering how Levinas talks of Blanchot's notion of art as a 'noire lumière'. I quote him at length here as this helps to connect several ideas discussed so far:

L'art, d'après Blanchot, loin d'éclairer le monde, laisse apercevoir le sous-sol désolé, fermé à toute lumière qui le sous-tend et rend à notre séjour son essence d'exil et aux merveilles de notre architecture — leur fonction de cabanes dans le désert. Pour Blanchot, comme pour Heidegger, l'art ne conduit pas — contrairement à l'esthétique classique — vers un monde derrière le monde, vers un monde idéal derrière le monde réel. Il est lumière. Lumière d'en-haut pour Heidegger, faisant le monde, fondant le lieu. Noire lumière pour Blanchot, nuit venant d'en-bas, lumière qui défait le monde, le ramenant à son origine, au ressassement, au murmure, au clapotement incessant, à un 'profond jadis, jadis jamais assez'. La recherche poétique de l'irréel est la recherche du fond dernier de ce réel.

[Art, according to Blanchot, far from elucidating the world, exposes the desolate, lightless substratum underlying it, and restores to our sojourn its exotic essence — and, to the wonders of our architecture, their function of makeshift desert shelters. Blanchot and Heidegger agree that art does not lead (contrary to classical esthetics) to a world behind the world, an ideal world behind the real one. Art is light. Light from on high in Heidegger, making the world, founding place. In Blanchot it is a black light, a night coming from below — a light that undoes the world, leading it back to its origin, to the over and over again, the murmur, ceaseless lapping of waves, a 'deep past, never long enough ago'. The poetic quest for the unreal is the quest for the deepest recess of that real.][53]

The Blanchotian function of art here detailed is comparable with our account of the *il y a* above.[54] Clearly what 'there is' under the world is precisely what is referred to by the 'sous-sol désolé' — 'fermé à toute lumière' being an evidently operative idea conveying the paradox of a black light. If what is underneath is a desert and the works that make up the world are, in a penetrating phrase, 'cabanes dans le désert', then the corollary is that to be fascinated by visual works is *to see what there is when there is nothing to see*. It is by the same token that the vocabulary of light as 'fondant le lieu' is consonant with how, as we saw earlier, the image causes things to 's'effondrer', to lose their ground. This idea is present in the word 'défait' above, while the sense of the deepest reality brings back the idea of the 'la réalité propre de l'irréel'.

This makes the image extremely complex to deal with in relation to representations. The motif of blindness might suggest the image's incompatibility with a theory of watching films, an eminently visual exercise. This is not to say that it is qua representation that things become image. We saw above that the initial doubling is what permits figuration. As Ropars-Wuilleumier writes: 'L'image s'oppose à la représentation, mais en s'inscrivant dans la représentation elle-même, voilà sans doute l'apport le plus fondamental de Blanchot à une pensée de l'image qui, par le regard, *affecterait toute vue*' [The image opposes representation, but by inscribing itself within representations; this is without doubt Blanchot's most fundamental contribution to a thinking about the image which, by means of the gaze, *would affect all sight*].[55] As we saw, the world as such can become image: in this it would affect all sight. It is in this way that Zenkine observes that the two senses of the word 'image' become blurred in Blanchot's novels and *récits*: 'la représentation artificielle est perçue avec l'intensité hallucinatoire d'un spectacle réel, et le spectacle effectivement donné est encadré comme un tableau ou une photographie' [the artificial representation is perceived with the hallucinatory intensity of a real spectacle, and the actual spectacle is framed like a painting or a photograph].[56] What I want to stress is that Blanchot's work conceives of the image as the condition of artistic production in general — not simply of writing.

Blanchot follows a genealogy of art in a key section of *L'Espace littéraire*, 'La Littérature et l'expérience originelle' [Literature and the Original Experience] (*EL* 219–60; *SL* 211–47). Here we read that art originally spoke the language of the gods, then of their disappearance, and now, the gods having long since departed, our time is one in which art speaks the language of the disappearance of the disappearance of the gods — that is, of forgetfulness itself. Blanchot is here drawing on the idea of a 'destitute time'. The poet Friedrich Hölderlin asks what *use* are poets in a destitute time, which Heidegger stresses in his essay 'What Are Poets For?' (1946) is 'the era to which we ourselves still belong'.[57] Now, for Blanchot, the destitute time is the time which 'en tout temps, est propre à l'art' (*EL* 259) ('in all times is proper to art', *SL* 246). The paragraph beginning 'L'œuvre qui a été parole des dieux' (*EL* 242) ('The work was once the language of the gods', *SL* 232) is crucial to the understanding of this section, for we see here the situational interplay between the historical and metaphysical arguments. Further, it is this interplay that gestures to how Blanchot brings Hegel into conversation with Heidegger. The paragraph forms a kind of summary of the historical development of Hegel's *Geist* through the figure of the work, with Heidegger's destitute time subsumed. There is however no grand culmination at the end of the dialectic. Blanchot writes on the foregoing page that, from the start, the work is *'le séjour de l'absence des dieux'* (*EL* 242) ('*the abode of the gods' absence*', *SL* 231). Art contains within itself what Blanchot variously refers to as a 'profonde *réserve*' or '*espace*', and this is found in the movement in which 'l'évidence et la dissimulation s'échangent sans arrêt, s'appellent et se saisissent là où pourtant ils ne s'accomplissent que comme l'approche de l'insaisissable' (*EL* 243) ('disclosure and dissimulation change places without cease, appealing and reaching to each other where, nevertheless, they are realized only as the approach of the unreachable', *SL* 233). This is the work's dialectic, which is to say its 'unité déchirée' (*EL* 239) ('torn unity', *SL* 229). Or again, we could find an extreme synecdoche of this entire debate in the formula: the work is 'l'intimité déchirée de sa propre essence' (*EL* 241) ('the torn intimacy of its own essence', *SL* 231), where 'l'intimité déchirée' stands for the ruined dialectic. The absence of the work here makes manifest the unworking of the work of history. It is thus that possibly the clearest statement of Blanchot's reading of Hegel is to be found when he writes of death, as discussed at the beginning of this chapter, that that which founds the dialectic also causes it to halt, falter, and persists as a 'sorte de souvenir' (*ED* 112; *WD* 68). Blanchot frequently dissociates the disaster from the dialectic, writing, for example, that 'rien ne lui soit plus étranger que la dialectique' (*ED* 63) ('nothing is more foreign to it than the dialectic', *WD* 36). Victoria Burke neatly summarizes this point: 'The Outside reconfigures the possibility of Hegelian absolute knowing into a "relation to impossibility"'.[58] The ideas connecting history, ontology, and art here start to coalesce. Fascination is a trace of this 'error' of history. By the same logic, the radical reworking of Hegel's formula 'art is a thing of the past' is found: art is a thing not of the simple historical past, but the immemorial past, the origin, the past of the return which has never been and never comes. The riposte to Heidegger's text 'The Origin of the Work of Art' (1950), with which 'La Littérature et l'expérience originelle' is in constant dialogue, is that art's essence 'est là où le non-vrai n'admet rien d'essentiel [...] elle ruine l'origine, elle la ramène à l'immensité errante de l'éternité dévoyée' (*EL* 256–57) ('lies where the nontrue admits of nothing essential [...] It ruins the origin by returning to it the errant immensity of directionless eternity', *SL* 244).[59] Forgetfulness relates to an origin that was never present, never possible to be remembered, yet is also our relation to the time of history, to the non-contemporaneity of time with itself. Blanchot is making a historical as well as a metaphysical argument, and an important point to draw out from this is that what Blanchot calls fascination is a particular kind of relation one has with art that is not necessarily eternal and true of all times but historical. So while art and our relation to it is always historical, it also relates to that which is outside history. In the context of the argument to come, therefore, film will both be of its historical time and bear a relation to that outside of time.

Blanchot, Film, and the Plastic Arts

Blanchot in his early and mid-period writings discusses visual arts more openly and frequently than he does in his later work. When he does, he often relates the plastic arts to writing according to a certain conceptual synaesthesia. The advantage of the plastic arts over writing, he says, is that they make manifest 'le vide exclusif à l'intérieur duquel elle semble vouloir demeurer, loin des regards' ('the exclusive void within which the work seems to want to dwell, far from every gaze'). He continues:

> Cette séparation décisive, dont la sculpture fait son élément, qui, au centre de l'espace, dispose un autre espace rebelle, un espace dérobé, évident et soustrait, peut-être immuable, peut-être sans repos, cette violence préservée, en face de laquelle nous nous sentons toujours de trop, semble manquer au livre. La statue qu'on déterre et qu'on présente à l'admiration, n'en attend rien, n'en reçoit rien, paraît plutôt arrachée à son lieu. (*EL* 201)

> [The book seems to lack this decisive separation, which sculpture makes its element and which places in the center of space another, rebel space — an inaccessible space both evident and withdrawn, perhaps immutable, perhaps ever restless, the constrained violence in the face of which we always feel in excess. The statue one digs up and presents for the public's admiration does not expect anything from this and does not receive anything; it seems, rather, torn from its place.] (*SL* 192–93)

Blanchot's example here happens to be Auguste Rodin's *Le Baiser* [The Kiss] (1889). Blanchot describes a restlessness and a violence that is both apparent and furtive.[60] Though Blanchot has just mentioned Rodin, with the reference to the unearthing of a statue, he seems to be referring equally to an archaeological object. Blanchot also gives an uncanny emphasis to the agency of the work itself — it seems to have a desire all of its own. The aspect that is under-noted in lines such as these is, in a book called *L'Espace littéraire*, the literal mention of space, as well as the metaphysical notion that Blanchot develops. As Ann Smock notes, the word 'space' is one of the key constants in the book (*SL* 12). The notion conveyed in the title is often taken to refer to the paradox of a space that is nowhere, and this is correct. But while most of the analysis of the book centres on literature, and the space sometimes reads like a metaphorical space in which the writer works and communication takes place, here Blanchot discusses analogically something like a reification of this space in sculpture.

A phrase that recurs in *L'Entretien infini* is the 'espace de l'image' (*EI* 475) ('space of the image', *IC* 324), and this formulation helps us to think the notion of the imaginary that Blanchot writes of in *L'Espace littéraire* as a space or as working by a 'spacing'. Blanchot will thus write elsewhere that images *designate a space* (*EI* 528; *IC* 360). In the text on Bachelard mentioned earlier, Blanchot stresses the sense that Bachelard arrives at 'une région de la phénoménologie la plus pure — une phénoménologie sans phénomènes' (*EI* 475, n. 1) ('a region of the purest sort of phenomenology — phenomenology without phenomena', *IC* 459, n. 6).[61] What Blanchot comes to think here is how fascination seems to open up a kind of space. A sense of this was given in reference to the experience of Irène, in which the actual space of the *salle* gave way to the both extended and distended space of phantasms. It is no surprise that when Deleuze talks of Blanchot in the context of film, it is with reference to 'le vertige de l'espacement' ('the vertigo of spacing'), which relates to the idea of 'la mise en question radicale de l'image' ('the radical calling into question of the image').[62] This vertigo is the unearthly feeling of the abandonment of the world, the abandonment of actual space and the exposure of a different space. We can connect these points to say that 'espacement' in Blanchot's writing of the 1950s names the movement of fascination, which is phenomenologically comparable to vertigo, and is constitutive of an hypostasization of the imaginary. There are therefore two spaces: firstly, physical space, and secondly, a metaphysical spacing. This can be phrased thus: a key dynamic in fascination is that in which the space of a site or location gives way through a spacing to the space of literature or the space of the image.

As with space, the word 'distance' is subject to a doubling — both physical distance conditioning a material relation and another distance that effectively dissolves the reality of that relation. On this point, one sculptor whom Blanchot mentions as paradigmatic is Alberto Giacometti. In a piece entitled 'Traces' (1963), about a book on Giacometti by Jacques Dupin, Blanchot writes that the relation one has with Giacometti's sculptures is one of distance, a distance which 'désigne une relation infinie' (*A* 247) ('designates an infinite relation', *F* 217). Blanchot writes:

> La présence n'est présence qu'à distance, et cette distance est absolue, c'est-à-dire infinie. Le don de Giacometti, celui qu'il nous fait, est d'ouvrir dans l'espace du monde l'intervalle infini à partir duquel il y a présence [...] Oui, Giacometti nous donne cela, il nous attire invisiblement vers ce point, point

unique, où la chose présente (l'objet plastique, la figure figurée) se change en
la pure présence, présence de l'Autre en son étrangeté, c'est-à-dire aussi bien
radicale non-présence. Cette distance (le vide, dit Jacques Dupin) n'est en rien
distincte de la présence à laquelle elle appartient [...] l'on pourrait dire que ce
que Giacometti sculpte, c'est la Distance, nous la livrant et nous livrant à elle,
distance mouvante et rigide, menaçante et accueillante, tolérante-intolérante,
et telle qu'elle nous est donnée chaque fois pour toujours et chaque fois s'abîme
en un instant: distance qui est la profondeur même de la présence, laquelle
étant toute manifeste, réduite à sa surface, semble sans intériorité, pourtant
inviolable, parce que identique à l'infini du Dehors. (*A* 248)

[Presence is only presence at a distance, and this distance is absolute — that
is, irreducible; that is, infinite. The gift of Giacometti, the one he makes us,
is to open, in the space of the world, the infinite interval from which there is
presence [...] Yes, Giacometti gives us this, he draws us invisibly towards this
point, a single point at which the present thing (the plastic object, the figured
figure) changes into pure presence, the presence of the Other in its strangeness,
that is to say, also radical non-presence. This distance (the void, says Jacques
Dupin) is in no way distinct from the presence to which it belongs [...] one
could say that what Giacometti sculpts is Distance, surrendering it to us and
us to it, a moving and rigid distance, threatening and welcoming, tolerant-
intolerant, and such that it is given to us each time forever and each time is
swallowed up in an instant: a distance that is the very depth of presence, which,
being completely manifest, reduced to its surface, seems without interiority, yet
inviolable, because identical to the infinite of the Outside.] (*F* 218–19)

Distance is clearly not simply physical distance, presence is not what is physically
present. Presence comes from an infinite interval, and it is to this extent that the
sculptures are 'dons'. At the same time as the reference to the Other anticipates
Blanchot's later, more heavily Levinas-inflected lexicon (to which I will return
in Chapter 4), the example of sculptures of figures makes this idea of an Other
very vivid here: the Other has a concrete form and recognizability. This passage
is a fully expanded explication of the idea that fascination is 'quand voir est un
contact à distance' (*EL* 23) ('when seeing is *contact* at a distance', *SL* 32); again, 'la
fascination se produit, lorsque, loin de saisir à distance, nous sommes saisis par la
distance, investis par elle' (*EI* 41) ('fascination arises when, far from apprehending
from a distance, we are apprehended by this distance, invested by it and invested
with it', *IC* 30). This reversibility brings out the idea that the work of art can be
the place of an encounter. Martin Crowley has highlighted the interpenetration of
the motifs of distance and contact in Blanchot's work, writing: 'Le toucher devient
le propre du voir, l'éloignement l'essence de la proximité' [touching becomes the
characteristic of seeing, and remoteness the essence of proximity].[63] This is the
sense of the capitalized 'Distance' as both something surrendered to us and us to
it; in other words, both sides of the relation of the image are in play. This is not,
however, to say that the image itself can be touched. One characteristic of the
image is its irrefrangibility. As Wall writes: 'I can dismantle the temple, build a
road with the marble, but I cannot dismantle the *image* the temple eminently *is*. I
can cast the celluloid into the fire but I cannot manipulate the motion picture *itself*.

I cannot even touch it'.[64] It is for this reason that Blanchot writes that the image is 'incorruptible' (*ED* 196; *WD* 128).

In *Écrire l'espace* (2002), Ropars-Wuilleumier asks why it is that literature is connected to space in Blanchot and tries to think how the literary space can be thought as a mode of access to works of art.[65] Her book seeks to find 'dans et par l'écriture, l'invention d'un mode paradoxal dans lequel l'espace, devenant "vertige de l'espacement", serait perçu selon sa contradiction essentielle' [in and through writing, the invention of a paradoxical mode in which space, becoming the 'vertigo of spacing', would be sensed in its essential contradiction].[66] Here she highlights that space is both an abstraction and a means by which actual, physical domains can be measured and specified. Space is not the same as place, but rather space is activated within a relation to place and its laws of orientation. There is always a subject in space observing it who can be exposed to this contradiction or discontinuity of space.[67] This can be testified to in writing and, referring to texts by Blanchot and Kafka, including *L'Instant de ma mort*, Ropars-Wuilleumier writes that they are haunted by 'la loi d'extériorité' [the law of exteriority] leading not only to the default of time (as previously discussed in reference to the problem of the instant), but also 'l'espacement du lieu' [spacing of place].[68] This phenomenon of 'espacement' is her real concern and can be rephrased in terms of the following question: what is it that happens when place seems to become estranged from itself?

Giacometti is in many ways an exemplary figure for Blanchot.[69] He is given a crucial place when Blanchot comes close to a definition of what it means to write:

> Quand nous regardons les sculptures de Giacometti, il y a un point d'où elles ne sont plus soumises aux fluctuations de l'apparence, ni au mouvement de la perspective. On les voit absolument: non plus réduites, mais soustraites à la réduction, irréductibles et, dans l'espace, maîtresses de l'espace par le pouvoir qu'elles ont d'y substituer la profondeur non maniable, non vivante, celle de l'imaginaire. Ce point, d'où nous les voyons irréductibles, nous met nous-mêmes à l'infini, est le point où ici coïncide avec nulle part. Écrire, c'est trouver ce point. Personne n'écrit, qui n'a rendu le langage propre à maintenir ou à susciter contact avec ce point. (*EL* 41)

> [When we look at the sculptures of Giacometti, there is a vantage point where they are no longer subject to the fluctuations of appearance or to the movement of perspective. One sees them absolutely: no longer reduced, but withdrawn from reduction, irreducible, and, in space, masters of space through their power to substitute for space the unmalleable, lifeless profundity of the imaginary. This point, whence we see them irreducible, puts us at the vanishing point ourselves; it is the point at which here coincides with nowhere. To write is to find this point. No one writes who has not enabled language to maintain or provoke contact with this point.] (*SL* 48)

This quotation is close to the one above, in which Giacometti draws us towards a point at which the thing turns into the presence of the Other. In this second quotation, Blanchot is describing the sculptures from this point. Is this a vantage point we can adopt? Reduction here signifies the phenomenological reduction, so the suggestion is that this is outwith ordinary phenomenological understanding.

The result is the opening of the space of the image where here meets nowhere. The idea of spacing is wonderfully reified above in the description of these sculptures as 'maîtresses de l'espace', capturing at once their actual dimensionality as well as their affective charge. Ropars-Wuilleumier stresses the idea that the space of art does not work according to an ordinary phenomenological understanding, in which one might spatially apprehend the approach of being. On the contrary, the more one tries to approach and penetrate it, the more it turns into non-being. Being itself seems to Giacometti to be transparent.[70] As he says: 'Si je vois une tête de très loin, j'ai l'idée d'une sphère. Si je la vois de très près elle cesse d'être une sphère pour devenir une complication extrême en profondeur' [If I see a head from very far away, I have the idea of a sphere. If I see it very close it ceases to be a sphere and becomes an extremely deep and complex problem].[71] It is therefore that one has to *create* space. This is one way in which one can understand the sense of the sculptures being masters of space: the sense of the transparency of being is brought out through the creation of space. Thus for Ropars-Wuilleumier, the space invented by Giacometti is 'Mobile, et cependant arrêté, multidirectionnel parce que sans unité centrale' [Mobile, and yet halted, multidirectional because without central unity]; it 'soustrait la forme à la possibilité d'une perception achevée' [takes form away from the possibility of a completed perception].[72] She writes that 'des œuvres figuratives peuvent rendre sensible l'espace, mais en cela précisément qu'il ne se résout pas à la figure' [figurative works of art can make space manifest, but precisely in the sense that space itself does not consist in a figure].[73] They always depend on an abstraction. If phenomenology deals with the objects that can be objects for a representing consciousness, and the 'object' of art is this impossible point — if it, as Simon Critchley writes of Blanchot's account of dying, exceeds 'the noetico-noematic correlative structures of phenomenology' — then the approach to art indicated here is not strictly phenomenological but 'meta-phenomenological'.[74] The object opens an attraction, but it cannot strictly be 'experienced'. Experience always means contact with being, even if it is non-being. Blanchot is not so often approached for his analyses of 'non-/experiences', or if he is it is typically with direct reference to literature. By such experiences or states I am referring to, for example, the reading of suicide in *L'Espace littéraire*, waiting in *L'Attente l'oubli* [Awaiting Oblivion] (1962), the encounter with the Other in *L'Entretien infini*. There is sometimes a sense in which the crucial moments for Blanchot are the moments, in an ordinary vocabulary, in which we stop paying attention, are tired, bored, and lose focus. There is a faintness bordering on ecstasy reminiscent of illness. It might also be argued that these states are inseparably related to the aesthetic experience. With the space of the image, Blanchot is not writing about a space outside of all time and space, but rather suggesting the possibility of a dislocation from the space we make use of in day-to-day life. There is a strong sense of dissociation and isolation in Blanchotian spacing. Writing puts one at this vanishing point within oneself. So when Blanchot writes of the possibility of living an event as an image, he is writing about a capacity inherent to our relation to the real itself and which is perhaps the defining mode of that relation. Blanchot writes: 'Le "réel" est ce avec quoi notre relation est toujours vivante' (*EL* 267) ('The "real" is that with which our relationship is always alive', *SHB* 418).[75] The logic of this is that the importance of art lies in bringing this out. While the thinking of space by way of Ropars-Wuilleumier is useful in thinking about space as an aspect of the visible and therefore visibility as such, subsequent chapters will show, as Ropars-Wuilleumier does, how Blanchot's literary space can help us to think through space in film. Our search will be to find the vantage point discussed above when dealing with film.

In *L'Évidence du film* [The Evidence of Film] (2001), Jean-Luc Nancy seems to evoke something of this 'point'. Nancy uses as his key example the work of Abbas Kiarostami. Just over halfway through his text he contends that 'le regard cinématographique devient une condition bien plutôt qu'une représentation' ('the cinematographic gaze becomes a condition much more than a representation'). Describing 'la forme d'un certain regard' ('the form of a certain look') that characters have in Kiarostami's films and how this look is varied with that looked at, he posits an 'invariant' behind all of the motion of the film such that 'l'immobilité photographique est-elle le véritable moteur du cinéma' ('the true motor of cinema is photographic immobility'). Nancy adds a footnote on this point, suggesting the presence of this 'affirmation' in the work of other contemporary filmmakers, thinking of *Beau Travail* (1999) by Claire Denis and *Yi Yi* (2000) by Edward Yang. Nancy writes:

> Chaque fois il s'agit d'un cinéma qui ouvre sur sa propre image comme sur un réel — ou sur un sens — que l'image seule peut aller prendre, et qu'elle prend depuis une visée au-delà de tout 'point de vue', depuis un regard dépourvu de subjectivité, depuis un objectif qui viserait la vie depuis le secret de la mort comme secret d'une évidence.

> [In each instance one deals with a cinema opening onto its own image as onto something real — or meaningful — that can only be taken by images, aiming from somewhere beyond any 'point of view,' with a look devoid of subjectivity, with a lens that would aim for life from the vantage point of the secret of death as the secret of something evident.][76]

Between the translation and the original we can see the essential ambiguity at work between the singular image as concept and the multiple, actual images of a film. The image as something film can open onto is paralleled with 'un réel' and 'un sens' as that which cinema can also open onto. The antecedent of that which can only be 'taken' by the image (or images) is that real or sense. That image must come from a paradoxical *visée* or 'sight' that is not a 'point de vue', which suggests it is something like a view or vantage point without a location. *Visée* here carries the sense of a viewfinder in a camera or a position behind a lens. This impersonal locus is like the place of the 'le secret de la mort': a poetic formula that, coming towards the end of a complex sentence, evokes the vanishing or un-locatable nature of the point itself. As in Blanchot's writing, death is that which suspends the relation to place. The sentence ends on the notion of 'évidence'. As Ian James shows more generally of *L'Évidence du film*, Nancy 'uses the term evidence in order to maintain an insistence upon the presentation of an image as a relation to worldly existence'.[77]

In other words, evidence is to be understood in the sense of that which is manifest, even as Nancy explores the way in which it conceals something in reserve. Thus, Nancy writes elsewhere: 'L'image est l'évidence de l'invisible' ('The image is the obviousness of the invisible').[78] The way the sentence quoted above winds from the cinema and its image through the viewpoint to death and its secret considered as the secret of the evident as such brings out the idea that what is hidden is hidden in plain sight. (One might compare the line quoted from Blanchot above, which stated that the space of art's reserve is found in the movement in which 'l'évidence et la dissimulation s'échangent sans arrêt' (*EL* 243; *SL* 233).) It is appropriate that the *visée* suggests the viewfinder of a camera as this was an idea touched upon in relation to Derrida's metaphor of the movie camera — this hiding in plain sight is another statement of the problem of *clarity*, of the capacity of that which is apparently transparent to maintain an opacity. This implies the whole question of this study, the problem of the image as such. Nancy writes: 'Il ne s'agit pas de la fascination de l'image: il s'agit de l'image en tant qu'elle ouvre sur le réel et en tant qu'elle seule ouvre sur lui. La réalité de l'image est l'accès au réel *même*' ('This is not about the fascination of images: it is about images insofar as they open onto what is real and insofar as they alone open onto it. The reality of images is the access to the real *itself*').[79] Again, the use of the singular 'image' in each case in the original strengthens the abstract import of the thought. Without necessarily reading into this an allusion to Blanchotian fascination, this statement effectively reframes the question from the Nancean perspective of finitude (Blanchot does not often speak of 'le réel'). At the same time, it cannot help but evoke Blanchot's earlier problematic of the image, which as we have seen, in a strikingly similar phrasing, gives 'l'accès à la réalité propre de l'irréel'. The image is a relation with the real — however defined — and it is a relation which takes the form of a seemingly impossible 'point'. It is a potentiality that inheres in the world and in art yet which opens a metaphysical relation, which is figured as a vantage point without a place. What is crucial is that while this vantage point was said by Blanchot to be opened by Giacometti's sculptures, in Nancy's more recent account of the point it is not only opened by cinema but that point itself is actually figured through the imagery of film technology, namely the camera. Like the passivity at the core of Stieglerian cinematic consciousness, Blanchot seems to stand as a concealed presence within Nancy's account of cinema, which is also an account of a relation to the world. Nancy's footnote in this way bears out my argument that cinema can offer a way of thinking the Blanchotian image today, where the image is both a mode of relation with and constitutive of the world. Whether or not Nancy has in mind Blanchot's 'point', it clearly persists in French philosophical writing on art — and it appears to have migrated to a new home in film.

Fascination and Analysis: 'Primal Scenes'?

One of the few texts that explicitly invokes Blanchot in relation to film theory is Steven Shaviro's *The Cinematic Body* (1993), a book in fact better known for its use of

Deleuze. Shaviro writes that 'Blanchot is not writing specifically about cinema, but his description [of the image] powerfully evokes what actually happens when I am sitting in a dark room, confronted by a parade of images moving across a screen'.[80] This association with darkness has been a suggestive connection for scholars looking to connect Blanchot to cinema, such as Oliver Harris; as Harris puts it, Blanchot's philosophy is 'fundamentally nocturnal'.[81] Shaviro refers to Blanchot to argue, expressly contra Lacanian psychoanalysis and Lacanian film theory, that the visual order is not dependent on the order of the signifier. Shaviro observes that the nontruth of the Blanchotian image is defined by its radical disjunction from language, consisting of a 'resemblance that has nothing to resemble'.[82] Shaviro also appreciates the way the image engenders a disruption of intentionality and the metaphysics of presence, much as we have discussed above. He draws out how fascination disrupts the relation in which seeing can be understood as an initiative and a power of the subject and causes the distance between subject and object to disappear.[83] For Shaviro, this contradicts the film-theoretical notions of scopophilia and voyeurism and can be understood in opposition to them as 'passion for the image' and as 'radical passivity'.[84]

As suggestive as it is, the problem with Shaviro's account is that it occludes the extent to which passivity does in fact have psychoanalytic associations for Blanchot, in addition to the phenomenological ones already discussed. Passivity as a notion is in danger of being understood too much according to its dictionary definition and not enough with these more specific associations. Shaviro is persuasive when he writes that, although much film theory has been concerned with the notion of the cinematic image as characterized by *lack* — the loss of, quoting Kaja Silverman, 'the absent real and the foreclosed site of production' — in fact the problem for the cinematic spectator, according to Shaviro, is that the object is *never quite lost enough*.[85] On this point he quotes Blanchot's comparison between the image and the cadaver. The image is not a substitute (the re-presentation of an object) but 'the material trace or residue of the object's failure to vanish completely'.[86]

Shaviro argues apropos of the films of Andy Warhol that such images as found in those films are perfect traces of a 'real' understood in a Blanchotian sense. This would be to say that, rather than marking a Bazinian transference of reality from the object to the representation, the real is in fact '*altered* by the very fact of passive, literal reproduction — of what could better be called hypermimetic simulation'.[87] Simulation is here understood in the Deleuzian/Guattarian sense, in which the real itself is said to be actually produced by simulation; but Shaviro also alludes to the notion of 'dissimulation' in 'Les Deux Versions de l'imaginaire': the originary split in being, before representation, discussed earlier in this chapter. Shaviro draws from this that we cannot speak of lack with images, for they make no reference to an anterior presence that has been lost. Shaviro writes:

> [Images] have always already subtracted themselves from the psychoanalytic narrative of traumatic separation, disavowal, phobic projection, and compensatory, fetishistic reconstruction. *Visual fascination is thus a precondition for the cinematic construction of subjectivity, and not a consequence of it.* It is not the gaze that demands images, but images that solicit and sustain — while remaining indifferent to — the gaze.[88]

Shaviro here draws out a crucial consequence of Blanchot's account of the image. The image is already present in things, rather than simply being given in films; in this way we could say that the image is re-opened and *perpetuated* by film. There is a certain logic in which it makes sense to speak less of the images in film than it does to say that, in film, the world becomes image. These lines also point to how the relationship of cinematic subjectivity to fascination may be one in which the former is a version of the latter, rather than the latter as an effect of the former.

Shaviro's central claim here is sound, but in his zeal to counter the Lacanians and to find in Blanchot a counter model to the perceived predominance of psychoanalysis he perhaps eschews the extent to which Blanchot himself in fact thinks the notions of image, fascination, and passivity through a certain strand of psychoanalysis. A key text on this subject is 'La Parole analytique' [The Speech of Analysis] (1956) in *L'Entretien infini*. Blanchot says there that the 'force' of analysis consists in the way it dissolves everything into 'une antériorité indéfinie' ('an indefinite anteriority'). The 'substance' of analysis consists less in the ancient conflicts sought in truth or imagination, or even whether they took place at all, than in the distance to that anteriority. It is this that renders it 'insaisissable comme fait et fascinant comme souvenir' (*EI* 347) ('ungraspable as fact and fascinating as remembrance', *IC* 232). It is really the effect of fascination that Blanchot is interested in. It is also in this way that he observes shortly before this that psychoanalysis originates close to hypnosis, magnetism, and suggestion, which are also characterized in passing by fascination (*EI* 344; *IC* 230). Analysis opens fascination much as the artwork does; fascination is itself a constitutive facet of psychoanalysis, and perhaps, as with cinema, also its precondition. Blanchot will argue somewhat sweepingly that the key contribution of Freud is the dialogue of analysis and the speech that is produced by the analysand, which is understood by Blanchot to be a form of errant speech with a relation to the neuter. Indeed, Blanchot, in what is to my mind one of his most pellucid moments, discusses the neuter in terms of other writers, notably psychoanalysts: while Freud reads it in terms of drives and instincts, Jung reads it under the name of the archetype (recuperating it 'pour le compte d'une spiritualité de bonne compagnie' ['on behalf of a respectable spirituality']), and Heideggerian philosophy can be understood as 'une tentative pour s'en approcher d'une manière non conceptuelle' (*EI* 441) ('an attempt to approach it in a non-conceptual manner', *IC* 299). We thus have the beginnings of a notion of fascination, related to psychoanalysis, based around a structure of anteriority perhaps comparable to loss — but, as we shall see, a loss without a lost object.

Similarly, Blanchot may not engage in classical Freudian conceptualization in 'Les Deux Versions de l'imaginaire', but that text nevertheless bears traces of an engagement with psychoanalysis. Bellour has drawn attention to a critical passage in a connected section of *L'Espace littéraire* in which fascination is related to childhood.[89] The passage, subheaded 'L'Image', comes from the first part of the book and it is at the end of this part that Blanchot refers us to the appendix, 'Les Deux Versions de l'imaginaire'. Blanchot writes that 'l'enfance est le moment de la fascination, *est elle-même* fascinée' ('childhood is the moment of fascination, *is itself* fascinated'). It follows: 'C'est *parce que* l'enfant est fasciné que la mère est fascinante' (*EL* 24, my emphases) ('It is *because* the child is fascinated that the mother is fascinating', *SL* 33).[90] These lines are remarkable as evidence of the way fascination disrupts established order. While the first line strangely suggests that a time period can itself take on the attribute of being 'fascinée', the latter formulation reverses causal and even semantic logic, almost as if in passing, to indicate that fascination is firstly a condition on the part of viewer or subject, before it is an effect of a fascinating object. Again we are referred back to the double nature of the image. Aside from the context of its psychoanalytic implications, this is just one localized example of the way Blanchot makes the concept of fascination his own at the textual level by detaching and stretching the word and its cognates from their ordinary functioning — the verb is transitive and ordinarily denotes an action whereby something enchants or transfixes something else, yet in Blanchot's usage it is possible that there is apparently no thing that does the fascinating, that that 'by which' one is fascinated is precisely *nothing*.

Bellour notes that it is difficult to read these lines without thinking of what will be said in Lacan's celebrated seminar ten years later in 1964, 'Les Quatre Concepts fondamentaux de la psychanalyse' [The Four Fundamental Concepts of Psychoanalysis].[91] Bellour carefully centres the difference between Lacan and Blanchot around the question of hypnosis. Lacan opposes hypnosis to the circuit of desire.[92] It is inversely invoked by Blanchot in *L'Espace littéraire*, writing that it is not about sending one to sleep, but in maintaining 'au sein de la nuit rassemblée, une lumière passive, obéissante, le point, incapable de s'éteindre, de la lucidité paralysée, avec laquelle la puissance qui fascine est entrée en contact, qu'elle touche dans ce lieu séparé où tout devient image' (*EL* 194) ('within concentrated night a passive, obedient light, the point of light which is unable to go out: paralyzed lucidity. The power that fascinates has come into contact with this point, which it touches in the separated place where everything becomes image', *SL* 185). As a 'point', this can be compared with the point discussed in relation to Giacometti. This night is an experience of being put out of touch with the world. Bellour tantalizingly suggests that with regard to the notions of contact at a distance, the gaze as light, the gaze in the mirror, and fascination, it is necessary to consider 'une façon possible de désigner la part la plus fondamentale et la plus obscure de l'expérience même de l'image' [a possible way of designating the most fundamental and the most obscure part of the very experience of the image], which Bellour names 'l'image-cinéma' [the cinema-image] and the 'corps-image propre au cinéma' [the body-image proper to cinema], 'bien que ce soit là une expérience à laquelle Blanchot a préféré demeurer étranger' [even if it would be an experience that Blanchot preferred to remain strange].[93] Bellour has expanded upon this essay in a more recent work, making more explicit that the discussion of hypnosis in Blanchot's text captures 'avec une exactitude étrange la situation de la salle obscure et de la projection, et du spectateur librement capturé dans ce dispositif, quand il devient un spectateur pensif, que sa passivité même porte à penser' [with a strange exactitude the situation of the dark auditorium and projection, and of the spectator freely caught up in the apparatus when he becomes a pensive spectator, which their very passivity suggests].[94] For Bellour, the fascination of childhood is re-opened in adult life through art in general and particularly through cinema. We can see here how cinema may be a way to understand the Blanchotian image as determined by a prior fascination. Even if Blanchot preferred the experience of the image to 'demeurer étranger', we shall attempt to open it up.

Bellour argues that the only psychoanalytic references that could make sense in relation to Blanchot's fascinated child would be ones that conceive of 'la réalité vivante de l'enfant' [the living reality of the child], such as found in D. W. Winnicott or Daniel Stern, rather than a Lacanian model.[95] This would be how to understand the 'corps-image' above and would point to a nexus of connections between childhood, fascination, and cinema.[96] Though Bellour does not mention it, this reflection on the fascinated gaze of the child also looks forward to Blanchot's more explicit reflections on Winnicott, as well as Serge Leclaire, in *L'Écriture du désastre*. Blanchot writes three particularly enigmatic passages in *L'Écriture du désastre* bearing the name: '(Une scène primitive?)' [A Primal Scene?] (*ED* 117, 176–79, 191–96; *WD* 72, 114–16, 125–28). A number of other fragments, including those on Winnicott and Leclaire and especially others written in italics, appear to form commentaries on these passages. Though the name 'une scène primitive' might seem to allude to that witnessing of parental coitus Freud details in the case of the Wolfman, Blanchot's primal scene is distinct from this.[97] Much like the myth of Orpheus in *L'Espace littéraire* (which we will come to in the next chapter), *L'Écriture du désastre* is structured around a parable of what can be understood as fascination, giving it the character of an essential motif in Blanchot's thought.

In the first of the fragments marked '(Une scène primitive?)', Blanchot describes in two paragraphs a small boy who is '*debout, écartant le rideau et, à travers la vitre, regardant*' ('*standing by the window, drawing the curtain and, through the pane, looking*'). He sees a garden, trees, the wall of a house, and slowly looks up to '*le ciel ordinaire*' ('*the ordinary sky*'):

> *Ce qui se passe ensuite: le ciel, le même ciel, soudain ouvert, noir absolument et vide absolument, révélant (comme par la vitre brisée) une telle absence que tout s'y est depuis toujours et à jamais perdu, au point que s'y affirme et s'y dissipe le savoir vertigineux que rien est ce qu'il y a, et d'abord rien au-delà.* (*ED* 117)

> [*What happens then: the sky, the same sky, suddenly open, absolutely black and absolutely empty, revealing (as though the pane had broken) such an absence that all has since always and forevermore been lost therein — so lost that therein is affirmed and dissolved the vertiginous knowledge that nothing is what there is, and first of all nothing beyond.*] (*WD* 72)

This fragment opens with the enigmatic invitation: '*Vous qui vivez plus tard, proches d'un cœur qui ne bat plus, supposez, supposez-le*' ('*You who live later, close to a heart that beats no more, suppose, suppose this*'). It is addressed in this way, eschewing any present, to a future reader while relating a scene from a far anterior moment. In this strange episode, the child sees the black void of absence, which leads to a strange knowledge which lasts only a moment. This passage, with its reference to the 'au-delà', seems in part to refer back to Blanchot's previous fragmentary text, *Le Pas au-delà*, especially an early fragment in which the 'Moi' ('Self') is said to be 'comme fissuré, dès le jour où le ciel s'ouvrit sur son vide' (*PA* 9) ('as if fissured, since the day when the sky opened up its void', *SNB* 2). This black void, this 'vide', may also recall the 'Figures du vide' edition of the *Nouvelle Revue de Psychanalyse* of 1975, in which the important essay by Winnicott, 'Fear of Breakdown', that Blanchot alludes to in relation to the primal scene first appeared in French. (It was also in this key year that Leclaire published *On tue un enfant* [A Child Is Being Killed], discussed below.)[98] In the essay by his friend Roger Laporte in that edition, Blanchot would have recognized a commentary on his own work in relation to the void. Laporte cites the end of Blanchot's *récit*, *Celui qui ne m'accompagnait pas* [The One Who Was Standing Apart From Me] (1953), in which we read of 'un sourire infini, fascinant' ('an infinite, fascinating smile'), which is sensed 'comme un bonheur' ('as a happiness') and experienced as 'une ressemblance saisissante' ('a thrilling resemblance').[99] This certainly has echoes with the child in the primal scene who is said, after the quotation above, to be submerged in '*le sentiment de bonheur*' ('*a feeling of happiness*') and '*la joie ravageante*' ('*ravaging joy*'). This is a joy closely related to the moment of death, as the paratactic text, with its subsumed dialogue, shows: '*Mais qui raconte? — Le récit. — L'avant-récit, "la circonstance fulgurante" par laquelle l'enfant foudroyé voit — il en a le spectacle — le meurtre heureux de lui-même qui lui donne le silence de la parole*' (*ED* 177) ('*But who recounts? — The story. — The pre-story, "the flashing circumstance" whereby the dazzled child sees — he has the spectacle of it — the happy murder of himself which gives him words' silence*', *WD* 115). Blanchot's reference point here, Leclaire's *On tue un enfant*, describes a 'représentation narcissique primaire' ('primary narcissistic representation'), 'une représentation inconsciente primordiale où se nouent, plus denses qu'en toute autre, les voeux, nostalgies et espoir de chacun' ('the unconscious, primordial representation in which, more densely than anywhere else, our wishes, our nostalgia, and hopes come together').[100] This representation takes the figure of a cherubic child and is named the 'infans'. Leclaire notes that the child is fascinating.[101] This is an unconscious representation that must be destroyed; as Blanchot writes, 'il s'agit de détruire l'indestructible et même de mettre fin (non pas d'un coup, mais constamment) à ce à quoi on n'a pas, n'a jamais eu, ni n'aura accès — soit la mort impossible nécessaire' (*ED* 111) ('one must destroy the indestructible and even finish off (not at one blow, but constantly) that to which one has not now, nor has one ever had, nor will one ever have, access: impossible necessary death', *WD* 67). In this first of the primal scenes, then, the reference to Leclaire would seem to encourage a reading in which we are presented with a scene in which a child (not to be confused with the eponymous child of Leclaire's book) sees the sky open onto a void of some sort — a void strongly suggested by the phrase's presence in the text to be equivalent or related to the *il y a* — which leads to an ambiguous feeling of happiness, comparable to what Laporte read in the earlier *récit*. This opening of the void in turn bears a relation to a dazzling spectacle in which the child sees his own 'meurtre heureux'.

The text by Winnicott describes a child in an early state of development suffering agony. The word 'breakdown' refers to a breakdown of the child's selfhood and its sense of the real.[102] Breakdown is 'a defence organisation relative to a primitive agony'; 'the underlying agony is unthinkable'.[103] It is in this way that Winnicott suggests that fear of breakdown is '*the fear of a breakdown that has already been experienced*'.[104] The patient has to 'remember' this, 'but it is not possible to remember something that has not yet happened, and this thing of the past has not happened yet because the patient was not there for it to have happen to'.[105] Winnicott's text is, for Blanchot, 'une application fictive destinée [...] à fournir une représentation de l'irreprésentable, à laisser croire qu'on pourra, à l'aide du transfert, fixer dans le présent d'un souvenir (c'est-à-dire dans une expérience actuelle) la passivité de l'inconnu immémorial' (*ED* 109) ('a fictive application designed [...] to furnish a representation of the unrepresentable, to allow one to believe that one can, with the help of the transference, fix in the present of a memory (that is, in a present experience) the passivity of the immemorial unknown', *WD* 66). Blanchot's primal scene, with the invitation to 'suppose' it, is also 'fictive', but it does not have an obvious 'application', therapeutic or otherwise. The child may seem to be 'remembering' the breakdown that for Winnicott has always already occurred, but Blanchot's concern is with testing the very notion of representing this scene (or breakdown) *insofar* as it is by definition unrepresentable and impossible to recall.[106]

The question of the applicability of the word 'scène' to what is designated is addressed at the start of the second fragment marked '(Une scène primitive?)'. Blanchot writes that the word is not ideal for what it names escapes representability as well as fiction. The value of the term is that it does not imply a particular event taking place at a definable moment: ' — *Une scène: une ombre, une faible lueur, un 'presque' avec les traits du 'trop', de l'excessif en tout*' (*ED* 176) (' — *A scene: a shadow, a faint gleam, an 'almost' with the characteristics of 'too much,' of excessiveness, in sum*', *WD* 114). The word 'scène', like the notion of dying, suggests the impossibility of fixing what is referred to in an instant or definable present; the relation to it is always *après-coup*. Indeed, perhaps one should go further and designate the 'scène' as in a sense outside of time altogether. In Kevin Hart's gloss, 'the child's vision is, strictly speaking, not an event but the return of an event that has never actually occurred, that has never found a moment in which to present itself'.[107] A scene could almost be understood as something that does not happen, or, to put it conversely, a 'nothing' that does happen. Hill discusses the scene in terms of its function within the fragmentary text of *L'Écriture du désastre*. For Hill, the text endlessly repeats the scene, showing that no scene is 'properly primal': 'it was always either more or less than a scene, thus confirming, in radically abyssal fashion, the revelation — the absence of revelation or revealed absence — staged by Blanchot's text as belonging to its own (non)primal (non)scene'.[108] In short, the primal scene 'turns into an interminable, infinite, undelimitable, abyssal trace' of the revelation in the primal scene that *'nothing is what there is and, to begin with, nothing beyond'*.[109] The primal scene thus tends to draw towards it a number of Blanchotian motifs: the unfinished dying that cannot be accomplished; the unspent negativity that causes the dialectic to falter; and the titular disaster, in which history absents itself from itself. All of which would be ciphers of what is named as 'unrepresentable' in the quotation above, but the primal scene is unusual in being treated as something to be approached as a 'scène', which is to say as something which is normally understood as seen or witnessed. If it is 'une ombre' or 'une faible lueur', it may be something non-phenomenal that can only be described in phenomenal terms. Like the disaster which, in the first line of the book, leaves 'tout en l'état' (*ED* 7) ('everything intact', *WD* 1), the sky remains the same after the primal scene: ' — *Rien n'est changé. — Sauf le bouleversement de rien*' (*ED* 178) (' — *Nothing has changed. — Except the overwhelming overturning of nothing*', *WD* 115). In the continuing mutation of Blanchot's conceptual vocabulary, it could be argued that in this late text the notion of the 'scène' itself is the way in which the image returns as a motif.

Though one might understand the primal scene's relation to impossibility as necessitating a disavowal of the visual or mimetic sense of 'scène', Christopher Fynsk argues that 'the figure of seeing only insists all the more, as we recognize when one of the commentators explicitly refers to the child's *specular* relation to its own death'.[110] This refers to the 'spectacle' the child has of his murder quoted above. Fynsk writes thus: 'My suggestion would be that Blanchot is inscribing in that figuration, which he claims to be essential to speech and life, a form of reflection that is the abyssal origin and possibility of any speculation, as of any specular relation'.[111] Lacoue-Labarthe argues along similar lines, that if memory is nothing other than thinking in its possibility, then, at the same time as all thinking bears the trace of this impossible memory, the infinitely anterior death escapes thought.[112] To draw out a critical correlative implication from this, all relations of looking would bear a trace of the primal scene. Derrida's remarks apropos of Blanchot's text *La Folie du jour* are suggestive in this regard:

> Voir la vision, sur-voir, cette folie abyssale d'une scène absolument primitive, cette scène de la scène, se simule et dissimule dans le récit sous la forme rassurante, pour qui veut se rassurer, de spectacles circonscrits, de 'visions' ou de 'scènes' déterminées qui viennent en quelque sorte allégoriser l'abîme et contenir la folie. Le mot 'vision' lui-même est assez équivoque pour permettre cette économie.

> [To see vision, to see on beyond sight: this abyss-like madness of an utterly primal scene, the scene of scenes, stages, representations, is simulated and dissimulated in the *récit* in the reassuring form (for those who want to be reassured) of spectacles within bounds, determinate 'visions' or 'scenes' that come in a way to allegorize the abyss and contain the madness. The word 'vision' itself is ambiguous enough to make this economy possible.][113]

Derrida wrote these lines before the publication of *L'Écriture du désastre*, but versions of the primal scene texts had appeared in 1976 and 1978, making it reasonable to assume that Derrida is, with the words 'une scène absolument primitive', directly referring to these texts within the context of a commentary on a much earlier *récit*. The notion of economy is invoked to show how it is by the staging of spectacles or the delimiting of episodes of vision that the 'folie' of seeing beyond sight can be contained. Yet that 'scène de la scène' would remain fundamental to those subsequent stagings.

The third and final fragment marked '(Une scène primitive?)' strengthens the case for this specular relation, being a commentary on Ovid's myth of Narcissus. Not italicized as the previous fragments were, it nevertheless continues something of the themes explored in them. Blanchot suggests the presence of death in the myth, its appearance in 'le jeu floral d'un enchantement limpide qui n'ouvre pas sur le sans-fond effrayant du souterrain, mais qui le mire dangereusement (follement) dans l'illusion d'une proximité de surface' ('in the flowery shimmering of a limpid enchantment which does not open onto the frightfully unfathomable underground, but reflects it dangerously (crazily) in the illusion of a surface proximity'). Yet Narcissus does not die: 'devenu image, il se dissout dans la dissolution immobile de l'imaginaire où il se dilue sans savoir, perdant une vie qu'il n'a pas' ('having turned into an image, he dissolves in the immobile dissolution of the imaginary, where he is washed away without knowing it, losing a life he does not have'). It is in this way that Narcissus, says Blanchot, is similar to the child described by Leclaire, both of them being 'toujours déjà mort et cependant destiné à un mourir fragile' (*ED* 193) ('always already dead and nonetheless destined to a fragile, attenuated dying', *WD* 126). Thus:

> dans l'entre-deux tremblant d'une conscience qui ne s'est pas formée et d'une inconscience qui se laisse voir et ainsi fait du visible le fascinant, il nous est donné d'apprendre l'une des versions de l'imaginaire selon laquelle l'homme — est-ce l'homme? — , s'il peut se faire selon l'image, est plus certainement exposé au risque de se défaire selon son image, s'ouvrant alors à l'illusion d'une similitude, peut-être belle, peut-être mortelle, mais d'une mort évasive qui est toute dans la répétition d'une méconnaissance muette. (*ED* 194)
>
> [In the oscillating, intermediary zone between a consciousness not yet formed and an unconsciousness that lets itself be seen and thereby turns vision into fascination, one of the versions of the imaginary offers its lesson: man — is it man? — can make himself in accordance with the image, but this means that he is still more apt to unmake himself in accordance with the image, exposing himself to the illusion of a similitude which may be beautiful, or fatal, but which is in any case the illusion of an evasive death that consists entirely in the repetition of a mute misapprehension.] (*WD* 126)

This lightly-worn reference to 'Les Deux Versions de l'imaginaire', a text published twenty-five years earlier, is crucial for shoring up the continuity of Blanchot's concerns: one could even go as far as to say that there is a withdrawn meditation on the nature of vision forming a through-line across Blanchot's writings. What can be read in this particular quotation is how the notion of the imaginary is rethought in Blanchot's later work. The 'illusion d'une similitude' would refer to what in the earlier text is called 'ressemblance', and the 'mort évasive' to the impossibility of dying also already discussed. What is different in this account is in fact the notion of consciousness, which was conspicuously absent in the earlier reading. It is as if the word was banished to ensure no comparison with Sartre's account of the imaginary, which explicitly invoked a notion of psychology. Alternatively it could be that Winnicott and Leclaire finally provided the only adequate psychological framework within which the two versions could be thought, and it is thus that the vocabulary of consciousness appears: the 'conscience qui ne s'est pas formée' can be read as Winnicott's primitive child and the 'unconsciousness' Leclaire's *infans*. It would seem that the 'entre-deux' between the two (non-)consciousnesses is the place in which childhood can be said to be 'elle-même fascinée' as we discussed after Bellour. It is in this place that the visible can be made fascinating. Thus what Narcissus sees is not a fixed image or reflection, but:

> dans le visible l'invisible, dans la figure l'infigurable, l'inconnu instable d'une représentation sans présence, la représentation qui ne renvoie pas à un modèle: l'anonyme que le nom qu'il n'a pas pourrait seul maintenir à distance. C'est la folie et la mort. (*ED* 204)

> [the invisible in the visible — in the picture the undepicted, the unstable unknown of a representation without presence, which reflects no model: he sees the nameless one whom only the name he does not have could hold us at a distance. It is madness he sees, and death.] (*WD* 134)

This is not the place for a full analysis of the complex question of the primal scene. For the present study, the crucial aspect of the primal scene is its implications for a consideration of the place of vision in Blanchot's writing and in fascination in particular. The key text on Blanchot's primal scene in this regard is Fynsk's *Infant Figures* (2000). This text has already been quoted in reference to the specular relation, but another important aspect of Fynsk's work here is how it serves to work through the material, bodily implications of the 'thought of relation' itself. Fynsk writes:

> We must think a bodily suffering that is immemorial and perhaps irreducible even to the formal unity of a 'subjectivity without subject' *together with* the perpetuation or the survival of the relation of responsibility that opens as this interruption. We must think, in effect, a structure of exposure — a writing, let us say — that *perpetuates exposure* both as a reiterated, unsatisfiable exigency, and as the constant presence of an unfigurable material suffering.[114]

These lines are rich in association and make several apparently disparate conceptual motifs work together. Although the lines move towards the idea of material suffering, which in this context alludes to Winnicott's primal agonies, the reference to responsibility brings out the relevance of the primal scene to the Levinasian Other, while 'exposure' carries the sense of thinking this problematic in a Bataillean register. Fynsk understands the invitation to 'suppose' the primal scene to be an invitation to enter a relation with that non-event. It can, it seems, only be a 'fictive engagement', yet it would involve entering 'the space of the infant figure, a space of the imaginary that must have opened if there is to be any speech and life, and that *is there* inasmuch as we live "close to a heart that no longer beats"'.[115] Part of the ingenuity of what is a somewhat experimental text is the engagement with the paintings of Francis Bacon. There can be no figure that could capture the *infans*, yet the *figural* explicitly has for Fynsk a material relation to the immemorial suffering posited in the 'infant figures' of Leclaire and Winnicott — a relation that is unusual given that this material relation is '"before" or "otherwise than" Being'.[116] The singularity of the primal scene, insofar as it can be, and has been by Fynsk, developed from Blanchot's text as a concept, is that it can stand for an immemorial event, that did not strictly happen, and yet can persist in the form of a trace and appear as a 'referent' in a work (such as Bacon's paintings), that appearance of the trace — that 'ex-scription' — in the work being in effect the first time that event has *been*.[117] This structure, in which an 'effect' can have a material efficacy without having had an anterior and ontologically secure 'cause', is, crucially, the same as that of fascination we saw above. The language of the primal scene is much as we saw in Blanchot's discussion of Giacometti in the previous section above: the sculpture is a gift which opens up, in the space of the world, and draws us towards a point of absence or the void. This exposure opens to us and 'chaque fois s'abîme en un instant'. When Fynsk writes in the quotation above that the work can 'perpetuate exposure', perpetuate an exposure that is psychoanalytically constitutive of human life, in the context of my argument that is also what I am suggesting film can be said to do. The preceding discussion has thus been a discussion of the preconditions of the fascination of cinematic subjectivity.

Return to the *Instant*

We should now be in a position to answer some of the questions we left at the end of the Introduction and to address the question evoked by Derrida of death and film in Blanchot's text. We observed there a connection between the moment of the suspended death — as exemplary of the instant — and the moment of recording. 'En réalité, combien de temps s'était-il écoulé?' (*ID* 6) ('In reality, how much time had elapsed?', *ID* 7). How long does this 'instant' last? When is this instant of death that does not come? Just as death suspends the relation to place, so too it suspends the relation to time. As Derrida writes: 'Constamment "Blanchot" ou le narrateur souligne la durée, la non-durée, l'impossibilité de mesurer la durée ou la demourance' (*D* 104) ('"Blanchot" or the narrator is constantly underlining the duration, the non-duration, the impossibility of measuring the duration or the *demourance*', *ID* 79). Of course, Blanchot's title is paradoxical: according to his logic, an instant, a definable time in which it could occur, is precisely what death does not have.

With the notion of the freeze-frame and the ontological irreducibility of the instant, Derrida's metaphor echoes Bellour's remarks on the complicity between the *arrêt* of death and that of the image:

> Si l'arrêt sur image, ou de l'image [...] pose ou pause d'image exprimant la puissance de la captation par l'immobile, si cette expérience est si forte, c'est évidemment qu'elle joue avec *l'arrêt de mort* — son point de fuite et en un sens le seul réel [...] Mais il faut saisir ce qui se conjugue dans le titre exemplaire de Blanchot, et sert de fil à son récit: l'arrêt qui prononce la mort est aussi ce qui parvient à la suspendre, la retourne et la rend à la vie.

> [If the freeze-frame, or the stilled image [...] — a pose or pause of the image expressing the capturing power of immobility — if this experience is so strong, it is obviously because it touches upon *l'arrêt de mort*, the finality of death: its vanishing point and in a sense the whole of the real [...] But we must grasp what is conjugated in Blanchot's exemplary title, serving as the thread to his narrative: the ruling that pronounces death is also that halt that manages to hold it at bay, turn it around and give it back to life.][118]

Here we have a play on the senses of the title *L'Arrêt de mort* that has been suggestive for several French critics, such as Derrida. Didi-Huberman also invokes this idea when he remarks that this *récit* multiplies the paradoxes of the structure of resemblance, as if each time it marked 'un *arrêt sur l'image*, suspendu entre la jeune fille et la mort' [an *immobile image* suspended between the young girl and death].[119] Yet what Bellour evokes in the death at work in the freeze-frame is the same death that, as we have seen, initiates the dialectic while causing it to halt. It is death not as finality but as a non-experience of which we retain a 'sorte de souvenir'.

For Laura Mulvey, Bellour's notion of a 'pensive spectator' allows us to reconceive of the 'reverie' that Roland Barthes associated with the photograph in relation to phenomena in cinema.[120] When we return to Barthes's *La Chambre claire* [Camera Lucida], published in the same year (1980) as *L'Écriture du désastre*, several motifs join up. Barthes writes: 'Devant la photo de ma mère enfant, je me dis: elle va mourir: je frémis, tel le psychotique de Winnicott, *d'une catastrophe qui déjà a eu lieu*. Que le sujet en soit déjà mort ou non, toute photographie est cette catastrophe' ('In front of the photograph of my mother as a child, I tell myself: she is going to die: I shudder, like Winnicott's psychotic patient, *over a catastrophe which has already occurred*. Whether or not the subject is already dead, every photograph is this catastrophe').[121] The point is not only that both Barthes and Blanchot refer to Winnicott in thinking that which is catastrophic or disastrous, but more importantly that this casting back to an immemorial past is either inspired or figured by an image (the 'spectacle' of the primal scene). This recurring schema that is called 'reverie' or fascination is also that detailed in Derrida's analysis of *L'Instant de ma mort*.[122] This comparison becomes particularly suggestive when we consider that the text was published in 1994, exactly fifty years after the wartime episode in Quain supposedly took place.[123] Blanchot's complicated use of the pronoun in the *récit*, in which the first-person is exchanged with the third-person, gives the impression that he is looking back to this episode as if engaged in a reverie like Barthes before his photograph. That fascination is one in which the subjectivity named by the 'I' is put under erasure. While Blanchot is not a point of reference for Mulvey, she also conceives of fascination in terms of the intrusion of something from outside the present:

> Rather than a masking of cinema's essence, fiction can introduce the level of imaginative time that, once delayed, contributes to rather than detracts from cinema's aesthetics. When the presence of the past, the time of registration, rises to the surface, it seems to cancel the narrative flow. In almost any halt to a film, a sense of the image as document makes itself felt as *the fascination of time fossilized overwhelms the fascination of narrative progression*. But then, once the film begins to flow again and the action takes over, the temporal register shifts again and its fictional present reasserts itself.[124]

This repeated use of 'fascination' gives a sense of the activation of different temporalities in fascination we have discussed, and the 'time fossilized' can be considered in relation to the immemorial 'index' of the primal scene which animates and re-opens an exposure to the outside of time.

Lacoue-Labarthe suggests that *L'Instant de ma mort* be read as something like a 'scène primitive' whose lesson is one of writing, that writing is not about recounting what has happened to oneself or to others, it is rather about saying how one is already dead and the subject already dissolved.[125] This is partly the sense of the death that 'has' taken place, both in the instant and always already, as would be suggested by the repeated formulations in Derrida's commentary to the effect that we know what is going to happen *because* it has already happened. The young man standing awaiting the final order for his death is said to experience an untranslatable feeling: 'un sentiment de légèreté extraordinaire, une sorte de béatitude (rien d'heureux cependant), — allégresse souveraine? La rencontre de la mort et de la mort?' ('a feeling of extraordinary lightness, a sort of beatitude (nothing happy, however) — sovereign elation? The encounter of death with death?'). This in itself is said to be impossible to analyze, but it is then protracted. 'A cet instant, brusque retour au monde, éclata le bruit considérable d'une proche bataille' ('At that instant, an abrupt return to the world, the considerable noise of a nearby battle exploded'). The lieutenant goes off to see what is happening. However, the soldiers stay in their position, 'prêts à demeurer ainsi dans une immobilité qui arrêtait le temps' (*ID* 4) ('prepared to remain thus in an immobility that arrested time', *ID* 5). Even this phrasing — it is 'immobilité' that tautologically does the halting of time — suggests the repetitive temporality it names. As in the primal scene, there is a moment of a sort of bliss, taking place in an inaccessible space and time, followed by the feeling that 'nothing happened'.

The becoming-cinema of Blanchot's text in Derrida's reading is thus a figure of the experience of fascination with the image. The death that does not come is an event *lived as image*. If it seems unexpected that Derrida thinks of the fascination of that instant of death in terms of cinema, given that the lesson of the text is one of writing, this should be no more so than the appearance of Blanchot in relation to cinema in the work of Bellour, Nancy, Stiegler, or, as will be suggested in the next chapter, Deleuze. Blanchot's work has inspired others to think of fascination reawakening an always prior state of passivity, a passivity conceived in contemporary culture as cinematic. While we observed at the outset that Blanchot's concern is avowedly with literature, in our epoch it is as if his thinking of literature has persisted in a strain of French thought, by a kind of *displacement*, in the thinking of cinema.

Notes to Chapter 1

1. Ropars-Wuilleumier, *Le Temps d'une pensée*, p. 297; 'On Unworking: The Image in Writing According to Blanchot', trans. by Roland-François Lack, in *Maurice Blanchot: The Demand of Writing*, ed. by Carolyn Bailey Gill (London: Routledge, 1996), pp. 137–51 (p. 139).
2. Ropars-Wuilleumier mentions, in a piece considering filmic montage in relation to *L'Arrêt de mort*, that there is always a risk with Blanchot of explaining his writing by reference to his

theoretical concepts. This is a risk that equally applies to the present study, i.e. of appropriating concepts such as the neuter too readily in the discussion of specific films. Ropars-Wuilleumier, *Écraniques*, p. 36.

3. The essay is reprinted as 'The Rhetoric of the Image', in Roland Barthes, *Image-Music-Text*, trans. by Stephen Heath (London: Fontana Press, 1977), pp. 32–51.
4. Joseph Libertson, *Proximity: Levinas, Blanchot, Bataille and Communication* (The Hague: Martinus Nijhoff, 1982), p. 2. Thus '[u]nderneath the thematic disparity which distinguishes Bataille's world of excess, irony and violence, Blanchot's economy of impersonality and nocturnal dispersion, and the Levinasian universe of gravity, dissymetry and responsibility, a single configuration of communication insists' (p. 3).
5. Jean-Luc Nancy, 'Reste inavouable: entretien avec Mathilde Girard', *Lignes*, 43 (2014), 155–76 (p. 170, my emphasis).
6. Jean-Luc Nancy, *La Communauté désœuvrée* (Paris: Christian Bourgois, 1999 [1986]), p. 79; *The Inoperative Community*, ed. by Peter Connor and trans. by Peter Connor and others, with a foreword by Christopher Fynsk (Minneapolis: University of Minnesota Press, 1991), p. 31. On Nancy's use of the term *désœuvrement*, see Christopher Fynsk's comment in that text, p. 154, n. 23.
7. For a discussion of this term, see the translator's introduction (*SL* 12–13).
8. Philippe Lacoue-Labarthe and Jean-Luc Nancy, *L'Absolu littéraire: théorie de la littérature du romantisme allemand* (Paris: Seuil, 1978), p. 80.
9. For Agamben, the term refers to 'neither the simple absence of work nor (as in Bataille) a sovereign and useless form of negativity. The only coherent way to understand inoperativeness is to think of it as a generic mode of potentiality that is not exhausted (like individual action or collective action understood as the sum of individual actions) in a *transitus de potentia ad actum*'. Giorgio Agamben, *Homo Sacer: Sovereign Power and Bare Life*, trans. by Daniel Heller-Roazen (Stanford, CA: Stanford University Press, 1998), pp. 61–62.
10. Alexandre Kojève, *Introduction à la lecture de Hegel* (Paris: Gallimard, 1947), p. 178.
11. Leslie Hill, *Maurice Blanchot and Fragmentary Writing: A Change of Epoch* (London: Continuum, 2012), p. 49.
12. For a recent reading of the motifs of 'changement d'époque' and 'la fin du Livre' in relation to digital technologies, see Bernard Stiegler, *Dans la disruption: comment ne pas devenir fou?* (Paris: Les Liens qui libèrent, 2016), pp. 102–04.
13. Maurice Blanchot, *Desperate Clarity: Chronicles of an Intellectual Life, 1942*, trans. by Michael Holland (New York: Fordham University Press, 2013), pp. 7–8.
14. On the subject of the politics of the rupture in Blanchot, see *PW* xxv–xxvii, and Martin Crowley, *L'Homme sans: politiques de la finitude* (Paris: Lignes, 2009), pp. 121–25.
15. Christopher Fynsk, *Last Steps: Maurice Blanchot's Exilic Writing* (New York: Fordham University Press, 2013), p. 3.
16. Hill, *Maurice Blanchot and Fragmentary Writing*, p. 7.
17. Marlène Zarader, *L'Être et le neutre* (Lagrasse: Éditions Verdier, 2001), p. 21. Zarader has been criticized for considering Blanchot's writing nihilistic, see Michael Holland, *Avant dire: essais sur Blanchot* (Paris: Hermann, 2015), pp. 149–51.
18. Georges Bataille, *Choix de lettres*, ed. by Michel Surya (Paris: Gallimard, 1997), pp. 595–96; *PW* xxxi–xxxii. Compare also *WD* 20; *ED* 38.
19. Maurice Blanchot, 'Les Deux Versions de l'imaginaire', *Les Cahiers de la Pléiade*, 12 (1951), 115–25. For a discussion of the two versions of the text, see Calum Watt, 'The Tortoise and the Corpse: Two Excisions from Maurice Blanchot's "Les Deux Versions de l'imaginaire"', *French Studies Bulletin*, 38, 142 (2017), 4–7.
20. Martin Heidegger, *Being and Time*, trans. by John Macquarrie and Edward Robinson (Oxford: Blackwell, 1962), p. 98 (*Sein und Zeit* (Tübingen: Max Niemeyer Verlag, 1967), p. 69).
21. Ibid., pp. 102–03 (p. 73).
22. Jean-Paul Sartre, *L'Imaginaire* (Paris: Gallimard, 1940).
23. Marie-Claire Ropars-Wuilleumier, 'Le Saisissement imaginaire', *Hors Cadre*, 4, 'L'Image, l'Imaginaire' (1986), 27–37 (p. 33).

24. It has been noted by several scholars that in *De l'existence à l'existant* [Existence and Existents] (1947), the text to which Blanchot refers us, Levinas in turn refers us to *Thomas l'obscur* (first version, 1941). See Emmanuel Levinas, *De l'existence à l'existant* (Paris: Vrin, 1984), p. 103; *Existence and Existents*, trans. by Alphonso Lingis (Dordrecht: Kluwer Academic Publishers, 1995), p. 63.
25. Ropars-Wuilleumier, *Le Temps d'une pensée*, p. 297; 'On Unworking', p. 140.
26. Zarader, *L'Être et le neutre*, p. 215.
27. Georges Didi-Huberman, 'De ressemblance à ressemblance', in *Maurice Blanchot: récits critiques*, ed. by Christophe Bident and Pierre Vilar (Tours: Éditions Farrago, 2003), pp. 143–67 (p. 145, my emphasis).
28. Kevin Hart, *Postmodernism: A Beginner's Guide* (Oxford: Oneworld, 2004), pp. 56 & 58.
29. Heidegger, *Being and Time*, p. 220 (*Sein und Zeit*, p. 176). See also ibid., pp. 107 & 149 (pp. 76 & 113).
30. Ibid., p. 394 (p. 344).
31. Ibid., p. 230 (p. 186). For the discussion of anxiety, see ibid., pp. 228–35 (pp. 184–91).
32. Ibid., p. 231 (pp. 247–48).
33. Ibid., pp. 163–68 (pp. 126–30).
34. Jean-Luc Nancy, *Le Discours de la syncope: 1. Logodaedalus* (Paris: Aubier-Flammarion, 1976), p. 148; *The Discourse of the Syncope: Logodaedalus*, trans. by Saul Anton (Stanford, CA: Stanford University Press, 2008), p. 138.
35. Ibid., p. 148; p. 139. For Blanchot's essay, see 'Le "Discours philosophique"', *L'Arc*, 46 (1971), 1–4.
36. Leslie Hill, *Radical Indecision: Barthes, Blanchot, Derrida, and the Future of Criticism* (Notre Dame, IN: University of Notre Dame Press, 2010), p. 357, n. 73.
37. Françoise Collin, *Maurice Blanchot et la question de l'écriture*, 2nd edn (Paris: Gallimard, 1986), p. 162.
38. Ian Maclachlan, 'Blanchot and the Romantic Imagination', in *Blanchot Romantique: A Collection of Essays*, ed. by John McKeane and Hannes Opelz (Bern: Peter Lang, 2011), pp. 155–71 (p. 168).
39. Immanuel Kant, *Critique of Pure Reason*, trans. by Norman Kemp Smith, 2nd edn (Basingstoke: Palgrave Macmillan, 2007). All references of this type refer to the German pagination of A and B versions.
40. Maclachlan, 'Blanchot and the Romantic Imagination', p. 171.
41. Martin Heidegger, *Kant and the Problem of Metaphysics*, trans. by Richard Taft, 5th edn (Bloomington: Indiana University Press, 1997). For an account of Heidegger's reading, see Richard Kearney, *The Wake of Imagination: Toward a Postmodern Culture* (New York: Routledge, 1988), pp. 189–95.
42. Heidegger, *Kant and the Problem of Metaphysics*, pp. 85–87.
43. Thomas Carl Wall, *Radical Passivity: Levinas, Blanchot, and Agamben* (New York: State University of New York Press, 1999), pp. 138–62 (p. 152).
44. Bernard Stiegler, *La Technique et le temps 3: le temps du cinéma et la question du mal-être* (Paris: Galilée, 2001), p. 100; *Technics and Time, 3: Cinematic Time and the Question of Malaise*, trans. by Stephen Barker (Stanford, CA: Stanford University Press, 2010), p. 61.
45. Ibid., p. 35; p. 13.
46. Calum Watt, 'The Uses of Maurice Blanchot in Bernard Stiegler's *Technics and Time*', *Paragraph*, 39:3 (2016), 305–18. For an account of Stiegler's relation to cinema, see Patrick Crogan, 'Experience of the Industrial Temporal Object', in *Stiegler and Technics*, ed. by Christina Howells and Gerald Moore (Edinburgh: Edinburgh University Press, 2013), pp. 102–18.
47. Stiegler, *La Technique et le temps 3*, pp. 97–98; *Technics and Time, 3*, p. 59.
48. Marie-Claire Ropars-Wuilleumier, *L'Idée d'image* (Paris: Presses Universitaires de Vincennes, 1995), p. 160.
49. Zarader, *L'Être et le neutre*, p. 140.
50. Jacques Derrida, *Papier machine* (Paris: Galilée, 2001), p. 391; *Paper Machine*, trans. by Rachel Bowlby (Stanford, CA: Stanford University Press, 2005), p. 157.

51. Jacques Derrida, *Mémoires d'aveugle: l'autoportrait et autres ruines* (Paris: Louvre, 1990), p. 56; *Memoirs of the Blind*, trans. by Pascale-Anne Brault and Michael Naas (Chicago, IL: University of Chicago Press, 1993), pp. 51–52.
52. Oliver Harris, 'Film Noir Fascination: Outside History, but Historically So', *Cinema Journal*, 43:1 (2003), 3–24 (p. 5).
53. Emmanuel Levinas, *Sur Maurice Blanchot* (Montpellier: Fata Morgana, 1975), p. 23; *Proper Names*, trans. by Michael B. Smith (Stanford, CA: Stanford University Press, 1996), p. 137.
54. For a discussion of Blanchot and Levinas on vision, see Martin Jay, *Downcast Eyes: The Denigration of Vision in Twentieth-Century French Thought* (Berkeley: University of California Press, 1994), pp. 551–55.
55. Ropars-Wuilleumier, *Le Temps d'une pensée*, p. 298 (my emphasis); 'On Unworking', p. 141.
56. Zenkine, 'Blanchot et l'image visuelle', p. 215.
57. Martin Heidegger, 'What Are Poets For?', in *Poetry, Language, Thought*, ed. and trans. by Albert Hofstadter (New York: Harper Collins, 2001), pp. 89–139 (p. 89).
58. Victoria I. Burke, 'From Desire to Fascination: Hegel and Blanchot on Negativity', *MLN*, 114:4 (1999), 848–56 (p. 854).
59. Martin Heidegger, 'The Origin of the Work of Art', in *Basic Writings*, ed. by David Farrell Krell (London: Routledge, 2009), pp. 143–212.
60. One might compare Blanchot's description of sculpture with the commentary on Rodin's work as evincing a shifting surface in Jacques Rancière, *Aisthesis: scènes du régime esthétique de l'art* (Paris: Galilée), pp. 185–201. For a discussion of the echoes of Rilke's account of working for Rodin in Blanchot's writing and the language of sculpture in the *récits*, see Elizabeth Presa, 'White Work', in Hill, Nelson and Vardoulakis, *After Blanchot: Literature, Philosophy, Criticism*, ed. by Leslie Hill, Brian Nelson, and Dimitris Vardoulakis (Newark: University of Delaware Press, 2005), pp. 257–69. For a theory of the connection between Blanchot and more contemporary sculpture, see Emmanuelle Ravel, *Maurice Blanchot et l'art au XXème siècle: une esthétique de désoeuvrement* (Amsterdam: Rodopi, 2007).
61. See Gaston Bachelard, *The Poetics of Space*, trans. by Maria Jolas (Boston: Beacon Press, 1969), p. 184.
62. Gilles Deleuze, *Cinéma 2: l'image-temps* (Paris: Éditions de Minuit, 1985), p. 235; *Cinema 2: The Time-Image*, trans. by Hugh Tomlinson and Robert Galeta (London: Continuum, 2005), p. 174.
63. Martin Crowley, 'Touche-là', in *Blanchot dans son siècle*, ed. by Antelme and others, pp. 166–76 (p. 170).
64. Wall, *Radical Passivity*, p. 69.
65. Marie-Claire Ropars-Wuilleumier, *Écrire l'espace* (Paris: Presses Universitaires de Vincennes, 2002), p. 7.
66. Ibid., p. 10.
67. Ibid., p. 9.
68. Ibid., p. 89.
69. Nevertheless, Blanchot refused Giacometti's idea that he make a portrait of him, see Bident, *Maurice Blanchot*, p. 537.
70. Ropars-Wuilleumier, *Écrire l'espace*, p. 149.
71. Ibid., p. 148.
72. Ibid., p. 151.
73. Ibid., p. 12.
74. Simon Critchley, 'Il y a — Holding Levinas's Hand to Blanchot's Fire', in *Maurice Blanchot: The Demand of Writing*, ed. by Gill, pp. 108–22 (pp. 108 & 109).
75. Compare this translation from *SHB* with that from *SL* 255.
76. Jean-Luc Nancy, *The Evidence of Film: Abbas Kiarostami*, trans. by Christine Irizarry and Verena Andermatt Conley (Brussels: Yves Gevaert, 2001), pp. 52–53, n. 4.
77. Ian James, 'The Evidence of the Image', *L'Esprit créateur*, 47:3 (2007), 68–79 (p. 73).
78. Jean-Luc Nancy, *Au fond des images* (Paris: Galilée, 2003), p. 30; *The Ground of the Image*, trans. by Jeff Fort (New York: Fordham University Press, 2005), p. 12.
79. Nancy, *The Evidence of Film*, pp. 16–17.

80. Steven Shaviro, *The Cinematic Body* (Minneapolis: University of Minnesota Press, 1993), p. 48.
81. Harris, 'Film Noir Fascination', p. 6.
82. Shaviro, *The Cinematic Body*, pp. 28–29.
83. Ibid., pp. 46–47.
84. Ibid., p. 48.
85. As quoted in ibid., p. 16.
86. Ibid., pp. 16–17.
87. Ibid., p. 18.
88. Ibid., p. 20 (my emphasis).
89. Raymond Bellour, 'L'Image', in *Maurice Blanchot: récits critiques*, ed. by Bident and Vilar, pp. 133–41.
90. Bellour had previously (1982) connected this passage to photography, see Bellour, *L'Entre-Images*, p. 69; *Between-the-Images*, pp. 81–82.
91. Bellour, 'L'Image', p. 137.
92. Jacques Lacan, *Le Séminaire, Livre XI: Les Quatre Concepts fondamentaux de la psychanalyse* (Paris: Seuil, 1973).
93. Bellour, 'L'Image', p. 139.
94. Raymond Bellour, *Le Corps du cinéma: hypnoses, émotions, animalités* (Paris: P.O.L., 2009), p. 295.
95. Bellour, 'L'Image', p. 138.
96. For Christian Metz, the spectator's relation with film is an object relation inscribed in the Lacanian imaginary. The existence of the cinema presupposes the spectator's having passed through the mirror stage in which the ego was formed through the identification with an image. The pre-Oedipal imaginary stage is reactivated by cinema. The experience of being a spectator in a cinema is comparable to childhood for Metz in that in both cases one is in 'un état de sous-motricité et de surperception' ('a sub-motor and hyper-perceptive state') and is 'la proie de l'imaginaire' ('prey to the imaginary'). Christian Metz, *Le Signifiant imaginaire: psychanalyse et cinéma* (Paris: Christian Bourgois, 1984), pp. 69–70; *Psychoanalysis and Cinema: The Imaginary Signifier*, trans. by Celia Britton and others (Basingstoke: Macmillan, 1982), p. 49.
97. For the Wolfman, see Sigmund Freud, *The Standard Edition of the Complete Psychological Works of Sigmund Freud, Vol. XVII: An Infantile Neurosis and Other Works*, trans. by James Strachey (London: Vintage, 2001).
98. See D. W. Winnicott, 'La Crainte de l'effondrement', *Nouvelle Revue de Psychanalyse*, 11, 'Figures du vide' (1975), 35–44; Serge Leclaire, *On tue un enfant* (Paris: Seuil, 1975); *A Child Is Being Killed*, trans. by Marie-Claude Hays (Stanford, CA: Stanford University Press, 1998). Blanchot was writing *L'Écriture du désastre* from 1974–80, Bident, *Maurice Blanchot*, pp. 508–20. It is also striking that it is at exactly the same time as these texts by Winnicott and Leclaire, in 1975, that the celebrated edition of *Communications*, on psychoanalysis and cinema and featuring texts by Metz and Jean-Louis Baudry, was published, in which the 'scène primitive' is explicitly theorized according to a Freudian notion of voyeurism. As Metz writes: 'Le film, pour son spectateur, se déroule dans cet "ailleurs" à la fois tout proche et définitivement inaccessible où l'enfant *voit* s'ébattre le couple parental [...] Le cinéma garde en lui quelque chose de l'interdit propre à la vision de la scène primitive' ('For its spectator, the film unfolds in that simultaneously very close and definitively inaccessible "elsewhere" in which the child *sees* the amorous play of the parental couple [...] The cinema retains something of the prohibited character peculiar to the vision of the primal scene'). Metz, *Le Signifiant imaginaire*, pp. 89–91; *Psychoanalysis and Cinema*, pp. 64–65. Of course, looking back to our point of departure for this section, a concern with the primal scene in cinema is one Shaviro is keen to avoid. Compare Deleuze's dismissive reference to 'la psychanalyse, qui n'a jamais donné au cinéma qu'un seul objet, une seule rengaine, la scène dite primitive' ('psychoanalysis, which has only ever given cinema one sole object, one single refrain, the so-called primitive scene'). Deleuze, *Cinéma 2*, p. 54; *Cinema 2*, p. 36.
99. Roger Laporte, 'Au-delà de l'"Horror vacui"', *Nouvelle Revue de la Psychanalyse*, 11, 'Figures du vide' (1975), 117–26 (pp. 120–21). For the passage on the smile, see Blanchot, *Celui qui ne m'accompagnait pas* (Paris: Gallimard, 1953), pp. 168–70; *SHB*, pp. 337–38.

100. Leclaire, *On tue un enfant*, pp. 12–13.
101. Ibid.
102. D. W. Winnicott, 'Fear of Breakdown', in *Psycho-Analytic Explorations*, ed. by Clare Winnicott, Ray Shepherd and Madeleine Davis (London: Karnac Books, 1989), pp. 87–95 (p. 88).
103. Ibid., p. 90.
104. Ibid.
105. Ibid., p. 92.
106. See Watt, 'The Uses of Maurice Blanchot in Bernard Stiegler's *Technics and Time*'.
107. Kevin Hart, *The Dark Gaze: Maurice Blanchot and the Sacred* (Chicago, IL: University of Chicago Press, 2004), p. 60.
108. Hill, *Maurice Blanchot and Fragmentary Writing*, p. 335.
109. Ibid., p. 337.
110. Christopher Fynsk, *Infant Figures: The Death of the 'Infans' and Other Scenes of Origin* (Stanford, CA: Stanford University Press, 2000), p. 60.
111. Ibid., p. 59.
112. Lacoue-Labarthe, *Agonie terminée, agonie interminable*, p. 144.
113. Derrida, *Parages*, pp. 137–38; *Parages*, p. 120.
114. Fynsk, *Infant Figures*, p. 72.
115. Ibid., pp. 74–75.
116. Ibid., p. 1.
117. Ibid., pp. 44–45.
118. Bellour, *L'Entre-Images*, p. 13; *Between-the-Images*, p. 15.
119. Didi-Huberman, 'De ressemblance à ressemblance', p. 155. Didi-Huberman appears to be playing on, as well as *l'arrêt de mort* and *l'arrêt sur image*, Serge Daney's term 'arrêt sur l'image' or 'immobile image', see Serge Daney, 'From Movies to Moving', in *Art and the Moving Image: A Critical Reader*, ed. by Tanya Leighton (London: Tate Publishing and Afterall, 2008), pp. 334–39. With the motif of the young girl, Didi-Huberman is also alluding to the death mask 'L'Inconnue de la Seine'. For this, see Anne-Gaëlle Saliot, ' "Venir comme des profondeurs d'un tombeau": Maurice Blanchot, l'inconnue de la Seine et les images', in *Maurice Blanchot*, ed. by Hoppenot and Rabaté, pp. 217–25.
120. Laura Mulvey, *Death 24x a Second: Stillness and the Moving Image* (London: Reaktion Books, 2006), p. 196.
121. Roland Barthes, *La Chambre claire: note sur la photographie* (Paris: Gallimard, 1980), p. 150; *Camera Lucida*, trans. by Richard Howard (London: Vintage Books, 2000), p. 96.
122. Barthes quotes Blanchot on fascination later in the text, Barthes, *La Chambre claire*, p. 165; *Camera Lucida*, p. 106.
123. See Bident, *Maurice Blanchot*, p. 582.
124. Mulvey, *Death 24x a Second*, p. 187 (my emphasis).
125. Lacoue-Labarthe, *Agonie terminée, agonie interminable*, p. 94.

CHAPTER 2

❖

Appropriations of Blanchot in Godard's *Histoire(s) du cinéma* and Deleuze's *Cinéma* volumes

'...l'image est bonheur...'

> Le cinéma ne craignait donc rien des autres, ni d'elle-même. Il n'était pas à l'abri du temps, il était l'abri du temps. Oui, l'image est bonheur, — mais près d'elle le néant séjourne, et toute la puissance de l'image ne peut s'exprimer qu'en lui faisant appel. Il faut peut-être ajouter encore que l'image, capable de nier le néant, est aussi le regard du néant sur nous. Elle est légère, et il est immensément lourd. Elle brille, et il est cette épaisseur diffuse où rien ne se montre.
>
> [Thus the cinema did not fear anything from others, nor from itself. It was not protected from time; it was the protection of time. Yes, the image is joy — but close to it lies nothingness, and all the power of the image cannot be expressed except by calling to nothingness. Perhaps one must add that the image, capable of negating nothingness, is also the gaze of nothingness upon us. It is light, and it is immensely heavy. It shines, and it is this diffuse thickness in which nothing reveals itself.][1]

In a filmic text full of quotations from a diverse range of sources, it is remarkable that Jean-Luc Godard in his video history of the cinema, *Histoire(s) du cinéma* (1989–1998), affords Blanchot one of the final references in the piece (at the end of Chapter 4B, 'Les Signes parmi nous' [The Signs Among Us]). Godard also explicitly names and reproduces a (rare) photograph of Blanchot (Figure 2.1). The above lines are read by Godard, to a doleful piano melody, over the following images:

Within the context of this brief montage, 'le regard du néant sur nous' seems to refer to the eponymous monster from F. W. Murnau's *Nosferatu* (1922), played by Max Schreck, and his penetrating gaze at the camera. Yet in terms of this quotation in itself, it must be asked more rigorously: to what exactly does the 'image' refer? In other words, how does Godard relate the Blanchotian image (with all that would be implied by it, as we examined in the preceding chapter) to what is onscreen? Is the 'image' something that can be located within this sequence in Godard's film? Could it in some sense refer to the sequence as a whole? It might also be asked how we are to understand the idea that the image can only express itself by appealing to itself. Nor is the provenance of the cloaked figures immediately apparent, unlike the instantly recognizable Nosferatu. Are they the 'diffuse' element of this 'épaisseur'? Yet nothing here 'brille', nor is there any evident 'bonheur'. As Roland-François Lack notes, the texts in Chapter 4B are recited with 'mournful resignation'.[2] The piano music (from the album *The Sea* by Ketil Bjørnstad [1994]) is carried over from the previous quotation and only runs until the word 'bonheur'. At this point the image of Nosferatu fades and the remainder of this section of the sequence plays out in silence. This sequence comes amid a closing gallery of quotations, including one from Arthur Rimbaud and one from Jorge Luis Borges, and this is surely the darkest of them. It is also curious that Godard chooses to reproduce not just the words but also a photograph of Blanchot.[3] It is as if the ghoul of Nosferatu suggests a mortification at the heart of the askance look of Blanchot, the mirrored pose and profile of Nosferatu revealing an underside to that of Blanchot — as if death was present in that look itself, making the juxtaposition of images a visualization of the gaze of nothingness upon us.

After the discussion in the previous chapter of how the concepts of the image and fascination in Blanchot's writing can be understood in relation to cinema, this chapter will explore how these ideas are put into play in Godard's film. At the same time as he was making *Histoire(s) du cinéma*, in 1995, Godard averred apropos of his film *JLG/JLG: autoportrait de décembre* (1995) that he wanted to make a film 'qui ressemble aux livres que j'ai pu lire dans mon adolescence, ceux de Blanchot, de Bataille' [which resembles the books I read during my adolescence, those of Blanchot, of Bataille].[4] What could it mean for a film to 'resemble' a book by Blanchot or Bataille?

Malraux and the Museum

We must be careful with the opening lines quoted, for Blanchot's original does not refer to 'le cinéma' but 'l'œuvre', and this ostensibly highly unusual reference to film in Blanchot is in fact a Godardian interpolation (*A* 48–51; *F* 37–40). Godard frequently and silently amends quotations. Leslie Hill has demonstrated that these particular lines, and the work of Blanchot more generally, are an important reference for Godard.[5] The reference in Blanchot's original is to visual artworks found in a museum, such as painting and sculpture. However, Godard's implication that cinema can be understood as a Blanchotian *œuvre* is highly significant. According to one mode of thought, this would be to understand the individual film as the discrete work of an artist. According to another, we might understand 'cinema' as a concept, as a totality of films working towards its destiny as a medium (cinema becoming a version of the absence of the book). Both readings seem logical in the context of Godard's usage. Godard claims the status of *œuvre* for cinema, which already gives a sense of how a film can be like a book by Blanchot or Bataille. The quotation comes from Blanchot's essay 'Le Musée, l'art et le temps' [The Museum, Art, and Time], originally published in two parts in *Critique* in 1950–51 and only twenty years later collected in *L'Amitié* [Friendship] (1971). The essay in parts reads like an addendum to 'Les Deux Versions de l'imaginaire', with which it is contemporaneous. The image according to Blanchot is not only 'capable de nier le néant' (an idea associated with Sartre), but is also the regard of nothingness on us; Didi-Huberman has argued that the whole dialectic of 'Les Deux Versions de l'imaginaire' is implied in these words.[6] This is a reiteration of the point stressed in the previous chapter, that the relation engendered by the image is double: the image is both in relation to a thing (of which it is image) and to the one who experiences the image. Godard is quoting a concentrated statement of Blanchot's concept of the image. Blanchot's essay is about André Malraux's *La Psychologie de l'art* (1947–49), but it also provides a platform for his remarks on the wider relation between art and history, which are generally in opposition to Malraux's humanist conception of the *musée imaginaire*. 'Le Musée, l'art et le temps' is an extremely rich text and it is suggestive that a filmmaker calls attention to it.

In the essay on Malraux, Blanchot identifies a break in the history of art. This is the moment both of modern art and the Museum: it is when art becomes ubiquitous, when it is removed from life and put into the museum that it truly achieves self-consciousness. As often in Blanchot, what is at stake is the capacity of an art to embody its own concept and to attain consciousness of itself in relation to that concept. Classical aesthetics idealized the moment of appearance in a work of art which infinitely repeated itself — the statue which forever declared its presence being one example. This moment of appearance might seem to represent the capacity for an infinitely renewed presence. However, following the break, appearance itself is said to disappear and the present does not repeat itself, instead collapsing into an 'absence de temps' (*A* 43; *F* 32–33). The artwork becomes identified with its material and instead of smiling or appearing, it assures us that it is *not there*, that what appears is *nothing* as such, mere matter; this is what is called 'resemblance'. Much as we saw in the genealogy traced in the previous chapter, fascination as described by Blanchot is a historical rather than a timeless phenomenon: today we do not relate to art in the manner of classical aesthetics and Blanchot is trying to establish how it is we do relate to art today. We can see that with Malraux and Godard the question becomes one of how to approach both modern art in general and, in Godard's case, cinema.

In addressing this question, Blanchot is particularly concerned with Malraux's notion of the *musée imaginaire*. To begin with, this phrase refers to the idea of divorcing artworks from their original functions and their usual historical, contextual parentheses. In this sense the museum offers 'une confrontation de métamorphoses' ('a confrontation of metamorphoses').[7] It could be argued that, to the extent that Godard offers any kind of clue in citing Blanchot's text, the text offers a way of reading his project. This is to say that *Histoire(s)* can be read as a Museum in the Malrucian sense, but also — by the extended logic opened up by the quotation — that it is a work of the imaginary in Blanchot's sense. It is with something of this in mind that Michael Temple begins his essay, the most comprehensive account of the significance of Malraux's place in *Histoire(s)*, with a conceit (reflexive in light of Godard's interpolation in the Blanchot text) in which he rewords a passage from Blanchot's essay on Malraux so that the references to Malraux are all replaced with eerily pre-emptive references to Godard's *Histoire(s)*.[8] More generally it could be said that *Histoire(s)* reflects on the capacity of cinema to embody itself as concept. At the same time, it also reflects on itself as an individual cinematic artwork and its ability to deal with that question. The film thus opens an *abyme*-like structure of reflection.

Malraux is read by Blanchot as writing a history of art that can be broadly understood as Hegelian, and Malraux's concept of metamorphosis can be related to the dialectic (for example *A* 28; *F* 18). The end of art for Malraux is myth, and it is a myth that looks towards salvation. Malraux describes the temporality of the work as a process of metamorphosis, which he calls the present. Blanchot in his essay, however, flatly opposes this with the notion of the absence of time. The idea of the present is one he frequently deconstructs and so this is an expected move in his commentary. This absence of time is to be understood as not far from the genealogy of art sketched in the previous chapter — what was read then as a dialectic of art as first presencing the gods, then presencing their absence, and now presencing the absence of that presence is negotiated by Blanchot in relation to Malraux's conception of art. Modern art is said to be conscious of this truth of absence, but what Blanchot takes issue with in Malraux is the notion that this can represent any kind of eternalization of human powers over nature or death. Thus Blanchot writes that Malraux 'semble exclure de la genèse artistique la notion d'image' (*A* 31) ('seems to exclude from artistic genesis the notion of image', *F* 21). This, as we see from the opening lines quoted, is what he goes on to elaborate.

Reading Malraux and Blanchot, as well as others, Douglas Smith has demonstrated the importance of the conception of the imaginary as a space in post-war French thought generally. He argues that Malraux's imaginary museum 'resembles'

Blanchot's space of literature in being 'a kind of unmappable space that explodes the traditional notion of the canon'.[9] Blanchot agrees with Malraux that modern art is the product of the falling away of religion in which art takes on transcendent properties, but he sees this transcendence as misunderstood: for Blanchot 'art both transcends and does not transcend temporal human existence [...] Art [...] is an absolute contestatory self-affirmation that reveals the nature of human activity as negation and the consequent absence of a substantive self to affirm'.[10] While what is crucial for Malraux is the ability of art to negate death and in this way to open the timeless space of the museum, for Blanchot 'art is itself the ambiguous incarnation of death' which suspends time and space as such.[11] Through a reading of how Hegelian negation and the transcendence of art are understood in different ways by different writers (including Sartre and Merleau-Ponty), Smith shows how 'Blanchot's theory of the image recognizes the unfulfilled potential of Malraux's insights as well as their risks and on that basis proceeds to reconstruct the space of the imaginary. This reconstruction is, of course, a deconstruction'.[12]

The lines quoted by Godard from Blanchot's essay on Malraux come from the final pages of that essay, in particular its final paragraph. Blanchot is making something like a summative statement on the function of the image in the abstract, and in placing these lines where they come at the climax of *Histoire(s)*, Godard also is according them an exemplary status. According to Blanchot, the perfection of the work of art, the eternalizing motion that would admit it to Malraux's Museum, is also the moment of the return of the work to absence. It is thus that we are to understand the poetic idea that though the image is 'bonheur', it lies close to nothingness. Although the image comforts us by sheltering us from time (puts a halt to time), it is also at that stroke outside of time and made up of absence. Blanchot continues that it is necessary for us to add this darker notion of the image as the gaze of nothingness upon us, and that the image is 'l'interstice, la tache de ce soleil noir, déchirure qui nous donne, sous l'apparence de l'éclat éblouissant, le négatif de l'inépuisable profondeur négative' (*A* 51) ('the interstice, the spot of this black sun, a laceration that gives us, under the appearance of a dazzling brilliance, the negative in the inexhaustible negative depths', *F* 40). This is what is meant when he paraphrases Malraux that today art has arrived at a consciousness of itself that is 'surtout négative' (*A* 27) ('above all negative', *F* 18), a consciousness of that negativity. So Blanchot's reading is that the image must, in addition to Malraux's account of its splendour, be considered in terms of the effects of its, so to speak, underside — which is null and *désœuvré*. The reference to 'bonheur' thus seems to be partly ironic: the last thing the Blanchotian artwork appears to offer us is deliverance. These lines can be read as an extreme condensation of the argument in 'La Littérature et le droit à la mort' that the joy of the author comes in his being validated *as* an author as a result of the production of the work; more precisely, it consists in 'ce que Hegel appelle le pur bonheur de passer de la nuit de la possibilité au jour de la présence' (*PF* 298) ('what Hegel calls the pure joy of passing from the night of possibility into the daytime of presence', *WF* 305). What is crucial, then, is this back and forth motion of night and day, dark and light, understood as impossibility and possibility. It is also in this way that the relation to history — as we learn earlier in the piece quoted — is one of, again, an 'absence de temps', a phrase which alludes only to 'ce pouvoir que nous avons de mettre fin au monde' ('the power that we have of putting an end to the world'); 'pouvoir qui est peut-être une souveraineté, mais qui s'affirme aussi dans toutes les situations où l'homme renonce à se maîtriser, accepte de ne pas se ressaisir' (*A* 43–44) ('a power that is perhaps a sovereignty but that also asserts itself in all situations in which man gives up mastering himself and accepts that he will not recover himself', *F* 33). One might consider this absence a nothingness, Blanchot continues:

> mais néant qui est encore l'être, l'être dont on ne peut rien saisir ni rien faire, où jamais rien ne commence ni ne s'achève, où tout se répète à l'infini parce que rien n'y a jamais lieu vraiment, l'éternel, peut-être, mais alors le ressassement éternel. (*A* 44)

> [but a nothingness that is still being, being about which one cannot grasp anything or do anything, where nothing ever begins and nothing ever ends, where everything is repeated ad infinitum because nothing has ever truly taken place. The eternal, perhaps, but if so, the eternal recurrence.] (*F* 33)

Throughout much of Blanchot's work the Nietzschean eternal return is thought through the absence of time, in which this time is repetitive and evokes the ancient past (the primal scene of the previous chapter). In other words, and in contrast to Malraux, for whom art is in part a kind of repository for history, Blanchot sees history as in a sense liquidated by art, art being the place in which one can withdraw from history. The position is one of passivity, the end of meaningful action. This is the meaning, to reiterate, of the line Godard quotes above, that the work is a shelter *of* time, not a shelter *from* time.

It is furthermore thus that Blanchot writes of art's task, 'qui est d'accomplir l'absence et non seulement l'absence du monde, mais l'absence comme monde' (*A* 44) ('which is to achieve absence; not simply the absence of the world, but absence as world', *F* 34). Godard appears to stage this sense as the lines quoted above are set to a still of the mad gaze of Nosferatu and a silent, slow-motion procession of sinister, masked figures approaching the screen, as if to confirm both the irony of the image as 'bonheur' and the ineluctable logic of the image's relation to nothingness; Blanchot's concept of the image is in fact marked by a kind of muted horror. Godard's montage is itself thus an interpretation of the text. The dual movement of the fading visage of the vampire and the nearing ghouls before the film cuts to black enacts the idea of the image as the gaze of nothingness, coming from and negating nothingness, black as talismanic of nothingness. Thus, 'bonheur' becomes a very complex term both in Godard's sequence and Blanchot's text. 'Le Musée, l'art et le temps' is close to 'Les Deux Versions de l'imaginaire' and an example of this proximity is found in the echo of this idea of happiness. Blanchot writes: 'Le bonheur de l'image, c'est qu'elle est une limite auprès de l'indéfini' (*EL* 266) ('The gratifying aspect of the image is that it constitutes a limit at the edge of the indefinite', *SL* 254). The muted phrasing of the translation here itself suggests the ambiguity of 'bonheur'. Looking to subsequent occasions on which Blanchot uses this word, one might point to the sense in the primal scene of 'le sentiment de bonheur qui aussitôt submerge l'enfant, la joie ravageante dont il ne pourra témoigner que par les larmes' (*ED* 117) ('the feeling of happiness that straightaway submerges the child, the ravaging joy to which he can bear witness only by tears', *WD* 72). In both cases, we have the sense that fascination, through the exposure to an immemorial past, conveys us to a profoundly ambiguous feeling. In the context of the gallery of quotations, the idea of 'bonheur' opens up a further level of connection to Georges Bataille, who is the author of the quotation immediately preceding the one from Blanchot.[13] 'Le Musée, l'art et le temps' was collected as the second essay in *L'Amitié*, and this collection as a whole in many ways forms an extended homage to Bataille.[14] The final, eponymous essay of the collection is a personal tribute to Bataille. It would not be too much to suggest that Godard is in some way playing on this idea of friendship and homage in his choice of references in the closing sequence of quotations. The early essays in *L'Amitié* relate to Bataille's pre-war work on museological topics in *Documents* (1929–30), in which Bataille seeks to break down the image to its 'formless' or materialist ground, its opening onto nothing.[15] Taking in these intertextual connections, the notion of 'bonheur' here stands in close proximity to anxiety, fear, and silence, topics which will recur in the course of this book.[16] The conflicted sense of 'bonheur' is furthermore developed in different ways by Godard and evoked in the volumes accompanying his film when he writes, quoting the final line of Max Ophüls's *Le Plaisir* (1952), that 'le bonheur n'est pas gai' [happiness is not cheerful].[17]

Histoire(s) du cinéma finishes its almost four-and-a-half hour running time shortly after the quotation from Blanchot, but the use of Nosferatu looks back to his other grisly appearances in *Histoire(s)*. The same image of Nosferatu appears, for example, in Chapter 4A during Alain Cuny's reading of a text by Élie Faure.[18] Here is described a 'force centrale qui a gouverné le cinéma' [central force which has governed cinema], which we follow:

> avec l'ombre et le rayon qui rodent, illuminant ceci, cachant cela [...] Ce qui plonge dans la lumière est le retentissement de ce que submerge la nuit. Ce que submerge la nuit prolonge dans l'invisible ce qui plonge dans la lumière.
>
> [with the prowling shadow and beam, illuminating one thing, hiding another [...] That which plunges into light is the echo of what the night submerges. What the night submerges sustains in the invisible that which plunges into light.]

I draw attention to this to suggest how the tenebrous association of Nosferatu connects Blanchot as but one term in a wider system of references to light and dark at work in Godard's film. Reading beauty through the metaphor of light in Chapter 2B, Jacques Aumont explicitly invokes Blanchot, among others, in the context of 'the impersonal being, the impersonal existent of French phenomenology', in which 'light can be identified with this *there is*, this murmur of being'.[19] As interpreters of the film have noted, Godard's use of stills, clips, and other materials generates a double movement of invocation and decontextualization, from which an associative play between images and materials perpetually arises. The Cuny monologue is an example of original material filmed by Godard and not excerpted from elsewhere. This makes it anchor some of the surrounding material that has been drawn from other sources. Within a minute of the beginning of Cuny's reading, Nosferatu is the seventh image with which we have been presented, those preceding including an image of Frankenstein and a still from Philippe Garrel's *Le Révélateur* (1968) — all works of shadowplay.

Michael Witt makes an argument that similarly moves from Malraux to Nosferatu: that for Godard, following Malraux, the artist does not so much transcribe reality as seek to replace it. For Malraux the art of the past must be recreated and, says Witt, *sacrificed* in the present, which is the principle of metamorphosis.[20] Witt argues that there is in Godard an additional step beyond André Bazin and other early cinema theorists' arguments, such that cinema not only *resurrects* dead life in the moment of projection, after preserving it in recording, but that in the process of filming it has to drain, even kill that life, so that the resurrection contains an act of mourning. Within all films is contained a secret dirge. For Bazin, life is preserved in cinema's recordings, and the logic of this argument is that the use of clips effectively constitutes this metamorphosis, the sacrifice of this resurrected life.[21] It is thus that the imagery used to evoke the function of art is that of fire and the vampire, both of which work by consumption and destruction.[22] Hence the mad gaze of Nosferatu the vampire would be, by this reckoning, a metaphorical image of cinema gazing back at us. Hill discusses the images of Blanchot and Nosferatu as 'if you will, two versions of the filmic imaginary'. One is said to stand for the spectacularization of the media while the other is proof of (im)possibility of redeeming reality by recourse to an image (Nosferatu being cinematic shorthand for Nazism). 'The exploitative violence of spectacularization on the one hand, then, and the grace (without grace) of impossible redemption on the other — there is perhaps no better summary of Godard's history of cinema as a whole, and the irreducible ambiguity to which it bears witness.'[23] We must add the fact of Nosferatu as a ghoul, given the stress made by Blanchot in 'Les Deux Versions de l'imaginaire' on the *cadaverous* nature of the image. The ideas of light and dark are once again brought out in relation to 'forces' and figures of the shadows.

When asked directly about the quotation from Blanchot with which this chapter opened, it being put to him that with Blanchot the image does not have 'la plénitude immédiate que vous lui donnez d'habitude' ('the immediate plenitude that you habitually give it'), Godard replied: 'C'est difficile à penser que l'image est regard, parce qu'on pense toujours que l'image est regard mais à travers l'objectif' ('It is difficult to think that the image is gaze, because we always think that the image is gaze but through a lens'). In other words, it is very strange to think of the image as *looking back at us*; it is strange to think of our undoing. As Godard indicates, the *bonheur* at work in this is one far removed from ordinary conceptions of happiness.[24] All of this serves to ask again the question, which can be asked in many different terms and around which this study will orbit: what is it that is at work in the making and use of images?

Sacrifice

An important way in which Godard invites a conceptualization of the image is through the notion of sacrifice. One sequence from Chapter 1B, 'Une histoire seule' [A Solitary History], is particularly significant in this regard (see Figures 2.5–10).

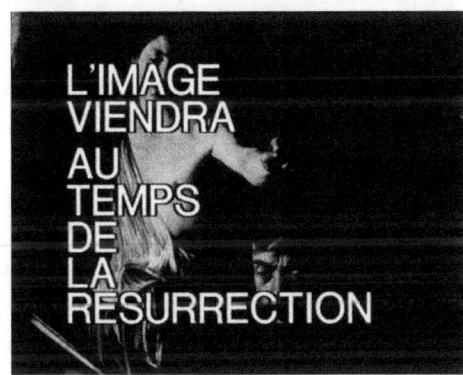
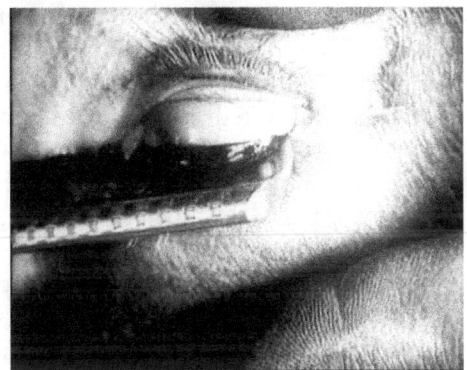

Figs. 2.5–2.10.

This line, 'L'IMAGE VIENDRA AU TEMPS DE LA RESURRECTION' [The image will come at the time of the Resurrection], is as Witt notes frequently misidentified as coming from St Paul (following Godard's misattributions).[25] About a minute earlier, the front cover of Samuel Beckett's *L'Image* (1988) repeatedly flashes on the screen as Godard is shown looking at books on his shelf, further signalling that this is a discursive moment in the film about the meaning of images in general.[26] Beckett's front cover doubles as a reference to his text and as an image in its own right: an image of the word 'image' which appears in the montage between black screens. Beckett's unpunctuated text describes someone in the dirt reminiscing about a past romance. The 'image' of the title and announced in the last line ('c'est fait j'ai fait l'image' [it's done I've made the image]) is thus an imagined or remembered image.

The images making up this brief sequence here themselves are of course well-known. The notorious moment from Luis Buñuel's *Un chien andalou* (1929) (Figure 2.8) is the only moving footage during this sequence, and the text appears only briefly over this and for slightly longer over Caravaggio's *David with the Head of Goliath* (1610) (Figure 2.9). The image of the eye being slit (Figure 2.10) is only very briefly shown, between black screens, after the main part of the sequence has finished. I have elided three stills from Carl Dreyer's *Ordet* (1955) from between Figures 2.7 and 2.8, which pass in quick succession and repeat the words 'OH TEMPS!'.

Perhaps the most striking feature linking these images is that they all depict the operations of hands. At a more abstract level, all pertain in some way to the idea of sacrifice. Let us first take the Giacometti (Figure 2.5), who is familiar from the previous chapter. The text crosses the thumb, as if to attach itself to it as a label. The text only appears after a second or two, then disappears. Giacometti only appears a few times in *Histoire(s)*, but for all that his usage is symptomatic of much of the material status of the images Godard uses. In sequences such as this we are more than simply presented with free-floating images. Godard's film works with images that are already cut out from other films, and we are often given a set detail from stills, or in this case an image of only part of the sculpture — only the hand, not the whole length of the arm, admittedly of a sculpture named *La Main* [The Hand] (1947).[27] Yet this would suggest a further level of appropriation beyond turning a three-dimensional object into a moment of a two-dimensional filmic image: *La Main*, which is to begin with a plaster sculpture of an arm starkly impaled on a stick, is subject to a further Orphic dismemberment and disintegration, as if this filmic quotation constituted an additional amputation. The sculpture is firstly an object before it is an image. If, as the superimposed text suggests, it is an archetypal image, if there is some equivalence between this image of part of Giacometti's sculpture and the word 'L'IMAGE', then it would suggest that the image is not simply derivative (qua reproduction), but something torn, separated, exposed.

Timothy Mathews's recent monograph on Giacometti is a suggestive reference, for *La Main* is read by Mathews as in itself a fragmentary work; in Godard's work it would be subject to a further fragmentation. Mathews writes that *La Main* 'shows a fragment', the notion of the fragmentary being understood according to Blanchot's terms as 'the gradually of the sudden'.[28] The fragment Mathews alludes to reads in full: '*Fragment: au-delà de toute fracture, de tout éclat, la patience de pure impatience, le peu à peu du soudainement*' (*ED* 58) ('Fragment: beyond fracturing, or bursting, the patience of pure impatience, the little by little suddenly', *WD* 34). For Mathews, this would speak to how the sculpture is in one's visual space 'suddenly', the sudden appearance of just part of a body, yet one which would gradually allude to the rest of its invisible body. It is simultaneously alive in its waving, yet dead in impalement. Suddenly then gradually, gradually then suddenly. There is something of this in the way *La Main* is presented in Godard's film, whereby the image appears suddenly, devoid of text for one second, the text present for five seconds, before the text disappears, the image stable and naked for a further, single second, before a transition over the course of five seconds to the following image of the hand on the floor. The transition begins with a sharp orchestral crash of snares and cymbals on the soundtrack — a sudden violent sound announcing a gradual visual dissolution.[29] The film mimics the movement of appearance and disappearance in which it would present itself were one to be physically present before the actual object.

Mathews writes that *La Main* gives form to the 'destiny of loss': 'The idea of a loss is not loss but representation, presence, here-ness. The immobility of *La Main* shows this, its material inevitability; it shows waving to the departed and not the departed themselves, the dead or the gone'.[30] This material destiny of the artwork has already been discussed, yet what happens when that materiality is then re-appropriated, the work put at a further remove as in this film? It would seem to bespeak a second death. Not only in these lines evoking the Blanchotian image as present in disappearance, Mathews's work speaks to the notion of *relation* more generally. This points to the connection between the themes I have been pursuing so far: the departed dead, a material object of art, the fragmentary and the notion of the image, all present in a moment of film.

Figures 2.6 and 2.7 are taken from Robert Bresson's *Procès de Jeanne d'Arc* [The Trial of Joan of Arc] (1962). Figure 2.6 shows the point at which a stone is thrown into Joan's cell, smashing the cell window as the mob outside are said to be 'clamouring for her death'. Figure 2.7 shows a detail from when Joan is ill in bed, she is attended to by the assembled churchmen and her chains are removed. Gestures in the image from Bresson are distinct, gentle, moulded (worked) as a Giacometti — the simplicity of gesture, in which the act is itself symbolic. With these images, Godard presents Joan of Arc as the paradigmatic martyr she is, the stone violently cast through the window prefiguring her burning at the stake, her outstretched hand in illness showing her submission to this sacrifice. In a speech by Malraux in 1961, on the anniversary of her death, he spoke of Joan as the 'first martyr of France'. This term is understood by Malraux in its consonance with the notion of sacrifice, declaring in a flourish that 'only sacrifice is equal to death'.[31]

Bresson's film is also a notable reference given the almost documentary nature it has by virtue of the source material of the actual historical trial transcripts. As Keith Reader observes, '[t]he sense that Bresson's *modèles* quote their lines rather than expressing them — like in a very different context the characters in a Brecht play — is thus more powerful in *Le Procès* than anywhere else in his work'.[32] As with the framing of the shots in Bresson's films in general, in which we tend not to be given to see the whole of a scene, but only the essential movements of it, there is a sense in which Bresson's films — like Giacometti's sculpture — are *already* subject to an operation of abstraction. Indeed, Deleuze elaborates the notion of the 'spiritual automaton' (discussed later in this chapter) by reference to Bresson's models as reduced to daily gestures that 's'empare la pensée du dehors, comme l'impensable dans la pensée' ('thought seizes from the outside, as the unthinkable in thought').[33]

Buñuel's shot (Figure 2.8), of course, is extremely famous. In this context, in which montage is the work of establishing a discursive meaning, the cutting of the eye would seem to signify the destruction of the condition of seeing. The montage separates the final image, containing two frames showing a single slicing motion, with black screens — black being what is 'seen' when nothing is seen. The montage points to both the sacrifice of seeing (the black screens) and the 'seeing' or the rendering visible of spectacular sacrifice (Caravaggio's classic decapitation in Figure 2.9). It is as if Godard wants to show the blackness as what lies behind the passing images, to show the nothingness that lies at the edge of the image, to evoke the quotation from the beginning of this chapter; as if to show it momentarily returning the gaze. In the previous chapter the motif of blindness was read as the impossibility of not seeing, as exposing the lightless interval between and behind images. This sequence, at the same time as presenting sacrificial images, replicates and evokes the sacrificial operation by which the sacrificed object enters into intimate relation with nothingness.

Histoire(s) du cinéma is a work to which Jacques Rancière has returned repeatedly in the course of recent years. In his book *La Fable cinématographique* [Film Fables] (2001), Rancière critiques *Histoire(s)* by saying its images have a tendency to turn into icons — icon understood as sacred. Rancière finds in *Histoire(s)* evidence of 'une sacralisation nouvelle de l'image et de la présence' ('a new sacralisation of the image and presence').[34] This is achieved by the way in which Godard extracts images from their narrative and subtracts their narrative function. This leaves the images to gain their power through their singularity, not by virtue of their combination, and this is a function of their decontextualization. It is for this reason that, for Rancière, Godard's method can be characterized as a kind of 'anti-montage'.[35] Godard's task is, according to Rancière, a soteriological one. *Histoire(s)* is:

> une entreprise de rédemption: fragmentation godardienne veut délivrer le potentiel des images de sa soumission aux histoires. En inventant des relations inédites entre films, photographies, peintures, bandes d'actualité, musiques, etc., elle fait jouer rétrospectivement au cinéma le rôle de révélateur et de communicateur qu'il a trahi en s'asservissant à l'industrie des histoires.
>
> [an enterprise of redemption: Godard's fragmentation is intended to deliver images and their potential from subjection to stories. By inventing original relationships between films, photographs, paintings, newsreels, music and so on, it retrospectively gives back to cinema its role of revelator and communicator which it had betrayed by enslaving itself to the storytelling industry.][36]

This argument revolves around the notorious sequence in Chapter 1A in which images from Nazi concentration camps, taken from footage shot by George Stevens during the war (one of the first to film the death camps), are edited together with shots of Elizabeth Taylor, taken from George Stevens's *A Place in the Sun* (1951), and a detail from Giotto's fresco of the Resurrection, *Noli me tangere* (1304–06).[37] Rancière is referring to how Godard rotates the image of Mary Magdalene in the fresco so that she appears to be coming from the sky and reaching down to Elizabeth Taylor. Through this montage, Godard seeks to sacralize the figure in the vividness of the moment of appearance. This 'cutting' would be the sacrifice Witt talks of, in which the image is taken from its place for exaltation. It would be a second death, and therefore, in the terms we are developing, the process by which a thing becomes image, even as Rancière argues that it brings the figure back to life. The question would then be the difference between icon and image. Most recently in the debate over this sequence, Céline Scemama has stressed the sense that the images are presented 'in a state of wandering and disconnection' in which there is 'no possibility of salvation'.[38] In a manner like the silence of the ghouls in the sequence featuring the photograph of Blanchot, Scemama writes that '[t]he halt in the music freezes the picture, which seems to remain forever repressed in time'.[39] The faces of the dead in this sequence will remain haunting figures in a limbo and will not be resurrected. Thus the principle of resurrection should be understood — and, Scemama argues, is understood by Godard — such that the dead only come back as image.[40] Eliciting the links to the Blanchot sequence, it could be argued that the word 'bonheur' echoes Godard's reference in voiceover to 'le bonheur d'Elizabeth Taylor': any redemptive joy is undercut with the ambiguity of the image.[41]

Douglas Morrey in this manner argues against Rancière's interpretation of Godard as partaking in a practice of iconization in *Histoire(s)*:

> What Godard seeks to do in this montage [the Georges Stevens sequence], as in others in *Histoire(s) du cinéma*, is thus not simply to raise the film image to the status of icon, but rather to stress that which, in the image, remains unapproachable, inexpressible; the image for Godard does not symbolise resurrection or the sacred, rather it evokes *as* sacred precisely that which cannot be symbolised, an absence which can never be made present.[42]

What emerges from the 'film image' is the 'unapproachable', which is the image in Blanchot's terms or the second version of the imaginary. Morrey concludes his treatment of this theme with a Blanchotian echo: 'In the image of that which it imagines, *Histoire(s) du cinéma* gives us to see the infinite regress of the image, that which first captivates us in the cinema and continues ever after to exert its fascination'.[43] What Morrey seems to be suggesting, contra Rancière, is that if the profane image would regress, then this would show the fascinating image in Blanchot's terms. The fascinating, 'unapproachable' aspect inheres as a potentiality of the image. In this way, the question of 'sacralisation' can be read in terms of a negative sacred, an infinite *absence* that is opened onto. Here again we are not far from Bataille. For Serge Zenkine, the notion of sacrifice in Bataille runs in parallel to the notion of the image in Blanchot. In both cases one is presented with the loss of an external form or physical destruction; the correlative is that 'intimacy' in Bataille's terms is related to the logic of resemblance in Blanchot. This parallelism indicates, for Zenkine, the place of the sacred in Blanchot's work, which is related to an elementary nature, a loss of form, an intimate nothingness, an 'auto-decomposition', and *effondrement*.[44] Rather than a raising to the empyrean, this model of sacrifice would be one of dissolution, a sacred that withdraws, and this may help us to come to a different sense from Rancière's resurrection as to how the sacred functions in *Histoire(s)*.

On the register of the sacred, we should note that for Giorgio Agamben, *Histoire(s) du cinéma* is 'an apocalypse of the cinema', in which 'apocalypse' is to be understood in the senses of catastrophe and revelation.[45] The messianic power of the image is a power of 'decreation' and a result of montage, which Agamben characterizes by 'repetition and stoppage':

> What becomes of an image wrought in this way by repetition and stoppage? It becomes, so to speak, 'an image of nothing.' Apparently, the images Godard shows us are images of images extracted from other films. But they acquire the capacity to show themselves qua images. They are no longer images of something about which one must immediately recount a meaning, narrative or otherwise. They exhibit themselves as such. The true messianic power is this power to give the image to this 'imagelessness,' which, as Benjamin said, is the refuge of every image.[46]

Both Morrey and Agamben are trying to reach the elusive nature of the image in Godard's film. Both have recourse to the word 'image' in more than one sense at a time, to the imaginary in its two versions. In one sense, this is not so far from Rancière's notion of anti-montage, according to which images are not animated by montage but suspended by it and in this suspension they show themselves without reference to narrative. However, in Agamben's account, montage is the power by which images find their relation to imagelessness.[47] Agamben's sense of imagelessness is close to Morrey's reading of the image as having an 'unapproachable' aspect and a core of 'absence'. James S. Williams evokes the sense that this 'decreation' has to be understood in terms of how concrete form and style allow the image to enter:

> A new realm of mystery and undecidability that lies within and beyond the literal image and is formed of opposites, as in montage which, if properly executed, can generate the flash and energy of the unexpected and unimagined — a sign of cinema's eternal self-renewal.[48]

In another context Williams has evoked how, at the same time as the image may be 'transformed metaphysically into a kind of epiphany, a manifestation of the mystery of cinematographic creation', what is crucial is the 'performability and transformability of the image within a larger signifying system rather than any innate expressivity it may possess'.[49] It is through the affective, formal, and figural connections that Godard sets up between images that the work resists its own conceptual totalization.[50] Close analysis of specific sequences will show how the specificity of literal images can undergo the transformation to become fascinating images.

In his essay on the place of Blanchot in *Histoire(s) du cinéma*, Hill argues that it is montage, not the image as such, which constitutes cinema: '"Speaking is not seeing", writes Blanchot in *L'Entretien infini*; to which Godard's film responds in (paradoxical) agreement: showing an image is not to say anything, since it is montage that speaks, not the image as such'.[51] It is remarkable that the major uses of Blanchot in the context of film theory often work around 'Parler, ce n'est pas voir', alluded to already and to which we will return. For Hill, what *Histoire(s)* brings out is that 'iterability, as Derrida calls it, not only governs so-called natural language; it names the possibility of cinematographic montage too. Quotation and montage in this regard are but two words for the same thing'.[52] Hill is addressing the sense of quotation as textual repetition which undermines its own putative original self-identity. The use of archive materials in *Histoire(s)* can, according to Hill, be read as a form of quotation: both 'address the moment in its essential repetition and its singularity, in its historicity and its contemporaneity, in relation to both the past and the future'.[53] Hill writes:

> By conceiving the image not as self-identity but as repetition and difference, the *neutre* also names that fold — not to be confused with self-reflexivity — by which cinema (among others), by dint of montage, is able to withdraw from itself to allow the singularity of its own trace to appear (or disappear). This movement of withdrawal and reinscription which the *neutre* designates in Blanchot simultaneously demands thought and resists it. It thereby affirms, so to speak, the necessary excess of textuality over positionality, of image and sound over thesis or argument. This excess is crucial. Without it, Godard's whole project of telling (and retelling) the history and histories of cinema by manipulating the historical archive would not be possible at all.[54]

Hill is here approaching the thought of the relation between the fragment and history. The fragment is unfinished and cannot be finished, and in this sense is very close to the notion of the historical moment or the instant. It is thus that Godard 'treats cinema as a form of fragmentary writing'.[55] What connects text and film is their common basis in a trace, rather than representation. There cannot be a resurrection of this trace or a return to the singularity of the instant, but only repetition. It is in this sense that quotation and the use of archive materials addresses the instant. What Hill refers to here as the trace appearing through repetition and difference is arguably not so far from Agamben's reading of the imagelessness that images are put into contact with through repetition and stoppage; this imagelessness is the 'excess' Hill writes of. Both readings appeal to a theoretical understanding of Godard's film in which its power lies in a repetitive movement in which the image reveals itself and withdraws.

This dynamic of appearance and disappearance is a movement which begins with the film's actual images in order to go beyond them, beyond specific sequences of montage to establish something like a general principle. As Hill says, it is not any individual image that speaks but montage. At a certain level, Godard's film works to show this movement as such and thus come to reflect on it. It is only by working at such a self-conscious level that it makes sense for Godard to invoke the quotation from Blanchot. The quotation's place in the film allows it in one sense to function as a commentary on what has gone before it in the film, a commentary on the dynamic at work in the film as a whole. It is in this self-consciousness, in which the film comes into contact with what could perhaps hyperbolically be called the essence of the image, that the film really attains the messianic quality identified by Agamben. If this involves, as Hill argues, an engagement with 'the moment' as such, we can observe the continuity with observations made earlier on the *instant*. The moment or instant comes out in the use of historical materials and the play of singularity implied through the practice of quotation; in other words, the instant emerges as a theme in the reference to and activation of previous *instances*, whether conceived of as the historical instances captured on film and replayed or the written word re-traced in quotation. In opening the past and a suspension of time, the instant opens up passivity and the relation to death. In the instant, the film in a manner of speaking is unworked. Hill's allusion to Derrida gives a clue to the answer to the question posed in the Introduction: the instant is cinematic in being unmoored from its own identity, like the ambiguity of the *déroulement* of film. This is also why Morrey is correct to argue that Godard's film presents not so much the work of the icon as it evokes absence as the sacred itself. The purpose of all of this — more than to take issue with Rancière as such — is to show how critics have been alive to what, it seems to me, in the terms developed so far, could be conceived of as a *Blanchotian filmic imaginary*. In other words, what is absolutely crucial is Hill's claim that Blanchot 'provides Godard, at least implicitly, with that theory of cinema which, paradoxically, cinema itself is alone able to supply'.[56] The precise extent to which Godard may or may not be aware of this operation is moot, for by definition this operation exceeds intention.

The Work of Hands

Giacometti appears on two further occasions in *Histoire(s)*, in Chapter 3B 'Une vague nouvelle' [A New Wave]. I am going to look at the first of these. On both occasions we are presented with images of hands. At the time of making *Histoire(s)*, in 1989, Godard himself likened his method of composition to that of the sculptor, and this, suggests Witt, explains the motif of hands in *Histoire(s)* more generally.[57] This idea can be expanded upon in relation to the analysis of Blanchot: Giacometti in the first place represents the presence of *work* in art, hands being in a synecdochic relation to work. The filmmaker Chris Petit has conveyed something of the 'massive, intensive labour' involved in the creation of *Histoire(s)*, especially the cutting with VHS.[58] Besides any individual reference, the sheer encyclopaedic range and wealth of Godard's panoply of sources in itself takes on, over the course of the series, its own kind of quality. As suggested in relation to Hill's point about iterability, there is a sense that in a work of this length, through repetition any dynamic has the tendency to present itself not merely as a unique instance but as a general principle. Godard sculpts a work of works from an immense morass, a text of palimpsestic accretion, a work of culture as a totality. Work becomes a governing idea. But the distinction of Giacometti, as discussed above, is also to expose worklessness; his hands show something other than work. His sculptures are avatars of the absence of the work

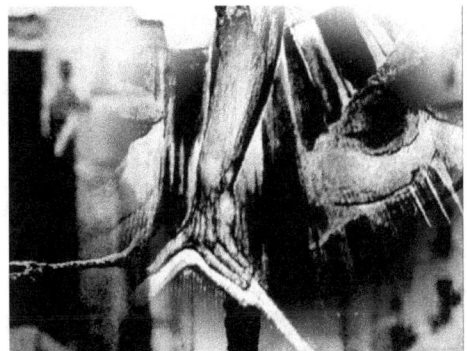

Figs. 2.11–2.13.

and they repeat the movement whereby at the same time as the art is made, it is also sacrificed. As in the argument made by Witt, Godard's film draws forth ideas of sacrifice — both in the film itself and in the criticism of the film.

In the first reference in Chapter 3B, Godard presents us with one of Giacometti's most celebrated works, *L'Homme au doigt* [Pointing Man] (1947) (Figure 2.11), and this is juxtaposed in the montage with a detail from William Blake's engraving used as a frontispiece in his book *Europe a Prophecy* (1794) (Figure 2.12). Blake's image is also known as a standalone image as 'The Ancient of Days', showing the figure Urizen's dividing hand of creation coming from the heavens. This is followed by a detail of Urizen's head and body (Figure 2.13).

These images appear as part of a sequence in which Godard engages with the ideas of the historian Fernand Braudel.[59] At the same time as Braudel can himself be heard on the soundtrack, we also hear Godard, who intones: 'Il ne raconte pas d'histoires. Ainsi qu'Étienne Jules Marey l'a demandé, le saint homme relève des traces et prend des mesures' [He does not tell stories. As Étienne Jules Marey asked him, the holy man looks for evidence and takes measures]. The Giacometti image here appears against an unidentified background that makes the sculpture look as if it is standing in the middle of a street.[60] The framing is not such as to emphasize the pointing gesture that is most striking when encountering the (almost six feet tall) sculpture 'in the flesh'; rather, it accentuates the torso and head, the top half of the sculpture. In Figure 2.12 it is as if, by virtue of the superimposition, the sculpture is being created by Urizen: the pointing arm appears to extend contiguously from Urizen's thumb. Like the edit between the photograph of Blanchot and the image of Nosferatu, the superimposition of the pictorial human forms of Urizen and *L'Homme au doigt* is an example of the '"horizontal" moments of confluence, contiguity, conjunction and coincidence within the "vertical" pull of Godard's rhetorical and imaginary manœuvres'.[61] The complexity of Godard's montage is augmented by the essential ambiguity of the artworks pictured. Of *L'Homme au doigt*, Yves Bonnefoy writes: 'The arms are outstretched, the hands seem to show or to incite or to forbid, but without upsetting the statue's balance, so that, on the whole, this balance is only enlarged, as if extended to take in what in life is speech, communication, civilization'.[62] Bonnefoy suggests that the statue's demonstrative gesture can be read in different ways, yet seems to pertain to a fundamental value. In Godard's sequence, the figure appears at the same time as Godard speaks the line 'relève des traces', as if the pointing gesture is to be read as a pointing at discovered evidence or 'traces'. In Blake's image, the hair and beard may at first suggest the Christian God, but Urizen is in Blake's elaborate and heterodox mythology a 'false deity [...] humanity's limited conception of God as the ultimate circumscriber and measurer'.[63] Creation in this image is a delimitation, a negative act or error which reduces the infinite to finiteness. Thus does the name Urizen derive from the Greek word for 'limit', which is the origin of the word 'horizon'. It is for this reason that Urizen is shown using a compass.[64] In the montage, this image appears in time with the soundtrack to illustrate Godard's 'prend des mesures'. Again it is a question of the ambiguity of hand gestures. The godlike figure Urizen appears here to create man not in his own image, but as a frail, reduced figure. Standing in the street, he is a man thrown into contemporary history. The words 'LE MUSÉE DU RÉEL' at once invoke the Malrucian museum where these artworks would dwell, but as 'real' these artworks are read against the real of history. Through his use of historical footage, Godard's film is a museum of the real. Mapping these concepts onto each other, Godard is showing how it is through the cinema — through the image — that man, art, and history are worked and unworked. The edit between the contemporary statue and the 'ancient' image blurs temporal register, showing how creation puts mankind both in and outside history.

Another case of hands at work comes with filmed acts of writing. One example we could draw attention to comes at the beginning of Chapter 2A, 'Seul le cinéma' [The Cinema Alone], when Godard announces the title of the episode by showing a hand writing it on a card. He does this with a thick black marker pen, slowly using a ruler to underline the words. The squeaking sound of the pen being pressed on this card is raised to the pitch of a piercing shriek, painful in contrast to the measured movement of the hand controlling it. Over the shrieks an atonal piano piece by Giacinto Scelsi evokes dread. There is a flickering superimposition that connects this writing to, among others, images of a man covering his eyes with his hands (Figure 2.14), a scientist looking through a microscope (Figure 2.16), fighters looking through rifle sights (Figure 2.17), and the Cyclops (Figure 2.18).

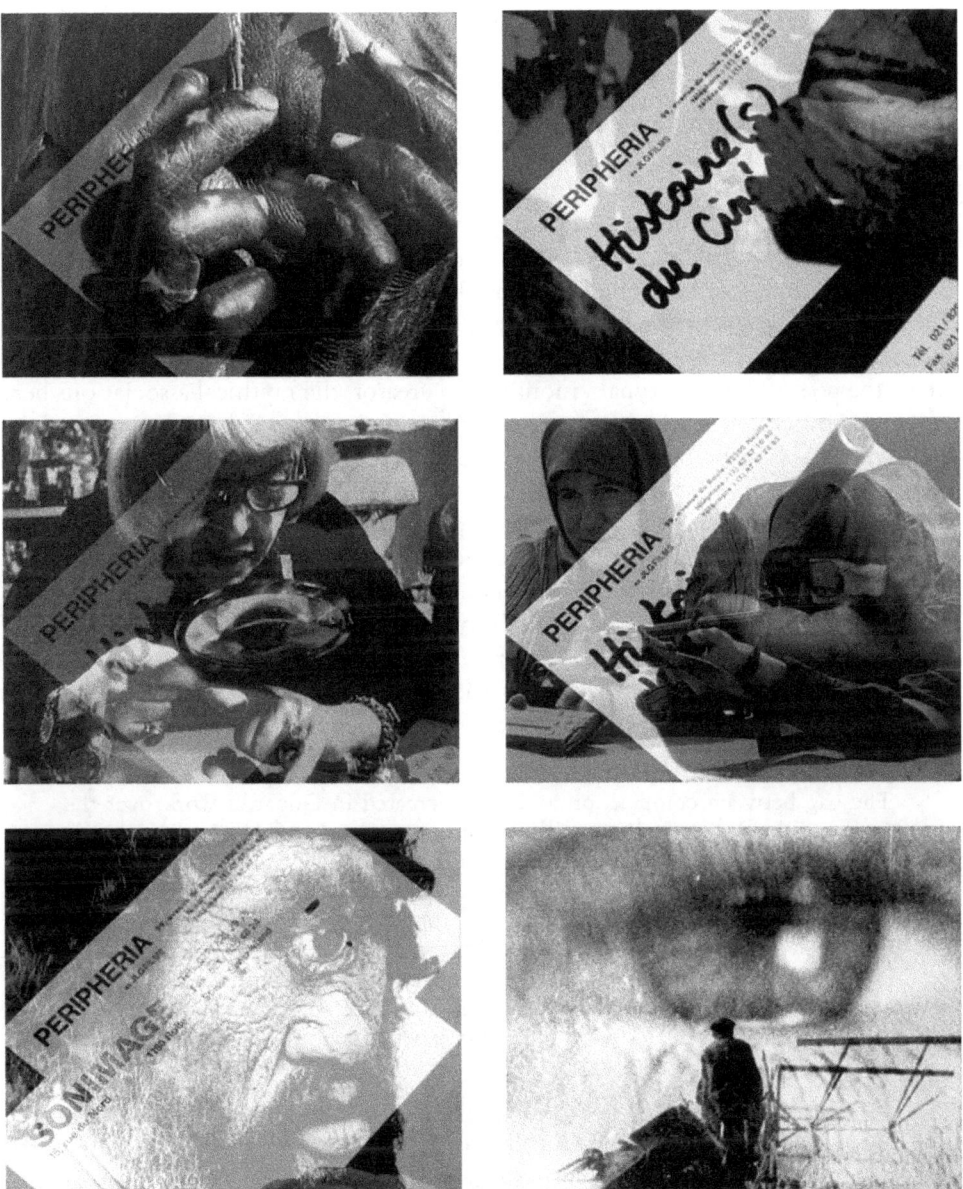

FIGS. 2.14–2.19.

Associations are here summoned by the act of writing: dread, pain, scientific calculation, violence, myth, the gaze. The sequence cuts between the writing hand and these other images with a constant hypnotic flashing. With the shrieking sounds, it is as if writing is here operating according to its etymological sense of cutting or tearing. There is also a sense here that, as Blanchot says, when the writer writes, it is not the hand moving the pen that is in control, it is the other, still hand

(EL 15; SL 25). By this he means that writing puts one in contact with an aleatory point over which one has no control, that apparently purposeful activity is always in relation to uncertainty. The writing hand makes a cut, and this introduces into the montage the other images, interrupting this action like visions of its truth. Writing here opens a gap or a rupture and with each underlining Godard affirms it. Writing here also conjures phantasms. As we saw in the previous chapter, the words 'image', 'imaginary', and 'imagination' 'ne désignent pas seulement l'aptitude aux phantasmes intérieurs, mais l'accès à la réalité propre de l'irréel' (*EI* 477) ('not only an aptitude for interior phantasms, but also access to the proper reality of the unreal', *IC* 325). In this sense Godard here dramatizes writing as the work of the imaginary. In evoking these phantasms, Godard's hand is *fascinated*. While for Blake the poet is the archetypal visionary and creator, the mythical associations here (the Cyclops) coupled with the very act of writing turn writing or creation into an intrusion, a cut or opening as if onto time itself, making the time of the film undecidable.[65]

Here is foregrounded what is Godard's own hand and, metonymically, his own work. The presence of Godard himself is here as elsewhere significant, for it gives a way of understanding the title of the second part of the series, 'Une histoire seule': that, as Godard says, cinema's 'way of working' is 'very solitary'.[66] The motif of writing in the film as it is given concrete expression here is both expressive and eminently ostensive of the working of the film as a whole. Here the palimpsest is literally being written. Alain Bergala has commented more generally about Godard's work of the 1980s:

> The gap between composition and attack created in Godard's work over the course of the decade [sic] one of those subterranean contradictions that secretly mark all creative advances, and that flicker occasionally on the surface of a film or a sequence, before plunging just as quickly back into that obscure zone where the work of negativity is as vital to the progress of the work as that which gives the superficial illusion of moving toward its accomplishment. I know of few cases as exemplary of this negativity at work in all acts of true creation, which Blanchot speaks of, as this refusal to submit on the part of the act of filming, which alone can make a true act of it, to the natural inclination of the visible.[67]

The notions of composition and attack (arranging the elements in a shot on the one hand, and on the other the considerations of angle, distance, and others in the shooting) are those of the actual conditions of making a film. Bergala's lines here bring out the centrality of the idea of creation as a solitary act, an idea that is visible in Godard's film, and which is abundantly present in the sequences described above. Reading this as the work of negativity shows how filmmaking can be understood in Blanchotian terms and what it would mean to make a film like a book by Blanchot or Bataille. In terms of *Histoire(s)*, Bergala writes that the shots Godard has chosen or 'set aside' for the film evince the quality of the 'visual' in which this gap can be seen, 'that of a fragile and moving hyperpresence of the beings and things on the screen'.[68] This gap that Bergala writes of, in which the negative both works and unworks itself in the image, is the rupture that Godard affirms in these sequences.

It is this unworking that the hands — the sacrificial hand of *La Main*, Urizen's measuring hand, and Godard's fascinated writing hand — all testify to.

Orpheus and Eurydice

We now turn to Godard's use of a myth embodying the idea of the work of the artist. At the climax of Chapter 2A we read the dispersed caption: 'LE CINEMA AUTHORISE ORPHÉE DE SE RETOURNER SANS FAIRE MOURIR EURYDICE' [Cinema allows Orpheus to turn around without causing Eurydice to die].[69] This is superimposed on a still from a lesser-known early silent work of Carl Dreyer, *The Bride of Glomdal* (1926), showing a man driving a barge with a deathly-looking woman laid out behind him. A concertina plays while a scoping effect conceals part of the image and moves from side to side to isolate the figures (Figures 2.20–21).

Dreyer's film was shot in Norway and is the story of a rural courtship. The two characters visible in these images, Tore and Berit, are thwarted lovers. The still comes from a sequence in which Berit has fallen ill and is being transported, giving Tore's role its first Orphic overtones. However, Godard seems to value this image for its pallor rather than its referential value; that is, he seems to fetishize the cadaverous image of the female Eurydice character and the aged, D. W. Griffith-era film image itself. Even by the standards of *Histoire(s)*, this is an old film image, and, at the simplest level, it presents us with, as Mulvey put it in the quotation from the previous chapter, the 'fascination of fossilized time'.[70]

Chapter 2A as a whole is about the relation between cinema and other visual arts; first as Godard discusses the relation between film's technical history and its relation to television with Serge Daney; and then in a longer section as Julie Delpy reads selected stanzas from Baudelaire's poem 'Le Voyage' over a variety of images, many of which are nineteenth-century paintings, thus bringing out a sense of the meaning of Godard's comment to Daney that cinema is 'l'affaire du XIXe siècle qui s'est résolue au XXe' [the affair of the nineteenth century which is resolved in the twentieth]. Cinema is this dreamt-of voyage of exoticism and horror away from terrestrial tedium. It is also for Godard a journey from the Underworld. Before

Orpheus is invoked, however, the final reading from Baudelaire is from the last stanza, the apostrophization of death. There is at least an element in the tenor of the sequence surrounding this last reading which undermines the buccaneering spirit of before. The travellers' tales in Baudelaire find their somewhat transposed correlative in footage from archive pornography and stills of concentration camps. The episode ends shortly after the Dreyer still with what looks like amateur footage taken from aboard a pleasure boat as it returns to land, providing at least a momentary repose. But there is a sense that this is a bitter return, and that the claim of cinema to turn around without causing Eurydice to die has been undercut. Yet what would it mean for cinema to be able to do this?

For Blanchot, the myth of Orpheus is an allegory of fascination and of the logic of the work of art. The central point of *L'Espace littéraire* is the section 'Le Regard d'Orphée' [The Gaze of Orpheus]. A brief reminder of the myth: Orpheus, a singer and player of the lyre, becomes mute with grief at the death of his wife, Eurydice. Orpheus visits the Underworld where Eurydice now dwells and plays his song. The guardians of the Underworld are spellbound by his playing and allow him to bring back Eurydice to the world on the condition that he leads his wife without looking back at her. But just as Orpheus is about to emerge from the Underworld, he is overcome with desire for Eurydice and turns to look upon her, thus losing her forever. In Blanchot's account, partly echoing Rilke's *Sonnets to Orpheus* (1922), she is the furthest point of art and his work is to bring her back to the day. Art opens the night of his descent. Looking back reveals the night's essence as 'l'inessential' (*EL* 180) ('the inessential', *SL* 172). Orpheus has always already turned towards Eurydice in Blanchot's reading, as soon as he descends: that which animates desire is that which puts a stop to it. His error is impatience, impatience to withdraw from the absence of time. Yet this gaze is part of the demand of the work, of the very moment of inspiration. At this instant the work is also compromised. This instant is a sacrifice. Orpheus's gaze is a gift through which he sacrifices the work (*EL* 183; *SL* 174); the sacred is given back in a 'sacrifice sans cérémonie' (*EL* 183) ('a sacrifice without ceremony', *SL* 175). Orpheus wants to bring the obscure origin of art to the light of day as art: he wants to see the blind spot, to have both Eurydice and Eurydice *as* lost object. As Didi-Huberman observes, we have here another double version: mortal Eurydice (personal, attainable) is to dead Eurydice (impersonal and infernal) what 'l'image-forme est à l'image-milieu, ou ce que la ressemblance-enchantement est à la ressemblance-dissolution' [the image-as-form is to the image-as-domain, or what resemblance-as-enchantment is to resemblance-as-dissolution].[71] It is thus that when Blanchot later reprises the theme, reading Eurydice as a figure of the Levinasian Other, he makes explicit that Orpheus's gaze represents violence and death (*EI* 86; *IC* 60). According to Blanchot: 'L'erreur d'Orphée semble être alors dans le désir qui le porte à voir et à posséder Eurydice, lui dont le seul destin est de la chanter. Il n'est Orphée que dans le chant' (*EL* 181) ('Orpheus's error seems then to lie in the desire which moves him to see and to possess Eurydice, he whose destiny is only to sing of her. He is Orpheus only in the song', *SL* 172).

In the context of this reference to the myth in *Histoire(s)*, if Eurydice represents 'le point profondément obscur vers lequel l'art, le désir, la mort, la nuit semblent tendre' (*EL* 179) ('the profoundly obscure point toward which art and desire, death and night, seem to tend', *SL* 171), would that make cinema the art which allows us to entertain a fascinated gaze halfway between the Underworld and the day, to grasp the very object of fascination?

Jacques Aumont has written most extensively on the theme of Orpheus in *Histoire(s)*. Looking across his œuvre as a whole, Aumont has gone so far as to suggest that several of Godard's earlier works are in fact remakes of the Orphic myth, that it is a recurring motif in Godard's work.[72] For Aumont, Orpheus's symbolic value in *Histoire(s)* is, at least, historiographical: Orpheus is cinema, 'qui a le pouvoir de regarder derrière lui et d'y faire, d'un même regard, à la fois advenir et disparaître l'Histoire' [which has the power to look behind itself and, in the same glance, to cause History to both open and dissolve].[73] It is thus that Aumont can complete Godard's fiat about how Orpheus can look back without killing Eurydice: 'mais en ne la laissant pas intacte: elle devient statue; débarrassée de son corps encombrant, on peut alors l'aimer ou l'adorer, à distance de mythe' [but not leaving her intact: she becomes statue: done with her cumbersome body, one can thus love her or adore her, from the distance of myth]. Aumont concludes: 'Filmé, le passé se fige, il cesse de vivre mais sans jamais plus pouvoir mourir; devenu statue "de sel", il continue de vivre sous la croûte translucide au goût amer' [Filmed, the past freezes, it ceases to live but without ever being able to die; having become a statue 'of salt', it continues to live under the translucent surface of a bitter taste].[74] It is thus that Aumont links the religious function of Malraux's Museum, of preservation, with Orpheus.[75] But Aumont argues, *pace* Bazin, that the ability to save is historical, not ontological, meaning that the work of preservation is one without end, one that must be repeated with each new era.[76] In a similar vein Scemama writes of the eye of cinema becoming the eye of History, with Orpheus figuring cinema and History at the same time.[77] In these ways, Godard's critics have regarded the motif of Orpheus — an essentially Blanchotian motif — as key to any theorization of *Histoire(s)*.

Further to his argument that was cited earlier on sacrifice, Witt writes that the 'Orphic-like challenge facing the historian' is that of bringing dead material back to life and making an image of the past, and he argues that for this reason we should see Godard as a 'cinema historian'.[78] Cinema's images would be this past life that, through cinema, is brought back from the dead. Bringing the past to life would be to recover Eurydice. Yet clearly here the question would be how literally to understand the notions of life and death. Is bringing the 'dead' material of the past back to 'life' on a screen a properly living life? Or is it to examine a dead life, to reanimate an indexical trace, a mode of preservation as in Bazin? For Aumont, the operation at issue here represents an historical preservation, which would suggest not only that the past 'cesse de vivre' [ceases to live], but that by extension the work of film is that of excavation and documentation; perhaps we could say of the order of archaeology rather than resurrection. It is the essential work of culture to preserve and understand the past, but that does not mean that we can return it to life.

Yet here the notion of the trace can also be read as referring back to an unreal index, as discussed in Chapter 1 in the structure of resemblance in the work of art and the cadaver. When we discussed how the work of art is 'unearthed', it was as if to suggest that the paradigmatic work of art would be like an ancient sculpture, serene in its untimely indifference. Would this be the same with film, such that a recording, always in the moment of recording becoming immediately a thing of the past, thus always presents itself in this archaeological perspective? If it is a statue, it is one, we could say, following Aumont, that is 'de sel', which would be one that is destined to ruination and always in a *process of disappearance*, appearing by way of disappearance. Connecting the threads with Witt's reading of Malraux, we could say that the sacrifice of past art in the new is structurally similar to this — the past itself is sacrificed in cinema on an archaeological altar, or rather Eurydice, as she 'becomes statue', must always be sacrificed in order to be looked at, can only be seen *as* disappearing. The sacrifice of Eurydice only represents a resurrection in the sense of becoming image that has been described above.

While *The Bride of Glomdal* presents the most explicit invocation of Orpheus in Godard's film, Jean Cocteau's film *Orphée* (1950), in which the myth is transposed to post-war France, is key to following through the other echoes of the myth throughout *Histoire(s)*. Figures 2.22 and 2.23 come from near the start of the previous chapter (1B) and show Orpheus (Jean Marais) pressing the mirror through which the Princess (Death) and two motorcyclists have just walked.

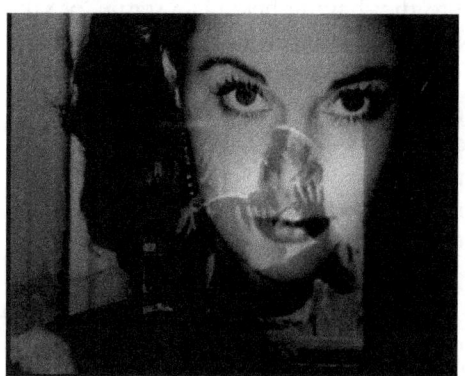 

While in the first image there is a woman's face superimposed over the footage from *Orphée*, in the latter image it is the footage that is superimposed over a still from Ingmar Bergman's *Prison* (1949), a frequently repeated image in this part of *Histoire(s)* showing a man and a woman at a projector, suggesting they are watching Marais. In the sequence from which the image is taken in *Prison*, the central protagonists Tomas and Birgitta watch a slapstick comedy film in a childhood attic, and shortly after this Birgitta has a nightmare. *Prison* is a particularly rich reference given that it in itself activates several levels of intertextuality. The central conceit is a film-within-a-film, in which *Prison* begins with one character suggesting an idea for a film — a somewhat existentialist film to show a world in which God is dead and Satan has taken over — which then appears to be what we are given to see: a narrator then tells us we are watching a film called 'Prison' and the credits are read.[79] Birgitta is a prostitute and Tomas is an alcoholic, both wandering through a figurative Underworld. The superimposed footage from *Orphée* speeds up and down, while Marlene Dietrich can be heard singing, before returning to a piece mentioned before, Hindemith's *Mathis der Maler*. Shortly before this moment, among other references to the film, we hear a snippet of dialogue from *Orphée*, in which Orpheus has been brought back to the Princess's ruined chalet after the brawl at the Café des Poètes. In the exchange, Orpheus demands to know what is going on. The Princess replies that the role of the dreamer is to accept their dreams. We hear as the Princess puts on the radio, on which can be heard a passage from Gluck's opera *Orpheus and Eurydice* (1762). In this way the work of intertextuality opens out onto several referential and temporal levels.[80]

A further suggestion of Orpheus and the withdrawn presence of Blanchot can be detected near the end of this chapter as Godard uses two quotations from Heidegger's essay 'What Are Poets For?', read out by Maria Casarès. Casarès is notable for her roles as the Princess in *Orphée* and *The Testament of Orpheus* (1960), thus suggesting a connection between these moments in Chapter 1B. This, like the Cuny performance, appears to be material that was recorded for *Histoire(s)* specifically and is not lifted from another source. Cocteau's film develops the myth of Orpheus such that Orpheus is as much in love with death, in the figure of the Princess, as he is with Eurydice. It would be an extremely sharp viewer/listener of *Histoire(s)* who recognized the same voice between these two moments in the episode within the polyphony — the first a crackly recording taken from a film, the second, a noticeably better quality recording and played across silence, and the actress's timbre itself altered by a lapse of thirty years. Yet there is here a continuity and a relation more obvious in the conceptual link of 'poets'. The passages quoted in Godard's film, taken together, read as follows:

> The default of God forebodes something even grimmer, however. Not only have the gods and the god fled, but the divine radiance has become extinguished in the world's history. The time of the world's night is the destitute time, because it becomes ever more destitute. It has already grown so destitute, it can no longer discern the default of God as a default. [...] Poets are the mortals who, singing earnestly of the wine-god, sense the trace of the fugitive gods, stay on the gods' tracks, and so trace for their kindred mortals the way toward the turning. The ether, however, in which alone the gods are gods, is their godhead. The element of this ether, that within which even the godhead itself is still present, is the holy. The element of the ether for the coming of the fugitive gods, the holy, is the track of the fugitive gods. But who has the power to sense, to trace such a track? Traces are often inconspicuous, and are always the legacy of a directive that is barely divined. To be a poet in a destitute time means: to attend, singing, to the trace of the fugitive gods.[81]

Godard would seem here to be connecting cinema with the work of poets and the failure of cinema with the default of God. In the books accompanying *Histoire(s) du cinéma*, Godard adds the line 'this is why at the time of the night of the world the poet speaks the sacred'. As with Godard's voiceover of the holy man who seeks 'traces', these traces are traces of the sacred. That which is evoked is a movement of withdrawal, as discussed in relation to Rancière, Morrey and Agamben. What is crucial in the context of my argument is that Godard is quoting the key text inspiring Blanchot's reflections on the destitute time in *L'Espace littéraire*. This, it seems to me, suggests the oblique presence of Blanchot, given that Blanchot discusses both Heidegger's text and the myth of Orpheus at length in *L'Espace littéraire*. I am suggesting that Blanchot's influential account of Orpheus is at some level imbricated in Godard's appropriation of the myth, consciously or otherwise. We have already seen that Godard was familiar with Blanchot's texts of the 1950s (contemporary with so much of the material Godard uses). Oliver Harris has also demonstrated Godard's use of the text of *L'Espace littéraire* in his earlier film, *Le Mépris* (1963), as well as persuasively arguing that Godard may be drawing on texts from *Le Livre à venir*.[82] What would be at stake in this is that Blanchot's reading implies the impossibility of bringing back Eurydice; that is, if we accept that Blanchot is a subterranean presence in *Histoire(s) du cinéma* and read this moment of the film through Blanchot, then cinema's powers do not extend as far as Godard sometimes triumphantly avers. Indeed, Godard seems to be aware of the contradiction, as he subsequently said in 1994 (speaking in an apparently eternal present) that sometimes Orpheus turns and sees nothing. Referring to gaps in the history of cinema, moments that cinema did not, or did not adequately, capture — thinking specifically of the Holocaust, the Resistance, and May 1968 — Godard says: 'I, too, had believed for a moment that the cinema authorized | Orpheus to look back without causing Eurydice's death. | I was wrong. Orpheus will have to pay'.[83] Cinema, as Orpheus, is damned for these lacunae.

In his exemplary essay 'L'Autre Cinéaste: Godard écrivain' [(Not) Just An Other Filmmaker] (1992), Bellour reflects on what it is that sets Godard apart as a filmmaker, a question which entails the whole, very complex question of the significance of the image for Godard.[84] Bellour throughout makes allusions to Orpheus, beginning with an epigraph taken from a statement by Godard:

> Pour moi, le cinéma c'est Eurydice. Eurydice dit à Orphée: 'Ne te retourne pas.' Et Orphée se retourne, Orphée c'est la littérature qui fait mourir Eurydice... Pour moi les images c'est la vie et les textes c'est la mort. Il faut les deux: je ne suis pas contre la mort. Mais je ne suis pas pour la mort de la vie à ce point-là, surtout pendant le temps où elle doit être vécue.

> [For me, cinema is Eurydice. Eurydice says to Orpheus, 'Don't look back.' And Orpheus looks back. Orpheus is literature causing Eurydice to die... For me, images are life, and texts are death. You need both — I'm not against death. But I'm not for the death of life to that extent, especially during the time when it needs to be lived.][85]

Bellour works through not only the Orphic metaphor, but also what is implicit in it, namely the relation between image and text, life and death. Bellour's entire essay is inflected with the thought of Blanchot, and these questions are discussed at times explicitly with quotations from Blanchot and at other points implicitly, through invocation of Blanchotian ideas, such as the lineage in which Bellour places Godard, a lineage which takes in key writers discussed by Blanchot, such as Mallarmé and Hölderlin. In terms of the relation between Godard's *Histoire(s) du cinéma* and Blanchot, Bellour's text exemplifies with rigour how one can read that relation *into* Godard's work more generally. That means that Bellour shows how perfectly Godard fits within a Blanchotian critical perspective: how his themes and philosophy bear out a Blanchotian agenda; how his self-conscious authorial statements outside the work itself seem to directly engage with Blanchot (such as the epigraph quoted above); and, perhaps most crucially, how his films play out at the formal level of image and sound the questions of writing and the image. While my discussion of the quotation from Blanchot that Godard uses at the end of *Histoire(s) du cinéma* proves an existant relation between Godard and Blanchot, Bellour's essay shows how one can use Blanchot to read Godard. While it is not a point that Bellour makes, I have suggested that the quotation discussed, in addition to the Orpheus material, not only lays open the possibility but *invites* this kind of reading.

What makes Godard an 'autre cineaste', according to Bellour, is that he has partly put himself in the place of a writer, which is to say that because of his relation to language and image he places himself in relation to 'Tout'. Bellour clarifies that by 'Tout' he means 'le rapport entre connaissance, expression et responsabilité, qui confère à l'écrivain la charge d'un monde toujours plus vaste et insaisissable, dans les limites d'un Moi qu'il ne connaît pas' ('the relation among knowledge, expression, and responsibility, which burdens the writer with a world forever more vast and ungraspable, within the limits of a Self the writer doesn't know').[86] Another way of saying this is to refer back to the ideas of the previous chapter where it was said that the writer is always in relation to the Book. For Bellour, this manifests itself in the problem of analysis: unlike musicians and painters (Godard's examples), those who are in the position of the writer have to 'analyze' the world and reality as such. We could gloss this by saying that language always entails a problem of discursive meaning. What is 'autre' about Godard, he writes, is that he brings in this problematic not only through the use of language but also 'entre les images'.[87]

The tension here that arises between word and image is one that Bellour places at the centre of his reading of Godard. Bellour notes how Godard has occasionally posited the image that was at work in silent cinema as a pure image free from writing and naming. It is this uncorrupted image that is to be opposed to words. At stake in this is the question of whether there was ever a kind of originary seeing prior to naming. In other words, was there ever a pure image uncontaminated by writing? This is also how to understand what Bellour means when he writes at another point that he sees Godard's paradox as seeking to return to an origin, 'une sorte de "scène primitive" du cinéma' ('a sort of "primal scene" of cinema').[88] Godard's work on the history of cinema involves trying to get to this origin. Again it would be thus that Bellour writes: 'Attaché avant tout à ce que cache et révèle ce que son mouvement découvre, il dépend du point fixe qui l'oriente, vers lequel *comme Orphée* il se retourne' ('Godard is attracted above all to the veil, to the thing that both hides and reveals what his movement unveils. He relies on the fixed point that orients him, toward which, *like Orpheus*, he looks back').[89] The desired state, or what we might call the object of this fascination of Godard's, is what resides in this moment of creation, this idea of there being a kind of element in the image testifying to an originary connection between thinking, creating, and speaking. A sense of this was evoked in the discussion of the montage of the writing hand. Bellour shows how, while the text 'Parler, ce n'est pas voir' allows us to think of a writing that would subsist within a speech that had no relation to seeing, Godard's films show something different: 'À la belle formule de *L'Entretien infini*, "parole d'écriture", on est tenté d'opposer chez Godard une "écriture de parole", qui rapporte ainsi par la parole l'écriture à l'image et les maintient dans une dépendance douloureuse, vitale, comme forcenée' ('To the neat formula of *L'Entretien infini*, "written speech," one is tempted to oppose Godard's "spoken writing," which brings writing to the image by way of speaking, and maintains them in a painful, vital, furious dependency').[90] We can understand this by thinking of all of the ways in which writing interacts with the image in the examples from *Histoire(s)* that we have considered, for example in the text that is superimposed on the images in the sacrifice sequence.

Bellour also notes how the implication of writing in the image is a reversible formula, such that writing can become image itself. There is in Godard the ability to 'traiter l'écrit comme l'image, une image, l'écran comme une page' ('to treat written texts as images, an image, and the screen as a page'). The connection between word and image in Godard implies 'de soustraire l'écriture elle-même à sa lisibilité propre pour en faire l'objet d'un visible-lisible, que garantit sa plasticité *in vivo* dans le temps d'inscription et de défilement (c'est entre autres ce qu'accomplit pleinement *Histoire(s) du cinéma*)' ('removing writing itself from its own readability in order to turn it into the object of a "seeable/readable," which its plasticity *in vivo* guarantees in the time of inscription and unfolding (this is what, among other things, *Histoire(s) du cinéma* fully achieves)').[91] With the phrase 'visible-lisible', Bellour is alluding to a formulation used by Deleuze to describe the way language can become part of the image after the end of the silent era. Bellour is describing here how writing can be something looked at rather than — or, as well as — read. This would be one way of considering the words that were part of the images in the sacrifice sequence, such as Beckett's book cover: at the same time as one reads them, they are also perceived as image. With 'plasticité *in vivo*', Bellour is pointing to how this capacity for the words to turn into image inheres in writing's living potential and animated, changing nature as such. The previously discussed sequence of the actual act of writing demonstrates this by presenting us with an instance of 'le temps d'inscription'.

The real complexity of Bellour's argument, and the real relevance of the Orpheus myth, comes in at this point. He argues that what Godard rejects is the solitude or detachment from life that is needed for writerly creation. Godard's pronouncements frequently threaten to view cinema and life as indistinguishable. In evoking this detachment Bellour refers to 'La Littérature et le droit à la mort' and the strange relation between the two terms in the title of that essay.[92] This is difficult in part because the relevance of the idea of solitude in Godard's film has already been suggested, and Bergala has also been quoted to this effect, when the point was made that Godard foregrounds how *Histoire(s)* is the product of work. But the point that Bellour is making is that this supposed rejection of detachment, this insistence of cinema as a constant, living work, as the matter of life itself, is really impossible. It is also what makes Godard great.[93] Godard wants cinema to be the equal of life and to have the plenitude of image imagined in the silent cinema, but he also wants to control everything in the manner of the global negation of the writer; he has to be both on set making films with others (in which the situation of filmmaking appears so entirely distinct from the work of the writer) and yet at the same time his will is such that he must partake of the solitude of the writer. The impossibility is to make these two scenarios coincide; what Godard aims for is 'l'éternel présent, toujours disjoint, de l'écriture' ('the eternal present, the always disjointed present of writing').[94] He wants to be present at the moment of creation.

At the end of his essay Bellour tries to resolve the problem of the figures of Orpheus and Eurydice in Godard's imagination. He argues that, rather than reading Orpheus as literature and Eurydice as cinema as Godard suggests (which would give us a model on which to read the whole foregoing problem of word and image), we should instead see Orpheus as cinema, with Eurydice as the 'beloved' to whom all films are written. This is a reconceptualization in which cinema is a struggle with impossibility, much as described at length above. In this struggle the solitude that Godard nominally rejects is one that cannot be renounced. This is resolved as Bellour introduces a conception of film as addressed from this solitude to 'l'autre' (gendered as woman in Godard's work).[95] Bellour here brings to the understanding of Godard's creative work a sense of its being animated by a kind of love. This is a love, of course, that can be found in the myth of Orpheus and Eurydice, and even if it is not one that Blanchot strongly plays towards it is one that helps us understand Godard's work. Bellour suggests that this is, ultimately, how to understand the line that 'le cinéma autorise Orphée de se retourner sans faire mourir Eurydice'.[96]

What I have tried to show in this extended engagement with Bellour's essay on Godard is how Blanchot can extensively inform the critical understanding of a work. Taking Bellour's reading with the question of the gaze of the image that is also a kind of *bonheur*, we can see not only how Godard uses Blanchot to think the conflicted intimacy of the artwork, but also how Blanchot's thought can help us to read this. What I have argued up to now in this chapter is that Blanchot is both a presence in, and hence an influence on, *Histoire(s) du cinéma* and critical approaches to it. I now move on to consider a different case of Blanchot's influence on the thought of cinema.

Deleuze's Use of Blanchot

Deleuze does not in his *Cinéma* volumes (1983–85) write on *Histoire(s)* — the film was made after the books — but what he says on the idea of the 'interstice' is clearly relevant to a discussion of montage in the film. At the same time, in a conjunction of themes, this is also the decisive moment at which Deleuze relies on Blanchot in his work on film, and thus we shall look here at his remarks. The appearance of Blanchot in Deleuze's influential *Cinéma* volumes is one of the most significant indicators of the relation between Blanchot and cinema to date.

Blanchot appears in *L'Image-mouvement* in a less developed role than he does in the *L'Image-temps*. In the first volume he appears alongside Charles Péguy to testify to what Deleuze calls the 'mystère du présent' ('mystery of the present'): 'C'est le même événement, mais dont une part s'est accomplie profondément dans un état de choses, tandis que l'autre est d'autant plus irréductible à tout accomplissement. [...] c'est la différence du procès et de la Passion' ('It is the same event but one part of it is profoundly realised in a state of things, whilst the other is all the more irreducible to all realisation [...] [It] is the difference between the trial and the Passion'). Deleuze is at this point thinking of Dreyer's film, *The Passion of Joan of Arc* (1928). This, he continues, is the difference between 'les causes actives' ('active causes') in things, on the one hand, and, on the other, 'l'événement lui-même, l'affectif, l'effet' ('the event itself, the affective, the effect').[97] The affect is like 'l'exprimé de l'état de choses' ('the expressed of the state of things'), an extraction which is related by the partitive 'de' — 'la colère *de* l'évêque' ('the anger *of* the bishop').[98] The affective aspect, which is the essence of Deleuze's concept of 'l'image-affection' ('the affection-image'), appears to be directly inspired by Blanchot, as Deleuze quotes from *L'Espace littéraire* the notion of 'la part de l'événement que son accomplissement ne peut pas réaliser' ('the aspect of the event that its accomplishment cannot realise').[99] Two filmmakers whom Deleuze associates with the affection-image have already been linked to Blanchot: Duras and Bresson. In the passage from which this quotation is taken, Blanchot is not writing about an abstracted 'affect' of an event — the brightness of light hitting a knife, as in Deleuze's example — but on the 'double death'. This is the idea according to which there are two relations with death: one in which death is that which is the force of meaning in the world (as my power and ultimate possibility), and one in which we are given over to the interminability of a dying that cannot be accomplished. This double relation is the correlative of the two versions of the imaginary. In other words, what Deleuze calls the 'exprimé' or 'l'image-affection' appears to be directly inspired by *le mourir*, and the affection-image is the corollary of fascination. It is as if, in the creation of a new ontology of images, Deleuze wants to subsume the Blanchotian image as but one of several variations in a taxonomy of images.

It can be demonstrated that Blanchot's notion of the double death was a long-term interest for Deleuze, as this line from *L'Espace littéraire* is also quoted in an earlier text, *Logique du sens* [The Logic of Sense] (1969), as part of Deleuze's discussion of 'la structure double de tout événement' ('the double structure of every event'). This doubleness is described as being 'comme l'effectuation et la contre-effectuation' ('like actualization and counter-actualization'), such that there is firstly the part of the event locatable in the present and then 'le futur et le passé de l'événement pris en lui-même, qui esquive tout présent, parce qu'il est libre des limitations d'un état de choses, étant impersonnel et pré-individuel, neutre, ni général ni particulier, *eventum tantum*' ('the future and the past of the event considered in itself, sidestepping each present, being free of the limitations of a state of affairs, impersonal and pre-individual, neutral, neither general nor particular, *eventum tantum*').[100] This temporal ambiguity is much as I have set out in the previous chapter under the name of the absence of time. Deleuze also quotes from these pages, but not specifically the same line ('la part de l'événement que son accomplissement ne peut pas réaliser'), earlier still in *Différence et répétition* [Difference and Repetition] (1968).[101] This time of pure events is concealed within ordinary time and released by cinema and art. While Blanchot's reading of death seems to be present as an aspect of Deleuze's theory of events, a more proximate reference is the chapter on A. N. Whitehead and Leibniz, 'Qu'est-ce qu'un événement?' [What Is An Event?], in *Le Pli* [The Fold] (1988). In this text, an event is conceived as a series of swarming intensities, and must be thought of as drawn on a tableau or opaque screen. However, Deleuze's translator Tom Conley has recently argued that this philosophical account does not preclude the cinema. For Conley, 'the principles of the seventh art are literally folded into' Deleuze's understanding of the Baroque in *Le Pli*.[102] Yet here again Blanchot appears. In light of Blanchot's description of a book as a kind of tableau in the preface to *L'Espace littéraire*, in which the eye is led to a 'virtual vanishing point' — the fascinating 'point' discussed in the previous chapter in relation to Giacometti — for Conley the title 'What Is An Event?' is as if grafted from Bazin's *Qu'est-ce que le cinéma?*. Events in this way provide the link between cinema and philosophy.[103] We also find Deleuze's recurrent quotation from Blanchot, discussed above, elsewhere in *Le Pli*.[104] In this light, the reference to Blanchot in reference to the affection-image is very suggestive.

Eleanor Kaufman picks up this link that Deleuze makes between his conceptions of Aion and Chronos and the two deaths in Blanchot. Deleuze calls the atemporal time of becoming, the time of pure events, 'Aion', while the static present time is 'Chronos'. Kaufman discusses this link via the notion of midnight in Blanchot's work. Midnight is particularly associated with the chapter on Mallarmé's *Igitur* in *L'Espace littéraire*. Midnight has no present, but is arrived at repetitively, every day, only to annul and restart time in a circular motion. In escaping the chronological time of the present, midnight may seem to correspond to Aion, the time of Deleuze's event which has no present, marked by seeming to be just about to happen and yet always having just happened. At the same time, according to Kaufman, it represents a state of presentness that is 'beyond becoming in that it is too unworkable, too inert'. There is running through Blanchot's work 'a fissure between the liminal atemporal, fleeting instant and the more weighty inertia of presentness, the inertia of being'.[105] The difference between the two thinkers is thus: 'If Deleuze redeems being by perceiving its hidden potential for movement, Blanchot affirms being by perceiving its disarming potential for inertia'.[106]

I am not so much concerned for now with Deleuze's larger debt to Blanchot (that would entail another project) so much as to draw out that *le mourir* has been directly influential as a concept in a theory of cinema. Deleuze takes from *le mourir* a temporal aspect and an 'affective' aspect. The temporal aspect is the idea of the absence of the present: Deleuze's theory of pure events is one that hinges on a becoming 'dont le propre est d'esquiver le présent' ('whose characteristic is to elude the present').[107] The affective aspect is the fascination with which the absence of the present is co-extensive. In short, *mutatis mutandis*, Deleuze's influential account of the affection-image in *L'Image-mouvement* is indebted to Blanchot's account of the image.

However, the major role Blanchot plays in Deleuze's *Cinéma* volumes is to be found in the second half of *L'Image-temps*, especially the chapter entitled, 'La Pensée et le cinéma' [Thought and Cinema]. This chapter considers the crisis of post-war cinema's confidence in logical or rational thought, which for Deleuze is exemplified in the works of Godard. It is when discussing Godardian montage that Deleuze invokes Blanchot to talk of the outside of images that appears in the interstices, or blanks, between images. The black screen is one way — along with the point-cut and relinkage — in which the interstice is made visible. According to Deleuze, in Godardian montage the 'tout' merges with what Blanchot calls the 'dispersion du Dehors' ('dispersal of the Outside') or 'le vertige de l'espacement' ('vertigo of spacing').[108] All films in this way are predicated on a gap, the gap between images which is their very constitution as an ensemble. This has the effect of calling the image itself in question. The notion of the whole can be understood, following Henri Bergson, according to an idea of becoming, such that it refers to the changing state of things as a kind of totality. Deleuze in this way equates the Blanchotian outside with the 'interval' characterizing the discontinuity of Godard's films. Deleuze is thus bringing Blanchotian ontology into his account of cinema. In terms of *Histoire(s)*, this would refer to the *abyme*-like structures alluded to above as well as the many interstices or black screens, such as those in the sequence with Blanchot's photograph and the sequence on sacrifice. It is necessary to look more closely at the idea of the interval in itself.

According to Ronald Bogue's gloss, in one sense the whole 'is a gathering together of individual images within a unifying concept (integration), but at the same time the whole is present in each image, the whole expressing or unfolding itself in the sequence of different images (differentiation)'.[109] In classical cinema, this whole can be understood as how each shot in a film has a relation to the film conceived as an organic whole. However, following the crisis that Deleuze posits in the history of cinema, this whole ceases to function. The outside, for Deleuze, is the modern counterpart of the classical whole, a whole conceived of as a gap and yet which is also 'l'entre-deux constitutif des images' ('the constitutive between-two of images'). In a crucial passage he writes:

> Le tout se confond alors avec ce que Blanchot appelle la force de 'dispersion du Dehors' ou 'le vertige de l'espacement': ce vide qui n'est plus une part motrice de l'image, et qu'elle franchirait pour continuer, mais qui est la mise en question radicale de l'image (tout comme il y a un silence qui n'est plus la part motrice ou la respiration du discours, mais sa mise en question radicale). Le faux-raccord, alors, prend un nouveau sens, en même temps qu'il devient la loi.
>
> [The whole thus merges with that [*sic*] Blanchot calls the force of 'dispersal of the Outside', or 'the vertigo of spacing': that void which is no longer a motor-part of the image and which the image would cross in order to continue, but

> is the radical calling into question of the image (just as there is a silence which
> is no longer the motor-part or the breathing-space of discourse but its radical
> calling into question). False continuity, then, takes on a new meaning, at the
> same time as it becomes the law.][110]

In classical cinema each image is an expression of the whole, but 'in modern cinema each interstice is an expression or unfolding of the outside, the outside dispersing itself in multiple interstices, constituting in each interstice non-rational links, spacing the world through the force of its generative intervals'.[111] It is thus that we can now understand how 'le tout devient la puissance du dehors qui passe dans l'interstice' ('the whole becomes the power of the outside that passes into the interstice').[112] Here Deleuze refers the reader to pages in *L'Entretien infini*. The texts in question are 'Le Grand Refus' [The Great Refusal] (1959) and 'L'Interruption (comme sur une surface de Riemann)' [Interruption: As on a Riemann Surface] (1964).[113] The pages from 'L'Interruption' posit a form of interruption in conversation in which the irreducible distance between the interlocutors is measured: 'séparation, fissure, intervalle qui le laisse infiniment en dehors de moi, mais aussi prétend fonder mon rapport avec lui sur cette interruption même, qui est une *interruption d'être*' (*EI* 109) ('a separation, fissure, or interval that leaves him infinitely outside me, but also requires that I found my relation with him upon this very interruption that is an *interruption of being*', *IC* 77). Once again, Blanchot emerges as the thinker of a fundamental interruption. Deleuze transposes the alien silence that can emerge in discourse into film. The interruption is now not between two speakers, but a gap between images in a montage. In the reference from 'Le Grand Refus', Blanchot gives a relatively clear statement of what he understands by the word 'dispersion':

> ce qui régit, ce n'est pas le recueillement immobile de l'unique, mais le renversement infini de la dispersion, mouvement non dialectique, où la contrariété est étrangère à l'opposition, à la conciliation, et où l'*autre* ne revient jamais au même: l'appellerons-nous le devenir, le secret du devenir? (*EI* 65)

> [What reigns in the experience of impossibility is not the unique's immobile collecting unto itself, but the infinite shifting of dispersal, a non-dialectical movement where contrariety has nothing to do with opposition or with reconciliation, and where the *other* never comes back to the same. Shall we call it becoming, the secret of becoming?] (*IC* 46)

It is from these pages that Deleuze appears to find the phrase 'dispersion du Dehors' and the 'vertige de l'espacement' which he also uses elsewhere in *Cinéma 2* but without citing them.[114]

Images are still said to 'shock' thought at this point in *Cinéma 2*, as they did in the account of the classical whole, but now without thought being able to assimilate that shock within coherent co-ordinates. Logical thought breaks down and experiences its own impotence (*impouvoir*). This reveals what Deleuze thinks of as an inability to think that is at the heart of thought and constitutive of thought as power. The outside is in this way experienced as a 'crack'. The unthought or unthinkable thoughts correspond to what Deleuze calls, borrowing from Antonin Artaud, 'l'automate spirituel' ('the spiritual automaton'). The spiritual automation in a sense refers to the central nervous system itself that Artaud theorizes cinema ought to affect directly. It is 'un contrôle supérieur unissant la pensée critique et consciente à l'inconscient de la pensée' ('a higher control which brings together critical and conscious thought and the unconscious in thought'); it is 'dans la situation psychique du voyant, qui voit d'autant mieux et plus loin qu'il ne peut réagir, c'est-à-dire penser' ('in the psychic situation of the seer, who sees better and further than he can react, that is, think').[115]

Patrick ffrench has demonstrated Artaud's significance for Deleuze as a thinker of cinema as producing shocks to thought and having a 'direct' impact on the brain. Artaud has also been shown as significant for conceiving of an impossibility or paralysis at the heart of thought, and most importantly for giving this idea in the figure of the paralyzed body. The paralysis of thought has its site in the body, particularly the body without sense or feeling as evidenced in the figures of the mummy or sleepwalker.[116] One might add to this analysis that, for Deleuze, Artaud's importance in this regard is in no small part thought in conjunction with and through Blanchot. In Deleuze's articulation, Artaud's premise of the innermost reality as not being a whole but a 'fêlure' ('crack') or 'fissure' is an idea with a strong Blanchotian resonance.[117] It is, however, even more notable that when these terms appear in Deleuze's text, Deleuze considers them by way of Blanchot, quoting them from Blanchot's essay on Artaud (1956) in *Le Livre à venir*.[118] Blanchot writes: 'Il a comme touché [...] le point où penser, c'est toujours déjà ne pas pouvoir penser encore: "*impouvoir*", selon son mot, qui est comme essentiel à la pensée, mais fait d'elle un manque d'extrême douleur' (*LV* 48) ('It is as if he has touched [...] the point at which thinking is always unable to think: it "uncan", to use his word, which is like the essential part of his thinking, but which makes it an extremely painful lack', *BC* 36). Summing up the relation, Deleuze writes:

> De Heidegger à Artaud, Maurice Blanchot sait rendre à Artaud la question fondamentale de ce qui fait penser, de ce qui force à penser: ce qui force à penser, c'est 'l'impouvoir de la pensée', la figure de néant, l'inexistence d'un tout qui pourrait être pensé. *Ce que Blanchot diagnostique partout dans la littérature se retrouve éminemment dans le cinéma*: d'une part la présence d'un impensable dans la pensée, et qui serait à la fois comme sa source et son barrage; d'autre part la présence à l'infini d'un autre penseur dans le penseur, qui brise tout monologue d'un moi pensant.
>
> [Between Heidegger and Artaud, Maurice Blanchot was able to give the fundamental question of what makes us think, what forces us to think, back to Artaud: what forces us to think is the 'inpower of thought', the figure of nothingness, the inexistence of a whole which could be thought. *What Blanchot diagnoses everywhere in literature is particularly clear in cinema*: on the one hand the presence of an unthinkable in thought, which would be both its source and barrier; on the other hand the presence to infinity of another thinker in the thinker, who shatters every monologue of a thinking self.][119]

This is a moment of interpretation that it is easy to pass over, but what is remarkable is the sleight of hand typical of Deleuzian interpretation. For Blanchot, literature is unusual, almost unique in its access to the silence of the unthinkable, yet Deleuze readily broadens this out. Deleuze is in effect imagining how fascination — explicitly related by Blanchot to literature — would work in cinema, going so far as to identify it with modern cinema. Again it is useful to compare Deleuze's other texts in order to see how important the idea is to him. In *Différence et répétition*, Deleuze again discusses:

> ce point dont Maurice Blanchot ne cesse de parler, ce point aléatoire, originel, aveugle, acéphale, aphasique, qui désigne 'l'impossibilité de penser qu'est la pensée', et qui se développe dans l'œuvre comme problème, et où 'l'impouvoir' se transmue en puissance.
>
> [that point of which Maurice Blanchot speaks endlessly: that blind, acephalic, aphasic and aleatory original point which designates 'the impossibility of thinking that is thought', that point at which 'powerlessness' is transmuted into power, that point which develops in the work in the form of a problem.][120]

As with the discussion of Giacometti in the previous chapter, it is once again a question of a 'point'. In the reading of Nancy we saw how images can 'aim from' a point that cannot be found. Here, Deleuze indicates a point in the viewer that is activated by the images, a 'penseur dans le penseur' that is like an other that emerges in the self, a new voice disturbing the unity of the subject. The positing of a point that can be accessed in the film (Nancy) and in the viewer (Deleuze) is entirely consistent with the idea of the image as a double relation outlined in the previous chapter. In a surviving recording of a lecture delivered at the time of the writing of the *Cinéma* volumes (1984), Deleuze can be heard averring that:

> beaucoup de thèmes de Blanchot, proches de Blanchot, sont comme devenus les lieux communs d'une espèce de manière de penser moderne; c'est-à-dire on y est immédiatement familier. Je veux dire que c'est des thèmes que même sans avoir lu Blanchot on a comme respirés.[121]
>
> [many of Blanchot's themes, close to Blanchot, have become like commonplaces in a strain of the modern manner of thinking. This is to say, we are immediately familiar with them. I mean there are themes that even without having read Blanchot it is as if one has breathed them in.]

This may be correct, but it slightly occludes the extent to which Deleuze himself is inspired by the texts.[122]

The lines quoted above linking Blanchot and Artaud also form an unusual reference to Heidegger, who is not a frequent presence in the *Cinéma* volumes. The link between Artaud, Blanchot, and Jean-Louis Schefer in Deleuze is described by D. N. Rodowick as 'a Heideggerianism', and is described thus in reference to the unthinkable, which in a Heideggerian register would be both that which we have not yet begun to think and that which means we have not yet begun to think. (This is also present in Blanchot's account of Artaud, *LV* 48; *BC* 36.) Awakening this is the essence of cinema, he continues, even though it is not apparent in most films, and that which awakens it is the spiritual automaton.[123] The relevant text by Heidegger is, as Rodowick observes, that which includes the famous lecture course of 1951–52, *Was Heisst Denken?*, or *What is Called Thinking?* The lectures have a historical significance for being the last given before Heidegger's retirement, as well as his first since 1944.¹²⁴ Once again, this is a text crucial for Blanchot. When Deleuze cites it, there is a danger of eliding the possibility that Heidegger is mediated by Blanchot, just as there is a sense that Godard may be reading Heidegger by way of Blanchot. Thus when Rodowick summarizes Deleuze to the extent that '[w]hat cinema contributes to the history of thought is a powerlessness — in fact, *a dispossession of thought in relation to the image* — that is equivalent to the division of the subject by the pure form of time', this sounds extremely close to saying that cinema's contribution to thought is fascination.¹²⁵ Richard Rushton has provided a clear statement of what is at stake in a Deleuzian spectatorship conceived of in this way. For him, Deleuze's spectator is 'ineluctably passive'.¹²⁶ The spectator's subject position is in Deleuze's account one which becomes fused with the film and does not exist prior to the film. To the extent that this subject has a body, it is one that is imaginarily projected into the image. 'Very few scholars in film studies,' he adds, 'have ever defended a passive spectator'.¹²⁷ To take Blanchot at his word, however, would be to *affirm* this very passivity.

A crucial text here is by Ropars-Wuilleumier, perhaps the most important writer to have considered the relation between Blanchot and film in detail.¹²⁸ For Ropars-Wuilleumier, Blanchot's role is 'systématique' thanks to 'la lecture biaisée' of Deleuze, 'qui retourne l'interprétation de Blanchot selon ses propres objectifs' ('who alters the interpretation of Blanchot according to his own objectives').¹²⁹ For Ropars-Wuilleumier, the crack of the unthinkable in thought as developed by Blanchot is a more radical notion than that allowed by Deleuze's *Cinéma* project and one which threatens to place the totalizing project of the two volumes as a whole in question. This problem quickly takes on the name of 'la pensée du dehors', thus indicating that the idea is to be understood according to its articulation by Michel Foucault.¹³⁰ According to Ropars-Wuilleumier, although there is a convergence between Blanchot's thought and the Deleuzian becoming of thought in *L'Image-temps*, Deleuze uses Blanchot to close off a line of flight that traverses the time-image and calls into question the possibility of inscribing the image in time. In this way she characterizes Blanchot's place in Deleuze's project as that of an '"attracteur étrange"' ('strange attractor').¹³¹ According to Ropars-Wuilleumier, the problem with Deleuze's reading is that the outside is subject to a 'régulation' ('regulation').¹³² In Chapter 8 of Deleuze's text, the outside is linked to the proximity of a 'dedans' ('inside') that it attracts; in Chapter 9, the outside is said to be made visible, coexisting with the 'dedans' of a film image, such that speech itself can be seen in the interval opened by Duras's off-screen, observational voices. This is for Deleuze a question of a new time-image coming out of the disjunction within the audio-visual as such, offering 'une forme de visibilité de l'invisible lui-même' ('a sort of visibility of the invisible itself').¹³³ Although as we have seen the visibility of the invisible is one of Blanchot's definitions of fascination, this is highly problematic. The outside, which is firstly a force of exclusion and upheaval, becomes in Deleuze's work a power for *including* the exteriority and incorporating it in the image. In contrast to the understanding of the space of the image set out in the previous chapter, in which the opening of that space can annul seeing, the logic of Deleuze's project requires him to salvage the visible. The recourse to the outside and then overturning it can be regarded as an attempt to delimit or contain the second version of the imaginary. Blanchot links this space of the image to a lack of the present, a deficiency of time that makes presence impossible. As Ropars-Wuilleumier writes:

> Telle une pensée du dehors, le devenir emporte, souterrainement ou de manière frontale, l'ensemble d'un dispositif où le présent ferait toujours défaut, si l'image n'en garantissait la présence en ramenant l'extériorité vers l'intimité, cristalline ou fissurée, de la visibilité elle-même. Dans *L'Image-temps*, l'image est là pour nous sauver du temps, cette ligne de fuite incessante. Et quand les circuits continus de Bergson ont explosé dans les courts-circuits de Godard, alors Blanchot prend la relève de Bergson pour répondre à la poussée du dehors en l'enfouissant au-dedans même de l'image. En ce sens, le dehors sert de contrefeu au devenir, qui traverse toutes les images-temps et rend insaisissable la présence du présent dans l'image présente.

> [Like a thought of the outside, becoming overcomes, head on or underground, the entirety of a system in which the present would always be lacking if the image did not guarantee presence by guiding exteriority back toward the intimacy, crystalline or fissured, of visibility itself. In *The Time-Image*, the image is there to save us from time, this endless line of flight. And when Bergson's continuous circuits have exploded in Godard's short-circuits, then Blanchot takes up where Bergson leaves off by responding to the advance of the outside by inserting it into the very inside of the image. In this sense, the outside serves as a backfire to the becoming that traverses all time-images and makes the presence of the present in the present image ungraspable.][134]

As we saw above in reference to 'Le Grand Refus', though it is a theme that abounds in Blanchot's texts, the outside disperses the present. Thus, as Ropars-Wuilleumier critically suggests, it might appear in the first instance that 'l'usage deleuzien de Blanchot n'est guère blanchotien' ('Deleuze's use of Blanchot is hardly Blanchotian'); one might even conclude that 'Deleuze a peu lu Blanchot, puisqu'il retourne les termes utilisés par celui-ci, ne retient pas ce qui concerne le temps dans la pensée de Blanchot et en refuse la logique radicale, qui remet en question l'ontologie' ('Deleuze has barely read Blanchot because he distorts his terms, does not retain what concerns time, and rejects the radical logic that places ontology into question').[135] What this brings us towards, at the risk of a tautological formulation, is the imaginary quality of the image, or what Ropars-Wuilleumier calls in another work, 'l'idée d'image' — the paradox by which the image takes on all the qualities of the invisible and yet can only be called an image on account of its visibility.[136]

Notes to Chapter 2

1. Godard's quotation is drawn with modifications from *A* 48 & 50–51, and the translation from *F* 37 & 40. Compare Jean-Luc Godard, *Histoire(s) du cinéma*, 4 vols (Paris: Gallimard/Gaumont, 1998), IV, 298–300.
2. Roland-François Lack, 'Sa voix', in *For Ever Godard*, ed. by Michael Temple, James S. Williams and Michael Witt (London: Black Dog, 2004), pp. 312–29 (p. 320).
3. This picture was taken by a paparazzo without Blanchot's consent in 1985. For an account of this image, and Godard's allusions to Blanchot in his work as a whole, see Leslie Hill, '"A Form that

Thinks"': Godard, Blanchot, Citation', in *For Ever Godard*, ed. by Temple, Williams and Witt, pp. 396–415 (p. 408). On questions surrounding representations of Blanchot, including Blanchot's personal resistance to photography and further background to this particular image, see Bident, *Maurice Blanchot*, pp. 531–40.

4. Jean-Luc Godard, *Jean-Luc Godard par Jean-Luc Godard*, ed. by Alain Bergala, 2 vols (Paris: Cahiers du cinéma, 1998), II, 301.
5. See Hill, '"A Form that Thinks"'. These lines appear in variegated forms in *Notre musique* (2003), *The Old Place* (1999), and *Éloge de l'amour* (2001). Most recently it can be observed that Godard uses a line from *L'Attente l'oubli* in his film *Adieu au langage* (2014).
6. Didi-Huberman, 'De ressemblance à ressemblance', p. 148.
7. André Malraux, *Le Musée imaginaire* (Paris: Gallimard, 1965), p. 12; *Museum Without Walls*, trans. by Stuart Gilbert and Francis Price (New York: Doubleday & Co., 1967), p. 10.
8. Michael Temple, 'Big Rhythm and the Power of Metamorphosis: Some Models and Precursors for *Histoire(s) du cinéma*', in *The Cinema Alone: Essays on the Work of Jean-Luc Godard 1985–2000*, ed. by Michael Temple and James S. Williams (Amsterdam: Amsterdam University Press, 2000), pp. 77–95 (pp. 77–78). Céline Scemama also substitutes the word 'cinéma' for 'livre' in a passage from Blanchot to make a comparable point, Céline Scemama, *'Histoire(s) du cinéma' de Jean-Luc Godard: la force faible d'un art* (Paris: L'Harmattan, 2006), p. 69. To give but two important examples of the way in which Malraux is used in *Histoire(s)*, Godard takes the title of 3A from the *Psychologie de l'art* series, 'Le Monnaie de l'absolu' [The Currency of the Absolute], while a recording of Malraux's famous speech to mark the transferral of Jean Moulin's ashes to the Panthéon in 1964 is played earlier in Chapter 4B. On this topic, see also Michael Witt, *Jean-Luc Godard: Cinema Historian* (Bloomington: Indiana University Press, 2013), pp. 85–90.
9. Douglas Smith, '(Un)Reconstructed Space?: The Imaginary in Post-War France (Sartre, Malraux, Merleau-Ponty, Blanchot', *Paragraph*, 27:3 (2004), 68–81 (p. 68).
10. Ibid., p. 76.
11. Ibid., p. 79.
12. Ibid., pp. 79–80.
13. Godard quotes from Georges Bataille, 'L'Amour d'un être mortel', in *Œuvres complètes*, 12 vols (Paris: Gallimard, 1970–88), VIII (1976), 496–503. Like the lines from Blanchot, this quotation from Bataille has been used by Godard elsewhere. On its use in *Éloge de l'amour*, see Patrick ffrench, *After Bataille: Sacrifice, Exposure, Community* (Oxford: Legenda, 2007), p. 188, and Douglas Morrey, 'History of Resistance/Resistance of History: Godard's *Éloge de l'amour* (2001)', *Studies in French Cinema*, 3:2 (2003), 121–30 (pp. 128–29).
14. For the relation between Blanchot and Bataille, see Bident, *Maurice Blanchot*, pp. 419–24, and Patrick ffrench, 'Friendship, Asymmetry, Sacrifice: Bataille and Blanchot', *Parrhesia*, 3 (2007), 32–42.
15. See 'Formless', in Georges Bataille, *Visions of Excess: Selected Writings 1927–1939*, ed. by Allan Stoekl, trans. by Allan Stoekl, Carl M. Lovitt and Donald M. Leslie Jr (Minneapolis: University of Minnesota Press, 1985), p. 31.
16. See ffrench, *After Bataille*, pp. 107–37 (pp. 123–24). The notion of *bonheur* may also suggest Georges Bataille, 'Dossier du *Pur Bonheur*', in *Œuvres complètes*, XII (1988), 525–47.
17. Godard, *Histoire(s) du cinéma*, I, 72–73. *Le Plaisir* is in turn based on short stories by Guy de Maupassant.
18. Compare with Godard, *Histoire(s) du cinéma*, I, 93.
19. Jacques Aumont, 'Mortal Beauty', in *The Cinema Alone*, ed. by Temple and Williams, pp. 97–112 (p. 99).
20. Witt, *Jean-Luc Godard: Cinema Historian*, p. 86.
21. Ibid., p. 25.
22. Ibid., p. 26.
23. Hill, '"A Form that Thinks"', p. 410.
24. Jean-Luc Godard and Youssef Ishaghpour, *Archéologie du cinéma et mémoire du siècle: dialogue* (Tours: Farrago, 2000), pp. 82–83; *Cinema: The Archaeology of Film and the Memory of a Century*, trans. by John Howe (Oxford: Berg, 2005), pp. 105–06 (translation modified).

him to salvage the visible. The recourse to the outside and then overturning it can be regarded as an attempt to delimit or contain the second version of the imaginary. Blanchot links this space of the image to a lack of the present, a deficiency of time that makes presence impossible. As Ropars-Wuilleumier writes:

> Telle une pensée du dehors, le devenir emporte, souterrainement ou de manière frontale, l'ensemble d'un dispositif où le présent ferait toujours défaut, si l'image n'en garantissait la présence en ramenant l'extériorité vers l'intimité, cristalline ou fissurée, de la visibilité elle-même. Dans *L'Image-temps*, l'image est là pour nous sauver du temps, cette ligne de fuite incessante. Et quand les circuits continus de Bergson ont explosé dans les courts-circuits de Godard, alors Blanchot prend la relève de Bergson pour répondre à la poussée du dehors en l'enfouissant au-dedans même de l'image. En ce sens, le dehors sert de contrefeu au devenir, qui traverse toutes les images-temps et rend insaisissable la présence du présent dans l'image présente.
>
> [Like a thought of the outside, becoming overcomes, head on or underground, the entirety of a system in which the present would always be lacking if the image did not guarantee presence by guiding exteriority back toward the intimacy, crystalline or fissured, of visibility itself. In *The Time-Image*, the image is there to save us from time, this endless line of flight. And when Bergson's continuous circuits have exploded in Godard's short-circuits, then Blanchot takes up where Bergson leaves off by responding to the advance of the outside by inserting it into the very inside of the image. In this sense, the outside serves as a backfire to the becoming that traverses all time-images and makes the presence of the present in the present image ungraspable.][134]

As we saw above in reference to 'Le Grand Refus', though it is a theme that abounds in Blanchot's texts, the outside disperses the present. Thus, as Ropars-Wuilleumier critically suggests, it might appear in the first instance that 'l'usage deleuzien de Blanchot n'est guère blanchotien' ('Deleuze's use of Blanchot is hardly Blanchotian'); one might even conclude that 'Deleuze a peu lu Blanchot, puisqu'il retourne les termes utilisés par celui-ci, ne retient pas ce qui concerne le temps dans la pensée de Blanchot et en refuse la logique radicale, qui remet en question l'ontologie' ('Deleuze has barely read Blanchot because he distorts his terms, does not retain what concerns time, and rejects the radical logic that places ontology into question').[135] What this brings us towards, at the risk of a tautological formulation, is the imaginary quality of the image, or what Ropars-Wuilleumier calls in another work, 'l'idée d'image' — the paradox by which the image takes on all the qualities of the invisible and yet can only be called an image on account of its visibility.[136]

Notes to Chapter 2

1. Godard's quotation is drawn with modifications from *A* 48 & 50–51, and the translation from *F* 37 & 40. Compare Jean-Luc Godard, *Histoire(s) du cinéma*, 4 vols (Paris: Gallimard/Gaumont, 1998), IV, 298–300.
2. Roland-François Lack, 'Sa voix', in *For Ever Godard*, ed. by Michael Temple, James S. Williams and Michael Witt (London: Black Dog, 2004), pp. 312–29 (p. 320).
3. This picture was taken by a paparazzo without Blanchot's consent in 1985. For an account of this image, and Godard's allusions to Blanchot in his work as a whole, see Leslie Hill, '"A Form that

Thinks"': Godard, Blanchot, Citation', in *For Ever Godard*, ed. by Temple, Williams and Witt, pp. 396–415 (p. 408). On questions surrounding representations of Blanchot, including Blanchot's personal resistance to photography and further background to this particular image, see Bident, *Maurice Blanchot*, pp. 531–40.
4. Jean-Luc Godard, *Jean-Luc Godard par Jean-Luc Godard*, ed. by Alain Bergala, 2 vols (Paris: Cahiers du cinéma, 1998), II, 301.
5. See Hill, '"A Form that Thinks"'. These lines appear in variegated forms in *Notre musique* (2003), *The Old Place* (1999), and *Éloge de l'amour* (2001). Most recently it can be observed that Godard uses a line from *L'Attente l'oubli* in his film *Adieu au langage* (2014).
6. Didi-Huberman, 'De ressemblance à ressemblance', p. 148.
7. André Malraux, *Le Musée imaginaire* (Paris: Gallimard, 1965), p. 12; *Museum Without Walls*, trans. by Stuart Gilbert and Francis Price (New York: Doubleday & Co., 1967), p. 10.
8. Michael Temple, 'Big Rhythm and the Power of Metamorphosis: Some Models and Precursors for *Histoire(s) du cinéma*', in *The Cinema Alone: Essays on the Work of Jean-Luc Godard 1985–2000*, ed. by Michael Temple and James S. Williams (Amsterdam: Amsterdam University Press, 2000), pp. 77–95 (pp. 77–78). Céline Scemama also substitutes the word 'cinéma' for 'livre' in a passage from Blanchot to make a comparable point, Céline Scemama, *'Histoire(s) du cinéma' de Jean-Luc Godard: la force faible d'un art* (Paris: L'Harmattan, 2006), p. 69. To give but two important examples of the way in which Malraux is used in *Histoire(s)*, Godard takes the title of 3A from the *Psychologie de l'art* series, 'Le Monnaie de l'absolu' [The Currency of the Absolute], while a recording of Malraux's famous speech to mark the transferral of Jean Moulin's ashes to the Panthéon in 1964 is played earlier in Chapter 4B. On this topic, see also Michael Witt, *Jean-Luc Godard: Cinema Historian* (Bloomington: Indiana University Press, 2013), pp. 85–90.
9. Douglas Smith, '(Un)Reconstructed Space?: The Imaginary in Post-War France (Sartre, Malraux, Merleau-Ponty, Blanchot', *Paragraph*, 27:3 (2004), 68–81 (p. 68).
10. Ibid., p. 76.
11. Ibid., p. 79.
12. Ibid., pp. 79–80.
13. Godard quotes from Georges Bataille, 'L'Amour d'un être mortel', in *Œuvres complètes*, 12 vols (Paris: Gallimard, 1970–88), VIII (1976), 496–503. Like the lines from Blanchot, this quotation from Bataille has been used by Godard elsewhere. On its use in *Éloge de l'amour*, see Patrick ffrench, *After Bataille: Sacrifice, Exposure, Community* (Oxford: Legenda, 2007), p. 188, and Douglas Morrey, 'History of Resistance/Resistance of History: Godard's *Éloge de l'amour* (2001)', *Studies in French Cinema*, 3:2 (2003), 121–30 (pp. 128–29).
14. For the relation between Blanchot and Bataille, see Bident, *Maurice Blanchot*, pp. 419–24, and Patrick ffrench, 'Friendship, Asymmetry, Sacrifice: Bataille and Blanchot', *Parrhesia*, 3 (2007), 32–42.
15. See 'Formless', in Georges Bataille, *Visions of Excess: Selected Writings 1927–1939*, ed. by Allan Stoekl, trans. by Allan Stoekl, Carl M. Lovitt and Donald M. Leslie Jr (Minneapolis: University of Minnesota Press, 1985), p. 31.
16. See ffrench, *After Bataille*, pp. 107–37 (pp. 123–24). The notion of *bonheur* may also suggest Georges Bataille, 'Dossier du *Pur Bonheur*', in *Œuvres complètes*, XII (1988), 525–47.
17. Godard, *Histoire(s) du cinéma*, I, 72–73. *Le Plaisir* is in turn based on short stories by Guy de Maupassant.
18. Compare with Godard, *Histoire(s) du cinéma*, I, 93.
19. Jacques Aumont, 'Mortal Beauty', in *The Cinema Alone*, ed. by Temple and Williams, pp. 97–112 (p. 99).
20. Witt, *Jean-Luc Godard: Cinema Historian*, p. 86.
21. Ibid., p. 25.
22. Ibid., p. 26.
23. Hill, '"A Form that Thinks"', p. 410.
24. Jean-Luc Godard and Youssef Ishaghpour, *Archéologie du cinéma et mémoire du siècle: dialogue* (Tours: Farrago, 2000), pp. 82–83; *Cinema: The Archaeology of Film and the Memory of a Century*, trans. by John Howe (Oxford: Berg, 2005), pp. 105–06 (translation modified).

25. Witt, *Jean-Luc Godard: Cinema Historian*, p. 25. Witt notes that this line is only apocryphally Pauline; it is in fact taken from a 1984 article by Jacques Henric. Compare Godard, *Histoire(s) du cinéma*, I, 205–14.
26. Beckett's text was first written in the 1950s and formed part of *Comment c'est* (1961). In 1988 it was published in a very slim edition by Minuit, which is the edition Godard shows. Samuel Beckett, *L'Image* (Paris: Éditions de Minuit, 1988).
27. For a reproduction, see Yves Bonnefoy, *Alberto Giacometti: A Biography of His Work*, trans. by Jean Stewart (Paris: Flammarion, 1991), p. 328.
28. Timothy Mathews, *Alberto Giacometti: The Art of Relation* (London: I. B. Tauris, 2013), p. 97.
29. The piece comes from Paul Hindemith's symphony *Mathis der Maler* (1933–34). On this piece of music, and Godard's use of music more generally, see James S. Williams, 'Music, Love, and the Cinematic Event', in *For Ever Godard*, ed. by Temple, Williams and Witt, pp. 288–311.
30. Mathews, *Alberto Giacometti*, p. 93.
31. André Malraux, 'Speech by André Malraux', *The Trial of Joan of Arc*, DVD (London: Artificial Eye, 2005).
32. Keith Reader, *Robert Bresson* (Manchester: Manchester University Press, 2000), p. 63.
33. Deleuze, *Cinéma 2*, p. 233; *Cinema 2*, p. 173.
34. Jacques Rancière, *La Fable cinématographique* (Paris: Seuil, 2001), p. 235/*Film Fables*, trans. by Emiliano Battista (Oxford: Berg, 2006), p. 185.
35. Ibid., p. 221; p. 174.
36. Jacques Rancière, *Les Écarts du cinéma* (Paris: La Fabrique éditions, 2011), pp. 43–44; *The Intervals of Cinema*, trans. by John Howe (London: Verso, 2014), p. 37.
37. For a discussion of this sequence, see Alan Wright, 'Elizabeth Taylor at Auschwitz: JLG and the Real Object of Montage', in *The Cinema Alone*, ed. by Temple and Williams, pp. 51–60.
38. Céline Scemama, 'Jean-Luc Godard's *Histoire(s) du cinéma* Brings the Dead Back to the Screen', in *The Legacies of Jean-Luc Godard*, ed. by Douglas Morrey, Christina Stojanova, and Nicole Côté (Ontario: Wilfrid Laurier University Press, 2014), pp. 99–124 (p. 103).
39. Ibid., p. 102.
40. Ibid., p. 104.
41. Douglas Morrey also connects this *bonheur* to Blanchot's account of the image, Douglas Morrey, 'Jean-Luc Godard and the Other History of Cinema' (unpublished PhD thesis, University of Warwick, 2002, pp. 54–55).
42. Ibid., p. 55.
43. Ibid., p. 60.
44. Zenkine, 'Blanchot et l'image visuelle', pp. 224–27.
45. Giorgio Agamben, 'Cinema and History: On Jean-Luc Godard', in *Cinema and Agamben: Ethics, Biopolitics and the Moving Image*, ed. by Henrik Gustafsson and Asbjørn Grønstad (New York: Bloomsbury, 2014), pp. 25–26 (p. 25).
46. Ibid. p. 26.
47. On the complex subject of Godard and montage more generally, see Michael Witt, 'Montage, My Beautiful Care, or Histories of the Cinematograph', in *The Cinema Alone*, ed. by Temple and Williams, pp. 33–50.
48. James S. Williams, 'Silence, Gesture, Revelation: The Ethics and Aesthetics of Montage in Godard and Agamben', in *Cinema and Agamben*, ed. by Gustafsson and Grønstad, pp. 27–54 (p. 44).
49. James S. Williams, 'European Culture and Artistic Resistance in *Histoire(s) du cinéma* Chapter 3A, *La Monnaie de l'absolu*', in *The Cinema Alone*, ed. by Temple and Williams, pp. 113–39 (p. 125).
50. Ibid., pp. 137–38.
51. Hill, '"A Form that Thinks"', p. 410.
52. Ibid., p. 400.
53. Ibid.
54. Ibid., pp. 414–15.
55. Ibid., p. 402.

56. Ibid., p. 414.
57. Witt, *Jean-Luc Godard: Cinema Historian*, p. 35. Hands are especially evident in Chapter 4A, see ibid., pp. 102–03, and Sally Shafto, 'On Painting and History in Godard's *Histoire(s) du cinéma*', *Senses of Cinema*, 40 (2006), <http://sensesofcinema.com/2006/the-godard-museum/histoires-du-cinema/> [accessed 27 June 2015]. For the sculptor reference, see Godard, *Jean-Luc Godard par Jean-Luc Godard*, II, 242.
58. Chris Petit, 'The History of Cinema and History in Cinema', *Vertigo*, 4:2 (2009), <https://www.closeupfilmcentre.com/vertigo_magazine/volume-4-issue-2-winter-spring-20091/the-history-of-cinema-and-history-in-cinema/> [accessed 5 June 2015].
59. For a discussion of this, see Witt, *Jean-Luc Godard: Cinema Historian*, pp. 83–85.
60. For a reproduction, see Bonnefoy, *Alberto Giacometti*, p. 325.
61. Williams, 'European Culture and Artistic Resistance in *Histoire(s) du cinéma*', p. 137.
62. Bonnefoy, *Alberto Giacometti*, p. 329.
63. William Blake, *Blake's Poetry and Designs*, ed. by Mary Lynn Johnson and John E. Grant, 2nd edn (New York: W. W. Norton & Company, 2008), p. 96. For a beautiful reproduction of this image, see Color Plate 9.
64. Ibid., p. 113.
65. Blanchot wrote perceptively on Blake during the war in which he stressed the unusual combination in Blake's imagination of a power of vision and a power of creation (see *FP* 37–41; 28–32).
66. As quoted in Colin MacCabe, *Godard: A Portrait of the Artist at Seventy* (London: Bloomsbury, 2003), p. 296. For MacCabe, although the work is made up of potentially esoteric references and filmic quotations, the 'real function' of this material is in its use in the telling of a personal story on Godard's part. As MacCabe writes, '[t]he advent of video technology means that there can be a new kind of reflection on the image in which the most private of identifications and the most public of images can be conjugated together' (p. 299).
67. Alain Bergala, 'The Other Side of the Bouquet', trans. by Lynne Kirby, in *Jean-Luc Godard: Son + Image, 1974–1991*, ed. by Raymond Bellour and Mary Lea Bandy (New York: MOMA, 1992), pp. 57–74 (p. 73).
68. Ibid., p. 70.
69. Compare Godard, *Histoire(s) du cinéma*, I, 188.
70. Mulvey, *Death 24x a Second*, p. 187.
71. Didi-Huberman, 'De ressemblance à ressemblance', p. 154.
72. Jacques Aumont, *Amnésies: fictions du cinéma d'après Jean-Luc Godard* (Paris: P.O.L., 1999), p. 36.
73. Ibid., p. 39.
74. Ibid., p. 40.
75. Ibid., p. 47.
76. Ibid., p. 42
77. Scemama, *'Histoire(s) du cinéma' de Jean-Luc Godard*, p. 190.
78. Witt, *Jean-Luc Godard: Cinema Historian*, p. 72. On the subject of Orpheus, see pp. 70–76.
79. The slapstick comedy viewed was later reprised by Bergman in the notorious opening sequence of *Persona* (1966).
80. The use of this moment from *Orphée* must be seen in the context of Godard's long and complex engagement with Cocteau. For this, see James S. Williams, *Jean Cocteau* (Manchester: Manchester University Press, 2006), pp. 190–96. For a discussion of *Orphée*, see pp. 110–35.
81. Heidegger, 'What Are Poets For?', pp. 89 & 92.
82. Oliver Harris, 'Pure Cinema? Blanchot, Godard, *Le Mépris*', *Critical Quarterly*, 53, 'Godard's Contempt: Essays from the London Consortium', ed. by Colin MacCabe and Laura Mulvey (2011), 96–106 (pp. 97 & 101). Harris writes that the only reference he has found which mentions the connection between *Le Mépris* and Blanchot is Kaja Silverman and Harun Farocki, *Speaking about Godard* (New York: New York University Press, 1998), p. 231, n. 12 (p. 104, n. 3). However, Ropars-Wuilleumier made this connection in an essay on Godard in 1988 called 'Totalité et fragmentaire: la réécriture selon Godard', see Ropars-Wuilleumier, *Le Temps d'une pensée*, pp. 153–66. Ropars-Wuilleumier is more interested in a theoretical connection between the works

than the question of how Godard is influenced by Blanchot, 'qu'il ne cite jamais' (p. 164). Godard's use of Blanchot has however become more evident in the last twenty years, as shown in the essay by Hill discussed in this chapter. More recently Hill has developed the connection between the Fritz Lang character's comments on Hölderlin in *Le Mépris* and Blanchot, see '"O himmlisch Licht!": Cinema and the Withdrawal of the Gods (Straub-Huillet, Hölderlin, Godard, Brecht)', *Angelaki: Journal of the Theoretical Humanities*, 17:4, 'Belief in Cinema: Themes after André Bazin', ed. by Lisa Trahair and Lisabeth During (2012), 139–55.
83. In extracts from the soundtrack published in *Le Monde*, as quoted in Witt, *Jean-Luc Godard: Cinema Historian*, p. 130. See for example Chapter 3A for Godard's identification of the absence of a cinema of the Resistance.
84. Raymond Bellour, *L'Entre-Images 2: mots, images* (Paris: P.O.L., 1999), pp. 113–38; '(Not) Just An Other Filmmaker', in Bellour and Bandy, *Jean-Luc Godard: Son + Image, 1974–1991*, pp. 215–31.
85. As quoted by Bellour, *L'Entre-Images 2*, p. 113; '(Not) Just An Other Filmmaker', p. 215.
86. Bellour, *L'Entre-Images 2*, p. 120; '(Not) Just An Other Filmmaker', p. 219.
87. Ibid., p. 120; p. 229.
88. Ibid., p. 134; p. 227.
89. Ibid. p. 116; p. 217 (my emphasis).
90. Ibid., p. 126; p. 222.
91. Ibid., p. 126; p. 222.
92. Ibid., p. 128; p. 223.
93. Ibid., p. 130; p. 223.
94. Ibid., p. 130; p. 224.
95. Ibid., p. 136; p. 228.
96. Ibid., p. 137; p. 230.
97. Gilles Deleuze, *Cinéma 1: l'image-mouvement* (Paris: Éditions de Minuit, 1983), pp. 150–51; *Cinema 1: The Movement-Image*, trans. by Hugh Tomlinson and Barbara Habberjam (London: Continuum, 2005), p. 109.
98. Ibid., p. 151; pp. 109–10.
99. As quoted in Deleuze, *Cinéma 1*, p. 146; *Cinema 1*, p. 105. See *EL* 161; *SL* 155.
100. Gilles Deleuze, *Logique du sens* (Paris: Éditions de Minuit, 1969), pp. 177–78; *The Logic of Sense*, ed. by Constantin V. Boundas, trans. by Mark Lester with Charles Stivale (London: Continuum, 2004), p. 172.
101. Gilles Deleuze, *Différence et répétition* (Paris: PUF, 1968), pp. 148–49; *Difference and Repetition*, trans. by Paul Patton (New York: Columbia University Press, 1994), p. 112.
102. Tom Conley, 'The Film-Event: from Bazin to Deleuze', paper given at the Maison française d'Oxford, 12 March 2015.
103. Ibid.
104. Gilles Deleuze, *Le Pli: Leibniz et le Baroque* (Paris: Éditions de Minuit, 1988), p. 141; *The Fold: Leibniz and the Baroque*, trans. by Tom Conley (London: Athlone, 1993), p. 105.
105. Eleanor Kaufman, 'Midnight, or the Inertia of Being', in *After Blanchot*, ed. by Hill, Nelson and Varoulakis, pp. 221–37 (p. 221).
106. Ibid., p. 222.
107. Deleuze, *Logique du sens*, p. 9; *The Logic of Sense*, p. 3.
108. Deleuze, *Cinéma 2*, p. 235; *Cinema 2*, p. 174.
109. Ronald Bogue, *Deleuze on Cinema* (New York: Routledge, 2003), p. 173.
110. Deleuze, *Cinéma 2*, p. 235; *Cinema 2*, p. 174.
111. Bogue, *Deleuze on Cinema*, p. 176.
112. Deleuze, *Cinéma 2*, pp. 236–37; *Cinema 2*, p. 175.
113. See ibid., p. 235, n. 44; p. 303, n. 44. Deleuze cites specifically *EI* 65 & 107–09; *IC* 45–46 & 75–77.
114. See Deleuze, *Cinéma 2*, p. 235; *Cinema 2*, p. 174. The 'vertige de l'espacement' appears on the following page, and Blanchot's footnote to it refers the reader back to his earlier usage in 'La Solitude essentielle' in *L'Espace littéraire*. See *SL* 31; *EL* 22, and also *EI* 66; *IC* 46.
115. Deleuze, *Cinéma 2*, pp. 215 & 221; *Cinema 2*, pp. 160 & 164.

116. Patrick ffrench, 'Belief in the Body: Philippe Garrel's *Le Révélateur* and Deleuze', *Paragraph*, 31:2 (2008), 159–72 (pp. 162–66).
117. Deleuze, *Cinéma 2*, p. 218; *Cinema 2*, p. 162. Notions of cracks and gaps abound in Blanchot's writing, for example: 'les fragments, destinés en partie au blanc qui les sépare, trouvent en cet écart non pas ce qui les termine, mais ce qui les prolonge, ou les met en attente de ce qui les prolongera, les a déjà prolongés, les faisant persister de par leur inachèvement' (*ED* 96) ('For fragments, destined partly to the blank that separates them, find in this gap not what ends them, but what prolongs them, or what makes them await their prolongation — what has already prolonged them, causing them to persist on account of their incompletion', *WD* 58).
118. See Deleuze, *Cinéma 2*, p. 218, n. 22; *Cinema 2*, p. 301. (In n. 20 Blanchot is also said to be close to Artaud.) Blanchot writes: 'Ce qui est premier, ce n'est pas la plénitude de l'être, c'est la lézarde et la fissure, l'érosion et le déchirement, l'intermittence et la privation rongeuse: l'être, ce n'est pas l'être, c'est ce manque de l'être' (*LV* 49–50) ('what is prime is the crack and the fissure, erosion and destruction, intermittence and gnawing privation: being is not being, it is the lack of being', *BC* 38). Deleuze also misquotes Blanchot at this point, giving: 'la totalité dont cette dépossession apparaissait' rather than Blanchot's 'la "*totalité immédiate*" dont cette dépossession apparaissait'.
119. Deleuze, *Cinéma 2*, pp. 218–19; *Cinema 2*, p. 162 (my emphasis).
120. Deleuze, *Différence et répétition*, pp. 257–58; *Difference and Repetition*, p. 199.
121. Gilles Deleuze, 'cinéma/pensée cours 70', lecture given 20 November 1984, <http://www.univ-paris8.fr/deleuze/article.php3?id_article=196> [accessed 27 June 2015].
122. The reference to the 'acéphale' above indicates that the same may be said vis-à-vis Bataille.
123. D. N. Rodowick, *Gilles Deleuze's Time Machine* (Durham, NC: Duke University Press, 1997), p. 189.
124. See Martin Heidegger, *What Is Called Thinking?*, trans. by Fred D. Wieck and J. Glenn Gray (New York: Harper & Row, 1968), p. xvii.
125. Rodowick, *Gilles Deleuze's Time Machine*, p. 190 (my emphasis).
126. Richard Rushton, 'Deleuzian Spectatorship', *Screen*, 50:1 (2009), 45–53 (p. 46).
127. Ibid., p. 48.
128. Ropars-Wuilleumier, *Le Temps d'une pensée*, pp. 401–17; 'Image or Time? The Thought of the Outside in *The Time-Image* (Deleuze and Blanchot)', trans. by Matthew Lazen with D. N. Rodowick, in *Afterimages of Gilles Deleuze's Film Philosophy*, ed. by D. N. Rodowick (Minneapolis: University of Minnesota, 2010), pp. 15–30.
129. Ibid., p. 402; p. 16.
130. See Michel Foucault and Maurice Blanchot, *Foucault/Blanchot*, trans. by Jeffrey Mehlman and Brian Massumi (New York: Zone Books, 1988), and Gilles Deleuze, *Foucault*, trans. by Seán Hand (Minneapolis: University of Minnesota Press, 1988).
131. Ropars-Wuilleumier, *Le Temps d'une pensée*, p. 402; 'Image or Time?' p. 16.
132. Ibid., p. 404; p. 17.
133. Ibid., p. 404; p. 17.
134. Ibid., pp. 410–11; p. 23.
135. Ibid., p. 406; p. 19.
136. Ropars-Wuilleumier, *L'Idée d'image*, p. 160.

CHAPTER 3

Experiencing the Absence of Time: *Satantango*

Satantango and Rancière's 'le temps d'après'

Unlike *Histoire(s) du cinéma*, there is in the Hungarian director Béla Tarr's work no direct evidence of a relation to Blanchot. The intellectual and artistic contexts of Blanchot and Tarr are quite distinct. In contrast to the intellectual discursiveness and the huge variety of references and materials making up *Histoire(s)*, Tarr's films have an austerely minimalist aesthetic and a concern with the materiality of the world, and as such are a demonstration of the relevance of Blanchotian fascination in a context removed from Blanchot. That said, it is however striking that in a recent collection of French essays on Tarr several pieces make allusions to Blanchot; some of these will be discussed in what follows.[1] What Tarr's films do — in a radically different way from *Histoires(s)* — is to put film itself in question, especially by subverting durational norms in individual takes. While avant-garde cinema had taken this to even more of an extreme at an earlier juncture (for example the work of Andy Warhol), I am interested in how Tarr's takes work within the context of a narrative and will argue that Tarr's film is not only resonant with Blanchotian themes — especially waiting and tiredness — but in its form it creates the effect of fascination detailed in the previous chapters. The extent of this will be clarified through continued engagement with the theoretical positions of Deleuze, Levinas, and Rancière, as well as the introduction of the ideas of Jean-François Lyotard. Particularly important in both this and the next and final chapter will be notions of temporality within film.

Satantango (*Sátántangó*, 1994) is Tarr's 432-minute masterpiece, set during the end of the Hungarian communist era. The film is a story of intrigues at a communal farm, the appearance of a false messiah, Irimiás (Mihály Vig), who leads the inhabitants to a new farm, and an alcoholic doctor as he surveys the scene. *Satantango* is structured identically to its original source novel by László Krasznahorkai, which takes the form of a 'dance': two parts, each of which has six episodes (or steps), the first part moving from I to VI, and the second back from VI to I. Thus derives the sense of the title, 'Satan's Tango'. For the purposes of referencing moments in this very long film I will use the chapter names and numbering from the Georges Szirtes translation of the novel.[2]

The secondary literature on Tarr has increased since he announced his retirement from filmmaking with *The Turin Horse* (*A torinói ló*) in 2011. The notion of 'slow cinema' with which he has been associated (rightly or wrongly) has received increasing academic attention.[3] The two key theoretical texts written on Tarr are those by András Bálint Kovács and Jacques Rancière, which I will refer to throughout the chapter.[4] Rancière's subtitle, 'le temps d'après', he tells us, refers not to some nihilistic aftertime, but to a concern with time itself. As Rancière writes: 'Le temps d'après n'est pas le temps uniforme et morose de ceux qui ne croient plus à rien. C'est le temps des événements matériels purs auxquels se mesure la croyance aussi longtemps que la vie la porte' ('The time after is not the morose, uniform time of those who no longer believe in anything. It is the time of pure, material events, against which belief will be measured for as long as life will sustain it').[5] This concern with time is crucial and inevitable when dealing with a film not merely of such length but also one whose major stylistic signature is the extensive use of the long take. For Bazin, the long take was to be championed for its supposed 'objective' qualities, associated with a form of realism.[6] The notions of belief and materiality in Rancière's lines above indicate that he is thinking about time in relation to a post-Deleuzian philosophy of cinema. *L'Image-temps* remains highly influential on the subject of the long take, and so further negotiation with Deleuze will be necessary, following on from the lines of argument developed in the previous chapter. I want to draw out the implications of interpreting Tarr's film through a Blanchotian lens by negotiating with Rancière's text on Tarr and Deleuze's *Cinéma* volumes. It is necessary to state Rancière's position in order to distinguish it from that of Blanchot, and also because he at times represents the persistence of a Deleuzian way of thinking about film. Thus Tarr is not influenced by Blanchot, but the key account of him is, indirectly, via Deleuze.

Rancière disavows the conventional consideration of Tarr's career, which identifies a split between an early focus on social issues in communist Hungary (conforming to conventional realism in Hungarian cinema) and a mature period marked by increasingly austere formalism and cosmic pessimism.[7] According to Rancière, the 'social' cannot be opposed to the 'cosmique' in this way, for they are both subtended by the continuum of realism. He understands the cosmic as 'un monde absolument réaliste, absolument matériel, dépouillé de tout ce qui émousse la sensation pure telle que le cinéma seul peut l'offrir' ('an absolutely realistic world, absolutely material, stripped of all that dulls pure sensation, as only cinema can offer it').[8] Despite the stylistic differences, he wants to stress their continuity. For Rancière, the essence of Tarr is a fidelity to life as it is lived by people and expressed in a cinema as an art of the *sensible*, not simply the visible. It is thus that Rancière works within an opposition between *réalisme* and *histoires*, arguing: 'Le réalisme oppose les situations qui durent aux histoires qui enchaînent et passent à la suite' ('Realism opposes situations that endure to stories that link together and pass from one to the next').[9] Realism must here be understood according to Rancière's definition. At the same time, Rancière is playing on the double sense of *histoire* much as Godard does: both 'story' and 'history'. It is in this way that Rancière's study of Tarr is in no way an aberration from his established writings on film, which revolve around a certain oppositional aesthetic thinking. Rancière outlines two regimes of art, the aesthetic and the representational. The former is broadly what could be termed the expressive and the latter is synonymous with narrative. Since Aristotle it has been the representational regime which has predominated and it is only with the romantic age that the aesthetic regime was articulated. The dichotomy between realism and *histoires* is a restatement of these two regimes, and it also corresponds to two ways of seeing: a relative mode, in which the visible is put to the service of chains of events, and an absolute mode, in which what is visible is given time to produce its own effect.[10] For Rancière, Tarr's films activate the latter category, and constitute a style in the Flaubertian sense of the word, which is to say the creation of an autonomous world.[11] Rancière's departure from Deleuze is that for him the contradiction between the two modes is found in the filmic image itself. He does not, it follows, see a separation between a movement-image and a time-image. Nor does Rancière privilege one regime over the other. Instead his writing is marked by an attendance to structural contradiction and its political implications. However, for the moment it is sufficient to say that Tarr's films have a 'realist' aesthetic in which there are moments of aesthetic suspension and time is made visible.

For Rancière, *Satantango*'s motifs of incessant rain, all-permeating fog, tramped mud, and ruined walls are to be understood as the way in which the exterior world inhabits individuals and their gaze. The affections of the exterior world convert themselves into accordion tunes, singers' lyrics, banal bar-room conversations, and idle reflections. It is thus that Tarr's art creates 'l'affect global où se condensent toutes ces formes de dissémination' ('the global affect in which all these forms of dissemination are condensed').[12] With this idea of a global affect, Rancière is postulating a vision of Tarr's world. Time is the medium of this affect. The lines quoted above are shortly followed by the decisive remark that each of Tarr's late films can be seen as taking the form of 'un assemblage de ces cristaux de temps où se concentre la pression "cosmique". Plus que toutes autres ses images méritent d'être appelées des images-temps' ('an assemblage of these crystals of time, in which the "cosmic" pressure is concentrated. More than all others, his images deserve to be called time-images').[13] This notion of the filmic image as infused with time is very clearly in line with *L'Image-temps*. This becomes essentially bound up with the question of the long take. The experience of duration is itself a key part of Tarr's aesthetic. The spectator is made to share in the waiting of the characters. As Ben Singer remarks, while Hollywood films tend to make time pass and in this way 'annihilate' it, '[i]t was Warhol who first showed in film that prolonged exposure to long periods of relatively unfaltering and thematically vacuous subject matter leads the viewer to experience duration as a "concrete" dimension of film'.[14] Tarr has stated in an existential fashion what might be at stake in this:

> In fact, nothing really happens as we flee from one condition to another. Because today there are only states of being — all stories have become obsolete and clichéd, and have resolved themselves. All that remains is time. This is probably the only thing that's still genuine — time itself: the years, days, hours, minutes and seconds.[15]

Tarr's stress here on actual time gives us to ask what the relation is between actual film running time and Blanchot's absence of time.

Waiting and the Tarr Style: Levinas and Immobility

Let us return to the subtitle of Rancière's book:

> Le temps d'après n'est ni celui de la raison retrouvée, ni celui du désastre attendu. C'est le temps d'après les histoires, le temps où l'on s'intéresse directement à l'étoffe sensible dans laquelle elles taillaient leurs raccourcis entre une fin projetée et une fin advenue [...] C'est le temps où l'on s'intéresse à l'attente elle-même.

> [The time after is neither that of reason recovered, nor that of the awaited disaster. It is the time after all stories, the time when one takes direct interest in the sensible stuff in which these stories cleaved their shortcut between an end to come and an end that has arrived [...] It is the time in which we take an interest in the wait itself.][16]

This focus on waiting itself is one of Rancière's more instructive insights. Firstly, Tarr's films are remarkable for offering representations of various forms of waiting, especially when waiting goes beyond being merely the defining mode of boredom and is refined into a deep acedia. Several sequences, especially towards the beginning of *Satantango*, are suggestive of the intense isolation of countryside afternoons. In an early indoors sequence, while the rain pours outside, the camera tracks across a room closely showing the patterns on the wallpaper, the windowpane, and the water running down the glass outside, through which can be seen pigs picking in the dirt. There is the sheer existential malaise of Karrer (Miklós B. Székely) in *Damnation* (*Kárhozat*, 1987) and Maloin (Miroslav Krobot) in *The Man from London* (2007), the crushing tedium of life in the remote collective in *Satantango*, the eschatological mood of *Werckmeister Harmonies* (*Werckmeister harmóniák*, 2000), and finally its apotheosis in *The Turin Horse*. Rancière seeks to discuss this waiting as a purely experiential time, but this is of course immediately complicated by the question of what it is the wait is for. If there is one thing that links these forms of waiting in particular, it is that they seem to be waits *for nothing*, or rather a wait, in all of their diverse manifestations, for something that will never come. Waiting means a dead or empty time, and to this extent it is necessary to side with Rancière rather than Kovács, who writes that *'temps mort'* ('extended periods of time between two events') is 'relatively rare' in Tarr's work and that characters 'are always busy doing something, however insignificant it may be. They very rarely just sit and wait, meditate or stare into nothingness'.[17]

The first scene of the 'Work of the Spider I' (1.IV) section is a suitable example of such waiting. The scene is set in the estate bar, silent save for a clock which ticks continually throughout the fourteen-minute duration. The landlord (Zóltan Kamondi) stands at the bar, the farmer Kerekes (István Juhász) sits by the door, and Halics (Alfréd Járai) in the corner. The scene consists of four shots, each of which forms a complex composition. The first is shot from behind Kerekes as he bickers with the landlord across the room. The shot begins with the landlord framed at the bar in a long shot and with Kerekes's shoulder out of focus occupying a large part of the right-hand side of the frame (see Figure 3.1). The landlord's footsteps can be heard as he paces to one end of the bar and fills up a glass, the sound of which can also be heard distinctly. The regular light thudding of the clock, which sounds like a grandfather clock, gives a certain rhythm to this otherwise inert shot. Kerekes and the landlord have a brief exchange across the room, with Kerekes asking for a fire to be lit. After almost two minutes Kerekes gets up and walks to the bar. At this point the room as a whole can be seen. Halics is initially hidden behind a curtain, but soon gets up and joins the two men at the bar. The men move from foot to foot, and some coins are dropped on the floor and picked up by Halics; again, the sound is unnaturally distinct and clear relative to the distant positioning of the camera in the corner of the room. Kerekes buys a litre bottle of beer and, after a brief testy exchange with the landlord, lumbers back to his seat. The initial framing, from behind his shoulder, is replicated. At this point the camera tracks right from behind his left shoulder to behind his right shoulder, which is leaning on a table on which is set his bottle (see Figure 3.2). In the course of the tracking, the shot becomes almost completely darkened as it moves past Kerekes's broad back. This moment conceals a racking of focus and, emerging at the right shoulder, the bar is now out of focus, seen in the background as he raises his arm to repeatedly fill up a glass from the bottle and drink from it. The camera remains still, with only the sounds of the creaking of Kerekes's chair and rubbing of his clothes as he drinks.

The second shot is static and framed like a still life, with Halics sat at a table in the left-hand side of the frame, a tablecloth or sheet of some kind hanging like a curtain from the roof in the middle, and a ruined appliance which looks like an old stove on the right (see Figure 3.3). Halics himself does not move for most of the shot, looking off-screen to the landlord, to whom he expounds a short monologue about the dire condition of his coat. While it used to be supple, it has been so soaked that, dried out, it is now stiff and brittle. He describes how the rain 'destroys everything'. In spite of an irascible rebuke from the landlord that he has been 'saying this for years', Halics talks not just of the incessant downpour outside but also about 'internal rains' which come from the heart to wash the body's organs. He eventually resolves that 'a glass of wine would help'. There is, he goes on, the 'incessant demand from the liver' and the other organs, which must work all the time without a break. At this point, some three minutes into the shot, Halics gets up, leaves the shot — which remains unchanged — before returning to his place with a glass of wine. When he is out of the shot, the off-screen sounds of footsteps, the clinking glass, and liquid being dispensed are again clear and distinct. Back in his seat, Halics observes that Kerekes has fallen asleep. There is a crash of thunder outside which lights up the face of Halics and the wall behind him. A door can be heard opening and there is a cut as the cart driver Keleman (Barna Mihók) enters. This third shot is from the point of view of the landlord as Keleman approaches, dripping wet, and tells of the fateful arrival of Irimiás and his sidekick Petrina (Putyi Horváth). The landlord shakes his head, out of focus in the foreground, and Keleman insists it is true. The landlord moves out of shot and Keleman relates the story of his seeing Irimiás in another bar earlier (see Figure 3.4). Finally there is a remarkable shot which slowly tracks backwards from a close-up of the landlord's impassive face to return to a long shot in the corner (without going behind Kerekes this time), while all in the shot remains still, frozen (see Figures 3.5 and 3.6). Here, as throughout the mature Tarr, shot-reverse shot is met with unusual resistance.

FIGS. 3.1–3.6.

These extended shots of inertia, needless to say, are marked by a consummate mood of boredom and waiting on the part of the protagonists, and this is only accentuated by the ticking clock. Halics is nominally waiting for Kráner and Schmidt to arrive in order to divide up money owed to him, but there appears to be no relative timescale in which this is to happen. In the post-synchronized sound, the ticking has a thudding quality, making it seem as if the passage of time itself has a vibration that can be felt. Even the close-up of Keleman, as he is clearly intended to be a tiresome character, carries a certain element of tedium in spite of his important news. Though it comes in a following scene, the landlord's remark that '[t]his is a pub, not a waiting room' truly sums up this sequence, precisely in being belied by it. Yet, as critics have stressed, this ostensible lack of anything 'happening' is never boring as such but on the contrary suspenseful.[18] I want to suggest that what is here conceived of as 'suspense' might be thought of as an aspect of fascination. The difference would be that while suspense implies an eagerness to find out what will happen next in a sequence of actions, in fascination there is a case rather of being rapt precisely by a lack of action. It is thus that there is one aspect of the fourth shot of the bar-room scene not mentioned earlier, which is the muffled, apparently extra-diegetic sound of bells tolling. At the point when Keleman has told the landlord of the arrival of Irimiás and Petrina, the ticking of the clock develops a reverberation which increases as the take goes on, contributing an untimely feel. The bells and the clock are also accompanied by a faint droning sound. This motif of bells is introduced at the beginning of *Satantango* and is one of the oddest recurring features of the film. Bells open the film, after the first scene of the rutting cattle emerging from a barn, as the troubled peasant Futaki awakes, and the conclusion of their mystery comes at the very end of the film. They are described in the novel as the sense of 'a sky that seemed to be full of ringing bells' and are clearly to be linked with the idea that, as Mrs Halics rants, 'we are living in apocalyptic times!'.[19]

One way in which fascination arises from inertia is through the use of speech in the film. Halics's speech on the rain is one of many monologues by a character in a Tarr film along the lines of ineluctable ruination. (Those of Karrer in *Damnation* are notable in this regard.) What sounds like an inner meditation is spoken aloud, and in spite of the landlord's irritation. This signifies the elevation of barroom talk to the status of something approximating poetry; in other words, the rendering strange of — or the exposure to the very strangeness of — everyday speech. Later in the film Irimiás (calling himself 'a sad researcher') dictates a letter to Petrina for his superiors which is not a prosaic account of what he has found out through his espionage, but rather a lofty monologue extending to metaphysical themes. Monologue is again an elevated form in Tarr, yet in this case one that is later cut down in bathos and irony by the penultimate episode in which two bureaucrats rewrite the letter for their official report. This freeing of speech from determined ordinary conditions and framing it in isolation is something Blanchot identifies in literature most obviously, but also in psychoanalysis and elsewhere.

The reverse-tracking shot of the frozen bar-room is not a naturalistic one, and it recalls another shot earlier in the film (that described by Keleman to the landlord, mentioned above) in which Irimiás, stopping in a bar with Petrina on the way to the collective, hears a strange humming sound and, calling abruptly for quiet, everyone in the bar freezes still ('We Are Resurrected' 1.II). He then announces that he shall 'blow everything up', but the staff and patrons simply look on and wait for them to leave. The camera tracks backwards to the corner of the room in exactly the same way as the shot with Keleman. This is not a freeze-frame (the actors are simply staying still), but it is as if the film's world itself stops. In a shot comparable to this, Rancière identifies the signature style of Tarr in the opening sequence of *Damnation*. Across a grey sky extends a long line of what look like coal carts being carried by cable overhead. Not seeing from whence they come or where they go, this forms 'la pure image d'un espace et d'un temps uniformes' ('the pure image of uniform space and uniform time'). More important, however, are the specific technical characteristics of the shot and how they are exemplary of the director's style: 'un mouvement dans un sens et la camera qui va en sens inverse; un spectacle et le lent déplacement qui nous conduit vers celui qui le regarde' ('a movement in one direction and the camera moving in the opposite direction; a spectacle and the slow displacement that leads us to the one who watches it').[20] To elaborate on Rancière's observation, we could say that the movement of the camera is on one level the slow formal unveiling of the scene (its diegetic purpose, even when there is little diegetic content) and at the same time an abandonment of it (an attitude of listlessness towards the diegetic exercise itself, especially when the camera comes to an extended halt before the next shot).

Things are slightly more complex in the shots discussed above. As an instance of waiting, the three crucial aspects are the ticking, the painterly composition of the static shot with Halics, and the enigmatic freezing of the scene in the reverse-tracking shot. Therefore within this sequence there is both an instance of stasis of the camera as it observes minimal diegetic movement (the second shot) as well as a dynamic camera movement observing diegetic stasis (the fourth shot). Using Rancière's vocabulary, we might be tempted to say that the shots' representational quality breaks down and we are left with the purely expressive aspect. However, this should be developed. The shot of Halics at the table is practically a still and it is as if he is part of the background. Again: not a shift between the representational cinematic flow and an expressive photographic stillness (this would contain its own dialectic of representation and expression), but between a cinematic, narrative being and the withdrawal of this. Thus, it is necessary to take Rancière further than his terms allow.

Some writers on Tarr's style have found in it an implied model of 'thinking'. In an interview with the film's cinematographer Fred Keleman about *The Turin Horse*, Robert Koehler outlines how the moving image in Tarr's work can be thought of as a 'thinking image':

> Perhaps because of its extreme intimacy and radical denial of much breathing room outside, the images in *The Turin Horse* become in many ways the inner thoughts of its two characters, even as the characters exist inside the images. A shot that begins with the father looking outside (we see what he sees at first) gradually evolves into a larger shot of the living space until it changes yet again into a view of the daughter sewing; the conventional film grammar would call for cuts [...] But Tarr/Kelemen's way with images argues for a different perspective: that instead of the cut, the ever-changing image in front of us produces a more mysterious, sometimes destabilizing effect, much like the way the mind can wander from thought to thought.[21]

Koehler considers this a form of 'anti-montage', but he does not intend this phrase in the same way as we saw Rancière did in the previous chapter apropos of *Histoire(s) du cinéma*, where it was a case of Godard extracting images from other films and, divorcing them from their narrative role, offering them up to exhibit their expressive power as singularities. Koehler here rather intends the idea of the sequence-shot, in which there is no need for editing as the camera moves through a series of framings without cuts. However, I want to suggest that while the notion of Tarr's shots as enacting thought may be persuasive to some extent, it occludes the degree to which the shots may also activate something that is other than thought, something that is, as he notes, 'mysterious and destabilizing'.

One way of gaining increased theoretical purchase on these ideas is to follow Matthew Flanagan in seeing slow cinema as exemplifying an 'extreme immobilisation' contrary to the contemporary post-continuity style of cinema, associated with neoliberalism, of increasing speed. Slow cinema can thus be thought of as a form of 'useless expenditure'.[22] Flanagan is referring here to the work of Jean-François Lyotard, particularly the 1973 essay 'L'Acinéma' [Acinema].[23] Lyotard's thinking on film, evidenced in a small number of essays, revolves around the problem of filmic material that does not fit easily into a narrative or representational paradigm, which in 'L'Acinéma' he argues is modelled on capitalist production. The work of the director is not only to make the film 'productive' in the sense of financially profitable, but to remove all sterile material in the film which does not contribute efficiently to the movement of a diegesis. Material that subverts this order typically takes the form of moments of either immobility or excessive movement: the former is associated with the *tableau vivant* and the latter with lyric abstraction.[24] These moments may be reincorporated or made to serve the dominant mode of representation, but in experimental and underground cinema they can lead out from this to form a new model of film based around sterile, non-productive elements. This is what Lyotard calls 'acinema'. In a later essay, 'Idée d'un film souverain' [Idea of a Sovereign Film] (1994), Lyotard uses the terms of Bataille to theorize such sterile moments as 'sovereign'.[25] Sovereignty is conceived here as that which is beyond utility and which allows for 'communication' in which subject and object fuse ecstatically.[26] In this time the camera is stuck in front of an object like a pensive gaze, giving the material object a sovereign quality.[27] While directors may conceive of the idea of a sovereign film, in which the real would be made palpable, for Lyotard this is a conception to which no film will actually correspond in reality: there are only moments of sovereignty in films.[28]

Recent work on Lyotard has indicated the need to move beyond 'L'Acinéma' to untranslated material in order to flesh out his contribution to the thinking of film as characterized by what Ashley Woodward calls a 'sacrificial economy of the image'.[29] With the notion of sacrifice, we can rethink more critically (and perhaps ironically) sequences in film which in Rancière's terms would be considered moments of aesthetic suspension in which an expressive aspect is brought out: the images are 'useless' and indifferent to the narrative, much as how film was theorized in relation to sculpture in the previous chapters. Sovereign materiality comes closer to Rancière, whose focus on the material, sensible world is borne out in *Satantango*, in which the material density of cracked faces, of pores and moles, seems to become one with the detail of damaged walls. The uselessness and indifference of images Lyotard describes is close to the rhetoric of abandonment used in Chapter 1, while the reference to communication discussed above gives a sense of what is at stake in the phrase 'moyens de communication'. In other words, the work of Lyotard represents an important articulation of what a cinema of fascination would look like.[30]

Given the increasing significance being placed on the notion of immobility, we should look to an essay by Reni Celeste on the idea of the 'frozen screen'.[31] In this article, Celeste considers, within the context of the action film, the idea of the 'entre-temps', as described in the key essay by Levinas, 'La Réalité et son ombre' [Reality and its Shadow] (1947).[32] This is a relatively early, albeit notorious, text by Levinas and must be seen in the context of post-war debates on the question of art's engagement in the world. Much like Blanchot's contemporaneous 'La Littérature et le droit à la mort', this piece is implicitly in dialogue with Sartre's polemics of the period. However, it is also an important piece in stating the implications of the thought of the *il y a* for the experience of art. In Levinas's *De l'existence à l'existant*, the *il y a* is described as an experience of the world come to an end, no longer populated, and in which the subject wanders among things in a state of disidentification. In 'La Réalité et son ombre', Levinas writes that art embodies the *il y a*, and what Levinas calls the *entre-temps* stands for the temporal state of art. In particular, this is said to be a function of the image (Blanchot's 'Les Deux Versions de l'imaginaire' is in part a response to this text). The *entre-temps* is art's tragic time, between the transcendent and the historical, and which exists in parallel with living time. It is ultimately a space without time, for it is exterior to time. 'For Levinas', Celeste writes, 'the tragic is not a narrative structure ending in fatality. It is the fixity inherent in all works of art, a fixity that *poses as time*'.[33]

Now, if anything, the films of Tarr are the opposite of the average action film, marked by a glacial pace and minimal recourse to editing. As we have identified stasis in Tarr, so we characterize the action film by its dynamism. Yet what Celeste reveals at the heart of the action film is almost precisely that which is brought out in Tarr's films. Could not it be said that the extended fixed shots described above evoke what Celeste calls the 'futureless landscape of suspended time'?[34] This would also be the opening, as suggested by Eleanor Kaufman in the previous chapter, of a horizon of absolute inertia. As we come to discuss landscape below, we will see how this is literally borne out, presenting the viewer with an emptied world. The difference between Rancière's notion of *le temps d'après* and this Levinasian reading is that while for Rancière what Tarr brings out is the nature of time in the diegetic world, in Celeste's account it is rather an aspect of the temporality of the film qua representation and thus an opening onto alterity.

Irimiás makes a rhetorical point comparable to this early on in the film. He and Petrina are first seen in some kind of official ministry building where they have a summons to attend. While awaiting this, Irimiás observes that the two clocks in the hallway tell different times, both wrong. One is very late, he says, while the other 'measures not so much time as, well, the eternal reality of the exploited, and we to it are as the bough of a tree to the rain that falls upon it: in other words we are helpless'. This is a speech, much like that of Halics discussed above, which begins almost apropos of nothing and launches the film into a realm of metaphysical speculation. In this case, Irimiás here seems to be describing his dramatic identity, existing within this Levinasian 'zone of frozen time, of terror, of a dream turned nightmare where characters live as doubles of themselves, prisoners of their fatality, between time, suffocating in their own infinite repetition'.[35] This suspended time is not simply as it were a screen behind the entire film, but one which is dramatized within the film itself. A temporality of infinite negation or absent time could not fit into either of Rancière's categories of realism or *histoires*, temporalities of duration or succession. As has been pointed out in the previous sequences discussed, there is the duration of the film and the duration represented in the film and there are moments in which each comes to stop respectively: a pause within the diegesis and a pause without. We will return to the implications of Levinas's thought for film in the next chapter.

Waiting, Tiredness, and Deleuze

The relevance of Blanchot becomes clear when considering some remarks of Deleuze. The eighth chapter of *Cinéma 2*, 'Cinéma, corps et cerveau, pensée' [Cinema, Body and Brain, Thought], opens with a highly suggestive disquisition on Michelangelo Antonioni and the function of the body in his films. Deleuze writes: 'Les catégories de la vie, ce sont précisément les attitudes du corps, ses postures [...] C'est par le corps [...] que le cinéma noue ses noces avec l'esprit, avec la pensée' ('The categories of life are precisely the attitudes of the body, its postures [...] It is through the body [...] that cinema forms its alliance with the spirit, with thought').[36] He goes on:

> Le corps n'est jamais au présent, il contient l'avant et l'après, la fatigue, l'attente. La fatigue, l'attente, même le désespoir sont les attitudes du corps. Nul n'est allé plus loin qu'Antonioni dans ce sens. Sa méthode: l'intérieur *par* le comportement, non plus l'expérience, mais 'ce qui reste des expériences passées', 'ce qui vient après, quand tout a été dit' [...] C'est une image-temps, la série du temps.
>
> [The body is never in the present, it contains the before and the after, tiredness and waiting. Tiredness and waiting, even despair are attitudes of the body. No one has gone further than Antonioni in this direction. His method: the interior *through* behavior, no longer experience, but 'what remains of past experiences', 'what comes afterwards, when everything has been said' [...] This is a time-image, a series of time.][37]

There are here certain affinities with and differences from Rancière's thought that we have been tracing. While Rancière talks of the exterior world that weighs down on and inhabits the body, Deleuze has the interior that is made manifest through the body. Deleuze's moods are 'catégories de la vie': 'la pensée' seems to be equated with 'l'esprit'. In Rancière's writing on Tarr, the body is that which is acted upon by things, by the world in general, and acted upon as if by way of thought itself — as if it were the moods of the world that are expressed by individuals. Halics's speech about the rain is indeed very close to the argument of Rancière about the 'l'affect global', as the weather seems to affect the very constitution of his soul. At first glance, this apparent concern with interiority in Deleuze's account might seem to constitute a reversal of Rancière's terms, but what Rancière calls *le temps d'après* — the time after stories in which we are left with pure material events — clearly bears some relation to the temporal structure in Deleuze's reading of Antonioni, such that the body relates to both past and future. However, we must follow Deleuze as he goes on to invoke Blanchot:

> L'attitude du corps met la pensée en rapport avec le temps comme avec ce dehors infiniment plus lointain que le monde extérieur. Peut-être la fatigue est-elle la première et la dernière attitude, parce qu'elle contient à la fois l'avant et l'après: ce que Blanchot dit, c'est aussi ce qu'Antonioni montre, non pas du tout le drame de la communication, mais l'immense fatigue du corps, la fatigue qu'il y a sous *Le cri*, et qui propose à la pensée 'quelque chose à incommuniquer', l'"impensé", la vie.
>
> [The attitude of the body relates thought to time as to that outside which is infinitely further than the outside world. Perhaps tiredness is the first and last attitude, because it simultaneously contains the before and the after: what Blanchot says is also what Antonioni shows, *not* the drama of communication, but the intense tiredness of the body, the tiredness there is beneath *The Outcry*, and which suggests to thought 'something to incommunicate', the 'unthought', life.]³⁸

The first line is curious. It might be understood how the attitude of the (actor's) body could constitute the manifestation of thought with regard to time (as an expression of thought taking place within time), but why would this be a correlative of thought's relation to the outside? The outside — perhaps the key idea for which Deleuze invokes Blanchot — is just that: outside everything, including time. Yet tiredness is, in this second quotation from Deleuze, accorded a privileged access to this outside; it seems only in this way that the body is never 'au présent' or can refer to 'l'avant et l'après'. The phrase 'l'"impensé", la vie' does not simply mean that which has hitherto not been thought of, but that life is as it were the opposite of thought. In contrast to Rancière's aesthetic regime, we have not this thought that is found outside *in* the world, but the *unthought* that is found *outside* the world.

Deleuze's footnote on this passage claims: 'Tout ce que Blanchot dit sur la fatigue, l'attente, convient particulièrement à Antonioni' ('Everything that Blanchot says about tiredness and waiting is particularly applicable to Antonioni') and refers the reader to the preface of *L'Entretien infini*.³⁹ This preface consists of about ten pages of fragments, many of which are dialogues between two anonymous figures and form a colloquy on the idea of *la fatigue* or weariness. Weariness seems to be that which makes possible the Blanchotian conception of thought, or the conversation, while simultaneously all but inhibiting it. Weariness is therefore in the same structural position as the interruption seen in Chapter 1 and the unthinkable seen in Chapter 2. Weariness is described as '*le plus neutre des neutres*' (*EI* xxi) ('*the most neutral of neutrals*', *IC* xx), and the fragments dramatize the association with repetition: '"*Être fatigué, être indifférent, c'est sans doute la même chose.*" — "*L'indifférence serait donc comme le sens de la fatigue.*" — "*Sa vérité.*" — "*Sa vérité fatiguée.*"' (*EI* xvi–xvii) ('"To be weary, to be indifferent, they are no doubt the same thing." — "Indifference, then, would be something like the meaning of weariness." — "Its truth." — "Its weary truth"', *IC* xvii). Not only repetition, in the increasing indistinction between weariness and 'indifference', the fragments here also register at the level of style the erasure to which weariness in Blanchot's account is necessarily submitted. Resignation or lack of thought seems here to constitute the very content of the 'thought' discussed above. In other words, it is a question of passivity. To this extent, tiredness is an 'expérience-limite' (*EI* 311) ('limit experience', *IC* 210) much like waiting: an experience which is not lived and is not undergone by a self; it is a non-event, or an event in which nothing happens. Both are exemplary as phenomena showing how we are ineluctably bound to existence, where that existence is defined according to a broader Blanchotian framework in which the 'subject' (for want of a better term and understood as above as not an experiencing self) is rendered passive, dispossessed, and lacking in self-identity vis-à-vis exteriority or the outside. It is for this reason that, while one might be inclined to understand his remarks as referring to the impassivity of the expressions of the protagonist Aldo (Steve Cochran) as he makes his itinerant progress through the Po Valley, Deleuze identifies a tiredness 'sous' Antonioni's film, *The Outcry* (*Il grido*, 1957), itself. In other words, while Deleuze can identify tiredness in 'le corps', that tiredness, like the 'l'impensée', is not discretely attached to the character but at a certain level becomes affectively indistinguishable from their surroundings.[40]

In the discussion of Deleuze's *Cinéma* volumes in the previous chapter, the interstice between images (in montage) was related to the Blanchotian outside, replacing the notion of the whole in classical cinema. This was said to call the image itself into question. With the breakdown of the sensory-motor schema, thought experiences itself as an *impouvoir* or a lack of power. What was found to be essential to Deleuze's thinking of the cinema was the postulation of this powerlessness at the heart of thought, an idea directly indebted to Blanchot. What is now observable, even in the few lines I have quoted above on Antonioni, is that, in contrast to the discussion of the interstices between images in relation to Godard, and as identified by Ropars-Wuilleumier, Deleuze seeks here to make the outside 'visible' in the image itself. The contradiction is precisely that which I have been working towards above: when tiredness is shown onscreen, what exactly is the relation between that and the outside? The previous section has by the same token discussed formally how moments of stasis or waiting are opened up in Tarr's film, and the question is again: how is it exactly and in what sense is it that these moments open the viewer to the outside?

Blanchot's most notable meditation on the phenomenon of waiting is to be found in the generically indefinable text *L'Attente l'oubli*. The book combines abstract lines on the phenomenon of waiting with a fragmented narrative, ostensibly concerning a man and a woman in a hotel room. This form prefigures the later fragmentary works of *Le Pas au-delà* and *L'Écriture du désastre*. Waiting, for Blanchot, escapes the opposition between active and passive. As Leslie Hill has shown, this is in part owing to the ambiguity of the French *attendre*, but owes more to the critique of the Heideggerian distinction between the transitive expecting (*erwarten*) and the intransitive anticipation (a slightly inadequate rendering of *vorlaufen*). The former is classed as inauthentic and the latter authentic, but given the deconstruction of the very notion of authenticity in Blanchot's work, this distinction dissolves.[41] It is with this in mind that we can understand the following apparently tautological line:

'L'attente est toujours l'attente de l'attente, reprenant en elle le commencement, suspendant la fin et, dans cet intervalle, ouvrant l'intervalle d'une autre attente' ('Waiting is always a wait for waiting, wherein the beginning is withheld, the end suspended, and the interval of another wait thus opened') (*AO* 38; 24). So when Rancière says that Tarr shows characters waiting for something that does not come, waiting for nothing, this is correct but not simply in his historical, even historical-existential argument. What Blanchot's discussion brings out is what Tarr shows intimately, namely that this waiting is constitutive of an interrupted existence.[42] It is thus that Irimiás's remarks on the two clocks seem to be symptomatic of what Blanchot names the impossibility of waiting in which time is not identical with itself: 'Dans l'attente règne l'absence de temps où attendre est l'impossibilité d'attendre' ('In waiting the absence of time reigns, where waiting is the impossibility of waiting') (*AO* 76; 52).

The Great Plain: Landscape and Seeing

In 'Heavenly Vision? Hallucination?' (2.IV) we see Irimiás, Petrina, and the delinquent they have enlisted into their service, Sanyi (András Bodnár), walk through the Hungarian Great Plain. That landscape which appears throughout the film is described by Rancière in a highly apt phrase as a 'désert gris' ('gray desert').[43] The three figures appear in a wide-shot, coming into the shot from behind a fixed camera (see Figure 3.7). They then continue walking straight along the path, into the centre of the shot and the distance until but specks and ultimately seeming to disappear into the horizon (see Figure 3.8).

FIGS. 3.7–3.8.

The take lasts more than two minutes, and by one minute in the characters are far in the distance. Here Tarr's love of letting the camera linger on empty frames (often showing empty rooms) after the action of a shot has been completed is taken to an extreme. This can create a sense of clarity, of letting events sink in for the viewer; yet it can also have the effect of suggesting the ethereality of the action itself.

One of the seminal writings on the long take is Pier Paolo Pasolini's 1967 essay 'Observations on the Long Take'. In this short text he conceives of cinema as 'an endless long take, as is reality to our senses for as long as we are able to see and feel (a long take that ends with the end of our lives)'.[44] Pasolini considers the Zapruder film of J. F. Kennedy's assassination as exemplary: 'the most typical long take imaginable'.[45] This is because it is subjective — coming from a fixed point of view — and is made of the present moment. Pasolini writes:

> Death performs a lightning-quick montage on our lives; that is, it chooses our truly significant moments [...] and places them in sequence, converting our present, which is infinite, unstable, and uncertain, and thus linguistically indescribable, into a clear, stable, certain, and thus linguistically describable past [...] Montage thus accomplishes for the material of film (constituted of fragments, the longest or the shortest, of as many long takes as there are subjectivities) what death accomplishes for life.[46]

Tarr's long take gives us this meaninglessness of the present for as long as possible — literally to the end of the strip of film in some cases — until the cut gives some meaning to the shot. It is as if to foreground the fact that the characters were not there before, and are not there after; as if to suggest the camera's sheer indifference towards the pro-filmic action. Taken to a logical extreme, the action before the camera is placed under erasure, such as to suggest that the characters are not — or might as well not be — really there at all.

As the characters walk along the path, on the soundtrack can be heard the crunch of footsteps on gravel and an exchange between Irimiás and Petrina. Petrina is expressing his fear and reservations about the plot that the three are engaged in. Irimiás is dismissive. With a somewhat limpid and desultory tone, characteristic for being simultaneously self-aggrandizing and casual, Irimiás remarks: 'Don't you see that we're partisans in this persistent and hopeless fight for human dignity?' The exchange tails off, with increasing gaps between the words spoken, and ends with Irimiás humming a tune. It does not, however, become quieter as the speakers recede into the distance. This aspect of the soundtrack, here as elsewhere in the film, masks — again, at the same time as it foregrounds — what is a silent visual composition. The film is constituted by a striking black-and-white aesthetic and a post-synchronized soundtrack. Given that the sound continues to be heard at the same volume throughout the take, even though the diegetic source of sound becomes increasingly distant, as the take goes on the sound, to use Michel Chion's terms, can here be said to become increasingly 'acousmatic' (as opposed to 'visualized').[47] A gap is thus opened between sound and image, as if to suggest that the world itself is silent and can only be synchronized *après coup*. The words spoken are set in play against the landscape dominating the visual image, as if implying their cosmic reverberation or perhaps their falling on the deaf ears of the ground. Looked at on a print, it seems the very emulsion of the celluloid image contributes to the revelling in the quiddity of the mud and dirt and gravel, rendered in a world of greys. The rain and cloud work to diffuse colour, as does the overcast sky. The pronounced detail of the ground in the shot is matched by the exaggerated crunching sound of the footsteps. It is by the same token that the camera seems to be tilted downwards, as if it wants to situate the viewer close to the ground, close to the real. (It is also thus that on more than one occasion in the film flies can be seen crawling on the surface of the lens.) Tarr is sometimes said to have a high-contrast, noir-style, but

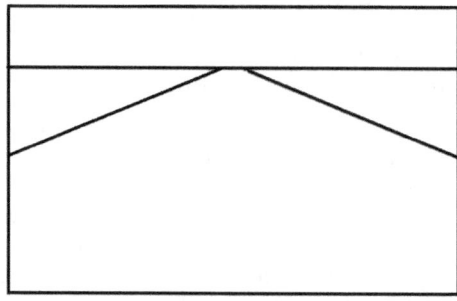

Fig. 3.9.

here the Tarr landscape is indeed a 'désert gris'. One effect of this is to produce a peculiar scopic depthlessness; if one were tempted to talk of deep focus here, it is one that abolishes itself in favour of disappearance. In the novel this path is seen by one of the three walkers as 'arrowing ahead into infinity', and this is borne out geometrically in the composition, with approximately 20% of the image taken up by the sky and about 60% of the shot given over to the path, the remaining 20% given over to the fields bordering the path (see Figure 3.9).[48]

Classical principles of filmmaking would dictate that more space ought to be afforded to the sky above the horizon. Given how painstaking the work is in Tarr's long takes, which effectively try to work as complete sequences within single takes, it seems appropriate to talk of them in this almost diagrammatic way, which is to say by referring to their planned visual composition at the expense of their narrative function. Critics are right to point to Tarr's early interest in installation filmmakers like Bill Viola and Michael Snow given that several sequences, by violating formal and narrative norms, at times seem to aspire to stand alone as short films.[49] Like the structural filmmakers, Tarr is interested in the physical properties of space itself. This is part of the reason, aside from *Satantango*'s runtime, for the film's curious quality of vastness, of occupying a vastness of space rather than, as we might say of other films of extraordinary length, covering an epic scope of time.

However, it must also be said that although this sequence may seem unusual, this kind of construction is repeatedly found in *Satantango*, as if Tarr is at pains to make it seem natural, and it becomes a standard set-up to show an unpeopled landscape into which characters walk, and then maintain the take over several minutes until they pass into specks and disappear. The effect of this extended duration and static camerawork is to present us with the starkness or even the obstinacy of the landscape. The landscape is here an immense static object through which characters pass, though there are many further variations, for example of dolly shots following characters along paths from behind or following in front of them. They all have subtly different senses and functions, but it is a common theme in writings on Tarr that the characters must be seen as part of the landscapes of his films, and this is a view that Tarr himself has put forward.[50] Tarr is constantly showing that his characters are in fact *in* this landscape. One further technique to this end is, for example, to follow a character from their discrete activity to track back to reveal this to be happening against a vast expanse. According to the set designer of *Damnation*, Gyua Pauer, the film's locations were created 'in such a way that they reflected the endgame of a world-era, the state of the last moment before the final disappearance'.[51] The duration of the take can make us see the world as abandoned or unworked.

Journey on the Plain (*Utazás az Alföldön*, 1995) was shot by Tarr soon after *Satantango* and is only half an hour in length. The mood, though still austere, is rather different from *Satantango*. The film opens with something like a replica of the shot described above, with Mihály Víg, who plays the central figure in the walking trio, the demonic Irimiás, now walking alone (see Figure 3.10).

FIG. 3.10.

In this film, which has little in the way of narrative, Víg walks through various parts of the Great Plain speaking the verse of the nineteenth-century Hungarian poet Sándor Petőfi in a quasi-documentary manner. He is not so much a character here as a voice. While here an extraction of speech is formed by the poetry, elsewhere in Tarr's work it is an effect of the deadpan and lapidary speech. This film, though rarely seen, forms something of a companion piece to *Satantango*, and I think by extension and association we should consider the echoes of Petőfi in *Satantango*. One of the things that comes out of this is the putting into focus of the Great Hungarian Plain in Tarr's work, which is to say how the landscape functions visually in the intense durational sequences of the films, as well as how the symbolic significance that the landscape had for the national poet Petőfi is refracted through the apocalyptic aesthetic of Tarr and Krasznahorkai. Tarr's use of such landscapes cannot but recall his master Miklós Jancsó's *The Round-Up* (*Szegénylegények*, 1965) with its extreme wide-angle shots of the Great Plain.

Common to the *mises en scène* of the shots from *Satantango* and *Journey on the Plain* is the composition in which approximately 60% is taken up by the path (even with the different aspect ratio). Though geometrically similar to the one before, chromatically this is radically different. Duration itself seems to be lost in the much less refined image, and the film works much more through its meditative and poetic voiceover. It is difficult to find much information on the film, though it appears (unusually for Tarr) to have been shot on video. It is not one of Tarr's most successful films, but is revealing in setting out his preoccupations in a less highly crafted manner than in his major works. Apocalyptic prophecies such as those in *Damnation* and *The Turin Horse* find a clear precedent in Petőfi's vision.[52] The verses of Petőfi that Tarr is most interested in are those of rustic sorrows, the praise of wine and prophecies of coming judgments. Death looms over the Plain, as a poem set over the image of a man with a scythe shows (see Figure 3.11).

FIG. 3.11.

Víg's voiceover says: 'Here I stand in the middle of the Plains, like a statue, stiffly. The Plain is covered by a grave-like silence, just as a corpse is covered with a shroud'. Petőfi's is here an existential landscape.

For Rancière the Great Plain is defined by its monotony and repetition, and it is through duration that he will identify, in a Deleuzian lexicon, 'lignes de fuite' [lines of flight] out from it. For Rancière such extended takes as the one here discussed would constitute a direct presentation of time, but I think they must also be considered as direct presentations of space, or perhaps the temporal dimension of that space. The logic of Rancière's argument would be to say that landscape is a means through which time is registered in *Satantango*. But the point I want to make is that *the reverse is also true*. By defining space by duration, one of the things Tarr seems to be stressing is geographic immemoriality. With Petőfi it is a national history, but it also accords with the theme of geological history.[53] Kovács has carried out a detailed quantitative analysis of the relative lengths of Tarr's takes, and though he does not suggest it himself such quantitative methods are reminiscent of the scientific illustrations of human presence on earth set against the scope of prehistory, such as those evoked by the doctor. We could consider the sequence referred to above as a visual correlative of such a scale and see Irimiás and Petrina's presence in the shot, qua humankind, as evoking their transience relative to the ancient and indifferent earth.

However, the precise length of Tarr's long takes is perhaps less important than their ability to give the viewer a blank space for projection and more broadly to activate what might be called the apophatic structure of the long take itself. This subject has been analyzed by Martin Lefebvre, for whom, in the cinema, 'landscape manifests itself in an interpretative gaze'.[54] In Lefebvre's account, the distinction between setting and landscape is that while setting is ultimately related back to narrative, landscape can become detached from narrative and take on an autonomy of its own.[55] Spectators play a role in this, in that it is their gaze that allows landscape to become autonomous, even if that gaze can be directed by the film. Lefebvre's account thus rests on a distinction between a 'narrative mode' and a 'spectacular mode' of spectatorial activity.[56] With the idea of the spectacular, Lefebvre is alluding to seminal debates in the history of film theory, such as that concerning the nature of early cinema before 1906. For Tom Gunning, cinema was originally founded not on mimetic principles and spectatorial absorption in a narrative, but on an 'act of showing and exhibition'. Early cinema can be considered as what he calls 'the cinema of attractions'. The 'exhibitionism' identifiable in early films 'does not disappear with the dominance of narrative, but rather goes underground, both into certain avant-garde practices and as a component of narrative films, more evident in some genres (for example, the musical) than in others'.[57] This begs the question of what the relation might be between what can broadly be considered 'spectacle' and fascination. With Lefebvre, we must add the interpretative gaze. Lefebvre's account of the 'autonomizing' gaze of the spectator suggests a degree of agency and intentionality absent in Blanchotian fascination, which tends to dispossess the subject as such. Landscape itself clearly exerts this kind of fascination in both the novel and film of *Satantango*. In the novel we read that the doctor 'particularly enjoyed looking through photo spreads of the wars in Asia, at scenes that never seemed very distant or exotic to him, and which, he was convinced, were photographed somewhere nearby'.[58] Such ideas in part inform the aesthetic of the film. In a shot very close to the end of the film, the doctor goes to seek the origin of the sound of the bells and looks out across a stretch of bog. The camera presents a vast panorama lasting one minute and which forms, very unusually in *Satantango*, almost a one hundred and eighty degree panning shot. Tarr seems to increase and then decrease the exposure of the film, as if to give the landscape a brief radioactive glow or to evoke the landscape's very *unearthliness*. What I want to hold on to from Lefebvre is the doubling of temporality instantiated by landscape — a narrative and spectatorial temporality — while rethinking the latter temporality as not an interpretative-spectacular gaze but a fascinated one.

'Parler, ce n'est pas voir'

In the shots discussed above, particularly the walking along the path, we see an almost literal manifestation of what Deleuze considers a characteristic of the voice in modern cinema, that is, its ability to reveal the 'les espaces quelconques' [any-spaces-whatever]. Deleuze writes that it is as if:

> La parole s'étant retirée de l'image pour devenir acte fondateur, l'image, de son côté, faisait monter les fondations de l'espace, les 'assises', ces puissances muettes d'avant ou d'après la parole, d'avant ou d'après les hommes. L'image visuelle devient *archéologique, stratigraphique, tectonique*.
>
> [Speech having withdrawn from the image to become founding act, the image, for its part, raised the foundations of space, the 'strata', those silent powers

of before or after speech, before or after man. The visual image becomes
archaeological, stratigraphic, tectonic.]⁵⁹

Deleuze compares this new aspect of the modern cinema to Cézanne's mountains, which have a sculptural quality at the same time as they reveal the mountains' geological aspect. When there is speech over this: 'L'acte de parole aérien crée l'événement, mais toujours posé de travers sur des couches visuelles tectoniques: ce sont deux trajectoires qui se traversent. Il crée l'événement, mais dans un espace vide d'événement' ('The ethereal speech-act creates the event, but always placed crosswise over tectonic visual layers: there are two trajectories crossing each other. It creates the event, but in a space empty of events').⁶⁰ Deleuze alludes to Chion's analyses of the voice-off in his discussion of a 'nouvelle asynchronie' ('new asynchrony') between the audio and the visual in the modern image. Thinking here of films such as Alain Resnais's *L'Année dernière à Marienbad* (*Last Year in Marienbad*, 1961) and Marguerite Duras's *India Song*, Deleuze argues that the voice-off does not, as it would in classical cinema, evince 'un hors-champ absolu comme rapport avec le tout' ('the absolute out-of-field or relation with the whole') but rather 'quelque chose d'indécidable entre les deux' ('something undecidable between the two'). In classical cinema the image can be imbued by the open whole by voiceover as it can indicate that which is outside the frame and therefore the continuity of the open whole. The new undecidability is effectively the result of the sound and image tracks now being conceived of as independent and autonomous. Between them is opened up an interstice.⁶¹ Deleuze towards the end of this discussion writes, with this relation of the audio and the visual in the modern image, that: 'C'est le cas de dire avec Blanchot: "parler, ce n'est pas voir". Il semble ici que parler cesse de voir, de faire voir et même d'être vu' ('we can say with Blanchot: "Speaking is not seeing". It seems here that speaking ceases to see, to make visible and also to be seen').⁶² The text referred to by Deleuze ('Parler, ce n'est pas voir') is crucial. In the first chapter this text was cited to strengthen the case that fascination takes place outside of the dichotomy of visible and invisible. In relation to *Histoire(s) du cinéma*, this was read, following the analyses of Hill and Bellour, as a way of conceiving: firstly, according to Hill, that it is montage, rather than the image itself, that speaks; and secondly, after the counter-reading of Bellour, that Godard incorporates speech into the image, making legible in the image an 'écriture de parole' (contra the 'parole d'écriture' of Blanchot's essay). Deleuze's reference to the piece goes between these various uses described. While Deleuze argues earlier in the chapter ('Les Composantes de l'image' [The Components of the Image]) that the arrival of sound in film had the apparently paradoxical effect of making speech visible, when he comes on to the modern image it is the case that: 'Ce que la parole profère, c'est aussi bien l'invisible que la vue ne voit que par voyance, et ce que la vue voit, c'est ce que la parole profère d'indicible' ('What speech utters is also the invisible that sight sees only through clairvoyance; and what sight sees is the unutterable uttered by speech').⁶³ For Deleuze, the new relation between seeing and speaking is born out of a certain non-relation; it is now 'un rapport indirect libre' ('a free indirect relationship') with 'deux faces dissymétriques, non totalisables' ('two dissymetric, non-totalizable sides') which form a time-image 'd'un dehors plus lointain que tout extérieur' ('of an outside more distant than any exterior').[64] Deleuze here seems to understand 'voir' and 'parler' as correlatives of vision and sound. This is arguably a productive misreading. As Ropars-Wuilleumier writes, Deleuze 'retourne radicalement' ('radically inverts') the argument of Blanchot's text into '"ne pas parler" (ou parler à la limite du sonore), "c'est voir"' ('"to not speak" (or a speaking at the limits of sound) "is to see"'). To do this Deleuze draws on Blanchot's critique of speech but 'en escamotant la critique de la vision que Blanchot y associe quand, du même mouvement, il met en question la possibilité de voir le visible' ('robs it of the critique of vision that Blanchot associates with it when, in the same motion, he calls into question the possibility of seeing the visible').[65] Ropars-Wuilleumier addresses the crucial issue here, which is the same as that which we identified in Deleuze's discussion of tiredness and Antonioni, and indeed is one of the animating questions of this study as a whole: what is the relation between vision and the outside? What happens to vision in fascination? How exactly does one get from time to the absence of time?

'Parler, ce n'est pas voir' is a dialogue of extraordinary density, even by Blanchot's standards. A full commentary on this text is beyond the scope of the present study, but I will attempt to evoke some of the key movements of the piece. The dialogue begins with a rumination on the meaning of knowledge. Blanchot writes that to search is to engage in a movement of turning (a phrasing reminiscent of the late dialogues of Heidegger on the approach to language). Searching is always in relation to a centre which is 'l'introuvable' (*EI* 36) ('cannot be found', *IC* 26), even as it exerts fascination over the one who seeks. The movement of turning is thus related to the movement of error, which in turn is conceived as a form of exile on an expanse without a horizon. (This rhetoric of turning and steps gives a sense of the essay's original title, 'La Marche de l'écrevisse' [The Walk of the Crayfish].) The next step is the association of error with speaking, with speaking characterized as a turning away from a path, and particularly from what is visible. It is from here that the title of the essay can be understood:

> Parler, ce n'est pas voir. Parler libère la pensée de cette exigence optique qui, dans la tradition occidentale, soumet depuis des millénaires notre approche des choses et nous invite à penser sous la garantie de la lumière ou sous la menace de l'absence de lumière. (*EI* 38)

> [Speaking is not seeing. Speaking frees thought from the optical imperative that in the Western tradition, for thousands of years, has subjugated our approach to things, and induced us to think under the guaranty of light or under the threat of its absence.] (*IC* 27)

This is not, one of the interlocutors is quick to say, to oppose hearing to sight, but it does bring out the question of writing.[66] Writing is related to turning, but also to its etymological sense of cutting or tearing. Speaking and writing both engage us in a dynamic of separation. Seeing, however, implies only a degree of separation:

> Voir, c'est certes toujours voir à distance, mais en laissant la distance nous rendre ce qu'elle nous enlève. La vue s'exerce invisiblement dans une pause où tout

> se retient. Nous ne voyons que ce qui d'abord nous échappe, en vertu d'une privation initiale, ne voyant pas les choses trop présentes ni si notre présence aux choses est pressante. (*EI* 39)

> [To see is certainly to see at a distance, but by allowing distance to give back what it removes from us. Sight is invisibly active in a pause wherein everything holds itself back. We see only what first escapes us by virtue of an initial privation, not seeing things that are too present, and not seeing them if our presence to things is pressing.] (*IC* 28)

Thus: 'Voir, c'est donc saisir *immédiatement* à distance' (*EI* 39) ('to see is to apprehend *immediately* from a distance', *IC* 28). This is a particularly dense moment, but must be understood according to the logic outlined in relation to this essay in Chapter 1, which is to say the optical imperative under which metaphysics operates, subordinating speech to vision. It is in this way we can say that the fascinating object is that which has been set apart or distinguished in some way. To become image in film, something must be framed or de-framed such as to activate this relation of distance or separation. It is this disjunction in which something appears as separate. This seems to be what Blanchot means by 'distance' and 'separation', terms to which he gives a metaphysical significance.

What is awaited, says one of the speakers, is a speech 'où parle l'"erreur": la parole du détour' (*EI* 40) ('in which "error" speaks: the speech of detour', *IC* 29). This is of course a gesture towards writing, and particularly the mode of fragmentary writing arrived at in Blanchot's late works. However, in a critical passage the notion of the image emerges, via a discussion of the function of light in dreams:

> Ce qui voile en révélant, le voile qui révèle en revoilant dans l'indécision ambiguë du mot révéler, c'est l'image. L'image est image en cette duplicité, non pas le double de l'objet, mais le dédoublement initial qui permet ensuite à la chose d'être figurée; plus haut encore que le doublement, c'est le ploiement, le tour du tournant [...]. La parole dont nous essayons de parler est retour à cette première tournure. (*EI* 42)

> [The image is what veils by revealing; it is the veil that reveals by reveiling in all the ambiguous indecision of the word reveal. The image is image by means of this duplicity, being not the object's double, but the initial division that then permits the thing to be figured; still further back than this doubling it is a folding, a turn of the turning [...]. The speech of which we are trying to speak is a return to this first turning.] (*IC* 30)

What one understands by 'parler, ce n'est pas voir', then, hinges on how 'voir' is conceptualized. The line can be understood as indicating that speech — suggesting communication in a strong sense — is not a mode of mastery, as seeing connotes in the classical tradition of metaphysics. To the extent that we are dealing with the relation entailed by the image, we are not dealing with seeing in a normal way. As Ropars-Wuilleumier writes in a different context, while the essay has been read as 'un désaveu du regard' ('a disavowal of the gaze'), in fact 'il ne rejette que le *pouvoir* de la vision, et non le recours au geste de voir' ('it is only the *power* of vision that is refused, and not the recourse to the gesture of seeing').[67] I want to press the question of visibility.

When the walkers are a certain way along the path, their relative movement becomes indiscernible. Reduced to a point in the distance, one *sees* a point a little above the centre of the image that oscillates slightly at the same time as seeming immobile. Movement and stillness are at a point of paradoxical equilibrium. At the same point, time is both passing and yet nothing is happening: no change or movement is registered. Furthermore, the bleeding of speech into the landscape brings a quality of strangeness. The divorcing of speech from its source works to erase the sense of a stable *hic et nunc* in which one could say that what passes 'is passing'. In this moment, the drawn-out nature of the take invites reflection on the timeframes at play. There is the actual running time of the shot (i.e. an uninterrupted two minutes and fourteen seconds) at the same time as the place of the shot within the running order of the film (i.e. just under six and a half hours into the film). There is the profilmic, indexical moment of the shoot at the same time as the diegetic time of the characters (this shot coming just after Irimiás's speech on Estike's death). There is also the time of the narrative structure, which both provides different perspectives on the same time (the two episodes before and after this are called 'The Perspective, as Seen from the Front' [2.V] and 'The Perspective, as Seen from the Back' [2.III]) at the same time as the relation to the history of the Earth implied in the geological vision. There is finally the time of the spectator. While for Lefebvre this can be read as inviting the interpretative gaze, we can say here that, with spatio-temporal co-ordinates in this way estranged from themselves, what seems to come to the fore as 'visible' is in fact the *imaginary* quality of physical existence itself. In an essay on landscape (2000), Ropars-Wuilleumier writes that:

> Le paysage mime et en même temps renverse le passage hors cadre où se déplie le dehors. Car le dehors [...] désigne moins l'ouverture de l'espace sur un monde extérieur au sujet [...] que l'impossibilité soudain reconnue de tracer le partage entre dedans et dehors, intimité et altération.[68]
>
> [Landscape imitates and at the same time upturns the passage out of the frame where the outside unfolds. Because the outside [...] designates less the opening of space onto a world exterior to the subject [...] than the impossibility suddenly recognized in tracing the division between inside and outside, intimacy and alteration.]

The Blanchotian filmic imaginary points to that world as preceded by its image.

When Bellour writes that reproducing a photograph within a film functions to create 'l'instant privilégié' ('a privileged instant') among 'l'instant quelconque' ('any-instant[s]-whatever'), he not only describes the opening of a time within time, but also notes the possession in this instant of 'une qualité d'abstraction et d'irréalité qui me semble introduire dans le film un saisissement comparable à celui qui transit d'emblée (dans) la peinture' ('a quality of abstraction and of irreality that seems to introduce a kind of paralysis — comparable to one that strikes (in) painting — into film').[69] Although he does not make the connection explicitly here, Bellour's description of the effect of the freeze-frame on the viewer is resonant with Blanchotian fascination. The 'privilege' of the privileged instant would be a somewhat ironic one in the time 'quand il n'y a de temps qu'entre-temps' (*EI* 617) ('when there is no time but the "meanwhile"', *IC* 420, translation modified). Indeed, the difficulty with Deleuze is precisely that identified by Bellour: Deleuzian time is 'unitaire, global' ('unitary and global') and 'sur lequel n'ont d'emprise ni le futur d'aucune utopie ni le passé d'aucune régression' ('on which neither the future of any utopia nor the past of any regression has a hold'). It is therefore one in which the film 'ne s'arrête jamais, ignore les mirages de l'instant, les points de vide de manque, en un mot la trace du négatif, et la hantise de la photographie' ('never comes to standstill, is oblivious to the mirages of the instant, the points of emptiness and lack, the trace of the negative and the specter of photography'). In short, it aims for a kind of total objectivity, at the expense of nostalgia and memory.[70] Deleuze as conceived in this way is at odds with a theory of film based around the experience of the viewer, with all of the subjective and psychoanalytic factors that this sets in place. This was discussed in Chapter 1 (especially in relation to Shaviro). The landscape from *Satantango*, at the same time as it is strongly evocative of certain passages from Deleuze, as has been shown above, cannot be reduced to the 'objectivizing' view, but must engage some notion of fascination.

The movement of these characters through space, getting further into the distance, is undercut by the motionlessness of the camera, which in a Deleuzian account would allow time to rise to the surface. The difference is that, for this argument, these images are not 'expressive' of time, as Rancière would have it. Although in a sense 'communicative' and engendering a kind of proximity with the outside, they are rather inexpressive, divested of direction and evacuative of spectatorial identification. They are not to show the weariness of the characters so much as a primordial weariness, a terminal inertia. It is not the protagonist's psychology that is dominant, but an impersonal lack of psychology. One might say it is less a temporal expression than a qualitative disjunction within the temporal relation itself, which is to say an opening to that which is *outside* time. While Deleuze may seem to allow for such a formulation, his philosophy must be pressed on this point in the manner of Ropars-Wuilleumier. If for Deleuze inert shots, such as those in his example of Antonioni's *The Outcry*, bring out an expression of intense tiredness, then what we are calling 'listlessness' or the indifference of the camera is perhaps more accurately an example of Blanchot's *désœuvrement*. We said above that this worklessness was foregrounded, but it would be better to say — with all of the ambivalence the word carries from 'Parler, ce n'est pas voir' — 'révélé'. Where Deleuze stresses the directorial composition of film, the present study seeks to bring out Blanchot's emphasis on how every work of art cannot but let this aspect appear. The image, for Blanchot, is both that which conceals and reveals the formless nothing behind each thing; it is in this sense that a shift in focus can be spoken of above. This follows from the double logic of the worklessness of the work as both that which inhibits its completion at the same time as it represents its *conditio sine qua non*. The worklessness of the work is precisely its animating paradox, and it is this model that can be posited against Rancière's dialectic of two regimes of visibility inhering in a single contradictory filmic image.

The reading pursued in the present study is one that moves between these alternative *temps* to conceive the fascinated, *disastrous* one: 'le hors de l'histoire historique'. There is in this time an implied messianism, but it is one with a '"maintenant" hors texte, d'un récit de sévère fiction' (*ED* 215) ('now of a severe, fictitious narrative', *WD* 142). This latter phrase is one that seems peculiarly appropriate to *Satantango*. It is the time of Tarr's cinematography, its extensions, movements, and fixations, the time after men in which comes 'l'infini calme (l'efferverscence) qui ne s'incarne pas et ne se rend pas intelligible' (*ED* 69) ('the infinite calm (the effervescence) which does not embody itself or make itself intelligible', *WD* 40). The bells in the barroom scene represent a phenomenon within the narrative structure of *Satantango* that suggests its relation to exteriority or alterity, and in this sense dramatizes the idea of an opening onto an absence of time that was identified above as being a typical effect of the film's long takes.

This tension between narrative and the image in Tarr's films is one that has also been developed by others in relation to Blanchot. Alluding to Nancy's *La Communauté désœuvrée*, Guillaume Sibertin-Blanc finds in Tarr's images the dynamics of excess and dissolution that characterize *désœuvrement*.[71] While he thematizes this in terms of community, his analysis of how the dilation of time in the travelling shots, the distended landscapes, and the density of weary bodies work to deprive the viewing gaze of its mastery accords with my reading of *Satantango* in terms of fascination.[72] More expansively than Sibertin-Blanc, Estelle Bayon refers to Blanchot to describe how Tarr's later films make palpable the experience of a disaster, the experience of a world in ruins. Bayon conceives of this as an ecological vision, which is to say a vision about being in the world. She argues that Tarr's is a disastrous ecology, showing an Earth that is uninhabitable and melancholy.[73] Tarr shows 'le lent désœuvrement du monde' [the slow *désœuvrement* of the world] by 'rendant visible le mouvement même du désastre' [making visible the very movement of the disaster], the metamorphosis of the landscape, for example that studied by the doctor, and the movement of the cosmos dramatized in the opening of *Werckmeister Harmonies*.[74] Elsewhere in Tarr's films we have visions of gales and torrential winds. In this way the images are imbued with the disaster, the estrangement from the sky described in the primal scene.

To the extent that we can talk of the valences of the disaster (Blanchot lends it attributes, even agency, at the same time as he disavows any descriptive or nominative approach to it), the disaster is something that *waits* and is *awaited*, although in a specialized sense. As Blanchot writes:

> Qu'il n'y ait pas attente du désastre, c'est dans la mesure où l'on pense que l'attente est toujours attente d'un attendu ou d'un inattendu. Mais l'attente, de même qu'elle ne se rapporte pas plus à l'avenir qu'à un passé accessible, est aussi bien attente de l'attente, ce qui ne nous fixe pas dans un présent, car 'J"ai toujours déjà attendu ce que j'attendrai toujours: le non mémorable, l'inconnu sans présent dont je ne puis pas plus me souvenir que je ne puis savoir si je n'oublie pas l'avenir, l'avenir étant ma relation avec ce qui, dans ce qui arrive, n'arrive pas et donc ne se présente, ne se re-présente pas. (*ED* 179–80)

[That there is no awaiting the disaster is true to the extent that waiting is considered always to be the awaiting of something waited for, or else unexpected. But awaiting — just as it is not related to the future any more than to an accessible past — is also the awaiting of awaiting, which does not situate us in a present, for 'I' have always already awaited what I will always wait for: the immemorial, the unknown which has no present, and which I can no more remember than I can know whether I am not forgetting the future — the future being my relation with what, in what is coming, does not come and thus does not present, or re-present itself.] (*WD* 117)

L'Écriture du désastre represents the furthest 'evolution' of Blanchot's thinking on waiting, and it is a text that will be of increased relevance in the next chapter, where the question will be not only of duration but also the direction of time. To a degree this concern is present in *Satantango*, in that its twelve sections several times overlap from different points of view. It can thus be said that the characters are awaiting something that has always already been, is still to come, and yet does not come. While the disaster is not the apocalypse, it nevertheless often takes on apocalyptic overtones. While what was apocalyptic in *Histoire(s)* was the sense of cinema's failed historical duty and, in Agamben's terms, the revelation of imagelessness, here it is the question of something that never arrives. Moving from the diegesis to the exposure opened by the film for the spectator, we can see why sequences such as those discussed in this chapter are so strange and leave a feeling of lightness in their wake.

Notes to Chapter 3

1. Corinne Maury and Sylvie Rollet, eds., *Béla Tarr: de la colère au tourment* (Crisnée: Yellow Now, 2016). See, for example, pp. 40 & 65.
2. László Krasznahorkai, *Satantango*, trans. by George Szirtes (London: Atlantic Books, 2012).
3. The best study remains Matthew Flanagan, '"Slow Cinema": Temporality and Style in Contemporary Art and Experimental Film' (unpublished PhD thesis, University of Exeter, 2012). For a recent collection, see *Slow Cinema*, ed. by Tiago de Luca and Nuno Barradas (Edinburgh: Edinburgh University Press, 2016).
4. András Bálint Kovács, *The Cinema of Béla Tarr: The Circle Closes* (New York: Wallflower Press, 2013); Jacques Rancière, *Béla Tarr: le temps d'après* (Paris: Capricci, 2011); *Béla Tarr: The Time After*, trans. by Erik Beranek (Minneapolis: Univocal Publishing, 2013).
5. Rancière, *Béla Tarr*, pp. 15–16; *Béla Tarr*, p. 9.
6. For an account of this and its relation to slow cinema, see Flanagan, '"Slow Cinema"', pp. 70–75.
7. For a broader account of Hungarian cinema in the period in which Tarr's filmmaking emerged, see John Cunningham, *Hungarian Cinema: From Coffee House to Multiplex* (London: Wallflower Press, 2004), pp. 142–59.
8. Rancière, *Béla Tarr*, p. 11; *Béla Tarr*, p. 5.
9. Ibid., p. 13; p. 7.
10. Ibid., p. 32; p. 26. For more on the two regimes, see Rancière, *Aisthesis*.
11. Rancière, *Béla Tarr*, p. 69; *Béla Tarr*, p. 63.
12. Ibid., p. 40; p. 34.
13. Ibid., p. 41; p. 34.
14. Ben Singer, '*Jeanne Dielman*: Cinematic Interrogation and "Amplification"', *Millennium Film Journal*, 22 (1989), 56–75 (p. 58). On the subject of Chantal Akerman, we can note in passing an example of this in the final shot of *News from Home* (1977), a very long but simple take taken from a boat as it leaves New York City. As the boat moves further into the distance away from the city, the New York skyline slowly comes to fill the screen. This hypnotic movement enacts

precisely the abandonment of the world I have been describing. It is no coincidence that Ivone Margulies refers to Blanchot at the outset of her study of Akerman, see Ivone Margulies, *Nothing Happens: Chantal Akerman's Hyperrealist Everyday* (Durham, NC: Duke University Press, 1996), p. 21.
15. As quoted in Erika Balsom, 'Saving the Image: Scale and Duration in Contemporary Art Cinema', *CineAction*, 72 (2007), 23–31 (p. 28).
16. Rancière, *Béla Tarr*, pp. 69–70; *Béla Tarr*, p. 63 (translation modified).
17. Kovács, *The Cinema of Béla Tarr*, p. 114.
18. Ibid., p. 115.
19. Krasznahorkai, *Satantango*, p. 88.
20. Rancière, *Béla Tarr*, p. 31; *Béla Tarr*, p. 25.
21. Robert Koehler, 'Interview — The Thinking Image: Fred Keleman on Béla Tarr and *The Turin Horse*', *Cinema Scope* (2012), <http://cinema-scope.com/cinema-scope-magazine/interview-the-thinking-image-fred-kelemen-on-bela-tarr-and-the-turin-horse/> [accessed 5 June 2015].
22. Flanagan, '"Slow Cinema"', pp. 120–22.
23. Jean-François Lyotard, 'L'Acinéma', in *Des dispositifs pulsionnels* (Paris: Galilée, 1994), pp. 57–69; 'Acinema', trans. by Paisley N. Livingston, in *The Lyotard Reader*, ed. by Andrew Benjamin (Oxford: Blackwell, 1989), pp. 169–80.
24. Ibid., pp. 60 & 66; pp. 172 & 177.
25. Jean-François Lyotard, 'Idée d'un film souverain', in *Misère de la philosophie* (Paris: Galilée, 2000), pp. 209–21 (p. 211).
26. For sovereignty, see for example Georges Bataille, *The Accursed Share: An Essay on General Economy, Volumes 2 and 3*, trans. by Robert Hurley (New York: Zone Books, 1991), pp. 197–211 (esp. p. 198); for communication, see for example Georges Bataille, *Inner Experience*, trans. by Leslie Anne Boldt (New York: State University of New York Press, 1988), pp. 93–98.
27. Lyotard, 'Idée d'un film souverain', p. 216.
28. Ibid., pp. 221 & 214.
29. Ashley Woodward, 'A Sacrificial Economy of the Image: Lyotard on Cinema', *Angelaki: journal of the theoretical humanities*, 19:4 (2014), 141–54.
30. Changing vocabulary for a moment, one might suggest that this idea of a recuperation of useless or sovereign images is resonant with the way in which Tarr has been read as exemplary of a move to 'save the image', a phrase of Bellour's which names the tactics of filmmakers to engage with the image itself in the face of increasing mediatization. While in the past cinema may have been a place of idle absorption of images in contrast to the outside world, today it is in the everyday world that one is absorbed in images, and only in the cinema is the image reinvested with its proper power, forcing one to engage with what one sees. See Balsom, 'Saving the Image', p. 28, and Raymond Bellour, 'Saving the Image', in *Saving the Image: Art After Film*, ed. by Tanya Leighton and Pavel Büchler (Glasgow: Centre for Contemporary Arts, 2003), pp. 52–77.
31. Reni Celeste, 'The Frozen Screen: Levinas and the Action Film', *Film-Philosophy*, 11:2 (2007), 15–36.
32. Emmanuel Levinas, 'La Réalité et son ombre', in *Les Imprévus de l'histoire* (Montpellier: Fata Morgana, 1994), pp. 123–48; 'Reality and its Shadow', in *Collected Philosophical Papers*, trans. by Alphonso Lingis (Pittsburgh: Duquesne University Press, 1987), pp. 1–13.
33. Celeste, 'The Frozen Screen', p. 23 (my emphasis).
34. Ibid., p. 31.
35. Ibid., pp. 18–19.
36. Deleuze, *Cinéma 2*, p. 246; *Cinema 2*, p. 182.
37. Ibid., pp. 246–47; p. 182.
38. Ibid., p. 247; p. 183.
39. Ibid., p. 246, n. 1; p. 305, n. 1. For the preface, see *EI* ix–xxvi; *IC* xiii–xxiii.
40. For an excellent article offering a wider perspective on weariness and waiting in art cinema, see Elena Gorfinkel, 'Weariness, Waiting: Endurance and Art Cinema's Tired Bodies', *Discourse*, 34, 2–3 (2012), 311–47.

41. Hill, *Maurice Blanchot and Fragmentary Writing*, p. 110. For Heidegger's distinction, see Heidegger, *Being and Time*, p. 306; *Sein und Zeit*, pp. 261–62.
42. It is worth noting that the epigraph for the source novel of *Satantango* reads as follows: 'In that case, I'll miss the thing by waiting for it'. This is in fact a reference to that most Blanchotian of texts, Kafka's *The Castle* (1926) (see Franz Kafka, *The Castle*, trans. by Willa and Edwin Muir (Harmondsworth: Penguin, 1957), p. 104.) This quotation comes about a third of the way into Kafka's novel and is the moment in which the protagonist, a land surveyor known as K., is waiting for the elusive official from the castle, Klamm. The novel as a whole is in a sense about waiting, as K. 'waits' interminably in the village to be admitted to the castle overlooking it. The relation between Kafka's text and that of Krasznahorkai — who, besides writing the novel on which it is based, also co-authored the film version of *Satantango* — is not immediately obvious, but the epigraph cannot but indicate the centrality of the motif of waiting to the story. Blanchot writes that K. 'tombe sans cesse dans la faute que Kafka désigne comme la plus grave, celle de l'impatience. L'impatience au sein de l'erreur est la faute essentielle, parce qu'elle méconnaît la vérité même de l'erreur qui impose, comme une loi, de ne jamais croire que le but est proche, ni que l'on s'en rapproche: il ne faut jamais en finir avec l'indéfini; il ne faut jamais saisir comme l'immédiat, comme le déjà présent, la profondeur de l'absence inépuisable' (*EL* 76–77) ('falls incessantly into the fault which Kafka designates as the gravest: impatience. The impatience at the heart of error is the essential fault, because it misconstrues the very trueness of error which, like a law, requires that one never believe the goal is close or that one is coming nearer to it. One must never have done with the indefinite; one must never grasp — as if it were the immediate, the already present — the profundity of inexhaustible absence', *SL* 79). Blanchot seems to be implying here that there is something like a correct response to waiting which would be called patience, in which one would not seek to command or comprehend the outside, but remain passive in relation to it.
43. Rancière, *Béla Tarr*, p. 46; *Béla Tarr*, p. 40.
44. Pier Paolo Pasolini, 'Observations on the Long Take', trans. by Norman MacAfee and Craig Owens, *October*, 13 (1980), 3–6 (p. 5).
45. Ibid., p. 3.
46. Ibid., p. 6.
47. Chion, *Audio-Vision*, pp. 71–72.
48. Krasznahorkai, *Satantango*, p. 207.
49. Kovács, *The Cinema of Béla Tarr*, p. 73.
50. Ibid., p. 60.
51. As quoted by Kovács in *The Cinema of Béla Tarr*, p. 63.
52. See especially the penultimate poem read out in the film, beginning 'I have leafed through history...'.
53. For a discussion of this idea in the doctor's episode, see Calum Watt, 'Alcoholism and the Doctor in Béla Tarr's *Satantango*', in *The Cinematic Bodies of Eastern Europe and Russia: Between Pain and Pleasure*, ed. by Matilda Mroz, Ewa Mazierska and Elzbieta Ostrowska (Edinburgh: Edinburgh University Press, 2016), pp. 53–66.
54. Martin Lefebvre, 'Between Setting and Landscape in the Cinema', in *Landscape and Film*, ed. by Martin Lefebvre (New York: Routledge, 2006), pp. 19–59 (p. 51).
55. Ibid., p. 35.
56. Ibid., p. 29.
57. Tom Gunning, 'The Cinema of Attractions: Early Film, Its Spectator and the Avant-Garde', *Wide Angle*, 8:3 (1986), 60–70 (p. 64).
58. Krasznahorkai, *Satantango*, p. 66.
59. Deleuze, *Cinéma 2*, p. 317; *Cinema 2*, p. 234.
60. Ibid., p. 322; p. 237.
61. Ibid., pp. 326–27; pp. 240–41.
62. Ibid., p. 339; p. 249 (translation modified).
63. See for example Deleuze, *Cinéma 2*, pp. 302–03; *Cinema 2*, pp. 223–24.
64. Deleuze, *Cinéma 2*, pp. 340–41; *Cinema 2*, p. 250. Deleuze is here drawing on Pier Paolo

Pasolini, 'The "Cinema of Poetry"', in *Heretical Empiricism*, ed. by Louise K. Barnett, trans. by Ben Lawton and Louise K. Barnett (Washington, DC: New Academia Publishing, 2005), pp. 167–86.
65. Ropars-Wuilleumier, *Le Temps d'une pensée*, p. 404; 'Image or Time?', p. 18.
66. It is thus notable that when Blanchot references the text in the letter to a filmmaker cited in the Introduction, he adds a word to the title: 'Parler (écrire), ce n'est pas voir'.
67. Ropars-Wuilleumier, *Le Temps d'une pensée*, p. 296; 'On Unworking', p. 138 (my emphasis).
68. Ropars-Wuilleumier, *Le Temps d'une pensée*, p. 390.
69. Bellour, *L'Entre-Images*, p. 119; *Between-the-Images*, p. 140.
70. Ibid., p. 132; pp. 154–55.
71. Guillaume Sibertin-Blanc, 'De la mélancolie à la résistance: communautés et désœuvrement', in *Béla Tarr: de la colère au tourment*, ed. by Maury and Rollet, pp. 150–64.
72. Ibid., esp. pp. 156–57.
73. Estelle Bayon, 'Un désastre écologique', in *Béla Tarr: de la colère au tourment*, ed. by Maury and Rollet, pp. 46–57 (p. 49).
74. Ibid., p. 50.

CHAPTER 4

Irréversible, Disidentification, and Disastrous Responsibility

Irréversible and its Critical Context

To pursue further the stylistic significance of the long take, this chapter discusses Gaspar Noé's film *Irréversible* (2002) and looks more closely at some aspects of the relation between Blanchot and Levinas and the implications this relation might have in thinking about film, and so attempts to address an *ethical* dimension — or the lack thereof — in film. This is to be considered through the idea of the relation with the Other, which can be conceptualized as a relation that can be opened up for the viewer in viewing the film, as it were through the screen itself. This is to be understood in terms of the model drawn up in previous chapters in which the spectatorial experience of filmic art can be said to involve contact with 'Otherness', and in which a relation with the Other is implicit in aesthetic experience.

Irréversible remains a controversial film, from its mention in James Quandt's now defining piece on the so-called 'New French Extremity', through David Edelstein's notorious contemporary review, in which he avers that the film itself 'rapes' the viewer.[1] It is in part the film's *maudit* status — that it can be regarded, far from being a masterpiece, as a symptom of anomie — that makes this film an object of a different order from those previously discussed. The ambivalent critical attention it continues to receive is due to its extremely violent imagery, its ambiguous politics with regard to homophobia and rape, and its director's signature stylistic heavy-handedness with which he overdetermines his film.[2] Many studies consider the key problem of *Irréversible* to lie in its gender politics, which is to say in whether the notorious rape scene engenders identification or an empathetic response to the rapist or the raped character, and whether the film's unusual reverse chronology logically entails a nihilistic determinism of such politics.[3] Another current has read it as in fact a 'moral' film, and the late critic Roger Ebert was the main proponent of this idea: the argument runs that, because of the way the narrative is organized in a reverse order, in the running of the film the consequences of actions are seen before those actions, and so the film is 'moral — at a structural level'.[4] Others have found in the presentation of the rape scene 'integrity and unflinching audacity'.[5] Most recently, the film has been the subject of a book-length study by Tim Palmer aiming to rehabilitate the film as an essential work within what he calls 'cinéma du corps' as well as the context of contemporary French film production more generally.[6] As Palmer points out, far from being an 'extreme' or unusual piece of cinema, the film was entirely French-funded, made with a budget typical for France at the time (4.6 million euros) and, what is more, selling over 500,000 tickets in France, can be counted as a reasonable success.[7] This chapter argues that questions of where identification lies in the film miss the 'disidentification' at work, particularly in Noé's use of the long take during the scenes of extreme violence. I will argue that these work rather to turn the characters into image in the Blanchotian sense. I will also discuss how the very word 'irréversible' is for Blanchot and Levinas a charged term appearing at crucial junctures in their work. It signifies a conception of time that is important in discussing the ontology of film as an art taking place in time. A key question, then, for the present chapter, both in terms of the film and the works of the two writers, will be: what is it that is 'irréversible'?

To give a brief synopsis of the film: *Irréversible* is a rape revenge story whose action is told in reverse chronological order and revolves around the events of a night in the life of three friends, Alex (Monica Bellucci), Marcus (Vincent Cassell), and Pierre (Albert Dupontel). Beginning with the end of the story represented, the film shows Marcus and Pierre searching a labyrinthine homosexual S&M nightclub for an elusive figure known as Le Ténia (Jo Prestia). Thinking they have found him, a fight ensues in which Pierre smashes the assailant's head to a pulp with a fire extinguisher. The film then proceeds back in time as the men demand of various passers-by where they might find the nightclub. The two men are then shown coming across Alex being stretchered into an ambulance, comatose, and in the following scene we see how this came about: she was the victim of a random attack, raped and beaten in an underpass by Le Ténia. The film goes back further to the party attended earlier in the evening by the three characters, where Alex, irritated at her lover Marcus, leaves early without him. Then comes their train journey en route to the party, and then back to Alex and Marcus in bed together before they set off for the evening. Finally, we see Alex sitting in an idyllic park reading, before a finale of strobe lighting and the closing caption: 'le temps détruit tout' [time destroys all].

So, structurally, the film is organized around two scenes of extreme violence with the counterpoint of a love scene. The reversal of linear chronology gives the viewer a distanced relation to characters, such that the violence is decontextualized, and this engenders a dispassionate, even ignorant attitude to the revenge. This also, however, implies that spectatorial identification with the diegetic characters is undermined — their motivations, for example, become alien as they are only revealed *après coup*. Ordinary narrative convention ruined, the segments of the story become not episodes in a narrative the viewer can follow, but discordant sequences that are divorced from regular continuity. The rape sequence in the underpass is the most notorious example of this phenomenon.

Todd McGowan discusses *Irréversible* in relation to what he calls 'atemporal cinema', by which he means contemporary films whose chronology is distorted. According to this psychoanalytical thesis, it is the atemporal structure of these films that shows the originary trauma constitutive of biological existence to be insoluble and irredeemable. In *Irréversible*, this notion of trauma is illustrated by the thematization of the misunderstanding of violence. So, for example, the film induces errors of judgment in the viewer, such as the way in which the graphic revenge viewed at the beginning of the film (but at the end of the diegetic sequence of events) is only later in the film shown to have been exacted on the wrong character, i.e. not the rapist. This dire and delayed dramatic irony serves, according to McGowan, to demonstrate that it is only in separating ourselves from the conventional order and direction of temporal existence that we might understand trauma as fundamental to existence. 'The implicit contention of *Irréversible*,' writes McGowan, 'is that though the systematic nature of knowledge may hide the temporality of knowing, temporality itself occasions its own deception, a deception that phenomenology aids in perpetuating'.[8] This deception, then, is the one that protects us from trauma and conceals the structure of the drive as circular. The meaning of the film's title within this Lacanian conceptual framework is therefore not to be understood with reference to time, but as characterizing the repetition of the drive, whose end can only come in individual biological death.

McGowan's argument is suggestive insofar as it can be split into a reading of the logic of the narrative (the idea that the film can have an 'implicit contention') and a critique of a mode of relation (i.e. phenomenology). I set out this argument here as it is a clear theoretical statement of what can be at stake in the construction of a film. The focus of the McGowan piece is on the structure of the film and it places less emphasis on the question of what we are to make of the extreme violence that, alongside the reverse chronology, defines *Irréversible*. The logic of his argument is that as a result of the narrative structure, the violence is shown always to inhere in the present: it is always ahead of itself, a fait accompli even before conception. What we here call 'violence' is really shorthand for trauma as being drive. However, the violence of the film is not abstract violence, especially if we take its manifestation in the underpass sequence, which is the motiveless brutality of one against another. I will return later to the structure of the film after addressing the question of violence.

The Underpass: Fascination and the Long Take

In a purely technical sense, this scene in the underpass resembles some of the Tarr shots that were discussed in the previous chapter. By this I mean that it is a long take and, after initial motion, the camera comes to be stationary for an extended period of time. The difference of course is that whereas in Tarr's shots we were presented with the fact of 'nothing happening', here something, it seems, definitely is happening; and this is made specific by the agonizing protraction of the shot. While the mind might have drifted in the previous examples, here it seems one wants to look away; what is presented is inescapable and viscerally offensive. Is the 'attitude' of the camera therefore clinical and indifferent or confrontational and provocative?

One of the most striking things about this sequence is the camera's immobility for most of the take. The sequence lasts almost thirteen minutes, of which nine consist of the rape and beating. This particular long take presents itself as an aesthetic problem. It could also be regarded as an ethical one, in the broader and non-specialized, non-Levinasian sense of that term. Part of this involves the inherent ambiguity of the long take in general, which can work to achieve a variety of different effects. Crucially, the long take can work to amplify the divergence between individual spectators' subjective evaluations of the same filmic material. As Kovács observes of critical readings of *Satantango*, the same long takes can for some be immersive and for others estranging.[9] In the case of *Irréversible* we have accounts of some viewers feeling unmoved and others feeling as if they have been violated.[10] Unlike a more typical sequence edited on the classical continuity principles, in which the viewer's gaze is directed by the changing images, in a static long take such as this there is a greater duration in which the viewer can engage with a particular image and in which individual, non-directed responses can develop. Noé insists that the point of this long duration is one of realism: this is the length of time a rape takes.[11] The duration suffered is in a sense one undergone both by Alex and the viewer. The apparent aspiration to verisimilitude suggests that Noé in some sense wants to put his viewer face to face with the real. However, this of course has stylistic effects, and this is an example of what McGowan is referring to when he notes that 'Noé edits the content of an exploitation film with editing more appropriate to an Italian Neorealist film'.[12]

Asbjørn Grønstad situates Noé's film in a cinematic tradition of 'confrontational sensibility' stretching from Lars von Trier back to Pasolini and ultimately Luis Buñuel.[13] I quote him at length as this is a useful statement of what is salient about *Irréversible* in the critical discourse surrounding the film and what is at stake in it:

> There is a fine line between, on the one hand, pictorial portrayals of human misery and anguish designed to stir the social consciousness and empathy of the viewers, and on the other, images that seem deliberately composed to make them uncomfortable [...] the acts of provocation that the images from this tradition perpetrate can be conceptualised as instances of what I have metaphorically termed razorblade gestures, the emotional, psychic and ethical slicing open of the gaze of the spectator. [...] these offensive images seem impervious to iconoclastic censure. Their taboo-breaking is of a different order. They challenge the moral integrity of the spectators and *put their subjectivity at risk*.[14]

Furthermore, writes Grønstad, with specific reference to the scene we are discussing, this could be seen as 'not about the violence but about the act of looking at painful images. It is another way of asking, in meta-spectatorial terms, how much of this sort of thing we can endure'.[15] This corresponds to the feeling that *Irréversible* perpetrates violence of a kind against the viewer as an attempt to create a correlative of a character's ordeal at the level of the film's visual style. A similar idea is articulated by Palmer when he argues that 'systematic distortion of the diegetic space' is a characteristic of the recent 'French cinema of the body', of which *Irréversible* is an outstanding example, and that this distortion of the image renders 'the stimulus directly from diegetic character to actual viewer'.[16] In the context of *Irréversible*, this could be understood to refer to the film's various visual and sonic effects including the frenetic hand-held camera movements and the use of low-frequency sound in the early parts of the film, both of which can inspire emetic effects. This, I think, in part explains the 'attraction' for some of this film — that it can be seen as something akin to an endurance test, much in the manner of horror films. Indeed, Noé's films have been read in relation to the scholarship of 'cinema of attractions', alluded to in the previous chapter.[17] However, as Grønstad argues, *Irréversible* is at the limit of the tradition of confrontational images and its effect on viewer subjectivity is in excess of that of horror. Indeed, its effect on subjectivity may even exceed that understood by Grønstad.

The sequence begins with Alex above ground, having left the party and looking to hail a taxi, wavering whether to cross the road until she is told by someone leaning on a nearby lamppost to take the underpass as the road is dangerous. The tunnel is long and crimson. The camera, handheld and operated by the director, follows a few steps behind Alex in a medium shot as she descends into the underpass and walks through. The rapist appears at the other end of the tunnel with a woman, whom he beats. Alex is stunned and looks to flee, but he sets on her and threatens her with a knife as the other woman (in fact the transgender prostitute Concha harassed later in the film by Marcus and Pierre) runs away. As he rapes her, the camera is fixed in place at ground level, near to Alex's head. The tunnel recedes into the background of the right-hand side of the shot. This frames her body, which lies across the centre of the shot, and accentuates her fearful eyes, which look out above the rapist's hand which covers her mouth. Le Ténia repeatedly grips Alex's ponytail with one hand and covers her mouth with the other. While to begin with she uses her hand to try and pry the rapist's hand from her mouth, in the end it is simply extended to the foreground, reaching out as it were from the screen to the viewer. When the rape ends, the camera moves slightly from the fixed position it has adopted for that duration and Le Ténia stands towering in the centre of the shot. Alex lies crumpled and sobbing before him. He suddenly and viciously kicks her in the face. He then repeatedly punches her, before finally turning her over to smash her face into the ground. At this point the handheld camera quickly tracks forward to frame this closely.

The early parts of the film are designed to give the illusion of the continuous motion of the camera as it flies through the night, but these sequences are in fact composed of many fragments edited together in postproduction. The underpass scene is notable, however, as in contrast to the earlier parts of the film it appears neither frenetic nor digitally altered. (*Irréversible* was shot on Super 16mm using a lightweight camera and edited digitally.)[18] When the camera drops to the ground during the rape, it brings the film to a halt both formally (in terms of camera movement) and narratively (by dwelling on the violence). After the urgency of Marcus and Pierre's pursuit of Le Ténia in the preceding scenes, this proceeds at a much slower pace. It is an unexpected intrusion of slowness into a film hitherto deliriously in motion.

The underpass scene is defined by its apparent relative simplicity, which is to say that the 'minimalism' of this represented violation is in complete contrast to the earlier sequences, minimalism in the sense that the camera is still and the scene depends almost exclusively on the actors for its effect. There is a sense that what we are seeing is unmediated by any effects of the camera. What this formal minimalism achieves — and this is where the 'unwatchable' aspect of it lies — is the stark, demonstrative gesture of the film towards itself ('look at this here'). This suggests a degree of self-consciousness on the part of the film, but Noé, who operated the camera during this scene, claims the stasis is the result of his having been physically unable to move during this shooting.[19] The effect of the shot, in any case, is to underscore the essential provocation, which is that what we are seeing should not be looked at and yet offers the imperative that we must. As Estelle Bayon argues, it is not so much the act itself that is depicted that makes a film 'obscene', so much as the *mise en scène*, that is, by the way in which it is presented.[20] This suggests that offensiveness in film is primarily a factor of style or the aesthetic. In Bayon's survey of 'le cinéma obscène', the scene in the underpass is the strongest example she finds of 'l'obscénité du plan long' [the obscenity of the long take], by which she means the use of duration in itself to exhaust the spectator, to render them powerless before that which is obscene.[21] The scene appears to exceed greatly its function in terms of the narrative, which is to show the event which prompts Marcus and Pierre to seek revenge. Even by comparison with other moments in the film, the grisly material is presented in such a drawn-out fashion as to stand out as particularly 'confrontational' in the manner identified by Grønstad. To this extent, the scene can be regarded as *excessive* in the Bataillean sense of going beyond required economic measure (in this case, in terms of the measure of time). Bataille is a key reference for Bayon and is also cited by Martine Beugnet, who suggests the relevance of Bataille's 'part maudite' [accursed share] to an understanding of what she calls the 'cinema of sensation'. She writes, citing films by directors such as Claire Denis, Philippe Grandieux, and Oliver Assayas, that the horror shown in such films 'is not made "better" with explanations and justifications; even if it offers a context, evokes the roots of a certain violence, it is a horror that denies the kind of functional-moral use that customarily befalls it in mainstream narratives'.[22] Beugnet is here suggesting that excessive material in a film can go so far as to negate its normal function and use, and this is what I mean by the idea that the scene in the underpass exceeds its narrative function: rather than being a piece in the narrative's larger chain, it seems instead to dismiss that chain as irrelevant. As for its 'moral' use, here too the violence seems beyond a rationale or explanation. Beugnet is touching on a key reason for so many varied responses to the film, and this is that the scene in the underpass renders null common ways of responding to violence in film, such as by appeal to its putative 'functional-moral use'. What this nexus of ideas from Grønstad, Bayon, and Beugnet gives us to think is that what, from a formal point of view, may be an apparently simple shot can have excessive effects and be obscene or unwatchable. In fact, it may be the case that this excess is actually a factor of that very simplicity, that — much as in the long takes of the previous chapter — these two poles are intimately related such that spareness has a way of translating itself into affective power, into fascination.

The question is not whether we are moved to reflection or sentimentality, or even particularly a question of the status of this suffering as fictional. As Libby Saxton argues, the scopic relationship one has with suffering onscreen is inherently ethically implicated whether or not it is real or artificial suffering (without of course creating an equivalence).[23] Perversely, and because of this, the scene is a moment of mimetic paradox par excellence. As a representation, what 'is happening' is of course not happening, but in appropriating the stylistic form of the long take, in its association with forms of unmediated record (one might suggest surveillance footage), there is a suggestion that it *is*. And therein is underscored the obscenity of it, that, as stated above, what we are seeing should not be looked at and yet offers the imperative that we *must*. Sex scenes in film typically involve close-ups of the face and frequent cuts for the purpose of the maintenance of the illusion that on the screen are real lovers and to sketch an emotional dimension, whereas those in pornographic films typically eschew these for voyeuristic effect, to exhibit precisely the fact that what is being shown is actually happening. Monica Bellucci is not raped in *Irréversible*, but an effort is made to show what it would look like if she were, and — this is the point — less for the purpose of the narrative than to show it for its own sake. It becomes a spectacle, like the landscapes of the previous chapter. This is what is fascinating. In Blanchot's quasi-phenomenological language, what is appearing is disappearance. It is this tension which creates the effect of unreality and the opening onto the imaginary. We can say in Blanchot's terms that this scene opens up a *strangeness*, a strangeness that is not simply a matter of distance or separation, but an *interruption* (*EI* 97; *IC* 68). With regard to the protraction of the scene, we are in a domain where, as we saw in Chapter 1, the image opens onto absence, onto the absence of the world (*EL* 25; *SL* 33).

There are several points to be made here, several aspects that must be distinctly enumerated to make clear why this scene bears such extended analysis. The simplest distinction might be to say that on the one hand we are technically interested in the precise effects of the length of the take, and on the other we need to address more rigorously the problem of what it is a take of, of what is onscreen.

The first point we have just intimated, but it needs a little more theoretical fleshing out. What we are particularly interested in is how, as a factor of protraction, the scene itself seems uncannily to withdraw from itself. We might say that this scene, in spite of — or because of? — its sheer 'visibility', brings out the failure of vision to capture the phenomenon of violence. This ambiguity is significant. The paradox is that even when presented with the most provocative imagery, imagery that aspires to be as 'real' as possible, the scene itself becomes image, unreal. Protraction, which asserts the unmediated 'reality' effect as discussed, is here attended by the suspension of ordinary relations of viewing, understood as spectatorial absorption in the flow of the narrative. To pick up on some key references from the previous chapter, we can say that in this scene, as discussed vis-à-vis Pasolini, the long take reproduces a meaningless present whose expression comes only with the cut. As in Lyotard's essay on sovereign film, there is a sense here that the camera is an absent gaze onto the ontological real. It is as if the darkness of the tunnel behind the actors seems to want to swallow them up.

Thomas Carl Wall uses the example of professional wrestling to describe how fascination with the Other can lead to the Other becoming a spectacle, 'a reality made up of nothingness'. In professional wrestling, the spectacle arises from 'the draining away of all "real" wrestling and competition'.[24] It is in a similar fashion that Bellucci seems to disappear into the scene, which is to say she becomes anonymous — not her sophisticated character with whom one might identify, not herself the famous actress, but simply a woman screaming, fragmented from the narrative, exposed, and become image. She is in a sense 'beside herself' for this extended duration, 'out of sync', a product of fascination, and this is why we must talk of the reverse of theories of spectatorial identification.

The psychoanalytic account of cinema given by Christian Metz, briefly discussed in Chapter 1, is relevant here in being an important statement of the idea of identification in film. In Metz's well-known account, when watching a film the spectator '*s'identifie à lui-même*, à lui-même comme pur acte de perception [...] comme une sorte de sujet transcendantal' ('*identifies with himself*, with himself as a pure act of perception [...] as a kind of transcendental subject').[25] This is what Metz calls 'l'identification cinématographique primaire' ('primary cinematic identification'), while identification with diegetic characters in a film, especially the direction of their looks, is secondary.[26] The identification at work is in the first place reminiscent of that which takes place during Lacan's mirror stage, with the difference that during the mirror stage the subject identifies with something *seen*, while in cinema that subject identifies with something *seeing*.[27] I am suggesting, however, that fascination involves the possibility that even Metz's primary cinematic identification may be broken, at least momentarily.[28] Blanchot writes of the effect of separation, in which the self becomes a kind of Other, as '*me désidentifiant*, m'abandonnant à une passivité' (*ED* 36, my emphasis) ('*dis-identifying me*, abandoning me to passivity', *WD* 19). This is an example where Blanchot's terms should be taken in a strong sense, to return to an idea introduced in Chapter 1.

In an essay on Bertolt Brecht that is not often discussed, 'L'Effet d'étrangeté' [The Effect of Strangeness] (1957), Blanchot discusses the Brechtian alienation effect in terms of fascination (Blanchot's title translates the German *Verfremdungseffekt*). Blanchot posits that Brecht tries to manipulate the imaginary as such, which is at work in the theatre and in life. Brecht wants to use theatre to break not only the fascination of the theatre but also 'la fascination du quotidien' (*EI* 535) ('the fascination of the everyday', *IC* 365). Blanchot argues that Brecht seeks to make the distance between spectacle and spectator 'maniable et disponible' (*EI* 537) ('workable and available', *IC* 366). There is thus 'une "bonne" et une "mauvaise" étrangeté' (*EI* 536) ('a 'good' strangeness and a 'bad' strangeness', *IC* 366). The first is the distance at work in making the object present for us and available in its absence; in other words, the work of the negative. The second is the reversal of the first, and is the basis of art. It is when 'l'image n'est plus ce qui nous permet de tenir l'objet absent, mais ce qui nous tient par l'absence même' ('the image is no longer what allows us to have the object as absent but is rather what takes hold of us by absence itself'); it is where the image 's'ouvre sur un espace neutre où nous ne pouvons plus agir, et nous ouvre, nous aussi, sur une sorte de neutralité où nous cessons d'être nous-mêmes et oscillons étrangement entre Je, Il et personne' (*EI* 536–37) ('opens onto a neutral space where we can no longer act, and also opens us upon a sort of neutrality where we cease being ourselves and oscillate strangely between I, He, and no one', *IC* 366). Blanchot is effectively recapitulating the two versions of the imaginary, but this reiteration fleshes out the dispersal of the subject at work in this. Blanchot's critique of Brecht is that, in seeking to set the spectator apart from the spectacle, he is at risk of adding to 'le pouvoir fascinant du spectacle' (*EI* 536) ('the spectacle's fascinating power', *IC* 365) for that power is in the first instance based on separation and distance.

To take this idea of the image seriously means reading Metz critically on the subject of identification. While it may be less contentious to argue that layers of Metz's secondary identification are peeled away in this scene (as I argued of Bellucci above), to say that primary identification is also undermined is more radical. The disidentification discussed in Blanchot's reading of Brecht points to the situation of the theatre (and the cinema) as one in which the subject is denatured. In this sense, referring back to the idea of a passive spectator raised in Chapter 2 by Richard Rushton, we are dealing here with a spectator more passive than passive. All we see is 'what there is', the filmic materials of the two actors. This, I will come to argue, in part explains the ambivalence aroused by the film under discussion.

The question of the length of the long take is ultimately one that cannot be measured in seconds and minutes. Blanchot asks in *L'Instant de ma mort*: 'En réalité, combien de temps s'était-il écoulé?' (*ID* 6) ('In reality, how much time had elapsed?', *ID* 7). The answer is that, like the exposure opened by Giacometti's sculpture, it is consumed in an instant (*A* 248; *F* 219). When Blanchot argues that the fascinated gaze exists in an *absence de temps*, this effectively refers to a time in which 'nothing' happens: 'ce qui apparaît, c'est le fait que rien n'apparaît' (*EL* 21) ('what appears is the fact that nothing appears', *SL* 30). This may seem an unusual way to describe the phenomenology of cinema, and insensitive when dealing with a scene featuring rape, but during this extended long take there is a sense of the spectator's exhaustion, to follow Bayon's reading. The correlative is that 'chaque chose se retire en son image et que le "Je" que nous sommes se reconnaît en s'abîmant dans la neutralité d'un "Il" sans figure' (*EL* 20–21) ('each thing withdraws into its image while the "I" that we are recognizes itself by sinking into the neutrality of a featureless third person', *SL* 30). Although the long take can bring about the experience of duration, much in the manner in which Noé wants to show how long a rape actually lasts, when it engenders fascination it abolishes that sense of time and opens the horizon of *l'absence de temps*, like the waiting of the previous chapter.

At the start of the sequence-shot the focus remains shallow, fixed on following Alex as she walks a few paces ahead of the camera, but in the underpass depth of field stretches out before us as we can see down to the end of the tunnel. (The only moment in which the camera is not completely trained on the body of Alex is as she descends, when the camera, still following her, tilts upwards briefly to register the sign above the underpass which reads, illuminated by red light, 'PASSAGE'.)

Above, the world in which Alex moves is a three-dimensional space in which the camera can, following her, turn three hundred and sixty degrees; underground, she moves only onward, forwards through a narrow space. Here, space emerges as a presence in the form of a one-dimensional distance, a paradoxical distance that is, in closing in on her, coming towards her as she moves through it. When the rape occurs, the camera is lowered and reframes to follow the attack, slightly panning to the left. This creates a composition in which the assault occupies the foreground while the end of the tunnel can be seen forming a square to the right. (See Figure 4.1.) So while the camera began moving directly forwards down the tunnel, at this point it is fixed such as to compose the space of the tunnel diagonally, as directed to the right of the screen. This serves to effect a change from the continuous depth of space, as Alex initially moves through the tunnel in this sequence, to a flattened image, in which the end of the tunnel appears side by side, rather than behind, the assault. This flattening creates an impression of encroaching space and depthlessness, which is proximal.

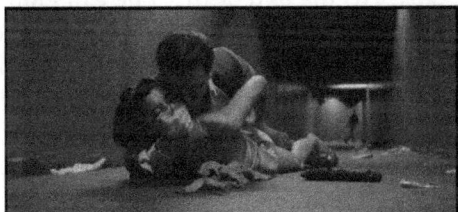

FIG. 4.1.

The cinematography and the Super 16mm film stock brings out the richness of the red walls of the underpass, a bloody, infernal tint reminiscent of the paintings of Francis Bacon.[29] Consonant with the spatial construction discussed above, the *mise en scène* of the underpass, with flickering lights on the ceiling of the tunnel, emerges as angular. Above ground the nocturnal Parisian air of passing cars is anonymous and distant, while in the underpass the space encroaches. While the redness may carry schematic or symbolic associations, its primary weight lies in its affective rawness, not as a bearer of meaning, but as something that bypasses meaning for affect. The redness functions, along with the reduction from three-dimensional space described above, to contribute to the sense of an abstraction of space. Ropars-Wuilleumier writes: 'L'espace ne se perçoit pas, sauf en cela qu'il inquiète ou qu'il brise le rapport entre la forme et la figurabilité' [Space cannot be perceived in itself, except insofar as it disturbs or breaks the relation between form and figurability].[30] What is developed here under the name of abstraction, Ropars-Wuilleumier might call the appearance of space as such.

Taken along with the duration of the long take, which abstracts itself from normal presentations of time in film, we are left with the two characters in an abstracted realm, two characters who are no longer characters but 'figures' present for a moment outside of the narrative, within a self-enclosed spectacle in a depthless place. This seems to me to be very close in effect to Deleuze's description, in his reading of Bacon, of the 'figural'. Beugnet suggests the relevance of the figural to her account of a 'cinema of sensation', writing that 'Deleuze's analysis seems equally, *if not more*, applicable to the medium of moving images because film is, first and foremost, a medium of time and change, where image and sound are in constant mutation'.³¹ Describing Bacon's techniques for isolating figures within his paintings, Deleuze writes that when it is isolated, the 'Figure' becomes 'une Image, une Icône' ('an Image, an Icon').³² The abstraction and isolation can be thought of as a work of exposure, exposing the assault. The build-up to the assault withdraws from immediate pertinence as we are simply left with the fact of the physical conflagration.

What we are exposed to is the representation of sexual violence in the abstract. How is one supposed to react to it? An effect of the duration is to allow time for what is happening to sink in. It is first viscerally offensive, before becoming psychologically disturbing. To try to think about what is happening in this scene is to come up against something that is sufficiently horrendous as to be almost, in a strong sense, unthinkable. To the extent that one can empathize or identify with the suffering, that identification can only be thrown back to one's own experiences and fears, one's own personal humiliation and pain at the hands of the cruel other, one's worst anxieties of physical violence and dissolution, *horror vacui*. Horror to which no theodicy would extend.

So much of Blanchot's work reflects on this essential experience. Art refers us to a fundamental anxiety. What Blanchot's writing offers us — in both the fiction and the critical writing — is something like an account *coming from within* this angst, this state of dissolution. As Blanchot puts it, in terms that are disarming by their apparent simplicity: it is through 'l'effroi' ('fright') that we are thrown from ourselves and experience the outside 'sous l'espèce de l'effrayant' ('in the guise of the frightening') (*EI* 70; *IC* 49). 'Peur' ('fear') in this text has a close relation to 'angoisse' ('anguish') (*EI* 70; *IC* 49). It is in such states that we have a sense of the Other, which 'nous ébranle, nous ravit, nous enlevant à nous-mêmes' (*EI* 72) ('seizes us, staggers and ravishes us, carrying us away from ourselves', *IC* 51). Looking back to the discussion of angst in Chapter 1, we can see how states of fear give way to an encounter with the Other qua Otherness.³³

One question of the assault's *mise en scène* is the idea of 'contingency'. In the case of *Irréversible* it can be said without ambiguity that the director felt it necessary to actually insert — artificially — an element of the apparently contingent into the scene in the underpass. Noé's visual effects supervisor, Rodolphe Chabrier, explains that although the scene in the underpass looks digitally untouched, in contrast to much of the rest of the film, there are in fact significant interpolations.³⁴ Firstly, the rapist's penis is a digitally added 3D CGI manipulation. Secondly, and more significantly, the passer-by who, halfway through the ordeal, appears at the end of the tunnel, takes one look and walks the other way, is also a digital addition. Noé was dissatisfied with the extra's performance in the cut in the film, so it — the square in the right of the screen — was excised and replaced with another take. The rape and the appearance of the bystander are taken from separate takes and morphed together. This is significant for more than simply technical reasons. The scene depends, as I have mentioned, for its effect on its apparent authenticity and immediacy, and this phantom bystander compromises the integrity of this take. Unlike the long takes of the previous chapter, chance is here artificially introduced. Of course as fiction the scene is not real, but the effect of the digital interpolations is to compound and confirm this imaginary quality. The sequence is not only phenomenologically haunted by absence, but, by virtue of the digital constitution of this spectral passer-by, absence is introduced into the sequence's very ontology.

The Face and the Faceless: Between Levinas and Blanchot

The other moment of extreme violence in *Irréversible* is the sequence at the beginning of the film in which a fight breaks out in the Rectum nightclub and Pierre smashes Marcus's assailant's face with a fire extinguisher. While what was so distressing about the scene in the underpass was the suffering of Bellucci's character, the cry of the tortured face, here it is the representation of the deforming effects of facial injury. Structurally this sequence is comparable with the rape in the sense that the violence is so spectacular that it brings about a halt to the preceding imbroglio. The anonymous figure assaulting Marcus — in fact attempting to rape him — is being cheered on by those present in the nightclub and the camera feverishly flies around this happening, but when Pierre in turn bludgeons him there is an abrupt change and the onlookers are stunned, the camera correspondingly following each blow as it clangs down. The handheld camerawork follows Marcus initially as he is on the ground, briefly framing him in a way comparable to Alex during the underpass scene, but when Pierre lands the first blow on his attacker the camera then follows the attacker, knocked to the ground and laid out. The gravitational axis shifts by ninety degrees, such that the camera's perspective is that of one lying next to the attacker. In just over a minute Pierre lands twenty-two blows. This is evidently another instance in which an assault is drawn out almost interminably to make both viewers and the event's diegetic onlookers within the sequence as uncomfortable with the violence as possible.

The face that appears onscreen being attacked is a composite of an actual latex head filled with false blood, receiving physical blows, digitally superimposed with a 3D rotoscopic face, the actor's face and progressively more gruesome matte injury effects.[35] Again I want to make not a technical point but a theoretical one. I am not drawing attention simply to the fact that the violence is a representation, a special effect, unreal — that is obvious — but to the way that the camera lingers on and is fixated by this brutality seemingly insofar as it is unreal. It is as if the multiple layering of digital artifice that constitutes the smashed face, and which becomes more and more palpably artificial with each impact, at some point becomes coterminous with the violence. The camera itself observes the violence in the manner of a fascinated gaze. Part of the reason for the fascination is that just as the destruction meted out seems never to satisfy the destroyer, so does the camera never seem to capture a final annihilation — the face can never be smashed enough. The parallel is that just as the film seeks to show that which is 'unwatchable' (to borrow Grønstad's term), so, as Levinas writes, does hatred seek to 'saisir l'insaisissable' ('grasp the ungraspable').[36] To rephrase that slightly, the scene is not just exemplary for showing the 'unwatchable', but also because that 'unwatchable' becomes conflated with 'l'insaisissable'. The suffering is the unwatchable, the violence is the ungraspable. It is this excessiveness that is crucial and it is in this way that Blanchot writes that:

> La présence échappe au pouvoir qui fait violence. La présence, face à la destruction qui veut l'atteindre, disparaît, mais reste intacte, se retirant dans la nullité où elle se dissipe sans laisser de traces [...] A l'expérience de la violence répond l'évidence de la présence qui lui échappe. (A 247)
>
> [Presence always escapes the power that does violence. Presence, in face of the destruction that wants to reach it, disappears but remains intact, withdrawing into nullity, where it is dissipated without leaving any trace [...] To the experience of violence there corresponds the evidence of the presence that escapes it.] (F 218)

Just as violence always fails in its aim, so the violence cannot be fully represented or grasped. Blanchot writes these lines in the context of a piece on Giacometti, and they form a brief aside on the 'cruelty' of the celebrated sculptor. What we should take from them is that violence always fails in its aim. This is not to say that art is a form of violence or hatred, but to note that both are in some sense tormented by that which escapes all mastery. It is for this reason that violence cannot be fully represented (perhaps in order to be denounced). The significance of the film's fixation on the violence is that both the vengeful Pierre smashing the face and the camera itself recording it are tormented by the ungraspable quality of the imaginary — as if excess, whether perpetrated or witnessed, could never be excessive enough. This is dramatized in *Irréversible* when, after the violence to the face is complete, the camera passes by Le Ténia, an onlooker to this scene and the one for whom the violence was intended, as he gazes, himself fascinated, from the brutalized face to Pierre. The face is almost no longer recognizably a face, yet still its ruined anonymous look has a kind of insistence, and that presence can be understood as a result of how 'La fascination est fondamentalement liée à la présence neutre, impersonnelle, le On indéterminé, l'immense Quelqu'un sans figure' (*EL* 24) ('Fascination is fundamentally linked to neutral, impersonal presence, to the indeterminate They, the immense, faceless Someone', *SL* 33). The facelessness of this Someone, this *Other*, seems to me to be precisely what these bloodied and unreal, digitally manufactured faces evoke.

The face is for Levinas the pre-eminent talisman of the Other. For Levinas, the Other is frequently figured by the weak and those in need of help. Recurring figures of the Other in his work include orphans, widows, strangers. With this Other, one is in a relation of responsibility. Levinas conceives the relation to the Other as a relation beyond power or possibility and beyond being or non-being. This pre-original and essentially ethical relation in fact structures subjectivity itself, such that a relation to the Other always comes before the Self. It is in this way that Levinas can write of 'la conjoncture Moi-Autrui' ('the I-Other conjuncture') and 'l'*orientation* inévitable de l'être "à partir de soi" vers "Autrui"' ('the inevitable *orientation* of being "starting from oneself" toward "the Other"'). The priority of this, Levinas indicates, is essential to the understanding of his text.[37] If *Totalité et infini* [Totality and Infinity] (1961) can be said to concern the structure of the relation to the Other, then *Autrement qu'être* [Otherwise than Being] (1974) concerns subjectivity itself, structured as responsibility for the Other. In this way the relation with the Other is always implicated and intricated in the structure of subjectivity and vice versa. When we discuss Blanchot's commentaries on these texts, we are primarily referring to three dialogues in *L'Entretien infini*: 'Connaissance de l'inconnu' [Knowledge of the Unknown], 'Tenir parole' [Keeping to Words], and 'Le Rapport du troisième genre (homme sans horizon)' [The Relation of the Third Kind: *Man without horizon*], all of which were originally published in *La Nouvelle Revue française* 1961–62 and *L'Écriture du désastre* respectively.

Although Blanchot is very close to Levinas in much of his writing and indeed could be said to effectively derive many of his notions from him, he departs from Levinas when the latter turns explicitly in the direction of the ethical. While for Levinas the relation with the Other is first and foremost an ethical one defined in terms of an obligation to the Other, Blanchot defines it in terms of its neutrality and impossibility, often placing the stress on the encumbering effect of the Other on myself and how this in itself opens the way to a relation to the Outside. Leslie Hill writes that Levinas's description in *Totalité et infini* of 'the relation of non-relation that obtains between the Same and the Other thus provides Blanchot with the means of re-inventing or re-articulating as the question of the Other the question of the impossibility of dying that is so crucial in his earlier work'. This is to say that Blanchot's reading of Levinas is an ongoing, occasionally sceptical one; a kind of 'unfaithful fidelity'.[38] The danger in interpretation here is that identified by Joseph Libertson: 'Many Blanchotian contexts, including the approach to the sirens, the approach to Eurydice, the fascination of the image, etc., lend themselves to a hasty dialectical reading which opposes the transitivity of consciousness or action to the escape of the absolutely other'.[39] What Libertson finds as a potential weakness in Blanchot's writing is equally by mirror image a potential flaw in reading Blanchot. In other words, while Libertson is wary that a dualistic structure can be detected in Blanchot's writing, we must be wary of falling into reading one into it.

To draw a distinction, we might say that Blanchot meditates on the unfathomability of the gap between myself and the Other at the expense of considering the impossible obligation to cross it. The quotation above also shows that Blanchot's language suggests an intimacy between violence itself and the Outside. It is at this point of departure from Levinas that Blanchot produces his original reading of the relation to the Other. Sometimes it seems that the Other is primarily of importance as a cipher of the Outside, while in the late texts it is in fact the relation with the Other that is of the essence, albeit crucially to be understood as conditioned by this connection to the Outside. These are different modalities of the same problem at the heart of Blanchot's entire *oeuvre*: the relation to alterity as such, whether opened by writing, art, the Other, or any other means. Perhaps the simplest formulation of the difference between Levinas and Blanchot is to be found in the following rhetorical question from Simon Critchley: 'Could one [...] accept Levinas's quasi-phenomenological descriptions of radical alterity whilst suspending or bracketing out their ethico-metaphysical consequences?'[40] It is precisely this neutrality that Blanchot places at the centre of his reading, at the expense of the ethical, that marks the crucial difference between his writings and those of Levinas. It is this difference that I will argue is useful when interpreting a film such as *Irréversible*, and the distance or 'remoteness' opened up in the underpass scene. By extension, it is this that would distinguish a reading of film based on his writings from the established precedent set by Levinasian scholars.

For Levinas, the relation between myself and the Other is strictly non-reversible. The word Levinas has for this is 'illéité', from the French *il*, meaning that the 'you' is not the simple reverse of the 'I'. The reason for this is that the notion of the command or appeal of the Other can only stand on the basis that the Other is not derived from the self. The Other cannot be recuperated within a dialectical logic as the mirror image of the self. The movement of 'illeity' named as God requires this irreversibility as a structural condition of subjectivity itself. I will return to the thematic of reversibility, but for now it suffices to observe that, while Levinas writes in *Totalité et infini* of an asymmetry between the Same and Other, Blanchot's relation is neutral and is described as a 'double dissymétrie' (*EI* 100; *IC* 70–71). In Blanchot's work, the relation takes the form of an interval belonging neither to being nor non-being, a space in which the distance from me to the Other is not the same as the Other to me. Blanchot multiplies the Otherness of the Other. This is a counter-intuitive idea. Blanchot comes to the lines quoted above by considering how, in contrast to the relation of myself to the Other, in which the Other is effectively a holy figure — described in an earlier text as the 'Très Haut' (*EI* 77) ('Most High', *IC* 54)[41] — in the relation of the Other to me, '*tout semble se retourner*' (my emphasis) ('*everything seems to reverse itself*'). When this happens, the Self is denatured and becomes a kind of Other itself. This, Blanchot writes, 'me sépare de moi, comme si la séparation (qui mesurait la transcendance de moi à Autrui) faisait son œuvre en moi-même, me désidentifiant, m'abandonnant à une passivité, sans initiative et sans présent' (*ED* 36) ('separates me from myself — as if separation (which measured the transcendence from me to the Other) did its work within me, dis-identifying me, abandoning me to passivity, leaving me without any initiative and bereft of present', *WD* 19). Levinas talks of the Other in the same, Blanchot talks of the Other in place of the I. This is how one should understand the notion of 'substitution', which is the core concept of *Autrement qu'être*. This is also how we should understand one of the very first lines of *L'Écriture du désastre*: '"je" ne suis pas sous sa menace [...] le désastre me menace qu'il menace en moi ce qui est hors de moi, un autre que moi qui deviens passivement autre' (*ED* 7) ('"I" am not threatened [...] the disaster threatens in me that which is exterior to me — an other than I who passively become other', *WD* 1). Blanchot's references to the self always imply that to be a self is to be a same, but the point is that there is no same, no identity except through relation to otherness. In *L'Écriture du désastre*, this

Otherness is conceived of as disastrous, for it means that there can be 'no identity, in other words, save by virtue of its ruination'.⁴² Another way of saying this would be that the same is always compromised by alterity. It is therefore that the Other becomes this tormentor figure who robs me of my identity, even an enemy (a term that seems inimical to Levinas). Although Levinas repeatedly writes in *Autrement qu'être* that the figure of being held hostage is an authentic expression of the bondage of responsibility to the Other, the bondage implied in this figure is a formal one in which the 'I' has no initiative and does not actively engage.⁴³ As we shall see, there is a reversibility here in which what is essentially a formal, metaphysical relation is dramatized in striking terms as sadomasochistic. Even in his abstraction Blanchot brings a visceral tone to his description of the Other. One might suggest that this is only natural in a text which deals with the concentration camps, but more fundamentally the point could be made that just as Blanchot arguably bases his metaphysics in aesthetics (as opposed to ontology or ethics), so what we might identify as 'concepts' in his writing seem frequently to be derived from the vividness of the terms in which they are described. This is one of the driving paradoxes of his work.

This is not to say that the idea of violence is absent from Levinas's philosophy. Levinas discusses the problem of violence and hatred in *Totalité et infini*. Hatred is that which 'cherche à saisir l'insaisissable, à humilier, de très haut, à travers la souffrance où autrui existe comme pure passivité' ('which seeks to grasp the ungraspable, to humiliate, from on high, through the suffering in which the Other exists as pure passivity').⁴⁴ This seems to be clear from the treatment of suffering, where Levinas writes: 'Dans la peur, la mort est encore future, à distance de nous; la souffrance, par contre, réalise dans la volonté la proximité extrême de l'être menaçant la volonté' ('In fear death is yet future, at a distance from us; whereas suffering realizes in the will the extreme proximity of the being menacing the will').⁴⁵ This is to say there is something like a temporal ambiguity in the moment of suffering. It is locked in a present that is impossible to flee and is thus protracted, and yet for consciousness the pain is nevertheless always still to come. It is an ambiguity matched by the paradox of the desire of the one who hates, who simultaneously in his abuse seeks to turn the victim into an object while also requiring that they bear witness to the cruelty, that their subjectivity is in fact elevated and maintained.

For Wall, what unites Levinas and Blanchot is the phenomenological mode of passivity, and it is to this end that the Levinasian *visage* is closely related to the image in Blanchot. In *Autrement qu'être*, passivity refers to the relation with the Other, an assignation prior to subjectivity that defines the subject by vulnerability and exposure. What is crucial is that it is also a term used by Blanchot to define the relation with the image, a relation in which one can have no agency. Wall conceives a synthesis of their ideas which renders each mutually comprehensible. In Wall's thesis, the 'aesthetic distance or Orphic glance' in Blanchot *is* what in Levinas is identified as an 'infinite responsibility, or even an uncontrollable compulsion to be for-the-other, which can never be satisfied or used up'. What conditions passivity is perspective, and it is the possibility of regarding the world or another person 'from the impossible perspective of an infinite distance, or a glacial remoteness, [that] is at the heart of Blanchot's *récits* and his writings on aesthetics, and it is also the kernel of Levinas's *éthique*'. It is thus that Wall suggests 'we might just as well grow accustomed to calling [this ethics] "imaginary" in Blanchot's sense, because it is an ethics that resists personal and familiar form'.[46] The significance of this is of course that it implies a mutual neutrality of ethics and aesthetics.

This connection between ethics and aesthetics is suggestive for thinking about how one might approach film, given the scholarship on Levinas and his relation to film. Sarah Cooper's commentary on the place of the *visage* in film is instructive here, especially in its focus on the limit of the phenomenal. The face of the Other, in Levinas's terms, does not mean — or at least cannot be limited to — actual or represented faces of individual human beings. It is a transcendent notion, and it must be borne in mind that vision is not for Levinas a relation of transcendence.[47] The encounter with Otherness is transcendent, and for Cooper film can open a space for such an encounter with alterity. It is precisely this gap between the film image, insofar as visible and phenomenologically palpable, and what escapes it that is at the heart of fascination in film. Cooper writes of a 'space of responsibility' as 'the difference between an excess of the image that we cannot know, and what we actually perceive,' and this cuts to the core of our concerns.[48] The word 'responsibility' in this context names the encounter with transcendent alterity. But while Cooper identifies in film the possibility of this call to responsibility, what I am identifying in the context of Blanchot is not such a call but the opening of the imaginary, in which one encounters the image and is fascinated. What Blanchot calls 'l'espace littéraire' or 'l'espace d'art' refers to a space in which the reading subject, or the subject contemplating, for example, a sculpture, is put into question by the work, and something similar can by extension be said to happen in film, much as Cooper argues in a Levinasian register. *Irréversible* does not put us 'face to face' with the Other in the Levinasian sense, but to the extent that we understand the Other to be the 'Quelqu'un sans figure', defined by strangeness (which is to say as being Outside), then it opens what we might in a Blanchotian manner call a 'space of neutrality'.

In an exchange between two interlocutors on Robert Antelme's *L'Espèce humaine* [The Human Race] (1947), his account of surviving the ordeal of the concentration camps, Blanchot provides something like an aphorism: 'L'homme est l'indestructible qui peut être détruit' (*EI* 192) ('Man is the indestructible that can be destroyed', *IC* 130).[49] In one sense, this is to say man as the Other qua presence remains even in death. Murder, in the emblematic case of Cain and Abel, is read as an attempt to react to the transcendence of the Other with the transcendence of murder. And as this necessarily fails — murder can never fully extinguish what it seeks to destroy — so there is no chance of relief from what Levinas calls 'responsibility'. To which one of the interlocutors responds: 'Comme si, plus terrible que l'universel désastre, était en l'homme l'inexorable affirmation qui toujours le maintient debout' (*EI* 192) ('As though the inexorable affirmation in man that always keeps him standing were more terrible than universal disaster', *IC* 130). This final term of course anticipates the later usage in the eponymous fragmentary text and demonstrates a certain thematic continuity between where Blanchot seeks to push the Levinas of *Totalité et infini* and where he will later ally the meditations on *Autrement qu'être* with those on the Holocaust.

When we say that the underpass scene seems to withdraw from itself, this is to be understood in the same way that affliction is described in the Antelme piece as a situation that tends to 'se désituer' (*EI* 194) ('de-situate itself', *IC* 132). Underlying this is the idea that the indestructible is the neuter. Extreme screen violence seems to gesture towards the fact that beneath it there lies this neutrality. In terms of the films associated with the 'new extremism', an argument can be made that what links so many otherwise diverse films in their myriad violent and excessive stylistic gestures and all manner of depictions of violence is the desire to get to what is, as it were, behind the screen, to bring out the imaginary quality that remains in spite of all and engenders fascination. To say these films are concerned with the unrepresentable is not very original, but to posit Blanchot's value here is to bring out what is at stake in this concern, how it is reflective of mimetic procedures in general. To be more explicit, this is to say that what is indestructible is the imaginary. In Chapter 1 we saw how, in Blanchot's argument, the tool, when damaged, is said to become its image. As Beugnet argues that the violence cannot be recovered by appeal to a 'functional-moral use', so here Blanchot describes how it is only by absenting itself from use that the image emerges. Blanchot continues by arguing: 'La catégorie de l'art est liée à cette possibilité pour les objets d'"apparaître", c'est-à-dire de s'abandonner à la pure et simple ressemblance derrière laquelle il n'y a rien — que l'être' (*EL* 271) ('the category of art is linked to this possibility for objects to "appear," to surrender, that is, to the pure and simple resemblance behind which there is nothing — but being', *SL* 259). Many studies of Noé are concerned either to justify or indict the violence, but in both cases overlook the strange work in which the violence 'appears' in Blanchot's sense above. The emphasis Blanchot gives to the word *apparaître* indicates the uncanniness of this event. The reason why this phenomenon might be considered alarming is that, while earlier in this chapter we observed that the violence was not abstract but visceral, we find now that the violence *does* abstract itself in its representation. The categories have shifted from their concrete, everyday usage to take on a new appearance. This goes back to Levinas's remarks in *De l'existence à l'existant*, in which art is rigorously described as essentially an operation of abstraction.[50]

All of this has troubling implications for a theory of spectatorship, for it is to this extent that when Grønstad says that these images put the subjectivity of their viewers at risk, he is more radically correct than the terms of his own argument permit. The opposition sketched above with which we would have liked to classify this scene from *Irréversible*, between the responses to the long take of boredom and of horror, of a lapse in focus, and of recoiling, is of course too straightforward. 'Subjectivity' can be understood in the more specific — (post-)phenomenological — sense than that implied by Grønstad, as in Levinas's account of how the encounter with the Other reveals the ontological priority of the Other and dissolves subjectivity into passivity.

This is troubling because, as we have seen, one of the chief ways in which one might seek to 'rehabilitate' or mitigate the offensiveness of a film like that of Noé is to demonstrate that it has some, for want of a better phrase, moral value. 'The screening of the unwatchable,' writes Grønstad, 'enacts a process of decommodification — of the body, of sexuality, even of aesthetic experience itself — out of which emerges an optical ethics for a renewed humanism'.[51] But as Blanchot never ceases to elaborate, art is in fact inhuman. It is linked to the imaginary and to neutrality and cannot be co-opted for humanist ends; rather than engaging subjectivity, it is rendered passive. *Irréversible* could hardly be further from the notion of a 'moral film', as mentioned with reference to Ebert at the beginning of this chapter, in which there could be anything resembling a practical ethical impetus resulting from its viewing. If we say that what happens in *Irréversible* is not spectatorial identification, this voids such arguments that would redeem films associated with the 'new extremism' by virtue of a putative empathetic response with characters suffering affliction. If we characterize the effect of the 'unwatchable' parts of *Irréversible* on spectatorship as that of fascination, then the model of spectatorship arrived at is one of a shorn and passive subject. If this can be called a 'process of decommodification', it is also one of metaphysical disintegration.

Irreversibility and *L'Écriture du désastre*

We must return to the theme of time and ask where this leaves the film's reverse chronology. To restate the question: what is it that is 'irreversible? Mary Ann Doane argues that the development of cinema was interrelated with the changes in scientific knowledge of the world in the nineteenth century, notably in the fields of evolutionary biology and physics. She points to how cinema as an apparatus can be conceived as the 'mechanical incarnation of irreversibility'.[52] More generally she demonstrates that irreversibility as a conceptualization of temporality is historically connected to the development of thermodynamics. The second law of thermodynamics states that, within a closed system, heat always dissipates towards cooler objects. This process is known as entropy, and from it follows the idea of the 'heat death' of the universe (the universe being itself a closed system). Crucially, this process cannot be reversed. This gives rise to the conception in physics of an 'arrow of time', the idea that time goes in a particular direction.[53] Doane notes that film has often been used as an example to make clear how this temporal directionality works: 'Film has become the privileged illustration of irreversibility in so many physics textbooks because its history in its mainstream forms so readily allies it with referentiality, realism, and an associated idea of "common sense," or the probable/plausible'.[54] Films always move forward, and even when they make use of repetition or run backwards, such experiments are predicated on the principle of irreversibility. Thus Ropars-Wuilleumier writes in a different context: 'Le plaisir filmique tient donc moins à l'irréversibilité du mécanisme, qu'au paradoxe d'une réversibilité dont la simulation accroît et dérobe en même temps l'irréversibilité' [The pleasure of film stems less from the irreversibility of the mechanism than from the paradox of a reversibility whose simulation augments at the same time as it conceals irreversibility].⁵⁵ *Irréversible* would be a case in point: even if the sequences are in reverse order in terms of the overall diegesis, the sequences themselves play out in the normal direction of time.

It is notable that the word *irréversible* comes up frequently in the writings of Blanchot and Levinas, particularly in relation to the Other. Levinas describes the obsession with the Other as an 'affection à sens unique irréversible comme la diachronie du temps qui coule entre les doigts de Mnémosyne' ('a one-way irreversible being affected, like the diachrony of time that flows between the fingers of Mnemosyne').⁵⁶ Diachrony is opposed to synchronic, linear time and is Levinas's term for the way in which the moment of the call of the Other is of a time antecedent to that of ordinary consciousness, such that consciousness is always marked by or even held by a kind of ur-instant and can never fully coincide with itself. Irreversibility is here another marker of the inaccessible, the infinitely anterior moment. Levinas concludes: 'Ne pas s'en aller en relations qui se retournent — l'irréversibilité — c'est la "subjectité" du sujet, *universel*' ('Not to turn into relations that reverse, irreversibility, is the universal subjectness of the subject').⁵⁷ What these quotations show is that Levinas uses the word *irréversible* to characterize both subjectivity and temporality. He writes furthermore: 'La transcendance de l'Infini est un écart irréversible par rapport au présent, comme celui d'un passé qui ne fut jamais présent' ('The transcendence of the Infinite is an irreversible divergency from the present, like that of a past that was never present').⁵⁸ The notion of responsibility as coming from a past that was never present is one that Levinas will frequently articulate. This is of course another way of saying that the temporality of the Other is outside of being, and that the call of the Other is a call from beyond. Irreversibility, then, characterizes the mode of that which is otherwise than being. This term is evidently a key, if underrated, watchword in Levinas's conceptual vocabulary.

It is remarkable that Heidegger also uses this concept. Levinas's usage is however quite distinct from Heidegger's, in which irreversibility is in fact associated with the banality of the putatively unilateral movement of time. In his critique of the 'vulgar conception of time', Heidegger writes:

> In the ordinary interpretation, the stream of time is defined as an *irreversible* [*nichtumkehrbares*] succession. Why cannot time be reversed [*umkehren*]? Especially if one looks exclusively at the stream of 'nows', it is incomprehensible in itself why this sequence should not present itself in the reverse direction. The impossibility of this reversal has its basis in the way public time originates in temporality, the temporalizing of which is primarily futural and 'goes' to its end ecstatically in such a way that it 'is' already towards its end.⁵⁹

Heidegger is discussing how the time of clocks is inadequate to the thinking of Dasein as a temporal being. The word 'ecstatically' indicates Heidegger's conception of time as a unity of 'ecstases' — the three ecstases being the past, the present, and the future. While Dasein is a temporal being, other beings simply exist 'within time'.⁶⁰ In other words, the ordinary conception of time does not take into account that, putting it in the simplest terms, Dasein relates to its past and future in a purposeful manner. It is for this reason that Heidegger writes:

> Temporalizing does not signify that ecstases come in a 'succession'. The future is *not later* than having been, and having been is *not earlier* than the Present. Temporality temporalizes itself as a future which makes present in the process of having been.[61]

For Heidegger, then, it is too simple to think of time as irreversible.

What is at stake in the reversal of time? The lines from Heidegger can be usefully compared with the following fragment from Blanchot:

> Le présent, s'il s'exalte en instants (apparaissant, disparaissant), oublie qu'il ne saurait être contemporain de lui-même. Cette non-contemporanéité est passage toujours dépassé, le passif qui, hors temps, le dérange comme forme pure et vide où tout s'ordonnerait, se distribuerait soit également, soit inégalement. Le Temps dérangé, sorti de ses gonds, se laisse encore attirer, fût-ce à travers l'expérience de la fêlure, en une cohérence qui s'unifie et s'universalise. Mais l'expérience inexpérimentée du désastre, retrait du cosmique [...] nous oblige à nous dégager du temps comme irréversible, sans que le Retour en assure la réversibilité. (*ED* 125)

> [The present, when heightened as successive instants (appearing, disappearing), forgets that it cannot be contemporaneous with itself. This noncontemporaneity is a passage already passed over; it is the passive which, outside time, disarranges time as pure and empty form wherein all would order and distribute itself either equally or unequally. Time that is deranged and off its hinges still lets itself be drawn — if only through the experience of the crack — into a coherence which unifies and universalizes itself. But the experience of the disaster — the experience none can have, the retreat of the cosmic [...] — obliges us to disengage ourselves from time as irreversible, without the Return's assuring its reversibility.] (*WD* 78)

Blanchot's fragment distinguishes a deranged or disastrous temporality from a synchronic conception of time, an example of which is Heidegger's ordinary conception of time. The 'instants' in the quotation above can be considered the equivalent of the 'nows' in the quotation from Heidegger. (We might note in passing an echo of the connection between the crack and the unthinkable discussed in relation to Deleuze in Chapter 2.) The disastrous time is a temporality in which the present is compromised and is not what it purports to be. In this time of the disaster, time is not exactly reversed, but it is no longer irreversible. It is as if the arrow of time is momentarily suspended or interrupted.

The idea of irreversibility is played on in another of Blanchot's later texts. The fragments in the early part of *Le Pas au-delà* suggest that if the present has no presence, all that is left are the directions of past and future, which too are 'infiniment vide' (*PD* 25) ('infinitely empty', *SNB* 14). The lack of presence means, furthermore, that there can be no crossing these two poles (*PD* 22; *SNB* 12). Blanchot writes that it is 'le mode narratif' that allows one to think the past as filled with events (conceived as 'fantômes') (*PD* 23; *SNB* 13). Thinking the idea of a narrative mode in relation to Pasolini's observations on the long take, we can see something of this in the phenomenology of the long take, in that it is the cut that instantiates the convention of narrative, of conferring meaning on that which passes, while the passing itself has no meaning, no 'present'. The narrative mode works because the past is both 'revoked forever' and 'irrevocable'. The figure of 'il' reflects on this:

> L'irrévocabilité serait le trait par lequel le vide du passé marque, en les donnant pour impossibles à revivre et donc comme ayant été déjà vécus dans un présent insituable, les semblants d'événements qui ne sont là que pour recouvrir le vide, l'enchanter en le dérobant, tout de même *en l'annonçant par l'indice d'irréversibilité*. (PD 24, my emphasis)

> [Irrevocability would be the trait by which the void of the past marks, by giving them as impossible to relive and as thus already having been lived in an unsituable present, the appearances of events that are there only to cover over the void, to enchant it in hiding it, while all the same *announcing it through the mark of irreversibility*.] (SNB 13)

Blanchot evokes this sensation by reference to a 'fall' or a 'slip', in which the immediately past seems to disappear — it falls into '"l'effroyablement ancien", là où rien ne fut jamais présent' (PD 24) ('"the terrifyingly ancient", there where nothing was ever present', SNB 14). When this 'happens', everything happens in 'non-temps'; in other words, the absence of time. In this, the motif of *le pas au-delà* is strikingly anticipated in *L'Espace littéraire*, and there also appears the notion of the irreversible. Discussing the two deaths, Blanchot writes that dying is not 'le passage irréversible au delà duquel il n'y aurait pas de retour, car il est ce qui ne s'accomplit pas, l'interminable et l'incessant' (EL 107) ('the irreversible step beyond from which there would be no return, for it is that which is not accomplished, the interminable and the incessant', SL 106, translation modified).

This time also defines the experience of passivity. In the quotation from *L'Écriture du désastre* above it is a substantive: the passive. Thus we can see the structural parallel between Levinas's diachrony and Blanchot's disaster by their common opposition to synchrony and being defined by passivity. The linkage between these temporal schemata and passivity is the correlative of the linkage identified by Wall between passivity and the Levinasian *visage* and the Blanchotian image; these schemata form the temporal dimensions implied by the *visage* and the image. On the sense of the temporal dimension of passivity, Levinas's comments on Blanchot's *La Folie du jour* are suggestive. He identifies in this text, and in Blanchot's whole œuvre, 'une non-liberté moins libre que toute déterminisme et que toute tragédie' ('an unfreedom less free than any determinism and any tragedy'). This 'non-liberté' is characterized by both renewal and repetition: 'Dans ce renouvellement qui est aussi une redondance, s'immobilise [...] la présence du présent. Jour qui ne passe pas. Au cœur du temps qui passe, rien ne se passe ni ne vient. Tout est toujours souvenir et menace' ('In this renewal that is also a redundance, the presence of the present is [...] immobilized. Day that does not pass. At the heart of the time that passes, nothing goes on, nothing comes up. All is memory and threat').[62] In *La Folie du jour*, there is something infernal about a day that does not pass. Levinas also associates it with Auschwitz: the very 'madness' of it happening, the way it eludes and ruins intelligibility. I am suggesting that there is a strong element of this happening in our long take from *Irréversible*, in which the assault is stuck in an immobilized (statically framed) present; drawn out, it 'ne passe pas'. Palmer writes more generally that '[i]nstead of a continuum from past to present, in the *cinéma du corps* there unfolds an anxious contiguous presentness, the terminus of today, a peculiar abstraction from history and a dissolved social contract'.[63] This comment evokes something of the madness of the take, even if that 'presentness' is for Blanchot defined by its lack of presence, or a hesitation between presence and absence. In the essay 'L'Absence de livre' [The Absence of the Book] (1969), Blanchot writes that the work can 'hésite' between 'l'œuvre comme présence et l'absence d'œuvre qui toujours échappe et *où le temps comme temps se dérange*' (*EI* 624, my emphasis) ('the work as presence and the absence of the work that constantly escapes, and *where time deranges itself as time*', *IC* 425). What is fascinating is that even in the midst of the assault 'nothing goes on'. To refer to Kaufman's discussion of Deleuzian and Blanchotian ontologies examined in Chapter 2, 'perhaps such movement, such infinite becoming, is equally the mask for the inertia that is so entrenched as to become invisible'.[64] This is also the correlative of the frozen screen discussed in the previous chapter. It is thus that Ropars-Wuilleumier writes that:

> L'image, loin d'échapper au temps, pourrait en figurer l'échappement; en d'autres termes, agissant entre présent et passé, creusant à la fois l'intervalle et l'attrait de l'un en l'autre, dans le reflet comme dans le regard, l'écart que Blanchot nomme 'entre-temps'.[65]
>
> [The image, far from escaping time, could give shape to that escape: in other words, moving between present and past, widening at the same time the interval and the attraction of one in the other, in reflection as in the gaze, the gap that Blanchot names 'the meanwhile'.]

Another dimension of this non-passing is the question of contingency that was raised in connection to the passer-by. As Doane suggests, irreversibility is also crucially connected to the idea of time as chance in the history of cinema. She argues that while later Hollywood films subordinate chance to narrative, early films, notably those of the Lumière brothers, accommodate the chance nature of the events they record:

> In its dominant historical development, [cinema] has become the narrativization of chance, the historicization of the present. A large part of its pleasure and fascination is no doubt due to the lure of contingency, the promise of its indexicality, and hence its access to the present. But such a lure and such a promise carry with them the threat of meaninglessness.[66]

In my account, it is in precisely that meaningless where the fascination lies.

The reason I dwell on these notions of temporality is that recent scholarship on Levinas and film has been attentive to the possibilities of engaging a relation with the Other through cinematic temporality. For the Levinasian film scholar Sam Girgus, regular synchronic time in film implies a philosophy of immanent subjectivity, but redemptive potentialities can be dramatized in film through diachronic temporal categories, such as flashback, in which an immanent and self-enclosed mode of being can turn towards ethics and the transcendent temporality of the Other.[67] Girgus opens his book by noting Levinas's reflection in *De l'existence à l'existant* on time as unhinged and discusses how this opens up and conditions the relation with the Other.[68] Girgus points to how something like a Levinasian narrative of redemption can be dramatized in film through such 'unhinged' temporal categories, which have an implicit relation with the temporality of the Other. The films in which such a narrative can be found open themselves to a new Messianic time. This time is not an eschatology in the sense of the end of the world, nor is it *le temps d'après* of Rancière, with its own messianic overtones. It does however go some way to giving us to understand the possibilities of an 'unhinged' time.

Given its own 'unhinged' time, it must be asked how *Irréversible* might fit with the schema in Girgus's work. For although Girgus discusses films of 'failed transcendence', Noé's film does not so much show a failed opportunity for a redemptive relation to the Other as an infernal madness of the day, a kind of reversed transcendence.[69] There may be a temporal opening in the underpass scene, but it is not one opening to Levinasian transcendent responsibility or being-for-the-Other so much as violence and sadism and the interminability implied by Blanchotian fascination: in other words, it corresponds precisely to that 'non-liberté' identified by Levinas in Blanchot's work. It might be noted here Wall's claim concerning temporality, that '[w]hen [...] Levinas speaks of *diachronie*, he means the "meanwhile"'.[70] This is an unexpected equivalence, as Levinas appears to set the two entirely in opposition. As discussed in the previous chapter, the meanwhile or *l'entre-temps* is the time of art, from which ethical time is distinct. To put that another way, diachrony can be understood to have two sides: an infinite messianic time, but also the timeless and infernal time of the outside. When we discussed the 'frozen screen' in the previous chapter, it was there said after Celeste that the tragic time of the *entre-temps* was not a structure of fatality but a basic fixity in artworks. Wall here offers a way of connecting these different readings by Blanchot and Levinas. It is thus that we can see not only the difference between the two thoughts, but also the particular relevance of Blanchot's reworking of the Levinasian relation with the Other for an understanding of *Irréversible*.

The madness of the day is not just contained in the moment of the underpass scene, but in a manner of speaking it is that which gives rise to the reversed narrative structure as a whole. The viewer is in a straightforward sense estranged from them, as indicated earlier in the chapter. The film stages events as having a lack of presence (this is the paradox I have tried to demonstrate in relation to the scene in the underpass). In a connected movement, the trajectory of the film wants to move towards an infinitely anterior past moment. The strobe and flicker effects at the end of the film indicate the impossibility of this movement the film begins to trace. This might sound like Deleuze's account of chronosigns as the manifestation of a problem, an event intervening from the outside. This is consonant with a reading of the scene in the underpass as 'l'expérience de la fêlure' that Blanchot describes, the crack being that which derails and reverses systems, and, we can say, the sequence of events depicted in this film. This gives some clue as to how we are to understand the line quoted from Levinas above that '[t]out est toujours souvenir et menace'. In the first place, this can be read in relation to the motif of presentiment in the film, which is signposted at the end of the film by showing Alex reading a copy of *An Experiment with Time* (1927), a book by the Irish aeronautical engineer and writer J. W. Dunne (1875–1949). For Dunne, all modes of time — past, present, and future — take place concurrently, such that there is an 'absolute Time' containing these moments.[71] The ordinary observer experiences their own time, but can be made aware of past and future times through experiences involving altered modes of consciousness, classically through dreams. It is thus that Alex, explaining to Marcus and Pierre before they catch the train to the party that she is currently reading a good book, summarizes: 'Il paraît que le futur est déjà écrit [...] et la preuve, c'est les rêves prémonitoires' [It seems that the future is already written [...] and the proof is in premonitory dreams]. This seems to be corroborated as the film moves back in diegetic time to the moment when she wakes, before they head out for the train station, and relates a dream she has just had to Marcus: 'J'étais dans un tunnel... un tunnel... tout rouge. Après, le tunnel s'est cassé en deux' [I was in a tunnel... a tunnel... completely red. Then the tunnel was broken in two]. This is a clear reference to her ordeal in the crimson underpass to come, but of course cannot be anticipated. It seems in this way that it is through Dunne that we are intended to read the line 'le temps détruit tout', the first line spoken in the film (by the 'Butcher' character from Noé's earlier film *Seul Contre Tous* (1998) in his appearance in the opening scene) and forming the film's closing caption (following a strobe finale and not succeeded by credits). However, the reverse structure of the film engenders this without the viewer necessarily following such esoteric clues: the conflicted temporal status of the filmic and the diegetic in *Irréversible* is such that, proceeding through the film, our memories of what has just passed filmically are those of what is to come next diegetically. All is already past yet still to come. Unlike a film such as *Memento* (2000), *Irréversible* does not use its structure to generate suspense or thrills. Although there are some moments that turn out to be prophetic, the effect in parts approaches the jarringly bathetic, as the evening before the rape and aftermath is marked by the levity of a social outing. To the extent that phenomenology implies a futural relation in the manner of Heidegger, McGowan is clearly correct that *Irréversible* runs counter to it. Without resorting to a meta-argument, we can note how in *Irréversible*, like the case of Irimiás and the conundrum of the two clocks and the cyclical structure of *Satantango* more generally, there is a sense in which the film's central long take only makes sense with reference to a theoretical temporal scheme stipulated elsewhere by the film itself.

It is striking that Ropars-Wuilleumier considers as her example of a film that can best be read in conjunction with Blanchot's notion of the outside one with a comparable narrative structure to *Irréversible*: Godard's *Éloge de l'amour* [In Praise of Love] (2001).[72] Godard's film is split into two halves, the first of which is set around two years after the second. *Éloge de l'amour*'s first half is shot in black-and-white, and is frequently evocative of a repressed memory, while the second looks further back to the failure to process adequately the events of the historical past. This suggests the inability to understand the present fully without reference to the past.

However, what is most fascinating about Ropars-Wuilleumier's piece, which plays out the differences between the meaning of the outside in Blanchot and Deleuze, is her argument that Blanchot's conception helps to understand the viewing of *Éloge de l'amour*. She writes:

> Il s'agit d'un film deleuzien en son principe d'organisation, mais seul le dehors blanchotien rend compte de l'impossibilité où se trouve le spectateur de le percevoir sans l'avoir déjà vu. L'avant sera après, l'après était avant, mais on ne le sait qu'après coup. Le film ne peut se voir au présent qu'en se revoyant comme déjà passé, donc dans le souvenir-effacement d'un passage par définition hors de soi. C'est ce temps du dehors, sans commencement ni fin, que Blanchot nomme 'vertige de l'espacement'.

> [*In Praise of Love* is a Deleuzian film in its organizing principle, but only Blanchot's outside takes into account the impossibility for the spectator of perceiving it without having already come to the end. The before comes after, the after was before, but this is only known after the fact. The film can only be viewed in the present by re-viewing it as already past, and thus in the memory-forgetfulness of a passage that is outside itself by definition. This is the time of the outside, without beginning or end, that Blanchot calls the *vertigo of spacing*.][73]

She concludes by remarking that 'le dehors tout à la fois empêcherait le temps et en déclarerait l'éventuel avènement' ('the outside, all at once, impedes time and declares it the eventual event').[74] This final line is particularly relevant to the discussion of Noé's film. If we have said that the underpass scene effectively stages an intrusion of the outside that derails the diegetic temporality, it is also clear that it occasions the close of the film and its Beethoven-scored journey to the sky. It announces the advent of time at the same moment as its dissolution. *Éloge de l'amour* suggests the need to understand the past to orient oneself in the present. *Irréversible* has a much stranger logic, and almost seems to suggest that the present cannot be understood without reference to the future, the future that annihilates the past. The presentiment that is also a memory that the viewer has by the end of *Irréversible*, especially during the penultimate scene in which Bellucci's and Cassell's characters engage in loveplay to an Étienne Daho cover of 'Mon manège à moi' before going out for the evening, illustrates Levinas's comment on Blanchot's *récit*, that it shows how in all joys and happiness — in all *bonheur* — there is this latent madness of the day, present in the temporality of time itself, 'comme un vrombissement lointain d'avions dans le silence' ('like a distant drone of aircraft in the silence').[75] As in *Éloge de l'amour*, in *Irréversible* we can say following Ropars-Wuilleumier that everything moves both towards 'le passé d'un futur et vers l'avenir d'une mémoire' ('the past of a future and toward the future of a memory'), placing the instant itself in a contradictory position.[76] The viewer both connects what they see to what has gone before and what is to come, but what has gone before is already what is to come and vice versa. The film does not so much make time visible, as the Deleuzian time-image would give us to understand, so much as it 'rend perceptible, avec et contre l'image-temps, le mouvement par lequel le temps échappe à l'image au moment même où celle-ci le vise' ('makes perceptible, with and against the time-image, the movement whereby time escapes the image at the very moment when the image aims for it').[77] Tying the three films discussed in this book together, each of which presents an unorthodox conception of time, we can observe how in this selection the image constantly announces in one way or another an annulment of time as linear, irreversible progression. As Blanchot writes:

> Toute l'ambiguïté vient de l'ambiguïté du temps qui entre ici en jeu et qui permet de dire et d'éprouver que l'image fascinante de l'expérience est, à un certain moment, présente, alors que cette présence n'appartient à aucun présent, détruit même le présent où elle semble s'introduire. (*LV* 16)

> [All the ambiguity stems from the ambiguity of time, which enters into play here, and which allows us to say and feel that the fascinating image of experience is, at a certain moment, present, while this presence does not belong to any present, and even destroys the present into which it seems to introduce itself.] (*BC* 9)

By putting events in reverse order, one thing the film does not do, though we might expect it to, is ask how the attack comes about. It is not a question of the 'responsibility' of any of the characters in what comes diegetically to pass — if Marcus did not offend Alex and cause her to leave the party early, if she did not take the underpass, and so on. Nor does the figure who stumbles into the underpass around halfway into the rape, takes one look, and then turns back signal a failure of any kind of Good Samaritan. The word 'responsabilité' in the context of Blanchot's writing, it is crucial to note, does not here have its normal meaning in the sense of circumspection and rectitude, which Blanchot dismisses as 'banal' (*ED* 45; *WD* 25). As Josh Cohen writes, 'Blanchot finds in this term a radical estrangement of its sedimented bourgeois associations — responsibility, far from the undertaking of a determinate and finite duty, is a term that can only annul itself'.[78] In this respect the term is much like many of Blanchot's terms in needing to be understood according to the specific use he makes of them. Taken from *Autrement qu'être*, responsibility is the name for Blanchot's revision of the Levinasian relation to the Other, which as we have seen is marked precisely by its neutrality. But while for Levinas the term refers to the infinite and unassumable obligation to the Other, Blanchot's use places more emphasis on the dispossession of the self that is implied by this. The Blanchotian Other does not imply the same exigency as the Levinasian. It is thus that we can see Blanchot's distinction from Levinas, particularly the thought that responsibility is 'elle-même désastreuse' (*ED* 47) ('itself disastrous', *WD* 27). There is nothing that could have been done to avert the attack in the underpass, but nor is there anything for the viewer to do having watched it. This is not the Levinasian argument that we examined in 'La Réalité et son ombre' that would consider 'moral film' to be a contradiction in terms, that art is inherently 'irresponsible'. Responsibility is disastrous as it does not lessen the burden of the Other, does not make us any more able to respond to the Other's appeal. Blanchot is clear that responsibility can only be spoken of by separating it from 'toutes les formes de la conscience-présente' (*ED* 46) ('all forms of present-consciousness', *WD* 25). The important thing is the (non-) experience of the viewing itself rather than any idea that one might derive from it. This bracketed 'non' before 'experience' means that it is an experience to which there is no reaction, at least no appropriate one. This is consonant with McGowan's argument that Noé's film offers an implicit critique of phenomenology, but it does not necessarily entail McGowan's thematic of the psychoanalytic theory of the death drive. When Blanchot writes that disastrous responsibility 'nous oblige à nous dégager du temps comme irréversible, sans que le Retour en assure la réversibilité', it is in this sense that we can answer our opening question: what is it in *Irréversible* that is irreversible? It is not only and as such the priority of the Other, but Levinas and Blanchot's common use of the word *irréversible* as conveying and relating to powerlessness and passivity — not only crucial aspects of fascination, but also ideas which I have argued pertain clearly to this film.

In conclusion, like disastrous responsibility, the experience of watching *Irréversible* divorces us from irreversible temporality and throws us into a time out of joint. This is particularly the case in the film's central long take in the underpass scene, which enters us into time's absence and fascination. This is how the question can be answered of what it is in *Irréversible* that is irreversible. It is also why, whether we want to rehabilitate Noé's film or not, the significance of *Irréversible* lies in raising the question of what is at work in disturbing aesthetic experiences. While Noé's critics take issue with its offensiveness and others find potential for its recuperation within an ethical framework, by introducing the film into discussion of Blanchot and Levinasian film theory it may tell us something about the passive relation of fascination we enter into before the image. The film is a case study that makes explicit the point that fascination is not the preserve of a canon of renowned masterpieces. To say that a film fascinates does not imply a value judgement about that film. In the sense in which I am using the term, terrible films can be fascinating just as much as fabulous ones. Indeed, fascination is a key reason for *Irréversible*'s *maudit* status. What seems to be so offensive for so many critics is that the film demands that one answer for one's response to the film. To theorize this, it could be argued that the film refers one back to one's own internal void, even to the primal scene itself. It could only be in this way that, for Ian Christie, '[i]f the film begins as an assault on the audience, then its movement back towards a serene Edenic image of Bellucci is experienced as therapeutic — a startling postmodern version of catharsis that purges us of the night's horrors'.[79] If it is therapeutic, or if it evokes some kind of *bonheur*, then in some sense this means we forget something of the horror. That horror or fearful passivity may only last a few moments of 'real time', and cannot be summoned by returning to the film at leisure or in study. What I have examined in this film and identified as the disquieting effect of the imaginary is for Blanchot constitutive of all art. If this is the case, then what is 'unwatchable' about Noé's film should perhaps mark it out not so much as an aberration in the history of European cinema, but rather as a film which gives us to ask what it is in art that is fascinating. As this book has argued throughout, the instant in which time dissolves cannot in itself be held. Like Orpheus, we ultimately emerge from the night, though without having captured the object of fascination.

Notes to Chapter 4

1. James Quandt, 'Flesh and Blood: Sex and Violence in Recent French Cinema', in *The New Extremism in Cinema: From France to Europe*, ed. by Tanya Horeck and Tina Kendall (Edinburgh: Edinburgh University Press, 2011), pp. 18–28; David Edelstein, 'Irreversible Errors', *Slate* (2003), <http://www.slate.com/articles/arts/movies/2003/03/irreversible_errors.html> [accessed 25 June 2015].
2. Though they are key issues in the secondary literature, I will not discuss here the potential problems of gender or homophobia in *Irréversible*. On these issues see the discussions of homophobia in Robin Wood, '*Irreversible*: Against and For', *Film International*, 1:5 (2003), <http://filmint.nu/?p=1475> [accessed 4 June 2015], and Todd McGowan, *Out of Time: Desire in Atemporal Cinema* (Minneapolis: University of Minnesota Press, 2011); and of violence against women in Martin Barker, '"Typically French"?: Mediating Screened Rape to British Audiences', in *Rape in Art Cinema*, ed. by Dominique Russell (New York: Continuum, 2010), pp. 145–58.
3. See for example Douglas Keesey, 'Split Identification: Representations of Rape in Gaspar Noé's *Irréversible* and Catherine Breillat's *A ma soeur!/Fat Girl*', *Studies in European Cinema*, 7:2 (2010), 95–107.
4. Roger Ebert, 'Irreversible', (2003), <http://www.rogerebert.com/reviews/irreversible-2003> [accessed 12 June 2015].
5. Wood, '*Irreversible*: Against and For'.
6. Tim Palmer, *Irreversible* (London: Palgrave, 2015). For an account of *cinéma du corps*, see Tim Palmer, *Brutal Intimacy: Analyzing Contemporary French Cinema* (Middletown: Wesleyan University Press, 2011).
7. For an account of *Irréversible* within the French film industrial context, see Palmer, *Irreversible*, pp. 1–30.
8. McGowan, *Out of Time*, p. 220.
9. Kovács, *The Cinema of Béla Tarr*, p. 50.
10. See the cases of the 'Embracers' and 'Refusers' in Barker, '"Typically French"?', pp. 156–57.
11. Jean Tang, '"There Are No Bad Deeds, Just Deeds"', *Salon* (2003), <http://www.salon.com/2003/03/12/noe/> [accessed 27 June 2015].
12. McGowan, *Out of Time*, p. 208.
13. Asbjørn Grønstad, 'On the Unwatchable', in *The New Extremism in Cinema*, ed. by Horeck and Kendall, pp. 192–205 (p. 205).
14. Ibid., pp. 204–05 (my emphasis).
15. Ibid., p. 202.
16. Tim Palmer, 'Style and Sensation in the Contemporary French Cinema of the Body', *Journal of Film and Video*, 58:3 (2006), 22–32 (p. 24).
17. Matt Bailey, 'Gaspar Noé', *Senses of Cinema* (2003), <http://sensesofcinema.com/2003/great-directors/noe/> [accessed 5 June 2015].
18. Palmer, *Irreversible*, p. 77.
19. David Cox, 'Masterclass with Gaspar Noé', BFI, (2009), <http://explore.bfi.org.uk/4fc75db652a32> [accessed 5 June 2015].
20. Estelle Bayon, *Le Cinéma obscène* (Paris: L'Harmattan, 2003), p. 80.
21. Ibid., pp. 152–53.
22. Martine Beugnet, *Cinema and Sensation: French Film and the Art of Transgression* (Edinburgh: Edinburgh University Press, 2007), p. 46. Beugnet makes only passing reference to *Irréversible*, saying it 'arguably harnesses an absence of substance to a display of technical virtuosity' (p. 36).
23. Libby Saxton, 'Spectatorship and Suffering', in *Film and Ethics: Foreclosed Encounters*, ed. by Lisa Downing and Libby Saxton (London: Routledge, 2010), pp. 63–75.
24. Wall, *Radical Passivity*, p. 54.
25. Metz, *Le Signifiant imaginaire*, p. 69; *Psychoanalysis and Cinema*, p. 49.
26. Ibid., p. 79; p. 56.
27. Ibid., p. 122; p. 97.

28. The priority Metz gives to pleasure in film might be thought to beg the question of the use of his theory when dealing with a film such as *Irréversible*, which challenges film as pleasure. For Metz, the spectator is 'aliéné et heureux, acrobatiquement raccroché à lui-même par le fil invisible de la vue' ('at once alienated and happy, acrobatically hooked up to himself by the invisible thread of sight') (*Le Signifiant imaginaire*, p. 119; *Psychoanalysis and Cinema*, p. 96). For Metz's account of 'déplaisir filmique' ('filmic unpleasure'), see ibid., pp. 135–36; pp. 111–12.
29. Palmer compares the underpass to an abattoir and suggests that the print has been digitally touched to enhance this colour scheme. Palmer, *Irreversible*, p. 126.
30. Ropars-Wuilleumier, *Écrire l'espace*, p. 152.
31. Beugnet, *Cinema and Sensation*, p. 65. My emphasis.
32. Gilles Deleuze, *Francis Bacon: logique de la sensation* (Paris: Éditions de la différence, 1981), p. 9; *Francis Bacon: The Logic of Sensation*, trans. by Daniel W. Smith (London: Continuum, 2003), p. 2. The notion of the figure is one that occasionally appears in Blanchot's work in connection to fascination. Looking back to the myth of Narcissus in Chapter 1, there it was argued that in this parable of fascination, what Narcissus sees is 'dans la figure l'infigurable' (*ED* 204) ('the unfigurable in the figure', *WD* 134, translation modified).
33. The motif of fear is one that is extensively analyzed in *Le Pas au-delà*.
34. Rodolphe Chabrier, 'SPX', *Irreversible*, collector's edn DVD (London: Tartan Video, 2006).
35. Ibid.
36. Emmanuel Levinas, *Totalité et infini: essai sur l'extériorité* (Paris: Livre de Poche, 1990), p. 266; *Totality and Infinity: An Essay on Exteriority*, trans. by Alphonso Lingis (The Hague: Martinus Nijhoff, 1979), p. 239.
37. Ibid., p. 237; p. 215.
38. Leslie Hill, *Blanchot: Extreme Contemporary* (London: Routledge, 1997), pp. 170 & 180. For accounts of the relationship between Blanchot and Levinas, see ibid., pp. 162–84, and Michael Holland, '"Let's Leave God Out of This": Maurice Blanchot's Reading of *Totality and Infinity*', in *Facing the Other: The Ethics of Emmanuel Levinas*, ed. by Seán Hand (Richmond: Curzon Press, 1996), pp. 91–106.
39. Libertson, *Proximity*, p. 275. Hill alludes critically to Libertson's reading.
40. Critchley, 'Il y a — Holding Levinas's Hand to Blanchot's Fire', p. 116.
41. See also Levinas, *Totalité et infini*, p. 23; *Totality and Infinity*, p. 34.
42. Ann Smock's note, *WD* 148, n. 5.
43. For the use of hostage imagery see for example Emmanuel Levinas, *Autrement qu'être, ou au-delà de l'essence* (Paris: Livre de Poche, 1990), pp. 185–86 & 202; *Otherwise than Being; Or, Beyond Essence*, trans. by Alphonso Lingis (Dordrecht: Kluwer Academic Publishers, 1991), pp. 117 & 127.
44. Levinas, *Totalité et infini*, p. 266; *Totality and Infinity*, p. 239.
45. Ibid., p. 266; p. 238.
46. Wall, *Radical Passivity*, p. 77.
47. Sarah Cooper, *Selfless Cinema? Ethics and French Documentary* (Oxford: Legenda, 2006), p. 17.
48. Ibid., p. 23.
49. For a discussion of the relation between Blanchot and Antelme, see Martin Crowley, *Robert Antelme: Humanity, Community, Testimony* (Oxford: Legenda, 2003), pp. 28–34.
50. Levinas, *De l'existence à l'existant*, pp. 81–105; *Existence and Existents*, pp. 52–64.
51. Asbjørn Grønstad, *Screening the Unwatchable: Spaces of Negation in Post-Millennial Art Cinema* (Basingstoke: Palgrave Macmillan, 2012), p. 163.
52. Mary Ann Doane, *The Emergence of Cinematic Time: Modernity, Contingency, the Archive* (Cambridge, MA: Harvard University Press, 2002), p. 112.
53. Ibid., p. 113.
54. Ibid., p. 131.
55. Ropars-Wuilleumier, *Le Temps d'une pensée*, p. 178.
56. Levinas, *Autrement qu'être*, p. 134; *Otherwise than Being*, p. 84.
57. Ibid.
58. Ibid., p. 241; p. 154.

59. Heidegger, *Being and Time*, p. 478 (*Sein und Zeit*, p. 426).
60. Michael Inwood, *A Heidegger Dictionary* (Oxford: Blackwell, 1999), pp. 220–22.
61. Heidegger, *Being and Time*, p. 401 (*Sein und Zeit*, p. 350).
62. Levinas, *Sur Maurice Blanchot*, p. 59; *Proper Names*, p. 159.
63. Palmer, *Irreversible*, p. 51.
64. Kaufman, 'Midnight, or the Inertia of Being', p. 236.
65. Ropars-Wuilleumier, *Le Temps d'une pensée*, p. 377.
66. Doane, *The Emergence of Cinematic Time*, p. 107.
67. Sam Girgus, *Levinas and the Cinema of Redemption* (New York: Columbia University Press, 2010), p. 154.
68. Ibid., pp. 1–4. See also Levinas, *De l'existence à l'existant*, p. 68; *Existence and Existents*, p. 45.
69. For a list of the examples considered by Girgus as 'failed transcendence', see Girgus, *Levinas and the Cinema of Redemption*, p. 7.
70. Wall, *Radical Passivity*, p. 104.
71. J. W. Dunne, *An Experiment with Time* (London: Faber and Faber, 1958 [1927]), p. 157.
72. *Éloge de l'amour* also has one of the characters quote a line from Blanchot which was discussed in Chapter 2: 'l'image, capable de nier le néant, est aussi le regard du néant sur nous'.
73. Ropars-Wuilleumier, *Le Temps d'une pensée*, pp. 412–13; 'Image or time?', p. 25.
74. Ibid., p. 413; p. 26.
75. Levinas, *Sur Maurice Blanchot*, p. 60; *Proper Names*, p. 160.
76. Ropars-Wuilleumier, *Le Temps d'une pensée*, p. 412; 'Image or time?', p. 25.
77. Ibid., p. 414; p. 26.
78. Josh Cohen, *Interrupting Auschwitz: Art, Religion, Philosophy* (London: Continuum, 2005), p. 81.
79. Ian Christie, 'Time Regained: The Complex Magic of Reverse Motion', in *Projected Shadows: Psychoanalytic Reflections on the Representation of Loss in European Cinema*, ed. by Andrea Sabbadini (London: Routledge, 2007), pp. 168–81 (pp. 177–78).

CONCLUSION

On a Disappearing Art

This study has demonstrated the relevance of Blanchot's conceptions of image and fascination in the thinking of film and, after a brief summary of its key arguments, will now conclude by sketching a broader horizon onto which they might fit.

Blanchotian fascination can be filmic. Put another way, film is a conduit, along with dreams, literature, and other Blanchotian topoi, for the perpetuation and continual re-opening of fascination. It has been shown in Chapter 1 and elsewhere how film can inform a theory of the image after Blanchot, gesturing towards the visual dimension of fascination as being of theoretical importance in the reading of Blanchot, not only in reference to the 'scène primitive' in *L'Écriture du désastre*, but through the writings on the image in the 1950s and after.

Chapter 2 explored the resonances of Blanchot's thought in Deleuze's *Cinéma* volumes and Godard's *Histoire(s) du cinéma* and drew connections between Godard's invocation of Blanchot at the end of the film and other moments in it, arguing that Blanchot is present in two of the most important works for thinking about film in the post-war period.

Close analysis of sequences of *temps mort* in which 'nothing happens' in the work of Tarr in Chapter 3 demonstrated the relevance of Tarr's work to the thinking of fascination. Developing the logic of this, Rancière's influential writing on Tarr, especially on the issue of temporality, was also considered, and in contrast to Rancière's two regimes of visibility it was argued that Tarr's films exhibit a disjunction within the image itself, an image prone to engendering fascination. The model arrived at considered thinking *temps mort* through the Levinasian *entre-temps*, itself thought through the *il y a*, a notion developed between Levinas and Blanchot.

A through-line of this study has been that cinema offers a way of thinking being itself, following through the ontological implications of Blanchot's essay 'Les Deux Versions de l'imaginaire', in which Blanchot posits an initial division or doubling that allows for representation, rather than representation being the cause of this. In other words, within the terms of a groundless ontology, the image is present at the base of being. By showing the world as an image, cinema makes palpable this sense, and Chapter 3 argued that the use of landscape in Tarr's film was a vivid way in which this is made manifest. In giving us abandoned landscapes in protracted long takes, these landscapes abandon themselves to the image and show the image as emerging when the world abandons itself.

This conception of time and space was used to rethink the Deleuzian time image as read by Rancière in Tarr's work. Conceiving landscape as a kind of 'spectacle' or image in Blanchot's terms, it was argued that, rather than opening lines of flight out from the characters' situations, this manner of filming offers the image itself as a source of fascination. More generally, the points in Deleuze's philosophy in the *Cinéma* volumes at which it invokes at the same time as it constrains the thought of Blanchot were probed, drawing on the work of Ropars-Wuilleumier. While Ropars-Wuilleumier thinks film through Blanchot's later work on writing and trace, the present study pursued Blanchot's earlier analyses of the image and fascination.

Chapter 4 turned to *Irréversible*, through which the figure of the Other in Blanchot's writing and film was discussed. This opened up the space for an encounter with the work of Levinas and Levinasian film theory, and also raised the question of violent images in film (as opposed to the 'slow' images of Tarr) and how this can be thought in relation to my theory of the image. Following other critics of the so-called 'new extremism' it was argued that *Irréversible* was a film seeking to confront the viewer and to expose them to violence. It was also shown that Noé's film — whatever we might think of its maligned status — touches on fundamental questions in art today and throughout history, questions that have been approached in the book as a whole through the theory of the image in Blanchot.

Blanchot does not address himself to aesthetics or criticism in their institutionalized forms, nor academic film studies. Nor does his writing deal in value judgements: it offers no scheme for relative evaluation of artistic merit. For Blanchot, the aesthetician reduces the work of art to 'un objet de réflexion et de savoir' (*EL* 245) ('an object of reflection and of knowledge', *SL* 234). To this extent, this study has necessarily engaged in aesthetics. However, it also offers a way of thinking with discontinuity. In an essay that has crucially informed this book, Ropars-Wuilleumier gives a clear statement summing up the function of art for Blanchot:

> L'*aisthésis* de Blanchot nous renvoie d'abord à l'insoutenable de l'idée d'image: une image littérale, et cependant jamais donnée; actuelle, sans virtualité; s'offrant à la vue et défiant la vision; une image qui serait incapable de soutenir sa propre présence autrement que par l'expansion du geste où elle se rend absente. S'il s'agit alors d'une esthétique, c'est parce qu'elle touche au regard, mais en proposant l'écart de tout sujet regardant; et si elle reste figurante, c'est dans la mesure où elle montre le retrait de la représentation sous l'attrait de l'image, qui s'incorpore à elle sans pour autant s'y substituer. C'est cette logique dé-figurante de l'image que Blanchot invite à regarder en face, et cela jusque dans les images les plus machiniques de la modernité: si celles-ci nous séduisent, ne serait-ce pas qu'elles dissimulent le détournement de la vue dans l'offre de vision? Nous appelant ainsi à nous retourner pour voir l'intervalle ouvert par l'image au cœur des œuvres mêmes de l'image.
>
> [Blanchot's aesthesis refers us first to the unsustainability of the idea of image: a literal image, and yet never given; actual yet without virtuality; offering itself to sight yet defying vision; an image that would be incapable of sustaining its own presence other than by an expansion of the gesture whereby it absents itself. If this is an aesthetic, it is because it touches on the gaze, while proposing

the removal of the gazing subject; and if it remains figuring, it is in so far as it shows the retraction of representation under the attraction of the image, which embodies itself in this aesthetic without substituting itself for it. Blanchot invites us to gaze directly upon this disfiguring logic of the image, even of modernity's most mechanical images: if such images seduce us, is it not because they dissimulate the turning away of sight in the offer of vision? Calling us to turn around to see the interval opened up by the image in the heart of the image's own works.][1]

Ropars-Wuilleumier in these lines points to how Blanchot's work puts aesthetics as such into question. In proposing a new understanding of the image, it not only asks us to rethink questions of representation, but of the subject and the gaze themselves. The implications of this bear a moment's reflection.

In the first chapter of this study I discussed what Blanchot calls 'l'absence de livre' as the way in which the book is always in the process of disappearing, the 'book' understood as referring to a notion of totality. Blanchot's debates about where literature is going seem oddly proleptic of the debates surrounding the ontology of film after the disappearance of celluloid. Cinema disappears in a much more literal and inexorable way than literature. Paolo Cherchi Usai has stressed how film is auto-destructive: celluloid disintegrates.[2] As Rodowick writes, 'the material basis of film is a chemically encoded process of entropy. This is one of many ways in which watching film is literally a spectatorship of death'.[3] Analogue film can thus be seen as a figure for the absence of the book, and in this strange way Blanchot echoes the anxiety surrounding the disappearance of celluloid, both within the spheres of filmmaking and film studies. To this extent, Blanchot's lack of engagement with film in his writings registers not so much a complete indifference as a thought that had perhaps already subsumed this anxiety before it even came about: film was already disappearing even as it was emerging. If film is the preeminent technological art — and even this seems perhaps quaint today — this is to say that it brings out most explicitly this disappearance in our time. Literature, by virtue of the written word, partakes in perhaps a purer erasure, but film, on account of its mechanical transmogrifications, is only too visible in betraying its disappearance. If disappearance is the (inessential) essence of art and indeed of our time as such, then by this reading the disappearance of film is only a measure of the change of epoch.

In an essay from 1991, 'L'Autre Vie' [The Other Life], Bellour discusses the text 'Parler, ce n'est pas voir', referred to throughout this book, in which Blanchot looks to a time to come in which there would be a speech without reference to light or seeing. He goes on:

> On peut imaginer — pure spéculation — que cette volonté accrue puisse avoir été favorisée par la pression toujours plus excessive des images des médias dans le monde contemporain. Ils semblent en effet incarner au plus près ce que Blanchot nommera la rumeur ou la voix étrangère, cette voix de la 'dictature' à laquelle l'écrivain impose silence — l'œuvre est ce silence.[4]

> [One can imagine — in a purely speculative way — that this heightened desire could have been enhanced by the ever more excessive pressure of media images

in the contemporary world. Indeed, they seem to incarnate as closely as possible that which Blanchot will name the rumour or the unfamiliar voice, this voice of the 'dictatorship' on which the writer imposes silence — the work is this silence.]

Bellour is here referring to Blanchot's 1955 essay 'Mort du dernier écrivain' [Death of the Last Writer]. In this essay, Blanchot tries to imagine a situation in which the last writer in the world dies. He imagines the world observing this and a kind of silence appearing to befall the world. This apparent silence is however a kind of language:

> C'est comme le vide qui parle, un murmure léger, insistant, indifférent, qui sans doute est le même pour tous, qui est sans secret et qui pourtant isole chacun, le sépare des autres, du monde et de lui-même, l'entraînant par des labyrinthes moqueurs, l'attirant sur place toujours plus loin, par une fascinante répulsion, au-dessous du monde commun des paroles quotidiennes. (*LV* 266)

> [It is like the void that speaks, a light murmur, insistant, indifferent, that is probably the same for everyone, that is without secret and yet isolates each person, separates him from the others, from the world and from himself, leading him through mocking labyrinths, drawing him always farther away, by a fascinating repulsion, below the ordinary world of daily speech.] (*BC* 219)

The emergence of this murmur is not an event which would only occur in the hypothetical scenario of the death of the last writer, but is something that has happened in every person's life, for it is 'en tiers dans chaque dialogue, en écho face à chaque monologue' (*LV* 266) ('the third part of each dialogue, the echo confronting each monologue', *BC* 219). Blanchot writes that this maddening voice must be silenced. This silencing is the work of writers, artists, and thinkers who enter into an intimacy with the voice by transforming it and expressing it. True works of art are reserves of this silence. The silence gives them the quality of a statue. In certain 'périodes de faiblesse' [periods of weakness], however, dictators take the place of writers. They appear to silence the voice with their word of command, but instead of silencing the voice they perpetuate it. In Chapter 1, I suggested the 'prolixité ressassante' that Blanchot claims is being exposed as the means of communication wear out is close to the media images that Bellour points to as today embodying this dictatorial voice. Bellour continues: 'On peut imaginer encore que le cinéma, dont Blanchot, semble-t-il, ne parle jamais, participe à ses yeux globalement de ce monde du "voir" dont la littérature devra se garder' [One can even imagine that the cinema, which Blanchot, it seems, never speaks of, in his eyes broadly takes part in this world of 'seeing' against which literature must protect itself].[5] Bellour notes that it was in the same decade as 'Parler, ce n'est pas voir' that cinema came more and more to regard itself as an art rather than a natural expression of the world. It came to understand itself not as presence, but as solitude. Bellour reflects on the solitude of works in which speech and writing and the image come together; in other words, in films. In Chapter 2, I suggested that *Histoire(s) du cinéma* represents this solitude. In this way, it is not only literature that withdraws from the world, but film often does too, sequestering itself in a space of the image. Bellour observes further that:

Dans ce lien si violent qui devient chez Blanchot tourment des corps, torsion des âmes et conception d'un sujet innommable, on peut sentir la préfiguration de formes d'art et de destin encore inconnues qui pourraient naître des nouvelles machines capables de transformer nos modes d'expression et de fascination — à condition qu'elles ne soient pas de pure terreur.[6]

[In this so violent connection that becomes in Blanchot the torment of bodies, the twisting of souls and the conception of an unnameable subject, one has the sense of a foreshadowing of forms of art and of destiny still unknown which could arise from new machines capable of transforming our modes of expression and of fascination — on condition that they are not simply terrifying.]

Bellour's essay is now twenty-five years old and in that time new machines have come, but fascination remains.[7]

This idea is much as in the first chapter, in which we saw that the 'moyens de communication' were wearing out, and it also bleeds over into Blanchot's suggestion in his texts in *L'Entretien infini* that fascination is an effect of the social, everyday world. The technologies of the image, it goes without saying, have developed enormously since the publication of these texts in the 1960s. This book has tried to gesture towards the relation with the image as implicit in the world itself, rather than discretely contained in any individual experience of going to the cinema or reading the newspaper. Furthermore, the discussion of the lesson Blanchot draws from Brecht in Chapter 4 sought to bring out how one cannot set the image against itself or pit fascination against fascination. If we understand the image as implicit in the idea of 'spectrality', I have effectively tried to demonstrate how Derrida is correct to write: 'La spectralité est partout à l'œuvre, et plus que jamais, de façon originale, dans la virtualité reproductible de la photographie ou du cinéma' ('Spectrality is at work everywhere, and more than ever, in an original way, in the reproducible virtuality of photography or cinema').[8] To answer the question posed in the Introduction of what is behind Derrida's use of filmic metaphors in his commentary on *L'Instant de ma mort*, it is that the image as such (of which cinema is an avatar) is involved in the constitution of the real as such, and therefore of the instant by extension.

Thus, to the extent that what has been discussed in the course of this work has been about film, it has been about film as an art form, and therefore about a diverse and diffuse cultural object with a pre-eminent access to the imaginary, the capacity of things to become image. Put more strongly, it has been about film insofar as film can act as a conduit for fascination, which is not only the real subject of this work but also, restating Blanchot, something like the real problem of existence. Film touches on what Blanchot calls 'l'expérience originelle'. One might go so far as to say that the specific films I have referred to in the course of this work are important to the extent that through them this essential experience is communicated; otherwise they are epiphenomenal. These films make us see, we can say with Ropars-Wuilleumier, that, even there where there is the most to see, 'ce n'est pas de voir qu'il s'agit, mais d'avancer, avec Blanchot, vers cette invisibilité de l'invisible que l'écriture ne cesse de frayer et que le film pourrait, paradoxalement, inscrire dans la visibilité elle-même' [it is not a case of seeing, but of moving, with Blanchot, towards this invisibility of the invisible which writing never stops opening up and which film can, paradoxically, inscribe in visibility itself].[9] As Ropars-Wuilleumier writes, this is at work in every shot, every montage, every image.

In this way, the study might even aspire to a reflection on the direction of film studies. Richard Rushton writes that, in contrast to the heyday of the journal *Screen*, today academic film studies too much consists in 'an *affirmation* of the commerce of cinema as an industry and apparatus'.[10] For Rushton, the discipline has lost its political purpose, and part of this consists in the increased study of audience reception when film criticism should be about '*potential* or *hypothetical* audiences'.[11] One is reminded of how Blanchot ponders in a parenthesis whether the spectator at the theatre is not 'souvent un homme très léger, c'est-à-dire très légèrement intéressé, aussi *incapable de fascination* que d'attention' (*EI* 530, my emphasis) ('often frivolous, that is, only slightly interested, as *incapable of fascination* as of attention', *IC* 362). For all that fascination is a passion, this line does imply a kind of competence or disposition — a capacity for passivity. Fascination is here something like the reverse of attention. If for Rushton the highest aim of film criticism is to 'encourage audiences to view differently', then this study has tried to encourage its reader to reflect on the passivity at work in spectatorship at the same time as indicating how particular films engender this.[12] It is not, following Rushton, cinema as commerce that should be affirmed, but cinema as fascination. As was shown in Chapter 4, even the most *maudit* of films may tell us truths about fascination.

In thinking fascination, I have sought to follow Fynsk's assertion that today it is necessary to put the notion of exposure at the heart of research in the humanities. For Fynsk, 'work that is *of* the humanities proceeds *from* the media and insistently *at the limits* of the media that belong to the domains that hold its concern'.[13] Such research:

> does not conceptualize questions such as community or freedom; rather, it draws them forth as questions, or exigencies, it shows they are there as exigencies as it limns their meaning. Such an endeavor does not abjure the concept, but it always tries to bring the concept back to its limits. It proceeds from the way such questions are given in the 'communicability,' 'legibility,' or 'translatability' of a text, and in an active form of critique.[14]

What I have tried to do in this book is to think this visually, in terms of the 'communicability' of film images, and to draw out, 'in an active form of critique', the question of fascination.

The stakes of this have been set out by Stiegler, for whom the work of the university — of thinking as such — involves the cultivation of attention. Looking back to Blanchot's link between attention and fascination above, we might add that fascination ought to be cultivated too. Yet today, owing to larger economic powers, ours is an age in which these are under threat.[15] Stiegler makes clear that we must recognize the cinematic nature of consciousness in order to deal with the problem of the industrialization of consciousness — a problem he argues that could lead to apocalypse.[16] Stiegler follows Theodor Adorno and Max Horkheimer in pointing to how, in the culture industry, the schematizing power of the imagination is exteriorized and reified, thus 'aliénant le plus radicalement qui soit le libre sujet de la raison — qu'elle assujettirait, précisément' ('radically alienating what should be the freely reasoning subject whom it subjugates — by de-subjectifying').[17] Reflecting on one's own passivity would in this way be to engage with wider forces at work in the world. While my examples have been art cinema, the power of fascination I have shown is at work in all forms of the image.

The film image exposes the viewer to *désœuvrement*. To echo Blanchot, this implies 'des degrés infinis'. Opening up a broader canvas, one might look to Agamben, who uses the term to discuss the very purpose and identity of mankind. The experience of worklessness or 'inoperability' opened by fascination touches on politics. For Agamben, politics:

> corresponds to the essential inoperability of humankind, to the radical being-without-work of human communities. There is politics because human beings are *argōs*-beings that cannot be defined by any proper operation — that is, beings of pure potentiality that no identity or vocation can possibly exhaust.[18]

If film opens up this inoperability, it also opens a possible politics of the image, a politics that would begin with the exposure in fascination. As suggested in Chapter 1, it would be a case of affirming the rupture, a rupture that is re-opened and perpetuated in film. Film would thus be another place where we encounter what Nancy thinks of as the 'exigence' of Blanchot: 'L'exigence de Blanchot est essentiellement celle-ci: faire droit sans réserve à l'au-delà du sens, cet au-delà qui n'est précisément *pas au-delà*, qui est le passage ici et maintenant, à chaque instant, en chaque lieu, vers le non-lieu ou le hors-lieu' [The demand of Blanchot is essentially this: to accede without reserve to the beyond of meaning, this beyond which is not exactly the *step (not) beyond*, which is the passage here and now, at every instant, in every place, to the non-place or the outside].[19]

Notes to the Conclusion

1. Ropars-Wuilleumier, *Le Temps d'une pensée*, pp. 309–10; 'On Unworking', p. 150.
2. Paolo Cherchi Usai, *The Death of Cinema: History, Cultural Memory and the Digital Dark Age* (London: BFI, 2001).
3. D. N. Rodowick, *The Virtual Life of Film* (Cambridge: Harvard University Press, 2007), p. 20.
4. Bellour, *L'Entre-Images 2*, p. 327.
5. Ibid.
6. Ibid., p. 328.
7. Bellour returned to the same text by Blanchot in a piece from 2011, also discussing the texts by Rodowick, Cherchi Usai, and Mulvey I have referred to, see Bellour, *Pensées du cinéma*, pp. 365–66.
8. Derrida, *Papier machine*, p. 392; *Paper Machine*, p. 158.
9. Ropars-Wuilleumier, *Le Temps d'une pensée*, p. 179.
10. Richard Rushton, 'The New Film Studies and the Decline of Critique', *CineAction*, 72 (2007), 2–7 (p. 3).
11. Ibid., p. 5.
12. Ibid.
13. Christopher Fynsk, *The Claim of Language: A Case for the Humanities* (Minneapolis: University of Minnesota Press, 2004), p. ix.

14. Ibid., p. 70.
15. Bernard Stiegler, *États de choc: bêtise et savoir au XXI*^{e} *siècle* (Paris: Mille et une nuits, 2012); *States of Shock: Stupidity and Knowledge in the Twenty-First Century*, trans. by Daniel Ross (Cambridge: Polity, 2015).
16. Stiegler, *La Technique et le temps 3*, pp. 118–23; *Technics and Time, 3*, pp. 74–78.
17. Ibid., p. 68; p. 37.
18. Giorgio Agamben, *Means Without End: Notes on Politics*, trans. by Vincenzo Binetti and Cesare Casarino (Minneapolis: University of Minnesota Press, 2000), p. 141.
19. Jean-Luc Nancy, 'Le Neutre, la neutralisation du neutre', *Cahiers Maurice Blanchot*, 1 (2011), 21–24 (pp. 21–22).

BIBLIOGRAPHY

Works by Blanchot in French

L'Amitié (Paris: Gallimard, 1971)
L'Attente l'oubli (Paris: Gallimard, 1962)
Celui qui ne m'accompagnait pas (Paris: Gallimard, 1953)
La Condition critique: articles 1945–1998, ed. by Christophe Bident (Paris: Gallimard, 2010)
'Les Deux Versions de l'imaginaire', *Les Cahiers de la Pléiade*, 12 (1951), 115–25
'Le "Discours philosophique"', *L'Arc*, 46 (1971), 1–4
Écrits politiques: 1958–1993 (Paris: Léo Scheer, 2003)
L'Écriture du désastre (Paris: Gallimard, 1980)
L'Entretien infini (Paris: Gallimard, 1969)
L'Espace littéraire (Paris: Gallimard, 1955)
Faux pas (Paris: Gallimard, 1943)
'Lettre à un jeune cinéaste', *Trafic*, 49 (2004), 139
Le Livre à venir (Paris: Gallimard, 1959)
Le Part du feu (Paris: Gallimard, 1949)
Le Pas au-delà (Paris: Gallimard, 1973)
Thomas l'obscur (Paris: Gallimard, 1950)
Thomas l'obscur: Première version, 1941 (Paris: Gallimard, 2005)

Works by Blanchot in English

Awaiting Oblivion, trans. by John Gregg (Lincoln: University of Nebraska Press, 1997)
The Book to Come, trans. by Charlotte Mandell (Stanford, CA: Stanford University Press, 2003)
Desperate Clarity: Chronicles of an Intellectual Life, 1942, trans. by Michael Holland (New York: Fordham University Press, 2013)
Faux Pas, trans. by Charlotte Mandell (Stanford, CA: Stanford University Press, 2001)
Friendship, trans. by Elizabeth Rottenberg (Stanford, CA: Stanford University Press, 1997)
The Infinite Conversation, trans. by Susan Hanson (Minneapolis: University of Minnesota Press, 1993)
Political Writings, 1953–1993, trans. by Zakir Paul (New York: Fordham University Press, 2010)
'Responses and Interventions (1946–98)', *Paragraph*, 30:3, 'Blanchot's Epoch', ed. by Leslie Hill and Michael Holland (2007), 5–45
The Space of Literature, trans. by Ann Smock (Lincoln: University of Nebraska Press, 1982)
The Station Hill Blanchot Reader, ed. by George Quasha, trans. by Lydia Davis, Paul Auster and Robert Lamberton (New York: Station Hill Press, 1999)
The Step Not Beyond, trans. by Lycette Nelson (New York: State University of New York Press, 1992)
A Voice from Elsewhere, trans. by Charlotte Mandell (New York: State University of New York Press, 2007)

The Work of Fire, trans. by Charlotte Mandell (Stanford, CA: Stanford University Press, 1995)

The Writing of the Disaster, trans. by Ann Smock, new edn (Lincoln: University of Nebraska Press, 1995)

BLANCHOT, MAURICE, and JACQUES DERRIDA, *The Instant of My Death/Demeure: Fiction and Testimony*, trans. by Elizabeth Rottenberg (Stanford, CA: Stanford University Press, 2000)

FOUCAULT, MICHEL, and MAURICE BLANCHOT, *Foucault/Blanchot*, trans. by Jeffrey Mehlman and Brian Massumi (New York: Zone Books, 1988)

Works by Other Authors

AGAMBEN, GIORGIO, 'Cinema and History: On Jean-Luc Godard', in *Cinema and Agamben: Ethics, Biopolitics and the Moving Image*, ed. by Henrik Gustafsson and Asbjørn Grønstad (New York: Bloomsbury, 2014), pp. 25–26

—— *Homo Sacer: Sovereign Power and Bare Life*, trans. by Daniel Heller-Roazen (Stanford, CA: Stanford University Press, 1998)

—— *Means Without End: Notes on Politics*, trans. by Vincenzo Binetti and Cesare Casarino (Minneapolis: University of Minnesota Press, 2000)

ALLOA, EMMANUEL, ed., *Penser l'image* (Dijon: Les Presses du réel, 2010)

AUMONT, JACQUES, *Amnésies: fictions du cinéma d'après Jean-Luc Godard* (Paris: P.O.L., 1999)

—— 'Mortal Beauty', in *The Cinema Alone: Essays on the Work of Jean-Luc Godard 1985–2000*, ed. by Michael Temple and James S. Williams (Amsterdam: Amsterdam University Press, 2000), pp. 97–112

BACHELARD, GASTON, *The Poetics of Space*, trans. by Maria Jolas (Boston: Beacon Press, 1969)

BAILEY, MATT, 'Gaspar Noé', *Senses of Cinema* (2003), <http://sensesofcinema.com/2003/great-directors/noe/> [accessed 5 June 2015]

BALSOM, ERIKA, 'Saving the Image: Scale and Duration in Contemporary Art Cinema', *CineAction*, 72 (2007), 23–31

BARKER, MARTIN, '"Typically French"?: Mediating Screened Rape to British Audiences', in *Rape in Art Cinema*, ed. by Dominique Russell (New York: Continuum, 2010), pp. 145–58

BARTHES, ROLAND, *La Chambre claire: note sur la photographie* (Paris: Gallimard, 1980)

—— *Camera Lucida*, trans. by Richard Howard (London: Vintage Books, 2000)

—— 'The Rhetoric of the Image', in *Image-Music-Text*, trans. by Stephen Heath (London: Fontana Press, 1977), pp. 32–51

BATAILLE, GEORGES, *The Accursed Share: An Essay on General Economy, Volumes 2 and 3*, trans. by Robert Hurley (New York: Zone Books, 1991)

—— 'L'Amour d'un être mortel', in *Œuvres complètes*, 12 vols (Paris: Gallimard, 1970–88), VIII (1976), 496–503

—— *Choix de lettres*, ed. by Michel Surya (Paris: Gallimard, 1997)

—— 'Dossier du *Pur Bonheur*', in *Œuvres complètes*, 12 vols (Paris: Gallimard, 1970–88), XII (1988), 525–47

—— *Inner Experience*, trans. by Leslie Anne Boldt (New York: State University of New York Press, 1988)

—— *Visions of Excess: Selected Writings 1927–1939*, ed. by Allan Stoekl, trans. by Allan Stoekl, Carl M. Lovitt and Donald M. Leslie Jr (Minneapolis: University of Minnesota Press, 1985)

BAYON, ESTELLE, *Le Cinéma obscène* (Paris: L'Harmattan, 2007)

—— 'Un désastre écologique', in *Béla Tarr: de la colère au tourment*, ed. by Corinne Maury and Sylvie Rollet (Crisnée: Yellow Now, 2016), pp. 46–57

BECKETT, SAMUEL, *L'Image* (Paris: Éditions de Minuit, 1988)
BELLOUR, RAYMOND, *The Analysis of Film*, ed. by Constance Penley (Bloomington and Indianapolis: Indiana University Press, [1979] 2000)
—— *Between-the-Images*, ed. by Lionel Bovier, trans. by Allyn Hardyck (Zurich: JRP/Ringier, 2012)
—— *Le Corps du cinéma: hypnoses, émotions, animalités* (Paris: P.O.L., 2009)
—— *L'Entre-Images: photo, cinéma, vidéo* (Paris: La Différence, 2002)
—— *L'Entre-Images 2: mots, images* (Paris: P.O.L., 1999)
—— 'L'Image', in *Maurice Blanchot: récits critiques*, ed. by Christophe Bident and Pierre Vilar (Tours: Éditions Farrago, 2003), pp. 133–41
—— '(Not) Just An Other Filmmaker', trans. by Lynne Kirby, in *Jean-Luc Godard: Son + Image, 1974–1991*, ed. by Raymond Bellour and Mary Lea Bandy (New York: MOMA, 1992), pp. 215–31
—— *Pensées du cinéma*, (Paris: P.O.L., 2016)
—— 'Saving the Image', in *Saving the Image: Art After Film*, ed. by Tanya Leighton and Pavel Büchler (Glasgow: Centre for Contemporary Arts, 2003), pp. 52–77
BERGALA, ALAIN, 'The Other Side of the Bouquet', trans. by Lynne Kirby, in *Jean-Luc Godard: Son + Image, 1974–1991*, ed. by Raymond Bellour and Mary Lea Bandy (New York: MOMA, 1992), pp. 57–74
BEUGNET, MARTINE, *Cinema and Sensation: French Film and the Art of Transgression* (Edinburgh: Edinburgh University Press, 2007)
BIDENT, CHRISTOPHE, *Maurice Blanchot: partenaire invisible* (Seyssel: Champ Vallon, 1998)
BIDENT, CHRISTOPHE, and PIERRE VILAR, eds., *Maurice Blanchot: récits critiques* (Tours: Éditions Farrago, 2003)
BLAKE, WILLIAM, *Blake's Poetry and Designs*, ed. by Mary Lynn Johnson and John E. Grant, 2nd edn (New York: W. W. Norton & Company, 2008)
BOGUE, RONALD, *Deleuze on Cinema* (New York: Routledge, 2003)
BONNEFOY, YVES, *Alberto Giacometti: A Biography of His Work*, trans. by Jean Stewart (Paris: Flammarion, 1991)
BRENEZ, NICOLE, *De la figure en général et du corps en particulier: l'invention figurative au cinéma* (Paris: De Boeck Université, 1998)
BRUNETTE, PETER, and DAVID WILLS, *Screen/Play: Derrida and Film Theory* (Princeton, NJ: Princeton University Press, 1989)
BURKE, VICTORIA I., 'From Desire to Fascination: Hegel and Blanchot on Negativity', *MLN*, 114:4 (1999), 848–56
CELESTE, RENI, 'The Frozen Screen: Levinas and the Action Film', *Film-Philosophy*, 11:2 (2007), 15–36
CHABRIER, RODOLPHE, 'SPX', on *Irreversible*, collector's edn DVD (London: Tartan Video, 2006)
CHERCHI USAI, PAOLO, *The Death of Cinema: History, Cultural Memory and the Digital Dark Age* (London: BFI, 2001)
CHION, MICHEL, *Audio-Vision: Sound on Screen*, ed. and trans. by Claudia Gorbman (New York: Columbia University Press, 1994)
CHRISTIE, IAN, 'Time Regained: The Complex Magic of Reverse Motion', in *Projected Shadows: Psychoanalytic Reflections on the Representation of Loss in European Cinema*, ed. by Andrea Sabbadini (London: Routledge, 2007), pp. 168–81
COHEN, JOSH, *Interrupting Auschwitz: Art, Religion, Philosophy* (London: Continuum, 2005)
COLLIN, FRANÇOISE, *Maurice Blanchot et la question de l'écriture*, 2nd edn (Paris: Gallimard, 1986)
CONLEY, TOM, 'The Film-Event: from Bazin to Deleuze', paper given at the Maison française d'Oxford, 12 March 2015

COOPER, SARAH, *Selfless Cinema ? Ethics and French Documentary* (Oxford: Legenda, 2006)
COX, DAVID, 'Masterclass with Gaspar Noé', BFI, 2009, <http://explore.bfi.org.uk/4fc75db652a32> [accessed 5 June 2015]
CRITCHLEY, SIMON, 'Il y a — Holding Levinas's Hand to Blanchot's Fire', in *Maurice Blanchot: The Demand of Writing*, ed. by Carolyn Bailey Gill (London: Routledge, 1996), pp. 108–22
CROGAN, PATRICK, 'Experience of the Industrial Temporal Object', in *Stiegler and Technics*, ed. by Christina Howells and Gerald Moore (Edinburgh: Edinburgh University Press, 2013), pp. 102–18
CROWLEY, MARTIN, *L'Homme sans: politiques de la finitude* (Paris: Lignes, 2009)
—— *Robert Antelme: Humanity, Community, Testimony* (Oxford: Legenda, 2003)
—— 'Touche-là', in *Blanchot dans son siècle*, ed. by Monique Antelme and others (Lyon: Parangon, 2009), pp. 166–76
CUNNINGHAM, JOHN, *Hungarian Cinema: From Coffee House to Multiplex* (London: Wallflower Press, 2004)
DANEY, SERGE, 'From Movies to Moving', in *Art and the Moving Image: A Critical Reader*, ed. by Tanya Leighton (London: Tate Publishing and Afterall, 2008), pp. 334–39
DELEUZE, GILLES, *Cinéma 1: l'image-mouvement* (Paris: Éditions de Minuit, 1983)
—— *Cinema 1: The Movement-Image*, trans. by Hugh Tomlinson and Barbara Habberjam (London: Continuum, 2005)
—— *Cinéma 2: l'image-temps* (Paris: Éditions de Minuit, 1985)
—— *Cinema 2: The Time-Image*, trans. by Hugh Tomlinson and Robert Galeta (London: Continuum, 2005)
—— 'cinéma/pensée cours 70', lecture given on 20 November 1984, <http://www.univ-paris8.fr/deleuze/article.php3?id_article=196> [accessed 27 June 2015]
—— *Différence et répétition* (Paris: PUF, 1968)
—— *Difference and Repetition*, trans. by Paul Patton (New York: Columbia University Press, 1994)
—— *Foucault*, trans. by Seán Hand (Minneapolis: University of Minnesota Press, 1988)
—— *Francis Bacon: logique de la sensation* (Paris: Éditions de la différence, 1981)
—— *Francis Bacon: The Logic of Sensation*, trans. by Daniel W. Smith (London: Continuum, 2003)
—— *Logique du sens* (Paris: Éditions de Minuit, 1969)
—— *The Logic of Sense*, ed. by Constantin V. Boundas, trans. by Mark Lester with Charles Stivale (London: Continuum, 2004)
—— *Le Pli: Leibniz et le Baroque* (Paris: Éditions de Minuit, 1988)
—— *The Fold: Leibniz and the Baroque*, trans. by Tom Conley (London: Athlone, 1993)
DE LUCA, TIAGO, and NUNO BARRADAS JORGE, eds., *Slow Cinema* (Edinburgh: Edinburgh University Press, 2016)
DERRIDA, JACQUES, *Demeure: Maurice Blanchot* (Paris: Galilée, 1998)
—— *Mémoires d'aveugle: l'autoportrait et autres ruines* (Paris: Louvre, 1990)
—— *Memoirs of the Blind*, trans. by Pascale-Anne Brault (Chicago, IL: University of Chicago Press, 1993)
—— *Papier machine* (Paris: Galilée, 2001)
—— *Paper Machine*, trans. by Rachel Bowlby (Stanford, CA: Stanford University Press, 2005)
—— *Parages* (Paris: Galilée, 1986)
—— *Parages*, ed. by John P. Leavey, trans. by Tom Conley and others (Stanford, CA: Stanford University Press, 2011)
DIDI-HUBERMAN, GEORGES, 'De ressemblance à ressemblance', in *Maurice Blanchot: récits critiques*, ed. by Christophe Bident and Pierre Vilar (Tours: Éditions Farrago, 2003), pp. 143–67

DOANE, MARY ANN, *The Emergence of Cinematic Time: Modernity, Contingency, the Archive* (Cambridge, MA: Harvard University Press, 2002)

DUNNE, J. W., *An Experiment with Time* (London: Faber and Faber, 1958 [1927])

EBERT, ROGER, 'Irreversible', 2003, <http://www.rogerebert.com/reviews/irreversible-2003> [accessed 27 June 2015]

EDELSTEIN, DAVID, 'Irreversible Errors', *Slate* (2003), <http://www.slate.com/articles/arts/movies/2003/03/irreversible_errors.html> [accessed 27 June 2015]

FFRENCH, PATRICK, *After Bataille: Sacrifice, Exposure, Community* (Oxford: Legenda, 2007)

—— 'Belief in the Body: Philippe Garrel's *Le Révélateur* and Deleuze', *Paragraph*, 31:2 (2008), 159–72

—— 'Friendship, Asymmetry, Sacrifice: Bataille and Blanchot', *Parrhesia*, 3 (2007), 32–42

FLANAGAN, MATTHEW, '"Slow Cinema": Temporality and Style in Contemporary Art and Experimental Film' (unpublished PhD thesis, University of Exeter, 2012)

FREUD, SIGMUND, *The Standard Edition of the Complete Psychological Works of Sigmund Freud, Vol. XVII: An Infantile Neurosis and Other Works*, trans. by James Strachey (London: Vintage, 2001)

FYNSK, CHRISTOPHER, *The Claim of Language: A Case for the Humanities* (Minneapolis: University of Minnesota Press, 2004)

—— *Infant Figures: The Death of the 'Infans' and Other Scenes of Origin* (Stanford, CA: Stanford University Press, 2000)

—— *Last Steps: Maurice Blanchot's Exilic Writing* (New York: Fordham University Press, 2013)

GILL, CAROLYN BAILEY, ed., *Maurice Blanchot: The Demand of Writing* (London: Routledge, 1996)

GIRGUS, SAM, *Levinas and the Cinema of Redemption* (New York: Columbia University Press, 2010)

GODARD, JEAN-LUC, *Histoire(s) du cinéma*, 4 vols (Paris: Gallimard/Gaumont, 1998)

—— *Jean-Luc Godard par Jean-Luc Godard*, ed. by Alain Bergala, 2 vols (Paris: Cahiers du cinéma, 1998)

GODARD, JEAN-LUC, and YOUSSEF ISHAGHPOUR, *Archéologie du cinéma et mémoire du siècle: dialogue* (Tours: Farrago, 2000)

—— *Cinema: The Archaeology of Film and the Memory of a Century*, trans. by John Howe (Oxford: Berg, 2005)

GODDARD, MICHAEL, 'Raymond Bellour', in *Film, Theory and Philosophy: The Key Thinkers*, ed. by Felicity Colman (Montreal & Kingston: McGill-Queens University Press, 2009), pp. 256–65

GORFINKEL, ELENA, 'Weariness, Waiting: Endurance and Art Cinema's Tired Bodies', *Discourse*, 34, 2–3 (2012), 311–47

GRØNSTAD, ASBJØRN, *Screening the Unwatchable: Spaces of Negation in Post-Millennial Art Cinema* (Basingstoke: Palgrave Macmillan, 2012)

—— 'On the Unwatchable', in *The New Extremism in Cinema: From France to Europe*, ed. by Tanya Horeck and Tina Kendall (Edinburgh: Edinburgh University Press, 2011), pp. 192–205

GUNNING, TOM, 'The Cinema of Attractions: Early Film, Its Spectator and the Avant-Garde', *Wide Angle*, 8:3 (1986), 60–70

HARRIS, OLIVER, 'Film Noir Fascination: Outside History, but Historically So', *Cinema Journal*, 43:1 (2003), 3–24

—— 'Pure Cinema? Blanchot, Godard, *Le Mépris*', *Critical Quarterly*, 53, 'Godard's *Contempt*: Essays from the London Consortium', ed. by Colin MacCabe and Laura Mulvey (2011), 96–106

HART, KEVIN, *The Dark Gaze: Maurice Blanchot and the Sacred* (Chicago, IL: University of Chicago Press, 2004)
—— *Postmodernism: A Beginner's Guide* (Oxford: Oneworld, 2004)
HEIDEGGER, MARTIN, *Kant and the Problem of Metaphysics*, trans. by Richard Taft, 5th edn (Bloomington: Indiana University Press, 1997)
—— 'The Origin of the Work of Art', in *Basic Writings*, ed. by David Farrell Krell (London: Routledge, 2009), pp. 143–212
—— *Sein und Zeit* (Tübingen: Max Niemeyer Verlag, 1967)
—— *Being and Time*, trans. by John Macquarrie and Edward Robinson (Oxford: Blackwell, 1962)
—— 'What Are Poets For?', in *Poetry, Language, Thought*, ed. and trans. by Albert Hofstadter (New York: Harper Collins, 2001), pp. 89–139
—— *What Is Called Thinking?*, trans. by Fred D. Wieck and J. Glenn Gray (New York: Harper & Row, 1968)
HILL, LESLIE, *Blanchot: Extreme Contemporary* (London: Routledge, 1997)
—— '"A Form that Thinks": Godard, Blanchot, Citation', in *For Ever Godard*, ed. by Michael Temple, James S. Williams and Michael Witt (London: Black Dog, 2004), pp. 396–415
—— *Marguerite Duras: Apocalyptic Desires* (London: Routledge, 1993)
—— *Maurice Blanchot and Fragmentary Writing: A Change of Epoch* (London: Continuum, 2012)
—— '"O himmlisch Licht!": Cinema and the Withdrawal of the Gods (Straub-Huillet, Hölderlin, Godard, Brecht)', *Angelaki: Journal of the Theoretical Humanities*, 17:4, 'Belief in Cinema: Themes after André Bazin', ed. by Lisa Trahair and Lisabeth During (2012), 139–55
—— *Radical Indecision: Barthes, Blanchot, Derrida, and the Future of Criticism* (Notre Dame, IN: University of Notre Dame Press, 2010)
HILL, LESLIE, BRIAN NELSON, and DIMITRIS VARDOULAKIS, eds., *After Blanchot: Literature, Philosophy, Criticism* (Newark: University of Delaware Press, 2005)
HOLLAND, MICHAEL, 'L'Archive introuvable', *Cahiers Maurice Blanchot*, 4 (2014), 164–74
—— *Avant dire: essais sur Blanchot* (Paris: Hermann, 2015)
—— '"Let's Leave God Out of This": Maurice Blanchot's Reading of *Totality and Infinity*', in *Facing the Other: The Ethics of Emmanuel Levinas*, ed. by Seán Hand (Richmond: Curzon, 1996), pp. 91–106
HOPPENOT, ÉRIC, and DOMINIQUE RABATÉ, eds., *Maurice Blanchot* (Paris: Éditions de l'Herne, 2014)
INWOOD, MICHAEL, *A Heidegger Dictionary* (Oxford: Blackwell, 1998)
JAMES, IAN, 'The Evidence of the Image', *L'Esprit créateur*, 47:3 (2007), 68–79
JAY, MARTIN, *Downcast Eyes: The Denigration of Vision in Twentieth-Century French Thought* (Berkeley: University of California Press, 1994)
KAFKA, FRANZ, *The Castle*, trans. by Willa and Edwin Muir (Harmondsworth: Penguin, 1957)
KANT, IMMANUEL, *Critique of Pure Reason*, trans. by Norman Kemp Smith, 2nd edn (Basingstoke: Palgrave Macmillan, 2007)
KAUFMAN, ELEANOR, 'Midnight, or the Inertia of Being', in *After Blanchot: Literature, Philosophy, Criticism*, ed. by Leslie Hill, Brian Nelson, and Dimitris Vardoulakis (Newark: University of Delaware Press, 2005), pp. 221–37
KEARNEY, RICHARD, *The Wake of Imagination: Toward a Postmodern Culture* (New York: Routledge, 1988)
KEESEY, DOUGLAS, 'Split Identification: Representations of Rape in Gaspar Noé's *Irréversible* and Catherine Breillat's *A ma soeur!/Fat Girl*', *Studies in European Cinema*, 7:2 (2010), 95–107

KOEHLER, ROBERT, 'Interview — The Thinking Image: Fred Keleman on Béla Tarr and *The Turin Horse*', *Cinema Scope* (2012), <http://cinema-scope.com/cinema-scope-magazine/interview-the-thinking-image-fred-kelemen-on-bela-tarr-and-the-turin-horse/> [accessed 5 June 2015]

KOJÈVE, ALEXANDRE, *Introduction à la lecture de Hegel* (Paris: Gallimard, 1947)

KOVÁCS, ANDRÁS BÁLINT, *The Cinema of Béla Tarr: The Circle Closes* (New York: Wallflower Press, 2013)

KRASZNAHORKAI, LÁSZLÓ, *Satantango*, trans. by Georges Szirtes (London: Atlantic Books, 2012)

LACAN, JACQUES, *Le Séminaire, Livre XI: Les Quatre Concepts fondamentaux de la psychanalyse* (Paris: Seuil, 1973)

LACK, ROLAND-FRANÇOIS, 'Sa voix', in *For Ever Godard*, ed. by Michael Temple, James S. Williams and Michael Witt (London: Black Dog, 2004), pp. 312–29

LACOUE-LABARTHE, PHILIPPE, *Agonie terminée, agonie interminable*, ed. by Aristide Bianchi and Leonid Kharlamov (Paris: Galilée, 2011)

LACOUE-LABARTHE, PHILIPPE, and JEAN-LUC NANCY, *L'Absolu littéraire: théorie de la littérature du romantisme allemand* (Paris: Seuil, 1978)

LAPORTE, JACQUELINE, and ÉRIC HOPPENOT, '"Le meilleur des amis": Jacqueline Laporte avec Éric Hoppenot', in *Maurice Blanchot*, ed. by Éric Hoppenot and Dominique Rabaté (Paris: Éditions de l'Herne, 2014), pp. 99–102

LAPORTE, ROGER, 'Au-delà de l'"Horror vacui"', *Nouvelle Revue de Psychanalyse*, 11, 'Figures du vide', (1975), 117–26

—— *Études* (Paris: P.O.L., 1990)

LECLAIRE, SERGE, *On tue un enfant* (Paris: Seuil, 1975)

—— *A Child Is Being Killed*, trans. by Marie-Claude Hays (Stanford, CA: Stanford University Press, 1998)

LEE, CRISPIN T., *Haptic Experience in the Writings of Georges Bataille, Maurice Blanchot and Michel Serres* (Bern: Peter Lang, 2014)

LEFEBVRE, MARTIN, 'Between Setting and Landscape in the Cinema', in *Landscape and Film*, ed. by Martin Lefebvre (New York: Routledge, 2006), pp. 19–59

LEVINAS, EMMANUEL, *Autrement qu'être, ou au-delà de l'essence* (Paris: Livre de Poche, 1990)

—— *Otherwise than Being; Or, Beyond Essence*, trans. by Alphonso Lingis (Dordrecht: Kluwer Academic Publishers, 1991)

—— *De l'existence à l'existant* (Paris: Vrin, 1984)

—— *Existence and Existents*, trans. by Alphonso Lingis (Dordrecht: Kluwer Academic Publishers, 1995)

—— *Proper Names*, trans. by Michael B. Smith (Stanford, CA: Stanford University Press, 1996)

—— 'La Réalité et son ombre', in *Les Imprévus de l'histoire* (Montpellier: Fata Morgana, 1994), pp. 123–48

—— 'Reality and its Shadow', in *Collected Philosophical Papers*, trans. by Alphonso Lingis (Dordrecht: Kluwer Academic Publishers, 1987), pp. 1–13

—— *Sur Maurice Blanchot* (Montpellier: Fata Morgana, 1975)

—— *Totalité et infini: essai sur l'extériorité* (Paris: Livre de Poche, 1990)

—— *Totality and Infinity: An Essay on Exteriority*, trans. by Alphonso Lingis (The Hague: Martinus Nijhoff, 1979)

LIBERTSON, JOSEPH, *Proximity: Levinas, Blanchot, Bataille and Communication* (The Hague: Martinus Nijhoff, 1982)

LYOTARD, JEAN-FRANÇOIS, 'L'Acinéma', in *Des dispositifs pulsionnels* (Paris: Galilée, 1994)

—— 'Acinema', in *The Lyotard Reader*, ed. by Andrew Benjamin, trans. by Paisley N. Livingston (Oxford: Blackwell, 1989), pp. 169–80

———'Idée d'un film souverain', in *Misère de la philosophie* (Paris: Galilée, 2000), pp. 209–21
MACCABE, COLIN, *Godard: A Portrait of the Artist at Seventy* (London: Bloomsbury, 2003)
MACLACHLAN, IAN, 'Blanchot and the Romantic Imagination', in *Blanchot Romantique: A Collection of Essays*, ed. by John McKeane and Hannes Opelz, (Bern: Peter Lang, 2011), pp. 155–71
MALRAUX, ANDRÉ, *Le Musée imaginaire* (Paris: Gallimard, 1965)
———*Museum Without Walls*, trans. by Stuart Gilbert and Francis Price (New York: Doubleday & Co., 1967)
———'Speech by André Malraux', *The Trial of Joan of Arc*, DVD (London: Artificial Eye, 2005)
MARGULIES, IVONE, *Nothing Happens: Chantal Akerman's Hyperrealist Everyday* (Durham, NC: Duke University Press, 1996)
MASCOLO, DIONYS, 'Naissance de la tragédie', *La Quinzaine Littéraire* 202, 15 January 1975
MATHEWS, TIMOTHY, *Alberto Giacometti: The Art of Relation* (London: I. B. Tauris, 2014)
MAURY, CORINNE, and SYLVIE ROLLET, eds., *Béla Tarr: de la colère au tourment* (Crisnée: Yellow Now, 2016)
MCGOWAN, TODD, *Out of Time: Desire in Atemporal Cinema* (Minneapolis: University of Minnesota Press, 2011)
MCMAHON, LAURA, *Cinema and Contact: The Withdrawal of Touch in Nancy, Bresson, Duras and Denis* (Oxford: Legenda, 2012)
METZ, CHRISTIAN, *Le Signifiant imaginaire: Psychanalyse et cinéma* (Paris: Christian Bourgois, 1984)
———*Psychoanalysis and Cinema: The Imaginary Signifier*, trans. by Celia Britton and others (Basingstoke: Macmillan, 1982)
MORREY, DOUGLAS, 'History of Resistance/Resistance of History: Godard's *Éloge de l'amour* (2001)', *Studies in French Cinema*, 3:2 (2003), 121–30
———'Jean-Luc Godard and the Other History of Cinema' (unpublished PhD thesis, University of Warwick, 2002)
MULVEY, LAURA, *Death 24x a Second: Stillness and the Moving Image* (London: Reaktion Books, 2006)
NANCY, JEAN-LUC, *Au fond des images* (Paris: Galilée, 2003)
———*The Ground of the Image*, trans. by Jeff Fort (New York: Fordham University Press, 2005)
———*La Communauté désœuvrée* (Paris: Christian Bourgois, 1999 [1986])
———*The Inoperative Community*, ed. by Peter Connor, with a foreword by Christopher Fynsk, trans. by Peter Conor and others (Minneapolis: University of Minnesota Press, 1991)
———*Le Discours de la syncope: 1. Logodaedalus* (Paris: Aubier-Flammarion, 1976)
———*The Discourse of the Syncope: Logodaedalus*, trans. by Saul Anton (Stanford, CA: Stanford University Press, 2008)
———*The Evidence of Film: Abbas Kiarostami*, trans. by Christine Irizarry and Verena Andermatt Conley (Brussels: Yves Gevaert, 2001)
———'Le Neutre, la neutralisation du neutre', *Cahiers Maurice Blanchot*, 1 (2011), 21–24
———'Reste inavouable: entretien avec Mathilde Girard', *Lignes*, 43 (2014), 155–76
ODIN, PAUL-EMMANUEL, *L'Absence de livre: Gary Hill et Maurice Blanchot — écriture, vidéo* (Marseille: La Compagnie, 2007)
PALMER, TIM, *Brutal Intimacy: Analyzing Contemporary French Cinema* (Middletown: Wesleyan University Press, 2011)
———*Irreversible* (London: Palgrave, 2015)

—— 'Style and Sensation in the Contemporary French Cinema of the Body', *Journal of Film and Video*, 58:3 (2006), 22–32
PASOLINI, PIER PAOLO, 'The "Cinema of Poetry"', in *Heretical Empiricism*, ed. by Louise K. Barnett, trans. by Ben Lawton and Louise K. Barnett (Washington, DC: New Academia Publishing, 2005), pp. 167–86
—— 'Observations on the Long Take', trans. by Norman MacAfee and Craig Owens, *October*, 13 (1980), 3–6
PETIT, CHRIS, 'The History of Cinema and History in Cinema', *Vertigo*, 4:2 (2009), <https://www.closeupfilmcentre.com/vertigo_magazine/volume-4-issue-2-winter-spring-20091/the-history-of-cinema-and-history-in-cinema/> [accessed 5 June 2015]
PRESA, ELIZABETH, 'White Work', in *After Blanchot: Literature, Philosophy, Criticism*, ed. by Leslie Hill, Brian Nelson, and Dimitris Vardoulakis (Newark: University of Delaware Press, 2005), pp. 257–69
QUANDT, JAMES, 'Flesh and Blood: Sex and Violence in Recent French Cinema', in *The New Extremism in Cinema: From France to Europe*, ed. by Tanya Horeck and Tina Kendall (Edinburgh: Edinburgh University Press, 2011), pp. 18–28
QUASHA, GEORGE, and CHARLES STEIN, '*Liminal Performance*: Gary Hill in Dialogue', in *Gary Hill*, ed. by Robert C. Morgan (Baltimore, MD: John Hopkins University Press, 2000), pp. 243–68
RANCIÈRE, JACQUES, *Aisthesis: scènes du régime esthétique de l'art* (Paris: Galilée, 2011)
—— *Béla Tarr: le temps d'après* (Paris: Capricci, 2011)
—— *Béla Tarr: The Time After*, trans. by Erik Beranek (Minneapolis: Univocal Publishing, 2013)
—— *Les Écarts du cinéma* (Paris: La Fabrique éditions, 2011)
—— *The Intervals of Cinema*, trans. by John Howe (London: Verso, 2014)
—— *La Fable cinématographique* (Paris: Seuil, 2001)
—— *Film Fables*, ed. by Emiliano Battista (Oxford: Berg, 2006)
—— *The Politics of Aesthetics*, trans. by Gabriel Rockhill (London: Continuum, 2004)
RAVEL, EMMANUELLE, *Maurice Blanchot et l'art au XXème siècle: une esthétique de désoeuvrement* (Amsterdam: Rodopi, 2007)
READER, KEITH, *Robert Bresson* (Manchester: Manchester University Press, 2000)
RODOWICK, D. N., *Gilles Deleuze's Time Machine* (Durham, NC: Duke University Press, 1997)
—— *Reading the Figural, or, Philosophy after the New Media* (Durham, NC: Duke University Press, 2001)
—— *The Virtual Life of Film* (Cambridge, MA: Harvard University Press, 2007)
ROPARS-WUILLEUMIER, MARIE-CLAIRE, *Écraniques: le film du texte* (Lille: Presses Universitaires de Lille, 1990)
—— *Écrire l'espace* (Paris: Presses Universitaires de Vincennes, 2002)
—— *L'Idée d'image* (Paris: Presses Universitaires de Vincennes, 1995)
—— 'Image or Time? The Thought of the Outside in *The Time-Image* (Deleuze and Blanchot)', trans. by Matthew Lazen with D. N. Rodowick, in *Afterimages of Gilles Deleuze's Film Philosophy*, ed. by D. N. Rodowick (Minneapolis: University of Minnesota, 2010), pp. 15–30
—— 'On Unworking: The Image in Writing According to Blanchot', trans. by Roland-François Lack, in *Maurice Blanchot: The Demand of Writing*, ed. by Carolyn Bailey Gill (London: Routledge, 1996), pp. 137–51
—— 'Le Saisissement imaginaire', *Hors Cadre*, 4, 'L'Image, l'imaginaire' (1986), 27–37
—— *Le Temps d'une pensée*, ed. by Sophie Charlin (Paris: Presses Universitaires de Vincennes, 2009)

Rushton, Richard, 'Deleuzian Spectatorship', *Screen*, 50:1 (2009), 45–53
——'The New Film Studies and the Decline of Critique', *CineAction*, 72 (2007), 2–7
Russell, Dominique, ed., *Rape in Art Cinema* (London and New York: Continuum, 2010)
Saliot, Anne-Gaëlle, '"Venir comme des profondeurs d'un tombeau": Maurice Blanchot, l'inconnue de la Seine et les images', in *Maurice Blanchot*, ed. by Éric Hoppenot and Dominique Rabaté (Paris: Éditions de l'Herne, 2014), pp. 217–25
Sartre, Jean-Paul, *L'Imaginaire* (Paris: Gallimard, 1940)
Saxton, Libby, 'Spectatorship and Suffering', in *Film and Ethics: Foreclosed Encounters*, ed. by Lisa Downing and Libby Saxton (London: Routledge, 2010), pp. 63–75
Scemama, Céline, *'Histoire(s) du cinéma' de Jean-Luc Godard: la force faible d'un art* (Paris: L'Harmattan, 2006)
——'Jean-Luc Godard's *Histoire(s) du cinéma* Brings the Dead Back to the Screen', in *The Legacies of Jean-Luc Godard*, ed. by Douglas Morrey, Christina Stojanova and Nicole Côté (Ontario: Wilfrid Laurier University Press, 2014), pp. 99–124
Shafto, Sally, 'On Painting and History in Godard's *Histoire(s) du cinéma*', *Senses of Cinema*, 40 (2006), <http://sensesofcinema.com/2006/the-godard-museum/histoires-du-cinema/> [accessed 27 June 2015]
Shaviro, Steven, *The Cinematic Body* (Minneapolis: University of Minnesota Press, 1993)
Sibertin-Blanc, Guillaume, 'De la mélancolie à la résistance: communautés et désœuvrement', in *Béla Tarr: de la colère au tourment*, ed. by Corinne Maury and Sylvie Rollet (Crisnée: Yellow Now, 2016), pp. 150–64
Silverman, Kaja, and Harun Farocki, *Speaking about Godard* (New York: New York University Press, 1998)
Singer, Ben, '*Jeanne Dielman*: Cinematic Interrogation and "Amplification"', *Millennium Film Journal*, 22 (1989), 56–75
Smith, Douglas, '(Un)Reconstructed Space?: The Imaginary in Post-War France (Sartre, Malraux, Merleau-Ponty, Blanchot', *Paragraph*, 27:3 (2004), 68–81
Stiegler, Bernard, *Dans la disruption: comment ne pas devenir fou?* (Paris: Les Liens qui libèrent, 2016)
——*États de choc: bêtise et savoir au XXIe siècle* (Paris: Mille et une nuits, 2012)
——*States of Shock: Stupidity and Knowledge in the Twenty-First Century*, trans. by Daniel Ross (Cambridge: Polity, 2015)
——*La Technique et le temps 3: le temps du cinéma et la question du mal-être* (Paris: Galilée, 2001)
——*Technics and Time, 3: Cinematic Time and the Question of Malaise*, trans. by Stephen Barker (Stanford, CA: Stanford University Press, 2010)
Tang, Jean, '"There Are No Bad Deeds, Just Deeds"', *Salon* (2003), <http://www.salon.com/2003/03/12/noe/> [accessed 27 June 2015]
Temple, Michael, 'Big Rhythm and the Power of Metamorphosis: Some Models and Precursors for *Histoire(s) du cinéma*', in *The Cinema Alone: Essays on the Work of Jean-Luc Godard 1985–2000*, ed. by Michael Temple and James S. Williams (Amsterdam: Amsterdam University Press, 2000), pp. 77–95
Temple, Michael, and James S. Williams, eds., *The Cinema Alone: Essays on the Work of Jean-Luc Godard 1985–2000* (Amsterdam: Amsterdam University Press, 2000)
Temple, Michael, James S. Williams and Michael Witt, eds., *For Ever Godard* (London: Black Dog, 2004)
Wall, Thomas Carl, *Radical Passivity: Levinas, Blanchot, and Agamben* (New York: State University of New York Press, 1999)
Watt, Calum, 'Alcoholism and the Doctor in Béla Tarr's *Satantango*', in *The Cinematic*

Bodies of Eastern Europe and Russia: Between Pain and Pleasure, ed. by Matilda Mroz, Ewa Mazierska and Elzbieta Ostrowska (Edinburgh: Edinburgh University Press, 2016), pp. 53–66
—— 'The Tortoise and the Corpse: Two Excisions from Maurice Blanchot's "Les Deux Versions de l'imaginaire"', *French Studies Bulletin*, 38, 142 (2017), 4–7
—— 'The Uses of Maurice Blanchot in Bernard Stiegler's *Technics and Time*', *Paragraph*, 39:3 (2016), 305–18
WILLIAMS, JAMES S., 'European Culture and Artistic Resistance in *Histoire(s) du cinéma* Chapter 3A, *La Monnaie de l'absolu*', in *The Cinema Alone: Essays on the Work of Jean-Luc Godard 1985–2000*, ed. by Michael Temple and James S. Williams (Amsterdam: Amsterdam University Press, 2000), pp. 113–39
—— *Jean Cocteau* (Manchester: Manchester University Press, 2006)
—— 'Music, Love, and the Cinematic Event', in *For Ever Godard*, ed. by Michael Temple, James S. Williams and Michael Witt (London: Black Dog Press, 2004), pp. 288–311
—— 'Silence, Gesture, Revelation: The Ethics and Aesthetics of Montage in Godard and Agamben', in *Cinema and Agamben: Ethics, Biopolitics and the Moving Image*, ed. by Henrik Gustafsson and Asbjørn Grønstad (New York: Bloomsbury, 2014), pp. 27–54
WINNICOTT, D. W., 'La Crainte de l'effondrement', *Nouvelle Revue de Psychanalyse*, 11, 'Figures du vide' (1975), 35–44
—— 'Fear of Breakdown', in *Psycho-Analytic Explorations*, ed. by Clare Winnicott, Ray Shepherd and Madeleine Davis (London: Karnac Books, 1989), pp. 87–95
WITT, MICHAEL, *Jean-Luc Godard: Cinema Historian* (Bloomington: Indiana University Press, 2013)
—— 'Montage, My Beautiful Care, or Histories of the Cinematograph', in *The Cinema Alone: Essays on the Work of Jean-Luc Godard 1985–2000*, ed. by Michael Temple and James S. Williams (Amsterdam: Amsterdam University Press, 2000), pp. 33–50
WOOD, ROBIN, '*Irreversible*: Against and For', *Film International*, 1:5 (2003), <http://filmint.nu/?p=1475> [accessed 4 June 2015]
WOODWARD, ASHLEY, 'A Sacrificial Economy of the Image: Lyotard on Cinema', *Angelaki: Journal of the Theoretical Humanities*, 19:4 (2014), 141–54
WRIGHT, ALAN, 'Elizabeth Taylor at Auschwitz: JLG and the Real Object of Montage', in *The Cinema Alone: Essays on the Work of Jean-Luc Godard 1985–2000*, ed. by Michael Temple and James S. Williams (Amsterdam: Amsterdam University Press, 2000), pp. 51–60
ZARADER, MARLÈNE, *L'Être et le neutre* (Lagrasse: Éditions Verdier, 2001)
ZENKINE, SERGE, 'Blanchot et l'image visuelle', in *Blanchot dans son siècle*, ed. by Monique Antelme and others (Lyon: Parangon, 2009), pp. 214–27

Filmography

Beau travail (Claire Denis, France, 1999)
The Bride of Glomdal (*Glomdalsbruden*, Carl Theodor Dreyer, Norway/Sweden, 1926)
Casque d'or (Jacques Becker, France, 1952)
Un chien andalou (Luis Buñuel, France, 1929)
Damnation (*Kárhozat*, Béla Tarr, Hungary, 1988)
Détruire dit-elle (Marguerite Duras, France, 1969)
Éloge de l'amour (Jean-Luc Godard, France/Switzerland, 2001)
Les Enfants du paradis (Marcel Carné, France, 1945)
Goodbye to Language (*Adieu au langage*, Jean-Luc Godard, France/Switzerland, 2014)
Histoire(s) du cinéma (Jean-Luc Godard, France/Switzerland, 1988–1998)
Incidences of Catastrophe (Gary Hill, USA, 1987–88)

India Song (Marguerite Duras, France, 1975)
Intervista (Federico Fellini, Italy, 1987)
Irréversible (Gaspar Noé, France, 2002)
JLG/JLG: autoportrait de décembre (Jean-Luc Godard, France, 1994)
Journey on the Plain (*Utazás az Alföldön*, Béla Tarr, Hungary, 1995)
Lecture du chapitre X de Thomas l'obscur *de Maurice Blanchot* (Benoît Jacquot, France, 1975)
The Man from London (*A londoni férfi*, Béla Tarr, France/Germany/Hungary, 2007)
Memento (Christopher Nolan, USA, 2000)
Le Mépris (Jean-Luc Godard, France/Italy, 1963)
News from Home (Chantal Akerman, France/Belgium/West Germany, 1977)
Nosferatu (F. W. Murnau, Germany, 1922)
Notre musique (Jean-Luc Godard, France/Switzerland, 2004)
The Old Place (Jean-Luc Godard and Anne-Marie Miéville, France/USA, 1998)
Ordet (Carl Theodor Dreyer, Denmark, 1955)
Orphée (Jean Cocteau, France, 1950)
The Outcry (*Il grido*, Michelangelo Antonioni, Italy/USA, 1957)
The Passion of Joan of Arc (*La Passion de Jeanne d'Arc*, Carl Theodor Dreyer, France, 1928)
Persona (Ingmar Bergman, Sweden, 1966)
A Place in the Sun (George Stevens, USA, 1951)
Le Plaisir (Max Ophüls, France, 1952)
Prison (*Fängelse*, Ingmar Bergman, Sweden, 1949)
Le Révélateur (Philippe Garrel, France, 1968)
The Round-Up (*Szegénylegények*, Miklós Jancsó, Hungary, 1966)
Satantango (*Sátántangó*, Béla Tarr, Hungary/Germany/Switzerland, 1994)
Seul contre tous (Gaspar Noé, France, 1998)
Shoah (Claude Lanzmann, France/UK, 1985)
The Silence (*Tystnaden*, Ingmar Bergman, Sweden, 1963)
The Testament of Orpheus (*Le Testament d'Orphée*, Jean Cocteau, France, 1960)
The Trial of Joan of Arc (*Procès de Jeanne d'Arc*, Robert Bresson, France, 1962)
The Turin Horse (*A torinói ló*, Béla Tarr, Hungary, 2011)
Werckmeister Harmonies (*Werckmeister harmóniák*, Béla Tarr, Hungary, 2001)
Yi Yi (Edward Yang, Japan/Taiwan, 2000)

INDEX

absence of time 63–64, 66, 82, 91, 105, 116, 123, 127, 140, 153
Adorno, Theodor 168
Agamben, Giorgio 18–19, 31, 56 n. 9, 74–76, 85, 128, 169
Akerman, Chantal 128 n. 14
Antelme, Robert 4, 148–49
Antonioni, Michelangelo 11, 113–15, 123, 126
anxiety 29–30, 67, 142, 165
Artaud, Antonin 93–95, 102 n. 118
Assayas, Oliver 137
Aumont, Jacques 67, 83–84

Bachelard, Gaston 26–27, 38
Bacon, Francis 53, 141–42
Barthes, Roland 16, 54, 60 n. 122
Bataille, Georges 21, 52, 56 nn. 4 & 9, 62–63, 67, 73–74, 80, 98 nn. 13, 14 & 16, 102 n. 122, 111, 129 n. 26, 137
Bayon, Estelle 127, 137, 140
Bazin, André 44, 68, 83, 91
Beckett, Samuel 70, 88, 99 n. 26
Bellour, Raymond 9, 12 n. 23, 22, 45–47, 52–55, 59 n. 90, 86–89, 122, 125–26, 129 n. 30, 165–67
Bergala, Alain 80, 88
Bergman, Ingmar 6, 84, 100 n. 79
Bergson, Henri 92, 97
Beugnet, Martine 137, 142, 149, 160 n. 22
Bident, Christophe 4
Blake, William 31, 77–78, 80, 100 n. 65
Blanchot, Maurice:
  L'Amitié 63, 67
  L'Arrêt de mort 3, 5, 10, 54, 55 n. 2
  L'Attente, l'oubli 41, 98, 115
  Celui qui ne m'accompagnait pas 48
  'Les Deux Versions de l'imaginaire' 23, 28, 33, 44–46, 51, 56 n. 19, 63, 66, 68, 112, 163
  L'Écriture du désastre 2, 21, 30, 33, 47, 49–50, 54, 59 n. 98, 115, 128, 145–47, 153, 163
  L'Entretien infini 2, 5, 14–15, 26, 33, 38, 41, 45, 75, 88, 93, 114, 145, 167
  L'Espace littéraire 15, 17–18, 23, 36, 38, 41, 46–47, 82, 86, 90–91, 153
  La Folie du jour 2, 50, 153
  L'Instant de ma mort 1–4, 10–11, 32, 40, 54–55, 140, 167
  'Lettre à un jeune cinéaste' 4–5
  'La Littérature et le droit à la mort' 15, 22, 25, 65, 88, 112
  Le Livre à venir 15, 86, 94
  'Parler, ce n'est pas voir' 5, 33, 75, 88, 121–24, 126, 165–66
  Le Pas au-delà 21, 30, 48, 115, 152, 161 n. 33
  Thomas l'obscur 5–9, 12 nn. 13, 14 & 20, 57 n. 24
Bogue, Ronald 92
Bonnefoy, Yves 78
Brecht, Bertolt 71, 139–40, 167
Brenez, Nicole 10
Bresson, Robert 71–72, 90
Buñuel, Luis 70, 72, 135
Burke, Victoria 36

Caravaggio 70, 72
Celeste, Reni 112, 155
Chion, Michel 5, 117, 122
Cocteau, Jean 84–85, 100 n. 80
Collin, Françoise 31
communication 14–18, 20, 23–24, 38, 56 n. 4, 111, 114, 124, 166–67
Conley, Tom 91
Cooper, Sarah 148
Crowley, Martin 39

Daho, Étienne 157
Daney, Serge 9, 60 n. 119, 81
death and dying 1–4, 28–30, 32, 36, 41–43, 48–55, 62, 65, 76, 83, 86, 90–91, 145, 148, 153
Deleuze, Gilles 10–11, 38, 43, 55, 59 n. 98, 88–97, 102 n. 118, 104–05, 113–15, 121–23, 126, 141–42, 152, 155, 157, 163–64
Denis, Claire 42, 137
Derrida, Jacques 1–4, 19, 33–34, 43, 50, 53–55, 75–76, 167
désœuvrement 16, 18–20, 56 n. 9, 126–27, 169
Didi-Huberman, Georges 27, 54, 60 n. 119, 63, 82
disaster 10, 19–20, 36, 50, 54, 127–28, 146–48, 152–53, 158–59
Doane, Mary Ann 150, 154
Dreyer, Carl 70, 81–82, 90
Dunne, J. W. 156
Duras, Marguerite 4, 12 n. 9, 90, 96, 122

Ebert, Roger 132, 150
Edelstein, David 132
Emard, Dominique 4
exposure 52–53, 55, 67, 140, 142, 147, 168–69

fascination 8–11, 20–21, 28–39, 43–47, 51–55, 67, 73, 81–83, 87, 90, 92, 95–96, 103, 109, 111, 121–27, 137–40, 143–45, 148–50, 154–55, 159, 163–69
ffrench, Patrick 94
Flanagan, Matthew 111
Foucault, Michel 19, 96
Freud, Sigmund 45, 47, 59 n. 98
Fynsk, Christopher 21, 50, 52–53, 168

Garrel, Philippe 68
Giacometti, Alberto 38–41, 43, 46, 53, 58 n. 69, 70–72, 76–77, 91, 95, 140, 144
Giotto 73
Girgus, Sam 154–55
Godard, Jean-Luc:
 Adieu au langage 98 n. 5
 Éloge de l'amour 98 nn. 5 & 13, 156–57, 162 n. 72
 Histoire(s) du cinéma 10, 61–89, 92, 103, 110, 122, 128, 163, 166
 JLG/JLG: autoportrait de décembre 62
 Le Mépris 86, 100 n. 82
 Notre musique 98 n. 5
 The Old Place 98 n. 5
Grandieux, Philippe 137
Grønstad, Asbjørn 135–37, 144, 149–50
Gunning, Tom 121

Harris, Oliver 44, 86, 100 n. 82
Hart, Kevin 29, 49
Hegel, Georg Wilhelm Friedrich 2, 15, 22, 36–37, 64–65
Heidegger, Martin 21–25, 29–32, 35–37, 45, 85–86, 94–96, 115, 123, 151–52, 156
Hill, Gary 5
Hill, Leslie 19, 21, 31, 49, 63, 68, 74–76, 100 n. 82, 115, 122, 145
Holland, Michael 19
Horkheimer, Max 168

il y a 25–27, 34–35, 49, 112, 163
image, concept of 9–10, 14–16, 20, 23–33, 35–36, 38–47, 50–52, 54–55, 62–76, 87–89, 90–97, 111–12, 124–26, 133, 136, 138–40, 147–48, 153–54, 158, 164–65, 167–69
imaginary, concept of 11, 24–29, 31, 38, 40, 51–52, 64–65, 68, 73–74, 76, 97, 125, 138–40, 143–44, 148–50, 159, 167

Jacquot, Benoît 5, 12 n. 13
James, Ian 42
Jancsó, Miklós 119

Kafka, Franz 27, 40, 130 n. 42
Kant, Immanuel 30–32
Kaufman, Eleanor 91, 154
Kennedy, J. F. 6, 117
Kiarostami, Abbas 42

Koehler, Robert 110
Kojève, Alexandre 19
Kovács, András Bálint 104, 106, 120, 135
Krasznahorkai, László 103, 119, 130 n. 42

Lacan, Jacques 44–47, 134, 139
Lack, Roland-François 62
Lacoue-Labarthe, Philippe 2, 18, 50
Lanzmann, Claude 4
Laporte, Jacqueline 5–6
Laporte, Roger 5–6, 48–49
Leclaire, Serge 47–48, 51–53, 59 n. 98
Lefebvre, Martin 120–21, 125
Levinas, Emmanuel 11, 22, 25–27, 29, 34, 39, 52, 57 n. 24, 82, 103, 112, 113, 131–32, 143–49, 151, 153–59
Libertson, Joseph 145
Lumière brothers 154
Lyotard, Jean-François 111, 138

MacCabe, Colin 100 n. 66
Maclachlan, Ian 31
Mallarmé, Stéphane 86, 91
Malraux, André 63–66, 68, 71, 83–84, 98 n. 8
Mascolo, Dionys 4
Mathews, Timothy 70–71
Maupassant, Guy de 98 n. 17
May 1968: 19–20, 86
McGowan, Todd 133–53, 156, 159
Merleau-Ponty, Maurice 30, 65
Metz, Christian 59 n. 96 & 98, 139–40, 161 n. 28
Morrey, Douglas 73–74, 76, 85
Mulvey, Laura 54, 81
Murnau, F. W. 6, 62

Nancy, Jean-Luc 17–18, 20, 22, 30, 42–43, 55, 95, 127, 169
Narcissus, myth of 27, 29, 51–52
Nietzsche, Friedrich 33, 66
Noé, Gaspar:
 Irréversible 133–38, 142–59
 Seul contre tous 156

Ophüls, Max 6, 67
Orpheus and Eurydice, myth of 47, 81–89, 159
Other, the 39–41, 132, 139, 142–55, 158–59, 164
Ozu, Yasujiro 6

Palmer, Tim 132, 135, 154
Pasolini, Pier Paolo 116–17, 135, 138, 152
passivity 27, 29, 32, 43–49, 55, 66, 76, 96, 115, 139–40, 146–50, 153, 159, 168–69
Petit, Chris 76
Petőfi, Sándor 119–20
phenomenology 23–24, 38, 40–41, 134, 138, 143, 146–49, 153, 156

Plato 26
primal scene 47–55, 59 n. 98, 66–67, 87, 127, 159
psychoanalysis 43–53, 59 n. 98, 109, 126, 133, 139, 159

Quandt, James 132

Rancière, Jacques 72–76, 85, 103–06, 109–14, 116, 120, 126, 155, 163–64
Resnais, Alain 122
responsibility 52, 144–45, 147–48, 151, 155, 158–59
Rilke, Rainer Maria 27, 36, 82
Rodin, Auguste 37, 58 n. 60
Rodowick, D. N. 95–96, 165
Ropars-Wuilleumier, Marie-Claire 9, 12 n. 9, 14, 22, 24, 27, 33, 35, 40–42, 55 n. 2, 96–97, 100 n. 82, 115, 123–26, 141, 150, 154, 156–57, 164–65, 167–68
Rushton, Richard 96, 140, 168

sacrifice 68–74, 77, 82–84, 111
Sartre, Jean-Paul 24, 27, 52, 63, 65, 112
Satantango, novel by Georges Szirtes 103, 109, 118, 121, 130 n. 42
Saxton, Libby 138
Scemama, Céline 73, 83, 98 n. 8
Shaviro, Steven 43–45, 59 n. 98, 126
Sibertin-Blanc, Guillaume 127
Silverman, Kaja 44
Smock, Ann 18, 38
Snow, Michael 118
Stevens, George 72–73
Stiegler, Bernard 32–33, 43, 55, 168–69

Szirtes, Georges 103

Tarr, Béla:
   Damnation 106, 109, 119–20
   Journey on the Plain 119–20
   The Man from London 106
   Satantango 10, 103–13, 116–21, 126–28
   The Turin Horse 103, 106, 110, 120
   Werckmeister Harmonies 106, 127
Temple, Michael 64
Trier, Lars von 135

Usai, Paolo Cherchi 165

Viola, Bill 118
violence 37, 132–38, 142–45, 147, 149, 155
vision 2, 9, 33–34, 44, 49–52, 72, 122–26, 138, 164–67

waiting 41, 105–10, 113–16, 127–28, 130 n. 42, 140
Wall, Thomas Carl 31–32, 39, 137–39, 147–48, 153, 155
Warhol, Andy 44, 103, 105
Welles, Orson 6
Williams, James S. 74
Winnicott, Donald 47–49, 52–54, 59 n. 98
Witt, Michael 68, 70, 73, 76–77, 83–84
Woodward, Ashley 111

Yang, Edward 42

Zarader, Marlène 21, 27, 33, 56 n. 17
Zenkine, Serge 4, 6, 35, 73–74

www.ingramcontent.com/pod-product-compliance
Lightning Source LLC
LaVergne TN
LVHW061251060426
835507LV00017B/2020

LEGENDA

LEGENDA is the Modern Humanities Research Association's book imprint for new research in the Humanities. Founded in 1995 by Malcolm Bowie and others within the University of Oxford, Legenda has always been a collaborative publishing enterprise, directly governed by scholars. The Modern Humanities Research Association (MHRA) joined this collaboration in 1998, became half-owner in 2004, in partnership with Maney Publishing and then Routledge, and has since 2016 been sole owner. Titles range from medieval texts to contemporary cinema and form a widely comparative view of the modern humanities, including works on Arabic, Catalan, English, French, German, Greek, Italian, Portuguese, Russian, Spanish, and Yiddish literature. Editorial boards and committees of more than 60 leading academic specialists work in collaboration with bodies such as the Society for French Studies, the British Comparative Literature Association and the Association of Hispanists of Great Britain & Ireland.

The MHRA encourages and promotes advanced study and research in the field of the modern humanities, especially modern European languages and literature, including English, and also cinema. It aims to break down the barriers between scholars working in different disciplines and to maintain the unity of humanistic scholarship. The Association fulfils this purpose through the publication of journals, bibliographies, monographs, critical editions, and the MHRA Style Guide, and by making grants in support of research. Membership is open to all who work in the Humanities, whether independent or in a University post, and the participation of younger colleagues entering the field is especially welcomed.

ALSO PUBLISHED BY THE ASSOCIATION

Critical Texts
Tudor and Stuart Translations • *New Translations* • *European Translations*
MHRA Library of Medieval Welsh Literature

MHRA Bibliographies
Publications of the Modern Humanities Research Association

The Annual Bibliography of English Language & Literature
Austrian Studies
Modern Language Review
Portuguese Studies
The Slavonic and East European Review
Working Papers in the Humanities
The Yearbook of English Studies

www.mhra.org.uk
www.legendabooks.com

INVENTION
THE LANGUAGE OF ENGLISH RENAISSANCE POETICS

EDITORIAL BOARD

Chair: Professor Jonathan Long (University of Durham)
For *Germanic Literatures*: Ritchie Robertson (University of Oxford)
For *Italian Perspectives*: Simon Gilson (University of Warwick)
For *Moving Image*: Emma Wilson (University of Cambridge)
For *Research Monographs in French Studies*:
Diana Knight (University of Nottingham)
For *Selected Essays*: Susan Harrow (University of Bristol)
For *Studies in Comparative Literature*:
Dr Emily Finer, University of St Andrews, and
Professor Wen-chin Ouyang, SOAS, London
For *Studies in Hispanic and Lusophone Cultures*:
Trevor Dadson (Queen Mary, University of London)
For *Studies in Yiddish*: Gennady Estraikh (New York University)
For *Transcript*: Matthew Reynolds (University of Oxford)

Managing Editor
Dr Graham Nelson
41 Wellington Square, Oxford OX1 2JF, UK

www.legendabooks.com

Invention

The Language of English Renaissance Poetics

Rocío G. Sumillera

Modern Humanities Research Association
2019

Published by Legenda
an imprint of the Modern Humanities Research Association
Salisbury House, Station Road, Cambridge CB1 2LA

ISBN 978-1-78188-320-4 (HB)
ISBN 978-1-78188-323-5 (PB)

First published 2019
Paperback edition 2021

All rights reserved. No part of this publication may be reproduced or disseminated or transmitted in any form or by any means, electronic, mechanical, photocopying, recording or otherwise, or stored in any retrieval system, or otherwise used in any manner whatsoever without written permission of the copyright owner, except in accordance with the provisions of the Copyright, Designs and Patents Act 1988, or under the terms of a licence permitting restricted copying issued in the UK by the Copyright Licensing Agency Ltd, Saffron House, 6–10 Kirby Street, London EC1N 8TS, England, or in the USA by the Copyright Clearance Center, 222 Rosewood Drive, Danvers MA 01923. Application for the written permission of the copyright owner to reproduce any part of this publication must be made by email to legenda@mhra.org.uk.

Disclaimer: Statements of fact and opinion contained in this book are those of the author and not of the editors or the Modern Humanities Research Association. The publisher makes no representation, express or implied, in respect of the accuracy of the material in this book and cannot accept any legal responsibility or liability for any errors or omissions that may be made.

Trademark notice: Product or corporate names may be trademarks or registered trademarks, and are used only for identification and explanation without intent to infringe.

© *Modern Humanities Research Association 2019*

Copy-Editor: Dr Alastair Matthews

CONTENTS

Acknowledgements		ix
Introduction: Situating Invention, Imitation, and Imagination		1
1	Invention from Classical to Medieval Times	7
	1.1 In Rhetoric and Dialectic	8
	1.2 In Grammar and Poetics	13
2	Rhetoric, Dialectic, and Poetics in the Renaissance	25
	2.1 The Dispute about the Concept of Invention	26
	2.2 Poetic Invention Introduced	34
3	Imitation and Emulation from Antiquity to the End of the Renaissance	49
	3.1 In Rhetoric	50
	3.2 In Poetics	55
	3.3 *Publica Materies* and Literary Theft	61
	3.4 Making and Creating: Brazen and Golden Worlds	67
4	Invention as a Distinguishing Factor	80
	4.1 In Poetry-Writing	81
	4.2 In Evaluating Composition	87
	4.3 In Translations	91
	4.4 Anti-Poetic Sentiment and the Reformation	96
5	The Development of the Concept of Imagination	107
	5.1 Before and during the Renaissance	108
	5.2 Against and for the Imagination	116
	Conclusion: Poetic Invention as a Transitional Stage	125
	Primary Sources	131
	Secondary Sources	138
	Index	155

ACKNOWLEDGEMENTS

The origins of this book are to be found in my doctoral dissertation on poetic invention in sixteenth-century England, defended at the University of Granada. In it, I gave particular thanks to José Luis Martínez Dueñas and José María Pérez Fernández, and I do so again here, for reasons old and new. To Andrew Hadfield goes my heartfelt gratitude for his involvement in this project. The book presents not only the distilled arguments of my dissertation, offered here in a far more precise way, but also a more solid intellectual scaffolding in support of them, as well as an updated bibliography. I have been able to complete this textual metamorphosis thanks to a research stay at University College London, specifically within the framework provided by UCL's Centre for Early Modern Exchanges; I have Alexander Samson to thank for his kind invitation, and the Plan Propio de Investigación of the University of Granada for the funding.

To my parents I dedicated my dissertation, and it is not through lack of inventiveness that I dedicate this book to them as well.

INTRODUCTION

Situating Invention, Imitation, and Imagination

> The first and most necessarie poynt that ever I founde meete to be cōsidered in making of a delectable poeme is this, to grounde it upon some fine invention. For it is not inough to roll in pleasant woordes, nor yet to thunder in *Rym, Ram, Ruff*, [...] nor yet to abounde in apt vocables, or epythetes, unlesse the Invention have in it also *aliquid salis*. By this *aliquid salis*, I meane some good and fine devise, shewing the quicke capacitie of a writer.[1]

Heir to the Latin *inventio* and the Greek εὕρεσις, invention is understood in the Renaissance not only as a mental capacity allowing for the devising of works of art (such as poems or plays), as well as artefacts unrelated to art,[2] but also as the idea in the deviser's mind that pictures such works and artefacts and thus guides the generative process. The Renaissance acknowledges that all arts and sciences, including poetry, are inventions, and that invention itself, a household term in the description and discussion of poetry-writing in the sixteenth century, is a necessary ingredient in exceptional poetic compositions. It ultimately indicates poetic excellence, and the lack of it suggests either the mediocrity of an author's personal undertaking, or close imitation or translation of a previous author. The centrality of this concept in Renaissance poetics is apparent, and it becomes a *sine qua non* condition for any significant poetic work, as well as an indispensable term for poets when describing the process of their art.

Within rhetoric and dialectic, 'invention' refers to the seeking out or selection of topics or arguments, and outside these fields it gradually acquires meanings related to devising or contriving, and thus to fabrication and fiction. It is the first of the five parts of classical rhetoric, and through it the orator finds arguments and proofs; the poet, for his part, exercises it when seeking the argument of his composition. In the late Middle Ages, when rhetoric instructed students in poetry-writing, *inventio*, along with other terms such as *dispositio* and *elocutio*, was introduced with slight modifications into the discourse of poetics; gradually, these concepts, originally rhetorical in nature, metamorphosed and bloomed in the field of poetics, developing new and more complex meanings. Dialectical or logical invention also had far-reaching relations with poetry,[3] and even at the end of the sixteenth century there were authors, such as the Italian refugee Alberico Gentili, who remained loyal to the medieval view that poetry is part of logic. In his *Commentatio ad Legem III Codicis de professoribus et medicis*, published in Oxford in 1593, Gentili affirmed that 'the poetic art, which hands down precepts about writing a poem, is no doubt a part of logic, since it is engaged in propounding the construction of examples'.[4] Rhetoric and logic thus bequeathed a variety of terms to poetics, which in its turn enriched the inherited terminology by giving it new implications and shades of meaning.[5]

'Invention' is commonly found in the vicinity of the concepts of imitation, or mimesis, and imagination, which are also inherited from theories stretching back to classical Antiquity and found in disciplines other than poetics. The Renaissance constitutes a key moment of conceptual transition between the omnipresent notion of imitation in Antiquity and the overwhelming significance assigned to the imagination by the Romantics. The distinct meaning of 'invention' in Renaissance poetics was non-existent in classical theory and was at best marginal after the shift initiated by Romanticism, as a result of which imagination was placed at the centre of an expanding network of concepts such as genius and originality that eventually superseded invention.[6] Thus, Renaissance invention, still imbued with rhetorical and dialectical nuances, helps to smooth the passage from the classical notion of poetry as imitation to the understanding that it is instead the product of the author's original thought and creative imagination. The conceptual richness of the term lies in this intermediary position, which captures many of the political, religious, and social tensions of the sixteenth and seventeenth centuries.

'Invention' refers not only to the most precious quality of a poetic composition but also to the essence that markedly distinguishes a work from its predecessors and distances it both from slavish imitation of established models and from translation. It is, in sum, what grants an author timeless recognition. Even if differentiating between a translation, a version, and a novel inventive work tends to prove challenging in practice,[7] the differences between the three are clear on the level of poetic theory. In fact, invention and imitation are often understood in opposition to each other. George Chapman, for instance, contrasts the unique invention of Homer's works, 'imitating none, nor euer worthily imitated of any', with Virgil's less admirable 'courtly, laborious, and altogether imitatorie spirit': 'not a *Simile* hee [Virgil] hath but is *Homers*: not an inuention, person, or disposition, but is wholly or originally built vpon *Homericall* foundations'.[8] Translations are believed to be mere copies of the invention of an author; solely for this reason, George Puttenham argues, translators cannot be called poets: 'the very poet makes and contrives out of his own brain both the verse and matter of his poem, and not by any foreign copy or example, as doth the translator, who therefore may well be said a versifier, but not a poet'.[9] Although the efforts of the translator and the imitator are acknowledged, if only because they elevate the status of the vernacular languages, the highest praise systematically goes to the inventive author. This explains why writers, in their prefaces, often take the opportunity to highlight their inventiveness, why imitators attempt to pass their works off as inventions, and why translators frequently advertise their translations as imitations in an attempt to make them appear less removed from true inventiveness. The praise of what is novel, non-mimetic, and non-translated in effect anticipates the even more overpowering praise for originality during the Romantic period and later.[10]

Until early modernity, imagination had been confined to studies of natural philosophy; suffice it to remember that phantasy is absent from Aristotle's *Poetics* and instead discussed in *De anima*. Ancient thought does not formulate a theory of the poetic mind, partly because of the prevalence of the belief in divine inspiration, and partly because the Greeks focus on the link between poetry and external reality rather than on the axis between the mind of the artist and the artistic object. A consistent and systematic theory of the faculty of poetic insight does not evolve in the Middle Ages either.[11] The transplantation of imagination into poetic discourse occurs inconspicuously, and in spite of the many prejudices which connect it to falsehood, irrationality, and the passions. Invention, by contrast, is spared much of this bias, possibly because it is rooted in a long and respected rhetorical and dialectical tradition which coated it with generally positive, rational, and orderly connotations. Nonetheless, with the gradual increase in occurrences of the term 'imagination' in poetics, and with the association of invention with the imagination, invention suffers from the bad press of the imagination, and steadily acquires some of the negative connotations associated with it. For instance, it has been noted that, in French poetics, the term 'imagination' does not play a dominant role, and that, in fact, the term is hardly ever used by poets when talking about poetry, so as 'to avoid associations with madness and frenzy'.[12] Yet it should be stressed that 'invention' is the standard term, while alluding to the imagination in poetic discourse is still a fairly recent phenomenon. In other words, the lower frequency of the word 'imagination' first and foremost reflects its comparative novelty within poetic discourse.

The following pages trace the concept of invention from classical Antiquity to the early modern period in the discourses of rhetoric, dialectic, and, from the late Middle Ages onwards, poetics, the focus being on sixteenth- and early seventeenth-century England. Thus, although considerable reference is made to early modern French and Italian sources (and, to a lesser degree, a selection of Spanish ones), English poetics remains at the centre of the study. The five chapters of this book show how, from the status of a newcomer in the discourse of poetics in the late Middle Ages, 'invention' has, by the sixteenth century, become a standard term in the description and discussion of poetry-writing. The place of invention within the disciplines of rhetoric, dialectic, and grammar from classical times to the Middle Ages is examined in Chapter 1. As will be seen, in ancient Greece the composition of poetry was not defined by the terms εὑρήσεις and εὑρίσκω, forerunners of the Latin *inventio* and *invenire*. Neither Cicero, Quintilian, nor Horace employed *inventio* to refer to the process of poetry-writing or to the work of the poet either. In fact, it would not be until the teachings on poetic composition contained in the medieval *artes poetriae*, a combination of rhetorical precepts of composition and versification and the grammatical *enarratio poetarum* (i.e. the art of interpreting, paraphrasing, or commenting on the poets), that *inventio* entered the discourse of poetics to denote the first stage in the process of poetry-writing. Even if it did so tentatively at first via treatises such as Geoffrey of Vinsauf's *Poetria nova* or John of Garland's *De arte prosayca, metrica et rithmica*, which instead emphasise concerns relating to style and ornamentation, invention had then entered poetics for good.

Chapter 2 summarises the history of rhetoric and dialectic and their interrelation with poetics in the Renaissance, when both were part of the curriculum in the universities and at grammar schools. It also discusses the dispute about the concept of invention in dialectic and rhetoric, the emergence of Ramism, and the new conceptualisation of poetry developed by humanism, inseparable from the recovery and translation into the vernacular of Aristotle's *Poetics*. The idea that Horace had read the *Poetics* and used it as a starting point for his own reflections on poetry in his *Ars poetica* became widespread, and many commentaries strove to find points of agreement between his postulates and those of Aristotle. The translation of the *Ars poetica* into the vernaculars in fact triggered the beginning of national poetic criticism at a time when poetry was generally conceived of as a *seconde rhétorique*.

The question of mimesis or imitation from Antiquity through the early modern period is addressed in Chapter 3. Issues such as the relation between works of art and nature, the debates between Ciceronians and eclectics regarding the models to imitate, and the anxiety of authors who attempt to emulate well-established models are considered here. Emphasis is placed on the need to select carefully the most appropriate models to imitate in order to reinterpret them personally, and to surpass them if possible. Slavish imitation is repeatedly rejected, and plagiarism and the conscious concealment of one's sources are reproved. Yet the existence of the concept of *publica materies*, supported by some, criticised by others, encourages the young poet to use to his advantage themes considered common property and part of the public poetic domain. Invention constantly appears in considerations of imitation, a common position being that, even if imitation of models is required in order to maintain tradition, to gain experience, and to train one's natural talents, imitation alone is not sufficient: no author of note was ever content with being a mere imitator. As is stated in *Love's labour's lost*, 'imitarie is nothing: So doth the Hound his maister, the Ape his keeper, the tyred Horse his rider'.[13]

Chapter 4 addresses invention as key to the process of poetry-writing, to evaluating a composition, and to distinguishing inventive works from translations. Works on poetics, defences of poetry, prefaces to translations, books of emblems, entries in dictionaries, and poems and dramatic texts, among other material, are studied as sources that suggest that, in the Renaissance, this concept was still associated with the rhetorical idea of 'finding' while new shades of meaning closer to imagination, phantasy, fancy, and wit were starting to become dominant.[14] Invention was made the heart and essence of poetry, understood in opposition to imitation and translation, associated with emulation and imagination, and underlined by the use of adjectives, invariably with positive connotations, which express oddity or novelty and hint at the extraordinary capacities of the artist. Yet the connection between anti-poetic sentiment and the discourse of the promoters of the Protestant Reformation in England led to attacks against invention; indeed, it was reviled and distrusted because of its potential to be uncooperative with reason and its connection with falsehood, sin, and heresy.

Chapter 5 deals with the development of the concept of imagination and discusses how, from the discourse of natural philosophy and discussions of the human soul, the imagination (or rather, phantasy) enters rhetorical discourse through the investigation of the emotions (*pathos*) and the orator's capacity to put into words vivid visual images for persuasive ends. In addition, the imagination is seen as the faculty of the soul that reshapes the images of sense perception and that holds an intermediary position between the senses and the intellect, as works such as Pico della Mirandola's *De imaginatione* explain in detail. The bond eventually established between invention and imagination in works on poetics, but also on natural philosophy, suggests that poetic composition began to be conceived of as a mentally demanding activity based on the complex mechanisms of the human brain. Yet, at the same time, the circumstances that favour a fertile imagination, and therefore enable poetry-writing, could, when taken to the extreme, lead to madness and frenzy, and to the disease of melancholy.

Early modernity was a time when the concepts of originality and creative genius as understood by Romanticism were still in their embryonic phase, and as Michael Mack notes, 'although the idea of human creativity reaches its full flourishing in the romantic period, it is the Renaissance that bears witness to its birth.'[15] It was thus a time when notions of icastic and fantastic art illustrated the complexity of the interrelation between the ideas of mimesis and imagination, and when the latter gradually gained ground against dominant invention-based definitions of poetry. Despite Harold Bloom's assertion that 'Shakespeare belongs to the giant age before the flood, before the anxiety of influence became central to poetic consciousness',[16] the remarkable importance that invention holds in reflections on poetry in the Renaissance nonetheless underlines the fact that ambitious authors were not spared from the pressure to emulate, to reject plain and unassuming imitation, and ultimately to search for a certain degree of novelty that would grant them everlasting poetic glory. Within the terminological galaxy of Renaissance poetics, the brightest heaven is, doubtless, that of invention.

Notes to the Introduction

1. George Gascoigne, 'Certayne Notes of Instruction Concerning the Making of Verse', in *The Complete Works of George Gascoigne*, 2 vols (Cambridge: Cambridge University Press, 1907–10), I, ed. by John William Cunliffe, pp. 465–73 (p. 465).
2. John M. Steadman, *The Lamb and the Elephant: Ideal Imitation and the Context of Renaissance Allegory* (San Marino, CA: Huntington Library, 1974), p. 180; Ullrich Langer, 'Invention', in *The Cambridge History of Literary Criticism*, 9 vols (Cambridge and New York: Cambridge University Press, 1989–2013), III: *The Renaissance*, ed. by Glyn P. Norton (2000), pp. 136–43 (p. 136).
3. See Rosemond Tuve, *Elizabethan and Metaphysical Imagery: Renaissance Poetic and Twentieth-Century Critics* (Chicago: University of Chicago Press, 1972); Rosemond Tuve, 'Imagery and Logic: Ramus and Metaphysical Poetics', *Journal of the History of Ideas*, 3.4 (1942), 365–400.
4. Alberico Gentili, 'Commentatio ad Legem III Codicis de professoribus et medicis' [1593], in *Latin Treatises on Poetry from Renaissance England*, ed. and trans. by J. W. Binns (Signal Mountain: Summertown, 1999), pp. 59–134 (p. 89).

5. Wesley Trimpi, 'The Quality of Fiction: The Rhetorical Transmission of Literary Theory', *Traditio*, 30 (1974), 1–118 (p. 1); see also Steadman, p. 183.
6. Grahame Castor, *Pléiade Poetics: A Study in Sixteenth-Century Thought and Terminology* (Cambridge: Cambridge University Press, 1964), p. 86; James Engell, *The Creative Imagination: Enlightenment to Romanticism* (Cambridge, MA: Harvard University Press, 1981), p. 173.
7. Robert John Clements, *Critical Theory and Practice of the Pléiade* (Cambridge, MA: Harvard University Press, 1942), p. 262.
8. George Chapman, *Achilles Shield Translated as the Other Seuen Bookes of Homer, Out of his Eighteenth Booke of Iliades* (London: printed by Iohn Windet, 1598), A2v.
9. George Puttenham, *The Art of English Poesy* [1589], ed. by Frank Whigham and Wayne A. Rebhorn (Ithaca and London: Cornell University Press, 2007), p. 93.
10. David Quint affirms that, by the end of the Renaissance, there had occurred a shift which led to 'the appreciation of a purely literary originality' in which the writer valued his own individuality and novel contributions (*Origin and Originality in Renaissance Literature: Versions of the Source* (New Haven: Yale University Press, 1983), p. 213).
11. Murray W. Bundy, 'Invention and Imagination in the Renaissance', *Journal of English and Germanic Philology*, 29 (1930), 535–45 (p. 536).
12. Suzanne Kooij, 'Poetic Imagination and the Paradigm of Painting in Early Modern France', in *Imagination in the Later Middle Ages and Early Modern Times*, ed. by Lodi Nauta and Detlev Pätzold (Leuven: Peeters, 2004), pp. 77–92 (p. 77).
13. William Shakespeare, 'Love's Labour's Lost' [1598], ed. by Francis X. Connor, in *The New Oxford Shakespeare: The Complete Works*, 2 vols (Oxford: Oxford University Press, 2017), I, 449–531 (IV. 2. 110–11; p. 496).
14. These complex terminological associations were common in the arts and the sciences in early modernity; for instance, Alexander Marr has pointed out, regarding the notions of curiosity and wonder, that there is a legion of related terms, each with its own historical and lexical development, that renders it 'difficult to disentangle' each one 'from its neighbour' ('Introduction', in *Curiosity and Wonder from the Renaissance to the Enlightenment*, ed. by Robert John Weston Evans and Alexander Marr (Aldershot: Ashgate, 2006), pp. 1–20 (p. 1)). See also Neil Kenny, *Curiosity in Early Modern Europe: Word Histories* (Wiesbaden: Harrassowitz, 1998). Marr has also discussed the term *ingegno* as employed in the sixteenth and early seventeenth centuries in Italy, particularly in the context of treatises on art and painting, and the difficulties of rendering it into English ('Pregnant Wit: *Ingegno* in Renaissance England', *British Art Studies*, 1 (2015) <http://dx.doi.org/10.17658/issn.2058-5462/issue-01/amarr> [accessed 25 January 2019]). *Logodaedalus: Word Histories of Ingenuity in Early Modern Europe*, ed. by Alexander Marr, Raphaële Garrod, José Ramón Marcaida and Richard J. Oosterhoff (Pittsburgh: Pittsburgh University Press, forthcoming) explores this concept as far as the eighteenth century.
15. Michael Mack, *Sidney's Poetics: Imitating Creation* (Washington: Catholic University of America Press, 2005), p. 157.
16. Harold Bloom, *The Anxiety of Influence: A Theory of Poetry*, 2nd edn (Oxford: Oxford University Press, 1997), p. 11.

CHAPTER 1

Invention from Classical to Medieval Times

This chapter reviews the meaning and the role of invention within the fields of rhetoric, dialectic, and grammar from Antiquity to the Middle Ages. From Aristotle and his theory of the topics to Cicero, Quintilian, and Boethius, the chapter traces the story of these three disciplines and their understanding of invention in two separate sections. The first focuses on the theory of the topics as articulating agents of invention both in rhetoric and dialectic. Aristotle's, Cicero's, and Quintilian's doctrines on them will be explored, as well as the impact of their texts throughout the Middle Ages. In addition, the role of Boethius in the transmission of topical theory will be covered, and the development of the concept of the commonplace will be connected to that of invention. Moreover, the manner in which both rhetoric and dialectic were taught at schools and universities until the end of the medieval period will be discussed, together with how the status of both disciplines in relation to each other varied through the centuries. Finally, the first section considers the history of the two fields specifically in England throughout the Middle Ages, which of course had an impact on the teaching of *inventio*.

The second section traces the history of this concept within grammar and poetics through classical and medieval times. In the Greek and Roman school systems, the reading and analysis of the figures and tropes and, more generally, of poetry pertained to the *ars grammatica*, whose thematic boundaries often blurred with those of the neighbouring field of rhetoric. However, neither Cicero nor Quintilian suggested a connection between *inventio* and poetry. It was only when poetic composition and versification became objects of instruction in the Middle Ages that teachers looked to rhetoric for terminology. The medieval *artes poetriae*, a crossover of rhetorical and grammatical precepts of composition, thus provide the circumstances for *inventio* to be added to the lexicon of poetics. The development of this concept throughout the Renaissance within the arena of rhetoric, logic, and, more significantly for the purposes of this volume, poetics is the object of study of the next chapter.

1.1. In Rhetoric and Dialectic

Aristotle's *Rhetoric* postulates that there are three parts to rhetoric: 'first, the sources of proofs; secondly, style; and thirdly, the arrangement of the parts of the speech'.[1] This Aristotelian tripartite division would subsequently metamorphose into the classical notions of invention, arrangement, style, and delivery. To these the Hellenistic period added memory. What Aristotle calls 'the sources of proofs' is truly a 'theory of argumentation' that becomes the backbone of rhetoric.[2] Roman rhetoricians would later identify it with *inventio*, the discovery of arguments and proofs, or, as defined by the pseudo-Ciceronian *Rhetorica ad Herennium*, the 'devising of matter, true or plausible, that would make the case convincing'.[3] Personal ability is channelled by technique, which provides the orator with the necessary systematisation to overcome the unreflective discovery of ideas; in other words, *ars* and *ingenium*, the technique and skills of the orator, are subsumed in *inventio*.

The 'chief engine of rhetorical invention' includes the topics or places (τόποι in Greek, *loci* in Latin),[4] which 'consist in basic "search" formulas which can lead to the discovery of a fitting idea'.[5] The topics are not arguments in themselves but rather heuristic devices, 'empty forms that can be of assistance in looking for arguments',[6] or 'points of departure which have to be available in a concrete situation for a discussion'.[7] Protagoras is for some the deviser of the *topoi*,[8] whereas for others Aristotle's *Topics* and *Rhetoric* systematise and develop a theory whose origins are to be found in Anaximander.[9] Aristotle distinguishes between rhetorical *topoi* and dialectical *topoi* (places such as definition, genus, species, and the like), of which the latter are appropriate for discussions of a philosophical and scientific nature. Dialectical *topoi* can be defined as 'logical principles to be used to examine an intellectual proposition', as strategies that 'take on a commonplacing function by which similarities and differences are created within a particular dispute',[10] or as relational principles 'enabling a person to locate and analyze the ways in which a specific predicate may be attributed to a subject'.[11] By contrast, rhetorical topics often appear as 'an amalgam of miscellaneous molds into which rhetorical arguments usually are cast'.[12] While dialectical places are traditionally seen as contributing to truth and knowledge, rhetorical places are generally related to ethics and the 'persuasion of the emotions', and thus are more appropriate 'for amplification and embellishment of the oration'.[13]

In the *Topica*, which contains Cicero's singular interpretation of Aristotle's *Topics* merged with his own beliefs, Cicero explains that the *Topics* 'contained a system developed by Aristotle for inventing arguments so that we might come upon them by a rational system without wandering about'.[14] Unlike the philosophical overtones of Aristotle's work, Cicero opts for a judicial and practical approach to the doctrine of the topics.[15] The fact that in the *Topica* Cicero deals with rhetorical matters, and that in *De oratore* he approaches the same selection of topics, seems to suggest that, for Cicero, the dialectician and the rhetorician draw their arguments from the same source and repertoire, and by means of the same method of topical invention.[16] Because of this, Cicero is considered the originator of a confusion around the demarcation between rhetorical and dialectical theories of invention which would extend throughout the early modern period. Not surprisingly, humanists would follow Cicero on this matter:[17] the rhetorical theory of the Middle Ages depended fundamentally on the Ciceronian juvenilia (i.e. *De inventione*, known as *rhetorica prima* or *rhetorica vetus*, and the pseudo-Ciceronian *Rhetorica ad Herennium*, called *rhetorica nova*) and on commentaries on these texts. The standard texts of Cicero's *Topica* and *De sophisticis*, used for introductory courses on dialectic from the end of the twelfth century, were known chiefly through Boethius, and it would not be until 1421 that Gerardo Landriani retrieved *De oratore*, *Orator*, and *Brutus*. Cicero is acknowledged in the Middle Ages as the *magister eloquentiae*, and when rhetoric enters the curriculum of medieval universities, it is essentially Ciceronian rhetoric. Aristotle is not in general popular in the theory of discourse during the Middle Ages, particularly in comparison to Cicero's enviable position.[18] Even if Aristotle's *Sophistical refutations* and *Topics*, both dealing with invention, enjoy popularity during the Middle Ages, his *Rhetoric* does not share the same success. *Rhetoric* becomes available in the Latin West in the thirteenth century through translations from Arabic such as William of Moerbeke's, completed c. 1270, but before the fifteenth century it does not play a significant role in Italy, then dominated by solid Ciceronianism, and not until 1431 is it mentioned in the statutes of Oxford University.

Quintilian's *Institutio oratoria* increases its presence and influence during the twelfth century and stands out in the fifteenth, when the humanist Poggio Bracciolini finds the complete text in the monastery of St Gall in 1416. Until then, Quintilian had been known for the greater part of the Middle Ages either through some fragments in florilegia, through the pseudo-Quintilian *Declamationes* (also known as *De causis*), or through the two versions of the *textus mutilatus* of the *Institutio*, which included the section on *inventio* close to Cicero's *De inventione*. Yet by that time, Quintilian's topics had become familiar quotations, recurrent sayings, or arguments, in sum, helpful training devices to exercise students' natural talents: topics were the means for students of rhetoric to improve their argument-building skills and ability to write persuasive discourses. Commonplaces were no longer used for invention but were memorised, and commonplace books 'became collections of aphorisms and verses rather than arts of invention'.[19]

During the so-called second sophistic period, from c. AD 100 to the fall of the Roman Empire in AD 410, rhetoric as a practical field of discourse loses strength. The stress is now on stylistic eloquence and decoration, with hardly any innovations in invention theory being introduced. In such circumstances, invention scarcely serves an epistemic purpose, but is rather treated as a means of exploring pathetic appeals in support of the imperial policy of the time. In fact, it has been argued that, by the end of Cicero's lifetime and throughout Quintilian's career, the political climate of the Empire 'became increasingly hostile to invention of any kind' and to 'open-ended inquiry'.[20] In addition, the spread of Christianity reorients rhetoric to the interpretation of the Scriptures and to enquiry into and communication of divine teachings. St Augustine of Hippo sees the benefit of rhetorical invention for theology: invention, as an art of exegesis, is conducive to the discovery of meaning in sacred texts. In his influential *De doctrina christiana* (396–426), Augustine in effect differentiates between the *modus inveniendi*, or means of discovering, based on exegesis, and the *modus proferendi*, or means of setting forth, which corresponds to style, or *elocutio*.[21]

In his *Consolatio philosophiae* (523–24) and another seven treatises on dialectical and rhetorical issues, Boethius summarises and systematises several traditions of topical theory. He aims to delimit the different arts of discourse, particularly dialectic and rhetoric. To this enterprise he devotes Book IV of his major rhetorical work, *De topicis differentiis*, widely known in the Middle Ages as *Topica Boetii* and used in the twelfth and thirteenth centuries as a textbook of rhetoric.[22] In addition, it becomes the source for the topical doctrine of medieval logic, based on Cicero's *Topica*, by virtue of the fact that Cicero's work is at this time known primarily through Boethius's commentary.[23] According to Boethius, topics are used both in dialectic and rhetoric for the purposes of invention, even if the nature of dialectical topics differs from that of rhetorical topics, partly because dialectic is concerned with universality whereas rhetoric focuses on the particular. Since Boethius considers dialectical topics prior to rhetorical topics, rhetoric for him cannot do without dialectical topics, whereas dialectical topics can indeed do without rhetoric. As a result, rhetoric becomes subordinate to dialectic, which explains why many medieval universities, including Paris and Oxford, consider dialectic a superior means of invention and omit rhetoric from their curricula.

Through the extremely popular *De nuptiis Philologiae et Mercurii et de septem artibus liberalibus libri novem* (c. 470), Martianus Capella's encyclopedic work, the Roman concept of the seven liberal arts passes to the Middle Ages during the Carolingian age, with a division into the trivium (grammar, rhetoric, and dialectic) and the quadrivium (geometry, arithmetic, astronomy, and music). Prior to the thirteenth century, the way each centre of knowledge organised and taught the trivium and the quadrivium, and the emphasis placed on them, was entirely independent.[24] Capella's work, which describes the marriage of Mercury (i.e. eloquence) to Philology before their bridesmaids, the seven liberal arts, survives in at least 243 manuscripts in European libraries, many of which date from the Carolingian age, when commentaries on the work began to be written. Although rhetoric is certainly one of the medieval liberal arts, 'Martianus's book on rhetoric was one of the least popular parts of his work'.[25] After all, when compared to the other arts of the trivium, rhetoric appears minor: university students would often learn grammar only to take up dialectic, without undergoing a course on rhetoric at all. John of Salisbury's defence of eloquence in the *Metalogicon* (1159) is scarcely undertaken on behalf of rhetoric, and focuses instead on grammar and non-sophistic logic, and the emphasis is on grammar in Henri d'Andreli's *Battle of the seven arts* (after 1236). What is more, after the twelfth century, logic and the Aristotelian *libri naturales* dominate the arts curricula in northern universities. In other words, rhetoric loses its pedagogical and cultural pre-eminence in the Middle Ages, first to grammar, then, after the twelfth century, to logic. With the founding of the great universities and their focus on law, medicine, and theology, logic is seen as remarkably useful in introductory courses to these three degrees.[26] Rhetoric, in the meantime, is taught exclusively at the school level alongside grammar, relegated to serving as the gateway to dialectic.[27]

The thirteenth century witnesses the culmination of the process by which rhetoric is made part of logic, in the sense that manuals of logic take over the *topoi* of rhetorical invention.[28] Logic receives the lion's share of attention and is made 'the most important university subject',[29] to the extent that, for instance, at Paris, the 'Mother of Universities', Book IV of Boethius's *Topica* and the *Rhetorica ad Herennium* are the only required texts on rhetoric mentioned in the middle of the thirteenth century;[30] this is also the case at Oxford.[31] If Plato was the philosopher par excellence of the twelfth century, Aristotle replaces him during the thirteenth and fourteenth centuries after the Aristotelian corpus enters Europe from the Arabic world in translation.[32]

The most representative contributions to rhetoric in the Middle Ages are the handbooks on *ars dictaminis*, or letter-writing (a rhetorical genre born in the 1080s), *ars poetriae*, or verse composition (which appeared in the 1170s), and *ars praedicandi*, or thematic preaching (c. 1200),[33] along with the many commentaries on *De inventione* and the *Rhetorica ad Herennium*. The three medieval rhetorical arts (*ars dictaminis, ars poetriae, ars praedicandi*) use the topics for amplifying and describing material for their own purposes. Curiously enough, it is the rediscovery of Quintilian's *Institutio oratoria* and Cicero's *De oratore*, of especial influence on Italian humanism, which accelerates the decline of the three medieval rhetorical arts ultimately based on Ciceronian notions.

The earlier humanists, understood as professional teachers of the disciplines of the *studia humanitatis* (grammar, rhetoric, poetry, history, and moral philosophy) or as writers of school and college textbooks,[34] devoted much of their time to philological and historical criticism. Through the study of texts, they ascertained that, in classical times, rhetoric had been 'a noble and creative art characteristic of human beings at their best' and not 'the arid study of the medieval trivium'.[35] What is more, the Middle Ages, they claimed, had been a dark period mainly because the revealing light of eloquence had been shunned.[36] This view has led contemporary criticism to place rhetoric at the heart of the definition of the Renaissance itself. For some 'the *renascentia litterarum*' was 'primarily a *renascentia rhetorica*';[37] for others, what truly united humanists 'was a conception of eloquence and its uses';[38] others emphasise that even the humanist *uomo universale* was expected to be an exceptional orator.[39] Eloquence became an ideal of the age, and speeches or works in oratorical form flourished. Unsurprisingly, the fifteenth century liberated rhetoric from dialectic and gave it renewed credit both at universities and at schools,[40] while humanists attacked scholastic logic on the grounds that it was abstract knowledge with no direct application and no real utility in human life, and unable to communicate important truths persuasively.[41]

The story of dialectic and rhetoric is no different in England. With the crystallisation of university curricula in the thirteenth century, the *ars rhetorica* is deliberately excluded from higher education and relegated to lower levels. For this reason, the commentaries on Cicero's rhetorical works are the products of schools and not of universities,[42] and the rhetorical genres of the *ars dictaminis*, *ars poetriae*, and *ars praedicandi* develop outside the university context. The limited knowledge of the classical tradition during the medieval period, which particularly affected those territories of Western Europe furthest from the Mediterranean basin, where the heritage of Antiquity was better preserved, accounts for the survival of the medieval tradition in England for over a hundred years longer than in Italy. Ascham's *Scholemaster* (1570) contains the first references in England to Cicero's *Orator* a century after the first printing of the book, and to Dionysius of Halicarnassus's *De compositione verborum*, first printed in 1508 by Aldus, then in 1546 by Estienne and in 1550 by Sturm, a friend of Ascham. Furthermore, no Elizabethan writer refers to *On the sublime*, by pseudo-Longinus, published in 1554 by Robortello, reissued three times, and cited as an authority in 1633 in Thomas Farnaby's *Index rhetoricus*; the work was eventually edited at Oxford by Langhorne as late as 1636.[43]

While in France and Italy a national rhetorical tradition developed, educational records, library catalogues, and literary allusions evince the lack of an English rhetorical tradition in the vernacular before the early fifteenth century.[44] The scant and generic references to rhetoric in some of Chaucer's works and in Gower's *Confessio amantis* (c. 1390) are exceptions in the literature of the time and attest the two writers' passing acquaintance with the principles of the art.[45] In fourteenth-century England it was to *ars grammatica* that the most popular works on the arts of discourse belonged (the rulebooks of Donatus, Priscian, and Alexandre de Villedieu). Moreover, the most common volumes in libraries and schools were the *Barbarismus* and *Graecismus*, for which reason some argue 'that Chaucer and his contemporaries may have participated in a "grammatical" rather than a "rhetorical" tradition'.[46] It is revealing that Caxton had no native English rhetoric to print: England had to wait another century for Stephen Hawes and Thomas Wilson, and a further century for Aristotle's *Rhetoric* to appear rendered into the English language. The only two works on rhetoric that Caxton ever published were the anonymous allegorical poem, long attributed to Lydgate, *The court of sapience* (c. 1481), which provides a medieval account of the seven liberal arts,[47] and Traversagnus's *Epitome margarita eloquentiae* (1479), mostly devoted to *inventio* after its treatment of the *Ad Herennium*. Traversagnus's work has the merit not only of being the first book on rhetoric ever published in England but also of partaking in a double revolution, 'one of subject matter and the other of pedagogy'.[48] Pedagogically, the *Epitome* became the first textbook in English history, for every student in the classroom had his own copy.[49] Upon arrival at Cambridge in 1476, at the time an Aristotelian university, Traversagnus lectured on the pseudo-Ciceronian *Rhetorica ad Herennium*. By introducing Ciceronian rhetoric into the curriculum, Traversagnus challenged the University's tradition and the ideology underlying it.

1.2. In Grammar and Poetics

The terms εὑρήσεις and εὑρίσκω were not part of the usual lexicon employed in ancient Greece to describe the work of the poet or to refer to the composition of poetic discourse or to the way the poet's mind operates. Instead, inspiration accounted for the origins of the poetic process, and εὑρήσεις and εὑρίσκω meant 'to discover' and 'to find'. Neither Cicero, Quintilian, nor Horace employ *invenire* or *inventio* to refer to the process of poetry-writing or to the work of the poet, and they never use *inventio* to allude to the poet's mental capacities or to the essence of poetry. No fragment in the work of Quintilian suggests a link between *inventio* and poetry, and there are few passages to that effect in the work of either Cicero or Horace. In *Brutus*, Cicero associates *invenire* with the invention of poetry as an art, but not to the composition of actual poetic works: 'nothing is brought to perfection on its first invention. We cannot doubt that there were poets before Homer'.[50] Likewise, in his *Orator*, Cicero affirms that 'in the realm of poetry verse was discovered [*inventus*] by the test of the ear and the observation of thoughtful men',[51] and Horace names Lucilius as the 'inventor' of satires: 'this satire [...] was what I could write with more success, though falling short of the inventor [*inventore*]'.[52] Horace again links invention with the origins of poems and poetic forms by affirming that 'Thespis is said to have discovered [*invenisse*] the Tragic Muse, a type unknown before',[53] and that the 'birth and creation [*natum inventumque*]' of a poem 'are for the soul's delight'.[54] The scant occurrences of *inventio* in the vicinity of discussions of poetry suggest the rarity of the term in the treatment of poetic matters, in which the theory of inspiration still prevails, even if at this point almost as a fossilised formula. For instance, Quintilian, who does not make a connection between invention and poetry, affirms that 'everyone agrees that it [poetry] came originally from the outpourings of inspiration',[55] and that 'the frequent practice of the greatest poets was to invoke the Muses'.[56]

If the ancient world produced myriad treatises on rhetoric, writings about poetry were comparatively scarce, and as a result 'rhetorical theory was both more fully developed and more widely understood than poetic theory'.[57] One reason for this is that students of rhetoric constituted a decent-sized educational market, whereas prospective poets were far fewer in number.[58] Second, because it was the theory of poetic inspiration that explained the origins of poetry, poetic composition was ultimately dependent on the mysterious intervention of divinity and not on the quality of poetic instruction.[59] When the matter of poetic composition and versification was addressed with a view to teaching it, rhetoric determined the approach of instructors. This seemed only logical, for both rhetoric and poetry address an audience and share concerns about style, figures, tropes, and rhythm. Metre and subject matter often appear as the main differences between rhetoric and poetry: while oratory has restrictions that tie it to reality, poetry enjoys greater freedom and licence (*licentia*). In the words of Longinus, poetry can 'show an exaggeration which belongs to fable and far exceeds the limits of credibility, whereas the most perfect effect of visualization in oratory is always one of reality and truth'.[60]

Oratory and poetry are generally understood as cognate arts.[61] Plato's *Phaedrus* treats poetry and rhetoric together; Aristotle alludes in Book III of the *Rhetoric* to the *Poetics*, and two of the six divisions of tragedy (thought and diction) are properly treated in the *Rhetoric* as well;[62] and Cicero commonly draws upon poetry and the plays of Terence to illustrate rhetorical principles, and in *De oratore* states that 'the poet is a very near kinsman of the orator'.[63] Quintilian affirmed that poetry could be helpful for the construction of oratorical discourses in terms of 'inspiration in thought, sublimity in language, every kind of emotional effect, and appropriateness in character-drawing',[64] even if the modus operandi of the orator was wholly different (for verse conditions the production of poetry), and even if the orator should avoid incorporating the poet's 'freedom of vocabulary' and 'licence to develop Figures'.[65] In addition, as Cicero claims in his panegyric *Pro Archia poeta*, reading the poets can be a source of inspiration for oratorical speeches and contribute to the strengthening of the abilities of the orator:

> Do you think that I could find inspiration for my daily speeches on so manifold a variety of topics, did I not cultivate my mind with study [...]? I am a votary of literature, and make the confession unashamed; [...] my devotion to letters strengthens my oratorical powers.[66]

In Horace, *decorum* is a shared virtue of rhetoric and poetry; Quintilian also illustrates observations on rhetoric with examples from the poets; and Aphthonius, author of the popular *Progymnasmata rhetorica*, admits in the first sentence of the book that, although 'Fabvla traxit à poëtis originē, qua Rhetores etiam communiter vtuntur, quòd admonitionibus fit idonea, & erudiendis imperitioribus apta' [the fable belonged to the poets originally, but because it was suitable for instruction and teaching, it was adopted by the rhetoricians].[67] The benefits that rhetoric and poetry obtained from each other were common knowledge, and Latin poetry is often called 'rhetorical' because it exhibits techniques learned in lessons on rhetoric.[68] Rhetoric served poetry for the purposes of characterisation (for instance, in the writing of speeches made by characters), and poetry was employed by the orator to enhance the vividness of speeches, to strengthen their persuasiveness, and to offer examples.

The best exponents of the close relationship between rhetoric and poetry in ancient times are the exercises of *progymnasmata*, exercises in composition intended to be a preparation for the writing and delivery of declamations, and aimed at training students in *inventio*.[69] Exercises of the *progymnasmata* kind involve fables, narratives, descriptions, and comparisons, of use for the study of both rhetoric and poetic composition. Chapter 28 of the anonymous treatise *Rhetoric for Alexander* (fourth century BC) contains the first reference to *progymnasmata*, and the Greek schoolmaster Aelius Theon of Alexandria wrote the earliest surviving textbook on their composition. After considerable popularity during the Hellenistic period, some of these exercises were adopted by Roman schools of grammar and rhetoric. The first extant Latin handbook of *progymnasmata* dates from the sixth century: it is Priscian's Latin paraphrase of a Greek work attributed to Hermogenes, the most important rhetorician of the second century. The *progymnasmata* treatise by Aphthonius of Antioch, who followed Hermogenes closely, became an authority in

Byzantine education, and in the late fifteenth century was translated into Latin by Rudolph Agricola. In the sixteenth and seventeenth centuries, there was a rise and fall of *progymnasmata*: they rose with the popularity of Priscian's grammar, together with which they frequently appeared, and fell with the boom of humanistic grammars by William Lily, Colet, and Erasmus that superseded Priscian. Next, the Latin Aphthonius 'rose with the Lily grammars as part of the new movement in humanistic grammar school training in Latin theme writing', and with the rise in the mid-sixteenth century of Ramism and its simplification of the topics.[70] In fact, the year 1681, which marks the end of the Ramist era, coincides approximately with the end of Aphthonian pre-eminence.[71]

In the Roman school system, as in the Greek one, the reading and analysis of poetry and its technical features was paramount. The study of versification and of figures and tropes pertained to the *ars grammatica*, concerned with the *ars recte loquendi*, or correctness in speaking or writing, and with the *enarratio poetarum*, or analysis and interpretation of renowned authors. Quintilian, who at first distinguished two parts of grammar, namely, the art of correct speech and the interpretation of the poets,[72] later added a third: the art of writing, that is, composition.[73] He dedicated an entire chapter to the *lectio*, the reading of the poets; in his view, only the morally valuable poets should be read, i.e. Homer and Virgil, and, with some exceptions, the lyric poets.[74] The end of *enarratio* was an overall judgement from an aesthetic viewpoint, and it encompassed commentaries on form (*verborum interpretatio*) and on content (*historiarum cognitio*). Grammarians would provide a quick and sketchy introduction followed by a detailed commentary on each word and line to explain the rhythm of the verses, difficult terms, and poetic constructions.[75] Roman teachers of grammar were thus in charge of teaching the dissemination, interpretation, imitation, and analysis of what we currently understand as literature,[76] and *enarratio* was often seen as preparatory for the learning of rhetoric. Indeed, the exercises employed in *enarratio* typically exceeded the limits of the discipline of grammar and the grammatical concept of correctness, and found their way into the domain of rhetoric. Quintilian denounced such a clash between grammar and rhetoric;[77] for him, the two disciplines were distinct in terms of method, and, if the *grammaticus* worked almost entirely through *imitatio*, understood as the copying or paraphrasing of models, the *rhetoricus* did so fundamentally through precepts.

Horace's didactic poem *Ars poetica*, a prescriptive body of fairly general precepts and a guide in composition meant for young poets-to-be, stands within the grammatical and rhetorical tradition stemming from the *enarratio poetarum*. 'Though I write naught myself,' says Horace, 'I will teach the poet's office and duty; whence he draws his stores; what nurtures and fashions him; what befits him and what not; whither the right course leads and whither the wrong.'[78] Horace recommends that prospective poets carefully choose a topic, for: 'Whoever shall choose a theme within his range, neither speech will fail him, nor clearness of order.'[79] Horace acknowledges that it is a challenge to approach in a personal manner a common topic and to make it one's own while avoiding the tempting force of slavish imitation. Yet dealing with themes never discussed previously seems to Horace even more complicated: 'It is hard to treat in your own way what is common: and you are doing better in spinning into acts a song of Troy than if, for the first time, you were giving the world a theme unknown and unsung.'[80] Innovation within tradition is the ideal, preferable to mere repetition of what is known.

With the consolidation of the Roman Empire and the virtual disappearance of opportunities for genuine political and judicial oratory, poetry became 'a natural outlet for rhetorical training'[81] and a rhetorisation of poetry occurred.[82] The Middle Ages inherited the idea 'that poetry was best understood from the precepts of rhetoric rather than those of grammar'.[83] Alcuin's *Versus de patribus regibus et sanctis euboricensis ecclesiae* (c. 782), the first medieval narrative poem, bears testimony to the application of rhetoric to poetry during the Carolingian Renaissance (late eighth to the ninth centuries), for Alcuin's work is in effect an instance of the elementary rhetorical exercise of *conversio*, to wit, the turning of verse into prose and vice versa. The confusion around the attributions of grammar and rhetoric was ongoing, for both disciplines taught the figures and tropes (essential in rhetorical *elocutio* and in grammatical *enarratio*), and both made use of exercises in textual paraphrase (rewriting texts in grammar lessons, and refining style and practising textual embellishment strategies in rhetoric classes).

The blurring of the boundaries of rhetoric and grammar became even more pronounced with the emergence of the medieval *artes poetriae*, nurtured through the legacies of Cicero, Quintilian, and Horace. The *artes poetriae*, which refer both to prose and verse composition, constitute a crossover of rhetorical precepts of composition and the grammatical *enarratio poetarum*.[84] Because the *artes poetriae* primarily taught composition, drawing on examples that worked as models for new texts, they came to function as preceptive grammars or rhetorics of versification. They were more practical than theoretical in nature insofar as they did not truly offer a disquisition on theoretical principles, despite being built upon them.[85] The fact that teachers of the *artes poetriae* were not rhetoricians but experts on grammar explains why composition fundamentally consisted of *enarratio* or textual exposition and exegesis, and was studied through the traditional *progymnasmata*.[86] It was these teachers, with their grammatical background, who wrote down the new poetic principles.

Medieval writers acknowledged that grammar prepared the way for the study of rhetoric and further learning. Grammar was in effect so central at elementary schools that 'grammar school' became synonymous with 'elementary school'. While the *ars rhetorica* was not studied at universities until almost the end of the medieval period, from the twelfth century onwards the *ars grammatica* was the primary subject at all European universities, for even logic demanded prior knowledge of grammar. Before 1200, grammar essentially meant syntax and *figurae*, and was dominated by Priscian, Donatus, and their commentators. After 1200, specialised grammatical works on *metricum* and *rithmicum* appeared together with two new textbooks: Alexandre de Villedieu's *Doctrinale* and Eberhard of Béthune's *Graecismus*. By that time, the commonplaces were no longer devices for the discovery of arguments but strategies for remembering, amplifying, describing, and constructing figures. After the twelfth century, the conceptualisation of poetry also changed, and mutated into a kind of versified rhetoric, a form of composition, a sort of argumentation or persuasion.[87] It was no longer a branch of grammar, and as such was treated in terms of style and rhetorical figures and subordinated to logic or morals (which is why poetry was recommended as school reading). Indeed, poetry was not an independent art, and proof of this lay in the fact that it lacked a separate place in the scheme of the seven liberal arts.[88]

Taking Horace's *Ars poetica* as their model, between 1175 and *c.* 1280 several teachers of grammar wrote works in Latin outlining precepts for verse composition. Matthew of Vendôme, Geoffrey of Vinsauf, John of Garland, John of Salisbury, Hugh of St Victor, Gervase of Melkley, Eberhard of Béthune, and Guilhem Molinier were among them. The underlying belief in their works was that verse composition could be taught in schools, and that such teachings gave shape to general poetic skills. Although instruction was virtually rhetorical (more precisely, Ciceronian), the fact that it was administered by teachers of grammar resulted in a further blending of grammar and rhetoric, and in additional emphasis on style and figures.[89] Matthew of Vendôme's *Ars versificatoria*, composed shortly before 1175, is the earliest surviving medieval handbook of poetry. Written in prose and addressed to beginners, it provided copious verse examples, tackling versification chiefly on an introductory level. Given that Matthew's focus is on the choice and arrangement of words and on rhetorical embellishment, the work supplies the student with *materia* for ornamentation, yet entirely overlooks *inventio* and *dispositio*. The versificatory treatise by Gervase of Melkley, and Eberhard of Béthune's *Laborintus* manual, likewise omit *inventio*.[90]

By contrast, *inventio* is in fact discussed in Geoffrey of Vinsauf's basic textbook, *Poetria nova*, also known as *Galfredi rethorica* (1200–15), written in the form of a hexameter poem and addressed to more advanced students. Its title might indicate Geoffrey's intention to present 'new doctrines to replace the older ones'.[91] Indeed, it brings to mind both Horace's *Ars poetica* (also known as *Poetria* during the Middle Ages) and the pseudo-Ciceronian *Rhetorica ad Herennium*, or *Rhetorica nova* (the *Rhetorica vetus*, Cicero's *De inventione*, was a great influence on Geoffrey's theory of poetic composition). Geoffrey's *Poetria* has been understood as a semi-conscious effort to update Horace's precepts to the context of medieval schools.[92] The *Poetria nova*, which appealed to both students and to a larger audience partly made up of contemporary writers in the vernacular,[93] became a complete success: there exist around two hundred manuscripts throughout Europe dating from the thirteenth to the fifteenth centuries, three manuscripts and two commentaries from the sixteenth century, and one seventeenth-century manuscript. In his *Ars versificaria* (*c.* 1213–16), Gervase of Melkley cites Geoffrey by name, and refers to the *Poetria nova* as well as to Geoffrey's manual for beginners *Documentum de modo et arte dictandi et versificandi* (*c.* 1180, revised *c.* 1210), which was of considerable influence in the late fourteenth and fifteenth centuries and in the teaching of rhetoric at Oxford.[94] Indeed, notes on certain manuscripts as well as some university charters indicate that Geoffrey's book was taught in medieval schools and in a few universities in Central Europe.[95]

It appears that Chaucer may have been influenced by Geoffrey,[96] and that, more generally, 'Vinsauf had a vogue among fifteenth-century English writers'.[97] Nonetheless, Stephen Hawes's allegorical poem *The pastime of pleasure* (1509) is perhaps the earliest to treat systematically the doctrines of Geoffrey in English.[98]

To write good poetry, Geoffrey argues, one ought to be acquainted with the *ars* (knowledge of precepts and rules), imitate the great writers (*imitatio*), and show diligent practice (*usus*). The five parts of classical rhetoric constitute the organising principles of the *Poetria nova*. Yet, even if style and ornament (*verba*) are subordinate and secondary to invention (*res*), when compared to his discussion of style, his reflections on *inventio* are limited:[99]

> let the poet's hand not be swift to take up the pen, nor his tongue be impatient to speak; trust neither hand nor tongue to the guidance of fortune. To ensure greater success for the work, let the discriminating mind, as a prelude to action, defer the operation of hand and tongue, and ponder long on the subject matter. Let the mind's interior compass first circle the whole extent of the material.[100]

Since the success of the poem depends mostly on its *materia*, and therefore on the process of invention, Geoffrey recommends time and again: "Give careful thought to the material, therefore, that there may be no possible grounds for reproach."[101] Invention is, for Geoffrey, a completely rational process, alien to the forces of inspiration that classical authors attributed to poetry: 'reason invents', he affirms.[102] Classical theories on inspiration and the irrationality of the poet seem a thing of the past: for these medieval authors, if reason is absent from the author's mind, nothing of worth can ever result from his textual efforts.[103] John of Salisbury, for instance, affirms in his verse work *Entheticus de dogmate philosophorum* that 'the powerful nature of intellect quickly masters all | the arts', including eloquence.[104] For him, a 'powerful intellect' should be accompanied by attentive study, attention to the sound of words, a patient and laborious disposition towards learning, strong Christian faith, good memory, powerful voice, and fluency and confidence when speaking in public. In a reference to Martianus Capella contained in the section 'The marriage of word and reason', John of Salisbury stresses the role of the intellect before any other quality of the mind (such as the imagination), since, like poetry for Geoffrey of Vinsauf, eloquence is a purely rational act.[105]

As the *Poetria nova* had previously done, John of Garland's *De arte prosayca, metrica et rithmica*, written in hexameters and originally composed c. 1229, also discusses (if briefly) the doctrine of invention — along with other issues such as amplification and abbreviation, memory, the selection of material, its arrangement and ornamentation, parts of letters and common faults when writing them, and rhythmical and metrical composition. Horace is the source of much of John of Garland's teachings about invention; in contrast to Geoffrey of Vinsauf, however, *inventio* becomes for John of Garland a purely verbal exercise that involves answering questions such as *ubi?*, *quid?*, *quale?*, *qualiter?*, or *ad quid?*, and inevitably leads to drawing on the lists of figures.[106]

The conditions for the transfer of the rhetorical notion of invention into the realm of poetics thus emanate from the confluence of the disciplines of rhetoric and grammar in the medieval *artes poetriae*. By the thirteenth century, authors such as Geoffrey of Vinsauf and John of Garland appropriate *inventio* together with other instances of rhetorical terminology to structure their discussions on poetry-writing. *Inventio* refers in such contexts to the application of reason to the first stage of the process of poetic composition. With this meaning invention enters the language of Renaissance poetics.

Notes to Chapter 1

1. Aristotle, *Art of Rhetoric*, ed. and trans. by John Henry Freese, 9th edn (Cambridge, MA: Harvard University Press, 2000), p. 345 (1403B).
2. Paul Ricoeur, 'Between Rhetoric and Poetics', in *Essays on Aristotle's Rhetoric*, ed. by Amélie Rorty (Berkeley: University of California Press, 1996), pp. 324–84 (p. 324).
3. Marcus Tullius Cicero, *Rhetorica ad Herennium*, trans. by Harry Caplan (Cambridge, MA: Harvard University Press; London: Heinemann, 1968), p. 7 (I. 2. 3).
4. John Monfasani, *George of Trebizond: A Biography and a Study of his Rhetoric and Logic* (Leiden: Brill, 1976), p. 243. Ever since Cicero and Quintilian, the theory of the topics seems to transcend the limits of *inventio* and *argumentatio*, affecting the other parts of discourse as well. See Belén Saiz Noeda, '*Inventio y dispositio*: Retórica y lingüística del texto: *Loci argumentorum* y "estructuras tópicas" en la *Institutio Oratoria* de Quintiliano', in *Quintiliano: Historia y actualidad de la retórica: Actas del Congreso Internacional: Madrid y Calahorra, 14 al 18 de noviembre de 1995*, ed. by Tomás Albaladejo Mayordomo, Emilio del Río, and José Antonio Caballero (Logroño: Instituto de Estudios Riojanos, 1998), pp. 733–42 (pp. 739–41).
5. Heinrich Lausberg, *Handbook of Literary Rhetoric: A Foundation for Literary Study*, trans. by Matthew T. Bliss, Annemiek Jansen, and David E. Orton, ed. by David E. Orton and R. Dean Anderson (Leiden: Brill, 1998), p. 119.
6. Samuel Ijsseling, *Rhetoric and Philosophy in Conflict: An Historical Survey* (The Hague: Nijhoff, 1976), p. 30.
7. Ernesto Grassi, *Rhetoric as Philosophy: The Humanist Tradition* (Philadelphia: Pennsylvania State University Press, 1980), p. 42–43.
8. Mario Untersteiner, *The Sophists*, trans. by Kathleen Freeman (Oxford: Blackwell, 1954), p. 29.
9. Geoffrey Ernest Richard Lloyd, *Polarity and Analogy: Two Types of Argumentation in Early Greek Thought* (Cambridge: Cambridge University Press, 1966). For more on the origins and historical development of the analytic *topoi*, see Friedrich Solmsen, 'The Aristotelian Tradition in Ancient Rhetoric', *The American Journal of Philology*, 62.1 (1941), 35–50 (p. 40); Frank J. D'Angelo, 'The Evolution of the Analytic Topoi: A Speculative Inquiry', in *Essays on Classical Rhetoric and Modern Discourse*, ed. by Robert J. Connors, Robert J. Ede, and Andrea A. Lunsford (Carbondale: Southern Illinois University Press, 1984), pp. 50–68.
10. Nola J. Heidlebaugh, *Judgment, Rhetoric, and the Problem of Incommensurability: Recalling Practical Wisdom* (Columbia: University of South Carolina Press, 2001), p. 85.
11. Donovan J. Ochs, 'Aristotle's Concept of Formal Topics', *Speech Monographs*, 36 (1969), 419–25 (p. 425).
12. Ochs, 'Aristotle's Concept of Formal Topics', p. 425.
13. J. M. Lechner, *Renaissance Concepts of the Commonplaces* (New York: Pageant Press, 1962), p. 228. For more on the difference between topical theory in rhetoric and dialectic in Aristotle, see Michael C. Leff, 'The Topics of Argumentative Invention in Latin Rhetorical Theory from Cicero to Boethius', *Rhetorica*, 1.1 (1983), 23–44 (p. 25). Aristotle also distinguishes between common or universal topics and special or subject-specific topics. The former are a group of twenty-eight lines of argument to be used in any type of discourse, regardless of any specific subject matter. The latter only apply to certain subjects and provide content for particular types of discourse, such as epideictic or ceremonial, deliberative or political, or judicial. See Ellen Quandahl, 'Aristotle's Rhetoric: Reinterpreting Invention', *Rhetoric Review*, 4.2 (1986), 128–37 (p. 128). For more on Aristotle's notion of the topics, see S. J. William Grimaldi, 'The Aristotelian Topics', *Traditio*, 14 (1958), 1–16.

14. Marcus Tullius Cicero, 'De inventione', 'De optimo genere oratorum', 'Topica', trans. by H. M. Hubbell (Cambridge, MA: Harvard University Press; London: Heinemann, 1960), p. 383 (*Topica*, I. 2).
15. Saiz Noeda, p. 738.
16. For more on Cicero's rhetorical system, see Donovan J. Ochs, 'Cicero's Rhetorical Theory: With Synopses of Cicero's Seven Rhetorical Works', in *A Synoptic History of Classical Rhetoric*, ed. by James J. Murphy and others (Mahwah: Hermagoras Press, 2003), pp. 151–200.
17. Gabriel González, *Dialéctica escolástica y lógica humanística de la Edad Media al Renacimiento* (Salamanca: Ediciones Universidad, 1987), p. 322.
18. James J. Murphy, *Rhetoric in the Middle Ages: A History of Rhetorical Theory from Saint Augustine to the Renaissance* (Berkeley: Dar Sadir, 1974), p. 107. See also George A. Kennedy, 'The Evolution of a Theory of Artistic Prose', in *Cambridge History of Literary Criticism*, I: *Classical Criticism*, ed. by George A. Kennedy (1989), pp. 184–99 (p. 190); Suzanne Reynolds, *Medieval Reading: Grammar, Rhetoric and the Classical Text* (Cambridge: Cambridge University Press, 1996).
19. Richard Peter McKeon, 'Creativity and the Commonplace', in *Selected Writings of Richard McKeon*, ed. by Zahava K. McKeon and William G. Swenson (Chicago: University of Chicago Press, 1998), pp. 42–50 (p. 44). For more on this subject, see Francis Goyet, *Le Sublime du 'lieu commun': L'Invention rhétorique dans l'Antiquité et à la Renaissance* (Paris: Champion, 1996).
20. Janice M. Lauer, 'Issues in Rhetorical Invention', in *Essays on Classical Rhetoric and Modern Discourse*, ed. by Connors, Ede, and Lunsford, pp. 127–39 (p. 134). For alternative explanations for this phenomenon, see Rita Copeland, *Rhetoric, Hermeneutics, and Translation in the Middle Ages: Academic Traditions and Vernacular Texts* (Cambridge: Cambridge University Press, 1995), p. 62; Janice M. Lauer, *Invention in Rhetoric and Composition* (West Lafayette: Parlor Press, 2003), pp. 37–38.
21. Augustine's understanding of invention has an impact on late medieval rhetorical poetics, the *artes poetriae*, where 'the *modus inveniendi* is achieved through — and is identical with — the *modus interpretandi*' (Copeland, p. 160).
22. On why *De topicis differentiis* had such an influence on later medieval rhetorical theory, see Michael C. Leff, 'Boethius' *De differentiis topicis*, Book IV', in *Medieval Eloquence: Studies in the Theory and Practice of Medieval Rhetoric*, ed. by James J. Murphy (Berkeley: Dar Sadir, 1978), pp. 3–24 (pp. 22–23); John O. Ward, 'Quintilian and the Rhetorical Revolution of the Middle Ages', *Rhetorica*, 13.3 (1995), 231–84 (pp. 233–34).
23. Otto Bird, 'The Tradition of the Logical Topics: Aristotle to Ockham', *Journal of the History of Ideas*, 23.3 (1962), 307–23 (p. 311).
24. Ralph McInerny, 'Beyond the Liberal Arts', in *The Seven Liberal Arts in the Middle Ages*, ed. by David L. Wagner (Bloomington: Indiana University Press, 1986), pp. 248–72 (p. 249).
25. George A. Kennedy, *Classical Rhetoric and its Christian and Secular Tradition from Ancient to Modern Times*, 2nd edn (Chapel Hill: University of North Carolina Press, 1999), p. 199.
26. Monfasani, *George of Trebizond*, p. 247.
27. R. R. Bolgar, 'The Teaching of Rhetoric in the Middle Ages', in *Rhetoric Revalued: Papers from the International Society for the History of Rhetoric*, ed. by Brian Vickers (Binghamton: State University of New York, Center for Medieval and Early Renaissance Studies, 1982), pp. 79–86 (p. 85).
28. Richard Peter McKeon and Mark Backman, *Rhetoric: Essays in Invention and Discovery* (Woodbridge: Ox Bow Press, 1987), p. 152.
29. Brian Vickers, 'Rhetoric and Poetics', in *The Cambridge History of Renaissance Philosophy*, ed. by Charles B. Schmitt and others (Cambridge: Cambridge University Press, 1988), pp. 715–45 (p. 725).
30. P. Osmund Lewry, 'Rhetoric at Paris and Oxford in the Mid-Thirteenth Century', *Rhetorica*, 1.1 (1983), 45–63 (pp. 45–46).
31. Lewry, p. 62. For more on the importance of logic at Paris from 1215 onwards, see James J. Murphy, 'Quintilian's Influence on the Teaching of Speaking and Writing in the Middle Ages and Renaissance', in *Latin Rhetoric and Education in the Middle Ages and Renaissance*, ed. by James J. Murphy (Aldershot: Ashgate Variorum, 2005), pp. 158–83 (p. 169).
32. McKeon and Backman, p. 170.

33. For more on rhetorical invention in some *ars praedicandi* manuals, see Harry Caplan, 'Rhetorical Invention in Some Mediaeval Tractates of Preaching', *Speculum*, 2.3 (1927), 284–95.
34. Hanna H. Gray, 'Renaissance Humanism: The Pursuit of Eloquence', *Journal of the History of Ideas*, 24.4 (1963), 497–514 (p. 500). For more on the term 'humanist', see Augusto Campana, 'The Origin of the Word "Humanist"', *Journal of the Warburg and Courtauld Institutes*, 9 (1946), 60–73; Donald Lemen Clark, 'Ancient Rhetoric and English Renaissance Literature', *Shakespeare Quarterly*, 2.3 (1951), 195–204 (p. 196).
35. Kennedy, *Classical Rhetoric and its Christian and Secular Tradition*, p. 227.
36. Donald Lemen Clark, 'Ancient Rhetoric', p. 196.
37. Heinrich F. Plett and Peter Heath, 'Aesthetic Constituents in the Courtly Culture of Renaissance England', *New Literary History*, 14.3 (1983), 597–621 (p. 598).
38. Hanna H. Gray, p. 498.
39. Donald Lemen Clark, 'Ancient Rhetoric', p. 196.
40. Vickers, 'Rhetoric and Poetics', p. 741.
41. Hanna H. Gray, p. 501.
42. James J. Murphy, 'The Double Revolution of the First Rhetorical Textbook Published in England: The *Margarita Eloquentiae* of Gulielmus Traversagnus (1479)', *Texte: Revue de critique et de théorie littéraire*, 8/9 (1989), 367–76 (p. 369).
43. The first printed editions of *On the Sublime*, of which around two thirds are extant today, date from 1554 to 1555, and the first printed Latin translations from 1566 to 1572, even though Latin translations in manuscript form had been circulating before those dates. See W. H. Fyfe 'Introduction', in Longinus, 'On the Sublime', ed. and trans. by W. H. Fyfe, in *Aristotle, 'Poetics'; Longinus, 'On the Sublime'; Demetrius, 'On Style'* (Cambridge, MA: Harvard University Press, 1995), pp. 145–58 (p. 155). The work, however, did not become influential until much later: Niccolò da Falgano's Italian translation of 1560 remained in manuscript form, and the first published English version (translated by John Hall) did not appear until 1652. Longinus had a profound impact on seventeenth-century English letters — see Dan Flory, 'Stoic Psychology, Classical Rhetoric, and Theories of Imagination in Western Philosophy', *Philosophy and Rhetoric*, 29.2 (1996), 147–67 (p. 160) — and it was from 1674 onwards, when the neoclassical French poet and critic Nicolas Boileau-Despréaux published his *Traité du sublime ou du merueilleux dans le discours, traduit du grec de Longin*, that *On the Sublime* enjoyed greater attention in poetic criticism. For more on the influence of Longinus on English literary criticism, see Thomas Rice Henn, *Longinus and English Criticism* (Cambridge: Cambridge University Press, 1934).
44. See James J. Murphy, 'A New Look at Chaucer and the Rhetoricians', *Review of English Studies*, n.s., 15 (1964), 1–20 (p. 2); James J. Murphy, 'Rhetoric in Fourteenth-Century Oxford', *Medium Ævum*, 34 (1965), 1–20.
45. James J. Murphy, 'John Gower's *Confessio Amantis* and the First Discussion of Rhetoric in the English Language', *Philological Quarterly*, 41 (1962), 401–11; James J. Murphy, 'New Look at Chaucer'.
46. James J. Murphy, 'New Look at Chaucer', p. 3.
47. James J. Murphy, 'Caxton's Two Choices: "Modern" and "Medieval" Rhetoric in Traversagni's *Nova Rhetorica* and the Anonymous *Court of Sapience*', *Medievalia et Humanistica*, n.s., 3 (1972), 241–55. For more on the early history of printed books on rhetoric, see James J. Murphy, 'Rhetoric in the Earliest Years of Printing, 1465–1500', *Quarterly Journal of Speech*, 70 (1984), 1–11.
48. James J. Murphy, 'Double Revolution', p. 367.
49. Ronald H. Martin, 'The *Epitome Margaritae Eloquentiae* of Laurentius Gulielmus de Saona', in *Proceedings of the Leeds Philosophical and Literary Society* (Leeds: Leeds Philosophical and Literary Society, 1971), pp 103–26.
50. Marcus Tullius Cicero, *'Brutus' and 'Orator'*, trans. by G. L. Hendrickson and H. M. Hubbell (Cambridge, MA: Harvard University Press; London: Heinemann, 1962), p. 67 (*Brutus*, 71).
51. Cicero, *'Brutus' and 'Orator'*, p. 457 (*Orator*, 178).
52. Horace, *'Satires', 'Epistles' and 'Ars Poetica'*, ed. and trans. by H. Rushton Fairclough (Cambridge, MA: Harvard University Press; London: Heinemann, 1978), p. 119 (I. 10. 46–49).
53. Horace, p. 473 (*Satires*, ll. 275–76).

54. Horace, p. 481 (*Satires*, ll. 378–79).
55. M. Fabius Quintilian, *The Orator's Education*, ed. and trans. by Donald A. Russell, 5 vols (Cambridge, MA: Harvard University Press, 2001), IV, 225 (IX. 4. 114).
56. Quintilian, II, 179 (IV. 4).
57. Kennedy, *Classical Rhetoric and its Christian and Secular Tradition*, p. 136.
58. Donald Andrew Russell, *Criticism in Antiquity* (London: Duckworth, 2001), p. 3.
59. Donald Lemen Clark, *Rhetoric and Poetry in the Renaissance: A Study of Rhetorical Terms in English Renaissance Literary Criticism* (New York: Columbia University Press, 1922), p. 6.
60. Longinus, 'On the Sublime', ed. and trans. by W. H. Fyfe, in *Aristotle, 'Poetics'; Longinus, 'On the Sublime'; Demetrius, 'On Style'* (Cambridge, MA: Harvard University Press, 1995), pp. 159–306 (pp. 221–23; XV. 8).
61. See Jeffrey Walker, *Rhetoric and Poetics in Antiquity* (Oxford: Oxford University Press, 2000). The term 'poetry' is here used throughout as encompassing drama as well. In this regard, Richard Harland explains that, 'in Greek culture, lyric poetry played a much smaller part than epic and drama', and so, 'when Plato and Aristotle theorise about *poiesis*, their conceptual framework derives from epic and drama' (*Literary Theory from Plato to Barthes: An Introductory History* (Basingstoke: Macmillan, 1999), p. 2).
62. 'Thought' is the only one of the two terms defined in the same way in both the *Rhetoric* and the *Poetics*.
63. Marcus Tullius Cicero, *De oratore*, 2 vols (London: Heinemann; Cambridge, MA: Harvard University Press, 1959–60), I, trans. by E. W. Sutton, completed by H. Rackham (1959), p. 51 (I. 16. 70).
64. Quintilian, IV, 267 (X. 1. 27).
65. Quintilian, IV, 267 (X. 1. 29).
66. Marcus Tullius Cicero, *The Speeches: Pro Archia. Post Reditum in Senatu. Post Reditum ad Quirites. De Domo Sua. De Haruspicum Responsis. Pro Plancio*, trans. by N. H. Watts (Cambridge, MA: Harvard University Press; London: Heinemann, 1923), p. 21 (VI. 12–13).
67. Aphthonius, *Aphthonii Progymnasmata* (London: Impensis Societatis Stationariorum, 1605), B1r.
68. George A. Kennedy, *The Art of Rhetoric in the Roman World: 300 B.C.–A.D. 300* (Princeton: Princeton University Press, 1972), p. 384.
69. John Hagaman, 'Modern Use of the *Progymnasmata* in Teaching Rhetorical Invention', *Rhetoric Review*, 5.1 (1986), 22–29 (p. 25); George A. Kennedy, *A New History of Classical Rhetoric* (Princeton: Princeton University Press, 1994), pp. 203–06.
70. Donald Lemen Clark, 'The Rise and Fall of *Progymnasmata* in Sixteenth Century Grammar Schools', *Speech Monographs*, 19 (1952), 259–63 (p. 262).
71. Clark, 'Rise and Fall', pp. 262–63.
72. Quintilian, I, 103 (I. 4. 2).
73. Quintilian, I, 103 (I. 4. 3).
74. Quintilian, I, 199–209 (I. 8). See also Richard Peter McKeon, 'Literary Criticism and the Concept of Imitation in Antiquity', *Modern Philology*, 34.1 (1936), 1–35; Francisco Luis Delgado Escolar, *Los poetas latinos como críticos literarios desde Terencio hasta Juvenal: Estudios estilísticos y lexicológicos* (Madrid: Universidad Complutense de Madrid, 1991).
75. Henri-Irenee Marrou, *Historia de la educación en la Antigüedad*, trans. by José Ramón Mayo (Buenos Aires: Editorial Universitaria de Buenos Aires, 1970), p. 342.
76. Kennedy, *Classical Rhetoric and its Christian and Secular Tradition*, p. 127; Terence Cave, 'The Mimesis of Reading in the Renaissance', in *Mimesis: From Mirror to Method, Augustine to Descartes*, ed. by John D. Lyons and Stephen G. Nichols, Jr (Aurora: Davies Group, 2004), pp. 143–58 (p. 158).
77. Quintilian, I, 265 (II. 1. 4–5).
78. Horace, p. 477 (*Ars poetica*, ll. 305–08).
79. Horace, p. 453 (*Ars poetica*, ll. 40–41).
80. Horace, p. 461 (*Ars poetica*, ll. 128–30).
81. Paul Prill, 'Rhetoric and Poetics in the Early Middle Ages', *Rhetorica*, 5.2 (1987), 129–47 (p. 131).
82. Ernst Robert Curtius, *European Literature and the Latin Middle Ages*, trans. by Willard R. Trask (London: Routledge and Kegan Paul, 1979), p. 148.

83. Prill, p. 133. See also Donald Lemen Clark, *Rhetoric and Poetry*, p. 43.
84. Copeland, p. 175.
85. Douglas Kelly, 'Definition of the Genre', in *The Arts of Poetry and Prose*, ed. by Douglas Kelly (Turnhout: Brepols, 1991), pp. 37–46 (p. 37).
86. See Erich Auerbach, *Literary Language and its Public in Late Latin Antiquity and in the Middle Ages*, trans. by Ralph Manheim (Princeton: Princeton University Press, 1993), for a standard discussion of many of these features of composition.
87. John William Hey Atkins, *English Literary Criticism: The Medieval Phase* (Cambridge: Cambridge University Press, 1943), pp. 183–84.
88. The Italian Benvenuto da Imola wondered why poetry was not counted among the liberal arts, to which Petrarch replied that poetry 'is beyond all the liberal arts and takes them all in', and that 'sometimes it is greater to be left out, just as the prince is left out of the number of great citizens' (*Letters of Old Age = Rerum senilium libri, I–XVIII*, trans. by Aldo S. Bernardo, Saul Levin, and Reta A. Bernardo, 2 vols (Baltimore: Johns Hopkins University Press, 1992), II, 588).
89. Charles Sears Baldwin, *Medieval Rhetoric and Poetic (to 1400): Interpreted from Representative Works* (New York: MacMillan, 1926), p. 195; Copeland, pp. 160–66.
90. See Edmond Faral, *Les Arts poétiques du XIIe et du XIIIe siècle* (Paris: Champion, 1924). *Laborintus* was the only one of the six most popular works of its kind to be printed (Leipzig) in the fifteenth century.
91. Jane Baltzell Kopp, 'Geoffrey of Vinsauf: *The New Poetics* (c. 1210 A.D.)', in *Three Medieval Rhetorical Arts*, ed. by James J. Murphy (Berkeley: University of California Press, 1985), pp. 27–108 (p. 30).
92. Ana María Calvo Revilla, 'La *Poetria nova* de Godofredo de Vinsauf', in Godofredo de Vinsauf, *Poetria nova*, ed. by Ana María Calvo Revilla (Madrid: Arco Libros, 2008), pp. 11–26 (p. 18).
93. Calvo Revilla, 'La *Poetria nova*', p. 23.
94. Marjorie C. Woods elaborates on Geoffrey's commentators in 'Literary Criticism in an Early Commentary on Geoffrey of Vinsauf's *Poetria nova*', in *Acta Conventus Neo-Latini Bononiensis: Proceedings of the Fourth International Congress of Neo-Latin Studies*, ed. by R. J. Schoeck (Binghamton: State University of New York, Center for Medieval and Early Renaissance Studies, 1985), pp. 667–73.
95. Marjorie C. Woods, 'A Medieval Rhetoric Goes to School — and to the University: The Commentaries on the *Poetria nova*', *Rhetorica*, 9 (1991), 55–65 (p. 55).
96. Karl Young, 'Chaucer and Geoffrey of Vinsauf', *Modern Philology*, 41.3 (1944), 172–82.
97. James J. Murphy, 'Caxton's Two Choices', p. 249.
98. Calvo Revilla, 'La *Poetria nova*', p. 23.
99. Ana María Calvo Revilla argues that, in lines 43–49, Geoffrey also comments on the rhetorical operation of *intellectio*, which would precede invention and the rest of the constituent operations of discourse ('El modelo retórico, entramado de la poética medieval: Análisis de la *Poetria Nova* de Godofredo de Vinsauf', *Helmantica: Revista de Filología Clásica y Hebrea*, 53 (2002), 281–307 (p. 288); 'La *Poetria nova*', pp. 32–34). For more on *intellectio*, see Tomás Albaladejo Mayordomo and Francisco Chico Rico, 'La *intellectio* en la serie de las operaciones retóricas no constituyentes de discurso', *Teoría/Crítica*, 5 (1998), 339–52; Stefano Arduini, *Prolegómenos a una teoría general de las figuras* (Murcia: Universidad de Murcia, 2000), pp. 59–72; Francisco Chico Rico, 'La teoría de la traducción en la teoría retórica', *Revista de Retórica y Teoría de la Comunicación*, 3 (2002), 25–40 (p. 25). See also Douglas Kelly, 'Topical Invention in Medieval French Literature', in *Medieval Eloquence*, ed. by Murphy, pp. 231–51 (p. 233).
100. Geoffrey of Vinsauf, *Poetria nova*, trans. by Margaret F. Nims (Toronto: Pontifical Institute of Mediaeval Studies, 1967), p. 17.
101. Geoffrey of Vinsauf, *Poetria nova*, p. 17.
102. Geoffrey of Vinsauf, *Poetria nova*, p. 87.
103. For more on the link between poetry and rhetoric in the English Middle Ages, see Donald Lemen Clark, 'Rhetoric and the Literature of the English Middle Ages', *Quarterly Journal of Speech*, 45 (1959), 19–28.
104. John of Salisbury, *Entheticus Maior and Minor*, ed. by Jan van Laarhoven, 3 vols (Leiden: Brill, 1987), I, 116.

105. John of Salisbury, I, 118.
106. Charles Sears Baldwin, p. 191.

CHAPTER 2

Rhetoric, Dialectic, and Poetics in the Renaissance

After following its passage from rhetoric, dialectic, and grammar into the discourse of poetics up to and through the Middle Ages, this chapter traces the history of invention from the fifteenth century to the first half of the seventeenth. In this period, invention is claimed to belong exclusively to the fields of rhetoric and dialectic, and rethought and redefined by highly influential authors such as Lorenzo Valla, Rudolph Agricola, Juan Luis Vives, and Petrus Ramus.

This chapter will also focus on the English adherence to Continental theories, as well as on the works for instruction in rhetoric and dialectic most widely used in the English school and university curricula. It will be seen how, in Tudor times, rhetoric still remained inferior to dialectic and was organised in the form of the medieval trivium, while a flood of works from the Continent coexisted with others written in English, or rendered into English, by national scholars. Cicero was the hero of rhetorical instruction in the sixteenth and seventeenth centuries, while Aristotle's *Rhetoric* was for the most part still unknown. In these works, invention continued to be associated with the finding of arguments. What exactly this search implied was nonetheless not generally agreed on: if some authors associated it with a process of discovering already existing ideas, others connected it to imagination and phantasy, suggesting that invention was equivalent not to recovery but rather to active construction.

In addition, the chapter will explore the close ties between rhetoric and poetics, and the implications of such strong links for the understanding of the concept of invention, in, particularly, Italy, France, and England from the fifteenth century onwards. It will show how Horace's *Ars poetica* and Aristotle's *Poetics* determined the development of humanist poetics in these countries. The poetic discourse in Italy and France, which often described poetic composition in rhetorical terms and structured the process of poetry-writing by drawing on *inventio*, *dispositio*, and *elocutio*, had a decisive impact upon English authors. Also asserting strong links between rhetoric and poetics, they eventually assimilated the Italian and French currents of thought, a fact that became apparent in their national poetic production.

2.1. The Dispute about the Concept of Invention

The Renaissance reignited the debate on the nature of invention. The first complete rhetoric of the period, George of Trebizond's *Rhetoricorum libri V* (1433–34), dedicates three out of its five books to invention. Trebizond tries to assemble the pieces resulting from the medieval fragmentation of rhetoric into the different *artes*, and hence he once again assigns the topics to rhetoric (after medieval logicians had appropriated them), and carries out a synthesis of the Byzantine and Latin traditions.[1] A year after the appearance of Trebizond's introductory textbook to logic, *Isagoge dialectica* (1438), his rival Lorenzo Valla, a critic of scholasticism, completes *Repastinatio dialecticae et philosophiae* (or at least the first version of the work, given that he will continue to revise it for the rest of his life). In it, Valla questions Aristotle and reviews what falls under the remit of dialectic and rhetoric. Valla's humanist dialectic, even if taken into consideration by contemporary Aristotelian logicians, becomes a serious competitor to traditional Aristotelian logic within the teaching system in the early sixteenth century.[2] Agricola is next in redefining the relationship between dialectic and rhetoric, as well as in bringing the humanist programme of classical studies from Italy to northern Europe. Not only does Agricola translate from Greek into Latin Aphthonius's *Progymnasmata*, which for hundreds of years would be the chief schoolbook of rhetorical composition in Byzantium, but he also authors *De inventione dialectica* (1479), which subordinates rhetoric to dialectic and displaces Peter of Spain's *Summulae logicales* and Paul of Venice's *Logica* as introductions to dialectic. In fact, from its first edition in 1515 until 1579, Agricola's work went through around forty editions, its circulation being particularly intense between 1515 and 1530, especially in France, where numerous commentaries on the work were published.[3] Agricola's claim is that rhetoric had usurped many of dialectic's traditional materials, that *inventio* as well as *dispositio* pertains to dialectic, and that *elocutio*, delivery, and memory alone are the proper parts of rhetoric. The three books of *De inventione dialectica* are concerned not with judgement, the second part of dialectic, but exclusively with invention. Agricola groups all places of invention under dialectic, and by so doing fully disregards the traditional theoretical distinction between rhetorical and dialectical *loci*. To his mind, there exists a single category of topics that can be turned to any discourse, and they are classified under dialectic. Agricola redefines and rearranges what Aristotle, Cicero, Quintilian, Boethius, and Themistius (as collected by Boethius and Trebizond) had postulated about the topics, to offer finally his own list of twenty-four, the foundation stones of rational thought and meaningful communication.[4] Ironically, the divorce of dialectic from rhetoric produces a type of dialectic greatly influenced by rhetorical models, to the extent that some argue that Agricola 'sees arguments in rhetorical, rather than traditionally dialectical terms in that he is concerned with probable, not absolute, truths'.[5] The new logic devised by humanists such as Valla and Agricola displaces almost entirely the logic of high scholasticism by 1530, and dominates the teaching of the discipline in northern Europe until the eighteenth century.[6] Indeed, Agricola's work exerts significant influence on some of the great scholars of the sixteenth and seventeenth centuries. Erasmus, Johannes

Sturm, Juan Luis Vives, Philipp Melanchthon, and Petrus Ramus, among others, owe much to Agricola.[7]

The five-part division of classical rhetorical theory is also questioned by Vives in *De disciplinis* (1531). According to him, this partition is imprecise and redundant, as both memory and invention are not restricted to rhetoric, and prove vital to all the arts instead. Vives attributes the invention of arguments solely to dialectic, and, in his reasoning, elocution is the only true constituent of rhetoric. Philipp Melanchthon, Protestant theologian and professor of Greek and rhetoric at Wittenberg, adopts Agricola's partition of dialectic and rhetoric in his *Elementorum rhetorices libri duo* (1531). Previously, however, his *Institutiones rhetoricae* (1521), a revision of his earlier *De rhetorica* (1519), had located judgement and arrangement within rhetoric. Taking Cicero and Quintilian as his main sources, Melanchthon applies rhetoric to theological ends, and his thought in this regard eventually contributes to the transformation of reading and interpretation practices.[8] The widespread dissemination of Melanchthon's textbooks on dialectic and rhetoric stimulates the conversion of German Protestant universities to his methodological convictions. Soon, his ideas also travel beyond German borders and pervade the thought of northern humanists.[9]

Petrus Ramus, or Pierre de la Ramée, a former student of Johannes Sturm, whom he had heard lecturing on Agricola's *De inventione dialectica*, is however the driving force for change in Renaissance rhetoric and dialectic. His goal is to put an end to the contamination between the two fields and to the repetition of material in them. With this objective in mind, Ramus reduces the question of their relationship to a method of teaching and searches for criteria to delimit their boundaries. Ramus, it has been said, took up the matter 'where Agricola had left it',[10] with the difference that, whereas Agricola's dialectic makes no issue of being anti-Aristotelian, that of Ramus does. With Ramus, rhetoric becomes *doctrina bene dicendi*, an adaptation of Quintilian's *scientia bene dicendi*, merely covering style (*elocutio*) and delivery (*pronunciatio*). The simple task of rhetoric is to take the truths arrived at through reason and present them vividly to the imagination of an audience in a manner that moves its will and appetites. On the other hand, Ramus divides the superior realm of dialectic into invention, which he bases on the theory of the topics, and judgement, which includes disposition and memory.[11] For the sake of clarity and simplicity, both of which are priorities for Ramus in order to facilitate memorisation of the theory, invention is limited to ten places; from these, all arguments for any subject could in principle be generated.[12] Ramism spreads rapidly throughout Europe and achieves great popularity in northern Europe, particularly in Protestant Germany, 'where almost every chair of philosophy eventually came to be occupied by a Ramist'.[13] Ramist ideas were opposed in Italy, except at Bologna, and met with general hostility in Spain, with exceptions such as Francisco Sánchez de las Brozas, 'el Brocense', who taught at the University of Salamanca and whom Ong identifies as the earliest disciple of Ramus outside France.[14]

In England, Ramism gains considerable popularity between the years 1574 and 1620, and Grafton and Jardine state that 'in the 1570s and 1580s in England it was a just-permissible sign of intellectual radicalism to profess Ramism — a somewhat voguish intellectual stance'.[15] In 1574, Roland McIlmain publishes, for the first time in Britain, the earliest Latin version of Ramus's *Dialecticae libri duo* as well as its first translation into English; Abraham Fraunce adapts Ramus's text in his *Lawier's logike* (1588); Dudley Fenner translates both Ramus and Talon in *The artes of logike and rhetorike, plainelie set foorth* (1584); Fraunce translates Talon in *The Arcadian rhetorike; or, The praecepts of rhetorike made plaine by examples* (1588); Charles Butler writes *Rameae rhetoricae libri duo* (1597), and Thomas Blundeville produces *The art of logike* (1599), which translates and adapts Melanchthon's treatise. Fifteen editions of the *Dialectic* and five of the *Rhetoric* are published in England between 1574 and 1600, not to mention the countless Continental printings also in circulation in the country. If Oxford remains the English bastion of Aristotelianism and overall proves hostile to Ramism, Puritanical circles in Britain, particularly in Scotland and at Cambridge, welcome it. The Earl of Murray, Regent of Scotland and former pupil of Ramus, spreads Ramist ideas in Scotland, with St Andrews becoming 'the first centre of Ramism in Britain',[16] and at Cambridge Ramism is greeted by figures such as Laurence Chaderton and Gabriel Harvey as an indicator of progress. Harvey, for instance, at this time a young professor of rhetoric, delivers in 1575 and 1576 three discourses with Ramist overtones, and publishes in 1577 his *Ciceronianus*, in which he explains his conversion to Ramism after years of blindly following Cicero. The confrontation between Aristotelians and Ramists reaches its peak at Cambridge in the 1580s and 1590s with the quarrels between, on the one hand, Everard Digby and the Ramist William Temple, and, on the other, Thomas Nashe and Harvey.

John Seton's *Dialectica* (1545), Thomas Wilson's *Rule of reason* (1551), and Peter Carter's *Annotationes* (1563) are the main English works on logic in the early Renaissance, and the three share the influence of Agricola's accounts of invention and place theory.[17] Seton's *Dialectica* targets the Cambridge schoolboy and makes explicit its author's dependence on Agricola to express either agreement or disagreement with the latter. From Agricola's *De inventione*, Carter appropriates the list and definition of the places, even if he then follows the Boethian rather than the Agricolan explanation of them. Wilson's *Rule of reason*, the only one of the three works written in English, assumes a broadly Aristotelian framework and divides logic into *judicium* (the discussion of which follows Melanchthon's *Erotemata dialectices*) and *inventio* (discussed through Agricola and Boethius).[18] Wilson defines *inventio* as 'finding out matter, and searchyng stuffe agreable to the cause'.[19] Logical invention becomes thus 'the store house of places',[20] and the places 'the restyng corner of an argumēt, or els a marke whiche giveth warnyng to our memory, what we maie speake probablie, either in the one parte or the other, upon all causes that fall in question'.[21] Agricola's distinction of twenty-four places, ten 'internal' and fourteen 'external', is appropriated and translated by Wilson without acknowledging its source.

Given that all candidates for degrees at the universities of Oxford and Cambridge have to participate in disputations, dialectic is treated as a pre-eminent practical skill with which students can invent arguments and organise persuasive discourses. Rhetoric, on the other hand, is not taught continuously or as an independent subject at Oxford or Cambridge until c. 1431, and is not firmly established in the curriculum even during the fifteenth century.[22] This is partly why Donald Lemen Clark asserts that, in England, 'the Renaissance university was still more medieval than humanistic'.[23] On the booklists of both universities, Cicero's *Orations* and his rhetorical works, including the pseudo-Ciceronian *Rhetorica ad Herennium*, occupy first place. Quintilian's *Institutio oratoria*, Cicero's *De oratore*, and Aristotle's *Rhetoric* follow. Lastly, the booklists reveal a modest but relevant number of copies of the Greek rhetorician Hermogenes, highly popular in the Middle Ages and widely known through Priscian's Latin translation.[24] Erasmus's *Ecclesiastes* and works by Melanchthon and Talon are the most abundant among the Renaissance manuals of rhetoric kept in the libraries.[25] John Rainolds's lectures on Aristotle's *Rhetoric* at Oxford, which constitute the 'only known complete text of an Elizabethan lecture course on rhetoric',[26] assume full knowledge of it on the part of students, and echo Agricola's and Vives's perspectives. In these university booklists, however, texts on dialectic comfortably outnumber those on rhetoric: Cicero's *Topica*, Agricola's *De inventione dialectica*, and Aristotle's *Topics* stand out among the listed books. Seton, Case, Sanderson, and Wilson author works on logic which are also used as textbooks at English universities. At Cambridge, the most widely used manuals in the second half of the sixteenth century are Agricola's *De inventione dialectica*, Melanchthon's *Dialectices* (1527) and *Erotemata dialectices* (1547), Caesarius's *Dialectica* (1532), Seton's *Dialectica* in Peter Carter's annotated edition (1572), and Ramus's *Dialecticae institutiones* (1543).[27]

In the school curriculum of Tudor England, rhetoric remains, as in the Middle Ages, inferior to dialectic, and at the beginning of the sixteenth century the teaching of rhetoric in English grammar schools such as Eton, Westminster, and St Paul's is still organised in the form of the medieval trivium, even if new handbooks coming from the Continent and written by Agricola, Melanchthon, Mosellanus, Susenbrotus, and Erasmus gradually begin to exert their influence. John Colet, accountable for formulating the backbone of literary humanism in England and for shaping the curriculum of St Paul's School,[28] encourages Erasmus to write a work that would make classical rhetoric palatable to young schoolboys and thus satisfy a pedagogical need that, far from being exclusive to England, existed throughout northern Europe. The result is Erasmus's *De duplici copia verborum et rerum* (1512), one of the most popular and widely used textbooks of the Renaissance, with eighty editions in the sixteenth century alone.[29] The statutes of St Paul's School (1512) have in fact often been taken to mark the beginning of English humanist poetics.[30]

Even when considered as a whole, the skills taught at the 360 grammar schools operating in England in 1575 do not represent the traditional full course in classical rhetoric, for there are omissions and adaptations that particularly affect invention. Indeed, there is no general treatment of invention, and the study of the forms of argument is deferred to university courses on dialectic.[31] Continental editions and translations are the major vehicles for rhetorical instruction both at grammar schools and at Oxford and Cambridge. Certainly, Cicero's rhetorical treatises are not printed in England until the 1570s (and even then with Continental commentaries), and Aristotle's *Rhetoric* not until the seventeenth century, even if the schoolmasters of Tudor England are beginning to engage with it: both Vives and Sir John Cheke know it, and Ascham studies it.[32] Yet the *Rhetoric* has virtually no influence on English rhetoric, and thus, although between 1572 and 1578 John Rainolds lectures on it, his rhetorical theory and style have been described as 'completely anti-Aristotelian'.[33] Instead, Cicero is the star of rhetorical instruction in the sixteenth and seventeenth centuries. He is unanimously hailed as a major authority, and his works have the advantage of being relatively easy to obtain. Moreover, an edition of his collected works was economical in practical terms, in that it could be used as a textbook for various levels and purposes.[34] The Ciceronian authorship of the *Rhetorica ad Herennium* is generally not questioned — with exceptions such as Clemens Timpler — until the beginning of the sixteenth century. Yet rhetoric teachers in that century remain fairly indifferent to its authenticity; in any case, the book is easily available, *en vogue*, and highly suitable for rhetorical instruction.[35]

As manuals for elementary levels, grammar schools use the works of Hermogenes and Aphthonius, whose *Progymnasmata*, with its fourteen kinds of introductory exercises such as the retelling of a fable or myth, becomes the textbook of Latin composition par excellence. The *Progymnasmata* is so successful that Richard Rainolde adapts into English Agricola's Latin translation of Aphthonius's work, edited by Reinhard Lorich in 1542, thus producing *A book called the foundacion of rhetorike* (1563).[36] Nonetheless, English students 'usually used Agricola's Latin translation',[37] and in England it is this composition handbook that stands out among the many available in print, to the extent that 'many, if not most, Renaissance English schoolboys learned the basic forms of composition from Aphthonius' in the Latin translation edited by Lorich.[38] Indeed, his edition of Aphthonius's *Progymnasmata* becomes 'one of the most printed textbooks of the sixteenth century'[39] and goes through twenty-eight editions in the sixteenth and seventeenth centuries.[40] Even at university level, 'the exercises taught by Aphthonius were never totally discarded as the formal bases for composition in the various rhetorical genres', and so, unsurprisingly, traces of Aphthonius's composition exercises can be found in the works of a great variety of early modern English playwrights.[41] Composition exercises such as the fable, which requires the student to compose 'a moral story by linking a narrative with a moral sentence',[42] and the *chreia*, which presents a saying or an action as a model for imitation and amplification, stand out as those that would appear to have provided the greatest scope for exploration and innovation to future poets and playwrights.[43] In addition, training in rhetoric relies to a considerable extent on commonplace textbooks, which supply young students of rhetoric with both ideas and words through collections of excerpts from the classics; their goal is to promote copious style and train the students' abilities in amplifying a theme.[44] Cato's *Disticha de moribus* (translated in 1477 as *The dictes and sayings of the philosophers*), Erasmus's *Adagia* (1500), and Lycosthenes's *Apophthegmatum* (1555), based primarily upon Erasmus, are the most popular Latin commonplace books. Among the English handbooks of collections of places, those which stand out are William Baldwin's *Treatise of morall phylosophie* (1547), Richard Taverner's *Garden of wysdom* and *Second booke of the garden of wysedome* (both 1539), Thomas Blage's *Schole of wise conceyts* (1569), William Phiston's *The welspring of wittie conceites* (1584), and Francis Meres's *Palladis tamia: Wit's treasury* (1598).

Texts on rhetoric written in English also begin to be printed partly because some English schoolmasters consider it advantageous to train their students in their native tongue. Not coincidentally, authorised English translations of the Bible start to appear at this time, when English is replacing Latin in the liturgies of the Church of England. The first rhetoric in English is Leonard Cox's *The art or crafte of rhethoryke* (1535), in part a translation of Melanchthon's *Institutiones rhetoricae* (1521) and in part a commentary by Cox, following a study guide written by a student of Melanchthon on certain features of rhetoric. The reason why Cox identifies four parts of rhetoric (judgement, invention, disposition, and style), and deals chiefly with invention without even discussing style, is that the 1521 version of Melanchthon's book that he uses as his model is an early work of Melanchthon which does not yet reflect the influence that Agricola would later have on him. Cox's book is followed by Richard Sherry's *A treatise of schemes and tropes, gathered out of the best grammarians and oratours* (1550), which appears in print with an appended translation of Erasmus's *On the education of children*.[45] Even if Sherry does not reduce rhetoric to style, his treatise deals solely with figures and tropes, and their use is illustrated by means of contemporary examples in English. Sherry's *Treatise* and Susenbrotus's *Epitome troporum ac schematum et grammaticorum et rhetorum* (1540) are the major influences on Henry Peacham's *The garden of eloquence* (1577), a manual of style that defines and illustrates a selection of figures of speech.[46] Angel Day's *The English secretary* (1586), on the duties of a secretary and the various types of letters, also gives an account of the figures and tropes based on Susenbrotus, and makes Erasmus's *De conscribendis epistolis* the chief model for its letter-writing manual. Ragsdale, in his discussion of English books on style published between 1600 and 1800, remarks that, even though these works lack a formal treatment of invention, 'there are many figures of speech which very closely correspond to the logical, emotional, and ethical modes of proof in the classical theory of invention'.[47]

Thomas Wilson's *Arte of rhetorique* is not only the first full-fledged book on rhetoric in English but also a great publishing success, going through eight editions between 1553 and 1585. The *Arte* was not conceived of as a textbook for school use, but was targeted instead at young adults with an interest in law, the Church, or public life, and was possibly intended for those studying law at the Inns of Court.[48] Cicero's *De inventione* and, above all, *Rhetorica ad Herennium* were Wilson's major sources, followed by Quintilian's *Institutio*, Melanchthon's *Elementorum rhetorices*, Erasmus's *De conscribendis epistolis* and *De copia*, Sherry's *Treatise of schemes and tropes*, and, for the treatment of emotional persuasion, Agricola's *De inventione dialectica*.[49] Wilson followed the five-part Ciceronian distinction, and, although he included a list of general and specific topics, he referred readers to his work on dialectic for detailed explanations. 'The findyng out of apte matter, called otherwise Invencion', understood as 'a searchyng out of thynges true, or thynges likely, the whiche maie reasonably sette furth a matter, and make it appere probable' is, according to Wilson, the ultimate end of humanist rhetoric.⁵⁰

Indeed, in non-Ramist English works on rhetoric, invention continues to be associated with the seeking of arguments for discussion and with the theory of the *loci*. This classical definition of rhetorical invention coexists with variations of it that suggest different interpretations. On the one hand, there is the stance adopted by authors such as Lydgate or Wilson: since arguments are housed within the human mind, invention implies a process of finding, searching, or seeking. On the other hand, some rhetoricians employ in their treatment of invention terms such as 'imagination', 'phantasy', 'fancy', or 'wit'. This suggests that, for the former group, arguments pre-exist in the human mind and, in consequence, orators only need to retrieve them in order to invent. By contrast, the latter group seems to conceive of the mind as an active mechanism, and of the process of inventing as pertaining to the domain of the imagination and fancy. From their perspective, when one invents, one does not simply recover a ready-made argument hidden in one's mind, but rather constructs it.

For John Lydgate, rhetorical invention is a mental process that is purely a matter of finding arguments already imprinted in one's mind. As he explains in *Here begynnethe the boke calledde Iohn bochas descriuinge the falle of princis princessis & other nobles* (1494), through invention

> [...] a man dothe in his hert *fynde*
> A secrete grounde founde on *reason*
> With circũstaũces ỹ nought be left behynde
> Fro poynt to poynt / imprīted in his mynde
> Touchyng ỹ mater / ỹ substaũce & the great
> Of whiche he cast / notably rentreat.⁵¹

Wilson's definition of invention as finding, quoted above, applies both to rhetorical as well as to dialectical invention, as made manifest in *The rule of reason*, where logical invention is defined as 'the store house of places wherein argumentes reste'. The task of the logician that invents is to 'finde argumentes, and reasons' after the manner of those 'that digge for golde in ỹ grounde, do searche narowly the vaynes of the yearth, and by diligent markyng the nature thereof, at length fynde out the mine'.⁵² In other words, inventing involves finding an argument in the 'store house of places', as if the logician were a gold-seeker working in the depths of the human mind in search of buried arguments to 'bryng to light and use, accordyng to his will'.⁵³ Inventing, thus, means unearthing already extant arguments. In similar terms, the Ramist *Art of logike* (1599) defines logical invention as that which 'findeth out meete matter to proove the thing that yee intend'.⁵⁴ Wilson further compares the logician with a hunter, and the argument he seeks with an animal hiding in its burrow:

> Those that be good hare finders, will sone finde by her fourme. For, when they se the grounde beaten flatte round about, & faire to the sight: thei haue a narow gesse by al likelihod that the hare was there a litle before. Likewyse the

hontesman in huntyng ỹ foxe, wil sone espie when he seeth a hole, whether it be a foxe borough, or not. So he ỹ will take profite in this parte of logique, must be like a hunter, and learne by labour to knowe the boroughes. For these places be nothyng els but couertes or boroughes, wherein if any one searche diligentlie, he maie fynde game at pleasure.[55]

Reminiscent of Wilson's comparisons is Richard Rainolde's reference in *A booke called the foundacion of rhetorike* (1563) to 'the secrete and hid wisedome' of the orator's mind. Rainolde says that to rhetoric 'wittie inuencion' is proper,[56] and that orators are trained so 'that thei might with all copiousnes and ingenious inuencion handle any cause': 'It is a goodly vertue in any one man, at a sodain, to vtter wittely and ingeniouslie, the secrete and hid wisedome of his mynde'.[57] 'Wittely' and 'ingeniouslie' in this case can mean either that the orator should reveal the hidden wisdom of his mind in a 'wittie' and 'ingenious' manner (and this suggests directions for elocution), or that 'the secrete and hid wisedome of his mynde' can only be recovered by means of wit and *ingenium*. Evidence of this traditional understanding of invention as finding can also be seen in the definition of *tŏpĭcē* and *inventio* in Thomas Thomas's *Dictionarium linguae latinae et anglicanae* (1587), where the former is said to mean 'invention or finding out of arguments',[58] and the latter 'an inventing, a finding'.[59] Similarly, John Florio's *A world of words* (1598) defines *tópica* as 'inuention or finding out of arguments';[60] Richard Perceval's *A dictionary in Spanish and English* (1599) defines *inventár* as 'to inuent, to finde out';[61] and Florio's *Queen Anna's new world of words* (1611) defines *inuentíua* as 'an inuention, a finding'.[62]

A second set of authors, by contrast, grant the human mind a more active role in the process of invention by acknowledging that imagination, phantasy, fancy, and wit contribute to manufacturing arguments. William Caxton, in *The myrrour: [and] dyscrypcyon of the worlde with many meruaylles* (1527, first published in 1481), sees rhetorical invention as an exercise of the imagination, for 'to invent' for him means 'to ymagyn the mater which thou intendest to shew / which must be of trew thyngs / or lyke to be trew'.[63] In *The art or crafte of rhetoryke* (1532), Leonard Cox states that the essential and 'moost difficile or harde' skill for an orator to possess is invention, for a rhetor 'must fyrst of all imagin or Inuent in his mynde what he shall say'. Even if Cox puts invention on a par with imagination by equating 'to imagine' with 'to invent', he later adds that judgement is also necessary to control invention, and in his explanation of this he introduces the idea of finding as well: '[one] must have wyt to deserne & iuge whether tho thynges that he hath founde in his mynde be conuenient to the purpose or nat'.[64] As a result, Cox combines the approach according to which invention involves finding something that seems to be hidden in one's mind, with the idea that the mind actively shapes what is invented. In keeping with the understanding of invention as finding, Cox goes on to say that 'Inuencion is comprehended in certayn places [...] / out of whom he that knoweth yᵉ faculty may fetche easely suche thynges as be mete for the mater that he shall speke of': 'I must for the Inuencyon of suche thynges as be for my purpose go to places of Rhetorique / where I shall easely finde (after I know the rules) that that I desyre.'[65]

Since Cox positions the places at the core of the theory of invention, 'finding' equals checking the list of places stored in one's mind (as the result of hours of study and memorisation) to 'fetche' that which is most appropriate depending on the theme at hand. The fact that Cox treats 'to invent' and 'to imagine' as synonyms suggests that imagination participates in inventing either during or after the finding of the proper place or *topos*. Hybrid understandings of invention, combining the idea of finding and other notions closer to the imagination or to devising, are also seen in some dictionary definitions. Florio's *A world of words* equates invention to the 'finding out of arguments', and defines *inuénia* as 'a deuice, an inuention, a newe found out thing' and *inuentione* as 'an inuention, a deuise, a forgerie, a surmise, a finding'.[66] Ralph Lever's *The arte of reason, rightly termed, witcraft* (1573) also implies that invention has to do with novelty, and that 'as time doth inuent a newe forme of building, a straunge fashion of apparell, and a newe kinde of artillerie, and munitions', so 'names are not giuen unto things afore the things themselues be inuented'.[67] Inventing here implies the devising of something 'newe' and 'straunge' that did not exist previously.

2.2. Poetic Invention Introduced

Poetry becomes a flourishing field in the second half of the thirteenth century in Italy (at this time experiencing a period of economic prosperity), and a constituent of the so-called *studia humanitatis* together with rhetoric, history, and moral philosophy. Humanist poetics is highly influenced by, on the one hand, the Latin rhetorical tradition (particularly by Cicero and Quintilian), and, on the other, Neoplatonism, whose theories on divine *furor*, poetic madness, and inspiration contribute to the strengthening of the connections between poetry and prophecy, and to the consolidation of the idea (traceable back to Homer and Hesiod) that the poet *vates* is born and not the product of hard training.[68] The general understanding of 'poetics' at this time typically suggests an *ars poetica*, to wit, a treatise on poetic composition following Horace's *Ars poetica*, or a manual on the techniques of verse composition that includes material on metre, stanza form, diction, and figures and tropes. There were three Horatian concepts that marked the development of humanist poetics: the civilising effect of poetry, the recognition of utility and delight as its ends, and the centrality of decorum. Horace's quasi-rhetorical theories proposed that the demands of the target audience of the poem condition the internal structure of the poem itself. The rhetorical readings that the humanists make of Horace's *Ars poetica* ultimately determine the relation between poetry and rhetoric in the sixteenth century.

Particularly in early humanism, poetry is seen as a form of eloquence (Petrarch is one of the main exponents of this view), and Dante's *De vulgari eloquentia* and *Convivio* also agree with the notion of the poet as orator.[69] Even Ramus admits commonalities between poetry and rhetoric — among others, a shared eagerness to deceive their audiences into drawing specific conclusions.[70] What is more, because Ramism believed poetry to be effective and useful in pedagogical terms, it made use of poetic examples to discuss and illustrate logical discourse. The decision to do so certainly turned out to be polemical, as the presence of poetry in this field 'transgressed the time-honored semantics of scholastic dialectic'.[71] while incorporating examples drawn from poetry for the purposes of illustration was customary within the field of rhetoric, it was anathema for dialectic. In employing poetic examples in dialectic, the Ramists were accused of violating 'the scholastic boundary between the figurative and the literal by effectively equalizing the status of dialectical and poetic languages'.[72] By contrast, since for Ramists 'both dialectical discourse and poetic discourse were believed to resemble — were taken as signs of — our natural habits of reasoning',[73] poetry could be put to this use.

The structure of the works on poetry produced in the sixteenth century also reveals the influence of rhetoric on poetics. For instance, Vida's *De arte poetica* (1527) is a verse treatise in the manner of Horace organised into three books dealing with, respectively, the training of the poet and the defence of poetry, *inventio* and *dispositio*, and *elocutio*. Minturno's *De poeta* (1559) discusses poetry, poetic genres, and style, mixing theories by Horace, Plato, Aristotle, Cicero, and Quintilian, and Scaliger's *Poetices* (1561) likewise fuses myriad sources and critical discourses, and treats a variety of topics such as genres, verse forms, poetic forms, style, and rhetorical figures. In Scaliger's *Poetices*, rhetoric is fundamental to understanding the theory of oratory and poetry, and to examining the practice of both. Yet by this point, poetry is more greatly differentiated from oratory, and — as a result of better knowledge of Aristotle's *Poetics*, unstoppable in its influence since the printing of Alessandro Pazzi's 1536 Latin version and Francesco Robortello's 1548 commentary on it — the field of poetics undergoes profound changes.

The intimate connection between rhetoric and poetics in the Renaissance has been repeatedly stressed by scholars such as Vickers[74] and Clark, for whom

> the renaissance theory of poetry was rhetorical in its obsession with style, especially the figures of speech, in its abiding faith in the efficacy of rules; and in its belief that the poet, no less than the orator, is occupied with persuasion.[75]

Kibedi Varga in addition argues that, in the Renaissance, poetics was seen as a 'versified rhetoric' and between the two there existed a relationship in which poetics was subordinated to rhetoric;[76] for Kennedy, 'poetry was not a matter of free expression but an application and development of the thought of the poet within the arts of grammar, rhetoric, and dialectic'.[77] This view has not gone uncontested: Howell, for instance, criticises the thesis that, in the Renaissance, 'rhetoric assumed control over poetics', and suggests instead that there existed 'common properties of rhetoric and poetics'.[78]

The role that Horace's and Aristotle's ideas on poetry play in humanist thought determines the humanist notion of poetics. Horace's *Ars poetica*, widely known in the late Middle Ages, becomes by far the most popular, comprehensive, and influential authoritative text on poetic composition for the humanists. It has in fact been remarked that Horace's *Ars poetica* exerted 'an almost uninterrupted influence on poetics from classical antiquity to the Renaissance'.[79] In the age of printing, it was usually read against the background of two sets of explanatory annotations, one by Porphyrion (third/fourth century) and another supposedly by Helenius Acron (fifth century). Further commentaries written by the humanists appear in the fifteenth and sixteenth centuries; the most important are those by Cristoforo Landino (1482) and Aulo Giano Parrasio (1531). Read against the background of these three commentators, Horace's *Ars poetica* 'becomes a vehicle for the whole range of views on poetic theory available up to about 1530'.[80] In England, it is from 1567 onwards that Horace's influence becomes extensive, thanks to Drant's rendering of the *Ars poetica* into English.

Unlike Horace's *Ars poetica*, Aristotle's *Poetics* was largely neglected in Antiquity, and in fact Aristotle's now fragmentary essay *On the poets* seems to have been better known.[81] The introduction of the *Poetics* to medieval Europe owes much to the twelfth-century abridged version of Averroes's *Middle commentary on Aristotle's Poetics*, translated into Latin by Hermannus Alemannus in 1256 and by Mantinus of Tortosa in the fourteenth century. The Averroes paraphrase in Alemannus's translation was published in Venice in 1481 and 1515, while new translations of Averroes based on the fourteenth-century Hebrew version appeared thanks to Abraham de Balmes (1523, 1560) and Jacob Mantino (1550, 1562). The book was known in the fifteenth and sixteenth centuries only in limited circles at European universities,[82] and despite Hermannus's early version, Dante and Boccaccio, and most likely Petrarch as well, never got to know the *Poetics*.[83] Aristotle's *Poetics* also re-entered the West through the 1278 translation of William of Moerbeke, bishop of Corinth, who rendered it from the Greek into Latin. Of this version, which was virtually ignored, there are only two extant manuscripts from the thirteenth century.

From around the 1470s, following the recovery of the original Greek texts, scholars no longer depended on these medieval commentaries and began to study the originals directly. Despite Giorgio Valla having translated the work into Latin in 1498, it would not be until the publication in 1536 of Pazzi's revised Latin version accompanying the original in Greek that Aristotle's *Poetics* became a landmark in poetic criticism.[84] During the sixteenth century, published commentaries on the *Poetics* proliferate. The *commenti maggiori*, or greater commentaries (by Robortello, Castelvetro, Vettori, Maggi and Lombardi, and Piccolomini) deal with the entire book, while partial commentaries dealing with specific passages also exist (by Trissino, G. B. Giraldi Cinthio, and Tasso, among others). Robortello's *In librum Aristotelis de Arte poetica explicationes* (1548), which accompanied the translation with a thorough commentary on every passage in the book, was the first of the *commenti maggiori*. In the vernacular, the commentaries that stand out are Castelvetro's (1570) and Piccolomini's (1575). These late sixteenth-century commentaries on Aristotle's *Poetics* tend to be deeply rhetorical, combine Aristotle with Cicero or Horace, and take it for granted that the goal of poetry and drama is to improve the audience morally by means of rhetorical devices. If Averroes had interpreted the *Poetics* as a treatise on epideictic rhetoric, Robortello re-emphasised this conclusion.[85] Many of the Italian commentaries endeavour to relate the *Ars poetica* to Aristotle's *Poetics*, and read one work in light of the other.[86] The idea that Horace had read the *Poetics* and used it as a starting point for his own reflections on poetry became widespread, and many commentaries (such as Maggi's) strove to find similarities and points of agreement between Aristotle's and Horace's postulates.[87]

These readings not uncommonly used Aristotle's *Poetics* and *Rhetoric* to interpret Horace's *Ars poetica*.[88] Indeed, the interpretation of the *Ars poetica* did not change substantially after Aristotle's *Poetics* re-entered the sphere of criticism.[89] It was only much later that, for example, Horace's alleged support for imitation as the essence of poetry was called into question,[90] and the belief that Horace made sense of Aristotle remained alive for a long time. For instance, in 1668 Dryden would affirm in his *Essay of dramatic poesy* that 'of that Book which *Aristotle* has left us, περὶ τες Ποιητικῆς, Horace his *Art of Poetry* is an excellent Comment'.[91] That Horace was acquainted with Aristotle's *Poetics* has been questioned by scholars such as Grube, who states that, even if various assertions in Horace's *Ars poetica* seem to derive from or coincide with Aristotle's *Poetics*, they are merely peripheral and not the main theories of Aristotle's work: 'it seems therefore most unlikely that Horace had read the *Poetics*. The same is true of the *Rhetoric*'.[92] Other scholars, such as La Drière, believe that, for Horace, *incitation*, rather than the idea of imitation, was 'the primary requisite of poetry'.[93] Atkins likewise doubts whether Horace's ideas on imitation coincide with those of Aristotle.[94]

Spingarn identifies the translation of Horace's *Ars poetica* into the vernaculars as the spur for the beginning of national poetic criticism: Dolce's Italian translation (1535) took the lead here, followed by Jacques Peletier du Mans's in France (1545), Drant's English version (1567), and Espinel's (1591) and Zapata's (1592) Spanish translations. In fact, Hardison distinguishes three stages in Italian criticism marked by the trajectories of Horace's and Aristotle's texts in Italy. First, he distinguishes a Platonic and rhetorical stage up to the end of the fifteenth century, in which the *Ars poetica* was read through the lens of Platonic and Neoplatonic doctrine and its ideas regarding *furor poeticus*.[95] The second phase of Italian criticism was inaugurated by Robortello's *Explicationes* (1548) and continued with other commentaries on Aristotle's work, such as those by Scaliger (1561) and Castelvetro (1570). Finally, the third phase, beginning in the late sixteenth century, was characterised by the emergence of various schools of criticism that differed in their consideration of Homer and Virgil, and in the legitimacy of literary forms such as the romance and the tragicomedy.[96]

Sixteenth-century English scholars and authors, with a few exceptions, such as Sir Philip Sidney,[97] had limited acquaintance with the rich critical work of their Italian contemporaries on the subject of poetics, and it is revealing in this respect that none of their previously mentioned works were rendered into English during the reign of the Tudors. Moreover, unlike their Italian counterparts, English critics were only slightly acquainted with Aristotle's ideas on poetry: Ascham's *Scholemaster* (1570) contains the first reference in early modern England to the *Poetics*, and Sidney's *Defence* represents its integration into English criticism. It is thanks to Sidney that 'the Aristotelianism of the Italian renaissance makes its first appearance in English criticism'.[98] Also contrasting with Italian criticism, despite closely following in its steps, sixteenth-century French criticism is less philosophical in its treatment of aesthetic matters and far more practical in its orientation, in the sense that it is more concerned with giving advice to prospective poets on how to write verse compositions.[99]

In the first half of the sixteenth century, economical and cultural relations between Lyon and Italy were so strong that the French city became a lively humanistic centre. In this renovating context, the poetic group of the Pléiade appeared, with Joachim Du Bellay's *Deffence et illustration de la langue françoyse* (1549) as its manifesto on the new poetry, written in response to Thomas Sébillet's *Art poétique françoys* (1548). Sébillet's treatise was still imbued with remnants of medieval conceptions of rhyme and versification, despite concurrently advancing a new set of ideas such as the replacement of the term *rimeur* with *poète*, the rejection of the notion that poetry is a superficial pastime, the belief that poetry is the result of divine inspiration, and the idea that art and training make the most of the natural gifts of the poet.[100] Du Bellay's *Deffence* demarcates the passage from the medieval stress on rhetorical and metrical structure to the Renaissance 'formation of a poetic language, the introduction of new *genres*, the creation of new rhythms, and the imitation of classical literature'.[101] Through the *Deffence*, Du Bellay introduces classical and Italian ideas into French linguistic and poetic criticism. Dante's *De vulgari eloquio* (1529, in the Italian version of Trissino) becomes the model for the *Deffence*,[102] and Speroni's *Dialogo delle lingue* (1542) and Ricci's *De imitatione libri tres* (1541) are some of his many other Italian influences. Following the Italian poetic doctrines stemming from Neoplatonism, Du Bellay proclaims the excellence of the poet and the quasi-sacred character of his creation. Nevertheless, the *Deffence* shows not direct signs of acquaintance with Aristotle's *Poetics* but, instead, indirect ones via Italian critics.[103] Indeed, Scaliger's *Poetices* is the work that would introduce the Aristotelian poetic canons into French criticism.[104] Curiously enough, despite the key role of Du Bellay within French humanism and the enormous influence of French critics in England, Du Bellay was not quoted by the English as a critical authority but rather known for his literary work, particularly in the 1580s. Instead, it was Du Bartas and Ronsard who primarily caught the attention of English criticism.[105] This is not to say, of course, that Du Bellay's poetic notions were not influential in England. On the contrary, his presence became pervasive in English letters, if only for the influence that he exerted on Spenser as far as the latter's theoretical approach to poetry, the uses and status of the vernacular language, and key concepts such as imitation are concerned (as will be seen in the next chapter).[106]

The poets of the Pléiade ponder the nature of poetry, wondering whether it is solely a branch of rhetoric (*la seconde rhétorique*) or whether it has independent status and an essence of its own. In contrast to the so-called *art de première rhétorique*, which focuses on prose and not on verse, relies heavily on classical erudition, and appears especially appropriate for the orator, the *art de seconde rhétorique* postulates that, although versification may be learned, poetry cannot be taught. Consequently, this *art* can only provide handy manuals of precepts for the would-be poet. By contrast, an *art poétique* is concerned with poetic inspiration, the essence of poetry, its proper subjects, the genres, poetic vocabulary, versification, and poetic translation and adaptation.[107] Sixteenth-century French criticism generally conceives of poetry as a *seconde rhétorique*, which has led some critics to assert that 'no modern European literature ever assumed a closer alliance between rhetoric and poetics than French literature did until the nineteenth century'.[108]

Pierre Fabri, for instance, in his *Le grand et vray art de pleine rhétorique* (1521), establishes the metrical and prosodic element as the sole difference between poetry and rhetoric. Otherwise, composition, for both the orator and the poet, means going through the operations of invention, disposition, and elocution. Similarly, Jacques Peletier, in the chapter of his *Art poétique* (1555) entitled 'De la Composition du Poème en général', states that 'toutes sortes d'Écrits s'accomplissent de trois parties principales, qui sont Invention, Disposition, Élocution' [all types of writings consist of three main parts, which are invention, disposition, elocution].[109] The rest of the major exponents of the French poetic scene (Sébillet, Du Bellay, Ronsard, among others) likewise describe poetic composition in rhetorical terms and refer to invention, disposition, and elocution in the process of poetry-writing. Sébillet, who would in fact go so far as to wonder, like Macrobius, whether Cicero or Virgil was the greatest rhetorician there had been, affirms that 'rhetoric is as present throughout the poem as it is throughout the oration', and that the invention of the poet matches, in terms of importance and nature, the invention of the orator:

> Le fondement et première partie du Poème ou carme, est l'invention. Et ne doit-on trouver étrange si je donne en l'art poétique les premières parties à celle, laquelle les Rhétoriciens ont aussi nombrée première part de tout leur art. Car la Rhétorique est autant bien épandue par tout le poème, comme par toute l'oraison. Et sont l'Orateur et le Poète tant proches et conjoints, que semblables et égaux en plusieurs choses [...]. Supposé donc que celui qui se veut exercer en la Poésie française, soit autrement bien versé et entendu en toutes les parties de Rhétorique, il doit toutefois être plus expert en l'invention, comme celle qu'il a particulièrement plus commune avec l'Orateur: et de laquelle résulte toute l'élégance de son poème.
>
> [The foundation and first part of the poem is invention. It should not be surprising that I give invention the first part in the art of poetry, when the rhetoricians have also named it the first part of their entire art. Indeed, rhetoric is as present throughout the poem as it is throughout the oration. And the orator and the poet are so close and linked that they are similar and alike in many things [...]. However well-versed and learned in all the parts of rhetoric is he who wants to practise French poetry, he nonetheless needs to be a greater expert in invention, as this is the part most closely shared with the orator, and the one from which all the elegance of his poem results.][110]

'Le surplus de l'invention qui consiste en l'art, prendra le poète des Philosophes et Rhéteurs' [The surplus of invention that is in the art, the poet will take from philosophers and rhetoricians],[111] Sébillet adds. Both rhetoric and poetry can learn profoundly from each other: 'Et tout ainsi que le futur Orateur profite en la leçon du Poète: aussi le futur Poète peut enrichir son style, et faire son champ autrement stérile, fertile, de la leçon des Historiens et Orateurs français' [and if the future orator benefits from the lesson of the poet, the future poet can likewise enrich his style, and make fertile his otherwise barren field, thanks to the lesson of French historians and orators].[112] Du Bellay in this respect affirms that 'the poet and the orator are as it were two pillars that support the structure of every language'.[113] Other authors, such as Peletier, acknowledge an independent realm for poetry in terms of language, the profile of its readership, and the subject matter of its compositions, which are more abstract and elevated in poetry than in rhetoric, in the sense that the latter is constrained by the immediate circumstances surrounding a speech:

> Ainsi voilà l'une des principales différences qu'il y a entre l'Orateur et le Poète, que cettui-ci peut s'ébattre en tous genres d'arguments, cettui-là est astreint aux choses particulières. Car l'Orateur ne pourra pas chercher l'occasion de faire parler les Dieux, de traiter l'Amour, les Jeux festifs, les Enfers, les Astres, les régions, les champs, les prés, les fontaines et telles beautés d'Écrits: Mais se tiendra dedans les causes de ses clients, mouvra les affects, déduira ses raisons, réfutera celles de son adversaire. Et en ces deux derniers points, le Poète y entre aussi: mais il les traite succinctement. Car lui qui parle à une éternité, doit seulement toucher le nœud, le secret et le fond d'un argument, et parler plus résolument, laissant les menues narrations. L'Orateur, qui parle aux hommes présents, et le plus souvent au peuple, fait assez s'il a une action, et une façon convenable à pouvoir gagner ses gens seulement pour une heure. [...] Les mots aussi doivent être différents au Poète et à l'Orateur. Comme par exemple, en Latin, l'Orateur ne dira pas *altum* pour la mer: ni la poupe pour toute la navire. Et autres semblables mots figurés, lesquels n'est ici commode de déclarer par le menu.

> [Thus, one of the principal differences between the poet and the orator is that one can play with all kinds of arguments, while the other is confined to specific things. For the orator will not have to make the gods talk, deal with love, festive games, Hades, the stars, regions, fields, meadows, fountains, and such beautiful things in writing, but will have to restrict himself to the causes of his clients, move feelings, deduce his reasons, and refute those of his adversary. In these last two points, the poet participates as well, but he discusses them succinctly, because he who speaks to eternity has to touch only the kernel, the secret and essence of an argument, and be more resolute, leaving small matters aside. The orator, who speaks to present men, and most frequently to the people, complies by having an effect, and using an appropriate fashion to gain his audience, if only for one hour. [...] Words also have to be different for the Poet and the Orator. Just as, for instance, in Latin the orator would never say *altum* for the sea, or the stern for the whole vessel. The same occurs with similar figurative words, inconvenient to enumerate here.][114]

As Ronsard summarises in his *Abrégé de l'art poétique français* and his 1572 preface to the *Franciade*, the orator ultimately seeks to persuade, while the goal of the poet is to represent the *vraisemblable*.[115]

The English were no different in asserting strong links between rhetoric and poetics. According to some critics, 'the literature of the English Renaissance was profoundly rhetorical', for 'verse and prose were conceived primarily as instruments of persuasion or proof'.[116] Others argue that 'the poet and the orator' were granted 'equal status, similar methods, identical goals — to move, to teach, to please', with the only distinction between them being made 'sometimes through the traditional dichotomy of media, prose against verse, sometimes through the presence or absence of fiction'.[117] Knowledge of rhetoric appears indispensable to an understanding of English prose fiction and in fully appreciating authors such as Thomas More and George Gascoigne, who manage to metamorphose rhetoric into a successful creative poetics.[118] For instance, Gascoigne's poetic production, inseparable from his work at the Inns, has been interpreted as the result of a 'curriculum that helped to prepare one for a life of service to the state'.[119] The grammar school academic assignments that Gascoigne would have had to do included exercises that involved poetic composition which he would subsequently knowingly imitate and parody as a poet.[120] In this regard, Lorna Hutson has shown how English Renaissance drama was significantly affected by 'new ways of thinking about the rhetorical invention of plot' that were tied to new ways of thinking about legal and administrative matters, as Gascoigne's works illustrate (particularly his *Supposes*, written in imitation of Ariosto's *I Suppositi*).[121] His contribution is thus a determining one in the imitation of forensic rhetoric by early modern drama.

English poetics makes clear an extensive use of rhetorical terminology. Lydgate, for instance, is responsible for the creation of 'a new critical language, coining words where none existed', and for 'assigning new meanings to terms that had been found in English before his time but that were not applied to poetry'.[122] These include terms such as 'enlumyne', 'adourne', 'enbelissche', 'aureate', 'goldyng', 'sugrid', 'rethorik', and 'eloquence', which became widespread in fifteenth-century critical language. Yet Lydgate does not stress the poet's powers of invention: the necessity to 'adourne', 'enbelissche', and 'enlumyne' the poetic composition captures his attention instead. He defines 'rethorik' as successful style in poetry or oratory, and 'rhetor' as 'a mark of distinction or skill, attained by only the best of poets, who combine the orator's mastery of language with a worthy vision and purpose'.[123] For Lydgate, that is to say, both 'rethorik' and 'elloquence' signal excellence in poetry, in contrast to previous authors such as Chaucer, who used these terms to refer to poetry only rarely, and negatively.[124]

Later works, such as Richard Rainolde's *A booke called the foundacion of rhetorike* (1563), similarly take for granted the connection between rhetoric and poetics. Of the three types of narration that Rainolde distinguishes ('historicall', 'ciuill, otherwise called Iudiciall,' and 'Poeticall'),[125] the poetical type is defined as an 'exposicion fained, set forthe by inuencion of Poetes, or other', 'other' here most likely meaning rhetors.[126] In addition, Rainolde understands fables, one of the products of poetic craft, as being advantageous for the orator: if 'Poetes firste inuented fables', 'Oratours also doe vse [them] in their perswasions, and not without greate cause, both Poetes and Oratours doe applie theim to their vse'.[127] Likewise, Thomas Wilson recommends orators to make use of fables, for 'sometymes feined Narrations and wittie invented matters (as though they were true in deede) helpe wel to set forwarde a cause, and have great grace in them, beyng aptely used and wel invented'.[128] Then, in *A discourse of English poetrie* (1586), one of the first attempts in England to write a systematic and comprehensive poetics, William Webbe describes rhetoric and poetry as sharing a concern with persuasion and style, their only difference being that oratory is in prose and poetry in verse: 'a good and allowable Poet must be adorned with words, plenteous in sentences and, if not equal to an orator, yet very near him'.[129] For Webbe, as for Puttenham and other authors like Harvey and Chapman, it is verse and not imitation the defining trait of poetry, what truly differentiates it from oratory. Puttenham exalts the value of poetry by explaining it in rhetorical terms and underlining its persuasive effects, inseparable from verse. According to Puttenham, 'speech by meter' surpasses eloquence at persuading because it is 'beside, a manner of utterance more eloquent and rhetorical than the ordinary prose, which we use in our daily talk':

> because it is decked and set out with all manner of fresh colors and figures, which maketh that it sooner inveigleth the judgment of man and carrieth his opinion this way and that, whithersoever the heart by impression of the ear shall be most affectionately bent and directed.[130]

As has been pointed out, 'much of what Puttenham says about poetry derives from or is identical with classical and Renaissance teachings about rhetoric'.[131] Their commonalities notwithstanding, the fact that rhetoric and poetry were different could not be denied. Sir Philip Sidney is one of the authors who discuss the implications of the much-repeated Latin saying *orator fit, poeta nascitur* regarding the dissimilar nature of the requirements proper to each art. Of poetry, he writes:

> the ancient-learned affirm it was a divine gift, and no human skill, since all other knowledges lie ready for any that hath strength of wit; a poet no industry can make, if his own genius be not carried unto it. And therefore is it an old proverb, *orator fit, poeta nascitur*.[132]

Thomas Lodge's words in *A defence of poetry, music and stage-plays* (1579) resound when reading Sidney's: 'I reson not that al Poets are holy, but I affirme that Poetry is a heauenly gift, a perfit gift, then which I know not greater pleasure.'[133] If proficiency in rhetoric is the result of training, study, and constant practice, poetry relies more heavily on the natural abilities of the poet. As a result, poetry seems to require a different kind of instruction, one that goes beyond the mimetic reproduction of models and that encourages personal innovation instead.

Notes to Chapter 2

1. Vickers, 'Rhetoric and Poetics', p. 729.
2. Lisa Jardine, 'Humanism and the Teaching of Logic', in *The Cambridge History of Later Medieval Philosophy: From the Rediscovery of Aristotle to the Disintegration of Scholasticism 1100–1600*, ed. by Anthony John Patrick Kenny and others (Cambridge: Cambridge University Press, 1982), pp. 797–807 (p. 800).
3. Jardine, 'Humanism and the Teaching of Logic', p. 801; Wayne A. Rebhorn, *Renaissance Debates on Rhetoric* (Ithaca: Cornell University Press, 2000), p. 42.
4. James Richard McNally, '"Prima pars dialecticae": The Influence of Agricolan Dialectic upon English Accounts of Invention', *Renaissance Quarterly*, 21 (1968), 166–77 (p. 167).
5. Rebhorn, *Renaissance Debates*, p. 42. See also Cesare Vasoli, 'L'Humanisme rhétorique en Italie au XVe siècle', in *Histoire de la rhétorique dans l'Europe moderne: 1450–1950*, ed. by Marc Fumaroli (Paris: Presses Universitaires de France, 1999), pp. 45–130 (p. 85).

6. Lisa Jardine, 'Lorenzo Valla and the Intellectual Origins of Humanist Dialectic', *Journal of the History of Philosophy*, 15 (1977), 143–64 (p. 144).
7. Anthony Grafton and Lisa Jardine, *From Humanism to the Humanities: Education and the Liberal Arts in Fifteenth- and Sixteenth-Century Europe* (London: Duckworth, 1986), p. 125. For more on Valla's and Agricola's thought on rhetoric and dialectic, see Peter Mack, *Renaissance Argument: Valla and Agricola in the Traditions of Rhetoric and Dialectic* (Leiden: Brill, 1993).
8. Robert E. Stillman, 'The Scope of Sidney's *Defence of Poesy*: The New Hermeneutic and Early Modern Poetics', *English Literary Renaissance*, 32 (2002), 355–85 (p. 368).
9. Paul Oskar Kristeller, *Renaissance Thought: The Classic, Scholastic, and Humanistic Strains* (New York: Harper & Row, 1961), p. 87.
10. Kennedy, *Classical Rhetoric and its Christian and Secular Tradition*, p. 250.
11. For more on the concept of judgement and its relationship with invention, see Richard Peter McKeon, 'The Methods of Rhetoric and Philosophy: Invention and Judgment', in *The Classical Tradition: Literary and Historical Studies in Honor of Harry Caplan*, ed. by Luitpold Wallach (Ithaca: Cornell University Press, 1966), pp. 365–73.
12. Kennedy, *Classical Rhetoric and its Christian and Secular Tradition*, p. 252.
13. G. A. Padley, *Grammatical Theory in Western Europe 1500–1700: Trends in Vernacular Grammar* (Cambridge: Cambridge University Press, 1985), p. 94. The Lutherans supported Philipp Melanchthon (himself a Lutheran) against Ramus on the grounds that Ramistic principles were an offshoot of Calvinism. Ramism remains influential in the universities until 1630. See Pierre Albert Duhamel, 'The Logic and Rhetoric of Peter Ramus', *Modern Philology*, 46.3 (1949), 163–71.
14. Walter J. Ong, *Ramus, Method, and the Decay of Dialogue: From the Art of Discourse to the Art of Reason* (Chicago: University of Chicago Press, 2004), p. 264. For a work that connects the thought of Ramus to poetic ideas in France, see Kees Meerhoff, *Rhétorique et poétique au XVIe siècle en France: Du Bellay, Ramus et les autres* (Leiden: Brill, 1986).
15. Grafton and Jardine, p. 195. For Wilbur Samuel Howell, Ramism enjoys its greatest vogue in Britain between 1574 and 1681 (*Poetics, Rhetoric and Logic: Studies in the Basic Disciplines of Criticism*, 2nd edn (Ithaca: Cornell University Press, 1980), p. 119). See also Wilbur Samuel Howell, 'Ramus and English Rhetoric: 1574–1681', *Quarterly Journal of Speech*, 37 (1951), 308–10.
16. Padley, p. 94.
17. Peter Mack counts twenty sixteenth-century English-language manuals dealing with discourse; these he groups into six categories according to specific types of teaching (*Elizabethan Rhetoric: Theory and Practice* (Cambridge and New York: Cambridge University Press, 2002), pp. 77–78).
18. Peter Mack, *Elizabethan Rhetoric*, p. 78.
19. Thomas Wilson, *The Rule of Reason, Conteinyng the Arte of Logique, Set Forth in Englishe* (London: printed by Richard Grafton, 1551), B1r.
20. Wilson, *Rule of Reason*, I4v.
21. Wilson, *Rule of Reason*, I5v.
22. James J. Murphy, 'Rhetoric at Oxford', p. 345.
23. Donald Lemen Clark, 'Ancient Rhetoric', p. 197.
24. Cicero's *De inventione* and the pseudo-Ciceronian *Rhetorica ad Herennium* flourished in the Renaissance. The *Ad Herennium* reached one hundred and forty editions with notes and commentaries, and *De inventione* about the same number. The *Topica* saw seventy-seven commentaries; *De partitione oratoria*, seventy-one; and *De oratore* (between the years 1477 and 1600), fifty-six. Quintilian's *Institutio oratoria* underwent eighteen editions by 1500, and another one hundred and thirty by 1600. See Vickers, 'Rhetoric and Poetics', pp. 720–21.
25. Peter Mack, *Elizabethan Rhetoric*, p. 52.
26. Peter Mack, *Elizabethan Rhetoric*, p. 52.
27. Lisa Jardine, 'The Place of Dialectic Teaching in Sixteenth-Century Cambridge', *Studies in the Renaissance*, 21 (1974), 31–62 (p. 50).
28. Pierre Albert Duhamel, 'The Oxford Lectures of John Colet: An Essay in Defining the English Renaissance', *Journal of the History of Ideas*, 14.4 (1953), 493–510 (p. 510). Colet was greatly valued, both in professional as well as personal terms, by other fellows and by his own students, on

whom he exerted an indelible influence; see Elizabeth Sweeting, *Early Tudor Criticism, Linguistic and Literary* (New York: Russell & Russell, 1964), p. 91.
29. See Thomas O. Sloane, 'Schoolbooks and Rhetoric: Erasmus's *Copia*', *Rhetorica*, 9.2 (1991), 113–29.
30. Arthur F. Kinney, *Humanist Poetics: Thought, Rhetoric and Fiction in Sixteenth-Century England* (Amherst: University of Massachusetts Press, 1986), p. 446.
31. Peter Mack, *Elizabethan Rhetoric*, p. 46.
32. See Marvin T. Herrick, 'The Early History of Aristotle's *Rhetoric* in England', *Philological Quarterly*, 5 (1926), 242–57.
33. Duhamel, 'John Colet', p. 501.
34. For a detailed study of the curriculum of sixteenth-century English grammar schools, see Thomas Whitfield Baldwin, *William Shakespere's Small Latine & Lesse Greeke* (Urbana: University of Illinois Press, 1944).
35. Joseph S. Freedman, 'Cicero in Sixteenth- and Seventeenth-Century Rhetoric Instruction', *Rhetorica*, 4.3 (1986), 227–54 (p. 242); John Monfasani, 'Three Notes on Renaissance Rhetoric', *Rhetorica*, 5.1 (1987), 107–18 (pp. 112–13); Ward, 'Quintilian and the Rhetorical Revolution', p. 248.
36. William G. Crane, *Wit and Rhetoric in the Renaissance* (New York: Columbia University Press, 1937), discusses at length Rainolde's treatise as a translation of Aphthonius. See also Francis R. Johnson, 'Two Renaissance Textbooks of Rhetoric: Aphthonius' *Progymnasmata* and Rainolde's *A Booke Called the Foundacion of Rhetorike*', *Huntington Library Quarterly*, 6.4 (1943), 427–44 (p. 443).
37. Mary Thomas Crane, *Framing Authority: Sayings, Self, and Society in Sixteenth-Century England* (Princeton: Princeton University Press, 1993), p. 89. For more on this, see particularly her Chapter 4, 'Educational Practice in Early Sixteenth-Century England' (pp. 77–92).
38. Charles O. McDonald, '*Decorum*, *Ethos*, and *Pathos* in the Heroes of Elizabethan Tragedy, with Particular Reference to *Hamlet*', *Journal of English and Germanic Philology*, 61.2 (1962), 330–48 (pp. 333–34).
39. Peter Mack, 'Rhetoric, Ethics and Reading in the Renaissance', *Renaissance Studies*, 19.1 (2005), 1–21 (p. 8).
40. Don Paul Abbott, 'Rhetoric and Writing in Renaissance Europe and England', in *A Short History of Writing Instruction from Ancient Greece to Twentieth-Century America*, ed. by James J. Murphy (Davis: Hermagoras Press, 1990), pp. 95–120 (p. 113).
41. McDonald, p. 334. It has been claimed that the introductory function of *progymnasmata* in England 'was uniquely institutionalised' to the extent that 'the burden of culture placed on the Aphthonian theme was augmented in England because of the disciplinary organisation of the grammar schools' themselves (William P. Weaver, *Untutored Lines: The Making of the English Epyllion* (Edinburgh: Edinburgh University Press, 2012), pp. 16, 23; see specifically Chapter 1, 'Progymnasmata: Humanist Rites of Passage').
42. Peter Mack, 'Rhetoric, Ethics and Reading', p. 8.
43. Peter Mack, 'Rhetoric, Ethics and Reading', p. 9.
44. See Lechner, p. 234; Walter J. Ong, 'Tudor Writings on Rhetoric', *Studies in the Renaissance*, 15 (1968), 39–69 (p. 58); Edward P. J. Corbett, 'The Theory and Practice of Imitation in Classical Rhetoric', *College Composition and Communication*, 22.3 (1971), 243–50 (p. 249).
45. When the second edition is published in 1555, it appears as a bilingual Latin–English version with a different subtitle: *Profitable for all that be studious of eloquence, and in especial for such as in grammar scholes doe reede most eloquent poets and orators*.
46. Wayne A. Rebhorn suggests that Peacham 'was affected by Ramus's methods as well as his redefinition of rhetoric that limited it to style' (*Renaissance Debates*, p. 223).
47. J. Donald Ragsdale, 'Invention in English "Stylistic" Rhetorics: 1600–1800', *Quarterly Journal of Speech*, 51.2 (1965), 164–67 (p. 167).
48. Ong, 'Tudor Writings', p. 54.
49. G. J. Engelhardt, 'The Relation of Sherry's *Treatise of Schemes and Tropes* to Wilson's *Arte of Rhetorique*', *Publications of the Modern Language Association of America*, 62.1 (1947), 76–82.

50. Thomas Wilson, *The Arte of Rhetorique* [1553], ed. by Thomas J. Derrick (New York: Garland, 1982), p. 31.
51. John Lydgate, *Here Begynneth the Boke of Iohan Bochas, Discryuing the Fall of Pri[n]ces, Princesses, and Other Nobles* (London: printed by Richard Pynson, 1527), GG2v (my emphasis).
52. Wilson, *Rule of Reason*, I5r.
53. Wilson, *Rule of Reason*, I5v.
54. Thomas Blundeville, *The Art of Logike* (London: printed by Iohn Windet, 1599), B1r.
55. Wilson, *Rule of Reason*, I5v.
56. Richard Rainolde, *A Booke Called the Foundacion of Rhetorike* (London: printed by Ihon Kingston, 1563), D1v, A1v.
57. Rainolde, D1v.
58. Thomas Thomas, *Dictionarium linguae Latinae et Anglicanae* (Cambridge: printed by Thomas Thomas, 1587), Nnnvii v.
59. Thomas Thomas, Hhvi v.
60. John Florio, *A VVorlde of Wordes; or, Most Copious, and Exact Dictionarie in Italian and English* (London: printed by Arnold Hatfield for Edw. Blount, 1598), Nn2v.
61. Richard Perceval, *A Dictionarie in Spanish and English* (London: printed by Edm. Bollifant, 1599), O1r.
62. John Florio, *Queen Anna's Nevv Vvorld of Words; or, Dictionarie of the Italian and English Tongues* (London: printed by Melch. Bradwood [and William Stansby] for Edw. Blount and William Barret, 1611), Z1v.
63. William Caxton, *The Myrrour: [And] Dyscrypcyon of the Worlde with Many Meruaylles* (London: printed by Laurence Andrewe, 1527), d3r.
64. Leonard Cox, *The Art or Crafte of Rhetoryke* (London: printed by Robert Redman, 1532), A4r.
65. Cox, A4v–A5r.
66. Florio, *A VVorlde of Wordes*, Q5v.
67. Ralph Lever, *The Arte of Reason, Rightly Termed, Witcraft* (London: printed by H. Bynneman, 1573), *iv v, *vi v.
68. Concetta Carestia Greenfield, *Humanist and Scholastic Poetics, 1250–1500* (London: Bucknell University Press, 1981), pp. 24–25.
69. Grassi, p. 76.
70. Ong, *Ramus*, p. 253.
71. Tamara A. Goeglein, '"Wherein Hath Ramus Been So Offensious?": Poetic Examples in the English Ramist Logic Manuals (1574–1672)', *Rhetorica: A Journal of the History of Rhetoric*, 14.1 (1996), 73–101 (p. 74).
72. Goeglein, p. 77.
73. Goeglein, p. 79.
74. Vickers, 'Rhetoric and Poetics', pp. 715–16, 718.
75. Donald Lemen Clark, *Rhetoric and Poetry*, p. 100.
76. Áron Kibédi Varga, *Rhétorique et littérature, études de structures classiques* (Paris: Didier, 1970), pp. 12–13.
77. Kennedy, *Classical Rhetoric and its Christian and Secular Tradition*, p. 249.
78. Howell, *Poetics, Rhetoric and Logic*, p. 105. See also Charles Sears Baldwin and Donald Lemen Clark, *Renaissance Literary Theory and Practice: Classicism in the Rhetoric and Poetic of Italy, France and England: 1400–1600* (Gloucester: Smith, 1959); Wayne A. Rebhorn, *The Emperors of Men's Minds: Literature and the Renaissance Discourse of Rhetoric* (Ithaca: Cornell University Press, 1995); Marc Fumaroli, *L'Âge de l'eloquence: Rhétorique et 'res literaria' de la Renaissance au seuil de l'époque classique* (Geneva: Droz, 2002).
79. Greenfield, p. 22.
80. Ann Moss, 'Horace in the Sixteenth Century: Commentators into Critics', in *Cambridge History of Literary Criticism*, III: *The Renaissance*, ed. by Glyn P. Norton (2000), pp. 66–76 (p. 71).
81. O. B. Hardison, *English Literary Criticism: The Renaissance* (London: Owen, 1967), p. 57.
82. O. B. Hardison, 'The Place of Averroes' Commentary on the *Poetics* in the History of Medieval Criticism', *Medieval and Renaissance Studies*, 4 (1970), 57–81 (p. 63).

83. Joel Elias Spingarn, *A History of Literary Criticism in the Renaissance*, 2nd edn (Westport: Greenwood Press, 1976), p. 16.
84. Spingarn, p. 138.
85. Vickers, 'Rhetoric and Poetics', p. 719.
86. According to Marvin T. Herrick, Parrhasius's commentary (1531) constitutes the first Horatian commentary to make any distinct use of Aristotle's *Poetics* (*The Fusion of Horatian and Aristotelian Criticism, 1531–1555* (Urbana: University of Illinois Press, 1946), p. 4). In 1555, the great Basle edition of Horace's works appeared, containing commentaries on the *Ars poetica* by various authors.
87. Bernard Weinberg, *A History of Literary Criticism in the Italian Renaissance*, 2 vols (Chicago: University of Chicago Press, 1961), I, 152.
88. Herrick, *Fusion*, p. 106. Nonetheless, 'after the revival of the *Rhetoric* and *Poetics*, the sixteenth-century commentators soon discovered the superior value of Aristotle's systematic theory of poetry as compared with that of Horace' (p. 107).
89. Weinberg, *History*, I, 155.
90. Craig La Drière, 'Horace and the Theory of Imitation', *American Journal of Philology*, 60.3 (1939), 288–300 (p. 288).
91. John Dryden, 'An Essay of Dramatick Poesie' [1668], in *The Works of John Dryden*, 20 vols (Berkeley: University of California Press, 1956–2000), XVII: *Prose 1668–1691: 'An Essay of Dramatick Poesie' and Shorter Works*, ed. by Hugh Thomas Swedenberg and Samuel Holt Monk (1971), pp. 3–82 (p. 17).
92. G. M. A. Grube, *The Greek and Roman Critics* (London: Methuen, 1965), p. 239.
93. La Drière, p. 297.
94. John William Hey Atkins, *Literary Criticism in Antiquity: A Sketch of its Development* (Cambridge: Cambridge University Press, 1934), pp. 75–76.
95. Henry Buckley Charlton asserts in this regard that 'although Platonism became a great force in thought through the labours of Marsilio Ficino (1433–1499), it did not become a definite component of the criticism of poetry until the time of Fracastoro's dialogue *Naugerius* (1555)' (*Castelvetro's Theory of Poetry* (Manchester: Manchester University Press, 1913), pp. 14–15).
96. Hardison, *English Literary Criticism*, p. 5.
97. John William Hey Atkins, *English Literary Criticism: The Renascence* (London: Methuen, 1947), pp. 344–45.
98. Clark, *Rhetoric and Poetry*, p. 83.
99. Spingarn, p. 172.
100. Eventually, Du Bellay as well as Ronsard developed a high regard for Sébillet; see Robert Sabatier, *La Poésie du XVIe siècle* (Paris: Michel, 1982), p. 130.
101. Spingarn, p. 173 (emphasis in original).
102. Spingarn, pp. 180–81.
103. 'There is indeed no well-established allusion to the *Poetics* in France before this time. None of the French humanists seems to have known it' (Spingarn, p. 184).
104. Spingarn, p. 177. In the seventeenth century, the Dutch scholars Daniel Heinsius and Gerardus Vossius crucially disseminated Aristotle's influence in France; see Edith Kern, *The Influence of Heinsius and Vossius upon French Dramatic Theory* (Baltimore: Johns Hopkins University Press, 1949). For more on the influences received by French poetics, see Perrine Galand-Hallyn and Fernand Hallyn, *Poétiques de la Renaissance: Le Modèle Italien, le monde Franco-Bourguignon et leur héritage en France au XVIe siècle* (Geneva: Droz, 2001).
105. Anne Lake Prescott, *French Poets and the English Renaissance: Studies in Fame and Transformation* (New Haven and London: Yale University Press, 1978), p. 42.
106. The study of the connections between Spenser and the Pléiade enjoys a long tradition in scholarship, going back at least to William Lindsay Renwick's article 'The Critical Origins of Spenser's Diction', *Modern Language Review*, 17 (1922), 1–16, and his book *Edmund Spenser: An Essay in Renaissance Poetry* (London: Arnold, 1925). Du Bellay's connection with Spenser is also discussed by Anne Lake Prescott in *French Poets*, pp. 39–52, and in 'Spenser (Re)Reading du Bellay: Chronology and Literary Response', in *Spenser's Life and the Study of Biography*,

ed. by Judith Anderson, Donald Cheney, and David A. Richardson (Amherst: University of Massachusetts Press, 1996), pp. 131–45. Alfred W. Satterthwaite also discusses Spenser's 'relationship to Ronsard, his contemporary and counterpart in the French Renaissance, whose career he paradoxically parallels, but whom he never mentions' (*Spenser, Ronsard, and Du Bellay: A Renaissance Comparison* (Princeton: Princeton University Press, 1960), p. 10).
107. Warner Forrest Patterson, *Three Centuries of French Poetic Theory: A Critical History of the Chief Arts of Poetry in France* (Ann Arbor: University of Michigan Press, 1935).
108. A. Donald Sellstrom, 'Rhetoric and the Poetics of French Classicism', *French Review*, 34.5 (1961), 425–31 (p. 425). See also Alex L. Gordon, 'The Ascendancy of Rhetoric and the Struggle for Poetic in Sixteenth-Century France', in *Renaissance Eloquence: Studies in the Theory and Practice of Renaissance Rhetoric*, ed. by James J. Murphy (Berkeley: University of California Press, 1983), pp. 376–84.
109. Jacques Peletier du Mans, 'Art poétique' [1555], in *Traités de poétique et de rhétorique de la Renaissance*, ed. by Francis Goyet (Paris: Librairie Générale Française, 1990), pp. 235–344 (p. 251). Unless otherwise stated, the translation of extracts from works by Sébillet, Peletier, Ronsard, and other French authors have been made by Rose Delale and me. In these cases, I reproduce the quotations in their original language as well.
110. Thomas Sébillet, 'Art poétique français' [1548], in *Traités de poétique et de rhétorique de la Renaissance*, ed. by Goyet, pp. 37–183 (p. 57).
111. Sébillet, pp. 58–59.
112. Sébillet, pp. 60–61.
113. Joachim Du Bellay, 'The Defence and Illustration of the French Language', in *Poetry & Language in 16th-Century France: Du Bellay, Ronsard, Sébillet*, ed. and trans. by Laura Willett (Toronto: Centre for Reformation and Renaissance Studies, 2004), pp. 37–96 (p. 65).
114. Peletier du Mans, pp. 249–50.
115. See Rita Guerlac, 'Rhetorical Doctrine and Some Poems of Ronsard', in *Essays on Renaissance Poetry*, ed. by James Hutton (Ithaca and London: Cornell University Press, 1980), pp. 291–310.
116. Richard Harrier, 'Invention in Tudor Literature: Historical Perspectives', in *Philosophy and Humanism: Renaissance Essays in Honor of Paul Oskar Kristeller*, ed. by Edward P. Mahoney (New York: Columbia University Press, 1976), pp. 370–86 (p. 370).
117. Brian Vickers, '"The Power of Persuasion": Images of the Orator, Elyot to Shakespeare', in *Renaissance Eloquence*, ed. by Murphy, pp. 411–36 (p. 412).
118. Arthur F. Kinney, 'Rhetoric as Poetic: Humanist Fiction in the Renaissance', *English Literary History*, 43.4 (1976), 413–43 (p. 440). Gascoigne's work, in particular, shows 'the extent to which sixteenth-century poetic theory draws on rhetorical theory' (Michael Mack, 'Sidney's Poetics: Imitating Creation', p. 35). In this regard, see Paul Salzman, 'Theories of Prose Fiction in England: 1558–1700', in *Cambridge History of Literary Criticism*, III: *The Renaissance*, ed. by Glyn P. Norton (2000), pp. 295–304.
119. Jessica Winston, *Lawyers at Play: Literature, Law, and Politics at the Early Modern Inns of Court, 1558–1581* (Oxford: Oxford University Press, 2016), p. 78; see specifically the section 'Gascoigne's Poetry: Imitation and Parody' (pp. 94–97).
120. Winston, p. 97.
121. Lorna Hutson, *The Invention of Suspicion: Law and Mimesis in Shakespeare and Renaissance Drama* (Oxford: Oxford University Press, 2007), p. 10.
122. L. A. Ebin, *Illuminator, Makar, Vates: Visions of Poetry in the Fifteenth Century* (Lincoln: University of Nebraska Press, 1988), p. 20.
123. Ebin, p. 32.
124. Ebin, p. 29
125. Narration is here understood as 'an exposicion, or declaracion of any thyng dooen in deede, or els a settyng forthe, forged of any thyng, but so declaimed and declared, as though it were doen' that contains 'inuencion of matter' (Rainolde, *Foundacion of Rhetorike*, C4r).
126. Rainolde, C4v.
127. Rainolde, A2v–A3r.
128. Wilson, *Arte of Rhetorique*, p. 394.

129. William Webbe, *A Discourse of English Poetry* [1586], ed. by Sonia Hernández-Santano (London: Modern Humanities Research Association, 2016), p. 140.
130. Puttenham, p. 98.
131. Rebhorn, *Renaissance Debates*, p. 203.
132. Philip Sidney, *An Apology for Poetry; or, The Defence of Poesy* [1595], ed. by Geoffrey Shepherd (Manchester: Manchester University Press, 2002), p. 109.
133. Thomas Lodge, *A Defence of Poetry, Music and Stage-Plays* [1579] (London: printed for the Shakespeare Society, 1853), p. 14.

CHAPTER 3

Imitation and Emulation from Antiquity to the End of the Renaissance

The growth of invention within poetics, and its evolution within the fields of rhetoric and dialectic, runs parallel to that of the concept of imitation, likewise present in the three disciplines and equally salient. Imitation is inescapable in rhetoric, and a constant in definitions of art from classical Antiquity to the end of the eighteenth century. Nevertheless, its prevalence in the discourse of poetics does not imply that all its forms are considered legitimate: in practice, borrowing is denounced whenever it turns secretive and servile. Slavish imitation and textual theft thus become serious accusations that call into question an author's skills and ethics. The four sections of this chapter explore imitation respectively in the context of rhetoric, in the context of poetics, in connection with ideas on plagiarism, and specifically among English authors, who view it as a forceful creative principle intertwined with invention.

The first section reviews the use of imitative exercises as part of rhetorical training from Antiquity to the end of the Renaissance. Isocrates, Cicero, and Quintilian among the ancients, and Erasmus among the moderns, acknowledge it as one of the most advantageous school activities for the teaching of rhetoric. Such becomes its importance that a heated debate of European dimensions springs up among the humanists over the most appropriate model (or models) to follow. Still, imitation does not seem to suffice for the renewal and perfection of tradition, for which invention is additionally required. As Quintilian puts it, 'whatever resembles another object is bound to be less than what it imitates'.[1] It will be thus seen how both *imitatio* and *inventio* are part of a web of concepts that also includes *aemulatio*, which stands for a more ambitious and inventive form of imitating that aims at outdoing the model.

Section two of this chapter traces the relevance of imitation within poetics from Plato and Aristotle's views to those widespread in sixteenth-century Italy and France, the two countries which England looks up to as an example. With the exception of Vida and his remarkable encouragement to steal from past authors, the prevalent opinion among the Italians and the French is that the theory of emulation should be applied to poetic composition. As will be seen, authors such as Petrarch, Erasmus, Du Bellay, Peletier, and Ronsard commonly employ two metaphors which go back to Seneca to illustrate the implications of transformative and emulative imitation: the apian metaphor and the metaphor of digestion.

The third section discusses the notion of *publica materies* as well as that of literary theft. The former is understood by Horace and Seneca, among others, as that which is common property and hence legitimately usable by authors in their own compositions. By contrast, again with exceptions such as Vida, critics advise against slavish imitation and the wrongful appropriation of somebody else's material. Petrarch's anxiety in this respect is illustrative of the fear of excessive and unconscious borrowing, and of ultimately becoming a mere imitator. The unnoticed influence of authorities thus becomes a source of distress which may lead to the questioning of a poet's own poetic practice. A connected fear is that of the misattribution of works, that is, of being assigned by mistake the works of another, and of not acknowledging one's literary debts; both possibilities are regarded as forms of stealing. The close of the section reflects on plagiarism and discusses attacks against some renowned authors (Shakespeare, Jonson, and Dryden among them), accused of it.

Finally, the fourth section focuses on views towards imitation in England in particular. More specifically, it considers Puttenham's and, above all, Sidney's complex stances. For Sidney, imitation is a creative process which not only copies nature but which, in addition, follows nature's creative powers. As a result, poetry appears to be a mimetic activity capable of producing improved natural realities or golden worlds. Sidney's belief, which elevates the artist to godlike status, constitutes a blend of the different philosophical currents articulating Renaissance poetics; his is no doubt among the most elaborate reflections on poetry in the England of his time.

3.1. In Rhetoric

Imitation was first and foremost a central pedagogical practice in the teaching of tongues, grammar, and rhetoric. In classical rhetoric, it becomes the object of reflection by authors such as Isocrates and Cicero. Both advocate the efficacy of the method of teaching rhetoric through it, and acknowledge it as the prime cause of stylistic growth and the source of continuity and development. In *Against the Sophists*, Isocrates argues that the teacher 'must in himself set such an example of oratory that the students who have taken form under his instruction and are able to pattern after him will, from the outset, show in their speaking a degree of grace and charm which is not found in others'.[2] Isocrates admits more than one good style, for, as Cicero also observes, personal talent and stylistic choice shape one's personal idiom. As a result, different pupils trained in the same school and following the same models under the supervision of the same teacher usually prove different from each other. For Cicero, imitation is a major driving force behind the evolution of oratory, and so each generation has a common style distinct from the previous one: 'nearly every age has produced its own distinctive style of oratory'.[3] Of course, imitation does not mean exact reproduction here, but rather the following of models to achieve personal improvement, which in the process leads to changes in and additions to tradition, and results in a form of 'evolution'.[4]

The product of a twenty-year teaching career, Quintilian's *Institutio oratoria* comments on the imitation of selected authors as a school exercise as well as a procedure for acquiring *copia rerum et verborum* for the orator. If Cicero saw the great benefits, at least for the young student, of imitating a single model, Quintilian is categorically against the slavish copying of one model, as also is Seneca.[5] *Imitatio* proves integral to the mastery of style as long as it is exclusively oriented to the excellences of each selected model and avoids its weaknesses and mannerisms. As Quintilian remarks, it 'makes the principles of everything so much easier for us than for those who had no antecedents to follow', although it can work 'to our disadvantage unless we handle it with caution and discrimination'.[6] An exercise in introspection on the part of the imitator is needed to discover the extent to which what he has learned from his model reflects or accommodates his own needs or limitations. Only by doing this will the imitator effectively incorporate the virtues of the model into his style and maximise his acquisition of *copia*. Translation, memorisation, and paraphrase (from verse to prose, or vice versa) are the major imitative exercises used by Greek and Roman teachers of rhetoric. Translation is so intimately related to imitation in Roman times that translating in fact becomes reinvention of the source and the production of a new text suited to the particular historical circumstances of the target audience. Ultimately, the Romans wished to displace through difference the much-admired Greek culture, and replication through translation conformed to this political agenda. In other words, translation was seen as 'an act of transference rather than of transmission', intended to achieve 'substitution, and ultimately displacement of the source'.[7]

Given the centrality of imitation in rhetorical instruction up to and through the Renaissance, it is unsurprising that heated debates sprung up around it, and that these raised questions about the best modes, methods, and model (or models) to imitate. The controversy that confronted the Ciceronians with the so-called eclectics, a burning issue among the humanists, revolved around whether there should be a single model to imitate or more than one in every genre. In the first place, the dispute was whether Cicero should be the exclusive model to follow in Latin prose. Ciceronians advocated replication of Ciceronian usage and style as the sole criterion of eloquence, whereas the anti-Ciceronians, or eclectics, believed it more advantageous to imitate the most admirable qualities of the best authors. In a parallel, though less polemic, argument, first Vida (in 1527) and later Scaliger (in 1561) argued that Virgil should be acknowledged as the absolute model for poetry. The roots of the controversy were traceable to the Quattrocento disagreement between Poggio Bracciolini, who embraced a theoretical notion of Cicero as the supreme model, and Lorenzo Valla. The quarrel revealed the differences between two generations of humanists, and anticipated the clashes between Poliziano, a convinced defender of eclecticism, and Paolo Cortese, a Ciceronian; between Gianfrancesco Pico della Mirandola, intellectual heir of Poliziano, and cardinal Pietro Bembo, promoter of a kind of vernacular Ciceronianism that would fix

Petrarch and Boccaccio as the models for poetry and prose respectively; and between Giraldi Cinthio and Celio Calcagnini. Erasmus's dialogue *Ciceronianus, sive, De optimo dicendi genere* (1528), a satire against radical Ciceronianism which alluded ironically to Cicero's *De optimo genere dicendi*, would export the argument beyond the Italian borders.[8]

Erasmus's objections to Ciceronianism originate in his ideal of historical decorum, or making speech suited to the general historical conditions of the present. Sixteenth-century eloquence, as a result, necessarily has to avoid Cicero's distant footsteps, and Erasmus underlines the impossibility of true Ciceronianism in discussions of realities unknown to Cicero, such as Christianity or the Church. Erasmus in this way stresses the Christian identity of the imitator in contrast to his pagan classical models. From this perspective, Ciceronians appear impious: right belief is a precondition for eloquence, true eloquence should be sustained on the imitation of Christ, and the final aim of the liberal arts (and thus of philosophy and oratory) is the achievement of better knowledge of Christ. A year before his death, Erasmus publishes *Ecclesiastes, sive De concionandi ratione libri IV* (1535), considered a logical sequel to his *Ciceronianus*, but on this occasion dealing with sacred eloquence. *Ecclesiastes* locates Christian eloquence in the imitation of Christ and the Apostles, orators in the name of the Father. That same year, the most virulent response to *Ciceronianus* is published: Etiènne Dolet's *De imitatione ciceroniana* (1535), which aspires to disassociate the religious component from discussions around *imitatio*.

Erasmus's vision of a uniquely Christian eloquence is disseminated in England through his *De duplici copia verborum et rerum* (1512) and by his friend John Colet.[9] This work also contains a defence of a liberating form of mimesis that favours the discovery of one's own personal style by considering several remarkable authors. Juan Luis Vives understands imitation in similar terms, insists on historical decorum, and recommends *aemulatio* instead.[10] Generally, scholars in England display a fairly moderate Erasmian approach to *imitatio* and do not engage so strongly in the Ciceronian controversy as their colleagues in Italy and France. For one thing, England joined the debate once it had passed its height. For another, the iconoclastic and anticeremonial features of English Protestantism, and its association of slavish copying with Catholicism and papistry, led almost unanimously to a restrained approach to *imitatio*. That moderation in imitation goes hand-in-hand with religious moderation is suggested, for example, by Hubert Languet's warning to his pupil Sir Philip Sidney in a letter sent from Vienna on 1 January 1574: 'beware of falling into the heresy of those who think that the height of excellence consists in the imitation of Cicero'.[11] Overall, English Protestant critics

> tend to associate *imitatio Christi* with the same excesses for which Erasmus castigates the Ciceronians: idolatry (typically defined as privileging the 'outward' humanity of Christ over His divine essence) and anachronism (understood in this context as a failure to recognize the unbridgeable gap between unfallen and fallen human nature).[12]

Yet, even if imitation is essential in oratorical instruction, it does not on its own ensure the development of rhetoric, and Quintilian reminds readers that no sharp wit can be satisfied solely with the words of others: 'It is a disgrace too to be content merely to attain the effect you are imitating. [...] what would have happened if no one had achieved more than the man he was following?'.[13] While mimesis secures the survival and continuity of tradition, invention accounts for its growth and renewal. If the former is *utile* and inescapable in the process of learning, the latter holds the pre-eminent position: 'It cannot be doubted that a large part of art consists of imitation. Invention of course came first and is the main thing, but good inventions are profitable to follow.'[14] *Imitatio* is thus not an end in itself but a means to cultivate one's own *inventio* by acquiring knowledge and skills, since 'nothing does grow by imitation alone':[15]

> only a lazy mind is content with what others have discovered [*aliis inventa*]. What would have happened in the days when there were no models, if men had decided to do and think of nothing that they did not know already? Nothing of course would have been discovered [*Nempe nihil fuisset inventum*].[16]

After all, 'the greatest qualities of an orator are inimitable: his talent, invention, force, fluency, everything in fact that is not taught in the textbooks'.[17] The higher regard that Quintilian has for invention is highlighted by the adjectives and phrases that accompany *imitatio* and *inventio/invenire*, which have far more positive connotations in the case of the latter two terms:

Imitatio	*Invenire (Inventio)*
utile (2.1)	praecipuum (2.1)
pigrum ingenium (2.4)	perfectus orator (2.9)
sequi (2.9)	contendere (2.9)
posterior (2.10)	prior (2.10)
idem facere (2.10)	plus facere (2.10)
alienum propositum (2.11)	exemplum (2.11)
imitatio facta est (2.11)	natura et uera uis (2.11)
declamationes (2.12)	orationes (2.12)
adsimulata materia (2.12)	uera materia (2.12)[18]

Dionysius of Halicarnassus's treatise *On imitation*, now preserved only in fragments, contains numerous references not only to *imitatio* but also to related concepts such as *similis* and *aemulatio*. If *similis* denotes the willingness to make something or someone similar to a model, *aemulari* expresses an endeavour to rival or surpass the model itself. 'Emulation will bring those great characters before our eyes, and their shining presence will lead our thoughts to the ideal standards of perfection', Longinus affirms.[19] Likewise, for Quintilian it is the eagerness of *aemulatio* to outdo one's models or *exempla* that works as the principle of growth and as the spur of invention. The perfect orator assimilates the best qualities of his models in order to surpass them; the imitator-emulator pursues not an exact reproduction of the model but its improvement through the personal contribution of his own invention.[20] Emulation, then, seems to embody a more determined and aggressive form of imitation, one which appropriates and displays the principles of invention.

Cicero recognises in *Tusculanae disputationes* that *aemulatio* can be understood 'in a twofold way, so that it has both a good and a bad sense'. On the one hand, 'rivalry is used of the imitation of virtue'; on the other, 'rivalry is distress, should another be in possession of the object desired and one has to go without it oneself'.[21] At the heart of emulation is the concept of *eris*: while good *eris* stimulates 'men, even lazy men, to increase their substance out of a desire to compete with their neighbors', bad *eris* stirs up 'war and suffering'.[22] That is, *aemulatio* points to the anxiety of desiring what somebody else possesses and one lacks, and so it can be envious and excessively competitive. As Erasmus observes in *Ciceronianus*, 'the goal of imitation is being like, of emulation, being better'; as a result, 'your intention is not merely to reproduce' your model 'but to outdo him'.[23] According to Erasmus, who seems to follow Quintilian on this point, it is both easier and more fruitful to imitate with aspirations to surpass the model than to pursue an exact copy of it.[24] In this regard, he rhetorically wonders

> what need is there always and in every way to be identical, when it would often be preferable to be as good but different, and would sometimes be easier to surpass than to equal, that is, to write something better rather than something similar?'[25]

Bartolomeo Ricci's *De imitatione* (1541) effectively distinguishes on a theoretical level between *sequi*, following or walking in somebody else's footsteps; *imitari*, which aims at equality; and *aemulari*, oriented towards surpassing the model. If *sequi*, which implies gathering or borrowing phrases, sentences, or passages from the model, is tantamount to non-transformative mimesis, *aemulari*, on the contrary, implies surpassing the model without disguising the achievement. Otherwise, the concealment of the existence of a model would also obscure the victory over it. In *Ciceronianus*, Erasmus had made similar remarks: *sequi*, or 'reproducing exactly', is different from 'producing something like' the model, for the former implies 'being a slave to it, always following behind it'.[26]

Sequi and *aemulari* correspond to what some present-day scholars refer to respectively as 'repetition-of-the-same' (or 'reproduction'), which attempts an absolutely faithful replica of the model, an 'exact duplication with no alteration', and 'repetition-of-difference', which, on the other hand, denies the possibility of identical reproduction of the model.[27] Within the typology developed by Greene, which takes into consideration the way texts address history and their models, *sequi* would parallel 'reproductive' or 'sacramental' imitation, which rehearses the model text liturgically in that the dignity of the model places it beyond alteration and criticism and elevates it to an almost sacred status. This quasi-religious reverence for the model leads, of course, only to literal repetition and sterile following.[28] *Aemulari*, by contrast, suggests what Greene calls 'heuristic' imitation, which manifests itself in texts that acknowledge their derivation from the models while, at the same time, distance themselves from their predecessors. By so doing, they overcome their dependence by realising a type of 'conditional independence'.[29]

Aemulari can be said to be 'a cardinal principle of Renaissance poetics', for, as Jonathan Bate has argued, it 'leaves room for dissimilitude as well as similitude' and 'ultimately comes down to matter, not mere words'.[30] Of course, emulation is acknowledged as a goal at times unattainable if the perfection of the model is beyond the reach of the imitator. Hubert Languet, Sir Philip Sidney's tutor, with a letter from Vienna dated 19 November 1573, sends Sidney 'an epistle of Pietro Bizarro of Perugia' so 'that you may have before your eyes his surpassing eloquence, and make it your model'.[31] On 5 December, Sidney responds from Venice: 'I read through the charming epistle of Pietro Bizarro of Perugia, and culled certain flowers, which, as I could do nothing better, I imitated.'[32] Emulation, then, might be an unreachable target; still, during the Renaissance, 'good imitation involves difference as well as similarity'.[33]

3.2. In Poetics

The ancient world developed contrasting ideas when it came to imitation in the arena of poetry. The Platonic doctrine understood mimesis as the production of images that copy an ideal and true realm into the sensible world. For Plato, truths in poetry imitated the Good; falsehoods, objects without external existence. If philosophers and other lovers of wisdom and beauty with knowledge of the ideal realm were to imitate, Plato implies, mimesis would produce truly beautiful and harmonious works. However, in Plato's eyes, poetry merely imitates the sensible world and the illusions of sense, and so he reduces poetry to an inferior degree of truth and knowledge, to feeding the passions as opposed to addressing reason.[34] An imitator consequently becomes a maker of images who only knows of appearances, as opposed to the maker of realities who possesses knowledge of being. Aristotle, however, understands mimesis as a natural faculty that facilitates human learning. Humans are not only the most imitative of all beings but also the ones that take a natural delight in the contemplation of works of imitation. Poetry is, for Aristotle, a mimetic art whose object is nature and human action, and the poet an 'image-maker', a 'mimetic artist' who may 'represent, in any instance, one of three objects: the kind of things which were or are the case; the kind of things that people say and think; the kind of things that ought to be the case'.[35] Mimesis does not posit a copy–original relation (i.e. simple reproduction of what already exists); in the Aristotelian sense, just as nature is dynamic and creative, art too has a margin of freedom from the actual.

The imitation of the greatness and wisdom of classical authors in the face of what was regarded as the rotting legacy of the medieval past is at the roots of humanism.[36] Humanist textual practices opposed the medieval model of interpretation that read texts allegorically and *in Christo*, and instead privileged a historical and philological approach.[37] The interpretation of texts, both sacred and secular, was made dependent on the recovery of the classical languages and the application of the philological method. In this context, imitation was not only a central pedagogical practice in the teaching of the classical tongues, grammar, and rhetoric, but also a key factor for understanding fields as varied as historiography, the visual arts, politics, music, philosophy, and, of course, poetics.[38] It provided in this scenario 'a model of continuity in change',[39] a means to negotiate the epistemological crisis in which early modern authors were immersed,[40] and 'a strategy for acknowledging and accommodating the historical distance separating early modern authors from the classical and sacred traditions that authorized their own aesthetic'.[41] The Renaissance inherited the Platonic doctrine of mimesis, revised and renewed by the Neoplatonics,[42] as well as the Aristotelian one and the rhetorical theories of *imitatio* which encouraged not only following but also surpassing outstanding models.

The views of sixteenth-century Italian critics regarding imitation oscillate between the position of eclectics, such as Francesco Patrizi and Castelvetro, vehemently against slavish replication, and authors with the highest admiration for Virgil and Cicero, such as Bembo and Scaliger and the servile Marco Vida, who goes as far as to advise new poets to steal from the ancients.[43] Vida's *De arte poetica* (1527) hails classical authors as indispensable in the education of young poets, crowns Virgil as the king of verse, and affirms, before the introduction of Aristotle's *Poetics* to the mainstream of Renaissance criticism,[44] that mimesis is the pivotal element in poetry-writing. According to Vida, 'art functions only by imitating nature', and 'poets have set Nature before them as their sole mistress, and in whatever their undertaking they always follow her footsteps'.[45] Indeed, Vida is far from condemning borrowing the invention and/or elocution of previous poets, as long as the disposition changes so as to conceal the theft:

> But when you are attempting thefts from the polished poets, proceed with particular caution: remember to conceal what you have stolen by altering the forms of the words and to escape detection by switching word order. Give everything a new countenance and a wholly new form. Once this task is complete (and it will not occupy you long), you yourself will scarcely recognize the altered words of the ancient poet.[46]

With exceptions such as Vida, imitation in the Renaissance usually means emulation of authors of reference. Most critics, Girolamo Muzio and Giraldi Cinthio, for instance, authors of *Arte poetica* (1551) and *Discorsi* (1554) respectively, criticise servility to past authors. Likewise, Castelvetro, in *Poetica d'Aristotele vulgarizzata et sposta* (1570), as will be seen in the next chapter, places the emphasis on invention instead, even if he believes, with Aristotle, that 'the mere use of metre does not make one a poet, and what distinguishes one kind of poet from another is not his kind of metre but his kind of imitation, and especially the kind of matter he imitates'.[47] It is significant in this respect that one of the few points of agreement between Pico and Bembo is their emphasis on surpassing models — in the plural for Pico — or a model — in the singular in the case of Bembo, for whom devotion to a single one is preferable:

> First, we should imitate the one who is best of all; next, we should imitate in such a way that we strive to overtake him; finally, all our effort should be devoted to surpassing him once we have overtaken him. Accordingly we should have in our minds those two outstanding accomplishers of very great matters, emulation and hope. But emulation should always be joined to imitation.[48]

Likewise, for Julius Caesar Scaliger, the success of the training of the young poet depends to a considerable extent on the appropriate selection of the best model to imitate: 'Neque enim aut imitandum sibi proponet quempiam aut imitationis inibit rationem, nisi et poetam elegerit et imitandi speciem probarit' [We will not attempt to imitate someone, we will not follow the path of imitation, unless we have chosen a poet as his model and experienced the value of a type of imitation].⁴⁹ This assertion is also accompanied by the revelation that 'ac tametsi non est imitatio necessaria; non enim primi quem sequerentur habuere' [after all, imitation is not indispensable: our forerunners had no-one to follow].⁵⁰ Still, for most authors, including the most renowned ones, Scaliger says, imitation has been a crucial tool for training and perfecting their composition skills. As a result, even if it is indeed possible to do without it, it ought to be acknowledged as a valuable practice for poets, one that they should not be ashamed to admit having employed in their writings: 'Alii vero inter quos Horatius cum universam irrident imitationem, sine illa non multum videntur potuisse. Ipse enim, qui *servum pecus* imitatores appellasset, in iis pedem locis posuit, e quibus vestigia sustulerat Lucilius' [Others, such as Horace, mocked all imitation, but we can very well see that without it they could not have done much. Horace even called imitators a 'servile flock', and yet he followed the footsteps of Lucilius].⁵¹

However, an outstanding capacity to imitate and assimilate may be mortifying for some authors, as Petrarch confesses in a letter to Boccaccio probably written in 1359. Petrarch specifically dreaded the 'impressionableness of youth and its readiness to admire everything', which he feared could turn him, 'perhaps unconsciously' and against his will, into a mere imitator: 'In the ardour of youth this thought filled me with aversion.'⁵² Petrarch tried to shun at all costs unconscious influences, out of fear that they be interpreted as 'secret or conscious imitation': 'this rock I have always endeavoured to avoid, especially in my writings in the vernacular', he admits in the same letter.⁵³ His emphasis on the necessity of contributing new approaches to poetry is recurrent, as is his insistence that 'nothing is so refined, so perfected that something cannot be added to it': 'Let us not be influenced either by that trite, vulgar saying that there is nothing new, or nothing new to be said.'⁵⁴ Enthusiastically, he encourages heuristic imitation as preferable to an unproductive unimaginative variety, for 'an imitator must see to it that what he writes is similar, but not the very same' as the model, in the sense that the similarity 'should be not like that of a painting or statue to the person represented, but rather like that of a son to a father, where there is often great difference in the features and members'.⁵⁵ This means that, even if authors 'may appropriate another's thought, and may even copy the very colours of his style', they 'must abstain from borrowing his actual words', for

> the one kind of imitation makes poets; the other — apes. It may all be summed up by saying with Seneca [...] that we must write just as the bees make honey, not keeping the flowers but turning them into a sweetness of our own, blending many very different flavours into one, which shall be unlike them all, and better.⁵⁶

Indeed, the mechanisms of mimesis are conceptualised from Latinity through the Renaissance through two extraordinarily popular metaphors: the apian metaphor, employed by Petrarch in the quotation above, and the metaphor of digestion. In *Epistulae morales* 84, Seneca formulates the question of whether bees collect honey from flowers or actually produce it themselves through some kind of process. By means of this metaphor he ponders whether the merit of poets resides in the simple act of gathering, or rather in production itself. Applied to poetry, the apian metaphor may or may not be used in a transformative sense, for the poet may appear as collector (hence following somebody else's work), or as maker (if he emulates it). The latter is precisely the reading Erasmus employs in *Ciceronianus*, where he links the apian metaphor to *aemulari*:

> Bees don't collect the material for making honey from just one bush [...]. And what they bring is not honey to begin with. They turn it into a liquid in their mouths and inner parts, and then reproduce it, transmuted into their own substance; in it one recognizes not the taste or smell of any flower or shrub the bee has sipped, but a creation of the bee itself, compounded from all the contributory elements.[57]

The apian metaphor also underlies Ronsard's sonnet to Monsieur des Caurres (LXXXVI), which exemplifies the parallelism between the work of the bees and the imitative-inventive practice of the poets. The 'ingenieuse abeille' [ingenious bee] (i.e. the poet), says Ronsard, flies 'De science en science et d'autheur en autheur, | De labeur en labeur, de merveille en merveille' [from science to science and from author to author, from hard work to hard work, from marvel to marvel], 'repaissant diversement l'oreille | Du François' [feeding in different ways the ear of the French].[58] The product of that gathering from myriad sources is not only much worthier than the individual sources themselves, but also a superior confection that renders the other works needless. Thus, Ronsard affirms that, thanks to the bees, 'Il ne faut plus charger du faix de tant de livres | Nos estudes en vain' [it is no longer necessary to vainly burden our studies with so many books]:

> [...] celuy que tu nous livres
> Seul en vaut un millier, des Muses approuvé,
> Qui peut à tous esprits doctement satisfaire.
> Sa clairté nous suffit, l'homme n'a plus que faire
> D'estoiles au matin, quand le jour est levé.

> [[...] the one that you [bees] bring to us is worth a thousand, approved by the Muses, and can learnedly satisfy all spirits. Its brightness is sufficient; men do not need stars in the morning once the sun has risen.][59]

The image of digestion is likewise used by Seneca and Erasmus to explain their stance on transformative imitation. In fact, it is only the transformative sort that Erasmus envisions as being of worth: 'I approve of imitation — but imitation not enslaved to one set of rules, from the guidelines of which it dare not depart'.[60] If what you imitate from your model 'suits your own cast of mind', and is run through your 'mind for inward digestion', Erasmus affirms, then you are on the right path. Inward digestion ensures that what you imitate will eventually become 'part of your own system', and so, the material that is digested 'gives the impression not of something begged from someone else, but of something that springs from your own mental processes, something that exudes the characteristics and force of your own mind and personality'.[61] In short, digestion grants that the distinctive style of every author, in agreement with the spirit of his contemporaries, transforms its models to produce a personal composition that behaves as 'a lifelike portrait of the person' the poet really is, so that the work of the poet is truly 'a child sprung from' the poet's 'own brain, the living image of its father' — a piece of advice similar to Petrarch's in its phrasing.[62]

In the vein of Erasmus, Du Bellay affirms that the Romans were 'able to enrich their language as they did' 'by imitating the best Greek authors, transforming themselves into them, consuming them, and after having digested them well, by converting them into blood and nourishment'.[63] For the French, who wished for their native tongue the same exuberant fruits that Italian was already collecting and exhibiting, imitation was unquestionably unavoidable. Unlike the Italians, who already had a prestigious body of literature written in the vernacular thanks to Dante, Petrarch, and Boccaccio, the poets of the Pléiade rejected the national poetic tradition in French, sought a new language more adequate for lyrical expression, and turned their eyes to Antiquity or to Italy for their models.[64] In the words of Du Bellay: 'without imitating the Greeks and Romans, we cannot give our language the excellence and brilliance of the more famous languages'.[65] Just as the Romans had done with the Greek past, the French were entitled to appropriate and assimilate the classical tongues to their advantage and for their own purposes: 'good imitation is the most useful [achievement], especially for those whose language is not yet particularly rich and abundant', says Du Bellay.[66] Its benefits for French letters were beyond question, despite the complexities of the process. Indeed, Du Bellay assures his readers that 'it is no simple matter to put oneself in the place of a good author and mimic his traits': 'Even Nature is unable to do as much, as can be discerned by some minute difference in things which seem otherwise nearly identical.'[67] Quintilian's and Erasmus's words resonate here.

As mentioned in the previous chapter, Du Bellay came to have a crucial influence on Spenser's poetic practice as well as on his understanding of poetic concepts, most significantly that of imitation. Spenser most likely discovered the work of Du Bellay through Richard Mulcaster, who is acknowledged as 'the principal source of Du Bellay's influence in England' and whose *The first part of the elementarie* owes much to the *Deffence*.[68] While still at school, and surely under the guidance of Mulcaster, Spenser translated several sonnets from *Un songe ou vision*, which were appended to Du Bellay's *Les antiquitez de Rome* (1558). Through these early translations of Du Bellay, Spenser internalised and personally refashioned some of the French author's poetic principles, to the degree that they became 'a pervasive influence on Spenser's style, vocabulary, and the themes of his major works, especially the dominant motifs of mutability, time, and imperial decline'.[69] Interestingly, Du Bellay's own understanding of imitation is, tellingly, based on a work of criticism written by another contemporary authority in a different vernacular: his *Deffence* draws extensively on Sperone Speroni's *Dialogo delle lingue* (1542) to argue in favour of imitation with a view to producing a national literature in France. However, Du Bellay's reliance on Speroni is not servile, but implies on the contrary 'a strong misreading that radically shifts the context of this interpretation from the Italian *questione della lingua* to the literary situation in France'. In so doing, it suggests 'a theory of literature that is not only absent from Speroni's work, but is also a genuine innovation in imitation theory'.[70] Du Bellay and Spenser do not fully agree here; they differ, for instance, in their perception of the status of the vernacular and the kinds of works that might be produced in it, for, despite his defence of the French language, Du Bellay ultimately considers it less refined than the classical ones, hence the importance of enriching it by imitating the classics and borrowing terms and notions of style from them. By contrast, Spenser appears to have a different attitude towards his models, perhaps a more challenging one towards sources and, as a result, one which is less pessimistic in its understanding of the process of what translating and imitating entails. It has been noted that, in translating Du Bellay's *Les antiquitez de Rome*, which he does in *Ruines of Rome*, Spenser is 'more explicitly occupied with his ambitions as a vernacular poet' than, for instance, when translating from Latin sources.[71] Here Spenser reveals more clearly his determination to present himself as a 'new' poet, and so, while paying homage to Du Bellay by refashioning him in English, he aims 'to inaugurate a new English form of poetry'.[72] Indeed, by imitating Du Bellay through translations, Spenser ends up constructing an understanding of imitation as transformation that becomes a pillar on which to sustain the far-reaching potential of a national poetry in the vernacular; the fact that he does so by translating *Les antiquitez* is even more significant in that this work, concerned as it is 'with the reappraisal of the European classical inheritance'[73] as embodied in the Roman Empire, itself becomes a statement of his optimism about the scope for poetic innovation and the possibilities thereof.[74] In other words, if Du Bellay was doubtful 'about the efficacy of the poet/translator's role', 'Spenser grants poets much greater powers against time', and in the process he also understands that translators 'do not "profane the sacred relics" but instead handle them',[75] and that this 're-handling of them' is precisely what is most valuable in the job of the poet/translator. Confirmation of Spenser's 'more optimistic attitude toward the poet's potential role in reviving the Classical past' has been read in his addition of the closing sonnet of *Ruines*, 'L'envoy', which is not a translation and which insists on his belief 'in a poet's power over time, as well as in a translator's power to sing for his nation'.[76] Spenser's translation of Du Bellay has thus been interpreted as 'a productive reworking' of the French author, not only of his poetry but moreover of his understanding of poetic imitation;[77] yet, like Du Bellay, Spenser aims to create a literature in the vernacular that competes, rivals, and ultimately surpasses that of the past, and for this, imitation of the works of Antiquity is required.[78] In this regard, the strategies that Spenser employs as a means of presenting *The faerie queene* as a model in itself are illustrative of his understanding of processes of poetic innovation.[79]

Also after the manner of Quintilian, Peletier in his *Art poétique* (1555) considers that imitation, a useful tool for new poets, ought not to be overused, because, on its own and without the final impulse of invention, it does not lead to the sweet laurels of fame and recognition:[80]

> Il ne faut pas pourtant que le Poète qui doit exceller, soit imitateur juré ni perpétuel. Ains se propose non seulement de pouvoir ajouter du sien, mais

encore de pouvoir faire mieux en plusieurs points. [...] *Par seule imitation rien ne se fait grand*: c'est le fait d'un homme paresseux et de peu de cœur, de marcher toujours après un autre. Celui sera toujours dernier, qui toujours suivra.

[The poet that has to excel should not be a faithful and permanent imitator. On the contrary, he should endeavour not only to add something of his own, but moreover to be able of doing better on various points. [...] *From sheer imitation, nothing great is ever achieved*: following somebody else's path is proper of a lazy man of little courage. He that follows will always be the last.][81]

In England, William Webbe similarly recommends in *A discourse of English poetrie* (1586) that 'an imitation should not be too servile or superstitious, as though one durst not vary one jot from the example', and that 'one should not altogether tread in the steps of others, but sometime he may enter into such ways as have not been haunted or used of others'.[82] From Webbe's viewpoint, poets 'may with discretion imitate the ancient writers',[83] but never slavishly. Robert Burton, conscious of the debates on rightful and illicit appropriation, provides in 'Democritus Junior to the reader', which opens *The anatomy of melancholy* (1621), a defence of his legitimate use of the sources employed in the composition of his work. To such an end, he draws on both the apian and the digestive metaphors. On the one hand, Burton affirms to 'have laboriously collected this *Cento* out of divers Writers', just as 'a Bee gathers Wax and Hony out of many Flowers, and makes a new bundle of all', 'and that *sine injuriâ*, I have wronged no Authors, but given every man his owne [...] I cite & quote mine Authors'.[84] That is to say, unlike some of his contemporaries, whom Burton disdains, he does not steal 'Verses, Pages, Tracts, as some doe now adaies, concealing their Authors names',[85] but instead openly acknowledges his debts and all those to whom he is indebted. On the other hand, Burton claims to 'incorporate, digest, assimilate' these sources, and so he says that he does with them just what 'nature doth with the aliment of our bodies'.[86] He concludes by affirming that his treatment of his models is justifiable as well as fair, for he plays by the rules of borrowing as an honest and lawful practice: 'I can say of my selfe, whom have I injured? The matter is theirs most part, and yet mine'.[87] Indeed, the undeniable relevance of the theory of imitation during the Renaissance does not mean that all forms of it are legitimate, for in practice borrowing is denounced if taken to the extreme of piracy. Ideally, existing material should be combined with the author's own, and the blend should be expressed in such a personal manner that the new treatment improves the previous one.[88]

3.3. *Publica Materies* and Literary Theft

In accordance with Quintilian, Horace recognises that imitating the best models is a secure way of guiding the new poet in his first attempts at poetic composition. Yet Horace does warn the would-be poet against slavish copying of tradition:

In ground open to all you will win private rights, if you do not linger along the easy and open pathway, if you do not seek to render word for word as a slavish translator, and if in your copying you do not leap into the narrow well, out of which either shame or the laws of your task will keep you from stirring a step.[89]

These lines of the *Ars poetica* encourage appropriation and reinterpretation of that — and only that — which is *publica materies* (common property), for the use of it cannot be considered theft. In Epistle 79.6, Seneca affirms that 'it makes a great deal of difference whether' young poets 'approach a subject that has been exhausted, or one where the ground has merely been broken; in the latter case, the topic grows day by day, and what is already discovered does not hinder new discoveries [*crescit in dies et inventuris inventa non obstant*]':

> Besides, he who writes last has the best of the bargain; he finds already at hand words which, when marshalled in a different way, show a new face. And he is not pilfering them, as if they belonged to someone else, when he uses them, for they are common property [*sunt enim publica*].[90]

In other words, the most advisable (because fruitful) subject matter for the compositions of young authors is, according to Seneca, one that is 'common property' with the potential for further development, previously treated by others (but not exhausted in its potential) and flexible enough to accept variations and novel arrangements in terms of *elocutio* and *dispositio*.[91] Seneca thus seems to agree with Isocrates that 'we should admire and honour [...] not those who seek to speak on subjects on which no one has spoken before, but those who know how to speak as no one else could'.[92] The underlying idea here is that what could be called independent fabrication easily leads the writer to mistakes and failure, whereas following an already extant path is far easier and less compromising. Seneca further recommends disguising the relationship between the model and the resulting text by means of dissimulative imitation: the poet's mind, he says, 'should hide away all the materials by which it has been aided, and bring to light only what it has made of them'.[93]

Of course, textual plunderers would always find encouragement and support in the works of Vida, whose stimulus to steal invention and elocution from past authors could not be more overt and unabashed. It is not that Vida incentives servile following, but rather the worst form of plagiarism:

> [the ancient poets'] golden words are our food and their best ornaments of style our eagerly sought plunder. Note how, that we may fit to our own use the spoils and noble trappings of the ancients, we appropriate in one instance their brilliant inventions, in another the order they employ, in others yet the spirit of their words, and even the words themselves — for one need not be ashamed of having sometimes spoken with another's tongue.[94]

For a young poet, the alternative to theft is, Vida assures his readers, failure, and so qualms about stealing the material of others jeopardise the chances of consolidating a successful career:

> Therefore, my pupils, let each of you follow my example; commit your thefts fearlessly and draw your booty from every quarter. For he is a hapless poet [...] who trusts rashly in his own powers and skill and, as though he stood in no need of another's aid, brashly refuses to follow the trustworthy steps of the ancients, abstaining, alas, too much from taking booty, having decided to spare 'others' property' — a vain scrupulosity this [...]. Their rejoicing on that

account is pitiably short-lived, [...] and, yet living, [they] have seen the funeral of their own fame.[95]

On the other side of the spectrum, we find an anxious Petrarch who worries in the extreme about dissimulation and unconscious reminiscences of models. In a letter to Boccaccio written from Pavia on 28 October 1365, Petrarch praises the inclination towards poetry of his young secretary Giovanni Malpaghini, in whom he happily observes 'a great deal of invention', 'a fine enthusiasm, and a heart that loves the Muses'.[96] Because of these traits, Petrarch is confident that the boy

> will develop vigour of thought and expression, and work out, as the result of his experiments, a style of his own, and learn to avoid imitation, or, better, to conceal it, so as to give the impression not of copying but rather of bringing to Italy from the writers of old something new.[97]

One day, this promising young secretary notes that the phrase *atque intonat ore* of Petrarch's sixth bucolic had first been employed by Virgil. Astonished, Petrarch confesses to having been unaware of the borrowing:

> I was astounded, for I realised, as he spoke, what I had failed to see when writing, that this is the ending of one of Virgil's lines, in the sixth book of his divine poem. I determined to communicate the discovery to you [Boccaccio]; not that there is room any longer for correction, the poem being well known by this time and scattered far and wide, but that you might upbraid yourself for having left it to another to point out this slip of mine [...]. I want you to join me in praying Virgil to pardon me, and not harden his heart against me for unwittingly borrowing — not stealing — these few words from him, — who himself has stolen outright, many and many a time, from Homer, and Ennius, and Lucretius, and many another poet.[98]

This 'unwittingly borrowing — not stealing' was particularly tormenting for Petrarch because he was an adamant critic of textual theft. In pondering over the ins and outs of imitation, Petrarch realises that he would always read and memorise authors like Ennius and Plautus with the feeling that their thoughts were alien to his own, in the sense that they were easily distinguishable from them. In contrast, he had digested so effectively the works of Virgil, Cicero, Horace, and Boethius that he had stored their words and thoughts in his memory without thinking them not his own. This would explain why some of their phrases came to his pen without his realising their original authorship.

Like Petrarch, in his essay 'Des livres' (1580) Montaigne affirms that constant reading facilitates the assimilation of models. Unlike Petrarch, however, Montaigne acknowledges being aware of his borrowings because of their extraordinary quality, superior to that of his own texts. The difficulty is rather to pinpoint their source with precision:

> Myself, who am constantly unable to sort out my borrowings by my knowledge of where they came from, am quite able to measure my reach and to know that my own soil is in no wise capable of bringing forth some of the richer flowers that I find rooted there and which all the produce of my own growing could never match.[99]

Even when Montaigne knows the sources of his appropriations, he often intentionally conceals them to protect his texts from fierce criticism:

> In the case of those reasonings and original ideas which I transplant into my own soil and confound with my own, I sometimes deliberately omit to give the author's name so as to rein in the temerity of those hasty criticisms which leap to attack writings of every kind, especially recent writings by men still alive and in our vulgar tongue.[100]

Nonetheless, this does not prevent Montaigne from criticising extensive borrowing and the practice of agglutinating arguments and fragments of previous works in order to guarantee the quality of a 'new' one. In this sense, Montaigne is critical of some contemporary playwrights 'who undertake to write comedies' by mixing 'three or four plots from Terence or Plautus to make one of their own'.[101] According to Montaigne, the reason why they do so is none other than 'their lack of confidence in their ability to sustain themselves with their own graces: they need something solid to lean on'.[102]

Among the French, Du Bellay was one of the authors accused of having stolen from past writers and of having attributed to himself words that in reality he had only translated. Overwhelmed by the magnitude of such shameful accusations of textual theft, he vehemently replies in the negative in the preface to the second edition of *L'olive* (1550). He was, indeed, a convinced defender of imitation in his theory of *innutrition*, and admitted that to some extent it was inevitable that, as a result of the perfect assimilation or digestion of models, authors would unconsciously draw on them in their writings without being fully aware that they were doing so:

> I am accused of bragging that I created what in fact I translated word for word from others. I am tempted to give them the answer that Virgil gave some vicious critic who accused him of borrowing Homer's poetry. [...] Those who would weigh the relative merits of ancient Latin and modern Italian writers, plucking out all those beautiful borrowed feathers by which the latter soar, risk leaving them dressed as Horatian crows. From reading good books, certain elements have become imprinted on my mind. When I then come to set out my own views on any given subject, rather than resurface in my memory as borrowings, these elements just flow readily through my pen. Must we therefore label them stolen property?[103]

Du Bellay additionally defends himself from these charges by vindicating his salient role as an inventor, arguing that in his writing 'there is far more original thought than there is artificial or fastidious emulation'.[104]

An entirely different problem raised by borrowing and appropriation is that of wrongly ascribing to an author the work of another, a delicate situation that poets such as Petrarch faced as well. In his letter from Venice to Angelo di Pietro Stefano dei Tosetti dated 9 April 1363, Petrarch complains that some poorly written short works have been mistakenly attributed to him. This misattribution is remarkably uncomfortable for Petrarch because he understands it as another form of theft: 'the people attributing them to me are doubly in the wrong: they rob their author of his work and burden me with what is not mine'.[105] 'I would rather that any grace of my own be hidden away than that another's disfigurements be stuck and stamped on my face', he goes on to state.[106]

Some writers strove to avoid misappropriation by carefully acknowledging all their sources. In England, Thomas Watson, author of the sequence of love poems *The hekatompathia; or, Passionate centurie of loue* (1582), was one such writer. Most of Watson's poems, which he calls 'passions' or, less frequently, 'sonnets', are eighteen lines long, written in iambic pentameter, and organised into three sextets.[107] Watson's passions are arranged in two sections: the first is made up of seventy-nine love poems built on Petrarchan tropes; the second, with a total of twenty-one passions, enunciates anti-Petrarchan sentiments. A short paragraph in prose preceding each passion explains classical allusions and identifies the sources of the themes sung in the poem. These prose explications, or headpieces, have clear didactic purposes, and are employed by Watson to make his borrowings explicit, to acknowledge his indebtedness to previous writers, or to label his poems as translations. Watson is careful to mention the author of the lines he translates or imitates, and highlights his own variations where these exist. 'My birdes are al of mine own hatching', Watson says, and adds proudly: 'I rather take vpon me to write better then *Charilus*, then once suppose to imitate *Homer*.'[108] Watson is honest enough to admit in passion V that 'all this Passion (two verses only excepted) is wholly translated out of *Petrarch*', or in XL that the poem 'is almost word for word taken out of *Petrarch* [...]. All, except three verses, which this Authour hath necessarily added'.[109] He does not even conceal that the invention of some of his poems is borrowed as well. The headpiece of passion LVII discloses that he has 'groundeth his inuention, for the moste part, vpon the old Latine Prouerbe *Consuetudo est altera natura*', and that of LXI that 'the inuention of this Passion is borrowed, for the most parte from *Seraphine Son. 125*'.[110]

Although it was not until 1709 that the first copyright legislation appeared in England,[111] Joseph Hall's *Virgidemiarum* (1598) is credited with the first recorded use of the English term 'plagiary'; 'plagiaries', meaning 'people who misappropriate texts', were indeed not uncommon at the time.[112] Thomas Heywood, for instance, denounces the third edition (1612) of the volume of poetry *The passionate pilgrime* (1599), published by the printer William Jaggard with the phrase 'By W. Shakespeare' on its title page, for not also including his name on the cover even though the volume printed material by him too. This made Heywood feel that his work was wrongly attributed to somebody else.[113] A likely allusion to Shakespeare as a plagiarist and a 'poor poet-ape' appears in Ben Jonson's 'On poet-ape' (*Epigrams*, 1616; LVI), where he builds an accusation against a poet that, by excessive appropriation of other authors' material, 'is become so bold a thief' that he shamelessly 'makes each man's wit his own' and gets away with it. The problem is then that 'He marks not whose 'twas first', and so 'after-times | May judge it to be his', thus failing to identify the plunder.[114] The irony about Jonson's angry denunciation of theft is that Jonson himself was repeatedly accused by other fellow writers of exactly the same crime. Aphra Behn, for instance, in 'An epistle to the reader', prefaced to *The Dutch lover* (1673), asserts that Jonson's 'Learning was but Grammar high; (sufficient indeed to rob poor Sallust of his best orations)'.[115] John Dryden, in *An essay of dramatic poesy*, is even fiercer in his criticism of Jonson for the same reasons:

> He [Ben Jonson] was not onely a professed Imitator of *Horace*, but a learned Plagiary of all the others; you track him every where in their Snow: If *Horace, Lucan, Petronius Arbiter, Seneca,* and *Juvenal*, had their own from him, there are few serious thoughts which are new in him; [...] I presume he lov'd their fashion when he wore their cloaths.[116]

Not only does Jonson clothe his works with garments of the ancients, but, according to Dryden, he also constantly pillages their works without fear of punishment, and so performs 'his Robberies' brazenly:

> He [Jonson] was deeply conversant in the Ancients, both Greek and Latine, and he borrow'd boldly from them: there is scarce a Poet or Historian among the Roman Authours of those times whom he has not translated in *Sejanus* and *Catiline*. But he has done his Robberies so openly, that one may see he fears not to be taxed by any Law. He invades Authours like a Monarch, and what would be theft in other Poets, is onely victory in him. With the spoils of these Writers he so represents old *Rome* to us, in its Rites, Ceremonies, and Customs, that if one of their poets had written either of his Tragedies, we had seen less of it then in him.[117]

As Ian Donaldson remarks, 'it is a further irony that throughout his long career Dryden himself also repeatedly faced accusations of plagiarism'.[118] For instance, Gerard Langbaine, author of the work revealingly entitled *Momus triumphans; or, The plagiaries of the English stage: Expos'd in a catalogue of all the comedies, tragi-comedies, masques, tragedies, opera's, pastorals, interludes, &c. [...] with an account of the various originals, as well English, French, and Italian, as Greek and Latine, from whence most of them have stole their plots* (1687), condemned Dryden's double standards:

> I cannot but blame him for taxing others with stealing Characters from him [...] when he himself does *the same*, almost in all the Plays he writes; and for arraigning his Predecessours for stealing from the *Ancients*, as he does *Johnson*; which 'tis evident that he himself is guilty of the same.[119]

Hall Bjørnstad, who defines 'plagiarism as imitation gone wrong, inappropriate appropriation, a transgressive practice of textual transfer', 'the "illicit sibling" of imitation',[120] rightly remarks that an accusation of plagiarism involves 'shifting the discussion of imitation from the realm of aesthetics to ethics, from a question of a text's literary quality to questioning the moral quality of the writer'.[121] As such, 'the accusation of plagiarism can function as a powerful polemical weapon able to sanction or even disqualify an adversary'.[122] In early modernity, as has been seen, appropriating the words of other poets without explicit acknowledgement of indebtedness leads to accusations of literary theft and plagiarism. These, in consequence, stain the reputation of an author and question the quality of his own work. As Florio says on borrowing in the address to the reader prefacing his translation of Montaigne's *Essays*, 'if with acknowledgement, it is well; if by stealth, it is too bad: in this, our conscience is our accuser; posteritie our iudge'.[123]

3.4. Making and Creating: Brazen and Golden Worlds

Sir Thomas Elyot, in *The boke named the governour* (1531), affirms that if a 'chylde were induced to make vearsis by the imytation of Virgile and Homere, it shulde mynister to hym moche dylectation and courage to study',[124] and Sir Thomas Wilson, who regards imitation a core training strategy for orators, explains in *The three orations of Demosthenes* (1570) that Demosthenes did 'imitate wholy Thucidides inuention' as well as 'his chiefe arguments and best reasons', and that 'by suche imitation and paynefull labor, came to that heigth of perfection, whereof he beareth the name, that is, to bee the chiefe Orator of all Greecelande'.[125] Nashe, in *Anatomie of absurditie* (1589), likewise recommends it for the improvement of the orator: 'let us [...] set before our eyes one of the excellentest to imitate, in whose example insisting, our industry may be doubled'.[126] In addition, Roger Ascham, in *The scholemaster* (1570), singles out imitation, 'a facultie to expresse liuelie and perfitelie that example: which ye go about to folow', as one of the 'six wayes appointed by the best learned men, for the learning of tonges, and encreace of eloquence'.[127] It can thus 'bring forth more learning, and breed vp trewer iudgement, than any other exercise that can be vsed' in these fields,[128] being moreover crucial in the writing of poetry. In this sense, Ascham distinguishes between two possible approaches to imitation in poetry: '*dissimilis materiei similis tractatio*' and '*similis materiei dissimilis tractatio*', as when '*Virgill* folowed *Homer*: but the Argument to the one was *Vlysses*, to the other *Aeneas*'.[129]

Sidney is convinced that a poet needs 'three wings to bear' himself 'up into the air of due commendation: that is, Art, Imitation, and Exercise'.[130] Following Aristotle, the second means for Sidney to 'borrow nothing of what is, hath been, or shall be; but range [...] into the divine consideration of what may be and should be'.[131] Also after Aristotle, Sidney defines poetry as 'an art of imitation' or '*mimesis*, that is to say, a representing, counterfeiting, or figuring forth — to speak metaphorically, a speaking picture'.[132] Mimesis implies for Sidney going beyond the mere copying of nature and activating the creative microcosm of the mind of the poet. Consequently, for Sidney the poet 'doth grow in effect into another nature, making things either better than Nature bringeth forth, or, quite anew, forms such as never were in Nature'.[133] Walter R. Davis, in fact, believes that, for Sidney, the poet does not appear to imitate or copy what exists in nature but rather what exists in his mind, thus 'producing an affective image'.[134] Poetic imitation becomes a godlike creativity, unlike the superficial copying proper to the rest of the arts, which solely reproduce external nature. This turns it into the purest and highest form of mimetic activity, and elevates the poet over the rest of the imitators. Indeed, for Sidney the poet can have glimpses of the ideal world by transcending the concrete and aiming at the absolutes: 'Nature never set forth the earth in so rich tapestry as divers poets have done [...]. Her world is brazen, the poets only deliver a golden.'[135] Only the poet exceeds nature and rivals it, for poetry is a force that works in parallel with nature:

> Only the poet, disdaining to be tied to any such subjection, lifted up with the vigour of his own invention, doth grow in effect into another nature, in

making things either better than Nature bringeth forth, or, quite anew, forms such as never were in Nature [...]: so as he goeth hand in hand with Nature, not enclosed within the narrow warrant of her gifts, but freely ranging only within the zodiac of his own wit.[136]

It is, then, poetic invention that enables the poet to reshape nature into a golden reality. Davis affirms that Sidney's poetic theory is 'Platonic in its origins, since it goes beyond Nature to Ideas for imitation, and Platonic in its status, since it mediates between Ideas of things as they should be and the material, things as they are'.[137] Yet Sidney's words have been also interpreted as an attempt to reconcile the Platonic and Aristotelian conceptions of mimesis. This is Ulreich's position,[138] which goes beyond Levao's argument that Sidney contrasts Aristotelian and Platonic theories against each other,[139] and against Craig's belief that Sidney holds them in tension.[140] Sidney does not appear to be a pure Aristotelian or a perfect representative of Neoplatonism either, despite employing some typically Neoplatonic notions.[141] Although the belief that the poet can create a new nature comes from Neoplatonism, the fact that Sidney does not endorse the theory of divine *furor* suggests that he is not a fully convinced Neoplatonic: Plato, he writes, 'attributeth unto Poesy more than myself do, namely, to be a very inspiring of a divine force, far above man's wit'.[142] For Sidney, the poet does not require divine inspiration to discover the divine truth of things. Also unlike the Neoplatonists, who admitted that artists could imitate ideas directly, but simultaneously thought that the work of art necessarily remained inferior to the transcendent idea, Sidney pictures the poet's composition as more than the blurred reflection of an idea. In this regard, Sidney's discussion of the fore-conceit might be closer to the art of conjecture of Nicholas of Cusa, who in *De coniecturis* (1442–43) writes that man is a human god, than to Neoplatonic art theory.[143]

Indeed, Sidney affirms that God, 'having made man to His own likeness, set him beyond and over all the works of that second nature'; this is particularly noticeable in the poet, who, 'with the force of a divine breath [...] bringeth things forth surpassing her doings'.[144] Sidney's argument is that, since nature is the product of God, and man is the product of God in 'His own likeness', man (and the poet specifically) exists above nature and its creative powers, and, consequently, poetry is placed at the top of the hierarchy of the arts and sciences: 'of all sciences [...] is our poet the monarch'.[145] Not coincidentally, Fulke Greville, friend and biographer of Sidney, begins his posthumously published *A treatie of humane learning* (1633) by underlining the capacity of the human mind to go beyond nature: 'the minde, in her vaste comprehension, | Containes more worlds than all the world can finde'.[146] Like Sidney, Greville suggests that man has the potential to become like God through the exercise of the sciences and the arts:

> [...] Sciences, and Arts;
> Which wee thirst after, study, admire, aduance,
> As if restore our fall, recure our smarts
> They could, bring in perfection, burne our rods;
> With *Demades* to make us like our Gods.[147]

The elevation of the artist to godlike status has its roots in Neoplatonic theory and not in the Aristotelian tradition, which tends to subordinate art to nature instead. C. S. Lewis affirmed in this regard that, in Neoplatonism, art and nature 'become rival copies of the same supersensous original, and there is no reason why Art should not sometimes be the better of the two'.[148] Although medieval thinkers repeatedly presented God as an author and the world as his book (one that could be read and interpreted by man), they never called poets or artists creators. This would have been blasphemous, as *creatio ex nihilo* was considered a privilege exclusive to God: the verb *poieo* was translated in the Middle Ages 'by *fingo* or *facio*, never by *creo*',[149] and poems were not deemed creations.[150] However, if in the fourteenth century the term 'maker' was used by poets almost exclusively to refer to God, a century later 'maker' began to designate the poet as craftsman as well.[151] In England, for instance, 'Chaucer employs "makere" and "makyng" to describe himself, his contemporaries, and their activity, and "poete" and "poetrie" to designate the ancients, the most revered moderns, and their work'.[152] A friend of Marsilio Ficino, Christophoro Landino is the first to compare the poet to God as creator, and in his *Commentary on Dante* (1481) he asserts that 'although the feigning of the poet is not entirely out of nothing, it nevertheless departs from making and comes very near to creating'.[153] Landino, that is, does not fully assert that the poet creates *ex nihilo* like God, although, when compared to the rest of men, the poet does seem a kind of semi-divinity. If Landino calls God 'the supreme poet', for Scaliger the poet is 'almost [...] a second deity',[154] a kind of semi-god able to perfect nature in the realm of art because, according to Scaliger, nature represents chaos, irregularity, and arbitrariness, whereas art equals harmony, elegance, order, and intellectual discipline.[155] In his *Commentatio* (1593), Alberico Gentili agrees that art can effectively surpass nature: 'art is the imitator of nature, yet it often excels nature'.[156]

George Puttenham is the first to suggest within the English tradition an incipient comparison between the human poet and God (i.e. the Maker). It is true, nonetheless, that in *The true order and methode of wryting and reading hystories, according to the precepts of Francisco Patricio and Accontio Tridentino* (1574), translated by Thomas Blundeville, it was already affirmed that 'of those that make anyethyng, some doe make much of nothing, as God dyd in creating the Worlde of naught, and as Poets in some respect also doe'.[157] Yet Puttenham is the first to employ the analogy of God and the poet to stress the uniqueness of the creative nature of poetry-writing:

> A Poet is as much to say as a maker. [...] Such as (by way of resemblance and reverently) we may say of God, who without any travail to his divine imagination made all the world of nought [...]. It is therefore of poets thus to be conceived, that if they be able to devise and make all these things of themselves, without any subject of verity, that they be (by manner of speech) as creating gods.[158]

Human invention applied to poetry resembles godly creation insofar as the poet does not employ 'any foreign copy or example' but 'makes and contrives out of his own brain'.[159] Nevertheless, unlike God the Maker, 'a poet may in some sort be said a follower or imitator' too, 'because he can express the true and lively of every thing is set before him [...] and so in that respect is both a maker and a counterfeiter: and poesy an art not only of making, but also of imitation'.[160] Poets are, according to Puttenham, like 'creating gods' (even if 'by manner of speech' only), for the poet's activity runs parallel with that of nature. If the poet takes his raw material from nature like every craftsman, unlike any other craftsman he transforms it into something different from nature, and so he works 'even as nature herself, working by her own peculiar virtue and proper instinct and not by example or meditation or exercise as all other artificers do'.[161] Poetry thus behaves like nature itself, and the poet is capable of creating in his poems a second nature more perfect than the sensory world.

Likewise, for Sidney, imitation of nature by poetry implies that poetry also imitates nature's creative powers. The poet's inventive powers are precisely what enable his production of a golden world,[162] a conclusion at which Sidney arrives after blending different and often contradictory currents of thought.[163] To the mix he adds the notion of the poet's 'idea or fore-conceit', which encapsulates two different traditions: while 'idea' brings to mind philosophy, truth, universals, and transcendent values, 'fore-conceit' ('fore-' potentially implying that the conceit pre-dates invention) is loaded with rhetorical and logical connotations, and instead 'suggests a realm of contingent relationships'.[164] It does not seem that for Sidney ideas are innate and pre-existent in the human mind;[165] on the contrary, it appears that the poet creates them by 'freely ranging only within the zodiac of his own wit'.[166] In this understanding of the notion of the idea, William Scott seems to follow Sidney when, in his *The model of poesy* (written c. 1599 and first published in Gavin Alexander's 2013 edition), he states that poetry involves both imitation and feigning because, given that poetic composition is a mental activity that originates in the mind of the poet, 'that which is in the conception of the mind only, men are said to feign or imitate equally: *feign* because it is nowhere in act or practice; *imitate* because in so expressing any thing or action they follow the idea or image modelled in their minds and reasonable apprehensions'.[167] The general belief in the sixteenth century was in fact that ideas had an *a posteriori* nature, and that they were connected to the power of the imagination. 'Idea' is, for instance, defined by Thomas Cooper and Thomas Thomas as 'the figure couceiued in Imagination',[168] by John Florio as the 'figure or forme of anything conceiued in imagination',[169] and by John Perceval as 'a forme or fashion, conceiued in imagination'.[170] The role of the imagination in shaping the understanding of poetry-writing, and the part that invention has in it, is the concern of the following chapters.

Notes to Chapter 3

1. Quintilian, IV, 327 (X. 2. 11).
2. Isocrates, 'Against the Sophists', in *Isocrates in Three Volumes*, 3 vols (Cambridge, MA: Harvard University Press, 1928–29), II, trans. by George Norlin (1929), pp. 160–80 (p. 175).
3. Cicero, *De oratore*, I, 267 (II. 22. 92).
4. Elaine Fantham, 'Imitation and Evolution: The Discussion of Rhetorical Imitation in Cicero

De oratore 2. 87–97 and some Related Problems of Ciceronian Theory', *Classical Philology*, 73.1 (1978), 1–16 (p. 11).
5. Quintilian, IV, 335 (X. 2. 26).
6. Quintilian, IV, 323 (X. 2. 3).
7. Copeland, p. 30.
8. Ángel García Galiano, *Teoría de la imitación poética en el Renacimiento* (Madrid: Universidad Complutense de Madrid, 1988), pp. 35–36. See also Izora Scott, *Controversies over the Imitation of Cicero as a Model for Style and Some Phases of their Influence on the Schools of the Renaissance* (New York: Teachers College, Columbia University, 1910).
9. Meyrick Heath Carré, *Phases of Thought in England* (Oxford: Clarendon Press, 1949), p. 180; Sweeting, p. 90.
10. G. W. Pigman III, 'Imitation and the Renaissance Sense of the Past: The Reception of Erasmus' *Ciceronianus*', *Journal of Medieval and Renaissance Studies*, 9 (1979), 155–77 (p. 168); Victoria Pineda, *La imitación como arte literario en el siglo XVI español* (Sevilla: Diputación Provincial de Sevilla, 1994), p. 42.
11. Letter from Languet to Sidney, Vienna, 1 January 1574, in *The Correspondence of Philip Sidney and Hubert Languet*, ed. by William Aspenwall Bradley (Boston: Merrymount Press, 1912), pp. 19–22 (p. 20).
12. Nandra Perry, '*Imitatio* and Identity: Thomas Rogers, Philip Sidney, and the Protestant Self', *English Literary Renaissance*, 35.3 (2005), 365–406 (pp. 373–74). Javier Gomá Lanzón also elaborates on the subject of imitation and Protestantism (*Imitación y experiencia* (Barcelona: Critica, 2005), p. 385).
13. Quintilian, IV, 325 (X. 2. 7).
14. Quintilian, IV, 323 (X. 2. 1).
15. Quintilian, IV, 325 (X. 2. 8).
16. Quintilian, IV, 323–25 (X. 2. 4–5).
17. Quintilian, IV, 327 (X. 2. 12).
18. Pernille Harsting, 'Quintilian, Imitation and "Anxiety of Influence"', in *Quintiliano*, ed. by Albaladejo Mayordomo, del Rio, and Caballero, pp. 1325–35 (p. 1331).
19. Longinus, p. 213 (14.2). Longinus bases successful mimesis on five principles: (*i*) 'the object must be worth imitating'; (*ii*) 'the spirit rather than the letter must be reproduced'; (*iii*) 'the imitation must be tacitly acknowledged, on the understanding that the informed reader will recognize and approve the borrowing'; (*iv*) 'the borrowing must be "made one's own", by individual treatment and assimilation to its new place and purpose'; and (*v*) 'the imitator must think of himself as competing with his model, even if he knows he cannot win' (Donald Andrew Russell, 'De imitatione', in *Creative Imitation and Latin Literature*, ed. by D. West and T. Woodman (Cambridge: Cambridge University Press, 1979), pp. 1–16 (p. 16)).
20. For more on Quintilian's notion of imitation, see Mª Victoria Utrera Torremocha, 'La imitación en la *Institutio Oratoria* de Quintiliano', in *Quintiliano*, ed. by Albaladejo Mayordomo, del Rio, and Caballero, pp. 1513–22.
21. Marcus Tullius Cicero, *Tusculan Disputations*, trans. by J. E. King (Cambridge, MA: Harvard University Press; London: Heinemann, 1966), pp. 345, 347 (IV.8.17-18).
22. G. W. Pigman III, 'Versions of Imitation in the Renaissance', *Renaissance Quarterly*, 33.1 (1980), 1–32 (p. 16).
23. Desiderius Erasmus, *Collected Works of Erasmus*, 89 vols (Toronto and Buffalo: University of Toronto Press, 1974–2019), XXVIII: '*Ciceronianus*', Notes, Indexes, trans. and ed. by Betty I. Knott (1986), p. 379.
24. Quintilian in this regard states that 'total similarity is so difficult to achieve that even Nature herself has failed to prevent things which seem to match and resemble each other most closely from being always distinguishable in *some* respect'; for this reason, 'it is generally easier to improve on something than simply to repeat it' (IV, 327; X. 2. 10; emphasis in original).
25. Erasmus, XXVIII, 366.
26. Erasmus, XXVIII, 379.
27. John Muckelbauer, 'Imitation and Invention in Antiquity: An Historical-Theoretical Revision',

Rhetorica, 21.2 (2003), 61–88 (p. 68).
28. Thomas M. Greene, *The Light in Troy: Imitation and Discovery in Renaissance Poetry* (New Haven and London: Yale University Press, 1982), p. 38.
29. Greene, p. 41.
30. Jonathan Bate, *Shakespeare and Ovid* (Oxford: Oxford University Press, 2001), p. 87.
31. *Correspondence of Philip Sidney*, pp. 1–3 (p. 2).
32. *Correspondence of Philip Sidney*, pp. 3–5 (p. 4).
33. Jonathan Bate, p. 87.
34. See J. Tate, '"Imitation" in Plato's *Republic*', *Classical Quarterly*, 22 (1928), 16–23 (p. 23); J. Tate, 'Plato and "Imitation"', *Classical Quarterly*, 26 (1932), 161–69. For more on the Platonic theory of poetry applied to the arts, see W. J. Verdenius, *Mimesis: Plato's Doctrine of Artistic Imitation and its Meaning to Us* (Leiden: Brill, 1962).
35. Aristotle, 'Poetics', ed. and trans. by Stephen Halliwell, in *Aristotle, 'Poetics'; Longinus, 'On the Sublime'; Demetrius, 'On Style'*, pp. 27–142 (pp. 125–27; 1460B).
36. For more on the Renaissance perception of the past, see Peter Burke, *The Renaissance Sense of the Past* (London: Arnold, 1969).
37. François Rigolot, 'The Renaissance Crisis of Exemplarity', *Journal of the History of Ideas*, 59.4 (1998), 557–63 (p. 561).
38. José Carlos Fernández Corte argues that, since rhetorical imitation is a common system of categories, it is more general, whereas poetic imitation can only be textual ('Imitación retórica e imitación poética en Quintiliano', in *Quintiliano*, ed. by Albaladejo Mayordomo, del Rio, and Caballero, pp. 1253–62). For Elaine Fantham, poetic imitation is more specific than rhetorical imitation partly because poetry is dependent on specific diction and genre conventions; and, while the poet typically extracts his subject matter from poetic tradition, the orator looks to reality or law for his oration instead ('Imitation and Evolution'). See also Elaine Fantham, 'Imitation and Decline: Rhetorical Theory and Practice in the First Century after Christ', *Classical Philology*, 73.2 (1978), 102–16.
39. Nancy S. Struever, *The Language of History in the Renaissance: Rhetoric and Historical Consciousness in Florentine Humanism* (Princeton: Princeton University Press, 1970), p. 64.
40. Richard Waswo, *Language and Meaning in the Renaissance* (Princeton: Princeton University Press, 1987).
41. Perry, p. 368.
42. See Stephen Halliwell, *The Aesthetics of Mimesis: Ancient Texts and Modern Problems* (Princeton and Oxford: Princeton University Press, 2002); although the book focuses on Plato and Aristotle, there is one chapter devoted to Neoplatonism and imitation: Chapter 11, 'Renewal and Transformation: Neoplatonism and Mimesis'.
43. For more on the theory and practice of imitation in Renaissance Italy, see Martin L. McLaughlin, *Literary Imitation in the Italian Renaissance: The Theory and Practice of Literary Imitation in Italy from Dante to Bembo* (Oxford: Clarendon Press, 1995).
44. Vida's judgement of poetry as an art of mimesis is independent from the Aristotelian theory on the same matter; see Ralf G. Williams, 'Introduction', in *The 'De arte poetica' of Marco Girolamo Vida*, ed. and trans. by Ralf G. Williams (New York: Columbia University Press, 1976), pp. xi–lii (p. xxix).
45. Marco Girolamo Vida, *The 'De arte poetica' of Marco Girolamo Vida*, ed. and trans. by Ralf G. Williams (New York: Columbia University Press, 1976), p. 73.
46. Vida, p. 99.
47. Ludovico Castelvetro, *On the Art of Poetry*, ed. and trans. by Andrew Bongiorno (Binghamton: State University of New York, Center for Medieval and Early Renaissance Studies, 1984), p. 16.
48. Quoted in English in Pigman, 'Versions of Imitation', p. 20.
49. Julius Caesar Scaliger, *Poetices libri septem = Sieben Bücher über die Dichtkunst, Band IV, Buch 5*, ed. by Luc Deitz and Gregor Vogt-Spira (Stuttgart and Bad Cannstatt: Frommann-Holzboog, 1998), p. 42 (214a). To my knowledge, only fragments of Scaliger's *Poetices* have been translated into English: Julius Caesar Scaliger, *Select Translations from Scaliger's 'Poetics'*, trans. and ed. by

Frederick Morgan Padelford (New York: Holt, 1905). Book v, Chapter 1 is not included in this selection; the translations from it here are my own.
50. Scaliger, *Poetices libri septem*, p. 42 (214a).
51. Scaliger, *Poetices libri septem*, p. 42 (214a).
52. Francis Petrarch, *Petrarch, the First Modern Scholar and Man of Letters: A Selection from his Correspondence with Boccaccio and other Friends, Designed to Illustrate the Beginnings of the Renaissance*, trans. by James Harvey Robinson with Henry Winchester Rolfe (New York: Haskell House, 1970), p. 183.
53. Petrarch, *Selection from his Correspondence*, p. 183.
54. Petrarch, *Letters*, I, 60, 59.
55. Petrarch, *Selection from his Correspondence*, p. 290.
56. Petrarch, *Selection from his Correspondence*, p. 291.
57. Erasmus, XXVIII, 402.
58. Pierre de Ronsard, *Œuvres complètes de P. de Ronsard*, 8 vols, ed. by M. Prosper Blanchemain (Paris: Jannet, 1857–67), V (1866), 357–58. For more on Ronsard's poetics, see Isidore Silver, 'Creative Imitation, Originality and Literary Tradition in Ronsard', in *Renaissance and Other Studies in Honor of William Leon Wiley* (Chapel Hill: University of North Carolina Press, 1968), pp. 215–27; François Rigolot, 'Between Homer and Virgil: *Mimesis* and *Imitatio* in Ronsard's Epic Theory', in *Renaissance Rereadings: Intertext and Context*, ed. by Maryanne Cline Horowitz, Anne J. Cruz, and Wendy A. Furman (Urbana: University of Illinois Press, 1988), pp. 67–79.
59. Ronsard, *Œuvres complètes*, V, 358.
60. Erasmus, XXVIII, 441.
61. Erasmus, XXVIII, 441.
62. Erasmus, XXVIII, 441–42.
63. Du Bellay, 'Defence and Illustration', p. 50.
64. Henri Weber, *La Création poétique au XVIe siècle en France: De Maurice Scève à Agrippa d'Aubigné* (Paris: Nizet, 1981), p. 118; Jean-Claude Carron, 'Imitation and Intertextuality in the Renaissance', *New Literary History: A Journal of Theory and Interpretation*, 19.3 (1988), 565–79 (p. 572). For more on imitation in the poetry written in Latin by the Pléiade, see Marc Bizer, *La Poésie au miroir: Imitation et conscience de soi dans la poésie latine de la Pléiade* (Paris: Champion, 1995).
65. Du Bellay, 'Defence and Illustration', p. 65.
66. Du Bellay, 'Defence and Illustration', p. 51.
67. Du Bellay, 'Defence and Illustration', p. 52.
68. Andrew Hadfield, *Edmund Spenser: A Life* (Oxford: Oxford University Press, 2012), p. 38.
69. Hadfield, p. 280.
70. Ignacio Navarette, 'Strategies of Appropriation in Speroni and Du Bellay', *Comparative Literature*, 41 (1989), 141–54 (p. 143).
71. Richard Danson Brown, *'The New Poet': Novelty and Tradition in Spenser's Complaints* (Liverpool: Liverpool University Press, 1999), pp. 63–95 (p. 63).
72. Brown, p. 63.
73. Brown, p. 64.
74. For an in-depth analysis of Spenser's *Ruines of Rome* translations and the manner in which Spenser explores the 'various problems of re-birthing the classical world with which his age was so concerned', see Anne Elizabeth Banks Coldiron, 'How Spenser Excavates Du Bellay's *Antiquitez*; or, The Role of the Poet, Lyric Historiography, and the English Sonnet', *Journal of English and Germanic Philology* 101.1 (2002), 41–67 (p. 46). See also Jean R. Brink, 'Who Fashioned Edmund Spenser?: The Textual History of "Complaints"', *Studies in Philology*, 88.2 (1991), 153–68; Margaret W. Ferguson, '"The Afflatus of Ruin": Meditations on Rome by Du Bellay, Spenser, and Stevens', in *Roman Images: Selected Papers from the English Institute*, ed. by Annabel Patterson (Baltimore: Johns Hopkins University Press, 1984), pp. 23–50. Ferguson argues that 'the experience of rereading and rewriting Du Bellay's Roman sonnets over a period of years led Spenser [...] to question the meaning of his own act of translating them' (p. 31).
75. Coldiron, p. 67.

76. Coldiron, pp. 48, 53.
77. Hassan Melehy, 'Spenser and Du Bellay: Translation, Imitation, Ruin', *Comparative Literature Studies*, 40.4 (2003), 415–38 (p. 416).
78. Melehy, 'Spenser and Du Bellay', p. 417. Melehy also stresses the thesis that 'Spenser borrows the notion of poetic imitation from the Pléïade in order to effect an imitative reworking of Du Bellay and the other poets, especially Virgil and Petrarch', in his *The Poetics of Literary Transfer in Early Modern France and England* (Farnham: Ashgate, 2010), p. 76.
79. For more on the process by which *The faerie queene* constructs 'authorization of its own canonical status on the basis of the prior poetry of another nation, namely the work of Du Bellay', see Hassan Melehy, 'Spenser's *Mutabilitie Cantos* and Du Bellay's Poetic Transformation', in *French Connections in the English Renaissance*, ed. by Catherine Gimelli Martin and Hassan Melehy (Burlington: Ashgate, 2013), pp. 51–64 (p. 55). For more on Spenser's understanding and use of imitation, see S. K. Heninger, *Sidney and Spenser: The Poet as Maker* (University Park: Pennsylvania State University Press, 1989), particularly Chapter 6, 'Spenser: Imitation as Harmonious Form'.
80. For more on literary imitation in sixteenth-century France, see Ann Moss, 'Literary Imitation in the Sixteenth Century: Writers and Readers, Latin and French', in *Cambridge History of Literary Criticism*, III: *The Renaissance*, ed. by Glyn P. Norton (2000), pp. 107–18.
81. Peletier du Mans, p. 256 (my emphasis).
82. Webbe, p. 138.
83. Webbe, p. 140.
84. Robert Burton, *The Anatomy of Melancholy* [1621], ed. by Thomas C. Faulkner, Nicolas K. Kiessling, and Rhonda L. Blair, 6 vols (Oxford: Clarendon Press; New York: Oxford University Press, 1989–2000), I (1989), 11.
85. Burton, I, 11.
86. Burton, I, 11. On the use of the metaphor of digestion in Burton's *Anatomy of melancholy*; see Claire Crignon-De Oliveira, '"Tout est à moi et rien n'est à moi": La digestion des sources dans l'*Anatomie de la mélancolie* de Robert Burton', in *Emprunt, plagiat, réécriture aux XVe, XVIe, XVIIe siècles: Pour un nouvel éclairage sur la pratique des lettres à la Renaissance*, ed. by Marie Couton and others (Clermont-Ferrand: Presses universitaires Blaise Pascal, 2006), pp. 235–50.
87. Burton, I, 11.
88. Harold Ogden White, *Plagiarism and Imitation during the English Renaissance: A Study in Critical Distinctions*, 2nd edn (New York: Octagon Books, 1973), p. 8.
89. Horace, p. 463 (*Ars poetica*, ll. 131–35).
90. Lucius Annaeus Seneca, *Ad Lucilium epistulae morales*, trans. by Richard M. Gummere, 3 vols (Cambridge, MA: Harvard University Press; London: Heinemann, 1917–25), II (1920), 203, 205.
91. In classical Antiquity, 'the material could be common, and even negligible, the manner of its application was to be individual; originality lay not at all in what you said but in the way you said it, or at least, in the new use you made of old matter' (A. J. Smith, 'Theory and Practice in Renaissance Poetry: Two Kinds of Imitation', *Bulletin of the John Rylands Library*, 47 (1964), 212–43 (p. 216)).
92. Isocrates, 'Panegyricus', in *Isocrates in Three Volumes*, 3 vols (Cambridge, MA: Harvard University Press, 1928–29), I, trans. by George Norlin (1928), pp. 115–242 (p. 125).
93. Seneca, II, 281.
94. Vida, p. 99.
95. Vida, p. 101.
96. Petrarch, *Selection from his Correspondence*, p. 288.
97. Petrarch, *Selection from his Correspondence*, pp. 289–90.
98. Petrarch, *Selection from his Correspondence*, pp. 292–93.
99. Michel de Montaigne, *The Complete Essays*, trans. and ed. by M. A. Screech (London: Penguin, 1993), p. 458.
100. Montaigne, p. 458.
101. Montaigne, p. 461.
102. Montaigne, p. 461.

103. Joachim Du Bellay, 'Second Preface to the *Olive*', in *Poetry & Language in 16th-Century France*, trans. by Willett, pp. 107–14 (pp. 111–12). Du Bellay's reference to 'Horatian crows' alludes to 'Horace's version of Aesop's fable of borrowed plumage: the crow who disguises himself with peacock's feathers. The image was deployed repeatedly in English literary criticism' (Nick Groom, 'Forgery, Plagiarism, Imitation, Pegleggery', in *Plagiarism in Early Modern England*, ed. by Paulina Kewes (Basingstoke: Palgrave Macmillan, 2003), pp. 74–89 (p. 77)).
104. Du Bellay, 'Second Preface to the *Olive*', p. 112. Margaret W. Ferguson explores 'the problems raised by Du Bellay's effort to combine a theory of invention with a theory (or theories) of imitation', and argues 'that this effort reveals an ambivalence toward the ancients that produces both an "offensive" and a "defensive" stance' ('The Exile's Defense: Du Bellay's *La Deffence et Illustration de la langue Françoyse*', *Publications of the Modern Language Association of America*, 93.2 (1978), 275–89 (p. 276)).
105. Petrarch, *Letters of Old Age*, I, 65.
106. Petrarch, *Letters of Old Age*, I, 66.
107. William M. Murphy, 'Thomas Watson's *Hecatompathia* (1582) and the Elizabethan Sonnet Sequence', *Journal of English and Germanic Philology*, 56 (1957), 418–28 (p. 419).
108. Thomas Watson, *The Hekatompathia; or, Passionate Century of Love, 1582* (Gainesville: Scholars' Facsimiles & Reprints, 1964), p. 7.
109. Thomas Watson, pp. 19, 54. Watson translates or closely imitates Petrarch on numerous occasions in the *Hekatompathia*, as in passions VI, 'a translation into latine of the selfe same sonnet of *Petrarch*' (p. 20); XXI, where Watson imitates '*Petrarch, Sonetto 221*' (p. 35); XXXIX, 'the fifte Sonnet in *Petrarch part. 1*' (p. 53); LXVI, the '*Petrarch Sonette 133*' (p. 80); XC (p. 104); and the epilogue, which Watson affirms was 'faithfully translated out of *Petrarch, Sonnet 314.2*' (p. 116). On other occasions, it is Ronsard who is translated or imitated in Watson's *Hekatompathia*, as in passions XXVII (p. 41), XXVIII (p. 42), LIIII (p. 68), and LXXXIII (p. 97). Furthermore, Watson states that he imitated other authors in passions VII (p. 21), XXII (p. 36), XXXIIII (p. 48), XXXVIII (p. 52), XLIII (p. 57), XLVII (p. 61), LI (p. 65), LIII (p. 67), LV (p. 69), LVI (p. 70), LXV (p. 79), LXVIII (p. 82), LXX (p. 84), LXXV (p. 89), LXXVII (p. 91), LXXVIII (p. 92), LXXIX (p. 93), LXXXV (p. 99), LXXXVI (p. 100), LXXXIX (p. 103), XCI (p. 105), XCIII (p. 107), XCIIII (p. 108), XCVI (p. 110), XCVIII (p. 112), XCIX (p. 114), and C (p. 115). Watson typically explains the extent of his imitation or the particularities of his translation.
110. Thomas Watson, pp. 71, 75.
111. It has been argued that Erasmus's collection of proverbs of Greek and Roman antiquity gathered in *Adages* (1508) marked a turning point in the Renaissance conception of literary property, for they simultaneously foreshadow the development of copyright while looking back to an ancient philosophical tradition according to which ideas should be universally shared in the spirit of friendship and hence viewed as common property; see Kathy Eden, *Friends Hold All Things in Common: Tradition, Intellectual Property, and the 'Adages' of Erasmus* (New Haven and London: Yale University Press, 2001); Neil Rhodes, 'Versions of the Common', in *Common: The Development of Literary Culture in Sixteenth-Century England* (Oxford: Oxford University Press, 2018), pp. 3-27.
112. The word *plagiarius*, which originally referred to someone who abducted the child or slave of another, a kidnapper, was used for the first time to refer to a literary thief by the Latin poet Martial in the first century. The following is William Cartwright's translation into English of Martial's Epigram 'Ad furem de libro suo', published posthumously in 1651: 'Th'art out, vile Plagiary, that dost think | A Poet may be made at th'rate of Ink, | And cheap-priz'd Paper; none e'r purchas'd yet | Six or ten Penniworth of Fame or Wit: | Get Verse unpublish'd, new-stamp'd Fancies look, | Which th'only Father of the Virgin Book | Knows, and keeps seal'd in his close Desk within, | Not slubber'd yet by any ruffer Chin; | A Book, once known, ne'r quits the Author; If | Any lies yet impolish'd, any stiff, | Wanting it's Bosses, and it's Cover, do | Get that; I've such, and can be secret too. | He that repeats stoln Verse, and for Fame looks, | Must purchase Silence too as well as Books' (William Cartwright, *Comedies, Tragi-Comedies, with Other Poems* (London: printed for [T. R. &] Humphrey Moseley, 1651), R1r). In France, the word *plagiat* was not in use 'until the late seventeenth century (first noted use 1697) [...]. However, [...] *repreneur, usurpation, rapiecer, rapetasser, contrerolleur*, etc. — all contain very

interesting metaphors that point to the notion of plagiarism' (Kristi Sellevold, 'Some "hardis repreneurs" in Sixteenth-Century France: Du Bellay, Aneau, Chappuys', in *Borrowed Feathers: Plagiarism and the Limits of Imitation in Early Modern Europe*, ed. by Hall Bjørnstad (Oslo: Unipub, 2008), pp. 53–65 (p. 65)).

113. Max W. Thomas, 'Eschewing Credit: Heywood, Shakespeare, and Plagiarism before Copyright', *New Literary History*, 31.2 (2000), 277–93 (p. 277). For more on the idea of plagiarism in Renaissance England before the passing of a copyright law to protect authors (or, rather, 'the rights of the printer or publisher'), see Brian Vickers, *English Renaissance Literary Criticism* (Oxford: Oxford University Press, 2003), p. 29. See also John Feather, *Publishing, Piracy and Politics: An Historical Study of Copyright in Britain* (London: Mansell, 1994), particularly Chapter 1, 'The Origins of Copyright 1475–1640'; Feather writes that 'the origin of copyright in England is clear enough: it began as a device developed within the London book trade in the sixteenth century to protect the investments of those involved in printing and publishing. There was no statutory framework for this device, although it was to some extent supported by the official status of the book trade's guild, the Stationers' Company, which was able to enforce its collective will on its members and had a wide range of monopolistic powers over the printing and selling of books. Authors had no significant part in these early developments, partly because the book trade excluded them from its own arrangements, but also because of their social and economic position' (p. 4). For more on the origins of copyright legislation, see Thomas Mallon, *Stolen Words: Forays into the Origins and Ravages of Plagiarism* (New York: Ticknor & Fields, 1989), particularly Chapter 1, 'Oft Thought, Ere Expressed: From Classical Imitation to International Copyright'; Mark Rose, *Authors and Owners: The Invention of Copyright* (Cambridge, MA: Harvard University Press, 1993); John Feather, 'From Rights in Copies to Copyright: The Recognition of Authors' Rights in English Law and Practice in the Sixteenth and Seventeenth Centuries', in *The Construction of Authorship: Textual Appropriation in Law and Literature*, ed. by Martha Woodmansee and Peter Jaszi (Durham and London: Duke University Press, 1994), pp. 191–210; Paul Goldstein, *Copyright's Highway: From Gutenberg to the Celestial Jukebox* (New York: Hill and Wang, 1994). More recent works on the history of plagiarism include Marilyn Randall, *Pragmatic Plagiarism: Authorship, Profit, and Power* (Toronto and Buffalo: University of Toronto Press, 2001); Hélène Maurel-Indart, *Plagiats, les coulisses de l'écriture* (Paris: Différence, 2007).

114. Ben Jonson, 'Epigrams' [1616], ed. by Colin Burrow, in *The Cambridge Edition of the Works of Ben Jonson*, 7 vols (Cambridge and New York: Cambridge University Press, 2012), v: *1616–1625*, pp. 101–98 (pp. 139–40).

115. Aphra Behn, 'The Dutch Lover' [1673], in *The Works of Aphra Behn*, ed. by Montague Summers, 6 vols (New York: Phaeton Press, 1967), I, 215–330 (p. 224).

116. Dryden, 'Essay', p. 21.

117. Dryden, 'Essay', pp. 57–58.

118. Ian Donaldson, '"The Fripperie of Wit": Jonson and Plagiarism', in *Plagiarism*, ed. by Kewes, pp. 119–33 (p. 127).

119. Gerard Langbaine, *Momus Triumphans; or, The Plagiaries of the English Stage* (London: printed for Nicholas Cox, 1687), a2v. For more on the practices of appropriation and borrowing of Jonson and Dryden, and accusations of literary theft, see David Bruce Kramer, *The Imperial Dryden: The Poetics of Appropriation in Seventeenth-Century England* (Athens and London: University of Georgia Press, 1994); Lynn Sermin Meskill, 'Tracks in other Men's Snow: Ben Jonson's Plagiary', in *Emprunt, plagiat, réécriture*, ed. by Couton and others, pp. 185–96. See also, more generally on the drama of the period, Laura Jean Rosenthal, *Playwrights and Plagiarists in Early Modern England: Gender, Authorship, Literary Property* (Ithaca and London: Cornell University Press, 1996); Janet Clare, *Shakespeare's Stage Traffic: Imitation, Borrowing and Competition in Renaissance Theatre* (Cambridge and New York: Cambridge University Press, 2014).

120. Hall Bjørnstad, 'Introduction', in *Borrowed Feathers*, ed. by Bjørnstad, pp. 5–17 (p. 6).

121. Bjørnstad, p. 7.

122. Bjørnstad, p. 7. See, in this regard, Harry Major Paull, *Literary Ethics: A Study in the Growth of the Literary Conscience* (London: Butterworth, 1928).

123. John Florio, 'To the Curteous Reader', in *The Essayes or Morall, Politike and Millitarie Discourses of*

Lo: Michaell de Montaigne [...]: The First Booke (London: printed by Val. Sims for Edward Blount, 1603), A5r–A6r (A5v).
124. Sir Thomas Elyot, *The Boke Named the Gouernour* (London: printed by Thomas Berthelet, 1537), D8r.
125. Thomas Wilson, *The Three Orations of Demosthenes Chiefe Orator among the Grecians, in Fauour of the Olynthians, a People in Thracia, Now Called Romania* (London: printed by Henrie Denham, 1570), *ivr.
126. Thomas Nashe, *The Anatomie of Absurditie* (London: printed by I. Charlewood for Thomas Hacket, 1589), E3v.
127. Roger Ascham, *English Works: 'Toxophilus', 'Report of the Affaires and State of Germany', 'The Scholemaster'*, ed. by William Aldis Wright (Cambridge: Cambridge University Press, 1970), pp. 264, 242. The other strategies are *translatio linguarum, paraphrasis, metaphrasis, epitome*, and *declamatio*.
128. Ascham, p. 268.
129. Ascham, pp. 266–67. For more on imitation in Ascham, see Marion Trousdale, 'Recurrence and Renaissance: Rhetorical Imitation in Ascham and Sturm', *English Literary Renaissance*, 6 (1976), 156–79.
130. Sidney, p. 109.
131. Sidney, p. 87. Ursula Kuhn discusses three kinds of imitation in Sidney's understanding of poetry: (*i*) that of 'authors dealing with religious subjects', (*ii*) that 'of authors dealing with philosophical (moral and natural) or historical subjects', and (*iii*) that 'of "real poets" (vates)' (*English Literary Terms in Poetological Texts of the Sixteenth Century* (Salzburg: Institut fur Englische Sprache und Literatur, University of Salzburg, 1974), pp. 148–49).
132. Sidney, p. 86 (emphasis in original). On this matter, see Thomas C. Kishler, 'Aristotle and Sidney on Imitation', *The Classical Journal*, 59.2 (1963), 63–64.
133. Sidney, p. 85.
134. Walter R. Davis, *Idea and Act in Elizabethan Fiction* (Princeton: Princeton University Press, 1969), p. 29.
135. Sidney, p. 85.
136. Sidney, p. 85.
137. Davis, p. 31.
138. John C. Ulreich, Jr, '"The Poets Only Deliver": Sidney's Conception of Mimesis', *Studies in Literary Imagination*, 15.1 (1982), 67–84.
139. Ronald Levao, 'Sidney's Feigned *Apology*', in *Sir Philip Sidney: An Anthology of Modern Criticism*, ed. by Dennis Kay (Oxford: Clarendon Press, 1987), pp. 127–46.
140. D. H. Craig, 'A Hybrid Growth: Sidney's Theory of Poetry in *An Apology for Poetry*', *English Literary Renaissance*, 10 (1980), 183–201.
141. Ronald Levao, *Renaissance Minds and their Fictions: Cusanus, Sidney, Shakespeare* (Berkeley: University of California Press, 1985), p. 137; Stillman, p. 373.
142. Sidney, p. 107.
143. See Ernst Cassirer and others, *The Renaissance Philosophy of Man* (Chicago and London: University of Chicago Press, 1948), p. 7; Levao, *Renaissance Minds*, pp. 67–68, 86. For more on Nicholas of Cusa, see Ferdinand Edward Cranz, *Nicholas of Cusa and the Renaissance* (Aldershot: Ashgate, 2000). For more on Neoplatonism in Nicholas of Cusa's and Marsilio Ficino's thought, see Maurice DeGandillac, 'Neoplatonism and Christian Thought in the Fifteenth Century (Nicholas of Cusa and Marsilio Ficino)', in *Neoplatonism and Christian Thought*, ed. by Dominic J. O'Meara (Norfolk, VA: International Society for Neoplatonic Studies; Albany: State University of New York Press, 1981), pp. 143–65; William J. Hoye, 'The Meaning of Neoplatonism in the Thought of Nicholas of Cusa', *Downside Review*, 104 (1986), 10–18. Dorothy Connell stresses Pico della Mirandola's unacknowledged influence on Sidney's recognition of man's creative powers, as well as the influence of other Renaissance humanists following Pico's *Oratio* (*Sir Philip Sidney's 'The Maker's Mind'* (Oxford: Clarendon Press, 1977), p. 2). On this, see also W. J. Bouwsma, 'The Renaissance Discovery of Human Creativity', in *Humanity and Divinity in the Renaissance and Reformation*, ed. by J. O'Malley and others (Leiden: Brill, 1993), pp. 17–34.

144. Sidney, pp. 85–86.
145. Sidney, p. 95.
146. Fulke Greville, Baron Brooke, 'A Treatie of Humane Learning', in *Certaine Learned and Elegant Workes of the Right Honorable Fulke Lord Brooke Written in his Youth, and Familiar Exercise with Sir Philip Sidney* (London: printed by E[lizabeth] P[urslowe] for Henry Seyle, 1633), d1r.
147. Greville, d3r (emphasis in original).
148. C. S. Lewis, *English Literature in the Sixteenth Century, Excluding Drama* (Oxford: Clarendon Press, 1966), p. 320.
149. E. N. Tigerstedt, 'The Poet as Creator: Origins of a Metaphor', *Comparative Literature Studies*, 20 (1970), 455–88 (p. 468).
150. There are a few isolated exceptions to this; the earliest are found in the commentaries of the medieval canonists and in the philosophy of Nicholas of Cusa (see Michael Mack, 'Sidney's Poetics: Imitating Creation', p. 18). Herodotus was the first to use the agent noun *poietés* and the verb *poiein* with regard to poetry, but the idea of creation then assumed in poetry was alien to the Greeks, who saw the poet as a producer of 'fabrication' rather than as an original creator (see Curtius, p. 398). The assimilation of *poietés* to *creator* derives, in fact, from Jewish and Christian theological speculations (see Luis Gil, *Los antiguos y la 'inspiración' poética* (Madrid: Guadarrama, 1966), p. 14).
151. Ebin, p. 198.
152. Glending Olson, 'Making and Poetry in the Age of Chaucer', *Comparative Literature*, 31.3 (1979), 272–90 (pp. 274–75).
153. Translated in Michael Mack, 'Sidney's Poetics: Imitating Creation', p. 20. See also Tigerstedt, pp. 456, 475.
154. Translated in Michael Mack, 'Sidney's Poetics: Imitating Creation', p. 22.
155. See Vernon Hall, Jr, 'Scaliger's Defense of Poetry', *Publications of the Modern Language Association of America*, 63.4 (1948), 1125–30.
156. Gentili, p. 97.
157. Thomas Blundeville, *The True Order and Methode of Wryting and Reading Hystories* (London: printed by VVillyam Seres, 1574), E4r.
158. Puttenham, pp. 93–94.
159. Puttenham, p. 93.
160. Puttenham, pp. 93–94.
161. Puttenham, p. 386.
162. Andrew D. Weiner, 'Sidney/Spenser/Shakespeare: Influence/Intertextuality/Intention', in *Influence and Intertextuality in Literary History*, ed. by Jay Clayton and Eric Rothstein (Madison and London: University of Wisconsin Press, 1991), pp. 245–70 (p. 248). Heninger also discusses theories of imitation put forward and applied by Sidney, particularly in Chapters 5 ('The defence of poesie: Language and Imitation') and 7 ('Sidney: Imitation as Image'). His essential argument regarding Sidneian imitation is that 'in *The defence of poesie* Sidney puts forward a radical poetics that marks an advance over the neoplantonist aesthetic of proportion and harmony' (p. 223), and that Sidney 'holds a pivotal position in the development of literary theory as the neoplantonist aesthetic shifted toward an aesthetic grounded in empiricism, as the criterion of harmony acceded to verisimilitude' (p. 306).
163. O. B. Hardison, 'The Two Voices of Sidney's *Apology for Poetry*', *English Literary Renaissance*, 2 (1972), 83–99; D. H. Craig, p. 197; Perry, p. 391.
164. Lawrence C. Wolfley, 'Sidney's Visual-Didactic Poetics: Some Complexities and Limitations', *Journal of Medieval and Renaissance Studies*, 6 (1976), 217–41 (p. 230).
165. Stillman, p. 380, instead argues that Sidney never acknowledged the poet as a maker of ideas, but rather that he saw the idea in close relationship with the poet's 'erected wit', very likely as something innate that would explain the connection between the poet and the divine maker. For his part, A. Leigh DeNeef argues that Sidney's conception of the idea is closer to Ficino than to any of the other Italian thinkers, even if 'no direct Ficinian influence need be assumed' ('Rereading Sidney's *Apology*', *Journal of Medieval and Renaissance Studies*, 10 (1980), 155–91 (p. 172)). The various influences that scholars have identified in the Sidneian understanding

of 'idea' include 'The Platonic form of the Good; Truths of Christian revelation; Mystical insights into the beauty of divine being; Images of Man's perfection in Eden, and similarly in the pagan Golden Age; Universal Aristotelian ethical conceptions, of magnanimity and of the various psychological and behavioral types; Stoic conceptions of the virtues and vices; The Four Cardinal Virtues and the Seven Deadly Sins; Theophrastian "characters"; Ciceronian models of political and oratorical virtue' (Wolfley, p. 230).
166. Sidney, p. 85.
167. William Scott, *The Model of Poesy* [*c.* 1599], ed. by Gavin Alexander (Cambridge: Cambridge University Press, 2013), p. 11. For more on Scott's treatise, see the special issue published by the *Sidney Journal* in 2015.
168. Thomas Cooper, *Thesaurus Linguæ Romanæ & Britannicæ* (London: printed by Henry Denham, 1578), Nnn4r; Thomas Thomas, Dd7v.
169. Florio, *A VVorlde of Wordes*, O4v.
170. Perceval, X5v.

CHAPTER 4

Invention as a Distinguishing Factor

In the Renaissance, 'invention' is consolidated as a central term for discussing and assessing poetry, and so becomes much more than the first stage in the crafting of a rhetorical or logical discourse, or the outcome of imitation, as the previous chapters have explored. The four sections of the present chapter approach this from various angles, tracing the process by which invention comes to be seen as the trigger of poetry-writing and as a renewing force that is believed to revisit tradition and encourage innovation in poetic compositions, despite being simultaneously distrusted by early English Reformers.

The first section examines how 'to invent' is taken to stand for the writing of fiction or the composition of fables. More generally, the term becomes one of the highest praise in poetics, as well as an indicator of the lifelike quality of the most outstanding poetry. It is envisioned as an organic fluid that imbues the written word with life, and some authors grant it supernatural provenance, regarding it to be in the hands of the gods and the Muses. Invention, it will be seen, requires the poet's wit and ingenuity to be at their best, coupled with a desire to go beyond what is clichéd. An analysis of the use of adjectives expressing rarity, oddity, and novelty when in the vicinity of this concept confirms that what is singular, unusual, and unexpected receives recognition and praise as extraordinary. What is run-of-the-mill and trite, by contrast, goes unnoticed. In the eyes of Thomas Nashe, poets 'take a pride in inuenting new opinions'.[1]

The second section of this chapter considers how invention works as a criterion for assessing poetic compositions, and how, as such, and for critics such as Castelvetro, it operates in direct opposition to imitation. In other words, the two are understood as mutually exclusive, and invention is thought to be the only one of the two indicative of poetic talent. Following this belief, the works of an array of authors, early modern as well as classical, are assessed by sixteenth- and seventeenth-century critics, often in a disheartening manner. The fact that imitation is widespread neither legitimises it in the eyes of these critics nor makes it any less disappointing. While imitation means playing it safe by reusing words and stories with a guarantee of success, the inventiveness of a poet 'quicker than his eye', as Nashe puts it, signals courageous skill. Precisely Nashe's confrontation with Gabriel Harvey over this concept opens up a discussion about plagiarism and the evils of illegitimate appropriation of another author's ideas.

The third section discusses the radical distinction that sixteenth-century authors establish between inventive works and translations on the level of poetic theory, even if in practice translation frequently acts as a spur to invention. As will be seen, this view is not exclusive to English authors but also shared by their Italian and French counterparts, who regard translation as a minor artistic activity because, they argue, the translator's invention is not put to use when translating. At best, translation is said to be the truest form of imitation, in the words of Peletier, and as such it carries all the negative connotations of imitation, while inventing is hailed as the ideal instead.

The chapter closes with a final section on the connection between anti-poetic sentiments and the discourse of the Protestant Reformation in England. Despite the merits attributed to invention, there exists a distrust against it which goes hand-in-hand with an anti-poetic sentiment fostered by Protestant thought. It is, after all, an active capacity of the mind that can be turned to a variety of purposes, including lying and deceiving, and is therefore believed to work to the advantage of idolatry and heresy, namely Catholicism. Thus, anti-poetic sentiment is intertwined in complex ways with religious matters, and this renders the relationship between poetry and truth and morality problematic.

4.1. In Poetry-Writing

Emblem books, which consisted of collections of pictures accompanied by a motto and an explanatory moral exposition typically written in verse, enjoyed immense popularity in England from the time of their introduction during the reign of Elizabeth I until the end of the seventeenth century. Whether they were translated into English or composed directly in that language, they revealed close connections with poetic works,[2] to the extent that 'the emblemata served up the rich iconography of poetry and poetic inspiration more abundantly than did the paintings or sculptures of the time'.[3] Horace's ideas, for instance, exerted an enormous influence on writers of emblem literature, since it was often his words that were reproduced verbatim as mottoes.[4] In Henry Peacham's emblem book *Minerva britanna* (1612), there appears an emblem with the motto *Tutissima comes* that depicts Pallas hand-in-hand with Ulysses on his return trip to Ithaca. The lines '*Homer* did invent it long agoe, | And we esteeme it as a fable'[5] illustrate the understanding of 'to invent' as synonymous with the devising of stories (fables) and the writing of fiction in general. With the same meaning in mind, George Gascoigne affirms at the beginning of the account of 'the adventures passed by Dan Bartholmew of Bathe' that 'To tell a tale without authoritye, | Or fayne a Fable by invencion' are activities proper to poets.[6]

Wilbur Samuel Howell argues that, in the Renaissance, many English authors identified poetry with fable — that is, with the Latin *fabula*, 'a narrative of imagined characters taking part in imagined events', which 'could be mythical, or legendary, or fictitious, or quasi-historical, or historical' and which could be narrated in 'realistic terms, or in terms of romance, or allegory'.[7] For such authors, the fable, which could shed light on truth and serious matters, was the essential principle

Emblem 1, 'Tutissima comes' (Peacham, *Minerua britanna*, L2v).

of poetry, that which made it distinct. As Thomas Wilson explains in his *Arte of rhetorique* (1553), 'the saiynge of Poets and all their fables [...] were not fayned of suche wise menne without cause', and so fables have a didactic purpose and can have persuasive ends, and by means of fables poets address issues of importance related to morals or the search for truth.[8] This didacticism of the fable acknowledged by Wilson is connected with the Horatian goal of teaching delightfully, thus fostering virtue and discouraging vice. According to Sidney, it was the poets who invented fables (i.e. the writing of fiction) as vessels for the dissemination of knowledge: 'it pleased the heavenly Deity, by Hesiod and Homer, under the veil of fables, to give us all knowledge, Logic, Rhetoric, Philosophy natural and moral'.[9]

In the sixteenth century, invention is generally understood not only as the writing of fiction, but more importantly as the element that adds quality and taste to a poet's composition and makes it worth reading. In France, the members of the Pléiade consolidated belief in its centrality in poetics before the English. In his *Art poétique françoys* (1548), Sébillet states that 'la sève et le bois' [the sap and the wood] of poetry 'sont l'invention et l'éloquence des Poètes' [are the poets' invention and elocution].[10] The image of poetry as a living organism in need of invention to grow and function also appears in Peletier's understanding of this concept, which he views in his *Art poétique* (1555) as flowing 'par tout le Poème, comme le sang par le corps de l'animal' [through the poem, like blood through the body of an animal]; for this reason, he says, it 'se peut appeler la vie ou l'âme du Poème' [can be called the life or soul of the poem].[11] Ronsard, in his *Abrégé de l'art poétique français* (1565), likewise

196 *Pennæ gloria perennis.*

To Edwarde Dier *Esquier.*

Emblem 2, 'Pennæ gloria perennis' (Whitney, *A choice of emblemes*, b2v)

envisions it as an essential element in poetry ('le principal point est l'invention') that springs 'tant de la bonne nature, que par la leçon des bons et anciens auteurs [both from good nature and the lesson of good and ancient authors],[12] and behaves as 'les nerfs et la vie du livre' [the nerves and life of a book].[13]

As the element that enlivens poetry, invention was not coincidentally understood as the trigger of poetic composition, just as it had been acknowledged in the past as the first stage in the crafting of a rhetorical or logical discourse. This is the reason why, fearing the lack of it, the poet pleads with the gods or Muses for quick and bright inventiveness, as in the powerful opening address of Shakespeare's *King Henry V* (1600), which requests 'a Muse of Fire' to share with the poet the delights of 'the brightest Heauen of Inuention'.[14] More fearful of his 'presumption', the poetic persona of Gascoigne's 'In prayse of a countesse' beseeches the gods for help in the form of a drop of invention to pursue the composition of a poem: 'I call the mighty Gods in ayd | To further forth some fine invention'.[15]

G. W. Senior, in a poem prefaced to Spenser's *Amoretti and Epithalamion* (1595), laments that 'while this Muse in forraine landes doth stay, | inuention weepes, and pens are cast aside', as consequently 'few do write'.[16] At times, the generous Muses even intervene before the poet experiences anxiety when facing the blank page, and provide unsolicited advice. This is the case for Sir Philip Sidney, 'whome mightie Ioue did blesse, with graces from aboue' from the moment of his birth, as stated in the lines accompanying an emblem with the Latin motto *Pennæ gloria perennis* included in Geoffrey Whitney's *A choice of emblemes and other devises* (1586):

'the pen, was by MERCVRIVS sente, | Wherewith, hee also gaue to him, the gifte for to inuente'.[17]

Thus, Sidney's godly poetic abilities explain why 'nowe, his workes of endlesse fame, delighte the worthie wittes'.[18] On other occasions, as in John Davies of Hereford's Epigram 26, 'Of wise fooles, or foolish wise men', the poet's desperate invocation is not to a muse or to a deity, but rather directly to a personification of invention: 'O *Inuention* rise, | And tickle wisest Heart-strings till they ake [of laughter]'.[19] Davies employs the same strategy in his ingenious poem 'Inuentions Life, Death, and Funerall', in which the poetic persona complains about the ill-functioning of his inventive faculty, unable to operate correctly in the sight of his beloved. She not only fails to nurture the poet's wit with love, as would be expected, but moreover manages to confuse, paralyse, and eventually kill it:

> This *Epitath* fix on his senslesse Head,
>   *Here lies Inuention*
> *That stood his louing Master in no steade*
>   *In Loues contention.*[20]

The belief that 'quicknes of invencion' was indispensable for a poet if he had ambitions of being 'crowned with Lawrell', as reads 'The letter of G. T. to his very friend H. W. concerning this worke', included in Gascoigne's *A hundreth sundrie flowres*,[21] is similarly echoed by sixteenth-century English lexicographers. As early as 1538, Thomas Elyot, in *The dictionary of Syr Thomas Eliot Knyght*, states that Homer's *Illiad* and *Odyssey* 'are worthy to be radde, for the meruailous inuention, and profytable sentences in them contayned'.[22] 'Invention' as a term is so central to the language of poetics that dictionary definitions of key words such as 'poetry', 'poem', and 'poet' inevitably include it. In the *Dictionarium linguae latinae et anglicanae* (1587), Thomas Thomas defines *pŏēma* as '*a poets inuention*, or worke';[23] for John Florio, *poéma* similarly means 'a composition or Poets worke or inuention', and *trouatore* 'an inuentor [...] a poet or auctor'.[24]

With few exceptions, works on poetics stress the unavoidable requirement of invention for a literary work to succeed.[25] John Hoskins's *Directions for speech and style* (c. 1599), which focuses on letter-writing, pronunciation, and elocution, briefly (and unexpectedly, given the Ramist tendencies of Hoskins) mentions it within the context of letter-writing. Prior to the discussion of disposition, Hoskins affirms that 'in writing of letters there is to be regarded the invention and the fashion',[26] even if for the former there are no fixed rules: 'there can be no rules of more certainty or precepts of better direction given you than conjecture can lay down'.[27] In his posthumously published *Timber; or, Discoveries made upon men and matter* (1641), Ben Jonson used Hoskins's words quasi-verbatim, and extended them to writing in general.[28] Thus, for Jonson, the precepts of the rhetoricians are of no avail to the poetic author, who can only trust his own 'conjecture' when devising the matter of his work.

In 'Certayne Notes of Instruction Concerning the Making of Verse', Gascoigne also underscores the difficulty of pinpointing and prescribing 'certayne and infallible rules' for invention, and yet he doubts that anything praiseworthy can be achieved without it: 'the first and most necessarie poynt', he writes, 'that ever I founde meete to be cōsidered in making of a delectable poeme is this, to grounde it upon some fine invention', which essentially relies on 'the quicke capacitie of a writer' and on his ability to avoid clichés and platitudes, the 'customes of commō writers'.[29] Topics ought to be approached in a novel fashion instead, for otherwise the poet risks mediocrity. Gascoigne suggests ways to escape from *'trita & obvia'* matters in, for example, the writing of love poetry, which at the time was a minefield of hackneyed phrases and overused Petrarchan conventions: 'if I should disclose my pretence in love, I would eyther make a straunge discourse of some intollerable passion [...] or use the covertest meane that I could to avoyde the uncomely customes of commō writers'.[30] Invention is so pivotal for Gascoigne that neither elocution nor rhyme should divert the poet from the supreme goal of soundly shaping it: 'beyng founde, pleasant woordes will follow well inough and fast inough'.[31] He insists: 'Your Invention being once devised, take heede that neither pleasure of rime, nor varietie of devise, do carie you from it'.[32] Elocution and rhyme are thus merely peripheral to the kernel of all poetic glory.

The most appealing poems are in fact, according to Gascoigne, those which present 'some rare invention and Methode before not commonly used'.[33] 'Rare', employed as a term of praise when accompanying 'invention', is not infrequent in the sixteenth century. The poem by G. W. Senior prefaced to Spenser's *Amoretti and Epithalamion* (1595) instantiates the favourable connotations of this collocation: 'thy muse hath got such grace, and power to please, | with rare inuention bewtified by skill'.[34] The phrase 'rare inuention' suggests a quest for innovation in poetic composition which stems from the awareness that difference is a must if a poetic work is to excel. The correspondence between Spenser and Gabriel Harvey published under the title *Three proper, and wittie, familiar letters* (1580) illustrates how adjectives expressing oddity acquire positive connotations when in the vicinity of 'invention'. For example, when Spenser reveals his intention to write a volume on the course of the River Thames, *Epithalamion Thamesis*, he remarks that the book 'wil be very profitable for the knowledge, and rare for the Invention, and manner of handling'.[35] Harvey in turn celebrates Spenser's *Dreames*, 'bicause they favour of that singular extraordinarie veine and inuention' of 'all the most delicate, and fine conceited Grecians & Italians [...] whose chiefest endeuour, and drifte was, to have nothing vulgare, but [...] rare, queint, and odde in euery pointe, [...] aboue the reache, and compasse of a common Schollers capacitie'.[36] In other words, while vulgarity (within the reach of 'a common Schollers capacitie') is marked as undesirable and altogether insufficient for poetic glory, whatever makes a composition 'rare, queint, and odde', singular or extraordinary 'in some respecte or other', deserves recognition and praise. Later on, Harvey affirms in regard to Spenser's *Nine comedies* that he is 'voyde of al iudgement' if they 'come not neerer *Ariostoes Comoedies*, eyther for the finenesse of plausible Elocution, or the rarenesse of Poetical Invention'.[37] In comparison to what is run-of-the-mill, the unusual and unexpected characterise the production of the poetic elite.

In his defence of poetry-writing, George Puttenham also acknowledges that 'rare invention' is an indicator of quality which confirms that a work deserves to 'be published' under the real name of the author, 'for reason serves it, and modesty doth not repugn' the recognition of authorship.[38] As a sign of novelty, 'rare' implies that what is of worth differs from what is ordinarily done and hence from what it is expected. The adjective 'new' is employed with identical connotations. In *Euphues and his England*, John Lyly opposes the 'inuention of *new* fables' to 'the reciting of old',[39] and in his *Summers last will and testament* (1600), Nashe states that a scholar 'going to his booke, or being about to inuent', 'sets a *new* poynt on his wit'.[40] Part of the task of the intellectual activity of scholars and authors is thus to covet what is new, that is, to surpass tradition. The search for novelty, indeed, constitutes a phenomenal source of concern and anxiety for authors, and leading figures such as Shakespeare are certainly not immune to it. Sonnet 59, for instance, describes the fear of the potential impossibility of writing anything new, or at least with the appearance of being new:

> If their bee nothing new, but that which is
> Hath beene before, how are our braines beguild,
> Which laboring for inuention beare amisse
> The second burthen of a former child?[41]

The frustration that goes hand-in-hand with the perspective of omnipresent repetition also pervades Sonnet 76:

> Why is my verse so barren of new pride?
> So far from variation or quicke change?
> Why with the time do I not glance aside
> To new found methods, and to compounds strange?
> Why write I still all one, euer the same,
> And keepe inuention in a noted weed,
> That euery word doth almost [tel] my name,
> Shewing their birth, and where they did proceed?[42]

'New pride', 'variation', 'quick change', 'new-found methods', 'compounds strange', and a new 'invention' underline the centrality of novelty in praiseworthy poetic compositions at the same time as suggesting that an absence thereof can only lead to artistic stagnation and the loss of recognition. Refashioning one's poetic style is thus brought to the fore as one of the greatest challenges of authors with a long career in poetry-writing. Gaining fame and recognition is an ephemeral success, for maintaining one's status as an authority in poetry demands a sustained effort to renew one's style and, with it, invention. As the emblem *Presidium et dulce decus* in Peacham's *Minerva britanna* (1612) also highlights, the greater their rarity and singularity, the more extraordinary the capacities of the artist. The emblem, an arm in armour which, appearing amidst the clouds, places a flag with a coat of arms on the summit of a mountain, is followed by the line 'For rar'st invention, and designe of wit'.[43] Indeed, nothing is as imperative as combining the two to climb the steep slopes of everlasting artistic fame.

Emblem 3, 'Presidium et dulce decus' (Peacham, *Minerua britanna*, P4v).

4.2. In Evaluating Composition

In *Love's labour's lost* (1598), Ovid is praised 'for smelling out the odoriferous flowers of fancie', 'the ierkes of inuention'.[44] Thanks to taking inspiration from the scent of previous authors, Ovid improved his own poetic skills, which would have otherwise become stagnant had he simply followed the *auctoritates* without having added his personal contribution. Imitation is despised partly because it is suggested that it demands no use of the intellectual capacities of rational beings and is, as such, proper to beasts: 'imitarie is nothing: So doth the Hound his maister, the Ape his keeper, | the tyred Horse his rider'.[45] The opposition between imitation and invention, one in which the latter has the upper hand, is a constant throughout the Renaissance. Edward Blount, editor of John Lyly's *Six court comedies*, in a letter prefixed to the volume, acclaims Lyly's works as 'six ingots of refined inuention' which owed nothing to imitation;[46] 'the *Lyre*' Lyly played on, says Blount, 'had no borrowed strings'.[47] Invention and renovation on the one hand, and slavish imitation and the immutable perpetuation of poetic tradition, on the other, are thus diametrically opposed.

One of the critics who proves more adamant in their discussion of this conceptual opposition is Castelvetro.[48] In his *Poetica d'Aristotele* (1570), he stresses that invention does not descend from a superior being but has its origins strictly within the human realm — yet does not come from another human source, that is, from another poet, either. Castelvetro thereby rejects theories of poetic inspiration and denies any form of imitation on the level of invention. The poet does not copy; instead, he is a qualified craftsman who makes the most of his natural talents by undergoing training and by learning the principles of the art of poetry. Unlike ordinary craftsmen, who simply assemble ready-made pieces, the poet 'invents not only the whole plot, i.e., its general design and the disposition of its parts, but also some of the particulars which give it body, not borrowing all of them from others'.[49] Castelvetro ponders the unacceptability of a conscious appropriation of the subject matter and the language of other authors, and concludes that 'a poet cannot legitimately fashion a plot that merely reproduces that of another poet, and if he does the resulting work would be not a poem but a history or a piece of stolen property'.[50] Such is the behaviour of thieves and not of poets, for the poet is first and foremost an inventor:

> the person who merely puts a known story into verse shirks the labor of invention; yet invention is the most difficult part of the poet's art, and it seems it was with an eye to the poet as inventor that the Greeks gave him a name that signifies 'maker'.[51]

Castelvetro envisions invention and imitation in mutually exclusive terms, with the texts constructed on imitation alone being not poetic but rather instances of cheeky fraud. Artificers, including poets, are of two kinds, Castelvetro says. First, there are 'those wise enough to discover the necessary principles of their art for themselves and by their precept and example to offer guidance to their fellows'; second, there are 'those who are unable to discover a single principle of the art they practice but can only follow the precepts and examples of others'.[52] While the former sort are true poets because they 'invent their own matter and their own modes of figurative speech', the second 'must never for a moment be tolerated' nor acknowledged as poets, for they 'ape the actions of others and acquire knowledge not by the exercise of their reason but mechanically, by imitation and practice'.[53] On this basis, Castelvetro makes the bold claim that Plautus, Terence, Virgil, Seneca, Petrarch, Ariosto, and Boccaccio, among others, are, strictly speaking, thieves, as their poetry lacks invention while heavily relying on imitation.[54] Of course, Virgil had already been accused of being a borrower of Homer, for instance by Sperone Speroni in his *Discorsi sopra Virgilio* (1563–64).[55] In England, Castelvetro's and Speroni's words are echoed by authors such as John Eliot and George Chapman. In *Ortho-epia gallica: Eliots fruits for the French* (1593), Eliot elevates Homer, the inventor par excellence, to the highest poetic glory, to a degree that resists imitation: 'Truly his wit was admirable, his inventions inimitable'.[56] Homer is thus praised on the grounds that he is unrepeatable and non-reproducible. In the preface to *Achilles shield, translated as the other seuen bookes of Homer out of his eighteenth booke of Iliades*, an instalment of his translation of Homer published in 1598,[57] Chapman contrasts the uniqueness of Homer's work, 'writ from a free furie, an absolute & full soule', with Virgil's 'altogether imitatorie spirit':

> not a *Simile* hee hath but is *Homers*: not an inuention, person, or disposition, but is wholly or originally built vpon *Homericall* foundations, and in many places

hath the verie wordes *Homer* vseth: [...] All *Homers* bookes are such as haue beene presidents euer since of all sortes of Poems: imitating none, nor euer worthily imitated of any.[58]

Indeed, for centuries Virgil's 'position went unchallenged but, with the rediscovery of Homer, humanists developed a greater awareness of Virgil's debt to his Greek predecessor', and many were particularly struck by how much Virgil 'had borrowed from Homer, down to the level of individual lines of verse'.[59] The same language that Eliot and Chapman employ to refer to Virgil, Dryden uses regarding Ovid and Chaucer in his *Preface to fables ancient and modern* (1700): 'neither were great Inventors: For *Ovid* only copied the *Grecian* Fables, and most of *Chaucer*'s Stories were taken from his *Italian* Contemporaries, or their Predecessors'.[60] 'Both of them built on the inventions of other men; yet, since Chaucer had something of his own', Dryden believes he should 'justly' give him 'the Precedence in that Part', for he 'can remember nothing of Ovid which was wholly his'.[61] Indeed, for Dryden, invention is central both in poetry as well as in painting: it is their 'first part, and absolutely necessary', he affirms in *A parallel betwixt painting and poetry* (1695).[62] Like Hoskins and Ben Jonson before him, Dryden regrets that 'no Rule ever was or ever can be given how to compass it'.[63] Much to the contrary, it relies solely on innate 'Genius', that is, 'the gift of Nature', 'the particular gift of Heaven',[64] and is consequently impossible to obtain if one is born without it, no matter how zealous one's training and learning are. Indeed, the Latin maxim *poeta nascitur, orator fit* had popularised for centuries the idea that nature constitutes the ultimate source of poetic talent, as Thomas Lodge, in *A defence of poetry, music and stage-plays* (1579), had explained a century before Dryden: 'Poetrye commeth from aboue, from a heauenly seate of a glorious God, unto an excellent creature man'.[65]

Dryden is in general of the opinion that 'the genius' of the English is inclined 'rather to improve an invention than to invent themselves',[66] a belief which Thomas Nashe shared. In 'To the gentlemen students of both universities', prefixed to Robert Greene's *Menaphon* (1589), Nashe laments that there exist few poets in England who do not have to 'borow inuention of *Ariosto*, and his Countreymen' to compose their works, and instead explore untrodden poetic paths divergent from the classics and the Italians.[67] Regrettably, however, Nashe finds the country brimming with imitators who, 'in disguised arraie', shamefully pass '*Ouids* and *Plutarchs* plumes as their owne'.[68] Nashe calls instead for a poet with an 'inuention quicker than his eye',[69] that is, for someone capable of employing his own creative powers as opposed to someone quick to see and take note of what others have done with a view to reproducing it. According to Nashe, 'the Adage, *Nil dictum quod non dictum prius*' was 'the most iudiciall estimate' about his contemporaries,[70] who, to his mind, did little more than copy what others had previously written. Some exceptions are to be noted, nonetheless, and Nashe singles out the poetic skill of, for example, George Peele, who 'goeth a step beyond all that write' because of 'his pregnant dexteritie of wit, and manifold varietie of inuention'.[71]

Lack of invention can only mean useless repetition of common knowledge and failure to contribute to the advancement of the arts and sciences. This is the argument of the physician and natural philosopher Juan Huarte de San Juan, author of the treatise *Examen de ingenios para las ciencias* (1575), first translated into English by Richard Carew as *The examination of mens wits* (1594).[72] His claim is that ignorance relies on imitation and plagiarism, whereas what is needed to make knowledge advance is instead 'to join the new invention of ourselves, who live now, with that which the ancients left written in their books'.[73] Otherwise, the authors who do not contribute anything new can only limit themselves to copying and unashamedly stealing from previous writers: 'such who want invention [...] do nought else save heap up matters already delivered and sentences of grave authors returning to repeat the self things, stealing one from hence, and taking another from thence'.[74]

The same applies to orators, who 'may not be wanting' either 'much invention, or much reading'.[75] Of course, the former is preferable to the latter, for it provides seemingly endless arguments, while the stock that comes from reading is finite: 'whatsoever books teach is bounded and limited, and the proper invention is a good fountain which always yieldeth forth new and fresh water'.[76] Should the fountain ever dry up, the orator would then, Huarte says, resemble that preacher who, 'not endowed with any invention of his own', 'was driven to fetch the same out of his books' to preach to his audience, who in three Lents got to know all his material.[77] By contrast, 'those who borrow their conceits out of their own brain stand not in need of study, time, or memory, for they find all ready at their fingers' ends'.[78] Leonard Cox, in *The art or crafte of rhetoryke* (1532), similarly comments on a preacher 'vnapt' to compose his sermons 'for lacke of inuencion and order with due elocucion'.[79] As a result of the 'great tediousnes' of his preaching, when he is not 'left almost aloon', 'the audience falleth for werynes of his ineloquent language fast on slepe'.[80] As one of the largest and most active groups of orators in the sixteenth century, it is unsurprising that preachers are the protagonists of numerous anecdotes of this sort. Interestingly, for Huarte there is yet another faculty an orator cannot do without: 'a very swift imagination'.[81] As if it were 'a brach', the imagination is needed 'to hunt and bring the game', and, if required, 'to devise somewhat as if it were material'.[82] Thomas Wilson's image of the orator as a hunter of arguments thus reappears in Huarte with a significant twist: for Huarte, the hound is none other than the faculty of the imagination, entirely absent from Wilson. The belief that the imagination can both 'devise somewhat as if it were material' and 'seek out arguments and convenient sentences'[83] combines the notions of invention as finding and as imaginative devising.

Precisely this concept lies at the heart of what has been considered 'the first English discussion in which accusations and denials of literary theft assumed importance',[84] to wit, the quarrel of many years between Gabriel Harvey and Nashe. The discord began with Nashe's previously mentioned epistle 'To the gentlemen students of both universities' and his criticism of those who 'feed on nought but the crummes that fal from the translators trencher' and of those who 'must borow inuention'.[85] Years later, in *Pierce pennilesse his supplication to the diuell* (1592), Nashe criticises 'some dul-headed ★ Diuines' whom he accuses of having censored his lofty work as a poet when they themselves have 'no eloquence' and 'no inuention'.[86]

Harvey, suspicious of Nashe's repeated claims to unborrowed invention, responds in *Pierces supererogation; or, A new prayse of the old asse: A preparative to certaine larger discourses intituled Nashes s. fame* (1593) by accusing him of slavishly following several authors, among them Greene, Gascoigne, and Marlowe: 'his gayest floorishes, are but Gascoignes weedes, or Tarletons trickes, or Greenes crankes, or Marlowes brauados'.[87] In sum, Harvey says that Nashe's 'freshest nippitatie' is 'but the froth of stale inuentiōs, long-since lothsome to quick tastes', and that his sole remarkable ability resides in his capacity to copy and deform his material:

> his only Art, & the vengeable drift of his whole cunning, to mangle my sentences, hack my arguments, chopp and change my phrases, wrinch my wordes, and hale euery sillable most extremely; euen to the disioynting, and maiming of my whole meaning.[88]

Harvey sarcastically underlines Nashe's 'fresh inuention from the tapp' and 'bottomlesse pitt of Inuention', and calls him 'the verye inuentor of Asses', a 'braue Columbus of tearmes', and the 'onely marchant venturer of quarrels; that detecteth new Indies of Inuention'.[89] Indeed, according to Harvey, Nashe lacks that 'super-excellent witt' which is 'the mother pearle of precious Inuention; and the goulden mine of gorgeous Elocution'.[90] Of course, Nashe did not stand idly by, and counter-attacked by accusing Harvey of, among other things, appropriating material from him and from other authors.[91] 'Nothing can be done without it', Dryden concludes with regard to invention, except to copy and plagiarise:

> Without Invention a Painter is but a Copier, and a Poet but a Plagiary of others. [...] Imitatours are but a servile kind of Cattle, says the Poet; or at best the Keepers of Cattle for other men: they have nothing which is properly their own.[92]

Similarly to Castelvetro, in Dryden's approach invention takes precedent over any other quality in the painter and the poet. Without it, painters and poets can only aspire to copy or plagiarise previous artists, and thus settle with being considered 'a servile kind of cattle' forever removed from the degree of perfection of their models. Inventiveness becomes the defining faculty of the poet, for it alone opens the doors to fame and defines the abyss between true poets and sheer imitators.[93]

4.3. In Translations

Translation exercises had been a common practice in the teaching of grammar and rhetoric since classical Antiquity. In grammar, translation was a special aspect of textual commentary or a form of commentary, and in rhetoric it was an exercise, a certain kind of imitation. Imitation via translation was a rhetorical practice of a heuristic nature, for, once a text is translated, it acquires a kind of primary status that turns it into a rhetorical model in itself. It would thus seem that translation can lead the way to invention. In the Roman context, translation 'generates new models' and 'displaces its Greek sources',[94] and the Roman model of translation as displacement and as the spur for rhetorical *inventio* reappears in the Middle Ages.

What Rita Copeland calls 'secondary' translations, Chaucer's *Legend of good women* and Gower's *Confessio amantis*, for instance, 'define themselves expressly in terms of difference: they call attention to their own position in a historical rupture and in so doing advance their own claims to displace their sources'.[95] They do this by employing the techniques of exegetical translation as strategies of topical invention, and thereby create a vernacular substitute for the source. In the prologue to the *Legend of good women*, Chaucer calls himself an *auctor*, therefore expressing his wish that his translations should not be read as translations or supplements to previous works, for they are specifically intended to efface their sources.[96]

In the Renaissance, the rediscovery of Greek and Latin texts fostered the *translatio studiorum* and led to engagement with the study of philology and the production of commentaries. In contrast to medieval theories and practices of translation, humanist translators were deeply concerned with the accuracy of their work because they were conscious of the special features of every language and of the idiosyncrasies of every author, which they strove to preserve in their translations.[97] Leonardo Bruni's *De interpretatione recta* (*c*. 1426), the first formal treatise on translation of the Renaissance, Étienne Dolet's *Manière de bien traduire d'une langue en l'autre* (1540), and Laurence Humphrey's *Interpretatio linguarum* (1559), recently translated into English for the first time,[98] contain the largest and most complete body of early Renaissance reflections on translation.[99]

Translation was also part of the English education system at the time; in grammar schools, for instance, it was used in the teaching of the classical languages. Roger Ascham's *The scholemaster* (1570) defines translation as the 'most common, and most commendable of all other exercises' for the purposes of teaching foreign tongues.[100] Ascham notes that this view was shared by both Quintilian, who 'preferreth translation before all other exercises' in the teaching of eloquence, and Pliny, also an advocate of 'double translating', an exercise which teaches 'not onelie all the hard congruities of Grammer, the choice of aptest wordes, the right framing of wordes and sentences, cumlines of figures and formes' but moreover 'inuention of Argumentes'.[101] Indeed, Ascham explains the benefits of translating in rhetorical terms, so that, to his mind, translation contributes to the formulation of arguments and to the perfection of the author's *dispositio* and *elocutio*.

Notwithstanding the many advantages derived from translation (from a useful classroom exercise to a tool for the dissemination of knowledge in works in the vernacular), the differences between it and inventive writing are constantly emphasised. To begin with, invention elevated poetic writings over translations, thus granting them a superior status. The reasoning was that, since translators do not invent but copy others, the outcome of translating inexorably remains inferior. Du Bellay, alluding in his *Deffence* (1549) to the Italian saying *traduttore, traditore*, attacks translators who, solely 'to make a scholarly name for themselves', choose to 'translate on trust languages of which they know nothing, such as Hebrew or Greek', and, 'to make a better impression, [...] take on the poets', who, in his opinion, are the most challenging of the writers.[102] As a result, they produce disastrous translations and in the process 'betray the authors they attempt to explain, depriving them of their glory'.[103] The particular difficulty of translating poets resides, Du Bellay explains, in their special inventive abilities, which turn true poets into a superior class of men: 'above all others, poets possess divine creativity', that is, *divinité d'invention*.[104] Naturally, Du Bellay is not unaware of the advantages of translation, and later adds that his remark 'does not apply to those who translate the greatest Greek and Latin poets on the command of princes and great lords', but instead applies 'to those translators who undertake such things frivolously and with a merry heart, as they say, and with the predictable results'.[105]

If, for Du Bellay, poets have been endowed with a *divinité d'invention* notably missing from translators, for Peletier, similarly, 'le Traducteur [...] s'asservit [...] à l'Invention d'autrui' [the translator [...] subjects himself [...] to the invention of another],[106] by which he becomes the truest kind of imitator. In Peletier's words: 'La plus vraie espèce d'Imitation, c'est de traduire: Car imiter n'est autre chose que vouloir faire ce que fait un Autre' [the truest form of imitation is translation: because to imitate is nothing but wishing to make what another does].[107] This subjection of the translator that Peletier mentions is also discussed by James I in 'To the favourable reader' preceding *The essayes of a prentise, in the divine art of poesie* (1584). For James I, it means lack of freedom: 'translations are limitat, and restraind in somethings, more then free inuentions are'.[108] The inherent restraints of translations render the job of the translator problematic in that no deviations from the path taken by the author are allowed — particularly when it comes to invention:

> Bot sen *Inuention*, is ane of the cheif vertewis in a Poete, it is best that ze inuent zour awin subiect, zour self, and not to compose of sene subiectis. Especially, translating any thing out of vther language, quhilk doing, ze not onely essay not zour awin ingyne of *Inuentioun*, bot be the same meanes, ze are bound, as to a staik, to follow that buikis phrasis, quhilk ze translate.[109]

As a poem prefaced to Robert Peterson's translation of *Galateo [...]; or rather, A treatise of the ma[n]ners and behauiours* (1576) puts it: 'Translatours can not mount: for though, ther armes with wings be spread, | In vaine they toile to take the flight, their feete are clogd with lead.'[110] For James I, poetry is not within everyone's reach, for to become a poet one needs to have '*Inuentioun*', which 'ze can not haue [...] except it come of Nature'.[111]

Gascoigne also makes invention the focal point of his distinction between a translator and an author, as the subtitle of his *A hundreth sundrie flowres bounde vp in one small poesie* (1573) indicates: *Gathered partely (by translation) in the fyne outlandish gardins of Euripides, Ouid, Petrarke, Ariosto, and others: And partly by inuention, out of our owne fruitefull orchardes in Englande*. In addition, in 'The letter of G. T. to his very friend H. W. concerning this worke', included in *A hundreth sundrie flowres* and possibly written by Gascoigne's acquaintance George Turbervile (G. T.), invention is systematically opposed to translation and imitation, and the former is invariably employed with more positive connotations. The work '*The clyming of an Eagles neast*', which Turbervile clarifies is 'of his [Master F. J.'s] owne invencion', is said 'to be a work worthy the reading'.[112] Regarding the sonnet 'Loue, hope, and death, do stirre in me such strife' by the same author, Turbervile speculates whether he 'borowed th'invention of an *Italian*', and states that 'were it a translation or invention [...] it is both prety and pithy'.[113] In the end, Turbervile concludes that he is 'sure that he [Master F. J.] wrote it, for he is no borrower of inventiõs'.[114] Nevertheless, when the time comes to judge the sonnet 'The stately dames of Rome, their pearles did weare', Turbervile is compelled to admit that it is 'but a translation': 'I am assured that it is but a translation, for I my selfe have seene the invention of an Italian'.[115]

After discussing the most prominent poets in English and their most renowned works, William Webbe in *A discourse of English poetrie* (1586) confesses that, having translated 'the two first Eclogues of Virgil', he could not think of a matter of his 'own invention' to 'lead to a less troublesome manner of writing'.[116] Likewise, when Puttenham is about to make his own inventory of some of the best English writers in the *Arte of English poesie* (1589), he asserts that the works of some of them 'appear to be but bare translations, other some matters of their own invention and very commendable'.[117] Undoubtedly, the fact that they are 'very commendable' has to do with them stemming from 'their owne inuention' as opposed to remaining simply on the level of 'bare translations'. In addition, Puttenham employs the expression 'to devise' as a close synonym for 'to invent', so as to contrast the inventing and translating of poetry: 'in Chaucer and Lydgate, the one writing the loves of Troilus and Cresseida, the other of the fall of princes, both by them translated, not devised'.[118] To Puttenham's mind, a translator cannot be upgraded to the category of poet precisely because of his lack of inventiveness: 'the very poet makes and contrives out of his own brain both the verse and matter of his poem, and not by any foreign copy or example, as doth the translator, who therefore may well be said a versifier, but not a poet'.[119] Yet, even if the merit of the translator/versifier is incomparably inferior to that of the poet, because translating enriches the English language Puttenham affirms that this activity deserves praise when carried out successfully: 'as I would wish every inventor which is the very poet to receive the praises of his invention, so would I not have a translator be ashamed to be acknown of this translation'.[120]

John Harington admits in *Orlando Furioso in English heroical verse* (1591) that he can claim no praise for the invention of his translation, 'having but borowed it'.[121] Like Peletier, who believed that 'une bonne Traduction vaut trop mieux qu'une mauvaise invention' [a good translation is worthier than a bad invention],[122] Harington 'would wish to be called rather one of the not worst translators then one of the meaner makers'.[123] In any case, he asserts, translating is as time-consuming as inventing: 'it is possible that if I would have employd that time that I have done upon this upon some invention of mine owne I could have by this made it have risen to a just volume'.[124] He bestows further dignity on his work by honestly presenting it as an actual translation rather than passing it off as an invention, and laments that many of his contemporaries frequently make such a deceitful claim and try to fly 'very high with stolen fethers': 'but I had rather men should see and know that I borrow all then that I steale any'.[125]

The French poet Agrippa d'Aubigné, in his Ode XIII, also defines as theft the full appropriation of the invention of others by concealing the fact that a text is a translation:

> C'est beaucoup de bien traduire,
> Mais c'est larcin de n'escrire
> Au dessus : traduction,
> Et puis on ne fait pas croire
> Qu'aux femmes et au vulgaire
> Que ce soit invention

[It is much to translate well, but it is a petty theft not to write 'translation' above, and so we only convince women and the common people that it is invention.][126]

Sébillet warns of the risks that invention entails, namely, attracting 'thieves of honour', which may eventually even discourage younger poets from inventing and lead them to opt for translation instead. In his words:

> chacun des Poètes famés et savants aime mieux en traduisant suivre la trace approuvée de tant d'âges et de bons esprits, qu'en entreprenant œuvre de son invention, ouvrir chemin aux voleurs de l'honneur dû à tout labeur vertueux.
>
> [every famous and wise poet prefers, by translating, to follow the path approved long ago and by great minds rather than to undertake a work of his own invention that will open a new path to the thieves of honour, as is the fate of every virtuous hard work.][127]

Versions and translations find in Sébillet a staunch advocate, for he defines them as 'le Poème plus fréquent et mieux reçu des estimés Poètes et des doctes lecteurs' [the more frequent and better received type of poem by great poets and learned readers alike].[128] Interestingly, the argument he puts forward to defend them is invention-based: after all, he says, they are 'de grand prix' [of great value] because they 'rendre la pure et argentine invention des Poètes' [render the pure and silvery invention of poets].[129]

Alexander Neville, in his preface to *The lamentable tragedie of Oedipus the sonne of Laius kyng of Thebes* (1563), also distinguishes between a translator and an author by means of the same criterion. Neville apologetically presents his tragedy as 'rudely translated', and begs the reader not to wonder 'at the grosenes of the Style: neither yet account the Inuentours dylygence disgraced by the Translators negligence'.[130] As if in an attempt to gain some recognition for his work, Neville states that his translation exhibits a margin of variation from the source, for 'he hath sometymes boldly presumed to erre frō his Author, rouynge at Randon where he lyst: adding and subtracting at pleasure', and in general carrying out considerable changes by 'rashly' employing his 'owne symple Invētion [...] wyshynge to please all'.[131] Neville's assertion is unusual for his time, considering that translation was then an activity allegedly alien to the inventive faculty. At the same time, one wonders to what extent such a confession might be intended not only as an explanation for the dissimilarities between the source text and his own rendering, but also as a strategy to claim, even if apologetically, extra recognition for his work: after all, it was more than a plain translation if it exhibited the fruits of his personal inventiveness.

4.4. Anti-Poetic Sentiment and the Reformation

Not infrequently, in contexts other than rhetorical, logical, or pro-poetic ones, 'invention' was employed with negative connotations. After all, it was an active capacity of the mind that could potentially be turned to a variety of purposes, including lying, feigning, and deceiving. In *The scholemaster* (1570), Ascham distrusts quick wits and 'inuentiuest heades', the reason being that 'quicke inuentors' tend to 'vse lesse helpe of diligence and studie than they ought to do', and in any case less than slower minds and tongues.[132] Anthony Munday's preface to *Zelavto* (1580) appears to share Ascham's suspicion when it says that 'secrete Serpentes' and 'ambicious heads' devise 'spitefull speeches' to 'confound' men with 'their craftyest inuentions'.[133] What is more, according to Ascham the 'fansies, opinions, errors, and faultes' proper to 'inward inuention' corrupt 'mens myndes' just like 'ill humors' corrupt 'mens bodies'.[134] The English dictionaries of the time record these negative views, which contrast with the impeccable image that, according to Grahame Castor (1964), the term still enjoyed in France. In Richard Huloet's *Abcedarium anglico latinum* (1552), *sycophantia* is defined as 'inuention of crafty accusations, & lies', and *sophisma* as 'inuention, or sophisticall oration, seamynge to be trewe, when it is false'.[135] John Baret for his part talks about 'a lye or leasing, a false inuention';[136] Cooper, Thomas Thomas, and Randle Cotgrave agree that calumny means 'a malicions inuention';[137] and, for Cooper and Thomas, *mendacium* signifies 'a lie: a leasing: a false inuention'.[138] *Machinatione* is understood by Florio as 'a complot, a conspiracie, a contriuing, a framing, a subtile inuention or deuising',[139] and by Cotgrave as 'a subtill plot, or conspiracie; a craftie inuention'.[140]

The distrust of invention is entangled in complex ways with attacks against poetry based on poetry's supposed connection with feigning, deceit, and the theatre, which is to say, immorality. Illustrative of this are Geoffrey Whitney's words: 'man is fraile, and all his thoughtes are sinne | And of him selfe he can no good inuent'.[141] For this reason, he says, authors 'before they oughte beginne, | Should call on GOD, from whome all grace is sent'.[142] Otherwise, if unsupervised by God, nothing of value can be expected to come from human inventiveness. A shared underlying idea surfaces in John Davies's 'T'insult vpon the wretched, is a crime', included in *A select second husband* (1616), which denounces 'some *idle Poets* of our *Time*' because they 'ouersee great *Reason*, for small *Ryme*', 'and from *Inuention*, take what comes vnwaigh'd', that is to say, unmediated 'by *Iudgement*, with the *Understandings* ayde',[143] and hence without the caution it requires.

In contrast to poets, orators received comparatively gentle treatment, and attacks against rhetoric took place on the grounds that it operated in the realm of opinion, probability, and contingency, and therefore could not promise absolute truths. Alberico Gentili's *Commentatio* (1593), cast in the form of a legal treatise, wonders why grammarians, logicians, painters, and rhetoricians enjoyed what he calls 'immunities' while these were denied to poets. After all, poets also had moral duties towards society as a whole, which they performed through 'invented deeds and fictitious actions'.[144] The typically medieval interpretation of poetry as the handmaiden of philosophy, still current in the Renaissance, neutralised the charges of immorality at the cost of subjecting poetry to ethics. The allegorical potential of poetry was used to defend it against charges of triviality, falsehood, and immorality, the argument being that poetry revealed concealed truths, and that it either set examples of virtue or attempted to dissuade from vice through negative exemplarity.

Platonic doctrine was still the source of many of the objections to poetry that circulated at the time, among them the ignorance of the artist (the poet was a mere imitator at three removes from the truth) and the appeal of poetry to the irrational part of the soul, and therefore to appearances and the sensuous world. On these premises, it is easy to see why the relationship between poetry on the one hand and truth and morality on the other was problematic. Poetry was effectively accused of exciting ignoble passions and lacking utility, and, as a result, of being an unprofitable occupation and a distracting idle force.[145] A common reply to Platonic objections was that, if according to Plato poets were divinely inspired, their poetry could by no means be immoral or false. The Horatian doctrine of poetry's ability to teach and delight was also employed by the advocates of poetry, who, in addition, and drawing on Aristotle, presented the mimetic character of poetry in a positive light. Neoplatonists even admitted that poets could directly imitate divine ideas by moving above the sensible and material world to the truer realm of the divine. Given that, for Neoplatonism, both art and nature copied the same original, it was possible that the products of art might sometimes excel nature itself.

Anti-poetic sentiment, which formed and shaped the works of authors like Sidney, Spenser, and Milton, was intertwined with religious matters when it was appropriated by the early English Protestants. From then on, the voices against poetry enjoyed extra authority and were held as a sign of moral credibility and respectability. Anti-poetic and anti-theatrical sentiment became dominant from the 1570s, which coincided with a revival of early English Protestantism. In 1573, for instance, the publisher John Day printed an edition of *The whole workes of W. Tyndall, Iohn Frith and Doct. Barnes*. Not coincidentally, works with the sole purpose of defending poetry and imaginative writing in general made an appearance in the 1570s. These defences of the art are in fact the earliest and most profound reflections on poetry of the English Renaissance.[146] Richard Willis's *De re poetica disputatio* (1573), appended to Willis's *Poematum liber*, was the first formal defence of poetry to appear in England.[147] Titles such as John Northbrooke's *A treatise against dicing, dancing, plays, and interludes* (c. 1577) and Stephen Gosson's *The schoole of abuse* (1579) are exponents of Puritan hostility to art in general, and to poetry and the stage in particular. Through moral arguments, for instance, Gosson encourages readers to refrain from practising or consuming poetry, music, and plays: 'Let us but shut uppe our ears to Poets, Pypers, and Players, pull our feete back from resort to Theaters, and turne away our eyes from beholding of vanitie'.[148]

Gosson accuses poets of being 'effeminate writers, unprofitable members, and utter enimies to vertue',[149] whose 'fables' 'unfold theyr mischiefe [...] and disperse their poyson through all the worlde'.[150] At the roots of Gosson's objection to poetry and drama lies their fictive character, which he interprets as sheer lying and thus finds unjustifiable, for 'every lye is sinne, for the deuill is the father of all lyes'.[151] Yet Gosson does not entirely dismiss poetry, for he recognises the 'right vse of aunciert Poetrie' in martial service to foster military courage in men.[152] Gosson appears to object to human poetry in part from the conviction that, on the one hand, the mere putting into words of poetry is an act of the senses that unavoidably spoils the ideal, and, on the other, that the pleasure derived from poetry is of a sensual type. Unlike the poetry of the Bible, directly inspired in man by God, human poetry is both made and perceived through man's infected senses.[153]

Indeed, the Puritans had to deal with the fact that poetry was present in the Scriptures as well. To this they responded either by arguing that human poetry was incomparable to that of the Scriptures irrespective of the poet's skills and efforts, or, contrariwise, by affirming that the poetry of the Bible sanctioned human poetry, even if the poetry of the Scriptures was *sui generis*.[154] The latter opinion was held by Robert Southwell, who wrote the following in *Saint Peters complaint, with other poemes* (1595):

> Poets by abusing their talent, and making the follies and faynings of loue, the customarie subiect of their base endeuours, have so discredited this facultie, that a Poet, a louer, and a Liar, are by many reckoned but three wordes of one signification. But the vanitie of men, cannot counterpoyse the authoritie of God, who deliuering many parts of Scripture in verse, and by his Apostle willing us to exercise our deuotion in Himnes and spirituall Sonnets, warranteth the Arte to bee good, and the use allowable.[155]

The Puritans distinguished between good and proper poetry, and what was immoral, idle, and dangerous amusement.[156] Although plays could be useful and acceptable provided that they disseminated Christian virtues and ideas, they were generally viewed with suspicion regardless of their moral qualities, particularly if they became too successful. Not by chance, throughout history, anti-theatrical prejudice has often emerged more strongly precisely when drama has enjoyed its greatest success, and hence when it has become a discourse competing with Church and state.[157] In 1577, drama was publicly condemned for the first time: on 3 November, in the context of a Sunday sermon at Paul's Cross in London, a city at the time gripped by the plague, the preacher identified sin as the cause of the plague, and plays as the origin of sin. In other words, plays were made accountable for the plague.[158]

Attacks against poetry on the part of preachers and divines spurred a wave of angry responses to such charges. Thomas Nashe, in *Pierce penilesse* (1592), admits having been 'censured among some dul-headed ★ Diuines', whom he considers 'enemies of Poetry'; for him it is clear that 'there goes more exquisite paines and puritie of wit, to the writing of one such rare Poem as Rosamond, than to a hundred of' their 'dunsticall ★ Sermons'.[159] Nashe accuses them of having 'no elquence but Tautologies', 'no wit to moue, no passion to vrge, but onely an ordinary forme of preaching, blowen vp by vse', which reveals 'no inuention'.[160] This forces them to commit plagiarism: 'I stole this note out of Beza or Marlorat', Nashe bids them to confess.[161] By contrast, the pressure to invent endured by authors is unknown to preachers: 'Should we (as you) borrow all out of others, and gather nothing of our selues, our names would be baffuld on euerie Booke-sellers stall, and not a Chandlers Mustard-pot but would wipe his mouth with our wast paper'. 'Newe Herrings new we must cry, euery time we make our selues publique, or else we shall be christened with a hundred new titles of Idiotisme', Nashe remarks.[162]

Likewise, when Lodge reprimands Gosson in his *Defence of poetry*, he does so by discrediting him for appropriating the material of others. In other words, Lodge disparages Gosson for lack of invention, and by doing so he simultaneously underlines the complexity and merit of the work of the poets which Gosson so ignorantly attacks:

> Tell me GOSSON was all your owne you wrote there? did you borow nothing of your neyghbours? Out of what booke patched you out Cicero's Oration? Whence set you Catulin's Inuectiue. Thys is one thing, *alienam olet lucernam, non tuam*; so that your helper may wisely reply upon you with Virgil:
>
>> *Hos ego versiculos feci: tulit alter honores.*
>> I made these verses, others bear the name.[163]

Religious discourse taints invention, deems it an ally of fancy, and understands it overall as a faculty that allows for man-made ideas in contradiction of, and in competition with, God's dictates. As such, it draws man away from salvation and closer to idolatry and heresy. For Hugh Latimer, it is altogether impossible that 'mans inuētions and fansies, coude plese god better than goddis preceptis, or straunge thinges better than his owne'.[164] Latimer fears 'these worldlynges' that 'pull downe the lyuely fayth, and full confidence that men haue in Christe, and sette up an other fayth, an other confidence of theyr owne makynge' based on 'workes of theyr owne inuention'.[165] For Latimer, heretical concoctions are the realm of Catholicism and its idolatrous rituals, including 'payntynge of ymages, candels, palmes, ashes, holie water, and new seruice of mennes inuentyng, as though man could inuente a better waye to honoure God with, then god hymselfe hath apoynted'.[166] John Foxe discusses in similar terms the relation between 'human inventions' and idolatry in his *Acts and monuments* (*The book of martyrs*, 1563). According to Foxe, for instance, in the reign of Edward III 'the light of the gospel of Christ was greatly eclipsed and darkened with human inventions, burthensome ceremonies, and gross idolatry',[167] and he refers to practices such as the selling of 'prayers for money' as 'foolish inventions'.[168] Likewise, in a deeply pessimistic sermon, John Knox claims that 'lies and men's inventions holden in authority' only lead to seeing 'the true religion of our God, and the zealous observers of the same [...] trodden under the feet of such as in their heart say that there is no God'.[169] That invention was associated with Catholicism, idolatry, and man-made ideas with no foundation in the Scriptures is again confirmed by Marlowe, who in *Massacre at Paris* (1593) makes the King of Navarre declare war 'Against the proud disturbers of the faith', that is, 'the *Guise*, the Pope, and King of *Spaine* | Who set themselves to tread us under foot, | And rent our true religion from this land' by means of 'their strange inventions'.[170] As will be discussed in the second section of the next chapter, such accusations and misgivings were shared by the closest of this concept's allies, the equally compelling faculty of the imagination.

Notes to Chapter 4

1. Thomas Nashe, *Pierce Penilesse his Supplication to the Diuell* (London: printed by Abell Ieffes for Iohn Busbie, 1592), I1r.
2. Rosemary Freeman, *English Emblem Books* (London: Chatto & Windus, 1948); Peter M. Daly, *The English Emblem and the Continental Tradition* (New York: AMS Press, 1988).
3. Robert John Clements, 'Iconography on the Nature and Inspiration of Poetry in Renaissance Emblem Literature', *Publications of the Modern Language Association of America*, 70.4 (1955), 781–804 (p. 781). See also Robert John Clements, 'The Cult of the Poet in Renaissance Emblem Literature', *Publications of the Modern Language Association of America*, 59.3 (1944), 672–85.
4. Clements, 'Iconography', p. 804. For more on the connection between emblem books and literature in the Renaissance, see Robert J. Clements, *Picta Poesis: Literary and Humanistic Theory in Renaissance Emblem Books* (Rome: Edizioni di Storia e Letteratura, 1960).
5. Henry Peacham, *Minerua Britanna; or, A Garden of Heroical Deuises* (London: printed by Wa: Dight, 1612), L2v (emphasis in original).
6. George Gascoigne, 'The Delectable History of Sundry Adventures Passed by Dan Bartholmew of Bathe', in *The Complete Works of George Gascoigne*, I, ed. by John William Cunliffe (1907), pp. 96-137 (p. 96).
7. Howell, *Poetics, Rhetoric and Logic*, p. 87. Howell distinguishes three types of literature: non-mimetic writings (orations, historical writings, and philosophical arguments), mimetic writings (tragedy, comedy, epic poetry, and prose narrative), and the literature of fable (which deals with imagined events and characters).
8. Wilson, *Arte of Rhetorique*, pp. 387–88.
9. Sidney, p. 116.
10. Sébillet, p. 56.
11. Peletier du Mans, p. 252.
12. Pierre de Ronsard, 'Abrégé de l'art poétique français' [1565], in *Traités de poétique et de rhétorique de la Renaissance*, ed. by Francis Goyet (Paris: Librairie Générale Française, 1990), pp. 465–93 (p. 468).
13. Ronsard, 'Abrégé', p. 471.
14. William Shakespeare, 'The Life of Henry the Fifth' [1623], ed. by Rory Loughnane, in *New Oxford Shakespeare*, II, 2301–85 (Prologue. 1–2; p. 2311).
15. George Gascoigne, 'In Prayse of a Countesse', in *The Complete Works of George Gascoigne*, I, ed. by John William Cunliffe (1907), pp. 336-37 (p. 336).
16. Edmund Spenser, 'Amoretti and Epithalamion' [1595], in *The Poetical Works of Edmund Spenser*, ed. by J. C. Smith and E. de Selincourt (Oxford: Oxford University Press, 1932), pp. 561–84 (p. 562). 'G. W. Senior' has been identified as Geoffrey Whitney, father; see Rudolf Gottfried, 'The "G. W. Senior" and "G. W. I." of Spenser's *Amoretti*', *Modern Language Quarterly*, 3 (1942), 543–46.
17. Geoffrey Whitney, *A Choice of Emblemes, and Other Deuises, for the Moste Parte Gathered Out of Sundrie Writers, Englished and Moralized* (Leyden: printed by Francis Raphelengius, 1586), b2v.
18. Whitney, b2v.
19. John Davies of Hereford, *The Scourge of Folly* (London: printed by E[dward] A[llde] for Richard Redmer, 1611), B6r (emphasis in original).
20. John Davies of Hereford, *Wittes Pilgrimage* (London: printed [by R. Bradock] for Iohn Browne, 1605), H4r (emphasis in original).
21. George Gascoigne, 'Appendix', in *The Complete Works of George Gascoigne*, I, ed. by John William Cunliffe (1907), pp. 474-502 (p. 491).
22. Thomas Elyot, *The Dictionary of Syr Thomas Eliot Knyght* (London: printed by Thomae Bertheleti, 1538), K1v.
23. Thomas Thomas, Yy5r (my emphasis).
24. Florio, *A VVorlde of Wordes*, Aa3v, Oo1v.
25. Henry Dethick's *Oratio in laudem poëseos* (c. 1575) and Alberico Gentili's *Commentatio* (1593) are among the few works that entirely overlook invention. For more on Dethick, see J. W. Binns,

'Henry Dethick in Praise of Poetry: The First Appearance in Print of an Elizabethan Treatise', *Library*, 30.5 (1975), 199–216. For an edition of Dethick, see Henry Dethick, 'Oratio in laudem poëseos' [c. 1575], in *Latin Treatises on Poetry from Renaissance England*, ed. and trans. by Binns, pp. 1–55.

26. John Hoskins, *Directions for Speech and Style* [c. 1599], ed. by Hoyt H. Hudson (Princeton: Princeton University Press, 1935), p. 4.
27. Hoskins, *Directions*, p. 4.
28. Ben Jonson, 'Discoveries' [1641], ed. by Lorna Hutson, in *Cambridge Edition of the Works of Ben Jonson*, VII: *1641, Bibliography*, pp. 495–596 (p. 572). According to John Aubrey, Ben Jonson called Hoskins 'father' ('*Brief Lives*': *A Modern English Version*, ed. by Richard Barber (Woodbridge: Boydell, 1982), p. 170). For more on the relationship between Jonson and Hoskins, see Gary R. Grund, 'Ben Jonson, John Hoskyns, and the Anti-Ciceronian Movement', *Studies in English Literature*, 54 (1977), 33–53.
29. Gascoigne, 'Certayne Notes of Instruction', pp. 465-66.
30. Gascoigne, 'Certayne Notes of Instruction', p. 466.
31. Gascoigne, 'Certayne Notes of Instruction', p. 466.
32. Gascoigne, 'Certayne Notes of Instruction', p. 466. Gillian Austen in fact believes that invention 'may be seen as the defining principle in his [Gascoigne's] writing' and that he 'reinterpreted Wilson's (and his predecessors') formal schema when he came to offer his own definition of invention' (*George Gascoigne* (Woodbridge: Brewer, 2008), p. 2).
33. Gascoigne, 'To Al Yong Gentlemen, and Generally to the Youth of England', in *The Complete Works of George Gascoigne*, I, ed. by John William Cunliffe (1907), pp. 9–14 (p. 13). These poems Gascoigne calls 'Floures', in opposition to 'Hearbes' and 'Weedes'. For more on Gascoigne's use of the gardening trope, and garden rhetoric in general in the sixteenth and early seventeenth centuries, see Susan Staub, 'Dissembling his Art: "Gascoigne's Gardnings"', *Renaissance Studies*, 25.1 (2011), 95–110.
34. Spenser, 'Amoretti and Epithalamion', p. 562.
35. Edmund Spenser, 'Three Proper, and Wittie, Familiar Letters' [1580], in *Poetical Works of Edmund Spenser*, ed. by Smith and de Selincourt, pp. 609–32 (p. 612).
36. Spenser, 'Letters', p. 628.
37. Spenser, 'Letters', p. 628. The *Nine comedies* have not survived. What is more, they may not even have existed at the time of Harvey's letter, in which case Harvey's words function as exhortation for their composition; see Allan Gilbert, 'Were Spenser's *Nine Comedies* Lost?', *Modern Language Notes*, 73.4 (1958), 241–43.
38. Puttenham, p. 113.
39. John Lyly, *Euphues and His England* (London: printed [by T. East] for Gabriell Cawood, 1580), Z2v (my emphasis).
40. Thomas Nashe, *A Pleasant Comedie, Called Summers Last Will and Testament* (London: printed by Simon Stafford for Walter Burre, 1600), F1r (my emphasis).
41. William Shakespeare, 'Shake-speares Sonnets [including "A Lover's Complaint"]' [1609], ed. by Francis X. Connor, in *New Oxford Shakespeare*, I, 1435–1516 (p. 1471).
42. Shakespeare, 'Sonnets', p. 1478.
43. Peacham, P4v.
44. Shakespeare, 'Love's Labour's Lost', IV. 2. 109 (p. 496).
45. Shakespeare, 'Love's Labour's Lost', IV. 2. 110–11 (p. 496).
46. John Lyly, *Sixe Court Comedies* (London: printed by William Stansby for Edward Blount, 1632), A4r.
47. Lyly, *Sixe Court Comedies*, A3v (emphasis in original).
48. For a summary of the importance of *inventio* in sixteenth-century Italian criticism, see Langer, pp. 137–38.
49. Castelvetro, p. 275.
50. Castelvetro, p. 42.
51. Castelvetro, p. 50.
52. Castelvetro, p. 41.

53. Castelvetro, p. 41.
54. For more on Castelvetro's ideas on poetry, see Bernard Weinberg, 'Castelvetro's Theory of Poetics', in *Critics and Criticism: Essays in Method*, ed. by R. S. Crane and others (Chicago: University of Chicago Press, 1957), pp. 146–68.
55. As David Wilson-Okamura explains, Castelvetro and Speroni 'prefer Homer' to Virgil 'for similar reasons': 'Like most of their contemporaries, Castelvetro and Speroni observed that Homer sows from the bag, Virgil from the hand. Castelvetro argues that this is a defect in Virgil, because brevity is inimical to wonder. In order to experience wonder, the reader of a poem must be able to visualize what is being described. Detailed descriptions — of thoughts, actions, costumes, scenery, and emotions — are therefore necessary. Homer provides these things in abundance, and in doing so shows himself a true poet; Virgil, however, mars all with his perverse addiction to minimalism. [...] For Speroni, ornament is the very essence of poetry; therefore flowery is good and brevity is bad' (*Virgil in the Renaissance* (Cambridge: Cambridge University Press, 2010), pp. 133–34).
56. John Eliot, *Ortho-Epia Gallica: Eliots Fruits for the French* (London: printed by [Richard Field for] Iohn VVolfe, 1593), G1r.
57. The extracts from the preface quoted here were not included in the prefaces to later editions, such as those of 1609 and 1611.
58. Chapman, A2v (emphasis in original).
59. Philip Ford, 'Virgil *versus* Homer: Reception, Imitation, Identity in the French Renaissance', in *Virgilian Identities in the French Renaissance*, ed. by Phillip John Usher and Isabelle Fernbach (Cambridge: Brewer, 2012), pp. 141–60 (pp. 141–42). Ford, p. 142, explains: 'The works of Homer were unknown in the West throughout the Middle Ages except by reputation, and it was not until around 1353 that Petrarch finally realized his ambition of obtaining a manuscript of the *Iliad* and the *Odyssey*. Even then, he was unable to read them, relying eventually on a word-for-word translation into Latin by Leontius Pilatus. It was not until the last decades of the fifteenth century, however, that the Homeric epics became known to a wider audience, thanks in part to the *editio princeps* of the Greek text in 1488, and also to the various Latin translations of Homer that found their way into print. Amongst other things, this led to a re-evaluation of Virgil.'
60. John Dryden, 'Fables Ancient and Modern: Preface' [1700], in *The Works of John Dryden*, 20 vols (Berkeley: University of California Press, 1956–2000), VII: *Poems, 1697-1700*, ed. by Vinton A. Dearing (Berkeley: University of California Press, 2000), pp. 24-47 (p. 31; emphasis in original).
61. Dryden, 'Preface', p. 558.
62. John Dryden, 'A Parallel between Painting and Poetry' [1695], in *Works of John Dryden*, xx: *Prose 1691–1698: 'De arte graphica' and Shorter Works*, ed. by A. E. Wallace Maurer and George R. Guffey (1989), pp. 38–77 (p. 61).
63. Dryden, 'Parallel', p. 61.
64. Dryden, 'Parallel', p. 61.
65. Lodge, p. 10.
66. Dryden, 'Preface', pp. 557–58.
67. Thomas Nashe 'To the Gentlemen Students of Both Universities', in Robert Greene, *Menaphon* (London: printed by T[homas] O[rwin] for Sampson Clarke, 1589), **1r–A3r (**1v).
68. Nashe, 'To the Gentlemen Students of Both Universities', **1v (emphasis in original).
69. Nashe, 'To the Gentlemen Students of Both Universities', **1v.
70. Nashe, 'To the Gentlemen Students of Both Universities', **2r.
71. Nashe, 'To the Gentlemen Students of Both Universities', A2v. Peele likewise employs 'invention' as a term of positive assessment of poetry in 'How George read a play booke to a gentleman', where George is said to possess 'a Poeticall inuention of his owne' (George Peele, *Merrie Conceited Iests of George Peele Gentleman* (London: printed by G[eorge] P[urslowe] for F. Faulkner, 1627), D2v).
72. Huarte was highly influential in English letters and thought; cf. Juan Huarte de San Juan, *The Examination of Mens Wits* [1594], trans. by Richard Carew, ed. by Rocío G. Sumillera (London:

Modern Humanities Research Association, 2014), pp. 23–30, 53–67. All references to Huarte's work are to this, Richard Carew's translation into English.
73. Huarte de San Juan, p. 131.
74. Huarte de San Juan, p. 131.
75. Huarte de San Juan, p. 178.
76. Huarte de San Juan, p. 178. The image of invention as a fountain was widely used in the sixteenth century. For instance, it appears in Rollo MacIlmaine, *The Logike of the Moste Excellent Philosopher P. Ramus Martyr, Newly Translated, and in Diuers Places Corrected, after the Mynde of the Author* (London: printed by Thomas Vautroullier, 1574), B1v ('invention is the fountayne of all sciences').
77. Huarte de San Juan, p. 179.
78. Huarte de San Juan, p. 179.
79. Cox, A3r.
80. Cox, A3r.
81. Huarte de San Juan, p. 177.
82. Huarte de San Juan, p. 178.
83. Huarte de San Juan, p. 177.
84. White, p. 84.
85. Nashe, 'To the Gentlemen Students of Both Universities', **1v.
86. Nashe, *Pierce Penilesse*, F1r.
87. Gabriel Harvey, *Pierces Supererogation; or, A New Prayse of the Old Asse: A Preparatiue to Certaine Larger Discourses, Intituled Nashes s. Fame* (London: printed by Iohn Vvolfe, 1593), H4v.
88. Gabriel Harvey, I1r.
89. Gabriel Harvey, B2v, E4r, B3r.
90. Gabriel Harvey, C1v.
91. For a full account of the Harvey–Nashe quarrel, see White, pp. 84–96.
92. Dryden, 'Parallel', pp. 61–62.
93. Still, Dryden's exaltation of invention runs parallel to his acknowledgement of the need to learn from the great models of the past and to acquire and respect the formal precepts established by tradition, within which invention should operate at all times. These should not be broken by, for example, daring proposals such as Lope de Vega's *Arte nuevo de hacer comedias* (1609), of which Dryden disapproves, for, he says, poets should after all 'be content to follow our Masters, who understood Nature better' (Dryden, 'Parallel', p. 62).
94. Copeland, p. 34.
95. Copeland, p. 180.
96. Copeland, p. 186.
97. Sweeting, p. 47. See also Valerie Worth-Stylianou, '*Translatio* and Translation in the Renaissance: From Italy to France', in *Cambridge History of Literary Criticism*, III: *The Renaissance*, ed. by Glyn P. Norton (2000), pp. 127–35 (p. 132).
98. Laurence Humphrey, 'Interpretatio linguarum' [1559], trans. by Gordon Kendal, in *English Renaissance Translation Theory*, ed. by Neil Rhodes, Gordon Kendal, and Louise Wilson (London: Modern Humanities Research Association, 2013), pp. 263–94.
99. For further analyses of Renaissance theories on translation, see Mauri Furlan, 'La retórica de la traducción en el Renacimiento: Elementos para la constitución de una teoría de la traducción renacentista' (unpublished doctoral dissertation, University of Barcelona, 2002); Massimiliano Morini, *Tudor Translation in Theory and Practice* (Aldershot: Ashgate, 2006); Neil Rhodes, 'Introduction', in *English Renaissance Translation Theory*, ed. by Neil Rhodes, Gordon Kendal, and Louise Wilson (London: Modern Humanities Research Association, 2013), pp. 1-67. See also Neil Rhodes, 'Translating for the Commonwealth', in *Common: The Development of Literary Culture in Sixteenth-Century England* (Oxford: Oxford University Press, 2018), pp. 111-156.
100. Ascham, p. 243.
101. Ascham, pp. 243, 244–45. Pliny actually 'seems to have had in mind alternative possibilities: translation from Greek into Latin *or* from Latin into Greek', and not Ascham's double-translation method (William E. Miller, 'Double Translation in English Humanistic Education', *Studies in the Renaissance*, 10 (1963), 163–74 (p. 168; emphasis in original)).

102. Du Bellay, 'Defence and Illustration', pp. 49–50.
103. Du Bellay, 'Defence and Illustration', p. 49.
104. Du Bellay, 'Defence and Illustration', p. 50; Joachim Du Bellay, *La Deffence, et Illustration de la langue françoyse (1549)*, ed. by Jean-Charles Monferran (Geneva: Droz, 2001), p. 90.
105. Du Bellay, 'Defence and Illustration', p. 50.
106. Peletier du Mans, p. 262.
107. Peletier du Mans, p. 262.
108. James I, King of England, *The Essayes of a Prentise, in the Divine Art of Poesie* (Edinburgh: printed by Thomas Vautroullier, 1584), C3v. J. J. Blanchot observes that James I's treatise does not partake of the tradition of the fifteenth- and sixteenth-century Scottish 'Makars' (it does not draw examples from Scottish poets of the previous century, for instance), but instead is fundamentally influenced by the French and the English ('L'Art poétique de Jacques VI d'Écosse', in *Recherches sur l'histoire de la poétique*, ed. by Marc-Mathieu Münch (Nancy: Lang, 1984), pp. 7–28). See also Ronald S. Jack, 'James VI and Renaissance Poetic Theory', *English*, 16 (1967), 208–11.
109. James I, M2v (emphasis in original).
110. Robert Peterson, *Galateo of Maister Iohn Della Casa, Archebishop of Beneuenta; or rather, A Treatise of the Ma[n]ners and Behauiours, it Behoueth a Man to Vse and Eschewe, in his Familiar Conuersation* (London: printed [by Henry Middleton] for Raufe Newbery, 1576), ¶2v.
111. James I, M3r.
112. Gascoigne, 'Appendix', p. 491.
113. Gascoigne, 'Appendix', p. 493.
114. Gascoigne, 'Appendix', p. 495.
115. Gascoigne, 'Appendix', p. 495.
116. Webbe, p. 123.
117. Puttenham, p. 147.
118. Puttenham, p. 155.
119. Puttenham, p. 93.
120. Puttenham, p. 339.
121. John Harington, 'Preface; or, Brief Apologie of Poetrie', in *Orlando Furioso: Translated into English Heroical Verse by Sir John Harington (1591)*, ed. by Robert McNulty (Oxford: Clarendon Press, 1972), pp. 2–16 (p. 14).
122. Peletier du Mans, p. 263.
123. Harington, p. 14.
124. Harington, p. 14.
125. Harington, p. 14.
126. Agrippa D'Aubigné, *Le Printemps: Stances et Odes* [composed 1570], ed. by Fernand Desonay (Geneva: Droz, 1952), p. 103 (ll. 181–86).
127. Sébillet, pp. 145–46.
128. Sébillet, p. 146.
129. Sébillet, p. 146.
130. Alexander Neville, *The Lamentable Tragedie of Oedipus the Sonne of Laius Kyng of Thebes Out of Seneca* (London: printed by Thomas ColWell, 1563), A5r.
131. Neville, A5r, A7v.
132. Ascham, p. 263.
133. Anthony Munday, *Zelauto: The Fountaine of Fame* (London: printed by Iohn Charlevvood, 1580), N2r –N2v.
134. Ascham, p. 263.
135. Richard Huloet, *Abcedarium Anglico Latinum* (London: [S. Mierdman] ex officina Gulielmi Riddel, 1552), R2r.
136. John Baret, *An Aluearie; or, Triple Dictionarie: In Englishe, Latin, and French* (London: printed by Henry Denham, 1574), Nn3r.
137. Cooper, P5v; Thomas Thomas, H6v; Randle Cotgrave, *A Dictionarie of the French and English Tongues* (London: printed by Adam Islip, 1611), N5v.
138. Cooper, Gggg5r; Thomas Thomas, Nn2v.

139. Florio, *A VVorlde of Wordes*, S3v.
140. Cotgrave, Ddd4r.
141. Whitney, ***2v.
142. Whitney, ***2v.
143. John Davies of Hereford, *A Select Second Husband for Sir Thomas Ouerburie's Wife, Now a Matchlesse Widow* (London: printed by Thomas Creede and Barnard Allsopp for Iohn Marriott, 1616), D8v (emphasis in original).
144. Gentili, p. 91.
145. Russell A. Fraser, *The War against Poetry* (Princeton: Princeton University Press, 1970), p. 9; Spingarn, pp. 5–6. Moreover, writing poetry was stigmatised as an effeminising activity capable of fostering political disorder. This distrust can be discerned even in emblem literature; see Robert John Clements, 'Condemnation of the Poetic Profession in Renaissance Emblem Literature', *Studies in Philology*, 43 (1946), 213–32.
146. G. Gregory Smith, *Elizabethan Critical Essays*, 2 vols (Oxford: Clarendon Press, 1904), I, xv–xvii.
147. For more on this subject, see Margaret W. Ferguson, *Trials of Desire: Renaissance Defenses of Poetry* (New Haven and London: Yale University Press, 1983).
148. Stephen Gosson, *The Schoole of Abuse* (London: printed [by Thomas Dawson] for Thomas Woodcocke, 1587), D6v.
149. Gosson, *Schoole of Abuse*, A7r.
150. Gosson, *Schoole of Abuse*, A6r.
151. Stephen Gosson, *Playes Confuted in Fiue Actions* (London: printed for Thomas Gosson, 1582), E4v.
152. Gosson, *Schoole of Abuse*, B3v. It has been argued that, behind Gosson's criticism of music and dancing, there exists a more general critique of English court life, its immoral idleness, its concern with leisure and pleasures, and its indifference to discipline and service. Gosson yearns instead for a warrior aristocracy; see Robert Matz, *Defending Literature in Early Modern England: Renaissance Literary Theory in Social Context* (Cambridge and New York: Cambridge University Press, 2000), p. 61.
153. Jacob Bronowski suggested that Sidney, whose *Defence* was meant as a reply to *The schoole*, understood poetry exactly as Gosson did, and that for both 'the poem is only the shadow of an ideal poetry: a shadow cast through the senses' (*The Poet's Defence* (Cambridge: Cambridge University Press, 1939), p. 39). By contrast, Andrew D. Weiner believes that, for Sidney, the best poetry managed to skip out sensual perception and thus man's corrupted senses, for it appealed directly to the imagination (*Sir Philip Sidney and the Poetics of Protestantism: A Study of Contexts* (Minneapolis: University of Minnesota Press, 1978), p. 40). For a discussion on the differing ideas of dramatic mimesis in Gosson and Sidney, see Cinta Zunino-Garrido, *Mimesis and the Representation of Experience: Dramatic Theory and Practice in Pre-Shakespearean Comedy (1560–1590)* (Frankfurt: Lang, 2012), pp. 21–57. Fraser, p. 7, notes that 'the hatred of poetry is not peculiar to the Puritan'.
154. Lawrence A. Sasek, *The Literary Temper of the English Puritans* (Baton Rouge: Louisiana State University Press, 1961), pp. 65–66.
155. Robert Southwell, *Saint Peters Complaint, with Other Poemes* (London: printed by [John Windet for] Iohn Wolfe, 1595), A2r.
156. Sasek, p. 110.
157. Jonas Barish, *The Antitheatrical Prejudice* (London and Berkeley: University of California Press, 1981), p. 191.
158. Fraser, p. 13.
159. Nashe, *Pierce Penilesse*, F1r.
160. Nashe, *Pierce Penilesse*, F1r.
161. Nashe, *Pierce Penilesse*, F1r.
162. Nashe, *Pierce Penilesse*, F1r.
163. Lodge, p. 28.
164. Hugh Latimer, *The Sermon that the Reuerende Father in Christ, Hugh Latimer, Byshop of Worcester,*

made to the Clergie, in the Co[n]uocatio[n], before the Parlyament Began, the 9. Day of June (London: printed by Thomas Berthelet, 1537), A7r.
165. Latimer, *Sermon [...] made to the Clergie*, C7r–C7v.
166. Hugh Latimer, *A Notable Sermo[n] of Ye Reuerende Father Maister Hughe Latemer* (London: printed by Ihon Day and Wylliam Seres, 1548), C3v–C4r.
167. John Foxe, *Fox's Book of Martyrs; or, The Acts and Monuments of the Christian Church* [1563], ed. by John Malham and T. Pratt (Philadelphia: Woodward, 1830), p. 513.
168. Foxe, p. 387.
169. John Knox, *The History of the Reformation of Religion in Scotland* [1559–66], ed. by William McGavin (Glasgow: Blackie & Son and A. Fullarton, & Co.; Dublin: WM. Curry Jun. & Co.; London: Simpkin & Marshall, 1832), p. 480.
170. Christopher Marlowe, 'Massacre at Paris' [1593], in *The Complete Works of Christopher Marlowe*, ed. by Fredson Bowers, 2 vols (Cambridge: Cambridge University Press, 1981), I, 353–417 (XIV. 700–05; p. 386).

CHAPTER 5

The Development of the Concept of Imagination

The Renaissance argument that the outcome of invention is better than the product of imitation is coupled with the widespread connection between the former and the faculty of the imagination. This link becomes apparent in the field of poetics, where imagination is said to engender invention. By extension, poetry is regarded as an art that relies on this faculty, and the poet is considered an imaginative artist. More generally, 'imagination', a term equating roughly to the Greek φαντασία, is understood in the Renaissance as a crucial influence on the way we apprehend, interpret, and respond to reality. The complexity of the concept has led Lodi Nauta and Detlev Pätzold to state that 'there is no such thing as *the* history of *the* imagination', only many conceptions and uses of it throughout history.[1]

The first of the two sections of this chapter begins by exploring the concept of phantasy as it develops from the thought of authors such as Plato and Aristotle, to the Stoics' rhetorical understanding of it. The section also explores imagination as it is conceived by natural philosophers engaged in the study of the workings of the mind: as a mental power dependent on the senses and bodily experience, and yet one required for rational thinking. Despite the fact that it is acknowledged as indispensable for rational processes, philosophical currents of thought such as Neoplatonism highly distrust it, to the extent that authors such as Pico della Mirandola hold it responsible for defective judgement and even bodily diseases. Still, it is hailed as the trigger of poetry, and as the mental faculty that defines the psycho-physiological profile of poets.

The second section considers, in particular, attacks against and defences of the imagination in Renaissance England. Precisely because its power is seen as extraordinary, it is distrusted on the grounds that it has enormous potential to lead reason astray, given its association with the fallen senses and its inclination towards falsehood and deception. The discourse of the English Reformers makes it an ally of Catholicism; by extension, poetry is distrusted as well. This section discusses the metaphorical language used to refer to the power of the imagination in poetry-writing, the arguments advanced in its favour by advocates of poetry, and the implications of the distinction between icastic and fantastic art put forward by its defenders. Sidney's complex views of the imagination in relation to poetry-writing inevitably come to the fore, and are among the most refined in the English context.

5.1. Before and during the Renaissance

The idea of man creating something from nothing was alien to ancient Greek thought,[2] and, consequently, the idea of the writer as a creator is generally absent from Antiquity.[3] Little is known about pre-Platonic and popular notions of *phantasia* (derived from φαίνω, 'to appear', 'to be apparent', 'to come to light'),[4] and it is from the fifth century BC onwards that *phantasia* begins to signify an active mental disposition and becomes philosophically complex,[5] particularly thanks to Plato and Aristotle. It appears in Plato's dialogues *Theaetetus*, *Sophist*, and *Republic*, in which he links it to the copying of the ideal world and thus relates it to deceptive images. By contrast, Aristotle envisions it as a mental capacity mediating between the senses and thought, thus tying the soul to the external world by providing the mind with phantasm (i.e. raw material for thought). In this manner, *phantasia* becomes necessary for perception and cognition, even if it is secondary to other mental capacities. Aristotle does not associate it with the activity of the poet or artist, and for this reason the word is never mentioned in the *Poetics*. Instead, the term is discussed in detail in *De anima*, in which Aristotle describes how phantasy mediates between sense experience and thought in beings that perceive, and differentiates between two types. As Murray W. Bundy explains, on the one hand, there is φαντασία αἰσθητική, the simple impression, a function of the lower soul, common to all animals, and associated with appetite and passion. On the other, φαντασία βουλευτική, the deliberative type which works with reason, operates in the higher soul and regulates the phantasms of the lower. If the former refers to the phantasy that works only with perception, the latter is a superior type that takes part in reasoning and deliberating, and in rational animals controls the φαντασία αἰσθητική. Without it, there is no thought. *Phantasia* is thus for Aristotle the intermediary between sensation and intellect, in that it houses the images collected from the senses which, when passed to the reasoning part of the mind, fuel conceptual thought.

Phantasy enters the rhetorical discourse through the investigation of the emotions (*pathos*) and the orator's capacity to put into words vivid visual images that may support his persuasive purposes. In other words, in rhetoric, 'phantasy' refers to the emotional states of the orator, the vivid mental pictures within his mind, and his ability to arouse emotions in his listeners. Although Stoicism dealt with it chiefly in terms of rhetoric,[6] it has been noted that 'the transformation of phantasia into a term for creative art was due to Platonic-Stoic syncretism' in the first century BC.[7] Influenced by Aristotle's *De anima* and Plato's *Philebus* and *Timaeus*, the Stoics described *phantasia* as a creative capacity actively operating within the process of cognition and intimately linked to language.[8] Mental images could be true (φαντασία καταληπτική) or false (φαντασματα). The former were based on real perception, and as such constituted the foundation of knowledge and right conduct; the latter, present for instance in dreams and hallucinations, were stigmatised as dangerous and were often associated with poetry.[9] The distinction between the true and the illusory types was at the root of an ethical problem for the Stoics, who claimed the supremacy of reason over phantasy and advocated a reasonable use of phantasies. Plotinus, attempting to combine Aristotle and Plato, differentiated two kinds of phantasy as well, one pertaining to the rational soul and to higher mental states, the other to the irrational or lower soul and connected with the passions and the body.[10] Like the Stoics, Plotinus brought this distinction into the ethical domain, attributing voluntary acts to the former type and untrustworthy instincts to the latter type.

In the Latin rhetorical tradition, *phantasia* became a standard term alluding to the power of the mind to envision the unsensed and the ability to convey it to an audience.[11] Everyone was able to cultivate such a capacity through training, for it was not a heavenly gift. Quintilian does not describe *phantasia* at length or offer many examples of it, but rather mentions it in passing as if it were a concept familiar to his readers. He explains that, for orators or poets to move the audience, they first need to feel the emotion they want to transmit, but, since emotions are out of our conscious control, orators or poets ought to resort to forming in their minds 'clear *phantasiai* — "visions" — of absent things; this means putting to practical use the faculty of day-dreaming and fantasy'.[12] The accuracy of the translation of the Greek φαντασία as *imaginatio* in Latin has often been doubted; it has been argued that *imaginatio* should have been used instead to render the concept of εἰκασία, which is 'derived from εἴκω, "to be like," or "capable of being compared"'.[13] This resulted in the medieval understanding of *phantasia* as the potentially dangerous 'free play' of 'combinatory functions'; when *imaginatio* was employed as a synonym for *phantasia*, it carried the same negative connotations, but otherwise it signified 'simpler presentative and reproductive powers', even if deemed capable of going beyond mere representation in aesthetic terms.[14]

In medieval thought, imagination was seen as the faculty of the soul that reshapes the images of sense perception and holds an intermediary position between the senses and the intellect. Many medieval authors distinguished five mental faculties or internal powers or senses hosted in brain chambers (*cellulae*) or ventricles (*ventriculae*). The frontmost ventricle hosted common sense and the imagination, the middle cell accommodated phantasy and judgement, and the rear one was home to memory.[15] *Margarita philosophica*, written by the German Carthusian Gregor Reisch in the 1490s, was an influential university textbook for the teaching of philosophy that acknowledged this fivefold distinction and described the workings of mental processes. First, it explained, the external senses passed their information to the common sense, which formed composite images that it subsequently sent to the imagination, which could then combine them to form new synthetic images of non-existent realities.[16]

In late medieval times this fivefold distinction was reduced to the imagination, common sense, and memory,[17] and the process would be described as beginning in the first cell, where the imagination resided. It would fashion an image, then pass it on to the *intellectus* in the central cavity, which used it to form opinions and ideas. The *intellectus* judged these mental images true or false, desirable or undesirable, good or evil, and then transmitted them to the will in order that they be treated correspondingly. The resulting idea was transferred to the rearmost ventricle, to the domain of memory (*vis memorativa*), where it was stored. This is the simplest formula, which became more complicated in some authors.[18] Indeed, as has been pointed out, 'there is no consistent mediaeval theory of imagination', but rather 'conflicting attitudes towards' it.[19]

Augustine discusses this notion at length in *De trinitate*, where imagination appears as an active faculty of the soul, working with memory-images and mediating between memory and the understanding. If for Platonism the images produced by phantasy could not be granted any truth, for Aristotle there is a degree of truth in materiality itself, in the physical world, and, as a consequence, in the images also. Thus, for scholasticism, the contemplation of particulars constitutes the starting point for the understanding of universals, and particular images thus have a kind of reality which the Platonic and Augustinian traditions deny them. Instead, Augustine places the idea before the particular, which means that an image of a particular thing in the mind is but an illustration of a universal that the mind already has and that only exists in the mind of God.[20] Because Augustine believes memory is independent of *imaginatio*, the latter has no intimate contact with ideas. By separating it so radically from the rest of the powers of the mind, medieval theorists ignore its participation in the higher processes of cognition and set it more definitively against reason and the intellect.[21] Augustine wholly distrusted and condemned *imaginatio* as a source of deceit, sin, and error due to its contact with the sensible world.[22] Following the Christian belief that God is the creator of all things, Augustine postulated that the imagination did not create but merely reflected, imitated, and discovered that which already exists.[23]

Philosophical reflections on the soul were, however, not exclusive to theology. They also fell within the scope of natural philosophy and medicine, and were influenced first and foremost by Aristotle's *Parva naturalia* and *De anima*, a work which in early modern Europe 'virtually all universities required [...] to be read for the degree of bachelor of arts, an honour it shared only with the *Physics* among Aristotle's non-logical works'.[24] Furthermore, they were understood in connection with the theory of the four elements (earth, water, air, and fire), according to which the elements along with their properties (heat, cold, moisture, and dryness) compose, in different proportions, all material things. If heat and moisture are the fundamental qualities for life, then cold and dryness are hostile to it. The four elements were additionally linked to the four bodily fluids (blood, phlegm, yellow bile, and black bile): blood was bound to heat and moisture and the element of air, phlegm was cold and moist and likened to water, yellow bile was hot and dry and related to fire, and black bile was thought to be cold and dry and associated with earth. A balance between the four humours guaranteed health, and an imbalance between them led to disease. Nevertheless, there was no consistent or unanimously agreed theory about the workings of the mind or about the human psyche in the early modern period. Instead, numerous psychological trends coexisted and merged, forming an asystematic blend of various traditions. As John Davies states when explaining the workings of the mind:

> *Imagination, Fancie,* Common-*sence,*
> In nature brooketh oddes or vnion,
> Some makes them one, and some makes difference.[25]

Likewise, when Florio attempts to define *ménte*, he does so by providing a long and confusing enumeration of terms related to the mind: 'the highe[s]t and chiefe[s]t part of the [s]oule, the mind, vnderstanding, memorie, iudgement, intent, thought, imagination, conceit, or foreknowledge'.[26] No wonder, then, that Renaissance (physiological) psychology has been described as 'a hodge-podge of utterly contradictory "facts," conflicting theories, hopelessly inter-mixed, overlapping terms, and extremely variable and ill-kept distinctions'.[27]

Imagination was, in the Renaissance, the image-making faculty that worked with what had already been experienced or perceived but was no longer before the senses, and the faculty that pictured, through the combination of images, new realities never even perceived. The price that it paid for its reliance on the senses was its connection to irrationality, deceitfulness, and the sins of the flesh. It was discussed at length in Neoplatonism, which accepted it as an intermediary between sense and intellect, and hence between the sensual world and the higher realm of forms of thought. Neoplatonism placed the intelligible above the sensible, regarded *phantasia* as the intermediary between the divine mind and the sensible substance, and consequently developed an interest in the possibility of transmitting transcendental knowledge through images in divination, prophecy, and dreams. Neoplatonists, though, were suspicious of *phantasia* due to its connection with the body. Although Marsilio Ficino does not develop an aesthetic system in the strict sense, in Book XIII, Chapter 3 of his *Platonic theology* he regards the arts to be conclusive proof of the superiority of man over animals, and a means for man to overcome dependence on the body and approach divinity.[28] Imagination allows communication between human souls and a superior realm and, what is more, becomes a pathway for the superior world to contact humans through images.[29]

Gianfrancesco Pico della Mirandola's *De imaginatione*, which takes Aristotle's *De anima* as its main source, even if often to disagree with it, defines imagination as a 'power of the mind' that receives 'through the instruments of the five exterior senses, of sight, hearing, smell, taste, and touch, the likenesses and impressions of things which are from without', and produces with this material 'a likeness and image of itself, in imitation of incorporeal and spiritual nature'.[30] According to Pico, it 'is placed on the border between intellect and sense, and holds the intermediate ground':

> It follows *sense*, by an act of which it is born; *intellection* it precedes. It coincides with sense in that, like sense, it perceives the particular, corporeal, and present; it is superior to sense in that, with no external stimulus, it yet produces images, not only present, but also past and future, and even such as cannot be brought to light by nature. It accords with sense in that it employs sensible forms as objects; but it surpasses sense in that at will it separates and in turn combines those forms which sense upon ceasing to function has abandoned. This activity can in no way be performed by sense.[31]

Like the intellect, imagination is 'free, unfixed, and devoted to no special object', yet 'it is surpassed by intellect, since it conceives and fashions the sensible and particular only, while intellect, in addition, conceives and fashions the universal and intelligible, and such things as are purified from all contact with matter'.[32] Nevertheless, without it reason cannot operate, and 'nor could the soul, fettered as it is to the body, opine, know, or comprehend at all, if phantasy were not constantly to supply it with the images themselves'.[33]

Yet, even if Pico acknowledged that reason could not function without the material provided by the imagination, his distrust of the latter was generally shared. According to Pico, this mental power 'is for the most part vain and wandering',[34] capable of deceit because it can produce images of non-existent objects, and altogether devoid of correct judgement and thus in need of the guidance of a superior force (reason) to lead man towards good and pull him away from beastliness and doom. The imagination can be affected by the temperament of the body, by sensual objects, by man's judgement (*arbitrium*), and finally, by good and bad angels. Remedies exist for all these, and Pico is meticulous in his explanations. Since it can corrupt reason and deceive the intellect, join with the passions, produce mental afflictions, and confuse judgement, it is not 'hard to prove that universal errors which occur as much in civil life as in the philosophic and Christian life, take their beginnings from the defect of the imagination':

> the depraved imagination is the mother and nurse of ambition [...] Cruelty, wrath, and passion are born from and nourished by the imagination of an ostensible but deceptive good, which one who is carried away by perfervid sense and rash imagination to insults, wounds, and murders, thinks inherent in retaliation. [...] And what else, if not the deceitful imagination, brings to the fore the other vices which for want of time I omit to mention? Neglecting reason, she gives precedence to injustice rather than to justice, to lust rather than to continence, to savagery rather than to clemency, to avarice rather than to generosity, to discord rather than to peace.[35]

In sum, Pico believes 'the faults of all monstrous opinions, and the defects of all judgment, are to be ascribed beyond all peradventure to the vices of phantasy', and that 'the Christian life, which consists in both belief and action, is ruined by a false imagination'.[36] His views were far from being an exception. Ronsard displays a variety of prejudices against imagination, including its capacity to shape 'les songes entrecoupés d'un frénétique, ou de quelque patient extrêmement tourmenté de la fièvre, à l'imagination duquel, pour être blessée, se représentent mille formes monstrueuses sans ordre ni liaison' [the broken dreams of a frenzied man, or of a patient extremely tormented by fever, whose ailing imagination sees a thousand monstrous forms without order or connection].[37] In his essay 'De la force de l'imagination', Montaigne, who admits to being 'one of those by whom the powerful blows of the imagination are felt most strongly',[38] proves distrustful of its great powers, of its irrational force, and of its links to superstition and psychosomatic diseases: 'It is likely that the credit given to miracles, visions, enchantments and such extraordinary events chiefly derives from the power of the imagination acting mainly on the more impressionable souls of the common people.'[39] Indeed, he affirms that, 'when imaginary thoughts trouble us we break into sweats, start trembling, grow pale or flush crimson; we lie struck supine on our feather-beds and feel our bodies agitated by such emotions'.[40] What is more, imagination can even 'bring fevers and death to those who let it act freely and who give it encouragement'.[41]

That the imagination was the mental power ultimately responsible for the composition of poetry was eventually taken for granted in the Renaissance. Stephen Hawes's *The pastime of pleasure* (1509) includes one of the earliest occurrences of the term in an English text on rhetorical/poetical themes. Hawes divides rhetoric into five parts: invention, imagination, 'fansy', good estimation (i.e. judgement), and 'retentise memory', each of them being distinct and separate forces. Reisch's *Margarita philosophica* may have been Hawes's main source, for Hawes follows Reisch in his enumeration of the five inward wits.[42] Imagination is acknowledged by Hawes as the virtue of 'famous poetes', and described as 'the operation | To make of nought, reason sentencious':

> And secondlye, by imagination
> To drawe a matter, ful facundious
> Full marveylous, is the operation
> To make of nought, reason sentencious
> Clokyng a trouthe, wyth coloure tenebrous.[43]

Hawes blends classical rhetorical notions with rhetoricised poetical ones, along with traditional ideas on the workings of the mind. He explains that the task 'Of famous poetes, ryght ymaginatife' was 'to fayne' fables, and at the same time says that poets 'had suche a fansy | In thys hye art' that moved them 'Newe thynges to fynde'.[44] What is unusual for his time is that Hawes does not understand 'imagination' and 'fancy' as synonymous, as many of his contemporaries did. For instance, Thomas Thomas defines *phantăsia* as 'the image of things conceiued in the minde: a vision, phantasie, appearance, representation or imagination';[45] Edmund Coote translates *phantasie* simply with 'imagination';[46] and Florio and Richard Perceval define *fantasia* as 'a fansie, a conceit, fantasie, humor, imagination' and as 'fantasie, light imagination' respectively.[47] Shakespeare likewise envisions imagination as that which the poet requires to compose his verses, which encapsulate and materialise the 'airy' images brought forth by it, as *A midsummer night's dream* (1600) puts it:

> And as imagination bodies forth
> The formes of things vnknowne, the Poets penne
> Turnes them to shapes, and giues to ayery nothing,
> A locall habitation and a name.[48]

Huarte de San Juan is one of the sixteenth-century authors who most consistently and systematically deals with the imagination, and he too connects it with poetry. Huarte explains the causes and variety of human abilities from a physiological point of view, drawing on Galen and the theory of the humours. He argues that the three faculties of the mind — understanding, imagination, and memory — are determined by the temperature and the dryness or moisture of the brain. Cold and dry are related to the first, heat to the second, and moisture to the third, and this set of correspondences furthermore correlates with specific professions, arts, sciences, and careers. Thus, 'from a good imagination spring all the arts and sciences, which consist in figure, correspondence, harmony, and proportion', to wit, 'poetry, eloquence, music, and the skill of preaching, the practice of physic, the mathematics, astrology, and the governing of a commonwealth, the art of warfare, painting, drawing, writing, reading'.[49] To explain the physiological source of poetry, which lies in the imaginative, Huarte gives the example of a man who is hopeless at poetry and who suddenly starts effortlessly writing verses in praise of his beloved. The reason for this is that 'love heateth and drieth his brain, and these are qualities which quicken the imagination'.[50] Yet, Huarte argues, the circumstances that favour it can also produce madness, frenzy, or melancholy when taken to the extreme. On top of that, the hot character of imaginative men inclines them to various vices: 'those who partake much heat are men of great imagination, and the same quality which maketh them witty traineth them to be naughty and vicious'.[51] From 'a forcible imagination' and a 'complexion very hot' thus 'spring three principal vices in a man: pride, gluttony, and lechery', 'for which cause men of great imagination are ordinarily bad and vicious, for they abandon themselves to be guided by their natural inclination'.[52]

Nonetheless, even if some men are more imaginative than others, which is what conditions them to become poets, imagination is at any rate a universal faculty shared by all. As such, it not only accounts for the production of poetic compositions, limited to a few lucky ones endowed with imaginative qualities, but also for the reception of such compositions. In other words, imagination is not only what enables the writing of poems and plays, but moreover what permits the understanding and enjoyment of them. This is precisely the reason why, for instance, authors such as Shakespeare argue that everyone can appreciate a play as a member of the audience. *King Henry V* (1600) famously demands that spectators activate this mental power to maximise the suspension of disbelief and transform the 'Wooden O' of the cockpit into 'the vastie fields of France':[53]

> Peece out our imperfections with your thoughts:
> Into a thousand parts diuide one Man,
> And make imaginarie Puissance.
> Thinke when we talke of Horses, that you see them,
> Printing their prowd Hoofes i'th' receiuing Earth;
> For 'tis your thoughts that now must deck our Kings.[54]

Unless the audience's 'imaginary forces' are engaged, or the cast by means of extraordinary dramatic skills facilitates that necessary suspension of disbelief only achievable through the imagination, the reception of the play results in catastrophe.[55] Faced with the poor performance of an amateurish company, Hippolyta and Theseus discuss in *A midsummer night's dream* (1600) the role of their imagination and that of the cast:

> HIPPOLYTA: This is the silliest stuffe, that euer I heard.
> THESEUS: The best, in this kinde, are but shadowes: and the worst are no worse, if imagination amend them.
> HIPPOLYTA: It must be your imagination, then; &not theirs.
> THESEUS: If we imagine no worse of them, then they of thēselues, they may passe for excellent men.[56]

Furthermore, the connection between the imagination and poetic invention is never questioned in the Renaissance. English lexicographers, for instance, define

Emblem 4, 'No passage can divert the Course, | of Pegasus, the Muses Horse' (Wither, *A collection of emblemes*, Q2r).

one in terms of the other. For John Baret, 'to inuent' means 'to imagine';[57] Thomas Thomas defines *invenio* as 'to deuise, invent, or imagine';[58] and Robert Cawdry and Randle Cotgrave talk respectively of invention as a 'deuise, or imagination' and 'a deuise, forgerie, conceit; [...] imagination'.[59] For Cotgrave too, *fantasier* means 'to imagine, deuise, conceiue, inuent', and *fantastiquer* 'to conceiue, imagine, deuise, [...] represent in the imagination'.[60] For Huarte, invention falls within the jurisdiction of the imagination, because, in his words, for an author to 'possess much invention', 'it behoveth that he have a very swift imagination'.[61] Likewise, both Peletier and Ronsard locate the source of invention in this faculty. For Peletier, 'Invention est un dessein provenant de l'imagination de l'entendement, pour parvenir à notre fin' [invention is a design born from the imagination of the understanding and conceived to achieve our ends].[62] For Ronsard, 'L'invention n'est autre chose que le bon naturel d'une imagination concevant les Idées et formes de toutes choses qui se peuvent imaginer tant célestes que terrestres' [invention is nothing but the natural capacity of an imagination that conceives of ideas and forms of all things that can be imagined, both heavenly as well as earthly].[63]

George Wither's emblem, preceded by the lines 'No passage can divert the Course, | Of Pegasus, the Muses Horse', found in *A collection of emblemes* (1635), shows in the foreground an image of a winged horse, Pegasus, 'the *Poets-horse*', 'on which the *Learned* mount their best *Invention*' to elevate over the sensible realm 'without rod or spurres'.⁶⁴ Pegasus, Wither says,

> [...] doth carry,
> Their *Fancie*, thorow *Worlds* imaginary;
> And, by *Idæas* feigned, shewes them there,
> The nature of those *Truths*, that reall are:
> By meanes of *this*, our *Soules* doe come to know
> A thousand secrets, in the *Deeps* below;
> Things, here on *Earth*, and, things above the *Skyes*,
> On which, we never fixed, yet, our eyes.⁶⁵

In other words, fancy (i.e. the imagination), is here presented as a means of knowing not only earthly things, but, in accordance with Ficino's thought, quasi-sacred ones. This end it is able to achieve thanks to its close collaboration with invention.

5.2. Against and for the Imagination

The faculty of the imagination was discredited in England first and foremost due to its association with the bodily senses, for they were what supplied it with raw material. Because the senses were seen as fallible and prone to immorality, the imagination became contaminated to its very roots, and therefore blamed for all kinds of false representations. In *A treatie of humane learning* (1633), Fulke Greville discusses the workings of the mind and traces the mistrust of the imagination all the way back to its connection with the fallen senses and its capacity to distort already problematic sensory material. The imagination can perversely confuse and misguide the understanding because it 'always cannot receiue | What sense reports, but what th' affections please', and so, 'as those Princes that doe leaue | Their State in trust to men corrupt with ease',

> So must th'Imagination from the sense
> Be misinformed, while our affections cast
> False shapes, and formes on their intelligence,
> And to keepe out true intromissions thence,
> Abstracts the imagination or distasts,
> With images preoccupately plac'd.
>
> Hence our desires, feares, hopes, loue, hate, and sorrow,
> In fancy make us heare, feele, see impressions,
> Such as out of our sense they doe not borrow;
> And are the efficient cause, the true progression
> Of sleeping visions, idle phantasmes waking,
> Life, dreames; and knowledge, apparitions making.⁶⁶

Likewise, in dictionary definitions of the term, 'imagination' appears at best as a toy and a trifle, and at worst as engendering falsehood, deceit, and evil schemes. 'To imagine' means for Baret to 'deuize or finde out some false tale or subtiltie';⁶⁷ Thomas Thomas, in defining *imāgo*, says that it is 'a likenes, a counterfaite, a vision, an idle toy, a fansie, an imagination';⁶⁸ and, for Cotgrave, *resverie* means 'idle talking, dotage, trifling, follie, vaine fancie, fond imagination'.[69] Florio defines *phantasma* as 'a vaine vision or false imagination, a fairie, a hobgoblin',[70] and Perceval describes *chiméra* not only as 'a monster with a head like a lyon, a belly like a goate, and taile of a serpent' but also as 'a fansie or imagination'.[71] Understandably, then, John Davies believes

> [...] it better farre
> Quite to distrust th' *Imagination*,
> Then to beleeue all which it doth auerre,
> Which breeds more false, then true opinion.[72]

The same view is repeated several times in Shakespeare as well. For example, in *Henry IV, Part 2* (1600), 'great imagination' is said to be 'proper to mad-men',[73] and in *A midsummer night's dream* (1600) Theseus repeats that 'The lunatick, the louer, and the Poet | Are of imagination all compact',[74] and that

> Louers, and mad men haue such seething braines,
> Such shaping phantasies, that apprehend
> More, then coole reason euer comprehends.[75]

To make matters worse, Tyndale and Coverdale, English translators of the Bible, stigmatised poetry as pernicious, and contrasted the partial truth conveyed by poetry with the whole truth of the Scriptures. In addition, reading poetry was presented not only as a potentially corrupting activity but also as a distraction from worthy pious readings. Tyndale's *An answer to Sir Thomas More's dialogue* (1530) responded to *A dialogue concerning heresies* (1529), More's refutation of Lutheranism in the form of a dialogue in which reality and fiction merge in complex ways. Tyndale rebuked More also because of his use of fictitious elements to deal with religious controversies. By linking fiction to Catholicism, Tyndale made anti-poetic sentiment part of the programme of Protestantism, and in consequence anti-poetic sentiment spread through all levels of society, fused to the discourse of religion.[76]

Tyndale, for instance, claimed that Catholics give 'thēselues onely unto poetrye, & shut up the scriptur'.[77] Puttenham confirms that 'poets as poesy are despised, and the name become of honorable infamous, subject to scorn and derision, and rather a reproach than a praise to any that useth it'.[78] This was partly because of the associations of poetry with phantasy: 'for commonly whoso is studious in the art or shows himself excellent in it, they call in disdain a "fantastical"; and a light-headed or fantastical man (by conversion) they call a poet'.[79] Anti-poetic sentiment fitted in nicely with the Reformers' insistence on the corruption of human faculties as a result of the Fall, after which products of the mind, particularly those of the imagination, were suspect. What is more, for the Reformers, the practices of the Catholic Church were based not on any direct scriptural authority but solely on the imagination, and as such were idolatrous. Tyndale, in fact, claims that until 'man cast away his owne imagynacyons', 'he can nat perceyue god / & understande the vertue and power of the blode of Christ'.[80] Furthermore, for him, Catholics replace worshipping God for 'a worshepinge of thine awne imaginacion',[81] an unforgivable mistake, for 'nothinge bringeth the wrath of god so sone and so sore on a man / as the ydolatry of his awne imagination'.[82] Frith, Coverdale, Joye, and Calvin, among others, likewise demonised the imagination in their writings and in their translations.[83]

'Imagination' appears in combination with, on the one hand, verbs such as 'feign' and 'forge', which underline its capacity to produce deceitful images, and, on the other, metaphors such as that of the fertile womb which forms fantasies, and of the glass or mirror capable of both reflecting and distorting appearances.[84] Puttenham explains that, in effect, 'fantasy may be resembled to a glass' in that some are 'false glasses and show things otherwise than they be indeed' (either 'things exceeding fair and comely', or 'figures very monstrous and ill-favored'), whereas other glasses show them 'right as they be indeed, neither fairer nor fouler, nor greater nor smaller'.[85] The metaphor of the glass illustrates the duality of 'the fantasticall part of man', which, 'if it be not disordered' is 'a representer of the best, most comely and beautifull images or appearances of things to the soul and according to their very truth'; 'if otherwise, then doth it breed chimeras and monsters'.[86] Puttenham later implicitly acknowledges that the phantasy that goes beyond the mirror which merely projects a faithful reflection of the world is of greater value and merit: 'to feign a thing that never was nor is like to be proceedeth of a greater wit and sharper invention than to describe things that be true'.[87] While everyone can describe reality, only the poet can describe the unseen.

Few were the voices in defence of the imagination. For instance, 'The letter of G. T. to his very friend H. W. concerning this worke', included in Gascoigne's *A hundreth sundrie flowres*, does state 'that Poets in their most feyned fables and imaginations, have metaphorically set forth unto us the right rewardes of vertues, and the due punishments for vices',[88] and Davies of Hereford identified the imagination as the origin of 'all maruellous *Inuentions*, | Which doe produce all *Artes* and *Sciences*'.[89] In his *Witty and witless*, John Heywood takes the 'resonabyll manns imagynashyon' as precisely a sign of humanity and intelligence, and as a strictly human quality, in the same way that reason is exclusive to humans as well: 'the beast in effecte hathe none'.[90] As long as it cooperates with the higher understanding, the imagination is considered a reputable faculty, and as such it is legitimised. Yet, since it was largely deemed to be an uncontrolled, distorting, and irrational power, the adherents of poetry faced the challenge of defending the art at a time when the prevalent opinion was that 'the truest poetrie is the most faining'.[91] Imagination was advocated on the grounds that the faculty was not wholly harmful: in poetry, it was disciplined, for the poet feigns and distorts reality in particular (rational) ways and for moral purposes. Imagining becomes, in the poetic context, the means of constructing plausible imitations of life that unmask the truth beneath appearances.

Plato had already distinguished in the *Sophist* between icastic, or 'likeness-making', and fantastic, or 'semblance-making', art. While the former occurs when 'anyone produces the imitation by following the proportions of the original in length, breadth, and depth, and giving, besides, the appropriate colours to each part', the latter does not represent the model faithfully.[92] That is, the icastic artist accurately copies the model without using his imagination, whereas the fantastic artist makes his own choices irrespective of the features of the model. Cinquecento critics such as Patrizi, Castelvetro, and Mazzoni employ Plato's distinction, and while the first two show a preference for icastic art, considering it more truthful and reliable, Mazzoni prefers the 'marvelous-credible' of fantastic art.[93] The two representatives par excellence of icastic and fantastic art in humanist Italy were, respectively, Tasso's *Gerusalemme liberata*, and Ariosto's *Orlando furioso*.

In England, apologists for poetry largely supported icastic over fantastic art. Puttenham distinguished between the 'fantastic' and the 'eufantastic', that is, between disordered art and ordered art, 'in whose exercises the inuentive part is most employed and is to the sound and true judgment of man most needful'.[94] According to Puttenham, 'such persons as be illuminated with the brightest irradiations of knowledge and of the verity and due proportion of things' are 'not *phantastici* but *euphantasiote*', 'and of this sort of fantasy are all good poets'.[95] Sidney attributes to fantastic art an 'infected will', and to icastic art an 'erected wit' that draws the poet closer to God: 'for I will not deny but that man's wit may make Poesy, which should be *eikastike*, which some learned have defined, "figuring forth good things", to be *phantastike* which doth contrariwise infect the fancy with unworthy objects'.[96]

Sidney is cautious about his use of the term 'imagination' in his *Defence*, for although he claims that the poet should deliver his ideas 'in such excellency as he had imagined them', he goes on to say that his 'delivering forth also is not wholly imaginative, as we are wont to say by them that build castles in the air'.[97] Sidney, then, summarises the arguments of the 'poet-whippers' by saying that they long for a past in which delight was taken 'upon action, and not upon imagination [i.e. poetry]', when the preference was more for 'doing things worthy to be written, than writing things fit to be done'.[98] In addition, if imagination is ultimately the image-making capacity, Sidney paraphrases its function on several occasions, as with his statement that 'it is not rhyming and versing that maketh a poet', but 'feigning notable images of virtues, vices, or what else, with that delightful teaching'.[99] Imagination put to the service of *docere* and *delectare* appears, thus, as the essence of poetry, as it distinguishes poets from philosophers: a poet produces 'a perfect picture' of things, 'for he yieldeth to the powers of the mind an image of that whereof the philosopher bestoweth but a wordish description'.[100] To those who wonder 'whether the feigned image of poesy or the regular instruction of philosophy hath the more force in teaching', Sidney responds that the philosopher's outcomes 'lie dark before the imaginative and judging power' of 'the speaking picture of poesy'.[101] Even 'the best and most accomplished kind of Poetry [i.e. the heroical]' is, according to Sidney, based on the imagination working through images for the achievement of virtue: 'as the image of each action stirreth and instructeth the mind, so the lofty image of such worthies most inflameth the mind with desire to be worthy, and informs with counsel how to be worthy'.[102]

Unsurprisingly, John Hoskins cannot avoid affirming, in a Sidneian fashion, that 'the conceits of the mind are pictures of things and the tongue is interpreter of those pictures'.[103] Although in Sidney there is no overt vindication of the imagination, he does, as has been seen, convey, whether consciously or unconsciously, the centrality of this concept in poetry-writing. Indeed, he has been thought to develop a landmark 'transitional theory', that is, of transition 'from poetry understood as imitation to poetry understood as creation',[104] as Abrams, who views Sidney's *Defence* as a turning point, has also argued, even if he does not recognise an actual theory of poetic creativity until the eighteenth century.[105]

A century later, Dryden places imagination at the core of poetry and affirms in *Annus mirabilis* (1667) that 'the composition of all Poems is or ought to be of Wit, and wit in the Poet, or wit writing, [...] is no other then the faculty of imagination'.[106] Dryden divides imagination into three parts: invention, 'or finding of the thought'; fancy, 'or the variation, deriving or moulding of that thought'; and elocution, 'or the Art of clothing and adorning that thought'.[107] For him, 'the quickness of the Imagination is seen in the Invention, the fertility in the Fancy, and the accuracy in the Expression'. Of the three, invention stands out, for 'the first happiness of the Poet's imagination is properly Invention, or finding of the thought'.[108] Thus, the relationship between the two concepts continues to be seen in the same manner in the second half of the seventeenth century, for invention is still made dependent on and subject to the poet's capacity to imagine.

Despite the widespread distrust of the imagination, it gradually began to gain ground against invention-based definitions of poetry, as will be seen in the Conclusion. In reflecting on the reasons for why the imagination flourished in poetics from the seventeenth century onwards, and on the nuances which invention lacked by comparison, it appears that 'the capacity for picture-making and image-forming' was the element that rendered 'imagination' such an appealing term for poetics.[109]

Notes to Chapter 5

1. Lodi Nauta and Detlev Pätzold, 'Introduction', in *Imagination*, ed. by Nauta and Pätzold, pp. ix–xiv (p. xiii; emphasis in original).
2. Michael Mack, 'Sidney's Poetics: Imitating Creation', p. 17.
3. Russell, *Criticism in Antiquity* p. 100.
4. M. Schofield, 'Aristotle on the Imagination', in *Aristotle on Mind and the Senses: Proceedings of the Seventh Symposium Aristotelicum*, ed. by G. E. R. Lloyd and G. E. L. Owen (Cambridge: Cambridge University Press, 1978), pp. 99–140 (p. 116).
5. Schofield, p. 132.
6. See Flory.
7. Gerard Watson, *Phantasia in Classical Thought* (Galway: Galway University Press, 1988), p. 91.
8. Ruth Webb, *Ekphrasis, Imagination and Persuasion in Ancient Rhetorical Theory and Practice* (Farnham and Burlington: Ashgate, 2009), p. 114.
9. Murray W. Bundy, *The Theory of Imagination in Classical and Mediaeval Thought* (Urbana: University of Illinois Press, 1927), p. 260; Webb, p. 116.
10. Gerard Watson, p. 102.
11. Flory, p. 156.
12. Russell, *Criticism in Antiquity*, p. 109.
13. Bundy, *Theory of Imagination*, p. 11. For more on the translation of φαντασία as *imaginatio*, see Schofield, p. 102.
14. Bundy, *Theory of Imagination*, p. 278.

15. Galen and other physicians criticised this rigid compartmentalisation into separate ventricles, and instead believed that each mental power could be found in all ventricles in approximately equal proportions; see Olaf Pluta, 'On the Matter of the Mind: Late-Medieval Views on Mind, Body, and Imagination', in *Imagination*, ed. by Nauta and Pätzold, pp. 21–34.
16. Katharine Park, 'The Organic Soul', in *Cambridge History of Renaissance Philosophy*, ed. by Schmitt and others, pp. 464–84.
17. Murray W. Bundy remarks that, during the Renaissance, there persisted a love, inherited from the Middle Ages (particularly from authors such as Augustine and Thomas Aquinas), for finding triads in the conceptualisation of the workings of the mind ('Shakespeare and Elizabethan Psychology', *Journal of English and Germanic Philology*, 23 (1924), 516–49 (p. 519)). For more on the Trinitarian analogy in the Renaissance, see Dennis R. Klinck, '*Vestigia Trinitatis* in Man and his Works in the English Renaissance', *Journal of the History of Ideas*, 42.1 (1981), 13–27 (p. 27).
18. Murray W. Bundy, 'Bacon's True Opinion of Poetry', *Studies in Philology*, 27.2 (1930), 244–64 (pp. 249–50).
19. Bundy, *Theory of Imagination*, p. 177.
20. Robert L. Montgomery, *The Reader's Eye: Studies in Didactic Theory from Dante to Tasso* (Berkeley: University of California Press, 1979), pp. 13–49 (p. 39).
21. Bundy, *Theory of Imagination*, pp. 179–80.
22. However, Jan R. Veenstra affirms that Augustine is 'the first to record the term *imaginatio* in Latin literature' ('The Subtle Knot: Robert Kilwardby and Gianfrancesco Pico on the Imagination', in *Imagination*, ed. by Nauta and Pätzold, pp. 1–20 (p. 1)).
23. Harry Berger, *Second World and Green World: Studies in Renaissance Fiction-Making* (Berkeley: University of California Press, 1988), pp. 50–53. For more on medieval notions of the workings of the mind and the role of images in mental processes, see Walter S. Melion, 'Introduction: Meditative Images and the Psychology of Soul', in *Image and Imagination of the Religious Self in Late Medieval and Early Modern Europe*, ed. by Reindert Falkenburg, Walter S. Melion, and Todd M. Richardson (Turnhout: Brepols, 2007), pp. 1–36.
24. Katharine Park and Eckhard Kessler, 'The Concept of Psychology', in *Cambridge History of Renaissance Philosophy*, ed. by Schmitt and others, pp. 455–63 (p. 456).
25. John Davies of Hereford, *Mirum in Modum: A Glimpse of Gods Glorie and the Soules Shape* (London: printed [by Valentine Simmes] for VVilliam Aspley, 1602), B3r (emphasis in original).
26. Florio, *Queen Anna's Nevv Vvorld of Words*, Cc5r.
27. Louise C. Turner Forest, 'A Caveat for Critics against Invoking Elizabethan Psychology', *Publications of the Modern Language Association of America*, 61.3, (1946), 651–72 (p. 656). Lawrence Babb argues that 'the physiological psychology of the Renaissance is a body of theory containing so many contradictions, semicontradictions, and disharmonies that any exposition of it is likely to misrepresent by introducing into it an orderliness which it does not really have' ('On the Nature of Elizabethan Psychological Literature', in *Joseph Quincy Adams: Memorial Studies*, ed. by James Gilmer McManaway, Giles Edwin Dawson, and Edwin E. Willoughby (Washington: Folger Shakespeare Library, 1948), pp. 509–22 (p. 510)). See also Edward Dowden, *Essays Modern and Elizabethan* (London and New York: Dent & Sons; Dutton, 1910), pp. 308–33; Francis R. Johnson, 'Elizabethan Drama and the Elizabethan Science of Psychology', in *English Studies Today: Papers Read at the International Conference of University Professors of English Held in Magdalen College, Oxford, August 1950*, ed. by C. L. Wrenn and G. Bullough (Oxford: Oxford University Press, 1951), pp. 111–19. A remarkable number of studies have approached the Elizabethan understanding of the workings of the human mind by drawing on, or alluding to, the poetry or drama of the period; among them are Bundy, 'Psychology'; Hardin Craig, *The Enchanted Glass: The Elizabethan Mind in Literature* (Oxford: Blackwell, 1950); Lawrence Babb, *The Elizabethan Malady: A Study of Melancholia in English Literature from 1580 to 1642* (East Lansing: Michigan State College Press, 1951); E. Ruth Harvey, *The Inward Wits: Psychological Theory in the Middle Ages and the Renaissance* (London: Warburg Institute, 1975); Kathy Eden, *Poetic and Legal Fiction in the Aristotelian Tradition* (Princeton: Princeton University Press, 1986), pp. 157–75.
28. John Martin Cocking, *Imagination: A Study in the History of Ideas*, ed. by Penelope Murray (London: Routledge, 1991), p. 172. The most recent edition of Ficino's work in English is Marsilio Ficino,

Platonic Theology, ed. by James Hankins with William Bowen, 6 vols (Cambridge, MA: Harvard University Press, 2001–06); cf. here IV: *Books XII–XIV*, trans. by Michael J. B. Allen (2004), pp. 169–83. See also Raphael Falco, 'Marsilio Ficino and Vatic Myth', *Modern Language Notes*, 122.1 (2007), 101–22.

29. It was also believed, nonetheless, that reason can be elevated over phantasy and contemplate the superior realm without any dependence on images.
30. Giovanni Francesco Pico della Mirandola, *'On the Imagination': The Latin Text with an Introduction, an English Translation, and Notes by Harry Caplan*, trans. by Harry Caplan (New Haven: published for Cornell University, Yale University Press; London: Milford, Oxford University Press, 1930), p. 25. Caplan's translation of *On the Imagination* uses the terms 'phantasy' and 'imagination' interchangeably.
31. Pico della Mirandola, p. 31 (emphasis in original).
32. Pico della Mirandola, p. 33.
33. Pico della Mirandola, p. 33.
34. Pico della Mirandola, p. 29.
35. Pico della Mirandola, pp. 45–47.
36. Pico della Mirandola, p. 49.
37. Ronsard, 'Abrégé', pp. 472.
38. Montaigne, p. 109.
39. Montaigne, pp. 111–12.
40. Montaigne, p. 110.
41. Montaigne, p. 109.
42. Yet Hawes does not follow Reisch with regard to invention, which is defined by Hawes as the first and principal part of rhetoric (Stephen Hawes, *The Historie of Graunde Amoure and La Bell Pucel, Called the Pastime of Plesure* (London: printed by Iohn Wayland, 1554), C4v). In fact, according to Jane Griffiths, 'Hawes' description of the part played by invention within the art of rhetoric is wholly his own' ('The Matter of Invention in Hawes' *Passetyme of Pleasure*', *SEDERI*, 13 (2003), 101–10 (p. 102)).
43. Hawes, D1r.
44. Hawes, D1r.
45. Thomas Thomas, Xx5v.
46. Edmund Coote, *The English Schoole-Maister* (London: printed by the Widow Orwin for Ralph Iackson and Robert Dextar, 1596), M4v.
47. Florio, *A VVorlde of Wordes*, L3r; Perceval, L5r. This understanding continues in the seventeenth century; cf. Robert Cawdry, *A Table Alphabeticall* (London: printed by I. R[oberts] for Edmund Weauer, 1604), E1r, G4r; Cotgrave, Zz2r, Nn5r, Ooo6v.
48. William Shakespeare, 'A Midsummer Night's Dream' [1600], ed. by Terri Bourus, in *New Oxford Shakespeare*, I, 859–922 (v. 1. 14–17; p. 912).
49. Huarte de San Juan, p. 156. Note the position of 'poetry' at the start of the enumeration.
50. Huarte de San Juan, p. 164.
51. Huarte de San Juan, p. 186.
52. Huarte de San Juan, pp. 185, 186. This negative presentation of imaginative men is inseparable from Huarte's claim that men from the north of Europe (Protestants) were dominated by the imagination, unlike Spaniards and peoples from the same latitudes (Catholics), typically ruled by the understanding and thus naturally prone to virtue. See Rocío G. Sumillera, 'Ingenios del norte e ingenios del sur en *Examen de ingenios para las ciencias* (1575) de Juan Huarte de San Juan', in *El sur también existe: Hacia la creación de un imaginario europeo sobre España*, ed. by Berta Raposo and Ferran Robles (Madrid: Iberoamericana, 2014), pp. 37–48.
53. Shakespeare, 'Henry the Fifth', Prologue. 12–13 (p. 2311).
54. Shakespeare, 'Henry the Fifth', Prologue. 23–28 (p. 2311).
55. Rocío G. Sumillera, 'Invention and Imagination in Sixteenth-Century English Literature', *Journal of Language, Literature and Culture*, 61.1 (2014), 21–32.
56. Shakespeare, 'Midsummer Night's Dream', v. 1. 205–10 (p. 917).
57. Baret, Ll1r.

58. Thomas Thomas, Hhvi v.
59. Cawdry, F2r; Cotgrave, Aaaiii v.
60. Cotgrave, Nn5v. Even I. A. Richards, in his study of six different senses in the present-day use of the term 'imagination', puts 'inventiveness' in fourth place ('The Imagination', in *Principles of Literary Criticism*, ed. by John Constable (London: Routledge, 2001), pp. 212–23 (pp. 212–14)).
61. Huarte de San Juan, p. 177. For more on the English context, see William Rossky, 'Imagination in the English Renaissance: Psychology and Poetic', *Studies in the Renaissance*, 5 (1958), 49–73.
62. Peletier du Mans, pp. 251–52.
63. Ronsard, 'Abrégé', p. 472. See also Brian Barron, 'Poetry and Imagination in the Renaissance', in *Poetry in France: Metamorphoses of a Muse*, ed. by Keith Aspley and Peter France (Edinburgh: Edinburgh University Press, 1992), pp. 61–82.
64. George Wither, *A Collection of Emblemes, Ancient and Moderne* (London: printed by A[ugustine] M[athewes] for Iohn Grismond, 1635), Q2r.
65. Wither, Q2r.
66. Greville, d2r.
67. Baret, Kk2r.
68. Thomas Thomas, Ee2r.
69. Cotgrave, Zzz4r.
70. Florio, *A VVorlde of Wordes*, Z5r.
71. Perceval, F5r.
72. Davies of Hereford, *Wittes Pilgrimage*, K4r (emphasis in original).
73. William Shakespeare, 'The Second Part of Henry the Fourth' [1600], ed. by Francis X. Connor, in *New Oxford Shakespeare*, I, 761–856 (I. 3. 27–28; p. 792).
74. Shakespeare, 'Midsummer Night's Dream', v. 1. 7–8 (p. 912).
75. Shakespeare, 'Midsummer Night's Dream', v. 1. 4–6 (p. 912).
76. Peter C. Herman, *Squitter-Wits and Muse-Haters: Sidney, Spencer, Milton, and Renaissance Antipoetic Sentiment* (Detroit: Wayne State University Press, 1996), p. 37.
77. William Tyndale, *The Practyse of Prelates* (London: printed by Anthony Scoloker and Willyam Seres, 1548), D2r.
78. Puttenham, p. 109.
79. Puttenham, p. 109.
80. William Tyndale, *A Path Way i[n]to the Holy Scripture* (London: printed by Tho[mas] Godfray, 1536), B4v.
81. William Tyndale, *The Obedie[n]ce of a Christen Man and How Christe[n] Rulers Ought to Governe* (Marlborow in the la[n]de of Hesse [i.e. Antwerp]: printed by Hans Iuft [i.e. J. Hoochstraten], 1528), P1r.
82. Tyndale, *Obedie[n]ce*, P8v. Herman, pp. 37–43, provides numerous instances from Tyndale's work of attacks on the imagination, which he directly opposes to God.
83. Herman, pp. 40–43.
84. See Jay L. Halio, 'The Metaphor of Conception and Elizabethan Theories of the Imagination', *Neophilologus*, 50 (1966), 454–61.
85. Puttenham, p. 110.
86. Puttenham, p. 110.
87. Puttenham, p. 323.
88. Gascoigne, 'Appendix', p. 491.
89. Davies of Hereford, *Mirum in Modum*, A4v (emphasis in original). See in this regard Ruth L. Anderson, 'A French Source for John Davies of Hereford's System of Psychology', *University of Iowa Philological Quarterly*, 6.1 (1927), 57–66.
90. John Heywood, 'Witty and Witless', in *The Plays of John Heywood*, ed. by Richard Axton and Peter Happé (Cambridge; Rochester: D.S. Brewer, 1991), pp. 55–73 (p. 67)
91. William Shakespeare, 'As You Like It' [1622], ed. by Francis X. Connor, in *New Oxford Shakespeare*, II, 1845–1922 (III. 3. 15; p. 1898).
92. Plato, *Theaetetus. Sophist*, trans. by Harold North Fowler (Cambridge, MA: Harvard University Press, 1921), p. 333 (235E).

93. Arthur F. Kinney. *Humanist Poetics*, p. 29.
94. Puttenham, p. 110.
95. Puttenham, p. 110.
96. Sidney, p. 104. For more on this extract, see Ronald Levao, 'Sidney's Feigned *Apology*', pp. 136–37.
97. Sidney, p. 85.
98. Sidney, p. 105.
99. Sidney, p. 87.
100. Sidney, p. 90.
101. Sidney, pp. 91, 90.
102. Sidney, p. 99. For more on the role of the image within Sidney's theory of poetry, see Davis, p. 37. For more on the visualist model of Sidney's theory, see Lawrence C. Wolfley, p. 233; Eden, *Poetic and Legal Fiction*, p. 174; Peter Mack, 'Early Modern Ideas of Imagination: The Rhetorical Tradition', in *Imagination*, ed. by Nauta and Pätzold, pp. 59–76 (pp. 69–72); Peter Mack, 'Rhetoric, Ethics and Reading', p. 15.
103. John Hoskins, 'Sidney's *Arcadia* and the Rhetoric of English Prose (c. 1599)', in *English Renaissance Literary Criticism*, ed. by Brian Vickers (Oxford: Oxford University Press, 2003), pp. 398–427 (p. 399).
104. Michael Mack, p. 14.
105. Abrams, M. H., *The Mirror and the Lamp: Romantic Theory and the Critical Tradition* (London: Oxford University Press, 1976), p. 272.
106. John Dryden, 'Annus Mirabilis' [1667], in *Works of John Dryden*, 1: *Poems 1649–1680*, ed. by Edward Niles Hooker and H. T. Swedenberg, Jr (Berkeley: University of California Press, 1956), pp. 48–105 (p. 53).
107. Dryden, 'Annus Mirabilis', p. 53.
108. Dryden, 'Annus Mirabilis', p. 53. For more on Dryden's understanding and use of the terms invention and imagination in the composition of poetry, see John M. Aden, 'Dryden and the Imagination: The First Phase', *Publications of the Modern Language Association of America*, 74.1 (1959), 28–40; Robert D. Hume, 'Dryden on Creation: "Imagination" in the Later Criticism', *Review of English Studies*, 21.83 (1970), 295–314.
109. Castor, p. 180.

CONCLUSION

Poetic Invention as a Transitional Stage

Poetic invention is a transitional stage between the classical concept of mimesis and the subsequent Romantic notion of creative imagination. Invention in Renaissance poetics no doubt owes its conceptual richness to the long and complex history of the concept. A rhetorico-logical notion in origin, it first appeared in medieval *artes poetriae*; during the Renaissance, it gradually dropped its purely logical and rhetorical connotations limited to the idea of 'finding', and came closer to imagination. Likewise, the latter was a newcomer in the discourse of Renaissance poetics because it initially pertained to the field of natural and moral philosophy and was mostly found in studies on the human mind. Thus, in the Renaissance, both concepts, coming from very different backgrounds, bore witness to the transformation of their respective home disciplines and the manner in which, over the centuries, those disciplines interacted with each other and borrowed from each other's language and concerns.

The conceptualisation of the process of poetry-writing in terms of imagination responded to a growing interest in understanding how the mind of the poet operated. Considering the theory of inspiration unsatisfactory and insufficient, Renaissance authors attempted to apply views from Antiquity and the Middle Ages regarding how the human mind works to the understanding of poetic activity. As a result, the old question of how a work of art relates to the real world began to compete with a rising curiosity about the mental process of invention and the potentially dangerous faculty of the imagination. Indeed, the question was not only that of how art related to nature, but how the poet's mind functioned in such a way as to allow the production of a superior golden world.

As Huarte acknowledged, 'from a good imagination spring all the arts and sciences',[1] beginning with poetry, and it is to this mental faculty that invention is affiliated. In his words, for an author to 'possess much invention', 'it behoveth that he have a very swift imagination'.[2] In Spain, this view was shared by the members of the Sevillian school of poetry of the late sixteenth century. In *Cisne de Apolo* (1602), Luis Carvallo acknowledges that, for poetry, 'es menester gran imaginativa, y esta es la diferencia de ingenio que a esta facultad pertenece' [great imagination is required, and that is the difference of wit that pertains to this faculty].[3] Juan Rengifo's *Arte poetica* (c. 1597, first dated edition 1607) closely follows Huarte's and Carvallo's perspectives. As Huarte and his followers illustrate, the connection between imagination, invention, and poetry in effect pervades not only the discourse of poetics but also that of medicine and natural philosophy, which the imagination had never abandoned. In other words, it not only happened that a term proper to natural philosophy entered poetics, but that, simultaneously, concerns about poetry-writing came to interest natural philosophers and physicians alike, who also argued that this faculty enabled poetic composition and that the poet by necessity was exceptionally imaginative.[4]

In agreement with Huarte, for the French physician Pierre Charron, author of the immensely successful *De la sagesse* (1601) and considered the 'most important conduit of Huarte's ideas' in France,[5] imagination is clearly the faculty of poetry. To it Charron attributes 'Fanciful Inventions, Pleasant Conceits, Witty Jests, Sharp Reflections, Ingenious Repartees; Fictions and Fables, Figures and Comparisons, Propriety and Purity of Expression', for which reason 'we may range under this Division, Poetry, Eloquence, Musick, Correspondence, Harmony, and Proportion'.[6] Charron provides a physiological explanation for poetry:

> The *Temperament* fittest for the *Imagination*, is, *Hot*, which makes Distracted, Hair-brain'd, and Feverish People, excel all others in bold and lofty Flights of Fancy. Thus *Poetry, Divination*, and all that depends upon *Imagination*, were always thought to proceed from a sort of Fury and Inspiration. This Faculty is for the same reason most Vigorous in Youth and the Flower of our Age: The Poets accordingly flourished at these Years.[7]

The year 1601 also saw the publication of one of the century's best known works on the human passions, Thomas Wright's *The passions of the mind in general* (1601). It too reflects on the imagination, and, unsurprisingly, was influenced by Huarte's theories.[8] A Catholic from York who taught at the English College in Valladolid after entering the Society of Jesus, Wright locates the origin of the passions in the imagination, from where 'the purer spirits flock from the brain by certain secret channels to the heart'.[9] For Wright, 'the diversities of complexions wonderfully increase or diminish Passions',[10] which means that a heated melancholic temperament, for instance, automatically determines an increase in the imaginative faculty and hence an increase in the passions of the heart too. And, vice versa, the latter can cause an alteration in human complexions: 'because when these imaginations are stirring in our minds they alter the humours of our bodies, causing some passion or alteration in them'.[11]

Later on in the seventeenth century, Robert Burton states similarly in *The anatomy of melancholy* (1621) that 'in Poets and Painters *Imagination* forcibly workes, as appears by their severall fictions',[12] and Edward Reynolds's *A treatise of the passions and faculties of the soule of man* (1640) also connects the strong powers of the imagination with poetry. Reynolds affirms, using his own characteristic wording, that 'the libertie of the Imagination', when it comes to poetry, manifests itself on three different levels, which he calls 'Creation', or 'new making of Objects'; 'Composition, or new mixing them; and Translation, or new placing them'. To these three are 'reduced all Poeticall Fictions', Reynolds affirms.[13] Of course, behind 'creation', 'composition', and 'translation' we can distinguish the notions of *inventio, dispositio*, and *elocutio* in classical rhetorical terminology. Again, therefore, invention is said to pertain to the poet's imagination.

The views on invention put forward by Renaissance natural philosophy and medicine are in agreement with those found in works on poetics. Furthermore, its rise in the field of poetics appears to coincide with the establishment of the pillars of empiricism and modern science.[14] Sir Francis Bacon, who believed in the refutation of traditional philosophy and the replacement of contemplative speculation with an active science, argued against the idea that scientific truths should be founded upon deductive knowledge, the opinions of consolidated authorities such as Aristotle, or the dictates of divine providence and religious doctrine. A new classification of knowledge was thus imperative, as well as new methods for acquiring knowledge. Bacon reversed the premises of deductive reasoning, and argued instead that general axioms should be the end and not the beginning of scientific inference. His view was that knowledge rises from lower propositions to general ones, so that it gradually becomes less empirical and more theoretical. In addition, he discussed invention and imagination at length in several of his works. In *Of the proficience and advancement of learning* (1605), the 'ARTS INTELLECTVALL' are classified into four groups 'according to the ends whereunto they are referred': 'ARTE of ENQVIRIE or INVENTION: ART of EXAMINATION or IVDGEMENT: ART of CVSTODIE or MEMORIE: and ART of ELOCVTION or TRADITION', for 'mans labour is to *inuent* that which is *sought* or *propounded*: or to *iudge* that which is *inuented*: or to *retaine* that which is *iudged*: or to *deliuer* ouer that which is *retained*'.[15] As Lisa Jardine explains, for Bacon, 'invention is the process of selection and collation of material', for which purpose it makes use of the places or topics.[16] Bacon understands that invention involves putting forward something new,[17] for, in his words, 'to Inuent is to discouer that, we know not, & not to recouer or resummon that which wee alreadie knowe'.[18]

Bacon also reflects on the imagination. In *Of the proficience and advancement of learning* and *De augmentis*, he divides all knowledge into history, poesy, and philosophy, and to each he attributes a specific mental faculty: memory to history, imagination to poesy, and reason to philosophy. 'Poesie faineth Acts and Euents', Bacon states, and in so doing it 'doth truly referre to the Imagination', which is the faculty that allows poetry to 'ioyne that which Nature hath seuered: & seuer that which Nature hath ioyned, and so make vnlawfull Matches & diuorses of things'.[19] The fact that the imagination is 'not tyed to the Lawes of Matter' grants poetry the freedom to escape the constrictions of reason.[20] By contrast, in rhetoric the former implements the latter's dictates.[21]

Bacon's philosophy entered the University of Cambridge's lecture halls in the 1640s together with that of Descartes, in just about 'the same years that Cambridge Platonism began as a distinct movement'.[22] Both the Cambridge Platonists and the rationalists discredited the imaginative faculty as part of the material realm, while claiming that true ideas were not subordinate to sensory images. As a result, to rationalist thinkers, the imagination seemed not only an inadequate means of attaining the highest kind of knowledge but also a force that dragged human thought towards materialistic stances. The British empiricists disagreed with Platonic idealism and the Cartesian rationalist school: if the latter advocated a dualistic type of psychology which marginalised and undervalued the imagination,[23] the former assigned to it a key role, and viewed it 'as a power that might replace or complement "reason"'.[24]

Empiricists acknowledged that it was necessary for cognition, for it gave meaning to the information gathered by the senses; for instance, in *Leviathan* (1651) and *Elements of philosophy* (1655–58), Hobbes regarded it a profoundly constructive power. For him, 'so farre forth as the Fancy of man, has traced the wayes of true Philosophy, so farre it hath produced very marvellous effects to the benefit of mankind'.[25] Indeed, the expansion of the imagination within the field of poetics does not seem to be disconnected from the incipient empirical science, which took experimentation and direct observation of nature as the starting point of all knowledge.

Despite the subsequent predominance of the imagination and its indisputable connection to creativity, genius, and originality in Romantic poetics, the notion of invention, which reached its peak in the Renaissance, was not dropped in Romanticism. In the preface to the 1831 edition of *Frankenstein*, Mary Shelley recalls the now-familiar events of the night in the summer of 1816 when Percy Shelley, Byron, and the physician John Polidori set out to write a ghost story. The challenge of that night would lead her to produce what would become one of the most enduring and representative novels of English Romanticism. Mary Shelley thus reflects on the origins of her novel by means of none other than the notion of invention, which, she affirms 'does not consist in creating out of void, but out of chaos', 'seizing on the capabilities of a subject, and [...] moulding and fashioning ideas suggested to it'.[26] In other words, invention does not entail that which is 'hitherto unknown'; that is, it does not signify the creation out of nothing of that which nobody has ever seen, considered, or fictionalised before, but rather refers to the innovative possibilities offered by the exploitation of fresh and unexpected 'relations and connections among things'.[27]

The implications of invention, rhetorical and logical in origin yet properly poetic in the Renaissance, thus surpass plain imitation, staunchly resist the temptations of slavish copying, disregard the ethically reproachable practice of literary theft, and instead involve emulation of the virtues and achievements of previous models. Inventing implies fully digesting the *auctoritates* and profiting from tradition, be it domestic or foreign, written in a classical tongue or in a vernacular, translated or in the original language. Tradition is in each case the supplier of raw material for complex heuristic processes that eventually lead to the composition of rare new literary products. Taken as an indicator of the poet's incisive mental acumen, invention alone makes a work worthy of being read, and as such is made a pre-eminent criterion for the assessment of literary merit. Despite the bad press ensuing from its alliance with the vigorous mental faculty of the imagination, invention could not deny its relation with the latter; as literary authors and natural philosophers and physicians acknowledged in their works, invention was in fact dependent on the imagination. Inventive poets were thus extremely imaginative, and their work a golden poetic universe capable of suggesting to the reader the striking mirage of what is entirely novel, previously unimagined, and ultimately created out of a void.

Notes to the Conclusion

1. Huarte de San Juan, p. 177.
2. Huarte de San Juan, p. 177.
3. Luis Alfonso de Carvallo, *Cisne de Apolo* [1602], ed. by Alberto Porqueras Mayo (Kassel: Reichenberger, 1997), p. 97.
4. Rocío G. Sumillera, 'From Inspiration to Imagination: The Physiology of Poetry in Early Modernity', *Parergon*, 33.3 (2016), 17-42.
5. Henry C. Clark, *La Rochefoucauld and the Language of Unmasking in Seventeenth-Century France* (Geneva: Droz, 1994), p. 42. See also Renée Kogel, *Pierre Charron* (Geneva: Droz, 1972), p. 43. Charron's work was translated into English by Samson Lennard as *Of Wisdome* (1608?), which had several editions (1615?, 1620, 1630, 1640, 1651, 1658, and 1670), before being retranslated in 1697 by George Stanhope. See F. Charles-Daubert, 'Charron et l'Angleterre', *Recherches sur le XVIIe Siècle*, 5 (1982), 53–56.
6. Pierre Charron, *Of Wisdom: Three Books [...] made English by George Stanhope* (London: printed for M. Gillyflower, M. Bently, H. Bornwick, J. Tonson, W. Freeman, T. Goodwin, M. Wotton, J. Waltboe, S. Manship, and R. Parker, 1697), I3v.
7. Charron, I2v.
8. Rocío G. Sumillera, 'Thomas Wright and Juan Huarte de San Juan', *Notes and Queries*, 63.1 (2016), 23–27.
9. Thomas Wright, *The Passions of the Mind in General* [1601], ed. by William Webster Newbold (New York and London: Garland, 1986), p. 123.
10. Wright, p. 123.
11. Wright, p. 94.
12. Burton, I, 152.
13. Edward Reynolds, *A Treatise of the Passions and Faculties of the Soule of Man: With the Severall Dignities and Corruptions thereunto Belonging* (London: printed by R. H[earne and John Norton] for Robert Bostock, 1640), D4v.
14. G. S. Rousseau, 'Science and the Discovery of the Imagination in Enlightened England', in *The Past as Prologue: Essays to Celebrate the Twenty-Fifth Anniversary of ASECS*, ed. by Carla H. Hay and Syndy M. Conger (New York: AMS Press, 1995), pp. 19–43 (p. 19).
15. Francis Bacon, *The Advancement of Learning* [1605], ed. by Michael Kiernan (Oxford: Clarendon Press, 2000), p. 107 (emphasis in original).
16. Jardine, 'Dialectic Teaching', p. 32.
17. Karl R. Wallace, *Francis Bacon on Communication and Rhetoric; or, The Art of Applying Reason to Imagination for the Better Moving of the Will* (Chapel Hall: University of North Carolina Press, 1943), p. 85.
18. Bacon, pp. 111–12.
19. Bacon, p. 73 (emphasis in original).
20. Bacon, p. 73. Among the scholars who have discussed Bacon's notions of poetry are Bundy, 'Bacon's True Opinion'; John L. Harrison, 'Bacon's View of Rhetoric, Poetry, and the Imagination', *Huntington Library Quarterly*, 20.2 (1957), 107–25; Hardison, *Literary Criticism*; Brian Vickers, 'Francis Bacon and the Progress of Knowledge', *Journal of the History of Ideas*, 53 (1992), 495–518; Brian Vickers, 'Bacon and Rhetoric', in *The Cambridge Companion to Bacon*, ed. by Markku Peltonen (Cambridge: Cambridge University Press, 1996), pp. 200–31; Brian Vickers, *Francis Bacon and Renaissance Prose* (Cambridge: Cambridge University Press, 2009). For more on Bacon and his idea of the imagination, see Karl R. Wallace, *Francis Bacon on the Nature of Man: The Faculties of Man's Soul: Understanding, Reason, Imagination, Memory, Will, and Appetite* (Urbana: University of Illinois Press, 1967); Todd Wayne Butler, *Imagination and Politics in Seventeenth-Century England* (Aldershot and Burlington: Ashgate, 2008), pp. 20–21.
21. In fact, according to Bacon, the duty of rhetoric is none other but '*To apply Reason to Imagination, for the better moouing of the will*' (p. 127; emphasis in original).
22. Tod E. Jones, 'From Pre-Reformation to Pre-Restoration: The Social-Historical and Theological Context', in *The Cambridge Platonists: A Brief Introduction*, ed. by Tod E. Jones (Lanham: University Press of America, 2005), pp. 3–14 (p. 8).

23. Descartes's views on this concept mostly appear in Rules XII and XIV of the *Rules for the Direction of the Mind* (1628), and in Meditations II and VI of the *Meditations on First Philosophy* (1641). W. Jackson Bate discusses the impact of the Cartesian principles of French neoclassicism on seventeenth-century England (*The Burden of the Past and the English Poet* (London: Chatto and Windus, 1971), p. 17). For more on the idea of imagination in seventeenth-century France, see Matthew W. Maguire, *The Conversion of Imagination: From Pascal through Rousseau to Tocqueville* (Cambridge, MA: Harvard University Press, 2006). See also Carson S. Duncan, *The New Science and English Literature in the Classical Period* (New York: Russell & Russell, 1972), which deals with Bacon and Descartes, among others.
24. Engell, p. 20.
25. Thomas Hobbes, 'The Answer of Mr. Hobbes to Sir Will. D'Avenant's Preface before Gondibert' [1650], in William D'Avenant, *Sir William Davenant's 'Gondibert'*, ed. by David F Gladish (Oxford: Clarendon Press, 1971), pp. 45–55 (p. 49). See further Donald F. Bond, 'The Neo-Classical Psychology of the Imagination', *English Literary History*, 4 (1937), 245–64; Engell. Eva T. H. Brann is more sceptical in attributing to the imagination a significant role in the philosophical postulates of Hobbes, Locke, and Leibniz (*The World of the Imagination: Sum and Substance* (Savage: Rowman & Littlefield, 1991), p. 78).
26. Mary Shelley, 'Introduction to *Frankenstein*, Third Edition (1831)', in *'Frankenstein': The 1818 Text, Contexts, Criticism*, ed. by J. Paul Hunter (New York: Norton, 2012), pp. 165–69 (p. 167).
27. Richard T. Gray, 'Introduction', in *Inventions of the Imagination: Romanticism and Beyond*, ed. by Richard T. Gray (Seattle: University of Washington Press, 2011), pp. 3–16 (p. 8).

PRIMARY SOURCES

APHTHONIUS, *Aphthonii Progymnasmata* (London: Impensis Societatis Stationariorum, 1605)
ARISTOTLE, *Art of Rhetoric*, ed. and trans. by John Henry Freese (Cambridge, MA: Harvard University Press, 1926)
—— 'Poetics', ed. and trans. by Stephen Halliwell, in *Aristotle, 'Poetics'; Longinus, 'On the Sublime'; Demetrius, 'On Style'* (Cambridge, MA: Harvard University Press, 1995), pp. 27–142
ASCHAM, ROGER, *English Works: 'Toxophilus', 'Report of the Affaires and State of Germany', 'The Scholemaster'*, ed. by William Aldis Wright (Cambridge: Cambridge University Press, 1970)
AUBREY, JOHN, *'Brief Lives': A Modern English Version*, ed. by Richard Barber (Woodbridge: Boydell, 1982)
BACON, FRANCIS, *The Advancement of Learning* [1605], ed. by Michael Kiernan (Oxford: Clarendon Press, 2000)
BARET, JOHN, *An Aluearie; or, Triple Dictionarie: In Englishe, Latin, and French* (London: printed by Henry Denham, 1574)
BEHN, APHRA, 'The Dutch Lover' [1673], in *The Works of Aphra Behn*, ed. by Montague Summers, 6 vols (New York: Phaeton Press, 1967), I, 215–330
BLUNDEVILLE, THOMAS, *The Art of Logike* (London: printed by Iohn Windet, 1599)
—— *The True Order and Methode of Wryting and Reading Hystories* (London: printed by VVillyam Seres, 1574)
BURTON, ROBERT, *The Anatomy of Melancholy* [1621], ed. by Thomas C. Faulkner, Nicolas K. Kiessling, and Rhonda L. Blair, 6 vols (Oxford: Clarendon Press; New York: Oxford University Press, 1989–2000)
CARTWRIGHT, WILLIAM, *Comedies, Tragi-Comedies, with Other Poems* (London: printed for [T. R. &] Humphrey Moseley, 1651)
CARVALLO, LUIS ALFONSO DE, *Cisne de Apolo* [1602], ed. by Alberto Porqueras Mayo (Kassel: Reichenberger, 1997)
CASTELVETRO, LUDOVICO, *On the Art of Poetry*, ed. and trans. by Andrew Bongiorno (Binghamton: State University of New York, Center for Medieval and Early Renaissance Studies, 1984)
CAWDRY, ROBERT, *A Table Alphabeticall* (London: printed by I. R[oberts] for Edmund Weauer, 1604)
CAXTON, WILLIAM, *The Myrrour: [And] Dyscrypcyon of the Worlde with Many Meruaylles* (London: printed by Laurence Andrewe, 1527)
CHAPMAN, GEORGE, *Achilles Shield Translated as the Other Seuen Bookes of Homer, Out of his Eighteenth Booke of Iliades* (London: printed by Iohn Windet, 1598)
CHARRON, PIERRE, *Of Wisdom: Three Books [...] Made English by George Stanhope* (London: printed for M. Gillyflower, M. Bently, H. Bornwick, J. Tonson, W. Freeman, T. Goodwin, M. Wotton, J. Waltboe, S. Manship, and R. Parker, 1697)
CICERO, MARCUS TULLIUS, *'Brutus' and 'Orator'*, trans. by G. L. Hendrickson and H. M. Hubbell (Cambridge, MA: Harvard University Press; London: Heinemann, 1962)

―― 'De inventione', 'De optimo genere oratorum', 'Topica', trans. by H. M. Hubbell (Cambridge, MA: Harvard University Press; London: Heinemann, 1960)
―― *De oratore*, 2 vols (London: Heinemann; Cambridge, MA: Harvard University Press, 1959–60)
―― *Rhetorica ad Herennium*, trans. by Harry Caplan (Cambridge, MA: Harvard University Press; London: Heinemann, 1968)
―― *The Speeches: Pro Archia. Post Reditum in Senatu. Post Reditum ad Quirites. De Domo Sua. De Haruspicum Responsis. Pro Plancio*, trans. by N. H. Watts (Cambridge, MA: Harvard University Press; London: William Heinemann, 1923)
―― *Tusculan Disputations*, trans. by J. E. King (Cambridge, MA: Harvard University Press; London: Heinemann, 1966)
COOPER, THOMAS, *Thesaurus Linguæ Romanæ & Britannicæ* (London: printed by Henry Denham, 1578)
COOTE, EDMUND, *The English Schoole-Maister* (London: printed by the Widow Orwin for Ralph Iackson and Robert Dextar, 1596)
The Correspondence of Philip Sidney and Hubert Languet, ed. by William Aspenwall Bradley (Boston: Merrymount Press, 1912)
COTGRAVE, RANDLE, *A Dictionarie of the French and English Tongues* (London: printed by Adam Islip, 1611)
COX, LEONARD, *The Art or Crafte of Rhetoryke* (London: printed by Robert Redman, 1532)
D'AUBIGNÉ, AGRIPPA, *Le Printemps: Stances et Odes* [composed 1570], ed. by Fernand Desonay (Geneva: Droz, 1952)
DAVIES, JOHN, OF HEREFORD, *Mirum in Modum: A Glimpse of Gods Glorie and the Soules Shape* (London: printed [by Valentine Simmes] for VVilliam Aspley, 1602)
―― *The Scourge of Folly* (London: Printed by E[dward] A[llde] for Richard Redmer, 1611)
―― *A Select Second Husband for Sir Thomas Ouerburie's Wife, Now a Matchlesse Widow* (London: printed by Thomas Creede and Barnard Allsopp for Iohn Marriott, 1616)
―― *Wittes Pilgrimage* (London: printed [by R. Bradock] for Iohn Browne, 1605)
DETHICK, HENRY, 'Oratio in laudem poëseos' [*c*. 1575], in *Latin Treatises on Poetry from Renaissance England*, ed. and trans. by J. W. Binns (Signal Mountain: Summertown, 1999), pp. 1–55
DRYDEN, JOHN, 'Annus Mirabilis' [1667], in *The Works of John Dryden*, 20 vols (Berkeley: University of California Press, 1956–2000), I: *Poems 1649–1680*, ed. by Edward Niles Hooker and H. T. Swedenberg, Jr (Berkeley: University of California Press, 1956), pp. 48–105
―― 'An Essay of Dramatick Poesie' [1668], in *The Works of John Dryden*, 20 vols (Berkeley: University of California Press, 1956–2000), XVII: *Prose 1668–1691: 'An Essay of Dramatick Poesie' and Shorter Works*, ed. by Hugh Thomas Swedenberg and Samuel Holt Monk (1971), pp. 3–82
―― 'Fables Ancient and Modern: Preface' [1700], in *The Works of John Dryden*, 20 vols (Berkeley: University of California Press, 1956–2000), VII: *Poems, 1697-1700*, ed. by Vinton A. Dearing (Berkeley: University of California Press, 2000), pp. 24-47
―― 'A Parallel between Painting and Poetry' [1695], in *The Works of John Dryden*, 20 vols (Berkeley: University of California Press, 1956–2000), XX: *Prose 1691–1698: 'De arte graphica' and Shorter Works*, ed. by A. E. Wallace Maurer and George R. Guffey (1989), pp. 38–77
DU BELLAY, JOACHIM, 'The Defence and Illustration of the French Language', in *Poetry & Language in 16th-Century France: Du Bellay, Ronsard, Sébillet*, ed. and trans. by Laura Willett (Toronto: Centre for Reformation and Renaissance Studies, 2004), pp. 37–96
―― *La Deffence, et Illustration de la langue françoyse (1549)*, ed. by Jean-Charles Monferran (Geneva: Droz, 2001)

—— 'Second Preface to the *Olive*', in *Poetry & Language in 16th-Century France: Du Bellay, Ronsard, Sébillet*, trans. by Laura Willett (Toronto: Centre for Reformation and Renaissance Studies, 2004), pp. 107–14

ELIOT, JOHN, *Ortho-Epia Gallica: Eliots Fruits for the French* (London: printed by [Richard Field for] Iohn VVolfe, 1593)

ELYOT, THOMAS, SIR, *The Boke Named the Gouernour* (London: printed by Thomas Berthelet, 1537)

—— *The Dictionary of Syr Thomas Eliot Knyght* (London: printed by Thomae Bertheleti, 1538)

ERASMUS, DESIDERIUS. *Collected Works of Erasmus*, 89 vols (Toronto and Buffalo: University of Toronto Press, 1974–2019), XXVIII: *'Ciceronianus', Notes, Indexes*, trans. and ed. by Betty I. Knott (1986)

FICINO, MARSILIO, *Platonic Theology*, ed. by James Hankins with William Bowen, 6 vols (Cambridge, MA: Harvard University Press, 2001–06)

FLORIO, JOHN, *Queen Anna's Nevv Vvorld of Words; or, Dictionarie of the Italian and English Tongues* (London: printed by Melch. Bradwood [and William Stansby] for Edw. Blount and William Barret, 1611)

—— 'To the Curteous Reader', in *The Essayes or Morall, Politike and Millitarie Discourses of Lo: Michaell de Montaigne [...]: The First Booke* (London: printed by Val. Sims for Edward Blount, 1603), A5r–A6r

—— *A VVorlde of Wordes; or, Most Copious, and Exact Dictionarie in Italian and English* (London: printed by Arnold Hatfield for Edw. Blount, 1598)

FOXE, JOHN, *Fox's Book of Martyrs; or, The Acts and Monuments of the Christian Church* [1563], ed. by John Malham and T. Pratt (Philadelphia: Woodward, 1830)

GASCOIGNE, GEORGE, 'Appendix', in *The Complete Works of George Gascoigne*, 2 vols (Cambridge: Cambridge University Press, 1907-10), I, ed. by John William Cunliffe (1907), pp. 474-502

—— 'Certayne Notes of Instruction Concerning the Making of Verse', in *The Complete Works of George Gascoigne*, I, ed. by John William Cunliffe (1907), pp. 465-73

—— 'The Delectable History of Sundry Adventures Passed by Dan Bartholmew of Bathe', in *The Complete Works of George Gascoigne*, I, ed. by John William Cunliffe (1907), pp. 96-137

—— 'To Al Yong Gentlemen, and Generally to the Youth of England', in *The Complete Works of George Gascoigne*, I, ed. by John William Cunliffe (1907), pp. 9-14

GENTILI, ALBERICO, 'Commentatio ad Legem III Codicis de professoribus et medicis' [1593], in *Latin Treatises on Poetry from Renaissance England*, ed. and trans. by J. W. Binns (Signal Mountain: Summertown, 1999), pp. 59–134

GOSSON, STEPHEN, *Playes Confuted in Fiue Actions* (London: printed for Thomas Gosson, 1582)

—— *The Schoole of Abuse* (London: printed [by Thomas Dawson] for Thomas Woodcocke, 1587)

GREVILLE, FULKE, BARON BROOKE, 'A Treatie of Humane Learning', in *Certaine Learned and Elegant Workes of the Right Honorable Fulke Lord Brooke Written in his Youth, and Familiar Exercise with Sir Philip Sidney* (London: printed by E[lizabeth] P[urslowe] for Henry Seyle, 1633), d1r–g3v

HARINGTON, JOHN, 'Preface; or, Brief Apologie of Poetrie', in *Orlando Furioso: Translated into English Heroical Verse by Sir John Harington (1591)*, ed. by Robert McNulty (Oxford: Clarendon Press, 1972), pp. 2–16

HARVEY, GABRIEL, *Pierces Supererogation; or, A New Prayse of the Old Asse: A Preparatiue to Certaine Larger Discourses, Intituled Nashes s. Fame* (London: printed by Iohn Vvolfe, 1593)

HAWES, STEPHEN, *The Historie of Graunde Amoure and La Bell Pucel, Called the Pastime of Plesure* (London: printed by Iohn Wayland, 1554)

HEYWOOD, JOHN, 'Witty and Witless', in *The Plays of John Heywood*, ed. by Richard Axton and Peter Happé (Cambridge; Rochester: D.S. Brewer, 1991), pp. 55-73

HOBBES, THOMAS, 'The Answer of Mr. Hobbes to Sir Will. D'Avenant's Preface before Gondibert' [1650], in William D'Avenant, *Sir William Davenant's 'Gondibert'*, ed. by David F Gladish (Oxford: Clarendon Press, 1971), pp. 45–55

HORACE, *'Satires', 'Epistles' and 'Ars poetica'*, ed. and trans. by H. Rushton Fairclough (Cambridge, MA: Harvard University Press; London: Heinemann, 1978)

HOSKINS, JOHN, *Directions for Speech and Style* [c. 1599], ed. by Hoyt H. Hudson (Princeton: Princeton University Press, 1935)

—— 'Sidney's *Arcadia* and the Rhetoric of English Prose (c. 1599)', in *English Renaissance Literary Criticism*, ed. by Brian Vickers (Oxford: Oxford University Press, 2003), pp. 398–427

HUARTE DE SAN JUAN, JUAN, *The Examination of Mens Wits* [1594], trans. by Richard Carew, ed. by Rocío G. Sumillera (London: Modern Humanities Research Association, 2014)

HULOET, RICHARD, *Abcedarium Anglico Latinum* (London: [S. Mierdman] ex officina Gulielmi Riddel, 1552)

HUMPHREY, LAURENCE, 'Interpretatio linguarum' [1559], trans. by Gordon Kendal, in *English Renaissance Translation Theory*, ed. by Neil Rhodes, Gordon Kendal, and Louise Wilson (London: Modern Humanities Research Association, 2013), pp. 263–94

ISOCRATES, 'Against the Sophists', in *Isocrates in Three Volumes*, 3 vols (Cambridge, MA: Harvard University Press, 1928–29), II, trans. by George Norlin (1929), pp. 160–80

—— 'Panegyricus', in *Isocrates in Three Volumes*, 3 vols (Cambridge, MA: Harvard University Press, 1928–29), I, trans. by George Norlin (1928), pp. 115-242

JAMES I, KING OF ENGLAND, *The Essayes of a Prentise, in the Divine Art of Poesie* (Edinburgh: printed by Thomas Vautroullier, 1584)

JONSON, BEN, 'Discoveries' [1641], ed. by Lorna Hutson, in *The Cambridge Edition of the Works of Ben Jonson*, 7 vols (Cambridge and New York: Cambridge University Press, 2012), VII: *1641, Bibliography*, pp. 495–596

—— 'Epigrams' [1616], ed. by Colin Burrow, in *The Cambridge Edition of the Works of Ben Jonson*, 7 vols (Cambridge and New York: Cambridge University Press, 2012), V: *1616–1625*, pp. 101–98

KNOX, JOHN, *The History of the Reformation of Religion in Scotland* [1559–66], ed. by William McGavin (Glasgow: Blackie & Son and A. Fullarton; Dublin: WM. Curry Jun.; London: Simpkin & Marshall, 1832)

LANGBAINE, GERARD, *Momus Triumphans; or, The Plagiaries of the English Stage* (London: printed for Nicholas Cox, 1687)

LATIMER, HUGH, *A Notable Sermo[n] of Ye Reuerende Father Maister Hughe Latemer* (London: printed by Ihon Day and Wylliam Seres, 1548)

—— *The Sermon that the Reuerende Father in Christ, Hugh Latimer, Byshop of Worcester, made to the Clergie, in the Co[n]uocatio[n], before the Parlyament Began, the 9. Day of June* (London: printed by Thomas Berthelet, 1537)

LEVER, RALPH, *The Arte of Reason, Rightly Termed, Witcraft* (London: printed by H. Bynneman, 1573)

LODGE, THOMAS, *A Defence of Poetry, Music and Stage-Plays* [1579] (London: printed for the Shakespeare Society, 1853)

LONGINUS, 'On the Sublime', ed. and trans. by W. H. Fyfe, in *Aristotle, 'Poetics'; Longinus, 'On the Sublime'; Demetrius, 'On Style'* (Cambridge, MA: Harvard University Press, 1995), pp. 159–306

LYDGATE, JOHN, *Here Begynneth the Boke of Iohan Bochas, Discryuing the Fall of Pri[n]ces, Princesses, and Other Nobles* (London: printed by Richard Pynson, 1527)

LYLY, JOHN, *Euphues and His England* (London: printed [by T. East] for Gabriell Cawood, 1580)
—— *Sixe Court Comedies* (London: printed by William Stansby for Edward Blount, 1632)
MACILMAINE, ROLLO, *The Logike of the Moste Excellent Philosopher P. Ramus Martyr, Newly Translated, and in Diuers Places Corrected, after the Mynde of the Author* (London: printed by Thomas Vautroullier, 1574)
MARLOWE, CHRISTOPHER, 'Massacre at Paris' [1593], in *The Complete Works of Christopher Marlowe*, ed. by Fredson Bowers, 2 vols (Cambridge: Cambridge University Press, 1981), I, 353–417
MONTAIGNE, MICHEL DE, *The Complete Essays*, trans. and ed. by M. A. Screech (London: Penguin, 1993)
MUNDAY, ANTHONY, *Zelauto: The Fountaine of Fame* (London: printed by Iohn Charlevvood, 1580)
NASHE, THOMAS, *The Anatomie of Absurditie* (London: printed by I. Charlewood for Thomas Hacket, 1589)
—— *Pierce Penilesse his Supplication to the Diuell* (London: printed by Abell Ieffes for Iohn Busbie, 1592)
—— *A Pleasant Comedie, Called Summers Last Will and Testament* (London: printed by Simon Stafford for Walter Burre, 1600)
—— 'To the Gentlemen Students of Both Universities', in Robert Greene, *Menaphon* (London: printed by T[homas] O[rwin] for Sampson Clarke, 1589), **1r–A3r
NEVILLE, ALEXANDER, *The Lamentable Tragedie of Oedipus the Sonne of Laius Kyng of Thebes Out of Seneca* (London: printed by Thomas ColWell, 1563)
PEACHAM, HENRY, *Minerua Britanna; or, A Garden of Heroical Deuises* (London: printed by Wa: Dight, 1612)
PEELE, GEORGE, *Merrie Conceited Iests of George Peele Gentleman* (London: printed by G[eorge] P[urslowe] for F. Faulkner, 1627)
PELETIER DU MANS, JACQUES, 'Art poétique' [1555], in *Traités de poétique et de rhétorique de la Renaissance*, ed. by Francis Goyet (Paris: Librairie Générale Française, 1990), pp. 235–344
PERCEVAL, RICHARD, *A Dictionarie in Spanish and English* (London: printed by Edm. Bollifant, 1599)
PETERSON, ROBERT, *Galateo of Maister Iohn Della Casa, Archebishop of Beneuenta; or rather, A Treatise of the Ma[n]ners and Behauiours, it Behoueth a Man to Vse and Eschewe, in his Familiar Conuersation* (London: printed [by Henry Middleton] for Raufe Newbery, 1576)
PETRARCH, FRANCIS, *Letters of Old Age = Rerum senilium libri, I–XVIII*, trans. by Aldo S. Bernardo, Saul Levin, and Reta A. Bernardo, 2 vols (Baltimore: Johns Hopkins University Press, 1992)
—— *Petrarch, the First Modern Scholar and Man of Letters: A Selection from his Correspondence with Boccaccio and other Friends, Designed to Illustrate the Beginnings of the Renaissance*, trans. by James Harvey Robinson with Henry Winchester Rolfe (New York: Haskell House, 1970)
PICO DELLA MIRANDOLA, GIOVANNI FRANCESCO, *'On the Imagination': The Latin Text with an Introduction, an English Translation, and Notes by Harry Caplan*, trans. by Harry Caplan (New Haven: published for Cornell University, Yale University Press; London: Milford, Oxford University Press, 1930)
PLATO, *Theaetetus. Sophist*, trans. by Harold North Fowler (Cambridge, MA: Harvard University Press, 1921)
PUTTENHAM, GEORGE, *The Art of English Poesy* [1589], ed. by Frank Whigham and Wayne A. Rebhorn (Ithaca and London: Cornell University Press, 2007)
QUINTILIAN, M. FABIUS, *The Orator's Education*, trans. and ed. by Donald A. Russell, 5 vols (Cambridge, MA: Harvard University Press, 2001)

Rainolde, Richard, *A Booke Called the Foundacion of Rhetorike* (London: printed by Ihon Kingston, 1563)

Reynolds, Edward, *A Treatise of the Passions and Faculties of the Soule of Man: With the Severall Dignities and Corruptions thereunto Belonging* (London: printed by R. H[earne and John Norton] for Robert Bostock, 1640)

Ronsard, Pierre de, 'Abrégé de l'art poétique français' [1565], in *Traités de poétique et de rhétorique de la Renaissance*, ed. by Francis Goyet (Paris: Librairie Générale Française, 1990), pp. 465–93

—— *Œuvres complètes de P. de Ronsard*, 8 vols, ed. by M. Prosper Blanchemain (Paris: Jannet, 1857–67)

Salisbury, John of, *Entheticus Maior and Minor*, ed. by Jan van Laarhoven, 3 vols (Leiden: Brill, 1987)

Scaliger, Julius Caesar, *Poetices libri septem = Sieben Bücher über die Dichtkunst, Band IV, Buch 5*, ed. by Luc Deitz and Gregor Vogt-Spira (Stuttgart-Bad Cannstatt: Frommann-Holzboog, 1998)

—— *Select Translations from Scaliger's 'Poetics'*, trans. and ed. by Frederick Morgan Padelford (New York: Holt, 1905)

Scott, William, *The Model of Poesy* [c. 1599], ed. by Gavin Alexander (Cambridge: Cambridge University Press, 2013)

Sébillet, Thomas, 'Art poétique français' [1548], in *Traités de poétique et de rhétorique de la Renaissance*, ed. by Francis Goyet (Paris: Librairie Générale Française, 1990), pp. 37–183

Seneca, Lucius Annaeus, *Ad Lucilium epistulae morales*, trans. by Richard M. Gummere, 3 vols (Cambridge, MA: Harvard University Press; London: Heinemann, 1917–25)

Shakespeare, William, 'As You Like It' [1622], ed. by Francis X. Connor, in *The New Oxford Shakespeare: The Complete Works*, 2 vols (Oxford: Oxford University Press, 2017), II, 1845–1922

—— 'The Life of Henry the Fifth' [1623], ed. by Rory Loughnane, in *The New Oxford Shakespeare: The Complete Works*, 2 vols (Oxford: Oxford University Press, 2017), II, 2301–85 (p. 2311, ll. 1–2)

—— 'Love's Labour's Lost' [1598], ed. by Francis X. Connor, in *The New Oxford Shakespeare: The Complete Works*, 2 vols (Oxford: Oxford University Press, 2017), I, 449–531

—— 'A Midsummer Night's Dream' [1600], ed. by Terri Bourus, *The New Oxford Shakespeare: The Complete Works*, 2 vols (Oxford: Oxford University Press, 2017), I, 859–922

—— 'The Second Part of Henry the Fourth' [1600], ed. by Francis X. Connor, in *The New Oxford Shakespeare: The Complete Works*, 2 vols (Oxford: Oxford University Press, 2017), I, 761–856

—— 'Shake-speares Sonnets [including] "A Lover's Complaint"' [1609], ed. by Francis X. Connor, in *The New Oxford Shakespeare: The Complete Works*, 2 vols (Oxford: Oxford University Press, 2017), I, 1435–1516

Shelley, Mary, 'Introduction to *Frankenstein*, Third Edition (1831)', in *'Frankenstein': The 1818 Text, Contexts, Criticism*, ed. by J. Paul Hunter (New York: Norton, 2012), pp. 165–69

Sidney, Philip, *An Apology for Poetry; or, The Defence of Poesy* [1595], ed. by Geoffrey Shepherd (Manchester: Manchester University Press, 2002)

Southwell, Robert, *Saint Peters Complaint, with Other Poemes* (London: printed by [John Windet for] Iohn Wolfe, 1595)

Spenser, Edmund, 'Amoretti and Epithalamion' [1595], in *The Poetical Works of Edmund Spenser*, ed. by J. C. Smith and E. de Selincourt (Oxford: Oxford University Press, 1932), pp. 561–84

—— 'Three Proper, and Wittie, Familiar Letters' [1580], in *The Poetical Works of Edmund Spenser*, ed. by J. C. Smith and E. de Selincourt (Oxford: Oxford University Press, 1932), pp. 609–32

THOMAS, THOMAS, *Dictionarium Linguae Latinae et Anglicanae* (Cambridge: printed by Thomas Thomas, 1587)
TYNDALE, WILLIAM, *The Obedie[n]ce of a Christen Man and How Christe[n] Rulers Ought to Governe* (Marlborow in the la[n]de of Hesse [i.e. Antwerp]: printed by Hans Iuft [i.e. J. Hoochstraten], 1528)
—— *A Path Way i[n]to the Holy Scripture* (London: printed by Tho[mas] Godfray, 1536)
—— *The Practyse of Prelates* (London: printed by Anthony Scoloker and Willyam Seres, 1548)
VIDA, MARCO GIROLAMO, *The 'De arte poetica' of Marco Girolamo Vida*, ed. and trans. by Ralf G. Williams (New York: Columbia University Press, 1976)
VINSAUF, GEOFFREY OF, *Poetria nova*, trans. by Margaret F. Nims (Toronto: Pontifical Institute of Mediaeval Studies, 1967)
WATSON, THOMAS, *The Hekatompathia; or, Passionate Century of Love, 1582* (Gainesville: Scholars' Facsimiles & Reprints, 1964)
WEBBE, WILLIAM, *A Discourse of English Poetry* [1586], ed. by Sonia Hernández-Santano (London: Modern Humanities Research Association, 2016)
WHITNEY, GEOFFREY, *A Choice of Emblemes, and Other Deuises, for the Moste Parte Gathered Out of Sundrie Writers, Englished and Moralized* (Leyden: printed by Francis Raphelengius, 1586)
WILSON, THOMAS, *The Arte of Rhetorique* [1553], ed. by Thomas J. Derrick (New York: Garland, 1982)
—— *The Rule of Reason, Conteinyng the Arte of Logique, Set Forth in Englishe* (London: printed by Richard Grafton, 1551)
—— *The Three Orations of Demosthenes Chiefe Orator among the Grecians, in Fauour of the Olynthians, a People in Thracia, Now Called Romania* (London: printed by Henrie Denham, 1570)
WITHER, GEORGE, *A Collection of Emblemes, Ancient and Moderne* (London: printed by A[ugustine] M[athewes] for Iohn Grismond, 1635)
WRIGHT, THOMAS, *The Passions of the Mind in General* [1601], ed. by William Webster Newbold (New York and London: Garland, 1986)

SECONDARY SOURCES

ABBOTT, DON PAUL, 'Rhetoric and Writing in Renaissance Europe and England', in *A Short History of Writing Instruction from Ancient Greece to Twentieth-Century America*, ed. by James J. Murphy (Davis: Hermagoras Press, 1990), pp. 95–120
ABRAMS, M. H., *The Mirror and the Lamp: Romantic Theory and the Critical Tradition* (London: Oxford University Press, 1976)
ADEN, JOHN M., 'Dryden and the Imagination: The First Phase', *Publications of the Modern Language Association of America*, 74.1 (1959), 28–40
ALBALADEJO MAYORDOMO, TOMÁS, and FRANCISCO CHICO RICO, 'La *intellectio* en la serie de las operaciones retóricas no constituyentes de discurso', *Teoría/Crítica*, 5 (1998), 339–52
ANDERSON, RUTH L., 'A French Source for John Davies of Hereford's System of Psychology', *University of Iowa Philological Quarterly*, 6.1 (1927), 57–66
ARDUINI, STEFANO, *Prolegómenos a una teoría general de las figuras* (Murcia: Universidad de Murcia, 2000)
ATKINS, JOHN WILLIAM HEY, *English Literary Criticism: The Medieval Phase* (Cambridge: Cambridge University Press, 1943)
—— *English Literary Criticism: The Renascence* (London: Methuen, 1947)
—— *Literary Criticism in Antiquity: A Sketch of its Development* (Cambridge: Cambridge University Press, 1934)
AUERBACH, ERICH, *Literary Language and its Public in Late Latin Antiquity and in the Middle Ages*, trans. by Ralph Manheim (Princeton: Princeton University Press, 1993)
AUSTEN, GILLIAN, *George Gascoigne* (Woodbridge: Brewer, 2008)
BABB, LAWRENCE, *The Elizabethan Malady: A Study of Melancholia in English Literature from 1580 to 1642* (East Lansing: Michigan State College Press, 1951)
—— 'On the Nature of Elizabethan Psychological Literature', in *Joseph Quincy Adams: Memorial Studies*, ed. by James Gilmer McManaway, Giles Edwin Dawson, and Edwin E. Willoughby (Washington: Folger Shakespeare Library, 1948), pp. 509–22
BALDWIN, CHARLES SEARS, *Medieval Rhetoric and Poetic (to 1400): Interpreted from Representative Works* (New York: MacMillan, 1926)
BALDWIN, CHARLES SEARS, and DONALD LEMEN CLARK, *Renaissance Literary Theory and Practice: Classicism in the Rhetoric and Poetic of Italy, France and England: 1400–1600* (Gloucester: Smith, 1959)
BALDWIN, THOMAS WHITFIELD, *William Shakespere's Small Latine & Lesse Greeke* (Urbana: University of Illinois Press, 1944)
BARISH, JONAS, *The Antitheatrical Prejudice* (London and Berkeley: University of California Press, 1981)
BARRON, BRIAN, 'Poetry and Imagination in the Renaissance', in *Poetry in France: Metamorphoses of a Muse*, ed. by Keith Aspley and Peter France (Edinburgh: Edinburgh University Press, 1992), pp. 61–82
BATE, JONATHAN, *Shakespeare and Ovid* (Oxford: Oxford University Press, 2001)
BATE, W. JACKSON, *The Burden of the Past and the English Poet* (London: Chatto and Windus, 1971)

BERGER, HARRY, *Second World and Green World: Studies in Renaissance Fiction-Making* (Berkeley: University of California Press, 1988)

BINNS, J. W., 'Henry Dethick in Praise of Poetry: The First Appearance in Print of an Elizabethan Treatise', *Library*, 30.5 (1975), 199–216

BIRD, OTTO, 'The Tradition of the Logical Topics: Aristotle to Ockham', *Journal of the History of Ideas*, 23.3 (1962), 307–23

BIZER, MARC, *La Poésie au miroir: Imitation et conscience de soi dans la poésie latine de la Pléiade* (Paris: Champion, 1995)

BJØRNSTAD, HALL, 'Introduction', in *Borrowed Feathers: Plagiarism and the Limits of Imitation in Early Modern Europe*, ed. by Hall Bjørnstad (Oslo: Unipub, 2008), pp. 5–17

BLANCHOT, J. J., 'L'Art poétique de Jacques VI d'Écosse', in *Recherches sur l'histoire de la poétique*, ed. by Marc-Mathieu Münch (Nancy: Lang, 1984), pp. 7–28

BLOOM, HAROLD, *The Anxiety of Influence: A Theory of Poetry*, 2nd edn (Oxford: Oxford University Press, 1997)

BOLGAR, R. R., 'The Teaching of Rhetoric in the Middle Ages', in *Rhetoric Revalued: Papers from the International Society for the History of Rhetoric*, ed. by Brian Vickers (Binghamton: State University of New York, Center for Medieval and Early Renaissance Studies, 1982), pp. 79–86

BOND, DONALD F., 'The Neo-Classical Psychology of the Imagination', *English Literary History*, 4 (1937), 245–64

BOUWSMA, W. J., 'The Renaissance Discovery of Human Creativity', in *Humanity and Divinity in the Renaissance and Reformation*, ed. by J. O'Malley and others (Leiden: Brill, 1993), pp. 17–34

BRANN, EVA T. H., *The World of the Imagination: Sum and Substance* (Savage: Rowman & Littlefield, 1991)

BRINK, JEAN R., 'Who Fashioned Edmund Spenser?: The Textual History of "Complaints"', *Studies in Philology*, 88.2 (1991), 153–68

BRONOWSKI, JACOB, *The Poet's Defence* (Cambridge: Cambridge University Press, 1939)

BROWN, RICHARD DANSON, *'The New Poet': Novelty and Tradition in Spenser's Complaints* (Liverpool: Liverpool University Press, 1999)

BUNDY, MURRAY W., 'Bacon's True Opinion of Poetry', *Studies in Philology*, 27.2 (1930), 244–64

—— 'Invention and Imagination in the Renaissance', *Journal of English and Germanic Philology*, 29 (1930), 535–45

—— 'Shakespeare and Elizabethan Psychology', *Journal of English and Germanic Philology*, 23 (1924), 516–49

—— *The Theory of Imagination in Classical and Mediaeval Thought* (Urbana: University of Illinois Press, 1927)

BURKE, PETER, *The Renaissance Sense of the Past* (London: Arnold, 1969)

BUTLER, TODD WAYNE, *Imagination and Politics in Seventeenth-Century England* (Aldershot and Burlington: Ashgate, 2008)

CALVO REVILLA, ANA MARÍA, 'El modelo retórico, entramado de la poética medieval: Análisis de la *Poetria Nova* de Godofredo de Vinsauf', *Helmantica: Revista de Filología Clásica y Hebrea*, 53 (2002), 281–307

—— 'La *Poetria nova* de Godofredo de Vinsauf', in Godofredo de Vinsauf, *Poetria nova*, ed. by Ana María Calvo Revilla (Madrid: Arco Libros, 2008), pp. 11–26

CAMPANA, AUGUSTO, 'The Origin of the Word "Humanist"', *Journal of the Warburg and Courtauld Institutes*, 9 (1946), 60–73

CAPLAN, HARRY, 'Rhetorical Invention in Some Mediaeval Tractates of Preaching', *Speculum*, 2.3 (1927), 284–95

CARRÉ, MEYRICK HEATH, *Phases of Thought in England* (Oxford: Clarendon Press, 1949)
CARRON, JEAN-CLAUDE, 'Imitation and Intertextuality in the Renaissance', *New Literary History: A Journal of Theory and Interpretation*, 19.3 (1988), 565–79
CASSIRER, ERNST, and OTHERS, *The Renaissance Philosophy of Man* (Chicago and London: University of Chicago Press, 1948)
CASTOR, GRAHAME, *Pléiade Poetics: A Study in Sixteenth-Century Thought and Terminology* (Cambridge: Cambridge University Press, 1964)
CAVE, TERENCE, 'The Mimesis of Reading in the Renaissance', in *Mimesis: From Mirror to Method, Augustine to Descartes*, ed. by John D. Lyons and Stephen G. Nichols, Jr (Aurora: Davies Group, 2004), pp. 143–58
CHARLES-DAUBERT, F., 'Charron et l'Angleterre', *Recherches sur le XVIIe Siècle*, 5 (1982), 53–56
CHARLTON, HENRY BUCKLEY, *Castelvetro's Theory of Poetry* (Manchester: Manchester University Press, 1913)
CHICO RICO, FRANCISCO, 'La teoría de la traducción en la teoría retórica', *Revista de Retórica y Teoría de la Comunicación*, 3 (2002), 25–40
CLARE, JANET, *Shakespeare's Stage Traffic: Imitation, Borrowing and Competition in Renaissance Theatre* (Cambridge and New York: Cambridge University Press, 2014)
CLARK, DONALD LEMEN, 'Ancient Rhetoric and English Renaissance Literature', *Shakespeare Quarterly*, 2.3 (1951), 195–204
—— 'Rhetoric and the Literature of the English Middle Ages', *Quarterly Journal of Speech*, 45 (1959), 19–28
—— *Rhetoric and Poetry in the Renaissance: A Study of Rhetorical Terms in English Renaissance Literary Criticism* (New York: Columbia University Press, 1922)
—— 'The Rise and Fall of *Progymnasmata* in Sixteenth Century Grammar Schools', *Speech Monographs*, 19 (1952), 259–63
CLARK, HENRY C., *La Rochefoucauld and the Language of Unmasking in Seventeenth-Century France* (Geneva: Droz, 1994)
CLEMENTS, ROBERT JOHN, 'Condemnation of the Poetic Profession in Renaissance Emblem Literature', *Studies in Philology*, 43 (1946), 213–32
—— *Critical Theory and Practice of the Pléiade* (Cambridge, MA: Harvard University Press, 1942)
—— 'The Cult of the Poet in Renaissance Emblem Literature', *Publications of the Modern Language Association of America*, 59.3 (1944), 672–85
—— 'Iconography on the Nature and Inspiration of Poetry in Renaissance Emblem Literature', *Publications of the Modern Language Association of America*, 70.4 (1955), 781–804
—— *Picta Poesis: Literary and Humanistic Theory in Renaissance Emblem Books* (Rome: Edizioni di Storia e Letteratura, 1960)
COCKING, JOHN MARTIN, *Imagination: A Study in the History of Ideas*, ed. by Penelope Murray (London: Routledge, 1991)
COLDIRON, ANNE ELIZABETH BANKS, 'How Spenser Excavates Du Bellay's *Antiquitez*; or, The Role of the Poet, Lyric Historiography, and the English Sonnet', *Journal of English and Germanic Philology*, 101.1 (2002), 41–67
CONNELL, DOROTHY, *Sir Philip Sidney's 'The Maker's Mind'* (Oxford: Clarendon Press, 1977)
COPELAND, RITA, *Rhetoric, Hermeneutics, and Translation in the Middle Ages: Academic Traditions and Vernacular Texts* (Cambridge: Cambridge University Press, 1995)
CORBETT, EDWARD P. J., 'The Theory and Practice of Imitation in Classical Rhetoric', *College Composition and Communication*, 22.3 (1971), 243–50
CRAIG, D. H., 'A Hybrid Growth: Sidney's Theory of Poetry in *An Apology for Poetry*', *English Literary Renaissance*, 10 (1980), 183–201

CRAIG, HARDIN, *The Enchanted Glass: The Elizabethan Mind in Literature* (Oxford: Blackwell, 1950)
CRANE, MARY THOMAS, *Framing Authority: Sayings, Self, and Society in Sixteenth-Century England* (Princeton: Princeton University Press, 1993)
CRANE, WILLIAM G., *Wit and Rhetoric in the Renaissance* (New York: Columbia University Press, 1937)
CRANZ, FERDINAND EDWARD, *Nicholas of Cusa and the Renaissance* (Aldershot: Ashgate, 2000)
CRIGNON-DE OLIVEIRA, CLAIRE, '"Tout est à moi et rien n'est à moi": La digestion des sources dans l'*Anatomie de la mélancolie* de Robert Burton', in *Emprunt, plagiat, réécriture aux XVe, XVIe, XVIIe siècles: Pour un nouvel éclairage sur la pratique des lettres à la Renaissance*, ed. by Marie Couton and others (Clermont-Ferrand: Presses universitaires Blaise Pascal, 2006), pp. 235–50
CURTIUS, ERNST ROBERT, *European Literature and the Latin Middle Ages*, trans. by Willard R. Trask (London: Routledge and Kegan Paul, 1979)
DALY, PETER M. *The English Emblem and the Continental Tradition* (New York: AMS Press, 1988)
D'ANGELO, FRANK J., 'The Evolution of the Analytic *Topoi*: A Speculative Inquiry', in *Essays on Classical Rhetoric and Modern Discourse*, ed. by Robert J. Connors, Robert J. Ede, and Andrea A. Lunsford (Carbondale: Southern Illinois University Press, 1984), pp. 50–68
DAVIS, WALTER R., *Idea and Act in Elizabethan Fiction* (Princeton: Princeton University Press, 1969)
DEGANDILLAC, MAURICE, 'Neoplatonism and Christian Thought in the Fifteenth Century (Nicholas of Cusa and Marsilio Ficino)', in *Neoplatonism and Christian Thought*, ed. by Dominic J. O'Meara (Norfolk, VA: International Society for Neoplatonic Studies; Albany: State University of New York Press, 1981), pp. 143–65
DELGADO ESCOLAR, FRANCISCO LUIS, *Los poetas latinos como críticos literarios desde Terencio hasta Juvenal: Estudios estilísticos y lexicológicos* (Madrid: Universidad Complutense de Madrid, 1991)
DENEEF, A. LEIGH, 'Rereading Sidney's *Apology*', *Journal of Medieval and Renaissance Studies*, 10 (1980), 155–91
DONALDSON, IAN, '"The Fripperie of Wit": Jonson and Plagiarism', in *Plagiarism in Early Modern England*, ed. by Paulina Kewes (Basingstoke: Palgrave Macmillan, 2003), pp. 119–33
DOWDEN, EDWARD, *Essays Modern and Elizabethan* (London and New York: Dent & Sons; Dutton, 1910)
DUHAMEL, PIERRE ALBERT, 'The Logic and Rhetoric of Peter Ramus', *Modern Philology*, 46.3 (1949), 163–71
——'The Oxford Lectures of John Colet: An Essay in Defining the English Renaissance', *Journal of the History of Ideas*, 14.4 (1953), 493–510
DUNCAN, CARSON S., *The New Science and English Literature in the Classical Period* (New York: Russell & Russell, 1972)
EBIN, L. A., *Illuminator, Makar, Vates: Visions of Poetry in the Fifteenth Century* (Lincoln: University of Nebraska Press, 1988)
EDEN, KATHY, *Friends Hold All Things in Common: Tradition, Intellectual Property, and the 'Adages' of Erasmus* (New Haven and London: Yale University Press, 2001)
——*Poetic and Legal Fiction in the Aristotelian Tradition* (Princeton: Princeton University Press, 1986)
ENGELHARDT, G. J., 'The Relation of Sherry's *Treatise of Schemes and Tropes* to Wilson's *Arte of Rhetorique*', *Publications of the Modern Language Association of America*, 62.1 (1947), 76–82

ENGELL, JAMES, *The Creative Imagination: Enlightenment to Romanticism* (Cambridge, MA: Harvard University Press, 1981)

FALCO, RAPHAEL, 'Marsilio Ficino and Vatic Myth', *Modern Language Notes*, 122.1 (2007), 101–22

FANTHAM, ELAINE, 'Imitation and Decline: Rhetorical Theory and Practice in the First Century after Christ', *Classical Philology*, 73.2 (1978), 102–16

—— 'Imitation and Evolution: The Discussion of Rhetorical Imitation in Cicero *De oratore* 2. 87–97 and some Related Problems of Ciceronian Theory', *Classical Philology*, 73.1 (1978), 1–16

FARAL, EDMOND, *Les Arts poetiques du XIIe et du XIIIe siècle* (Paris: Champion, 1924)

FEATHER, JOHN, 'From Rights in Copies to Copyright: The Recognition of Authors' Rights in English Law and Practice in the Sixteenth and Seventeenth Centuries', in *The Construction of Authorship: Textual Appropriation in Law and Literature*, ed. by Martha Woodmansee and Peter Jaszi (Durham and London: Duke University Press, 1994), pp. 191–210

—— *Publishing, Piracy and Politics: An Historical Study of Copyright in Britain* (London: Mansell, 1994)

FERGUSON, MARGARET W., '"The Afflatus of Ruin": Meditations on Rome by Du Bellay, Spenser, and Stevens', in *Roman Images: Selected Papers from the English Institute*, ed. by Annabel Patterson (Baltimore: Johns Hopkins University Press, 1984), pp. 23–50

—— 'The Exile's Defense: Du Bellay's *La Deffence et Illustration de la langue Françoyse*', *Publications of the Modern Language Association of America*, 93.2 (1978), 275–89

—— *Trials of Desire: Renaissance Defenses of Poetry* (New Haven and London: Yale University Press, 1983)

FERNÁNDEZ CORTE, JOSÉ CARLOS, 'Imitación retórica e imitación poética en Quintiliano', in *Quintiliano: Historia y actualidad de la retórica: Actas del Congreso Internacional: Madrid y Calahorra, 14 al 18 de noviembre de 1995*, ed. by Tomás Albaladejo Mayordomo, Emilio del Rio, and José Antonio Caballero (Logroño: Instituto de Estudios Riojanos, 1998), pp. 1253–62

FLORY, DAN, 'Stoic Psychology, Classical Rhetoric, and Theories of Imagination in Western Philosophy', *Philosophy and Rhetoric*, 29.2 (1996), 147–67

FORD, PHILIP, 'Virgil *versus* Homer: Reception, Imitation, Identity in the French Renaissance', in *Virgilian Identities in the French Renaissance*, ed. by Phillip John Usher and Isabelle Fernbach (Cambridge: Brewer, 2012), pp. 141–60

FOREST, LOUISE C. TURNER, 'A Caveat for Critics against Invoking Elizabethan Psychology', *Publications of the Modern Language Association of America*, 61.3 (1946), 651–72

FRASER, RUSSELL A., *The War against Poetry* (Princeton: Princeton University Press, 1970)

FREEDMAN, JOSEPH S., 'Cicero in Sixteenth- and Seventeenth-Century Rhetoric Instruction', *Rhetorica*, 4.3 (1986), 227–54

FREEMAN, ROSEMARY, *English Emblem Books* (London: Chatto & Windus, 1948)

FUMAROLI, MARC, *L'Âge de l'eloquence: Rhétorique et 'res literaria' de la Renaissance au seuil de l'époque classique* (Geneva: Droz, 2002)

FURLAN, MAURI, 'La retórica de la traducción en el Renacimiento: Elementos para la constitución de una teoría de la traducción renacentista' (unpublished doctoral dissertation, University of Barcelona, 2002)

FYFE, W. H., 'Introduction', in Longinus, 'On the Sublime', ed. and trans. by W. H. Fyfe, in Aristotle, *'Poetics'; Longinus, 'On the Sublime'; Demetrius, 'On Style'* (Cambridge, MA: Harvard University Press, 1995), pp. 145–58

GALAND-HALLYN, PERRINE, and FERNAND HALLYN, *Poétiques de la Renaissance: Le Modèle Italien, le monde Franco-Bourguignon et leur héritage en France au XVIe siècle* (Geneva: Droz, 2001)

GARCÍA GALIANO, ÁNGEL, *Teoría de la imitación poética en el Renacimiento* (Madrid: Universidad Complutense de Madrid, 1988)
GIL, LUIS, *Los antiguos y la 'inspiración' poética* (Madrid: Guadarrama, 1966)
GILBERT, ALLAN, 'Were Spenser's *Nine Comedies* Lost?', *Modern Language Notes*, 73.4 (1958), 241–43
GOEGLEIN, TAMARA A., '"Wherein Hath Ramus Been So Offensious?": Poetic Examples in the English Ramist Logic Manuals (1574–1672)', *Rhetorica: A Journal of the History of Rhetoric*, 14.1 (1996), 73–101
GOLDSTEIN, PAUL, *Copyright's Highway: From Gutenberg to the Celestial Jukebox* (New York: Hill and Wang, 1994)
GOMÁ LANZÓN, JAVIER, *Imitación y experiencia* (Barcelona: Critica, 2005)
GONZÁLEZ, GABRIEL, *Dialéctica escolástica y lógica humanística de la Edad Media al Renacimiento* (Salamanca: Ediciones Universidad, 1987)
GORDON, ALEX L., 'The Ascendancy of Rhetoric and the Struggle for Poetic in Sixteenth-Century France', in *Renaissance Eloquence: Studies in the Theory and Practice of Renaissance Rhetoric*, ed. by James J. Murphy (Berkeley: University of California Press, 1983), pp. 376–84
GOTTFRIED, RUDOLF, 'The "G. W. Senior" and "G. W. I." of Spenser's *Amoretti*', *Modern Language Quarterly*, 3 (1942), 543–46
GOYET, FRANCIS, *Le Sublime du 'lieu commun': L'Invention rhétorique dans l'Antiquité et à la Renaissance* (Paris: Champion, 1996)
GRAFTON, ANTHONY, and LISA JARDINE, *From Humanism to the Humanities: Education and the Liberal Arts in Fifteenth- and Sixteenth-Century Europe* (London: Duckworth, 1986)
GRASSI, ERNESTO, *Rhetoric as Philosophy: The Humanist Tradition* (Philadelphia: Pennsylvania State University Press, 1980)
GRAY, HANNA H., 'Renaissance Humanism: The Pursuit of Eloquence', *Journal of the History of Ideas*, 24.4 (1963), 497–514
GRAY, RICHARD T., 'Introduction', in *Inventions of the Imagination: Romanticism and Beyond*, ed. by Richard T. Gray (Seattle: University of Washington Press, 2011), pp. 3–16
GREENE, THOMAS M., *The Light in Troy: Imitation and Discovery in Renaissance Poetry* (New Haven and London: Yale University Press, 1982)
GREENFIELD, CONCETTA CARESTIA, *Humanist and Scholastic Poetics, 1250–1500* (London: Bucknell University Press, 1981)
GRIFFITHS, JANE, 'The Matter of Invention in Hawes' *Passetyme of Pleasure*', *SEDERI*, 13 (2003), 101–10
GRIMALDI, S. J. WILLIAM, 'The Aristotelian Topics', *Traditio*, 14 (1958), 1–16
GROOM, NICK, 'Forgery, Plagiarism, Imitation, Pegleggery', in *Plagiarism in Early Modern England*, ed. by Paulina Kewes (Basingstoke: Palgrave Macmillan, 2003), pp. 74–89
GRUBE, G. M. A., *The Greek and Roman Critics* (London: Methuen, 1965)
GRUND, GARY R., 'Ben Jonson, John Hoskyns, and the Anti-Ciceronian Movement', *Studies in English Literature*, 54 (1977), 33–53
GUERLAC, RITA, 'Rhetorical Doctrine and Some Poems of Ronsard', in *Essays on Renaissance Poetry*, ed. by James Hutton (Ithaca and London: Cornell University Press, 1980), pp. 291–310
HADFIELD, ANDREW, *Edmund Spenser: A Life* (Oxford: Oxford University Press, 2012)
HAGAMAN, JOHN, 'Modern Use of the *Progymnasmata* in Teaching Rhetorical Invention', *Rhetoric Review*, 5.1 (1986), 22–29
HALIO, JAY L., 'The Metaphor of Conception and Elizabethan Theories of the Imagination', *Neophilologus*, 50 (1966), 454–61
HALL, JR, VERNON, 'Scaliger's Defense of Poetry', *Publications of the Modern Language Association of America*, 63.4 (1948), 1125–30

HALLIWELL, STEPHEN, *The Aesthetics of Mimesis: Ancient Texts and Modern Problems* (Princeton and Oxford: Princeton University Press, 2002)
HARDISON, O. B., *English Literary Criticism: The Renaissance* (London: Owen, 1967)
—— 'The Place of Averroes' Commentary on the *Poetics* in the History of Medieval Criticism', *Medieval and Renaissance Studies*, 4 (1970), 57–81
—— 'The Two Voices of Sidney's *Apology for Poetry*', *English Literary Renaissance*, 2 (1972), 83–99
HARLAND, RICHARD, *Literary Theory from Plato to Barthes: An Introductory History* (Basingstoke: Macmillan, 1999)
HARRIER, RICHARD, 'Invention in Tudor Literature: Historical Perspectives', in *Philosophy and Humanism: Renaissance Essays in Honor of Paul Oskar Kristeller*, ed. by Edward P. Mahoney (New York: Columbia University Press, 1976), pp. 370–86
HARRISON, JOHN L., 'Bacon's View of Rhetoric, Poetry, and the Imagination', *Huntington Library Quarterly*, 20.2 (1957), 107–25
HARSTING, PERNILLE, 'Quintilian, Imitation and "Anxiety of Influence"', in *Quintiliano: Historia y actualidad de la retórica: Actas del Congreso Internacional: Madrid y Calahorra, 14 al 18 de noviembre de 1995*, ed. by Tomás Albaladejo Mayordomo, Emilio del Rio, and José Antonio Caballero (Logroño: Instituto de Estudios Riojanos, 1998), pp. 1325–35
HARVEY, E. RUTH, *The Inward Wits: Psychological Theory in the Middle Ages and the Renaissance* (London: Warburg Institute, 1975)
HEIDLEBAUGH, NOLA J., *Judgment, Rhetoric, and the Problem of Incommensurability: Recalling Practical Wisdom* (Columbia: University of South Carolina Press, 2001)
HENINGER, S. K., *Sidney and Spenser: The Poet as Maker* (University Park: Pennsylvania State University Press, 1989)
HENN, THOMAS RICE, *Longinus and English Criticism* (Cambridge: Cambridge University Press, 1934)
HERMAN, PETER C., *Squitter-Wits and Muse-Haters: Sidney, Spencer, Milton, and Renaissance Antipoetic Sentiment* (Detroit: Wayne State University Press, 1996)
HERRICK, MARVIN T., 'The Early History of Aristotle's *Rhetoric* in England', *Philological Quarterly*, 5 (1926), 242–57
—— *The Fusion of Horatian and Aristotelian Criticism, 1531–1555* (Urbana: University of Illinois Press, 1946)
HOWELL, WILBUR SAMUEL, *Poetics, Rhetoric and Logic: Studies in the Basic Disciplines of Criticism*, 2nd edn (Ithaca: Cornell University Press, 1980)
—— 'Ramus and English Rhetoric: 1574–1681', *Quarterly Journal of Speech*, 37 (1951), 308–10
HOYE, WILLIAM J., 'The Meaning of Neoplatonism in the Thought of Nicholas of Cusa', *Downside Review*, 104 (1986), 10–18
HUME, ROBERT D., 'Dryden on Creation: "Imagination" in the Later Criticism', *Review of English Studies*, 21.83 (1970), 295–314
HUTSON, LORNA, *The Invention of Suspicion: Law and Mimesis in Shakespeare and Renaissance Drama* (Oxford: Oxford University Press, 2007)
IJSSELING, SAMUEL, *Rhetoric and Philosophy in Conflict: An Historical Survey* (The Hague: Nijhoff, 1976)
JACK, RONALD S., 'James VI and Renaissance Poetic Theory', *English*, 16 (1967), 208–11
JARDINE, LISA, 'Humanism and the Teaching of Logic', in *The Cambridge History of Later Medieval Philosophy: From the Rediscovery of Aristotle to the Disintegration of Scholasticism 1100–1600*, ed. by Anthony John Patrick Kenny and others (Cambridge: Cambridge University Press, 1982), pp. 797–807
—— 'Lorenzo Valla and the Intellectual Origins of Humanist Dialectic', *Journal of the History of Philosophy*, 15 (1977), 143–64

—— 'The Place of Dialectic Teaching in Sixteenth-Century Cambridge', *Studies in the Renaissance*, 21 (1974), 31–62
JOHNSON, FRANCIS R., 'Elizabethan Drama and the Elizabethan Science of Psychology', in *English Studies Today: Papers Read at the International Conference of University Professors of English Held in Magdalen College, Oxford, August 1950*, ed. by C. L. Wrenn and G. Bullough (Oxford: Oxford University Press, 1951), pp. 111–19
—— 'Two Renaissance Textbooks of Rhetoric: Aphthonius' *Progymnasmata* and Rainolde's *A Booke Called the Foundacion of Rhetorike*', *Huntington Library Quarterly*, 6.4 (1943), 427–44
JONES, TOD E. 'From Pre-Reformation to Pre-Restoration: The Social-Historical and Theological Context', in *The Cambridge Platonists: A Brief Introduction*, ed. by Tod E. Jones (Lanham: University Press of America, 2005), pp. 3–14
KELLY, DOUGLAS, 'Definition of the Genre', in *The Arts of Poetry and Prose*, ed. by Douglas Kelly (Turnhout: Brepols, 1991), pp. 37–46
—— 'Topical Invention in Medieval French Literature', in *Medieval Eloquence: Studies in the Theory and Practice of Medieval Rhetoric*, ed. by James J. Murphy (Berkeley: University of California Press, 1978), pp. 231–51
KENNEDY, GEORGE A., *The Art of Rhetoric in the Roman World: 300 B.C.–A.D. 300* (Princeton: Princeton University Press, 1972)
—— *Classical Rhetoric and its Christian and Secular Tradition from Ancient to Modern Times*, 2nd edn (Chapel Hill: University of North Carolina Press, 1999)
—— 'The Evolution of a Theory of Artistic Prose', in *The Cambridge History of Literary Criticism*, 9 vols (Cambridge and New York: Cambridge University Press, 1989–2013), I: *Classical Criticism*, ed. by George A. Kennedy (1989), pp. 184–99
—— *A New History of Classical Rhetoric* (Princeton: Princeton University Press, 1994)
KENNY, NEIL, *Curiosity in Early Modern Europe: Word Histories* (Wiesbaden: Harrassowitz, 1998)
KERN, EDITH, *The Influence of Heinsius and Vossius upon French Dramatic Theory* (Baltimore: Johns Hopkins University Press, 1949)
KINNEY, ARTHUR F., *Humanist Poetics: Thought, Rhetoric and Fiction in Sixteenth-Century England* (Amherst: University of Massachusetts Press, 1986)
—— 'Rhetoric as Poetic: Humanist Fiction in the Renaissance', *English Literary History*, 43.4 (1976), 413–43
KISHLER, THOMAS C., 'Aristotle and Sidney on Imitation', *The Classical Journal*, 59.2 (1963), 63–64
KLINCK, DENNIS R., '*Vestigia Trinitatis* in Man and his Works in the English Renaissance', *Journal of the History of Ideas*, 42.1 (1981), 13–27
KOGEL, RENÉE, *Pierre Charron* (Geneva: Droz, 1972)
KOOIJ, SUZANNE, 'Poetic Imagination and the Paradigm of Painting in Early Modern France', in *Imagination in the Later Middle Ages and Early Modern Times*, ed. by Lodi Nauta and Detlev Pätzold (Leuven: Peeters, 2004), pp. 77–92
KOPP, JANE BALTZELL, 'Geoffrey of Vinsauf: *The New Poetics* (c. 1210 A.D.)', in *Three Medieval Rhetorical Arts*, ed. by James J. Murphy (Berkeley: University of California Press, 1985), pp. 27–108
KRAMER, DAVID BRUCE, *The Imperial Dryden: The Poetics of Appropriation in Seventeenth-Century England* (Athens and London: University of Georgia Press, 1994)
KRISTELLER, PAUL OSKAR, *Renaissance Thought: The Classic, Scholastic, and Humanistic Strains* (New York: Harper & Row, 1961)
KUHN, URSULA, *English Literary Terms in Poetological Texts of the Sixteenth Century* (Salzburg: Institut fur Englische Sprache und Literatur, University of Salzburg, 1974)

LA DRIÈRE, CRAIG, 'Horace and the Theory of Imitation', *American Journal of Philology*, 60.3 (1939), 288–300

LANGER, ULLRICH, 'Invention', in *The Cambridge History of Literary Criticism*, 9 vols (Cambridge and New York: Cambridge University Press, 1989–2013), III: *The Renaissance*, ed. by Glyn P. Norton (2000), pp. 136–43

LAUER, JANICE M., *Invention in Rhetoric and Composition* (West Lafayette: Parlor Press, 2003)

—— 'Issues in Rhetorical Invention', in *Essays on Classical Rhetoric and Modern Discourse*, ed. by Robert J. Connors, Robert J. Ede, and Andrea A. Lunsford (Carbondale: Southern Illinois University Press, 1984), pp. 127–39

LAUSBERG, HEINRICH, *Handbook of Literary Rhetoric: A Foundation for Literary Study*, trans. by Matthew T. Bliss, Annemiek Jansen, and David E. Orton, ed. by David E. Orton and R. Dean Anderson (Leiden: Brill, 1998)

LECHNER, J. M., *Renaissance Concepts of the Commonplaces* (New York: Pageant Press, 1962)

LEFF, MICHAEL C., 'Boethius' *De differentiis topicis, Book IV*', in *Medieval Eloquence: Studies in the Theory and Practice of Medieval Rhetoric*, ed. by James J. Murphy (Berkeley: Dar Sadir, 1978), pp. 3–24

—— 'The Topics of Argumentative Invention in Latin Rhetorical Theory from Cicero to Boethius', *Rhetorica*, 1.1 (1983), 23–44

LEVAO, RONALD, *Renaissance Minds and their Fictions: Cusanus, Sidney, Shakespeare* (Berkeley: University of California Press, 1985)

—— 'Sidney's Feigned *Apology*', in *Sir Philip Sidney: An Anthology of Modern Criticism*, ed. by Dennis Kay (Oxford: Clarendon Press, 1987), pp. 127–46

LEWIS, C. S., *English Literature in the Sixteenth Century, Excluding Drama* (Oxford: Clarendon Press, 1966)

LEWRY, P. OSMUND, 'Rhetoric at Paris and Oxford in the Mid-Thirteenth Century', *Rhetorica*, 1.1 (1983), 45–63

LLOYD, GEOFFREY ERNEST RICHARD, *Polarity and Analogy: Two Types of Argumentation in Early Greek Thought* (Cambridge: Cambridge University Press, 1966)

MACK, MICHAEL, *Sidney's Poetics: Imitating Creation* (Washington: Catholic University of America Press, 2005)

MACK, PETER, 'Early Modern Ideas of Imagination: The Rhetorical Tradition', in *Imagination in the Later Middle Ages and Early Modern Times*, ed. by Lodi Nauta and Detlev Pätzold (Leuven: Peeters, 2004), pp. 59–76

—— *Elizabethan Rhetoric: Theory and Practice* (Cambridge and New York: Cambridge University Press, 2002)

—— *Renaissance Argument: Valla and Agricola in the Traditions of Rhetoric and Dialectic* (Leiden: Brill, 1993)

—— 'Rhetoric, Ethics and Reading in the Renaissance', *Renaissance Studies*, 19.1 (2005), 1–21

MAGUIRE, MATTHEW W., *The Conversion of Imagination: From Pascal through Rousseau to Tocqueville* (Cambridge, MA: Harvard University Press, 2006)

MALLON, THOMAS, *Stolen Words: Forays into the Origins and Ravages of Plagiarism* (New York: Ticknor & Fields, 1989)

MARR, ALEXANDER, 'Introduction', in *Curiosity and Wonder from the Renaissance to the Enlightenment*, ed. by Robert John Weston Evans and Alexander Marr (Aldershot: Ashgate, 2006), pp. 1–20

——, Raphaële Garrod, José Ramón Marcaida and Richard J. Oosterhoff, eds., *Logodaedalus: Word Histories of Ingenuity in Early Modern Europe* (Pittsburgh: Pittsburgh University Press, forthcoming)

—— '*Pregnant Wit*: *Ingegno* in Renaissance England', *British Art Studies*, 1 (2015) <http://dx.doi.org/10.17658/issn.2058-5462/issue-01/amarr> [accessed 25 January 2019]

MARROU, HENRI-IRENEE, *Historia de la educación en la Antigüedad*, trans. by José Ramón Mayo (Buenos Aires: Editorial Universitaria de Buenos Aires, 1970)

MARTIN, RONALD H., 'The *Epitome Margaritae Eloquentiae* of Laurentius Gulielmus de Saona', in *Proceedings of the Leeds Philosophical and Literary Society* (Leeds: Leeds Philosophical and Literary Society, 1971), pp. 103–26

MATZ, ROBERT, *Defending Literature in Early Modern England: Renaissance Literary Theory in Social Context* (Cambridge and New York: Cambridge University Press, 2000)

MAUREL-INDART, HÉLÈNE, *Plagiats, les coulisses de l'écriture* (Paris: Différence, 2007)

McDONALD, CHARLES O., '*Decorum, Ethos,* and *Pathos* in the Heroes of Elizabethan Tragedy, with Particular Reference to *Hamlet*', *Journal of English and Germanic Philology*, 61.2 (1962), 330–48

McINERNY, RALPH, 'Beyond the Liberal Arts', in *The Seven Liberal Arts in the Middle Ages*, ed. by David L. Wagner (Bloomington: Indiana University Press, 1986), pp. 248–72

McKEON, RICHARD PETER, 'Creativity and the Commonplace', in *Selected Writings of Richard McKeon*, ed. by Zahava K. McKeon and William G. Swenson (Chicago: University of Chicago Press, 1998), pp. 42–50

—— 'Literary Criticism and the Concept of Imitation in Antiquity', *Modern Philology*, 34.1 (1936), 1–35

—— 'The Methods of Rhetoric and Philosophy: Invention and Judgment', in *The Classical Tradition: Literary and Historical Studies in Honor of Harry Caplan*, ed. by Luitpold Wallach (Ithaca: Cornell University Press, 1966), pp. 365–73

McKEON, RICHARD PETER, and MARK BACKMAN, *Rhetoric: Essays in Invention and Discovery* (Woodbridge: Ox Bow Press, 1987)

McLAUGHLIN, MARTIN L., *Literary Imitation in the Italian Renaissance: The Theory and Practice of Literary Imitation in Italy from Dante to Bembo* (Oxford: Clarendon Press, 1995)

McNALLY, JAMES RICHARD, '"Prima pars dialecticae": The Influence of Agricolan Dialectic upon English Accounts of Invention', *Renaissance Quarterly*, 21 (1968), 166–77

MEERHOFF, KEES, *Rhétorique et poétique au XVIe siècle en France: Du Bellay, Ramus et les autres* (Leiden: Brill, 1986)

MELEHY, HASSAN, *The Poetics of Literary Transfer in Early Modern France and England* (Farnham: Ashgate, 2010)

—— 'Spenser and Du Bellay: Translation, Imitation, Ruin', *Comparative Literature Studies*, 40.4 (2003), 415–38

—— 'Spenser's *Mutabilitie Cantos* and Du Bellay's Poetic Transformation', in *French Connections in the English Renaissance*, ed. by Catherine Gimelli Martin and Hassan Melehy (Burlington: Ashgate, 2013), pp. 51–64

MELION, WALTER S., 'Introduction: Meditative Images and the Psychology of Soul', in *Image and Imagination of the Religious Self in Late Medieval and Early Modern Europe*, ed. by Reindert Falkenburg, Walter S. Melion, and Todd M. Richardson (Turnhout: Brepols, 2007), pp. 1–36

MESKILL, LYNN SERMIN, 'Tracks in other Men's Snow: Ben Jonson's Plagiary', in *Emprunt, plagiat, réécriture aux XVe, XVIe, XVIIe siècles: Pour un nouvel éclairage sur la pratique des lettres à la Renaissance*, ed. by Marie Couton and others (Clermont-Ferrand: Presses universitaires Blaise Pascal: Centre d'études sur les réformes, l'humanisme et l'âge classique, 2006), pp. 185–96

MILLER, WILLIAM E., 'Double Translation in English Humanistic Education', *Studies in the Renaissance*, 10 (1963), 163–74

MONFASANI, JOHN, *George of Trebizond: A Biography and a Study of his Rhetoric and Logic* (Leiden: Brill, 1976)

—— 'Three Notes on Renaissance Rhetoric', *Rhetorica*, 5.1 (1987), 107–18

MONTGOMERY, ROBERT L., *The Reader's Eye: Studies in Didactic Theory from Dante to Tasso* (Berkeley: University of California Press, 1979)
MORINI, MASSIMILIANO, *Tudor Translation in Theory and Practice* (Aldershot: Ashgate, 2006)
MOSS, ANN, 'Horace in the Sixteenth Century: Commentators into Critics', in *The Cambridge History of Literary Criticism*, 9 vols (Cambridge and New York: Cambridge University Press, 1989–2013), III: *The Renaissance*, ed. by Glyn P. Norton (2000), pp. 66–76
—— 'Literary Imitation in the Sixteenth Century: Writers and Readers, Latin and French', in *The Cambridge History of Literary Criticism*, 9 vols (Cambridge and New York: Cambridge University Press, 1989–2013), III: *The Renaissance*, ed. by Glyn P. Norton (2000), pp. 107–18
MUCKELBAUER, JOHN, 'Imitation and Invention in Antiquity: An Historical-Theoretical Revision', *Rhetorica*, 21.2 (2003), 61–88
MURPHY, JAMES J., 'Caxton's Two Choices: "Modern" and "Medieval" Rhetoric in Traversagni's *Nova Rhetorica* and the Anonymous *Court of Sapience*', *Medievalia et Humanistica*, n.s., 3 (1972), 241–55
—— 'The Double Revolution of the First Rhetorical Textbook Published in England: The *Margarita Eloquentiae* of Gulielmus Traversagnus (1479)', *Texte: Revue de critique et de théorie littéraire*, 8/9 (1989), 367–76
—— 'John Gower's *Confessio Amantis* and the First Discussion of Rhetoric in the English Language', *Philological Quarterly*, 41 (1962), 401–11
—— 'A New Look at Chaucer and the Rhetoricians', *Review of English Studies*, n.s., 15 (1964), 1–20
—— 'Quintilian's Influence on the Teaching of Speaking and Writing in the Middle Ages and Renaissance', in *Latin Rhetoric and Education in the Middle Ages and Renaissance*, ed. by James J. Murphy (Aldershot: Ashgate Variorum, 2005), pp. 158–83
—— 'Rhetoric in the Earliest Years of Printing, 1465–1500', *Quarterly Journal of Speech*, 70 (1984), 1–11
—— 'Rhetoric in Fourteenth-Century Oxford', *Medium Ævum*, 34 (1965), 1–20
—— *Rhetoric in the Middle Ages: A History of Rhetorical Theory from Saint Augustine to the Renaissance* (Berkeley: Dar Sadir, 1974)
MURPHY, WILLIAM M., 'Thomas Watson's *Hecatompathia* (1582) and the Elizabethan Sonnet Sequence', *Journal of English and Germanic Philology*, 56 (1957), 418–28
NAUTA, LODI, and DETLEV PÄTZOLD, 'Introduction', in *Imagination in the Later Middle Ages and Early Modern Times*, ed by Lodi Nauta and Detlev Pätzold (Leuven: Peeters, 2004), pp. ix–xiv
NAVARETTE, IGNACIO, 'Strategies of Appropriation in Speroni and Du Bellay', *Comparative Literature*, 41 (1989), 141–54
OCHS, DONOVAN J., 'Aristotle's Concept of Formal Topics', *Speech Monographs*, 36 (1969), 419–25
—— 'Cicero's Rhetorical Theory: With Synopses of Cicero's Seven Rhetorical Works', in *A Synoptic History of Classical Rhetoric*, ed. by James J. Murphy and others (Mahwah: Hermagoras Press, 2003), pp. 151–200
OLSON, GLENDING, 'Making and Poetry in the Age of Chaucer', *Comparative Literature*, 31.3 (1979), 272–90
ONG, WALTER J., *Ramus, Method, and the Decay of Dialogue: From the Art of Discourse to the Art of Reason* (Chicago: University of Chicago Press, 2004)
—— 'Tudor Writings on Rhetoric', *Studies in the Renaissance*, 15 (1968), 39–69
PADLEY, G. A., *Grammatical Theory in Western Europe 1500–1700: Trends in Vernacular Grammar* (Cambridge: Cambridge University Press, 1985)

PARK, KATHARINE, 'The Organic Soul', in *The Cambridge History of Renaissance Philosophy*, ed. by Charles B. Schmitt and others (Cambridge: Cambridge University Press, 1988), pp. 464–84
PARK, KATHARINE, and ECKHARD KESSLER, 'The Concept of Psychology', in *The Cambridge History of Renaissance Philosophy*, ed. by Charles B. Schmitt and others (Cambridge: Cambridge University Press, 1988), pp. 455–63
PATTERSON, WARNER FORREST, *Three Centuries of French Poetic Theory: A Critical History of the Chief Arts of Poetry in France* (Ann Arbor: University of Michigan Press, 1935)
PAULL, HARRY MAJOR, *Literary Ethics: A Study in the Growth of the Literary Conscience* (London: Butterworth, 1928)
PERRY, NANDRA, '*Imitatio* and Identity: Thomas Rogers, Philip Sidney, and the Protestant Self', *English Literary Renaissance*, 35.3 (2005), 365–406
PIGMAN III, G. W., 'Imitation and the Renaissance Sense of the Past: The Reception of Erasmus' *Ciceronianus*', *Journal of Medieval and Renaissance Studies*, 9 (1979), 155–77
—— 'Versions of Imitation in the Renaissance', *Renaissance Quarterly*, 33.1 (1980), 1–32
PINEDA, VICTORIA, *La imitación como arte literario en el siglo XVI español* (Sevilla: Diputación Provincial de Sevilla, 1994)
PLETT, HEINRICH F., and PETER HEATH, 'Aesthetic Constituents in the Courtly Culture of Renaissance England', *New Literary History*, 14.3 (1983), 597–621
PLUTA, OLAF, 'On the Matter of the Mind: Late-Medieval Views on Mind, Body, and Imagination', in *Imagination in the Later Middle Ages and Early Modern Times*, ed. by Lodi Nauta and Detlev Pätzold (Leuven: Peeters, 2004), pp. 21–34
PRESCOTT, ANNE LAKE, *French Poets and the English Renaissance: Studies in Fame and Transformation* (New Haven and London: Yale University Press, 1978)
—— 'Spenser (Re)Reading du Bellay: Chronology and Literary Response', in *Spenser's Life and the Study of Biography*, ed. by Judith Anderson, Donald Cheney, and David A. Richardson (Amherst: University of Massachusetts Press, 1996), pp. 131–45
PRILL, PAUL, 'Rhetoric and Poetics in the Early Middle Ages', *Rhetorica*, 5.2 (1987), 129–47
QUANDAHL, ELLEN, 'Aristotle's Rhetoric: Reinterpreting Invention', *Rhetoric Review*, 4.2 (1986), 128–37
QUINT, DAVID, *Origin and Originality in Renaissance Literature: Versions of the Source* (New Haven: Yale University Press, 1983)
RAGSDALE, J. DONALD, 'Invention in English "Stylistic" Rhetorics: 1600–1800', *Quarterly Journal of Speech*, 51.2 (1965), 164–67
RANDALL, MARILYN, *Pragmatic Plagiarism: Authorship, Profit, and Power* (Toronto and Buffalo: University of Toronto Press, 2001)
REBHORN, WAYNE A., *The Emperors of Men's Minds: Literature and the Renaissance Discourse of Rhetoric* (Ithaca: Cornell University Press, 1995)
—— *Renaissance Debates on Rhetoric* (Ithaca: Cornell University Press, 2000)
RENWICK, WILLIAM LINDSAY, 'The Critical Origins of Spenser's Diction', *Modern Language Review*, 17 (1922), 1–16
—— *Edmund Spenser: An Essay in Renaissance Poetry* (London: Arnold, 1925)
REYNOLDS, SUZANNE, *Medieval Reading: Grammar, Rhetoric and the Classical Text* (Cambridge: Cambridge University Press, 1996)
RHODES, NEIL, *Common: The Development of Literary Culture in Sixteenth-Century England* (Oxford: Oxford University Press, 2018)
—— 'Introduction', in *English Renaissance Translation Theory*, ed. by Neil Rhodes, Gordon Kendal, and Louise Wilson (London: Modern Humanities Research Association, 2013), pp. 1-67

RICHARDS, I. A., 'The Imagination', in *Principles of Literary Criticism*, ed. by John Constable (London: Routledge, 2001), pp. 212–23

RICOEUR, PAUL, 'Between Rhetoric and Poetics', in *Essays on Aristotle's Rhetoric*, ed. by Amélie Rorty (Berkeley: University of California Press, 1996), pp. 324–84

RIGOLOT, FRANÇOIS, 'Between Homer and Virgil: *Mimesis* and *Imitatio* in Ronsard's Epic Theory', in *Renaissance Rereadings: Intertext and Context*, ed. by Maryanne Cline Horowitz, Anne J. Cruz, and Wendy A. Furman (Urbana: University of Illinois Press, 1988), pp. 67–79

—— 'The Renaissance Crisis of Exemplarity', *Journal of the History of Ideas*, 59.4 (1998), 557–63

ROSE, MARK, *Authors and Owners: The Invention of Copyright* (Cambridge, MA: Harvard University Press, 1993)

ROSENTHAL, LAURA JEAN, *Playwrights and Plagiarists in Early Modern England: Gender, Authorship, Literary Property* (Ithaca and London: Cornell University Press, 1996)

ROSSKY, WILLIAM, 'Imagination in the English Renaissance: Psychology and Poetic', *Studies in the Renaissance*, 5 (1958), 49–73

ROUSSEAU, G. S., 'Science and the Discovery of the Imagination in Enlightened England', in *The Past as Prologue: Essays to Celebrate the Twenty-Fifth Anniversary of ASECS*, ed. by Carla H. Hay and Syndy M. Conger (New York: AMS Press, 1995), pp. 19–43

RUSSELL, DONALD ANDREW, *Criticism in Antiquity* (London: Duckworth, 2001)

—— '*De imitatione*', in *Creative Imitation and Latin Literature*, ed. by D. West and T. Woodman (Cambridge: Cambridge University Press, 1979), pp. 1–16

SABATIER, ROBERT, *La Poésie du XVIe siècle* (Paris: Michel, 1982)

SAIZ NOEDA, BELÉN, '*Inventio* y *dispositio*: Retórica y lingüística del texto: *Loci argumentorum* y "estructuras tópicas" en la *Institutio Oratoria* de Quintiliano', in *Quintiliano: Historia y actualidad de la retórica: Actas del Congreso Internacional: Madrid y Calahorra, 14 al 18 de noviembre de 1995*, ed. by Tomás Albaladejo Mayordomo, Emilio del Rio, and José Antonio Caballero (Logroño: Instituto de Estudios Riojanos, 1998), pp. 733–42

SALZMAN, PAUL, 'Theories of Prose Fiction in England: 1558–1700', in *The Cambridge History of Literary Criticism*, 9 vols (Cambridge and New York: Cambridge University Press, 1989–2013), III: *The Renaissance*, ed. by Glyn P. Norton (2000), pp. 295–304

SASEK, LAWRENCE A., *The Literary Temper of the English Puritans* (Baton Rouge: Louisiana State University Press, 1961)

SATTERTHWAITE, ALFRED W., *Spenser, Ronsard, and Du Bellay: A Renaissance Comparison* (Princeton: Princeton University Press, 1960)

SCHOFIELD, M., 'Aristotle on the Imagination', in *Aristotle on Mind and the Senses: Proceedings of the Seventh Symposium Aristotelicum*, ed. by G. E. R. Lloyd and G. E. L. Owen (Cambridge: Cambridge University Press, 1978), pp. 99–140

SCOTT, IZORA, *Controversies over the Imitation of Cicero as a Model for Style and Some Phases of their Influence on the Schools of the Renaissance* (New York City: Teachers College, Columbia University, 1910)

SELLEVOLD, KRISTI, 'Some "hardis repreneurs" in Sixteenth-Century France: Du Bellay, Aneau, Chappuys', in *Borrowed Feathers: Plagiarism and the Limits of Imitation in Early Modern Europe*, ed. by Hall Bjørnstad (Oslo: Unipub, 2008), pp. 53–65

SELLSTROM, A. DONALD, 'Rhetoric and the Poetics of French Classicism', *French Review*, 34.5 (1961), 425–31

SILVER, ISIDORE, 'Creative Imitation, Originality and Literary Tradition in Ronsard', in *Renaissance and Other Studies in Honor of William Leon Wiley* (Chapel Hill: University of North Carolina Press, 1968), pp. 215–27

SLOANE, THOMAS O., 'Schoolbooks and Rhetoric: Erasmus's *Copia*', *Rhetorica*, 9.2 (1991), 113–29

SMITH, A. J., 'Theory and Practice in Renaissance Poetry: Two Kinds of Imitation', *Bulletin of the John Rylands Library*, 47 (1964), 212–43
SMITH, G. GREGORY, *Elizabethan Critical Essays*, 2 vols (Oxford: Clarendon Press, 1904)
SOLMSEN, FRIEDRICH, 'The Aristotelian Tradition in Ancient Rhetoric', *American Journal of Philology*, 62.1 (1941), 35–50
SPINGARN, JOEL ELIAS, *A History of Literary Criticism in the Renaissance*, 2nd edn (Westport: Greenwood Press, 1976)
STAUB, SUSAN, 'Dissembling his Art: "Gascoigne's Gardnings"', *Renaissance Studies*, 25.1 (2011), 95–110
STEADMAN, JOHN M., *The Lamb and the Elephant: Ideal Imitation and the Context of Renaissance Allegory* (San Marino, CA: Huntington Library, 1974)
STILLMAN, ROBERT E., 'The Scope of Sidney's *Defence of Poesy*: The New Hermeneutic and Early Modern Poetics', *English Literary Renaissance*, 32 (2002), 355–85
STRUEVER, NANCY S., *The Language of History in the Renaissance: Rhetoric and Historical Consciousness in Florentine Humanism* (Princeton: Princeton University Press, 1970)
SUMILLERA, ROCÍO G., 'From Inspiration to Imagination: The Physiology of Poetry in Early Modernity', *Parergon*, 33.3 (2016), 17–42
—— 'Ingenios del norte e ingenios del sur en *Examen de ingenios para las ciencias* (1575) de Juan Huarte de San Juan', in *El sur también existe: Hacia la creación de un imaginario europeo sobre España*, ed. by Berta Raposo and Ferran Robles (Madrid: Iberoamericana, 2014), pp. 37–48
—— 'Invention and Imagination in Sixteenth-Century English Literature', *Journal of Language, Literature and Culture*, 61.1 (2014), 21–32
—— 'Thomas Wright and Juan Huarte de San Juan', *Notes and Queries*, 63.1 (2016), 23–27
SWEETING, ELIZABETH, *Early Tudor Criticism, Linguistic and Literary* (New York: Russell & Russell, 1964)
TATE, J., '"Imitation" in Plato's *Republic*', *Classical Quarterly*, 22 (1928), 16–23
—— 'Plato and "Imitation"', *Classical Quarterly*, 26 (1932), 161–69
THOMAS, MAX W., 'Eschewing Credit: Heywood, Shakespeare, and Plagiarism before Copyright', *New Literary History*, 31.2 (2000), 277–93
TIGERSTEDT, E. N., 'The Poet as Creator: Origins of a Metaphor', *Comparative Literature Studies*, 20 (1970), 455–88
TRIMPI, WESLEY, 'The Quality of Fiction: The Rhetorical Transmission of Literary Theory', *Traditio*, 30 (1974), 1–118
TROUSDALE, MARION, 'Recurrence and Renaissance: Rhetorical Imitation in Ascham and Sturm', *English Literary Renaissance*, 6 (1976), 156–79
TUVE, ROSEMOND, *Elizabethan and Metaphysical Imagery: Renaissance Poetic and Twentieth Century Critics* (Chicago: University of Chicago Press, 1972)
—— 'Imagery and Logic: Ramus and Metaphysical Poetics', *Journal of the History of Ideas*, 3.4 (1942), 365–400
ULREICH, JR, JOHN C., '"The Poets Only Deliver": Sidney's Conception of Mimesis', *Studies in Literary Imagination*, 15.1 (1982), 67–84
UNTERSTEINER, MARIO, *The Sophists*, trans. by Kathleen Freeman (Oxford: Blackwell, 1954)
UTRERA TORREMOCHA, Mª VICTORIA, 'La imitación en la *Institutio Oratoria* de Quintiliano', in *Quintiliano: Historia y actualidad de la retórica: Actas del Congreso Internacional: Madrid y Calahorra, 14 al 18 de noviembre de 1995*, ed. by Tomás Albaladejo Mayordomo, Emilio del Rio, and José Antonio Caballero (Logroño: Instituto de Estudios Riojanos, 1998), pp. 1513–22
VARGA, ÁRON KIBÉDI, *Rhétorique et littérature, études de structures classiques* (Paris: Didier, 1970)

VASOLI, CESARE, 'L'Humanisme rhétorique en Italie au XVe siècle', in *Histoire de la rhétorique dans l'Europe moderne: 1450–1950*, ed. by Marc Fumaroli (Paris: Presses Universitaires de France, 1999), pp. 45–130
VEENSTRA, JAN R., 'The Subtle Knot: Robert Kilwardby and Gianfrancesco Pico on the Imagination', in *Imagination in the Later Middle Ages and Early Modern Times*, ed. by Lodi Nauta and Detlev Pätzold (Leuven: Peeters, 2004), pp. 1–20
VERDENIUS, W. J., *Mimesis: Plato's Doctrine of Artistic Imitation and its Meaning to Us* (Leiden: Brill, 1962)
VICKERS, BRIAN, 'Bacon and Rhetoric', in *The Cambridge Companion to Bacon*, ed. by Markku Peltonen (Cambridge: Cambridge University Press, 1996), pp. 200–31
—— *English Renaissance Literary Criticism* (Oxford: Oxford University Press, 2003)
—— 'Francis Bacon and the Progress of Knowledge', *Journal of the History of Ideas*, 53 (1992), 495–518
—— *Francis Bacon and Renaissance Prose* (Cambridge: Cambridge University Press, 2009)
—— '"The Power of Persuasion": Images of the Orator, Elyot to Shakespeare', in *Renaissance Eloquence: Studies in the Theory and Practice of Renaissance Rhetoric*, ed. by James J. Murphy (Berkeley: University of California Press, 1983), pp. 411–36
—— 'Rhetoric and Poetics', in *The Cambridge History of Renaissance Philosophy*, ed. by Charles B. Schmitt and others (Cambridge: Cambridge University Press, 1988), pp. 715–45
WALKER, JEFFREY, *Rhetoric and Poetics in Antiquity* (Oxford: Oxford University Press, 2000)
WALLACE, KARL R., *Francis Bacon on Communication and Rhetoric; or, The Art of Applying Reason to Imagination for the Better Moving of the Will* (Chapel Hall: University of North Carolina Press, 1943)
—— *Francis Bacon on the Nature of Man: The Faculties of Man's Soul: Understanding, Reason, Imagination, Memory, Will, and Appetite* (Urbana: University of Illinois Press, 1967)
WARD, JOHN O., 'Quintilian and the Rhetorical Revolution of the Middle Ages', *Rhetorica*, 13.3 (1995), 231–84
WASWO, RICHARD, *Language and Meaning in the Renaissance* (Princeton: Princeton University Press, 1987)
WATSON, GERARD, *Phantasia in Classical Thought* (Galway: Galway University Press, 1988)
WEAVER, WILLIAM P., *Untutored Lines: The Making of the English Epyllion* (Edinburgh: Edinburgh University Press, 2012)
WEBB, RUTH, *Ekphrasis, Imagination and Persuasion in Ancient Rhetorical Theory and Practice* (Farnham and Burlington: Ashgate, 2009)
WEBER, HENRI, *La Création poétique au XVIe siècle en France: De Maurice Scève à Agrippa d'Aubigné* (Paris: Nizet, 1981)
WEINBERG, BERNARD, 'Castelvetro's Theory of Poetics', in *Critics and Criticism: Essays in Method*, ed. by R. S. Crane and others (Chicago: University of Chicago Press, 1957), pp. 146–68
—— *A History of Literary Criticism in the Italian Renaissance*, 2 vols (Chicago: University of Chicago Press, 1961)
WEINER, ANDREW D., 'Sidney/Spenser/Shakespeare: Influence/Intertextuality/Intention', in *Influence and Intertextuality in Literary History*, ed. by Jay Clayton and Eric Rothstein (Madison and London: University of Wisconsin Press, 1991), pp. 245–70
—— *Sir Philip Sidney and the Poetics of Protestantism: A Study of Contexts* (Minneapolis: University of Minnesota Press, 1978)
WHITE, HAROLD OGDEN, *Plagiarism and Imitation during the English Renaissance: A Study in Critical Distinctions*, 2nd edn (New York: Octagon Books, 1973)
WILLIAMS, RALF G., 'Introduction', in *The 'De arte poetica' of Marco Girolamo Vida*, ed. and trans. by Ralf G. Williams (New York: Columbia University Press, 1976), pp. xi–lii

WILSON-OKAMURA, DAVID SCOTT, *Virgil in the Renaissance* (Cambridge: Cambridge University Press, 2010)
WINSTON, JESSICA, *Lawyers at Play: Literature, Law, and Politics at the Early Modern Inns of Court, 1558–1581* (Oxford: Oxford University Press, 2016)
WOLFLEY, LAWRENCE C., 'Sidney's Visual-Didactic Poetics: Some Complexities and Limitations', *Journal of Medieval and Renaissance Studies*, 6 (1976), 217–41
WOODS, MARJORIE C., 'Literary Criticism in an Early Commentary on Geoffrey of Vinsauf's *Poetria nova*', in *Acta Conventus Neo-Latini Bononiensis: Proceedings of the Fourth International Congress of Neo-Latin Studies*, ed. by R. J. Schoeck (Binghamton: State University of New York, Center for Medieval and Early Renaissance Studies, 1985), pp. 667–73
—— 'A Medieval Rhetoric Goes to School — and to the University: The Commentaries on the *Poetria nova*', *Rhetorica*, 9 (1991), 55–65
WORTH-STYLIANOU, VALERIE, '*Translatio* and Translation in the Renaissance: From Italy to France', in *The Cambridge History of Literary Criticism*, 9 vols (Cambridge and New York: Cambridge University Press, 1989–2013), III: *The Renaissance*, ed. by Glyn P. Norton (2000), pp. 127–35
YOUNG, KARL, 'Chaucer and Geoffrey of Vinsauf', *Modern Philology*, 41.3 (1944), 172–82
ZUNINO-GARRIDO, CINTA, *Mimesis and the Representation of Experience: Dramatic Theory and Practice in Pre-Shakespearean Comedy (1560–1590)* (Frankfurt: Lang, 2012)

INDEX

Acron, Helenius 36
Aelius Theon of Alexandria 14
aemulatio 49, 52–54
Agricola, Rudolph 15, 25–31, 43, 146
Alcuin of York 16
Anaximander 8
Aneau, Barthélémy 76, 150
Angelo di Pietro Stefano dei Tosetti 64
Aphthonius of Antioch 14, 15, 22, 26, 30, 44, 131, 145
appropriation 50, 61, 62, 64–66, 73, 76, 80, 88, 94, 142, 145, 148
Ariosto, Ludovico 41, 85, 88, 89, 93, 119
Aristotle 3, 4, 7–9, 11, 12, 14, 19–22, 25, 26, 29, 30, 35–38, 42, 44, 46, 49, 55, 56, 67, 72, 77, 97, 107, 108, 110, 111, 120, 127, 131, 134, 139, 142, 144, 145, 148–50
arrangement 8, 17, 18, 27
ars dictaminis 11, 12
ars grammatica 7, 12, 15, 16
ars poetriae 11, 12
ars praedicandi 11, 12, 21
ars rhetorica 11, 16
art de première rhétorique 38
art de seconde rhétorique 38
Ascham, Roger 12, 30, 37, 67, 77, 92, 96, 103, 104, 131, 151
Aubrey, John 101, 131
auctor 84, 92
auctoritates 87, 128
Augustine of Hippo 9, 10, 20, 22, 110, 121, 140, 148
authorship 30, 63, 76, 86, 142, 149, 150
Averroes 36, 45, 144

Bacon, Francis 121, 127, 129–31, 139, 144, 152
Balmes, Abraham de 36
Baret, John 96, 104, 115, 116, 122, 123, 131
Behn, Aphra 65, 76, 131
Bembo, Pietro 51, 56, 72, 147
Benvenuto da Imola 23
Beza, Theodore 98
Bible 31, 98, 117
Blage, Thomas 31
Blount, Edward 45, 77, 87, 101, 133, 135
Blundeville, Thomas 28, 45, 69, 78, 131
Boccaccio, Giovanni 36, 52, 57, 59, 63, 73, 88, 135
Boethius 7, 9–11, 19, 20, 26, 28, 63, 146
Boileau-Despréaux, Nicolas 21

borrowing 49, 50, 54, 56, 57, 60, 61, 63–66, 71, 76, 88, 140
brain 2, 5, 59, 69, 86, 90, 94, 109, 113, 114, 117, 126
Bruni, Leonardo 92
Burton, Robert 61, 74, 126, 129, 131, 141
Butler, Charles 28
Byron, George Gordon 128

Caesarius, Johann 29
Calcagnini, Celio 52
Calvin, John 117
Calvinism 43
Carew, Richard 90, 102, 103, 134
Carter, Peter 28, 29
Cartwright, William 75, 131
Carvallo, Luis Alfonso de 125, 129, 131
Castelvetro, Ludovico 36, 37, 46, 56, 72, 80, 87, 88, 91, 101, 102, 119, 131, 140, 152
Catholicism 52, 81, 99, 107, 117
Cato, Dionysius 30
Cawdry, Robert 115, 122, 123, 131
Caxton, William 12, 21, 23, 33, 45, 131, 148
Chaderton, Laurence 28
Chapman, George 2, 6, 42, 88, 89, 102, 131
Chappuys, Claude 76, 150
Charron, Pierre 126, 129, 131, 140, 145
Chaucer, Geoffrey 12, 18, 21, 23, 41, 69, 78, 89, 92, 94, 148, 153
Cheke, John 30
Cicero, Marcus Tullius 3, 7–14, 16, 17, 19–22, 25–31, 34–36, 39, 43, 44, 49–53, 56, 63, 70, 71, 99, 131, 142, 146, 148, 150
Ciceronianism 9, 51, 52
Colet, John 15, 29, 43, 44, 52, 141
Columbus, Christopher 91
commonplace 7, 9, 16, 19, 20, 30, 146, 147
Cooper, Thomas 70, 79, 96, 104, 132
Coote, Edmund 113, 122, 132
copy 2, 12, 54, 55, 57, 67, 69, 88, 89, 91, 92, 94
copyright 65, 75, 76, 142, 143, 150, 151
Cortese, Paolo 51
Cotgrave, Randle 96, 104, 105, 115, 116, 122, 123, 132
Coverdale, Miles 117
Cox, Leonard 31, 33, 34, 45, 90, 103, 132
creativity 5, 20, 67, 77, 93, 120, 128, 139, 147
Cusa, Nicholas of 68, 77, 78, 141, 144, 146

D'Aubigné, Agrippa 73, 94, 104, 132, 152
D'Avenant, William 130, 134
Dante Alighieri 34, 36, 38, 59, 69, 72, 121, 147, 148
Davies, John, of Hereford 84, 96, 100, 105, 110, 117, 118, 121, 123, 132, 138
Day, Angel 31
Day, John 97, 106, 134
decorum 14, 34, 44, 52, 147
delectare 119
delivery 8, 14, 26, 27
Demetrius 21, 22, 72, 131, 134, 142
Demosthenes 67, 77, 137
Descartes, René 22, 127, 130, 140
Dethick, Henry 100, 101, 132, 139
dialectic 1, 3, 4, 7–11, 19, 25–29, 31, 35, 42, 43, 49, 129, 144–47
Digby, Everard 28
Dionysius of Halicarnassus 12, 53
dispositio 1, 17, 19, 25, 26, 35, 62, 92, 126, 150
disposition 2, 18, 27, 31, 39, 56, 84, 88, 108
docere 119
Dolce, Lodovico 37
Dolet, Etiènne 52, 92
Donatus, Aelius 12, 16
drama 22, 36, 41, 47, 76, 78, 97, 98, 121, 144, 145, 146
Drant, Thomas 36, 37
Dryden, John 37, 46, 50, 66, 76, 89, 91, 102, 103, 120, 124, 132, 138, 144, 145
Du Bellay, Joachim 38–40, 43, 46, 47, 49, 59, 60, 64, 73–76, 92, 93, 104, 132, 133, 140, 142, 147–50

Eberhard of Béthune 16, 17
Eliot, John 88, 89, 102, 133
elocutio 1, 10, 16, 25–27, 35, 62, 92, 126
elocution 27, 33, 39, 56, 62, 82, 84, 85, 91, 120
eloquence 9–11, 18, 20, 21, 23, 31, 34, 41, 42, 44, 45, 47, 51, 52, 55, 67, 90, 92, 113, 126, 142, 143, 145, 146, 152
Elyot, Thomas 47, 67, 77, 84, 100, 133, 152
emblem 4, 81–83, 86, 87, 100, 105, 115, 123, 137, 140–42
emotion 5, 8, 102, 108, 109, 112
empiricism 78, 127
emulation 4, 49, 53–56, 64, 128
enarratio poetarum 3, 15, 16
Enlightenment 6, 142, 146
Ennius, Quintus 63
Erasmus, Desiderius 15, 26, 29–31, 44, 49, 52, 54, 58, 59, 71, 73, 75, 133, 141, 149, 150
eris 54
Espinel, Vicente Gómez Martínez 37
Euripides 93
exegesis 9, 10, 16

fable 13, 14, 30, 41, 75, 80–82, 86, 89, 97, 100, 102, 113, 118, 126, 132

Fabri, Pierre 39
fabrication 1, 62, 78
fabula 81
Falgano, Niccolò da 21
fancy 4, 32, 33, 99, 113, 116, 119, 120, 126, 128
fantasia 113
Farnaby, Thomas 12
Fenner, Dudley 28
Ficino, Marsilio 46, 69, 77, 78, 111, 116, 121, 122, 133, 141, 142
fiction 1, 6, 41, 44, 47, 77, 80–82, 117, 121, 124, 126, 139, 141, 145, 146, 150, 151
figure of speech 7, 13–18, 31, 34, 35, 42, 92, 126
finding 4, 25, 28, 32–34, 90, 120, 125
Florio, John 33, 34, 45, 66, 70, 76, 79, 84, 96, 100, 105, 111, 113, 117, 121–23, 133
fore-conceit 68, 70
Foxe, John 99, 106, 133
Fracastoro, Girolamo 46
Fraunce, Abraham 28
frenzy 3, 5, 114
Frith, John 97, 117
furor 34, 37, 68

Gascoigne, George 5, 41, 47, 81, 83–85, 91, 93, 100, 101, 104, 118, 123, 133, 138, 151
genius 2, 5, 42, 89, 128
Gentili, Alberico 1, 2, 5, 69, 78, 96, 100, 105, 133
George of Trebizond 19, 20, 26, 147
Gervase of Melkley 17
Giraldi Cinthio, Giovanni Battista 36, 52, 56
Gosson, Stephen 97–99, 105, 133
Gower, John 12, 21, 92, 148
grammar 3, 4, 7, 10, 11, 13–18, 20, 22, 25, 29, 30, 35, 41, 43, 44, 50, 55, 65, 91, 92, 140, 148, 149
Greene, Robert 89, 91, 102, 135
Greville, Fulke 68, 78, 116, 123, 133

Hall, John 21
Hall, Joseph 65
Harington, John 94, 104, 133
Harvey, Gabriel 28, 42, 80, 85, 90, 91, 101, 103, 133
Hawes, Stephen 12, 18, 113, 122, 134, 143
Heinsius, Daniel 46, 145
Hermannus Alemannus 36
hermeneutics 20, 140
Hermogenes 14, 29, 30
Herodotus 78
Hesiod 34, 82
Heywood, John 118, 123, 134
Heywood, Thomas 65
Hobbes, Thomas 128, 130, 134
Homer 2, 6, 13, 15, 34, 37, 63–65, 67, 73, 81, 82, 84, 88, 89, 102, 131, 142, 150
Horace 3, 4, 13–18, 21, 22, 25, 34–37, 45, 46, 50, 57, 61, 63, 66, 74, 75, 81, 134, 146, 148

Hoskins, John 84, 89, 101, 119, 124, 134
Huarte de San Juan, Juan 90, 102, 103, 113–15, 122, 123, 125, 126, 129, 134, 151
Hugh of St Victor 17
Huloet, Richard 96, 104, 134
humanism 4, 11, 21, 29, 34, 38, 42, 43, 47, 55, 72, 143, 144, 147, 151, 152
humour 96, 110, 113, 126
Humphrey, Laurence 92, 103, 134

image 5, 47, 55, 58, 59, 67, 70, 73, 75, 78, 79, 82, 90, 96, 103, 108–13, 115, 116, 118–22, 124, 127, 142, 147, 152
imaginatio 109, 110, 120, 121
imagination 1–6, 18, 21, 25, 27, 32–34, 69, 70, 77, 90, 99, 105, 107, 109–30, 135, 138–40, 142–52
imitatio 15, 18, 49, 51, 52, 53, 56, 57, 71, 73, 149, 150
imitation 1, 2, 4, 5, 15, 22, 30, 37, 38, 41, 42, 44, 46, 47, 49–64, 66–68, 70–78, 80, 81, 87, 88, 90, 91, 93, 102, 107, 111, 118, 120, 128, 139, 140, 142–52
ingenium 8, 33, 53
ingenuity 6, 80, 146
innutrition 64
inspiration 3, 13, 14, 18, 34, 38, 68, 81, 87, 88, 100, 125, 126, 129, 140, 151
intellect 5, 18, 108–12
intellectio 23, 138
intellectus 109
invenire 3, 13, 53
inventiveness 2, 3, 80, 83, 91, 94–96, 123
inventor 13, 64, 84, 88, 89, 91, 94–96
Isocrates 49, 50, 62, 70, 74, 134

Jaggard, William 65
James I, King of England 93, 104, 134
John of Garland 4, 17–19
John of Salisbury 10, 17, 18, 23, 24, 136
Jonson, Ben 50, 65, 66, 76, 84, 89, 101, 134, 141, 143, 147
Joye, George 117
judgement 15, 19, 26, 27, 31, 33, 42, 43, 67, 72, 85, 96, 107, 109, 111–13, 119, 144, 147
Juvenal 22, 66, 141

Knox, John 99, 106, 134

Landino, Cristoforo 36, 69
Landriani, Gerardo 9
Langbaine, Gerard 66, 76, 134
Languet, Hubert 52, 55, 71, 132
Latimer, Hugh 99, 105, 106, 134
Leibniz, Gottfried Wilhelm 130
Lennard, Samson 129
Lever, Ralph 34, 45, 134
Lily, William 15
loci 8, 19, 26, 32, 150
Locke, John 130

Lodge, Thomas 42, 48, 89, 99, 102, 105, 134
logic 2, 5, 7, 10, 11, 16, 17, 19, 20, 26, 28, 29, 42, 43, 45, 82, 100, 141, 143, 144, 147, 151
Lombardi, Bartolomeo 36
Longinus 12, 13, 21, 22, 53, 71, 72, 131, 134, 142, 144
Lope Félix de Vega Carpio 103
Lorich, Reinhard 30
Lucan 66
Lucilius, Gaius 13, 57
Lucretius 63
Lutheranism 117
Lycosthenes, Conrad 30
Lydgate, John 12, 32, 41, 45, 94, 134
Lyly, John 86, 87, 101, 135

MacIlmaine, Rollo 103, 135
Macrobius Ambrosius Theodosius 39
Maggi, Vinzenzo 36, 37
maker 55, 58, 69, 70, 74, 77, 78, 88, 94, 140, 144
Malpaghini, Giovanni 63
Mantino ben Samuel, Jacob 36
Mantinus of Tortosa 36
Marlorat, Augustin 98
Marlowe, Christopher 91, 99, 106, 135
Martial 75
Martianus Capella 10, 18
Matthew of Vendôme 17
Mazzoni, Jacopo 119
McIlmain, Roland 28
medicine 10, 110, 126, 127
melancholy 5, 61, 74, 114, 126, 131
Melanchthon, Philipp 27–29, 31, 43
memory 8, 18, 26–28, 63, 64, 90, 109, 110, 113, 127, 129, 152
Meres, Francis 31
metaphor 49, 50, 57, 58, 61, 74, 76, 78, 118, 123, 143, 151
metre 13, 34, 56
Milton, John 97, 123, 144
mimesis 2, 4, 5, 22, 47, 52–57, 67, 68, 71–73, 77, 105, 125, 140, 144, 150–53
mind 1, 3, 13, 14, 17, 18, 26, 27, 32–34, 45, 53, 56, 58, 62, 64, 67, 68, 70, 77, 81, 89, 92, 94–96, 103, 107–11, 113, 116, 117, 119–21, 125, 126, 129, 130, 137, 140, 141, 146, 149, 150
Minturno, Antonio Sebastiano 35
Molinier, Guilhem 17
Montaigne, Michel de 63, 64, 66, 74, 77, 112, 122, 133, 135
More, Thomas 41, 117
Mosellanus, Petrus 29
Mulcaster, Richard 59
Munday, Anthony 96, 104, 135
music 10, 42, 48, 55, 89, 97, 105, 113, 126, 134
Muzio, Girolamo 56

Nashe, Thomas 28, 67, 77, 80, 86, 89–91, 98–103, 105, 133, 135
natural philosophy 3, 5, 110, 126, 127
Neoplatonism 34, 38, 68, 69, 72, 77, 97, 107, 111, 141, 144
Neville, Alexander 95, 104, 135
Northbrooke, John 97

oratory 13, 14, 16, 35, 41, 42, 50, 52
originality 2, 3, 5, 6, 73, 74, 128, 149, 150
Ovid 72, 87, 89, 138

painting 6, 57, 81, 89, 102, 114, 132, 145
paraphrase 14, 16, 36, 51, 119
Parrasio, Aulo Giano 36
Patrizi, Francesco 56, 119
Paul of Venice 26
Pazzi de' Medici, Alessandro 35, 36
Peacham, Henry 31, 44, 81, 82, 86, 87, 100, 101, 135
Peele, George 89, 102, 135
Peletier du Mans, Jacques 37, 39, 40, 47, 49, 60, 74, 81, 82, 93, 94, 100, 104, 115, 123, 135
Perceval, Richard 33, 45, 70, 79, 113, 117, 122, 123, 135
Peter of Spain 26
Peterson, Robert 93, 104, 135
Petrarch, Francis 23, 34, 36, 49, 50, 52, 57, 59, 63–65, 73–75, 88, 102, 135
Petronius Arbiter, Gaius 66
phantasia 108, 109, 111, 120, 152
phantasy 3–5, 25, 32, 33, 107–10, 112, 117, 118, 122
philosophy 3, 5, 11, 19–21, 27, 34, 42, 43, 47, 52, 55, 70, 77, 78, 82, 96, 109, 110, 119, 121, 125–28, 130, 140, 142–44, 147, 149, 152
Phiston, William 31
Piccolomini, Alessandro 36
Pico della Mirandola, Giovanni Francesco 5, 51, 56, 77, 107, 111, 112, 121, 122, 135, 152
Pietro Bizarro of Perugia 55
Pilatus, Leontius 102
piracy 61, 76, 142
plagiarism 4, 49, 50, 62, 66, 74–76, 80, 90, 98, 139, 141, 143, 146, 149–52
Plato 11, 14, 22, 35, 49, 55, 68, 72, 97, 107, 108, 118, 119, 123, 135, 144, 151, 152
Plautus 63, 64, 88
Pléiade 6, 38, 46, 59, 73, 82, 139, 140
Pliny 92, 103
Plotinus 108, 109
poetics 1–7, 13, 14, 18–23, 25, 29, 34–47, 49, 50, 54–56, 72–74, 76, 78, 80, 82, 84, 100, 102, 105, 107, 108, 120, 124–28, 131, 134, 136, 140, 142–47, 149–53
poetry 1–7, 11, 13–19, 22, 23, 25, 34–42, 45, 46–48, 50–52, 55–58, 60, 63–65, 67–70, 72–75, 77, 78, 80–86, 88, 89, 93, 94, 96–102, 105, 107, 108, 113, 114, 117–27, 129, 131, 132–34, 136–45, 148, 149, 151
Poggio Bracciolini, Gian Francesco 9, 51
poiein 78
poiesis 22
poietés 78
Polidori, John 128
Poliziano (Agnolo Ambrogini) 51
Porphyrion 36
preaching 11, 21, 90, 98, 113, 139
Priscian 12, 14–16, 29
progymnasmata 14–16, 22, 26, 30, 44, 131, 140, 143, 145
Protagoras 8
Protestantism 52, 71, 97, 105, 117, 152
publica materies 4, 50, 61, 62
Puttenham, George 2, 6, 42, 48, 50, 69, 70, 78, 85, 94, 101, 104, 117–19, 123, 124, 135

Quintilian 3, 7, 9, 11, 13–16, 19, 20, 22, 26, 27, 29, 31, 34, 35, 43, 44, 49, 51–54, 59–61, 70–72, 92, 109, 135, 142, 144, 148, 150–52

Rainolde, Richard 30, 33, 41, 44, 45, 47, 136, 145
Rainolds, John 29, 30
Ramism 4, 15, 27, 28, 34, 43
Ramus, Petrus 5, 25, 27–29, 34, 43–45, 103, 135, 141, 143, 144, 147, 148, 151
Reformation 4, 47, 77, 81, 96, 106, 129, 132–34, 139, 145
Reisch, Gregor 109, 113, 122
Rengifo, Juan 125
Reynolds, Edward 126, 129, 136
rhetoric 1–4, 7–23, 25–47, 49–52, 55, 72, 78, 82, 91, 96, 100, 101, 108, 113, 120, 122, 124, 127, 129, 131, 134, 138–53
rhyme 38, 85
Ricci, Bartolomeo 38, 54
Robortello, Francesco 12, 35–37
Rogers, Thomas 71, 149
Romanticism 2, 5, 6, 128, 130, 142, 143
Ronsard, Pierre de 38–40, 46, 47, 49, 58, 73, 75, 82, 100, 112, 115, 122, 123, 132, 133, 136, 143, 150

Sallust 66
Sánchez de las Brozas, Francisco 27
Sanderson, Robert 29
Scaliger, Julius Caesar 35, 37, 38, 51, 56, 57, 69, 72, 73, 78, 136, 143
scholasticism 26, 42, 110, 144
Scott, William 70, 79, 136
Scriptures 9, 98, 99, 117
Sébillet, Thomas 38, 39, 46, 47, 82, 95, 100, 104, 132, 133, 136
Seneca, Lucius Annaeus 50, 51, 57, 58, 62, 66, 74, 88, 104, 135, 136
sequi 53, 54

Seton, John 28, 29
Shakespeare, William 5, 6, 21, 47, 48, 50, 65, 72,
    76–78, 83, 86, 100, 101, 113, 114, 117, 121–23, 134,
    136, 138–40, 144, 146, 151, 152
Shelley, Mary 128, 130, 136
Shelley, Percy 128
Sherry, Richard 31, 44, 141
Sidney, Philip 6, 37, 42, 43, 47, 48, 50, 52, 55, 67, 68,
    70–72, 74, 77–79, 82–84, 97, 100, 105, 107, 119,
    120, 123, 124, 132–34, 136, 140, 141, 144–46, 149,
    151–53
similis 53, 67
soul 5, 13, 82, 88, 97, 108–12, 116, 118, 121, 126, 129,
    132, 136, 147, 149, 152
Southwell, Robert 98, 105, 136
Spenser, Edmund 38, 46, 47, 59, 60, 73, 74, 78, 83,
    85, 97, 100, 101, 136, 139, 140, 142–44, 147, 149,
    150, 152
Speroni, Sperone 38, 59, 60, 73, 88, 102, 148
Stanhope, George 129, 131
studia humanitatis 11, 34
Sturm, Johannes 12, 27, 77, 151
style 4, 8, 10, 13, 16–18, 21, 22, 27, 30, 31, 35, 39–42,
    44, 50–52, 57–60, 62, 63, 71, 72, 84, 86, 95, 101,
    131, 134, 142, 150
Susenbrotus, Johannes 29, 31

Talon, Omer 28, 29
Tarleton, Dick 91
Tasso, Torquato 36, 119, 121, 148
Taverner, Richard 31
Temple, William 28
Terence 14, 64, 88
theatre 76, 96, 140
theft (literary / textual) 49, 50, 56, 61–66, 76, 90, 94,
    95, 128
Themistius 26
theology 9, 10, 110, 111, 122, 133
Thomas, Thomas 33, 45, 70, 79, 84, 96, 100, 104, 113,
    115, 116, 122, 123, 137
Thucidides 67
Timpler, Clemens 30

topics 1, 7–11, 14, 15, 19, 20, 26, 27, 29, 31, 35, 85, 127,
    139, 143, 146, 148
translation 1, 2, 4, 9, 11, 20, 21, 28–31, 36, 37, 39, 44, 47,
    51, 59, 60, 65, 66, 72–75, 81, 88, 91–95, 102, 103,
    109, 118, 120, 122, 126, 134–36, 140, 147–49, 153
translator 2, 60, 61, 81, 90, 92–95, 117
Traversagnus, Gulielmus 12, 21, 148
Trissino, Gian Giorgio 36, 38
trope 7, 13, 15, 16, 31, 34, 44, 65, 101, 141
Turbervile, George 93, 94
Tyndale, William 117, 123, 137

Valla, Giorgio 36
Valla, Lorenzo 25, 26, 43, 51, 144, 146
versification 3, 7, 13, 15–17, 38, 39
versifier 2, 94
version 2, 6, 9, 21, 26, 28, 31, 35–38, 44, 71, 72, 75, 95,
    101, 131, 149
Vettori, Piero 36
Vida, Marco Girolamo 35, 49–51, 56, 62, 72, 74, 137, 152
Villedieu, Alexandre de 12, 16
Vinsauf, Geoffrey of 4, 17–19, 23, 137, 139, 145, 153
Virgil 2, 15, 37, 39, 51, 56, 63, 64, 67, 73, 74, 88, 89,
    94, 99, 102, 142, 150, 153
Vives, Juan Luis 25, 27, 29, 30, 52
Vossius, Gerardus 46, 145

Watson, Thomas 65, 75, 137, 148
Webbe, William 41, 42, 48, 61, 74, 94, 104, 137
Whitney, Geoffrey 83, 96, 100, 105, 137
William of Moerbeke 9, 36
William of Ockham 20, 139
Willis, Richard 97
Wilson, Thomas 12, 28, 29, 31–33, 41, 43–45, 47, 67,
    77, 82, 90, 100, 101, 137, 141
wit 4, 6, 31–33, 42, 44, 53, 65, 68, 70, 75, 76, 78, 80,
    84, 86, 88, 89–91, 96, 98, 100, 102, 113, 118–21,
    123, 125, 132, 134, 141, 144, 146
Wither, George 115, 116, 123, 137
Wright, Thomas 126, 129, 137, 151

Zapata, Luis de 37

www.ingramcontent.com/pod-product-compliance
Lightning Source LLC
La Vergne TN
LVHW061252060426
835507LV00017B/2039